£39-50
Som

International Macroeconomic Stabilization Policy

Uncertainty and Expectations in Economics

Series Editors: J. L. Ford, John D. Hey and Mark Machina

Surveys in the Economics of Uncertainty

Edited by John D. Hey and Peter Lambert

Production and Decision Theory under Uncertainty

Karl Aiginger

Economics of Search

Steven Lippman and John J. McCall

Time, Uncertainty and Information

Jack Hirshleifer

International Macroeconomic Stabilization Policy

Stephen J. Turnovsky

International Macroeconomic Stabilization Policy

STEPHEN J. TURNOVSKY

Basil Blackwell

First published 1990

Basil Blackwell, Inc.
3 Cambridge Center
Cambridge, Massachusetts 02142, USA

Basil Blackwell Ltd
108 Cowley Road, Oxford, OX4 1JF, UK

Library of Congress Cataloging in Publication Data

International macroeconomic stabilization policy/Stephen J.
Turnovsky . . . [et al].
p. cm.
ISBN 0-631-17335-8
1. Economic stabilization. 2. Economic policy. 3. International finance.
4. Macroeconomics. I. Turnovsky, Stephen J.
HB3732.I68 1990
339.5–dc20 89-49714
CIP

British Library Cataloguing in Publication Data
A CIP catalogue record for this book is available from the British Library.

Typeset in 10 on $11\frac{1}{2}$pt Times
by Keytec Typesetting Ltd, Bridport, Dorset
Printed in Great Britain by T.J. Press (Padstow) Ltd, Padstow, Cornwall.

Contents

Series Editors' Preface

Over the past decade, and increasingly so over the past five years, a large number of significant contributions have been made in the general area of uncertainty and expectations in economics. These cover the whole range of core economics, from the modeling of individual decision-making under uncertainty to the implications of rational expectations in temporary general equilibrium and macro models. These advances have contributed to a significant transformation in economic theory, and in economists' understanding of the economic world.

Until now, the majority of these advances have been published in prestigious academic journals, written by experts for fellow experts. In a few areas, books have appeared, but these have been scattered and isolated – lacking a central focus. The series *Uncertainty and Expectations in Economics* aims to provide that focus. Moreover, it will provide an outlet so that the experts may synthesize and pass on their important new findings to interested non-experts.

We believe that developments in uncertainty and expectations will continue to set the pace for advances in economic theory generally over the coming years. We also believe that these developments should be quickly made accessible to the profession at large, and hence we believe that this series will serve as an important forum for intellectual debate on issues of great importance.

We envisage books in a variety of areas within the general umbrella of *Uncertainty and Expectations in Economics*. Some examples are: criticisms and appraisals of subjective utility theory; alternative theories of individual and group behavior under risk and uncertainty; the formulation and adaptation of expectations; the implications of different expectational schemes within different areas of economics; psychological theories of behavior under uncertainty and expectations; asymmetric information; consumer and firm behavior under uncertainty; insurance; contract theory; labor markets under uncertainty; job search; consumer search; learning and adaptive behavior; auctions, contracts and bidding; value of life and safety; duopoly, oligopoly and monopolistic competition; strategic models; R&D; game theory; bounded rationality; rules of thumb; reasonable behavior; fix price "disequilibrium" general equilibrium models; the principal/agent problem; macro disequilibrium models;

conjectures and conjectural equilibrium; expectations in financial markets; models of monetary sequence economies; Keynesian models; econometric modeling and investigation of disequilibrium and search models; rational expectations.

The type of volume will vary from survey and synthesis, to collection of influential papers and research monographs. The level of books will range from undergraduate text to academic treatise.

J. L. Ford
University of Birmingham

John D. Hey
University of York

Mark Machina
University of California, San Diego

Acknowledgments

These essays were written over the past decade or so, during which I was at the Australian National University, the University of Illinois at Urbana-Champaign, and the University of Washington. I am grateful to these institutions, their faculty, and students for providing a productive environment in which the underlying research could be carried out. Several of the papers are co-authored and in this regard I gratefully acknowledge the contributions of Tamer Basar, Jonathan Eaton, Malcolm Gray, Vasco d'Orey, and Partha Sen. All essays appear in their originally published form, except that typographical errors have been corrected and minimal editorial changes have been made. I acknowledge with thanks the permission of the original publishers of all these essays to reproduce them here; a note giving information on first publication appears at the opening of each chapter.

Stephen J. Turnovsky
University of Washington, Seattle

Overview

International macroeconomics has been an area of intensive research activity during the last two decades or so. For many years, macroeconomics as taught and studied in the United States dealt almost exclusively with a closed economy. International aspects were neglected, or at best were treated in passing. Recently, however, the role of the United States in the world economy has become increasingly recognized and now international transactions are treated as a much more integral part of the relevant macroeconomic relationships. This in turn has stimulated research activity in this area.

At least two considerations have led to the growing interest in international macroeconomics. First is the increased integration of world financial markets. Second is the interdependence between fiscal deficits, on the one hand, and trade deficits, on the other. The focal issues themselves, and the resulting attention that they have received, have evolved over the period. The international macroeconomic models of the 1970s were primarily motivated by monetary issues and the transmission of monetary shocks. In contrast, the 1980s has seen a decided switch in interest toward fiscal issues. No doubt this can be attributed to a large degree to the recent magnitude of the US government deficit and its implications for the trade deficit.

The analytical models employed to study these issues have evolved over the past two decades and become increasingly sophisticated. Throughout the 1960s the standard framework was the Mundell–Fleming model. Since this was an extension of the basic IS–LM macroeconomic model, it was essentially static. Subsequent models have focused much more on dynamics, and in particular on the role of exchange rate expectations. These models can be usefully grouped into several categories.

First, there are sticky price models of the type originating with Rudiger Dornbusch's seminal 1976 contribution. These models are characterized by continuous clearance of the money market, brought about by instantaneous adjustments in the exchange rate, accompanied by only gradual clearance of the goods market, owing to the sluggish behaviour of prices. The fundamental dynamics of these models are in terms of the evolution of the price level and exchange rate, although these can be, and have been, extended to include asset dynamics as well.

A second class of models employed to analyse issues in international macroeconomics consists of stochastic rational expectations models. These are basically extensions of the new classical rational expectations models to the open economy. This has proved to be a particularly fertile area of application of this framework, because the underlying assumptions concerning market efficiency and information are particularly appropriate insofar as the foreign exchange market is concerned. This stochastic approach is convenient for categorizing disturbances according to characteristics such as whether they are temporary or permanent, anticipated or unanticipated, all of which are factors which affect how they will impact on the economy.

Thirdly, and more recently, there is a growing literature in macroeconomics in general, and in international macroeconomics in particular, directed at deriving macroeconomic equilibrium relationships from the intertemporal optimizing behavior of the representative agents in the economy. The purpose of this is to eliminate the arbitrariness of macroeconomic models, which has been a frequent source of criticism, and instead to base them on firm microeconomic foundations. But the extent to which this approach is successful in meeting this objective is not entirely clear, since the objective function to be optimized, together with some of the underlying constraints, is itself subject to some degree of arbitrariness. But despite this reservation, this approach is proving fruitful and providing insight in tackling a variety of policy issues.

This book contains a collection of 15 papers which I have published in the area of international macroeconomics over the past decade or so. The papers are divided into five groups. While these correspond to the above characterization of the literature, two other sections, dealing with two types of policy issues, have been added. The first of these deals with the issue of exchange market intervention, or more generally monetary policy in an open economy, studying how it interacts with other forms of policy, such as wages policy. The second considers questions related to strategic policy-making and policy coordination in a two-country setting. Generally, these types of issues have been discussed within the context of the stochastic models noted above. In selecting these papers for inclusion in this volume, I have attempted to ensure that each contains some new aspect of the model, or some different methodological aspect. The objective of the volume is primarily to develop analytical approaches and modeling strategies which hopefully can be usefully applied to a variety of issues in international macroeconomics.

I STICKY PRICE MODELS

Chapter 1 develops a basic sticky price model almost identical with that of the original Dornbusch model. In his original contribution, Dornbusch assumed that exchange rate expectations, which are a key ingredient of the model, are determined regressively; that is, the exchange rate is always expected to revert to its long-run equilibrium level. The case where exchange rate expectations are formed rationally was treated as a special case. In this chapter the rational expectations assumption is built in at the outset. Within this framework, we allow the domestic money supply to follow a quite general exogenous time path. The chapter presents a general approach to solving saddlepoint-type rational expectations models, in which the exchange rate is a forward-looking variable while prices move sluggishly. It analyses the effects of both current and anticipated future monetary disturbances upon the current exchange rate. It also points out that the assumption of regressive expectations may in fact be consistent with rational expectations under only very restrictive assumptions.

Like the bulk of the recent literature in international macroeconomics, the basic model assumes perfect international capital mobility in the sense of uncovered interest parity. That is, the differential between the domestic and world interest rate equals the expected rate of depreciation of the domestic currency. The empirical evidence in support of this hypothesis, which is based on risk neutrality, is not strong. However, the weaker assumption of covered interest parity, which is consistent with risk-averse speculators and where the interest differential equals the premium on forward exchange, is much more strongly supported by empirical evidence. Chapter 2 extends the model of chapter 1 to allow for covered interest parity. The critical modification that this introduces is that the dynamics of asset accumulation now become interdependent with that of price and exchange rate dynamics. A particularly simple form of savings behavior is introduced in this model. However, one important implication is that the overshooting of the exchange rate in response to a monetary disturbance, an important feature of the original Dornbusch model (and also obtained in chapter 1), may, or may not, obtain. Risk-averse market participants may play a stabilizing role insofar as fluctuations in the exchange rate are concerned.

Chapter 3 introduces a simple term structure of interest rates into the basic model. This is done by assuming that real aggregate demand depends upon the long-term real rate of interest, while the portfolio decision, essentially the demand for money, depends upon the short-term nominal interest rate. These rates are linked by arbitrage conditions and, as in the original model, uncovered interest parity is again assumed. The resulting dynamic system involves the exchange rate and the long-term real interest rate, both of which may respond instantaneously to new information, together with the price level, which continues to adjust gradually. The analysis highlights the short-run divergence between the short-term and long-term interest rates. The former responds primarily to current influences, while the latter is dominated by long-term expectational effects. Expectational influences can give rise to seemingly perverse short-run behavior. For example, an announced future fiscal expansion may lead to an immediate rise in the long-term real rate. This leads to a short-run contractionary effect on the economy, although this is eventually reversed when the anticipated fiscal expansion eventually occurs. It is also possible for the long and short rates initially to move in opposite directions, thereby twisting the yield curve in the short run.

The models of chapters 1–3 deal with a small open economy. Chapter 4 presents a two-country extension. In so doing, it assumes, as a reasonable first approximation, that the two countries are symmetric in the sense of having identical parameters. This assumption leads to an enormous analytical simplification, enabling us to adopt a solution introduced by Masanao Aoki. This procedure enables the dynamics to be decoupled into (a) averages and (b) differences of the relevant variables. In the model presented, the latter, but not the former, respond to announcements of future disturbances, and this in turn has important consequences for the dynamics. Specifically, the domestic and foreign economies are affected in precisely offsetting ways during the initial phase of the adjustment following the announcement of any future policy (or other) change. This means that an announced domestic future monetary expansion say, which initially keeps world output fixed by generating a short-run depreciation of the domestic currency (appreciation of the foreign currency), causes an immediate recession abroad. Two special features of this model should be noted. First, the fact that the effects in the two economies are exactly offsetting during the initial phase is a consequence of the perfect symmetry being assumed. Also, the failure of the average world economy to respond to announcements would no longer apply if, say, a long-term interest rate, with its forward-looking behavior, were introduced into the model. But the symmetric framework is a useful one, offering insight, and has become widely used in two-country analyses, particularly in the recent literature dealing with strategic aspects of policy-making.

II STOCHASTIC MODELS

Part II presents two stochastic monetary models of a small open economy. The first of these, discussed in chapter 5, is based on uncovered interest parity. Most of the attention is devoted to analysing stochastic disturbances in the domestic money supply, although foreign price shocks are also briefly treated. The model assumes rational expectations and the solution for current output is obtained in terms of (a) the unanticipated change in the current money supply and (b) the discounted sum of revisions to forecasts of future money supplies, updated between time $t-1$ and t on the basis of new information forthcoming at time t. In addition to depending upon both (a) and (b), the current price level and the exchange rate also depend upon the discounted sum of all expected future money supplies based on the information available at time $t-1$.

This form of model is very convenient for categorizing the monetary disturbances on the basis of (a) the extent that they are anticipated or unanticipated and (b) the extent to which they are perceived as being temporary or permanent. Various cases are discussed and a general conclusion is that the impact of these disturbances on the economy depends critically upon how they are perceived and their resulting impact on exchange rate expectations.

Chapter 6 basically extends this model to the case of covered interest parity, where speculators are risk-averse. The forward exchange market therefore assumes a central role. The model focuses on the effects of various monetary disturbances on both the current spot and current forward exchange rates. Both domestic and foreign disturbances are considered. In many respects, this model can be viewed as being a stochastic analogue to that presented in chapter 2.

III EXCHANGE MARKET INTERVENTION AND WAGE INDEXATION

Part III contains four chapters dealing with different aspects of macroeconomic stabilization policy in a small open economy. All are based on some variant of the stochastic models discussed in part II.

Chapter 7 considers the important question of exchange market intervention. For expositional purposes, the economy considered is the simplest one in which there is a single traded bond and a single traded good, with both uncovered interest parity and purchasing power parity being assumed to hold. The objective of the stabilization authority is to minimize some weighted average of the variances of domestic output and price movements. The policy instrument is described by a parameter μ, which describes the degree of intervention by the monetary authority in the foreign exchange market. The values of $\mu = 0$ and $\mu \to \infty$ correspond to the polar cases of perfectly flexible and perfectly fixed exchange rates respectively. There are two main conclusions to come out of this analysis. The first is that neither fixed nor flexible rates will in general be optimal, except in very special circumstances. Secondly, the optimal exchange rate policy rule may involve "leaning against the wind" or "leaning with the wind," depending upon the relative magnitudes of the underlying stochastic disturbances and the objective of the policy-maker.

Exchange market policy is but one instrument available for conducting macroeconomic stabilization policy in a small open economy. Chapter 8 considers the role of wage indexation and focuses on its interaction with exchange market intervention. The two types of rules are parallel. On the one hand, the exchange market rule of the type considered in chapter 7 assumes that the policy-maker adjusts the money supply in response to current stochastic disturbances insofar as they are reflected in the observed value of the current nominal exchange rate. On the other hand, the wage indexation rule as introduced in this chapter allows the policy-maker to respond to current stochastic disturbances, insofar as they are reflected in observed current price movements. The former impacts on the demand side of the economy, while the latter operates through the supply function. This chapter stresses the interdependence between these two forms of rules. It is shown how the choice of either policy instrument impinges on the effectiveness of the other. If the domestic wage is fully indexed to any arbitrary weighted average of the domestic and foreign price level, then exchange market intervention becomes completely ineffective in stabilizing real output. Likewise, there is a specific degree of exchange market intervention, which renders wage indexation ineffective. The tradeoffs between the two policy instruments, which arise in between these two extremes, are also highlighted.

The next chapter builds on the last, by developing an optimal combination of wage policy and monetary policy under a variety of assumptions regarding (a) the relative information available to private agents and the stabilization authority and (b) the perceived nature of the disturbances impinging on the economy. The distinctions between unanticipated and anticipated disturbances, on the one hand, and permanent and transitory disturbances, on the other, are emphasized. The extent to which stabilization can be achieved is shown to depend critically upon the nature of the disturbances and the available information. Optimal policies are often shown to involve redundancy, implying that the optimal rule can frequently be specified in many equivalent ways.

The final chapter of part III relaxes the assumption of uncovered interest parity and risk neutrality, and assumes instead that investors are risk-averse with covered interest parity holding. If it is assumed that underlying asset demands are derived from maximizing a two-period mean–variance utility function, the demand for forward exchange by speculators can be shown to depend inversely upon the one-period variance of the spot exchange rate. The coefficient describing speculative behavior therefore becomes endogenously determined, along with this variance. Moreover, since the distribution of the spot rate is a function of government intervention policy, this coefficient becomes dependent upon the policy regime. This chapter analyses intervention in both the spot and forward exchange markets, taking account of the endogeneity of private speculative behavior and how it is influenced by government policy. The endogeneity of the speculative coefficient renders the model nonlinear, thereby raising questions of the existence and possible nonuniqueness of equilibrium. The main conclusion of this analysis is that any structural change to the economy, whether truly exogenous or due to a change in policy regime, has two effects: (a) the direct effect of the change itself; (b) induced effects which operate through the changes in private speculative behavior. In some instances the two partial effects are mutually reinforcing; in other cases they are offsetting. But both need to be taken into account.

IV INTERTEMPORAL OPTIMIZING MODELS

Much of the current research being undertaken in international macroeconomics is based on the intertemporal optimizing representative agent model. Part IV contains two chapters based on this approach.

The first of these, chapter 11, is a monetary model in which there is a single traded good and labor is the only factor of production. If, in addition, there is a single traded bond which is perfectly mobile internationally, in the sense of uncovered interest parity holding, then the economy must be continuously in steady state equilibrium. In response to any shock, the economy moves instantaneously to a new steady state – the transitional dynamic degenerates.

In order to restore dynamics to this system system some sluggishness must be introduced and this is done by introducing domestic bonds which are imperfect substitutes for traded bonds. The procedure by which this is done is to introduce quadratic costs on the holdings of foreign bonds. This is meant to capture in a certainty framework the imperfect substitutability between domestic and foreign bonds. While this representation is arbitrary, it does yield a perfectly sensible demand function for traded bonds. Basically, it is proportional to the uncovered interest differential, with the proportionality depending upon the cost.

The results obtained in this chapter have a bearing on a general issue. Macroeconomic models, based on *ad hoc* relationships, are often criticized as being arbitrary. If the model is changed, the results change. The analysis of this chapter suggests that models grounded in intertemporal optimization are not entirely immune from this criticism either. The implications are shown to depend upon the specification, which to some degree is also arbitrary. This is particularly so in the case of the precise assumptions being made with respect to the cost of holding foreign bonds.

A good deal of the recent work in international macroeconomics focuses on the transmission of real disturbances. Chapter 12 constructs and analyses such a model. The critical feature of the model is the role of capital accumulation which, because of a convex, cost-of-adjustment function, can occur only gradually. This mechanism has become a standard means of introducing dynamics into this type of framework. The particular shock studied here is that of a tariff on the imported good, and we analyse the effect that this has on both the rate of capital accumulation and on the current account deficit. However, the model is more general than that and lends itself to the analysis of various fiscal, terms of trade and other disturbances.

The model assumes a single traded world bond. One interesting feature of this assumption is that in order to have a well-defined steady state, the rate of consumer time discount in the domestic economy (assumed to be small) must equal the given world interest rate. This in turn means that the marginal utility of consumption must be constant, and this introduces a zero root into the dynamics. As a consequence, the steady state of the economy depends upon the initial conditions in existence at the time any policy change is introduced. The effect of this in turn is that a temporary policy change – in this case a temporary change in the tariff – will lead to a permanent effect. This rather striking result can be identified with the phenomenon of "hysteresis" which has been receiving a lot of attention in connection with various European economies.

The specific results obtained in chapter 12 are also of interest and contrast with existing literature analysing the macrodynamic adjustments to tariffs. The present analysis shows that a tariff is contractionary in both the short and the long run, so that the intertemporal tradeoff emphasized by previous authors does not really exist. The initial reduction in investment leads to a current account surplus, while savings may or may nor rise.

V STRATEGIC ASPECTS OF POLICY-MAKING

The increasing interdependence between countries in the world economy has led to an interdependence in international macroeconomic policy-making. A policy implemented in one country will generate effects abroad, leading to appropriate policy responses. This has led to recent interest in the strategic aspects of macroeconomic policy-making in an international context. Part V contains three chapters dealing with these questions.

Chapter 13 uses a simple two-country monetary model, analogous to that developed in chapter 4, to consider the analysis of strategic monetary policy. The model is static, with each country being subjected to stochastic demand and supply shocks. Each policy-maker has an objective, which is to maximize a weighted average of the variances of output and the consumer price index. The stochastic disturbances introduce a conflict and each policy-maker is assumed to react in accordance with his objective function.

Two types of equilibria are considered – noncooperative and cooperative – and, within each class, three alternative outcomes are discussed. In the basic noncooperative equilibrium, the Cournot equilibrium, each agent takes the behavior of his rival as given and assumes that his rival does not react to his actions. However, each agent is shown to respond in accordance with a reaction function, so that *ex post* the assumption of no response is incorrect. In contrast, we also consider the so-called consistent conjectural variations equilibrium, in which each policy-maker, in determining his own actions, correctly conjectures the response of his opponent. Thirdly, we discuss the Stackelberg equilbrium in which one of the two policy-makers acts as a leader.

The basic cooperative equilibrium considered is the Pareto optimal, where the agents choose to maximize their joint welfare. In addition, two alternative forms of monetary systems are considered, namely the familiar perfectly fixed and perfectly flexible exchange rate regimes. These represent two forms of cooperative behavior where the policy-makers agree to follow particular monetary rules.

Several general conclusions are obtained. Demand shocks are much less problematic than supply shocks from the viewpoint of macroeconomic stabilization. The superiority of the Pareto optimal cooperative equilibrium over the various noncooperative equilibria is small, and almost negligible, when the relative price elasticity of demand is reasonably large. The strategic equilibria all show substantial margins of superiority over the traditional regimes of fixed and flexible exchange rates.

Chapter 14 extends this type of analysis to an intertemporal optimizing context. In this analysis dynamic strategic monetary rules are employed using the methods of dynamic game theory. Many possible strategic equilibria are candidates for consideration, depending upon the formation structure. This chapter compares three feedback solutions, namely feedback Nash, feedback Stackelberg, and a cooperative equilibrium. The policy rules are expressed in terms of adjustments in the real money supplies to movements in the real exchange rate. The welfare implications are analysed primarily using numerical simulation methods. The gains from cooperation are computed and found to be substantially larger than those obtained in the previous single-period analysis.

One important point concerning the specification of the model should be noted. The welfare costs, summarizing the solution, are expressed in terms of the current real exchange rate, which we denote s_1. If the current nominal exchange rate is permitted to jump instantaneously, then, with prices being predetermined as they are in this model, the real exchange rate may jump, thereby driving the economy instantaneously to steady-state equilibrium. In this case there would be no transitional dynamics. This of course is precisely how the economy is assumed to react when there is just one unstable root and no active stabilization policy is in effect.

However, there is a question of whether such a jump is optimal. Consider an economy which starts out from some inherited nominal and real exchange rate. The jump we have just been describing presumably imposes some initial adjustment costs on the economy, and these need to be taken into account in determining the desirability of such a jump. In fact, whether such a jump is desirable or not depends upon the nature of these costs. Under a broad class of cost functions, it is perfectly plausible for no initial jump in the exchange rate to be optimal, in which case the exchange rate can be treated as being predetermined. Thus while the model developed in chapter 14 does not include suich initial costs explicitly, they nevertheless implicitly underlie the dynamic adjustments being discussed.

The final chapter examines the gains from fiscal cooperation using a real trade model. The framework here is very different from that employed in the previous two chapters in that the welfares are assessed in terms of underlying utility functions of consumption, rather than in terms of macroeconomic quadratic loss functions. The analysis emphasizes the adjustments in the terms of trade and focuses on determining the effects in moving from a noncooperative Cournot–Nash equilibrium to a cooperative Pareto optimal outcome. In comparing the two, it finds that a noncooperative equilibrium leads to an over-expansion of government expenditure on export goods and an under-expansion of government expenditure on import goods, relative to the Pareto optimal outcome. A logarithmic example is used to compare the magnitudes of the gains as well as the welfare effects resulting from the formation of a coalition of two economies among a group of three. Extensions of this type of analysis, considering strategic behavior among more than two economies, would seem to be a fruitful area for future research.

Part I

Sticky Price Models

1 The Stability of Exchange Rate Dynamics under Perfect Myopic Foresight

(WITH M. R. GRAY)

1 INTRODUCTION

The stability of financial markets under conditions of perfect foresight has recently been a subject discussed extensively by monetary economists (see for example Sidrauski, 1967; Burmeister and Dobell, 1970; Nagatani, 1970; Olivera, 1971; Sargent and Wallace, 1973; Black, 1974). One of the main findings to come out of this literature is that the dynamics of such markets under perfect foresight will typically be associated with "saddlepoint-type" instability. That is, unless the initial conditions happen to place the system somewhere on the stable arm of the saddlepoint, the system will tend to arch around the equilibrium and ultimately to diverge from it.

One financial market of particular importance is the foreign exchange market. In a recent article, Dornbusch (1976) has developed an interesting model analysing the role of exchange rate expectations in the dynamic adjustment of the exchange rate following an exogenous change in monetary policy. While most of his analysis is based on an arbitrary regressive expectations hypothesis, he also considers what he calls "consistent expectations," when the hypothesis he introduces is consistent with a form of perfect myopic foresight.[1] This is obviously desirable since, as he argues, perfect myopic foresight is the only assumption which is not arbitrary and does not in general involve systematic forecasting errors.

At first sight, the stability of the Dornbusch model under consistent expectations may appear to contradict the above monetary literature.

Originally published in *International Economic Review*, 20 (3), October 1979, 643–60. We are indebted to W. A. Brock and E. Sieper for helpful discussions on the general approach underlying this chapter and to R. Dornbusch, G. Fane, D. Roper, and E. Sieper for their comments on earlier drafts.

The purpose of this chapter is therefore to investigate more fully the relationship of the Dornbusch analysis to the perfect foresight model. It is shown how the introduction of perfect myopic foresight into his model does indeed generate saddlepoint-type behavior. Stability of the system can then be achieved by following a procedure originally outlined by Sargent and Wallace (1973).[2] Essentially this involves integrating the system forwards in time and imposing certain terminal conditions which systems embodying optimizing behavior are known to satisfy (see for example Brock, 1974, 1975). These conditions ensure that the system is always on the stable arm of the saddle and is therefore always converging towards equilibrium. This approach can be justified on the grounds that it is desirable for any descriptive model (such as the Dornbusch model) to be consistent with optimizing behavior, at least to the extent of having comparable stability properties (see Brock). An important consequence of this approach is that any unanticipated discrete jump in the money supply will lead to an immediate discrete jump in the exchange rate. The magnitude of this jump is precisely that necessary to move the system from its present state onto the stable arm associated with the new equilibrium corresponding to the increased money supply. Thereafter, in the absence of additional monetary disturbances, the system will converge toward the new equilibrium. This jump is exactly identical with that obtained by Dornbusch and, as in his analysis, involves an initial overshooting of the exchange rate.

We also consider the effect of a pre-announced change in the money supply and show how the subsequent adjustment in the exchange rate consists of three phases. Following an initial jump, the exchange rate will continue to rise in a continuous exponential manner until the stable arm of the saddle is reached, which is then followed towards the new equilibrium. The announcement moderates the initial jump and indeed, with sufficient lead time, the *initial* overshooting may no longer occur. In this case, a lesser degree of overshooting will take place during the second (unstable) phase of the adjustment path.

In the latter part of the chapter we deal briefly with two further issues pertinent to the modeling of perfect myopic foresight. First, while the regressivity of expectations as modeled by Dornbusch can be consistent with perfect myopic foresight as long as the instability is of the saddlepoint type, not all instabilities associated with this assumption need to be of this kind. This is illustrated with a simple extension to the basic model in which the (single) root of the dynamic system is unstable, and regressivity can never be made consistent with perfect myopic foresight. Secondly, it is often thought that instability in financial markets is due solely to perfect myopic foresight. This is not so. Rather, it is due to the conjunction of this assumption with the instantaneous adjustment of the variables which are being predicted. Thus we are able to show how the system can be made unambiguously stable if the rate of adjustment in the exchange rate is sufficiently slow.

2 SADDLEPOINT BEHAVIOR UNDER PERFECT MYOPIC FORESIGHT

The Dornbusch model, modified to allow for perfect myopic foresight in predicting exchange rate changes, can be summarized by the following set of equations

$$R = R^* + X \tag{1.1a}$$

$$X = \dot{E} \tag{1.1b}$$

$$M - P = \alpha_1 Y + \alpha_2 R \qquad \alpha_1 > 0, \alpha_2 < 0 \tag{1.1c}$$

$$\dot{P} = \rho\{\beta_0 + (\beta_1 - 1)Y + \beta_2 R + \beta_3(E - P)\} \tag{1.1d}$$

$$0 < \beta_1 < 1, \beta_2 < 0, \beta_3 > 0, \rho > 0$$

where R^* is the foreign (nominal) rate of interest, taken to be exogenous, R is the domestic (nominal) interest rate, X is the expected rate of exchange depreciation, E is the logarithm of the current exchange rate (measured in units of domestic currency per unit of foreign currency), M is the logarithm of the domestic nominal money supply, taken to be exogenous, P is the logarithm of the domestic price level, Y is the logarithm of domestic real output, taken to be fixed.[3]

Equation (1.1a) asserts that, through arbitrage, the domestic interest rate is kept equal to the exogenous world rate plus the expected rate of change of the domestic currency price of foreign exchange. The second equation embodies the assumption of perfect myopic foresight. The demand for money is of the conventional type, with (1.1c) specifying continuous equilibrium in the domestic money market. Finally, (1.1d) is a price adjustment equation according to which the rate of domestic price adjustment is proportional to excess demand. This is given by the term in parentheses and is seen to vary negatively with income and the domestic interest rate and positively with the relative price $E - P$.

In order to simplify notation it is convenient to define an initial exogenous level of the money supply $\bar{M}$ and to consider subsequent changes in the money supply relative to this base level. By setting first derivatives to zero, the stationary equilibrium corresponding to $\bar{M}$ is attained where

$$\bar{R} = R^* \tag{1.2a}$$

$$\bar{X} = 0 \tag{1.2b}$$

$$\bar{M} - \bar{P} = \alpha_1 Y + \alpha_2 \bar{R} \tag{1.2c}$$

$$\beta_0 + (\beta_1 - 1)Y + \beta_2 \bar{R} + \beta_3(\bar{E} - \bar{P}) = 0 \tag{1.2d}$$

which determines the equilibrium levels of the endogenous variables, $\bar{R}$, $\bar{X}$, $\bar{E}$, $\bar{P}$ in terms of the exogenous variables and parameters. Taking total differentials of these equations and setting $\mathrm{d}Y$, $\mathrm{d}R^*$ equal to zero, it follows that

$$\mathrm{d}\bar{P} = \mathrm{d}\bar{E} = \mathrm{d}\bar{M} \tag{1.3}$$

implying that a *ceteris paribus* 1 percent increase in the domestic money supply will lead to a 1 percent increase in the equilibrium rate of exchange and in the domestic price level.

Subtracting (1.2) from (1.1), we can express the dynamics of the system about the initial equilibrium (1.2) in the form[4]

$$\begin{bmatrix} \dot{e} \\ \dot{p} \end{bmatrix} = \begin{bmatrix} 0 & -1/\alpha_2 \\ \rho\beta_3 & -\rho(\beta_3 + \beta_2/\alpha_2) \end{bmatrix} \begin{bmatrix} e \\ p \end{bmatrix} + \begin{bmatrix} 1/\alpha_2 \\ \rho\beta_2/\alpha_2 \end{bmatrix} m(t) \tag{1.4}$$

where $e = E - \bar{E}$, $p = P - \bar{P}$, and $m(t) = M(t) - \bar{M}$, so that $\dot{e} = \dot{E}$, $\dot{p} = \dot{P}$, and $\dot{m}(t) = \dot{M}(t)$. If the domestic money supply remains fixed at its initial level $\bar{M}$, then obviously $m(t) = 0$ and (1.4) is a homogeneous system. However, as we wish to consider changes in monetary policy (possibly with a time profile), we choose to introduce $m(t)$ explicitly, recognizing that it may be a function of time. The advantage of defining the system about its initial equilibrium is that it enables us to incorporate the constants and exogenous parameters of the system (such as R^*, Y, etc.) in $\bar{E}$, $\bar{P}$.

The usual approach to modeling dynamic systems of this type is to treat the initial values of e and p, e_0 and p_0, say, as exogenously given. With this assumption, it is clear from (1.4) that the assumption of perfect myopic foresight constrains the rate of change of the exchange rate; e is not free to jump instantaneously. From the first equation in (1.4), which is derived from the money market equilibrium condition, it is seen that an increase in M will lead to an instantaneous reduction in the rate of exchange depreciation $\dot{e}$, and not an increase in the level of the exchange rate e, as under the Dornbusch expectations assumption (see below), or for that matter as in the traditional Mundell–Fleming model.[5]

The characteristic equation for (1.4) is given by

$$\alpha_2\lambda^2 + \rho(\beta_2 + \beta_3\alpha_2)\lambda + \rho\beta_3 = 0 \tag{1.5}$$

the roots of which are both real and of opposite sign, implying the familiar saddlepoint property of the stationary equilibrium.[6] Denoting these roots by $\lambda_1 < 0$, $\lambda_2 > 0$, for fixed m, the dynamics of the system can be solved to yield

$$e(t) = \frac{1}{\alpha_2(\lambda_2 - \lambda_1)} \{\alpha_2\lambda_2 e_0 + p_0 - (1 + \alpha_2\lambda_2)m\} \exp(\lambda_1 t)$$

$$- \frac{1}{\alpha_2(\lambda_2 - \lambda_1)} \{\alpha_2\lambda_1 e_0 + p_0 - (1 + \alpha_2\lambda_1)m\} \exp(\lambda_2 t) + m \tag{1.6a}$$

$$p(t) = \frac{-\lambda_1}{\lambda_2 - \lambda_1} \{\alpha_2\lambda_2 e_0 + p_0 - (1 + \alpha_2\lambda_2)m\} \exp(\lambda_1 t)$$
$$+ \frac{\lambda_2}{\lambda_2 - \lambda_1} \{\alpha_2\lambda_1 e_0 + p_0 - (1 + \alpha_2\lambda_1)m\} \exp(\lambda_2 t) + m \tag{1.6b}$$

where e_0, p_0 are the exogenously given initial conditions. Hence both $e(t)$ and $p(t)$ will be unbounded unless[7]

$$\alpha_2\lambda_1 e_0 + p_0 - (1 + \alpha_2\lambda_1)m = 0 \tag{1.7}$$

Equations (1.6a) and (1.6b) are formal descriptions of the saddlepoint behavior. The stable arm is described by the locus

$$\alpha_2\lambda_1 e(t) + p(t) - (1 + \alpha_2\lambda_1)m = 0 \tag{1.8}$$

along which the dynamics can be described by

$$\dot{e} = \lambda_1(e - m) \qquad \lambda_1 < 0 \tag{1.9}$$

implying a stable first-order adjustment path. Likewise, the unstable arm is given by

$$\alpha_2\lambda_2 e(t) + p(t) - (1 + \alpha_2\lambda_2)m = 0 \tag{1.10}$$

or equivalently

$$\dot{e} = \lambda_2(e - m) \qquad \lambda_2 > 0 \tag{1.11}$$

so that e follows an unstable first-order path. In either case the dynamics can be expressed in terms of p and $\dot{p}$ rather than e and $\dot{e}$. Moreover it is obvious that if the system begins on either of the branches it will remain on that branch indefinitely.

In Figure 1.1 we illustrate the behavior of the system by considering a once-and-for-all change in the money supply. Assume initially that $M = \overline{M}$ $(m = 0)$ and that at the time of the increase in the money supply, given by m say, the system is in stationary state. Hence $e = p = 0$, so that this initial equilibrium is represented by the origin O. From equations (1.3) we see that in the steady state corresponding to the new money supply $m > 0$, say, P and E will increase in the same proportion as the money stock, so that the new equilibrium will be at the point Q where $p = m$, $e = m$. The values of the interest rate and the expected rate of exchange depreciation are of course unchanged in this new equilibrium. The lines XX and YY represent the stable and unstable arms respectively of the saddlepoint about the new equilibrium, with the directions of motion along the arms indicated by the arrows. Moreover, it is easily shown from (1.5) that $\lambda_1 + \lambda_2 < 0$ implying that

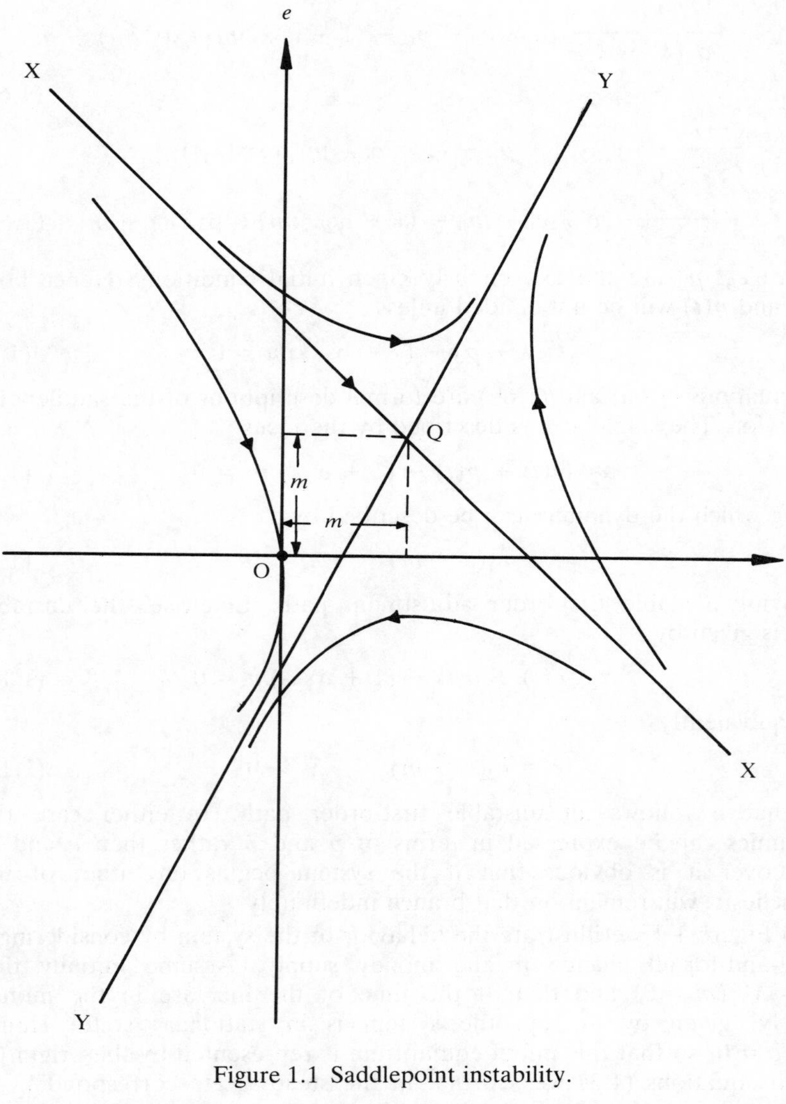

Figure 1.1 Saddlepoint instability.

the positively sloped line is relatively steeper as it has been drawn.[8]

Suppose that the increase in m occurs at time 0. At that exact instant of time, if the system begins from equilibrium, we must have

$$R(0) = \bar{R},$$
$$X(0) = \dot{e}(0) = \dot{p}(0) = e(0) = p(0) = 0. \tag{1.12}$$

However, with the money supply increased by m, these values are no longer consistent with money market clearance (equation (1.1c)) and since, by (1.1d), $\dot{p}$ cannot be infinite, R must jump to a value m/α_2 in order to clear the money market. This in turn requires similar jumps in X and $\dot{e}$, so as to clear the foreign exchange market and ensure that exchange rate changes are perfectly foreseen. The rate of inflation will also jump. Hence immediately after the increase in money stock at time 0, we must have

$$\begin{aligned} R(0+) = X(0+) = \dot{e}(0+) &= \frac{m}{\alpha_2} \\ e(0+) = p(0+) &= 0 \\ \dot{p}(0+) &= \frac{\rho\beta_2 m}{\alpha_2} \end{aligned} \tag{1.13}$$

so that with $\dot{e} < 0$, $\dot{p} > 0$, the exchange rate will start to fall and the price level start to rise. In figure 1.1 this is illustrated by a movement towards the unstable branch of the saddlepoint. Hence with e_0, p_0 thus constrained, a once-and-for-all change in the money stock generates an unstable adjustment process.

3 INTRODUCTION OF TERMINAL CONDITIONS TO ACHIEVE STABILITY

The result obtained above is the only solution that satisfies all the conditions thus far imposed, namely that equations (1.1a)–(1.1d) should hold for all $t \geqslant 0$, with $e(0)$ and $p(0)$ taking their given values e_0, p_0 respectively.[9] We now consider whether these requirements, which follow conventional methods for solving differential equations, make economic sense. Indeed upon reflection one of them seems to us to be somewhat unrealistic. One of the objectives of the analysis carried out above was to investigate the response of the system to a shock occurring at time zero (taken to be a jump in the money stock). Since shocks are by their very nature unanticipated events, it seems excessively stringent to require that expectations be perfectly accurate at the time that a shock is impinging on the system. But this is precisely the consequence of requiring (1.1b) to hold at $t = 0$.

In the light of these considerations we propose to modify the conditions to be satisfied by the solution as follows. Equations (1.1a), (1.1c), and (1.1d) are still required to hold for all $t \geqslant 0$, but now (1.1b) need apply only for $t > 0$; (1.1b) need not hold at $t = 0$. This frees E to jump at time 0, thereby rendering the predetermined value e_0 irrelevant for the future evolution of the system. This respecification of the system, while more in accord with the underlying economic behavior, does involve some complications. First there is the mathematical difficulty that the solution to the new conditions is not unique. In fact there is a separate solution for each initial jump in $e(0)$ one might care to specify. Secondly, it is feasible only as long as E is free to jump. If, as in section 4.2 below, E is constrained to continuous adjustments, this solution method is no longer applicable. For the present, however, we abstract from this latter complication.

To resolve the problem of the initial jump, we turn to the literature on monetary models derived from optimizing behavior. In this literature we find that an important role in the solution procedure is played by the transversality conditions. These state that only solutions satisfying certain terminal conditions represent optimizing behavior. The effect of imposing these conditions is typically to force the system onto the stable arm of the saddle, thereby ensuring stability of the resulting dynamic system. While it may not necessarily be feasible to derive behavioral relationships in macroeconomic models from a full dynamic optimization, it is desirable for descriptive models (such as this) to be generally consistent with corresponding optimizing models, insofar as their stability properties are concerned.

The transversality condition which some systems embodying optimizing behavior are known to satisfy (see Brock, 1974, 1975), and which we will invoke, is that the long-run level of the real money stock is strictly positive and finite. Since we will be concerned with analysing the system for various finite levels of the nominal money stock, this boundedness condition in effect means that the equilibrium price level is finite. This condition added to those respecified as above, is sufficient to ensure a unique solution as we will now show.

To begin, we write the solutions to (1.4) in their most general form, i.e.

$$e(t) = \exp(\lambda_1 t)\left\{A_1 + B_1\int_0^t m(\tau)\exp(-\lambda_1\tau)\,d\tau\right\} + \exp(\lambda_2 t)\left\{A_2 + B_2\int_0^t m(\tau)\exp(-\lambda_2\tau)\,d\tau\right\} \quad (1.14a)$$

$$p(t) = -(\lambda_1\alpha_2)\exp(\lambda_1 t)\left\{A_1 + B_1\int_0^t m(\tau)\exp(-\lambda_1\tau)\,d\tau\right\} - (\lambda_2\alpha_1)\exp(\lambda_2 t)\left\{A_2 + B_2\int_0^t m(\tau)\exp(-\lambda_2\tau)\,d\tau\right\} \quad (1.14b)$$

where as before $\lambda_1 < 0$, $\lambda_2 > 0$ are the two solutions to the characteristic equation (1.5).[10] The coefficients B_1, B_2 are the solutions to

$$B_1 + B_2 = 1/\alpha_2 \quad (1.15a)$$

$$\lambda_1 B_1 + \lambda_2 B_2 = -\frac{\rho\beta_2}{\alpha_2^2} \quad (1.15b)$$

while the remaining constants A_1, A_2 are arbitrary. In the previous section these were obtained by imposing initial conditions $e(0) = e_0$, $p(0) = p_0$. In the present context they will be determined by a combination of initial and terminal conditions.

With $p(t)$ evolving sluggishly, we continue to impose the initial price level p_0 as an initial condition for (1.14a) and (1.14b). Setting $t = 0$ in (1.14b), we obtain

$$\lambda_1 A_1 + \lambda_2 A_2 = -p_0/\alpha_2 \tag{1.16a}$$

In order to impose our second condition, that the real money supply remain strictly positive and finite for all t, we let $t \to \infty$ in (1.14). Assuming $m(t)$ is bounded, we can apply L'Hôpital's rule to find that the limit of the first term is

$$\lim_{t\to\infty}\left[-(\lambda_1\alpha_2)\exp(\tau_1 t)\left\{A_1 + B_1\int_0^t m(\tau)\exp(-\lambda_1\tau)\,\mathrm{d}\tau\right\}\right] = \alpha_2 B_1 m(\infty)$$

which, as long as $m(\tau)$ is bounded, will be finite.[11] Turning to the second term, with $\lambda_2 > 0$, a necessary condition for the price level to be bounded is

$$\lim_{t\to\infty}\left\{A_2 + B_2\int_0^t m(\tau)\exp(-\lambda_2\tau)\,\mathrm{d}\tau\right\} = 0$$

or

$$A_2 = -B_2\int_0^\infty m(\tau)\exp(-\lambda_2\tau)\,\mathrm{d}\tau \tag{1.16b}$$

In this case the term

$$-(\lambda_2\alpha_2)\exp(-\lambda_2 t)\left\{A_2 + B_2\int_0^t m(\tau)\exp(-\lambda_2\tau)\,\mathrm{d}\tau\right\} \to \alpha_2\beta_2 m(\infty)$$

which, with $m(\tau)$ bounded, will also remain finite.

Solving (1.16a) and (1.16b) for the constants A_1, A_2, we can express the final solution for the system in the form

$$\begin{aligned} e(t) = {} & \exp(\lambda_1 \mathrm{t})\left\{\frac{-p_0}{\alpha_2\lambda_1} + \frac{\lambda_2}{\lambda_1}B_2\int_0^\infty m(\tau)\exp(\lambda_2\tau)\,\mathrm{d}\tau\right. \\ & \left. + B_1\int_0^t m(\tau)\exp(-\lambda_1\tau)\,\mathrm{d}\tau\right\} \\ & - B_2\exp(\lambda_2 t)\int_t^\infty m(\tau)\exp(-\lambda_2\tau)\,\mathrm{d}\tau \end{aligned} \tag{1.17a}$$

$$\begin{aligned} p(t) = {} & \exp(\lambda_1 t)\left\{p_0 - \lambda_2\alpha_2 B_2\int_0^\infty m(\tau)\exp(-\lambda_2\tau)\,\mathrm{d}\tau\right. \\ & \left. - \lambda_1\alpha_2 B_1\int_0^t m(\tau)\exp(-\lambda_1\tau)\,\mathrm{d}\tau\right\} \\ & + \lambda_2\alpha_2 B_2\exp(\lambda_2 t)\int_t^\infty m(\tau)\exp(-\lambda_2\tau)\,\mathrm{d}\tau \end{aligned} \tag{1.17b}$$

where B_1, B_2 are given by (1.15). These two equations express the time path for the exchange rate and price level in terms of the initial price level p_0 and the time path of money supply $m(\tau)$.[12] Because of the way that A_1, A_2 have been chosen, provided that $m(\tau)$ remains finite, both $e(t)$ and $p(t)$ will be bounded.

Of particular interest is the initial jump in the exchange rate. In terms of the notation introduced in eqn (1.13), this is denoted by $e(0+)$ and is obtained by considering the limit of (1.17a) as $t \to 0$. This gives

$$e(0+) = \frac{-p_0}{\alpha_2\lambda_1} + B_2\frac{\lambda_2 - \lambda_1}{\lambda_1}\int_0^\infty m(\tau)\exp(-\lambda_2\tau)\,\mathrm{d}\tau \tag{1.18}$$

and depends upon the initial price level p_0 as well as the time path of the (expected) future money supply. If the money supply remains constant at m say, (1.18) integrates to

$$e(0+) = \frac{-p_0}{\alpha_2\lambda_1} + B_2\frac{\lambda_2 - \lambda_1}{\lambda_1\lambda_2}m \tag{1.19}$$

By direct calculation it can be shown that

$$B_2\frac{\lambda_2 - \lambda_1}{\lambda_1\lambda_2} = \frac{\rho\beta_2 + \alpha_2\lambda_1}{\rho\beta_3\alpha_2} = 1 + \frac{1}{\alpha_2\lambda_1} \tag{1.20}$$

the latter equality following from the fact that λ_1 is a root of (1.5).[13] Substituting (1.20) into (1.19) yields

$$e(0+) = \frac{-p_0}{\alpha_2\lambda_1} + \left(1 + \frac{1}{\alpha_2\lambda_1}\right)m \tag{1.21}$$

and comparing (1.21) with (1.7) it is seen that $e(0+)$, p_0 lies on the stable arm of the saddle passing through the equilibrium corresponding to m. In other words, whatever the fixed money supply happens to be, the initial value of the exchange rate adjusts so as to place the system on the stable arm of the saddle passing through the corresponding equilibrium. This is illustrated in figure 1.2.

Consider now a (previously) unanticipated expansion in the money supply of m at time 0, but which is now expected to continue indefinitely. As we have seen this causes the equilibrium levels of both e and p shift by m. As a consequence the stable arm of the saddle will undergo a parallel shift equal to $(1 + 1/\alpha_2\lambda_1)m$ from XX to X′X′. If initially the system is at point A on XX, it is seen from (1.21) that the exchange rate will immediately jump by an amount

$$\frac{\mathrm{d}e(0+)}{\mathrm{d}m} = 1 + \frac{1}{\alpha_2\lambda_1} > 1 \tag{1.22}$$

which is precisely that necessary to reach the new stable arm at A′.[14] Thereafter, in the absence of any additional monetary disturbances, the system will follow X′X′ until the new equilibrium Q is reached.

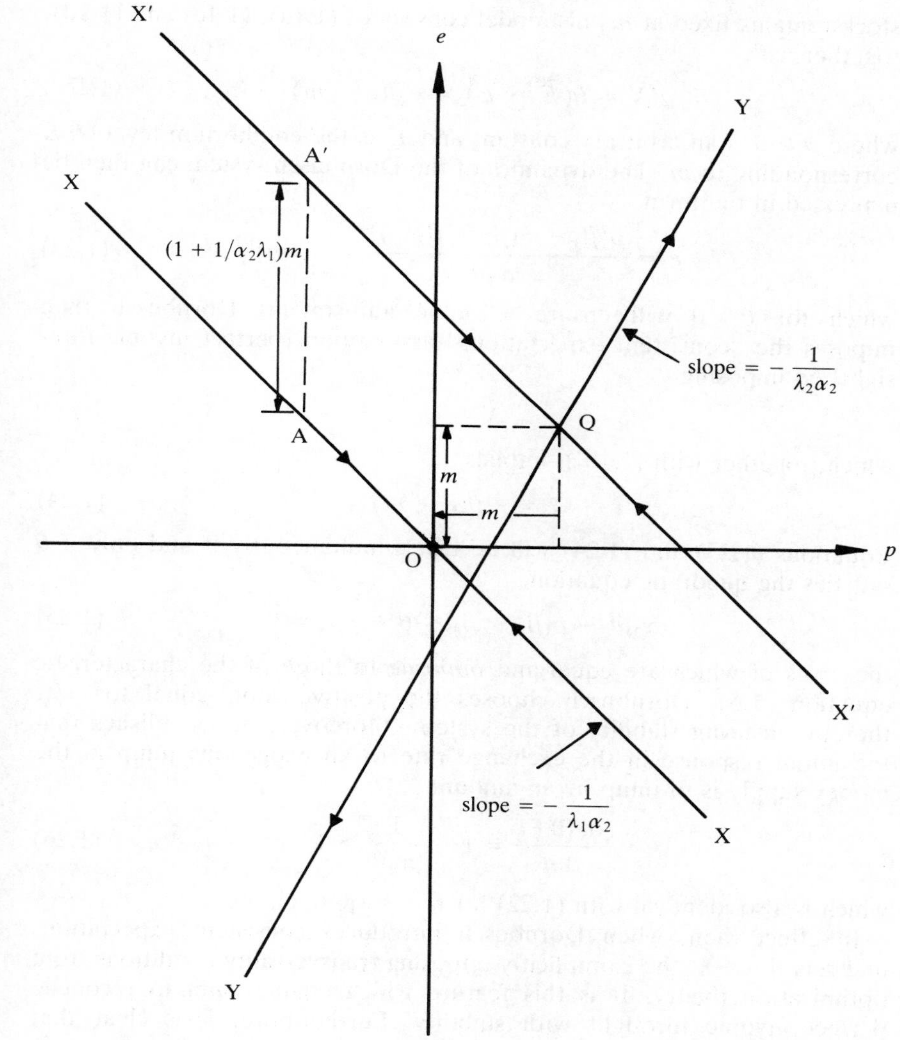

Figure 1.2 Response to expansionary monetary policy.

Comparing (1.22) and (1.3) it is seen that the initial jump involves an overshooting in the exchange rate.

This response to an expansionary monetary policy is precisely the same as that obtained by Dornbusch. He initially replaces the assumption of perfect myopic foresight (1.1b) with the assumption that expectations are formed regressively. If it is assumed that the nominal money stock remains fixed at m, his model consists of (1.1a), (1.1c) and (1.1d), together with

$$X = \theta(\widetilde{E} - E) = -\theta(e - m) \tag{1.1b'}$$

where $\theta > 0$ is an arbitrary constant and $\widetilde{E}$ is the equilibrium level of E corresponding to m. The dynamics of the Dornbusch system can then be expressed in the form

$$\dot{e} = \frac{\rho\{\beta_3 - \theta(\beta_2 + \beta_3\alpha_2)\}}{\alpha_2\theta}(e - m) \tag{1.23}$$

which for $\theta > 0$ will ensure a stable adjustment. Dornbusch then imposes the "consistent expectations" assumption (perfect myopic foresight) by imposing

$$X = \dot{e}$$

which, together with (1.1b′), implies

$$\dot{e} = -\theta(e - m) \tag{1.24}$$

Equations (1.23) and (1.24) will be true simultaneously if and only if θ satisfies the quadratic equation

$$\alpha_2\theta^2 - \rho(\beta_2 + \beta_3\alpha_2)\theta + \rho\beta_3 = 0 \tag{1.25}$$

the roots of which are equal and *opposite* to those of the characteristic equation (1.5). Dornbusch chooses the positive root, equal to $-\lambda_1$, thereby ensuring stability of the system. Moreover, he establishes that the initial response in the exchange rate to an exogenous jump in the money supply is to jump by an amount

$$\frac{de(0+)}{dm} = 1 - \frac{1}{\alpha_2\theta} > 1 \tag{1.26}$$

which is also identical with (1.22) for $\theta = -\lambda_1$.

In effect then, when Dornbusch introduces consistent expectations and sets $\theta = -\lambda_1$, he is implicitly imposing transversality conditions from optimization theory. It is this feature which enables him to reconcile perfect myopic foresight with stability. Furthermore, it is clear that (1.1b′) is the *only ad hoc* expectations hypothesis which can be made consistent with perfect myopic foresight in a model involving saddlepoint-behavior.

In this regard one further point should be noted. It is apparent that under the Dornbusch expectations assumption, as in our formulation, perfect myopic foresight must be suspended for the instant during which the jump in m and hence e occurs; $\dot{e}$ must momentarily become *infinite* and clearly cannot equal the *finite* expected rate of exchange depreciation implied by the Dornbusch hypothesis. Perfect myopic foresight is restored immediately after the completion of the jump.

The fact that an increase in the money stock will lead to an initial overshooting in the exchange rate is an important feature of the Dornbusch model which he discusses at some length. This is associated with a *monotonic* adjustment in the price level to its new equilibrium. Our relationship (1.17) enables us to determine the impacts of a whole time profile of monetary policies on the system in general and on the exchange rate in particular.

As an example, it is of some interest to consider the effect of an increase in m which is announced at time 0 to take effect at a future time $t = T$ say. In this situation it is natural to have the jump take place when the information on which individuals' expectations are based changes; i.e. at $t = 0$ rather than when the by now perfectly anticipated change actually takes place at $t = T$. The effect of this policy on the exchange rate over the period $(0, T)$ (before the policy is put into effect) can be written in the form[15]

$$\frac{\mathrm{d}e(t)}{\mathrm{d}m} = \frac{(1 + 1/\alpha_2\lambda_1)\{\lambda_2 \exp(\lambda_1 t) - \lambda_1 \exp(\lambda_2 t)\} \exp(-\lambda_2 T)}{\lambda_2 - \lambda_1} > 0 \tag{1.27}$$

In particular, the initial impact on the exchange rate is

$$\frac{\mathrm{d}e(0+)}{\mathrm{d}m} = \left(1 + \frac{1}{\alpha_2\lambda_1}\right) \exp(-\lambda_2 T) < \left(1 + \frac{1}{\alpha_2\lambda_1}\right) \tag{1.28$'$}$$

from which it can be seen that the announcement moderates the initial jump in the exchange rate: the longer is the lead time, the smaller is the initial jump.[16] Moreover, for

$$T > \frac{\ln(1 + 1/\alpha_2\lambda_1)}{\lambda_2} \tag{1.28}$$

the *initial* overshoot will no longer apply. However, overshooting at some other intermediate time point T_1 say $(0 \leqslant T_1 \leqslant T)$ will still occur. From (1.27) it is seen that the exchange rate will continue to rise in an essentially exponential fashion until it reaches the stable arm of the saddle, which it will do at time T. Thereafter it will follow this stable trajectory into the new equilibrium.

The fact that overshooting in the exchange rate must eventually occur can be established as follows. Differentiating (1.17a) with respect to t it is readily shown that $e(t)$ increases monotonically over the time interval $0 \leqslant t \leqslant T$. Hence for such overshooting not to occur we must have

$$\frac{\mathrm{d}e(T)}{\mathrm{d}m} < 1$$

and therefore

$$\exp\{(\lambda_1 - \lambda_2)T\} < \frac{\lambda_1(1 + \alpha_2\lambda_2)}{\lambda_2(1 + \alpha_2\lambda_1)} \tag{1.29}$$

The left-hand side of (1.29) is positive. Give $\lambda_1 < 0$, $\lambda_2 > 0$, $(1 + \alpha_2\lambda_1) > 0$, the sign of the right-hand side depends upon that of $1 + \alpha_2\lambda_2$, which from the characteristic equation (1.5) can be shown to be unmbiguously positive. The right-hand side of (1.29) is therefore negative, so that the inequality (1.29) can never hold, implying that there is no lead time for which overshooting can be avoided. In other words, even if the monetary expansion is announced some time in

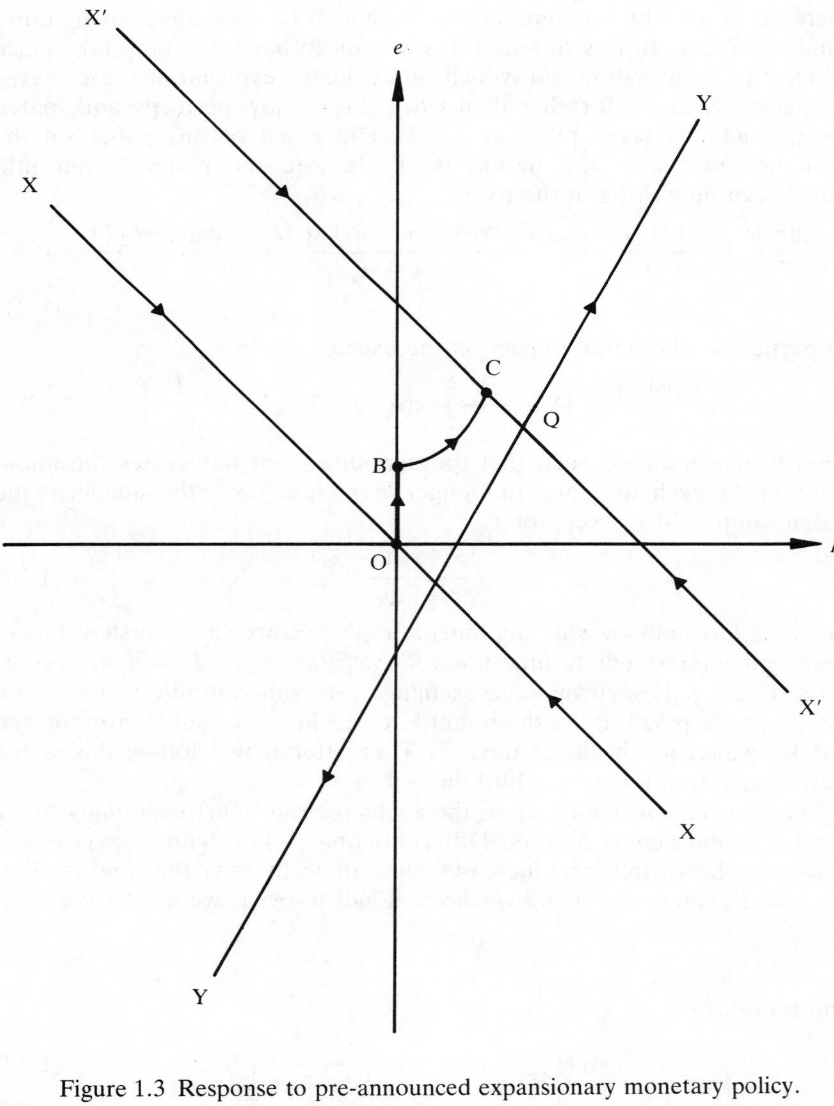

Figure 1.3 Response to pre-announced expansionary monetary policy.

advance, overshooting in the exchange rate must ultimately occur during the transition to the stable branch. This is illustrated in figure 1.3 by the path OBCQ which also illustrates how the lead time moderates the amount of overshooting.

4 SOME FURTHER ISSUES

In this section we briefly consider two further issues pertaining to the stability properties of perfect myopic foresight. These concern (a) the possibility that the instability may not be of the saddlepoint variety, and (b) how the introduction of appropriate sluggish adjustment in the system may convert a saddlepoint into a fully stable system.

4.1 Nonsaddlepoint instability

One way of viewing the Dornbusch procedure of requiring a relationship such as (1.1b′) to hold is that it imposes a structure on the system which may or may not be consistent with perfect myopic foresight. In the present context it turns out that, at least along the stable arm, perfect myopic foresight can be consistent with regressive expectations as specified by (1.1b′).[17]

However, this is possible only if the instability is of the saddlepoint variety. Instabilities associated with perfect foresight are not always of this kind; to illustrate the limitations of the above procedure we introduce a simple modification to the price adjustment equation, when consistency of perfect myopic foresight with this form of regressivity is no longer obtained.

Specifically we replace (1.1d) in the system (1.1a)–(1.1d) above by

$$\dot{P} = \rho\{\beta_0 + (\beta_1 - 1)Y + \beta_2 R + \beta_3(\mathrm{E} - \mathrm{P})\} + Q \qquad (1.1\mathrm{d}')$$

$$0 < \beta_1 < 1,\ \beta_2 < 0,\ \beta_3 > 0,\ \rho > 0$$

where Q denotes the anticipated rate of price inflation. Equation (1.1d′) embodies the Friedman–Phelps explanation of price determination, in which the rate of price information depends on the anticipated rate of inflation as well as on the state of excess product demand.[18] In accordance with the accelerationist hypothesis the coefficient of Q in this relationship is set equal to unity. Specifying that inflationary expectations also exhibit perfect myopic foresight, i.e.

$$Q = \dot{P} \qquad (1.1\mathrm{e})$$

completes a fairly conventional extension of the basic model, now comprising (1.1a), (1.1b), (1.1c) (1.1d′), and (1.1e), to incorporate inflationary expectations.

Proceeding as above, the dynamics can be written in the following form

$$(\alpha_2\beta_3 + \beta_2)\dot{e} + \beta_3 e = \beta_3 m(t) \tag{1.30}$$

the characteristic root λ of which is

$$\lambda = \frac{-\beta_3}{\alpha_2\beta_3 + \beta_2} > 0 \tag{1.31}$$

This equilibrium does not have a saddlepoint property and there is no stable locus which will move the system into the origin. The only way to stabilize the model is to set $X = Q = 0$. For unanticipated changes this imposes instantaneous adjustment to the steady state.[19] In effect, perfect myopic foresight is inconsistent with regressive expectations, at least as they are specified by (1.1b′).

4.2 Sluggish adjustment

Since saddlepoint-type instability has been widely obtained for models incorporating perfect myopic foresight, it might be thought that these two phenomena are inevitably associated.[20] This impression would be reinforced if we were to replace the assumption of perfect myopic foresight with regressive expectations in either of the unstable models above, for such a modification would restore stability. It is our aim in this section to show that this impression is misleading. Rather, saddlepoint behavior is caused by the conjunction of the assumptions of perfect myopic foresight and instantaneous adjustment of the variables about which expectations are being formed.[21] We illustrate this by modifying the original model to make exchange rate adjustment sluggish. Although the interest rate also adjusts instantaneously, this does not destabilize the system because interest rate expectations play no part in the model. Moreover, had we chosen to make interest rate adjustment sluggish, while allowing exchange rates to adjust instantaneously, the instability would still have remained. For the model incorporating price expectations the modification discussed below is also sufficient to ensure stability, since prices are already assumed to adjust sluggishly according to (1.1d).

Thus in the system (1.1a)–(1.1d), we replace (1.1a) by

$$\dot{E} = \gamma(R^* + X - R) \qquad \gamma > 0 \tag{1.1a′}$$

describing the sluggish adjustment in the exchange rate. In effect (1.1a′) asserts that the incipient capital flows, which Dornbusch assumes will ensure that (1.1a) holds at all times, take place at a finite rate over time. If $R > R^* + X$, so that the domestic interest rate exceeds the expected return to domestic residents on holding foreign securities, there will be a tendency for a capital inflow, leading to an appreciation of the domestic currency. The adjustment is reversed if $R < R^* + X$.

Proceeding as before, we deduce that the characteristic equation describing the evolution of this system is

$$\alpha_2\lambda^2 + \rho(\beta_2 + \beta_3\alpha_2)\lambda - \frac{\beta_3\gamma\rho}{1-\gamma} = 0 \tag{1.32}$$

which is stable if and only if[22]

$$\gamma < 1 \tag{1.33}$$

That is, the rate of exchange depreciation must be less than the degree of interest rate disequilibrium. In this case it follows that the jump in $\dot{e}$ stemming from an increase in the money stock is given by

$$\frac{\partial \dot{e}}{\partial m} = \frac{-\gamma}{(1-\gamma)\alpha_2}$$

implying that an increase in m will lead to an *increase* in the rate of exchange depreciation, rather than a decrease as was the case in (1.4). Since the domestic currency will be overvalued at this point, the system is moving back toward equilibrium whereas in the original model it was moving away. The Dornbusch regressivity hypothesis acts by causing a jump in the exchange rate so that the currency is undervalued and the appreciation that takes place subsequently along the stable arm of the saddle is moving the system back toward equilibrium.

If $\gamma > 1$, however, the usual saddlepoint property will be obtained; in particular, as $\gamma \rightarrow \infty$ the model will converge to the previous case. The borderline case $\gamma = 1$ implies that the domestic interest rate is pegged at the exogenous world rate. With price movements constrained by (1.1d), there is nothing to ensure continuous equilibrium in the money market and the logical consistency of the model breaks down.

The stability condition $\gamma < 1$ is of course an empirical matter. If it is believed that the arbitrage process whereby interest rate parity is attained operates quickly, then this condition will presumably not be met. However, the main point of this example is to illustrate how sluggish adjustment in the appropriate market may avoid the saddle-point problem even though perfect myopic foresight is assumed.[23]

As a final point we can observe that the analysis of section 4.1 can also be expressed in these terms. Dornbusch's original specification featured sluggish adjustment of the price of goods (see (1.1d)). Our modification to (1.1d′) caused the price of goods to adjust instantaneously. To see this, combine (1.1d′) and (1.1f), which gives

$$\beta_0 + (\beta_1 - 1)Y + \beta_2 R + \beta_3(E - P) = 0 \tag{1.34}$$

The expression on the left-hand side of (1.34) is the excess demand for goods, and this equation asserts that the price of goods adjust so that this quantity is always zero. Thus the model of section 4.1 incorporated perfect myopic foresight in forming expectations about both the exchange rate and the price of goods together with the assumption that both these markets should adjust instantaneously. As we have shown, it is the combination of these assumptions which eliminates the saddlepoint, and with it the possibility of a stable gradual adjustment.

NOTES

1. We say that forecasts of a given variable satisfy perfect myopic foresight if the expected instantaneous rate of change of that variable equals its actual instantaneous rate of change. This relationship is not always defined explicitly in the literature; see Turnovsky and Burmeister (1977) for further discussion of this issue.
2. In this regard we should also note the related contribution by Stanley Black (1973) to the analysis of exchange markets under rational expectations.
3. Dornbusch also briefly discusses an extension to his model in which real output is determined endogenously. Clearly a similar extension is possible here.
4. For notational convenience we sometimes drop the time argument from $e(t)$, $p(t)$. However, for the money supply m denotes a constant level, with $m(t)$ being used where the time path is arbitrary.
5. See for example Mundell (1960), Fleming (1962).
6. The saddlepoint-type instability of the exchange rate under perfect myopic foresight has been previously discussed by Kouri (1976). He comments how, in his model, perfect myopic foresight renders the exchange rate indeterminate, analogous to a similar indeterminacy in the price level obtained elsewhere by Black (1974). In both cases, these indeterminacies in the steady state exchange (price) level are consequences of the monetary growth rule that they adopt. With the money supply fixed, this indeterminacy does not arise in the present context. Both the steady state level of the exchange rate and given initial conditions, the (unstable) adjustment path are uniquely determined.
7. We should note that if one extends this kind of model to an inflationary environment and includes such aspects as the accumulation of financial wealth and the inflation tax on financial wealth, it is possible for the system to be stable under perfect myopic foresight. For an example of such a model, see Turnovsky and Kingston (1977).
8. It can also be shown that slope of YY exceeds unity so that O lies above the line YY.
9. We understand these conditions to subsume the requirement that all variables entering the system, e.g. R, X, E, etc., should be defined for $t \geqslant 0$. It is in order to satisfy this requirement that we rule out jumps in P and E which would leave $\dot{P}$ and $\dot{E}$ undefined.
10. This is a standard formula (see for example Kaplan, 1958, ch. 6).
11. If we write this term formally as

$$\frac{-(\lambda_1\alpha_2)\{A_1 + B_1\int_0^t m(\tau)\exp(-\lambda_1\tau)\,d\tau\}}{\exp(-\lambda_1 t)}$$

it is seen to be of the form ∞/∞ as $t \to \infty$, to which L'Hôpital's rule is directly applicable.

12. It should be noted that since we are integrating forward in time, the term $m(\tau)$ for $t > \tau$ strictly speaking refer to *expectations* of the money supply for time τ held at time t.
13. The essential steps involve solving for B_2 from (1.15) and applying standard results from the theory of equations to the characteristic equation (1.5).
14. If the expansion in the money supply at time 0 is anticipated through some previous announcement, there will be no jump at time 0. In this case the jump will occur at the time that the announcement is made and expectations are revised (see below).
15. This expression if obtained by setting $m(\tau) = 0$, $0 \leq \tau < T$ and $m(\tau) = m$, $\tau > T$ in (1.17a) and differentiating the resulting expression for $e(t)$ with respect to m.
16. This parallels a similar result obtained with respect to jumps in the price level by Sargent and Wallace (1973).
17. There are, however, other possible specifications of regressive expectations, and these may not be consistent with perfect myopic foresight. One obvious case is the adaptive hypothesis which is necessarily inconsistent with perfect myopic foresight for any finite rate of adaptation.
18. See Friedman (1968) and Phelps (1968). We might also wish to include Q in the money demand function as representing the expected yield of stocks of good relative to the yield on money. This yields a model with two possibly complex roots, both of which are unstable, so that our conclusions would not be affected.
19. Such jumps can also be justified by the methods of section 3 (see Sargent and Wallace, 1973).
20. Here we are using stability to characterize the results of the standard solution techniques, exemplified by (1.4)–(1.7).
21. Our discussion here is an application of ideas developed in greater detail by Burmeister and Turnovsky (1978).
22. If stable, the convergence will be monotonic or cyclical according as

$$\rho(1 - \gamma)(\beta_2 + \beta_3\alpha_3)^2 + 4\alpha_2\beta_3\gamma \gtreqless 0.$$

For very low values of γ the former case will occur; cyclical adjustment will tend to occur as γ approaches unity.

23. This same procedure can be used to stabilize the Sargent–Wallace (1973) model.

REFERENCES

Black, F. (1974) Uniqueness of the price level in monetary growth models with rational expectations. *Journal of Economic Theory* 7, 53–65.

Black, S. W. (1973) *International Money Markets and Flexible Exchange Rates*. Princeton Studies in International Finance, no. 32.

Brock, W. A. (1974) Money and growth: the case of long-run perfect foresight. *International Economic Review*, 15, 750–77.

—— (1975) A simple perfect foresight monetary model. *Journal of Monetary Economics*, 1, 133–50.

Burmeister, E. and Dobell, A. R. (1970) *Mathematical Theories of Economic Growth*. New York: Macmillan.

—— and Turnovsky, S. J. (1978) Price expectations, disequilibrium adjustments, and macro-economic stability. *Journal of Economic Theory*, 17, 287–311.

Dornbusch, R. (1976) Exchange rate expectations and monetary policy. *Journal of Political Economy*, 84, 1161–76.

Fleming, J. M. (1962) Domestic financial policies under fixed and floating exchange rates. *IMF Staff Papers*, 9, 369–79.

Friedman, M. (1968) The role of monetary policy. *American Economic Review*, 58, 1–17.

Kaplan, W. (1958) *Ordinary Differential Equations* Reading, MA: Addison-Wesley.

Kouri, P. J. K. (1976) The exchange rate and the balance of payments in the short run and in the long run: A Monetary Approach. *Scandinavian Journal of Economics*, 78, 280–304.

Mundell, R. A. (1960) The monetary dynamics of international adjustment under fixed and flexible exchanges rates. *Quarterly Journal of Economics*, 74, 227–57.

Nagatani, K. (1970) A note on Professor Tobin's money and economic growth. *Econometrica*, 38, 171–75.

Olivera, J. H. (1971) A note on passive money, inflation and economic growth. *Journal of Money, Credit and Banking*, 3, 137–44.

Phelps, E. S. (1968) Money-wage dynamics and labor-market equilibrium. *Journal of Political Economy*, 76, 678–711.

Sargent, T. J. and Wallace, N. (1973) The stability of models of money and growth with perfect foresight. *Econometrica*, 41, 1043–48.

Sidrauski, M. (1967) Inflation and economic growth. *Journal of Political Economy*. 75, 796–810.

Turnovsky, S. J. and Burmeister, E. (1977) Perfect foresight, expectational consistency and macroeconomic equilibrium. *Journal of Political Economy*, 85, 379–93.

—— and Kingston, G. H. (1977) Monetary and fiscal policies under flexible exchange rates and perfect myopic foresight in an inflationary world. *Scandinavian Journal of Economics*, 79, 424–41.

2 Covered Interest Parity, Uncovered Interest Parity, and Exchange Rate Dynamics

(WITH J. EATON)

1 INTRODUCTION

The advent of floating rates among the major currencies has led to the development of increasingly sophisticated models of open economies in which exchange rates are market determined. As was pointed out in the early work of Fleming (1962) and Mundell (1963), the degree of international capital mobility is crucial in determining the response of an economy to both monetary and fiscal actions. While the Fleming–Mundell analysis is based on the traditional static short-run model, the importance of the degree of capital mobility applies to the long-run response as well.

Perhaps because capital does seem to be very mobile among the major industrial countries, the polar assumption of perfect capital mobility has received most attention. This assumption can be interpreted in two different ways, however. The first, weaker, version is that bonds that are free of default risk domestically are also free of default risk abroad; in Aliber's (1973) terminology, there is no "political" risk. When capital mobility of this degree obtains, foreign bonds on which forward cover has been obtained are perfect substitutes for domestic bonds and arbitrage brings the domestic interest rate R into equality with the foreign interest rate R^* plus the forward premium F on foreign exchange. Thus *covered* interest parity (CIP) obtains:

$$R = R^* + F \tag{2.1}$$

Originally published in *The Economic Journal*, 93, September 1983, 555–75. We wish to thank Gene M. Grossman, a referee, and an Associate Editor for some helpful comments on this paper.

where R, R^*, and F are defined over the same time interval. In fact, empirical evidence suggests that, among the major industrial nations, deviations from CIP are not significant (see for example Aliber, 1973; Frenkel and Levich, 1975, 1977).

A stronger definition of capital mobility is one that adds to the criterion for the first, the requirement that attitudes towards exchange risk be characterized by risk neutrality, either because there exists a sufficient number of risk-neutral speculators or because exchange risk is perfectly diversifiable. In this case speculation will bring the forward premium on foreign exchange into equality with the expected rate of appreciation of the foreign currency:

$$F = (\dot{E}/E)^{e} \tag{2.2}$$

where E denotes the price of foreign currency in terms of domestic currency, and where, for any variable X, we define $\dot{X} \equiv \mathrm{d}X/\mathrm{d}t$, and X^{e} denotes the expectation of X. Substituting (2.2) into (2.1) yields the condition

$$R = R^* + (\dot{E}/E)^{e} \tag{2.3}$$

a condition that is referred to as *uncovered* interest parity (UIP) and requires both (2.1) and (2.2) to hold.[1]

However, the empirical evidence in support of (2.2) is not as strong as it is for (2.1). Bilson (1978), Levich (1978) and Hansen and Hodrick (1980) report some systematic deviations for several exchange rates over long periods.[2] These findings are consistent with financial models of foreign investment which suggest that risk aversion among rational fully informed speculators will create a risk premium, thereby causing (2.2) to break down. Solnik (1973), Kouri (1976), Adler and Dumas (1977), Frankel (1979), and Eaton and Turnovsky (1981) derive various expressions for this premium based on expected utility maximization.

However, despite the lack of theoretical justification for UIP and the empirical evidence against it, most well-known results about the behavior of macroeconomic models with perfectly mobile capital require this stronger definition to apply. This chapter develops a model of a small open economy under the more general assumption that the forward premium on foreign exchange is determined by risk-averse speculative behavior. Capital is still perfectly mobile in the weaker sense that CIP obtains and a special case of our model is one in which the degree of risk aversion tends to zero, in which case UIP applies as well. We use this model to examine several propositions about the behavior of a small open economy with a flexible exchange rate. These pertain to the effects of changes in domestic asset supplies and foreign interest rate on the steady-state levels of the domestic interest rate and exchange rate, the effects of ongoing government deficits, and the dynamic behavior of the exchange rate between steady states. Our purpose in this analysis is twofold. First we wish to illustrate the implications, some of them rather implausible, of assumptions that have been prominent in the literature. Second we wish to examine the behavior of the exchange rate under a more general specification which is consistent with a more plausible set of outcomes.

In section 2 we develop a dynamic model of an open ecomomy in which the exchange rate, interest rate, and forward premium are determined at each instant by money market and forward market equilibrium conditions together with CIP. At any moment, the price of nontraded goods and asset supplies are predetermined, while we treat the foreign interest rate and price level as exogenous. Over time, the price of nontraded goods adjusts gradually to the price of traded goods and the supplies of domestic assets change through the government deficit, while the balance of payments on current account determines the change in foreign asset supplies. With risk-averse speculative behavior, exchange rate and price dynamics on the one hand become inherently linked with asset supply dynamics on the other. For the system as a whole, and the exchange rate and interest rate in particular, to be in steady state, all asset accumulation must cease and, for this to occur, both the budget deficit and the balance of payments on current account must equal zero.

In the limiting case in which speculators are risk neutral, the conditions for the exchange rate and price level to attain steady state may be relaxed. For example, with a bond-financed government deficit, it is necessary only for the budget deficit and current account surplus to sum to zero. Thus the exchange rate and price level can be in steady state even if the government deficit is perpetually unbalanced, as long as it is offset by an appropriate imbalance on the current account. Thus when UIP obtains a small country can run a perpetual current account deficit without affecting its exchange rate or its interest rate.[3] If, in addition to UIP, asset supplies do not affect the demand for money, the exchange rate and the price level evolve independently of the government deficit and the balance of payments on current account outside of steady state. In this case, the exchange rate and price level can be in steady state even if these two quantities do not sum to zero.[4]

These observations are of relevance to a number of recent studies of exchange rate and price dynamics (e.g. Dornbusch, 1976; Gray and Turnovsky, 1979, this volume, ch. 1; Wilson, 1979) in which domestic and foreign bond supplies play no explicit role. This exclusion is legitimate only under the strong assumption of UIP (an assumption that all these authors make). Furthermore, Mundell's (1963) finding that under flexible rates of government deficit will not disturb the steady state exchange rate or interest rate (because its effect on the total bond supply is offset by the current account) also requires UIP to hold.

In section 3 we examine the properties of the steady state itself. An important aspect of the income determination models of Mundell (1963) and Fleming (1962), and of the exchange rate dynamics of Dornbusch (1976) and others, is that in steady state the domestic interest rate equals the foreign interest rate and is independent of domestic asset supplies.[5] In addition, the steady state exchange rate and domestic price level are homogeneous of degree 1 in the domestic money supply. None of these results is preserved when speculators are risk-averse. Thus, even if CIP obtains, the domestic interest rate can be affected by domestic policies in steady state, something that is not possible under UIP. Also, the exchange rate and domestic price level are homogeneous of degree 1, and the interest rate is homogeneous of degree 0, in the supplies of both nominal domestic assets taken together, and not just money.[6]

Sections 4 and 5 examine the transition between steady states, a subject which has been receiving extensive treatment recently. In section 4 we show that once-and-for-all proportional unannounced increases in the supplies of money and domestic bonds introduced simultaneously can, on impact, cause either a smaller than or greater than proportional response in the exchange rate. This result contrasts with the previous models in which, under similar assumptions but with UIP holding, the exchange rate necessarily 'overshoots' its steady state value.[7] The change in the exchange rate on impact can vary inversely with the degree of risk aversion. Our model thus suggests a sense in which speculation (or, more properly, less risk-averse speculation) destabilizes exchange rates; this is in the sense of increasing their short-run sensitivity to changes in domestic asset supplies. Finally, in section 5 we consider the dynamic effects of once-and-for-all unannounced changes in the money supply, achieved via open market operations.

2 A DYNAMIC MACROMODEL

We consider a small open economy in which private agents may hold as assets domestic (outside) money, domestic government bonds, and foreign bonds, all of which, we assume, they regard as components of their net wealth. The first two assets are denominated in domestic currency and the third in foreign currency. Thus, at any moment, private nominal wealth W is given by

$$W = M + A^{\mathrm{d}} + EB^{\mathrm{d}} \tag{2.4}$$

where M denotes the supply of domestic money (which we assume is held only domestically), A^{d} the number of domestic bonds held domestically, and B^{d} the number of foreign bonds held domestically.

We assume that there is no perceived risk of default on domestic to foreign bonds so that CIP obtains:

$$R = R^* + F \tag{2.5}$$

Since our analysis is in continuous time, F measures the instantaneous rate of forward premium on foreign exchange and is defined formally by

$$F(t) \equiv \lim_{h\to 0}\left\{\frac{E^{\mathrm{f}}(t, t+h) - E(t)}{hE(t)}\right\} \tag{2.6}$$

where $E^{\mathrm{f}}(t, t+h)$ is the price at time t of one unit of foreign exchange in period $t+h$. Since, as the time unit $h \to 0$, the spot and forward rates must converge, $E(t) = E^{\mathrm{f}}(t, t)$, in which case the limit in (2.6) can be expressed by the following partial derivative:

$$F(t) = \frac{E_2^{\mathrm{f}}(t, t)}{E^{\mathrm{f}}(t, t)} \tag{2.6$'$}$$

Since domestic and covered foreign bonds are perfect substitutes, we will assume that all domestic bonds are held domestically. Thus we let $A^{\mathrm{d}} = A$ where A denotes the total supply of domestic bonds. We allow B^{d} to assume negative values when domestic agents issue liabilities denominated in foreign currency.

Individuals consume both traded and nontraded goods, which are imperfect substitutes. Perfect goods arbitrage ensure that the prices of traded goods are determined by the law of one price. We assume that, because of long-term contracts, the prices of nontraded goods at any instant are fixed at P say. An index of the domestic cost of living C is therefore

$$C = P^{\delta}(EP^*)^{1-\delta} \qquad 0 \leqslant \delta \leqslant 1 \tag{2.7}$$

where δ denotes the share of nontraded goods in consumption and P^* is the exogenously given foreign price level (i.e. the foreign price of traded goods). For notational simplicity we set $P^* = 1$.

We assume a demand-for-money function of the form

$$\frac{M}{C} = L(Y, R, H) \qquad L_Y \geqslant 0,\ L_R \leqslant 0,\ 0 \leqslant L_H \leqslant 1 \tag{2.8}$$

where Y is real oputput and $H \equiv W/C$ denotes real wealth. Note that we have deflated by C, reflecting the fact that real wealth depends upon the price of both traded and nontraded goods in accordance with their shares in consumption. Note that only the domestic interest rate R is included in the money demand function. Elsewhere (Eaton and Turnovsky, 1981) we have derived optimal savings and portfolio behavior for a single consumer in a two-period model in which money provides utility via its transactions services. In this analysis, since domestic bonds and money are assumed to be equally risky, the division of assets denominated in *domestic* currency depends only upon the domestic interest rate.[8]

Together, equations (2.4), (2.5), (2.7) and (2.8) determine, at any moment, equilibrium values of C, R, F and W as functions of P, E, Y, A, B^{d}, M and the exogenous foreign variables R^* and P^*.

We now turn to the dynamic equations of the system. First, consider forward market equilibrium. Participation in the forward market may be for two reasons, speculation and arbitrage.[9] We assume that the real demand for speculative foreign exchange forward, denoted by J, is an increasing function of the expected rate of return on speculation, given by the difference between the expected rate of depreciation of the domestic currency $(\dot{E}/E)^{e}$ and the forward premium F. We will assume that expectations are realized on average. Since we suppress stochastic elements in our model, except for unanticipated once-and-for-all changes in asset supplies, this is equivalent to assuming perfect foresight. Thus $(\dot{E}/E)^{e} = \dot{E}/E$ except at the moment when asset supplies change.[10] Forward market equilibrium requires that J equal the supply of foreign exchange forward for arbitrage, i.e. that which is sold to cover domestic holdings of foreign bonds:

$$\frac{EB^{d}}{C} = J\left(\frac{\dot{E}}{E} - F\right) \qquad J' \geqslant 0 \tag{2.9}$$

Such a specification follows from financial micromodels of the forward market (see for example Kouri, 1976; Adler and Dumas, 1977; Eaton and Turnovsky, 1981). Frankel (1979) has emphasized that this specification relies on the assumption that domestic government debt constitutes a component of private national wealth, an assumption that we make here. As shown by previous authors, J embodies attitudes to risk-taking. In particular, J' varies inversely with the degree of risk aversion, with $J' \to \infty$ in the limitating case of risk neutrality when UIP obtains.

By appropriate choice of units, the steady state price of nontraded goods can be equated to the domestic price of traded goods. We assume that the price of nontraded goods is determined by long-term contracts, so that the price of nontraded goods cannot jump instantaneously to its equilibrium level, but can adjust only continuously over time as contracts expire. When the average price of nontraded goods exceeds its normal level, we assume that their output exceeds their steady state supply, and conversely. Consequently, we specify a relationship for the *supply* of real output as

$$Y - \widetilde{Y} = Z(E/P) \qquad Z' > 0,\ Z(1) = 0 \tag{2.10}$$

where $\widetilde{Y}$ denotes the steady state value of Y, which we treat as exogenous. We also assume that when $Y > \widetilde{Y}$ the price of nontraded goods is revised upwards, and conversely. This adjustment is specified by the relationship[11]

$$\dot{P} = G(E/P) \qquad G' > 0,\ G(1) = 0 \tag{2.11}$$

The rate of change in the supply of domestic assets is determined by the government budget constraint

$$\dot{M} + \dot{A} = PG_{\mathrm{d}} + EG_{\mathrm{m}} - T + RA \equiv g \tag{2.12}$$

where G_d and G_m represent real government expenditures on nontraded and traded goods respectively and T' denotes nominal tax revenues. The rate of change in the domestic holdings of foreign assets is equal to the balance of payments on current account:

$$E\dot{B}^d = EX(.) - EG_m + R^* EB^d \equiv b \tag{2.13}$$

where $X(.)$ denotes the real net exports of the private sector.

Together with an assumption about the government finances its expenditures, equations (2.9), (2.10), (2.11), (2.12) and (2.13) determine the evolution of E, P, Y, A, M, and B^d. From the description of the system it might appear that the spot rate E is constrained always to move continuously. This is not so. Because of the assumption of perfect foresight embodied in (2.9), the dynamics will usually involve (at least) one unstable root. Following the rational expectations methodology, this root can be eliminated by allowing the exchange rate to undergo an endogenously determined initial jump at points where the system is subjected to an unanticipated exogenous disturbance. Simple examples of this are given in sections 4 and 5.

Define the total nominal bond holdings B as

$$B \equiv A + EB^d$$

Adding (2.12) and (2.13) and using the CIP condition (2.5), we obtain

$$\dot{M} + \dot{B} = PG_d - T + EX + RB + (\dot{E}/E - F)\, EB^d \tag{2.14}$$

From this equation it is evident that in general the evolution of the system depends upon the breakdown of B between domestic and foreign bonds. Thus, for example, if $\dot{M} = 0$ (the deficit is bond financed), E, P, and B cannot assume their steady state values unless $\dot{B}^d = \dot{A} = 0$, i.e. unless both the government deficit g and the balance of payments on current account b are zero. The same applies in the case of money financing.

Consider, however, the limiting case in which $J'(.) \to \infty$, i.e. the speculative demand for foreign exchange forward becomes infinitely elastic. In order for the speculative demand to remain bounded, (2.2) must hold. In this case (2.5) and (2.9) reduce to the UIP condition (2.3), so that (2.14) becomes

$$\dot{M} + \dot{B} = PG_d - T + EX + RB \tag{2.14'}$$

If we write (2.4) as

$$H = \frac{M + B}{C} \tag{2.4'}$$

equations (2.4), (2.7), (2.3), (2.8), (2.10), (2.11) and (2.14′) constitute a dynamic system in which A and B^d do not appear (assuming of course that A and B^d do not enter separately in the specifications of G_d, G_m,

T, or X). If the government deficit is bond financed, $\dot{M} = 0$. The dynamics depend only upon the sum of the government deficit and the current account deficit $g + b$ and not on the separate components. Steady state now only requires that $\dot{B} = \dot{E} = \dot{P} = 0$. The government can sustain a deficit in steady state as long as it is offset by a current account deficit of equal size, since the steady state requirement $\dot{B} = 0$ is equivalent to $\dot{A} = -E\dot{B}^{d}$. With money financing, both components must be zero.

A special case widely adopted in the literature, and therefore of importance, arises if the demand for money is assumed to be independent of real wealth H. Consider first the limiting assumption of risk-neutral speculation. If the government deficit is bond financed, the dynamics of P and E become independent of $g + b$ and these variables can attain steady state equilibrium with wealth, in the form of bonds, being accumulated indefinitely.[12] With a money-financed deficit, steady state for E and P requires only that the government deficit be zero; the current account balance can be nonzero, with domestic residents continually accumulating (or decumulating) foreign bonds. In the general case where J' is finite, no variable can be in steady state unless $g = b = 0$. However, under bond financing E and P can attain steady state with only $b = 0$, provided that we impose the additional restriction that net exports be independent of H.[13]

In formulating dynamic macromodels such as the one above, it is often convenient to specify real savings behavior (or asset accumulation) directly. Thus, if we postulate

$$\frac{E\dot{B}^{d} + \dot{M} + \dot{A}}{C} = S(.) \tag{2.15}$$

if follows from (2.4), (2.13) and (2.15) that the rate of net capital inflow $E\dot{B}^{d}$ can be derived as

$$\begin{aligned} E\dot{B}^{d} &= CS(.) - (\dot{M} + \dot{A}) \\ &= CS(.) - (PG_{d} + EG_{m}) + T - RA \end{aligned} \tag{2.16}$$

Comparison of (2.13) and (2.16) makes it clear that $S(.)$, $X(.)$, and the government financing decision cannot be specified independently.

These observations about the appropriate specification of dynamic models under perfect capital mobility have important implications for various models appearing in the literature. First, the model of exchange rate dynamics introduced by Dornbusch (1976) and studied by other authors ignores the balance-of-payments and savings behavior in analysing the dynamics of the exchange rate. This is possible only because they assume UIP and that there are no asset supply effects on money demand. Under the less restrictive condition of CIP, however, the dynamic adjustment of the exchange rate, on the one hand, and asset accumulation, on the other, are jointly determined, even in the absence of wealth effects in the demand for money.

Second, a well known result of Mundell (1963) is that a government deficit has no effect on the steady state of a small open economy under conditions of perfect capital mobility and flexible exchange rates. This is certainly true under the conditions of UIP when any change in the deficit will be offset by a change in the current account deficit, leaving the system unchanged. However, it is not generally true under CIP, when indeed steady state requires the deficit to be zero.

3 STEADY STATE PROPERTIES

Models of exchange rate determination based on the assumption of UIP and the absence of an ongoing inflation yield the following steady state relationship:

$$\tilde{R} = R^* \tag{2.17}$$

where the tilde denotes the steady state value of a variable. Thus the domestic interest rate is completely tied to the world rate, from which we immediately infer:

(1) changes in the foreign interest rate yield equal changes in the domestic interest rate;
(2) the domestic interest rate is independent of the supply of domestic money or domestic bonds.

Other steady state properties depend upon the policy specification and the dynamic system so generated. If in addition to (2.17) we adopt the frequently postulated savings function[14]

$$S = \phi\{\bar{H}(Y, R - \dot{C}/C) - H, Y\} \tag{2.18}$$

where $\bar{H}$ is some long-run desired level of real wealth, the steady state monetary equilibrium relationship becomes[15]

$$\frac{M}{E} = L\{\tilde{Y}, R^*, \bar{H}(\tilde{Y}\ R^*)\} \tag{2.19}$$

From this equation, two further propositions follow:

(3) a given change in the domestic money supply leads to a proportionate change in the exchange rate;
(4) the exchange rate is independent of the supply of domestic bonds.

None of properties 1–4 characterizes the steady state of the model presented in section 2 except in the limiting case when the speculative demand for foreign exchange forward is perfectly elastic.[16]

We adopt the saving function (2.18) and assume, for simplicity and without essential loss of generality, that $\bar{H}$ is exogenous and independent of the interest rate. The steady state of the model presented in section 2 is attained when $\dot{E} = \dot{P} = \dot{A} = \dot{M} = \dot{B}^{\mathrm{d}} = 0$. Imposing these conditions yields the equations

$$\bar{H} = \frac{\widetilde{M} + \widetilde{A}}{\widetilde{E}} + \widetilde{B}^{\mathrm{d}} \qquad \widetilde{R} = R^{*} + \widetilde{F} \tag{2.20a, b}$$

$$\frac{\widetilde{M}}{\widetilde{E}} = L(\widetilde{Y}, \widetilde{R}, \bar{H}) \qquad \widetilde{B}^{\mathrm{d}} = J(-\widetilde{F}) \tag{2.20c, d}$$

$$\widetilde{E}(G_{\mathrm{d}} + G_{\mathrm{m}}) - \widetilde{T} + \widetilde{R}\widetilde{A} = 0 \tag{2.20e}$$

Given $\bar{H}$, these five equations involve the seven variables $\widetilde{M}$, $\widetilde{A}$, $\widetilde{B}^{\mathrm{d}}$, $\widetilde{E}$, $\widetilde{R}$, $\widetilde{F}$, $\widetilde{T}$. We will assume initially that the monetary authorities peg $M = \bar{M}$ and $A = \bar{A}$, continuously adjusting T to balance the budget.

Thus $\bar{M}$ and $\bar{A}$, along with R^{*}, may be treated as exogenous parameters. Totally differentiating the system with respect to these variables we obtain the following effects on the domestic interest rate $\widetilde{R}$:

$$\frac{\mathrm{d}\widetilde{R}}{\mathrm{d}\bar{M}} = -\frac{\bar{A}}{\widetilde{E}\Delta} < 0 \qquad \frac{\mathrm{d}\widetilde{R}}{\mathrm{d}\bar{A}} = \frac{\bar{M}}{\widetilde{E}\Delta} > 0 \qquad 0 < \frac{\mathrm{d}\widetilde{R}}{\mathrm{d}R^{*}} = \frac{J'\bar{M}}{\Delta} < 1 \tag{2.21a, b, c}$$

where $\Delta \equiv J'\bar{M} - L_{\mathrm{R}}(\bar{M} + \bar{A}) > 0$. Thus a once-and-for-all increase in the domestic money supply reduces the steady state domestic interest rate, while an increase in the domestic supply of bonds increases it. An increase in the foreign interest rate leads to a reduction in the forward premium, causing the domestic interest rate to rise by a smaller amount. In the limiting case when $J' \to \infty$, the response becomes proportional and in this extreme case changes in $\bar{M}$ and $\bar{A}$ have no effect on R. Thus, unless speculators are risk-neutral or perceive no exchange risk, the domestic interest rate is not totally determined by the interest rate abroad and responds to domestic asset supplies in the manner indicated.

Multiplying (2.21a) by $\bar{M}$ and (2.21b) by $\bar{A}$ and summing yields an expression equal to zero. Thus an increase in the domestic money supply accompanied by a proportional increase in the domestic bond supply is neutral in its effect on the steady state domestic interest rate.

Changes in $\bar{M}$ and $\bar{A}$ have the following proportional effect on the steady state spot rate E:

$$\frac{\mathrm{d}\widetilde{E}}{\mathrm{d}\bar{M}}\frac{M}{\widetilde{E}} = \frac{\bar{M}(J' - L_{\mathrm{R}})}{\Delta}\begin{cases} > 0 \\ < 1 \end{cases} \tag{2.22a}$$

$$\frac{\mathrm{d}\widetilde{E}}{\mathrm{d}\bar{A}}\frac{\bar{A}}{\widetilde{E}} = -\frac{\bar{A}L_{\mathrm{R}}}{\Delta}\begin{cases} > 0 \\ < 1 \end{cases} \tag{2.22b}$$

Both elasticities are positive and less than unity, while summing to unity. Thus, contrary to propositions 3 and 4, an increase in the money supply leads to a less than proportional increase in the exchange rate, while the supply of domestic bonds also affects the exchange rate. Proportional increase in the supplies of the two nominal assets together lead to proportional increases in the exchange rate and the domestic price level. As $J' \rightarrow \infty$, (2.22a) tends to unity and (2.22b) tends to zero. Thus only in the limiting case do propositions 3 and 4 hold.

Fiscal policy involves changing $\bar{A}$.[17] A well-known proposition of Mundell (1963) and Fleming (1962) is that under flexible rates and perfect capital mobility fiscal policy has no effect on the steady state of a small open economy. It is evident from our analysis that, again, for the result to apply, perfect capital mobility must be interpreted to mean that UIP obtains, i.e. that foreign exchange speculation requires no risk premium.

The same general characteristics of the steady state described by (2.20a)–(2.20e) obtain under alternative policy specifications. If, for example, tax receipts are held at a constant real level, say τ, and the government finances its deficit with bonds, the steady state relations (2.20a)–(2.20e) will continue to determine the steady state values of $\widetilde{B}^{\mathrm{d}}$, $\widetilde{R}$, $\widetilde{F}$, $\widetilde{E}$ and $\widetilde{A}$. Now, however (2.20e) requires the stock of domestic bonds to adjust in proportion to the exchange rate, since $\widetilde{T} = \widetilde{E}\tau$. Under UIP propositions 1 and 4 still obtain, but if UIP does not hold these propositions will be violated as before. The responses of $\widetilde{R}$ and $\widetilde{E}$ to changes in propositions will be violated as before. The responses of $\widetilde{R}$ and $\widetilde{E}$ to R^* and $\bar{M}$ can be calculated (A is now endogenous) and will generally differ from the expressions given in (2.21) and (2.22) because of the difference in policy specification.

4 EXCHANGE RATE DYNAMICS: PROPORTIONAL INCREASES IN MONEY AND DOMESTIC BOND SUPPLIES

We now consider an economy in which steady state is disturbed by unanticipated once-and-for-all increases in the money supply and domestic bond supply of equal proportion and examine the behavior of the exchange rate during its transition to the new steady state. For convenience, we assume a log-linear version of the model developed in section 2. Other simplifications are introduced not only to expedite the dynamic analysis, but also to make our results as comparable as possible with the existing literature.

Following Driskill (1980) for example, we take the following log-linear approximation to wealth:

$$h = \mu_1 a + \mu_2(e + b^{\mathrm{d}}) + (1 - \mu_1 - \mu_2)m - c \equiv w - c \quad (2.23)$$

where μ_1 is the share of domestic bonds in domestic wealth and μ_2 is the share of foreign bonds.[18] We set $r \equiv R - \widetilde{R}_0$ and $f \equiv F - \widetilde{F}_0$, and for all other variables let $x \equiv \ln X - \ln \widetilde{X}_0$, where for any variable $\widetilde{X}_0$ denotes the values of X in the initial steady state. Thus x is the percentage deviation in X from its initial steady state value.

If it is assumed that the foreign interest rate remains unchanged at R^*, the interest rate parity condition (expressed in deviation form) is

$$r = f \tag{2.24}$$

while the price index now becomes

$$c = \delta p + (1 - \delta)e \tag{2.25}$$

A log-linear approximation to the supply function (2.10) is

$$y = \rho(e - p) \qquad \rho \geqslant 0 \tag{2.26}$$

and a similar approximation to money market equilibrium is given by

$$m - c = -\alpha_1 r + \alpha_2 h + \alpha_3 y \qquad \alpha_i \geqslant 0. \tag{2.27}$$

If the assumption of perfect foresight is imposed (except at points where asset supplies change unexpectedly) the log-linear approximation to the condition for forward market equilibrium becomes

$$e + b^{\mathrm{d}} - c = \gamma(\dot{e} - f) \qquad \gamma \geqslant 0 \tag{2.28}$$

where γ is the elasticity of speculative demand for foreign exchange forward with respect to the risk premium. γ varies inversely with the degree of risk aversion, with $\gamma \rightarrow \infty$ as risk neutrality is approached.[19] The adjustment of prices is specified by[20]

$$\dot{p} = \theta(e - p) \qquad \theta > 0 \tag{2.29}$$

Since our analysis treats the nominal supplies of money and domestic bonds as fixed everwhere except at one instant, savings must take the form of accumulating foreign bonds. Assuming that interest rates do not affect desired wealth, we approximate the asset acculumation function (2.16) by

$$\dot{b}^{\mathrm{d}} = -\sigma_1 h + \sigma_2 y \qquad \sigma_1 \geqslant 0, \qquad \sigma_2 \geqslant 0 \tag{2.30}$$

This expression can also be interpreted as a log-linear approximation to the current account equation.

Equations (2.23)–(2.30) constitute a complete dynamic system. Equations (2.23)–(2.27) determine at any moment values of h, c, r, y and f as functions of e, p and b^{d}, whose dynamic behavior is described by equations (2.28)–(2.30).

For the special case in which $\alpha_2 = 0$ (zero wealth effects in the demand for money), $\rho = 0$ (fixed real output), and $\gamma \rightarrow \infty$ (currency speculation requires no risk premium), the model outlined in equations

(2.23)–(2.30) reduces in essence to that examined by Dornbusch (1976), Gray and Turnovsky (1979, this vol, ch. 1) and Wilson (1979). As we mentioned in section 2, when $\gamma \to \infty$, exchange rate dynamics are independent of B^{d} and A. For this reason these earlier studies did not require any assumptions about the bond-financed conponent of the government deficit or about savings behavior.

Dornbush and other authors consider the effects of a once-and-for-all change in the money supply on the path of the exchange rate and price level. As we pointed out in section 3, in the special case that they consider, the steady state effect of such change is a proportional change in the exchange rate and the price level, with the domestic interest rate remaining unchanged. To maintain this long-run neutrality in our more general model, the change in the money supply must be accompanied by a proportional change in the supply of domestic bonds. Thus the policy of a once-and-for-all transfer of money *and* bonds is considered in this section.

Consider an initial steady state in which all variables in equations (2.23)–(2.30) are zero (i.e. $\ln X = \ln X_0$ etc.) and assume that the supplies of money and domestic bonds increased once and for all by $\bar{m}$ percent.[21] In the new steady state $\tilde{e} = \tilde{p} = \tilde{c} = \bar{m}$, while all other variables return to their initial (zero) levels.

Solving equations (2.23)–(2.27) for h, c, r, f and y, and substituting the resulting expressions into (2.28)–(2.30) allows us to describe the equations as a third-order system of differential equations in e, p, and b^{d}[22]

$$\begin{bmatrix} \dot{e} \\ \dot{p} \\ \dot{b}^{\mathrm{d}} \end{bmatrix} = \begin{bmatrix} a_1 & a_2 & a_3 \\ \theta & -\theta & 0 \\ c_1 & c_2 & c_3 \end{bmatrix} \begin{bmatrix} e \\ p \\ b^{\mathrm{d}} \end{bmatrix} + \begin{bmatrix} a_0 \\ 0 \\ c_0 \end{bmatrix} \tag{2.31}$$

$$a_1 \equiv \frac{\delta}{\gamma} + \frac{\alpha_3\rho + \alpha_2\mu_2 + (1-\alpha_2)(1-\delta)}{\alpha_1}$$

$$a_2 \equiv \frac{-\delta}{\gamma} - \frac{\alpha_3\rho - (1-\alpha_2)\delta}{\alpha_1}$$

$$a_3 \equiv \frac{1}{\delta} + \frac{\alpha_2\mu_2}{\alpha_1} \qquad a_0 \equiv \frac{\alpha_2(1-\mu_2) - 1}{\alpha_1}\bar{m}$$

$$c_1 \equiv \sigma_1(1-\delta-\mu_2) + \sigma_2\rho \qquad c_2 \equiv \sigma_1\delta - \sigma_2\rho$$

$$c_3 \equiv -\sigma_1\mu_2 \qquad c_0 \equiv \sigma_1(\mu_2 - 1)\bar{m}$$

The solution to the system is

$$e(t) = \bar{m} + A_1\exp(\lambda_1 t) + A_2\exp(\lambda_2 t) + A_3\exp(\lambda_3 t) \tag{2.32a}$$

$$p(t) = \bar{m} + B_1\exp(\lambda_1 t) + B_2\exp(\lambda_2 t) + B_3\exp(\lambda_3 t) \tag{2.32b}$$

$$b^{\mathrm{d}}(t) = C_1 \exp(\lambda_1 t) + C_2 \exp(\lambda_2 t) + C_3 \exp(\lambda_3 t) \tag{2.32c}$$

where λ_1, λ_2, and λ_3 are the solutions to the characteristic equation of (2.31)

$$\lambda^3 - (a_1 + c_3 - \theta)\,\lambda^2 - \{\theta(\alpha_1 + a_2 + c_3) - a_1 c_3 + c_1 a_3\}\lambda$$
$$- \theta\{(c_1 + c_2)a_3 - (a_1 + a_2)c_3\} = 0 \tag{2.33}$$

and where, given the arbitrary constants A_1, A_2, and A_3, the remaining constants B_i, C_i, $i = 1, 2, 3$, are determined by the relationships

$$\begin{bmatrix} B_i \\ C_i \end{bmatrix} = \begin{bmatrix} a_2 & a_3 \\ c_2 & c_3 - \lambda_i \end{bmatrix}^{-1} \begin{bmatrix} \lambda_i - a_i \\ -c_1 \end{bmatrix} A_i \qquad i = 1, 2, 3 \tag{2.34}$$

The constant term in (2.33) can be shown from the definitions of a_i and c_i to be unambiguously negative, implying that the product $\lambda_1\lambda_2\lambda_3$ of the roots is greater than zero.[23] Thus (2.31) has either one or three positive eigenvalues. Moreover, the coefficient of λ in (2.33), which equals $-(\lambda_1\lambda_2 + \lambda_2\lambda_3 + \lambda_3\lambda_1)$, is almost certainly positive, in which case some of the roots must be negative, so that in fact there can be only one unstable root. A sufficient, but by no means necessary, condition for this to be so is $\mu_2 < \alpha_2/\alpha_1$, which imposes an upper limit on the fraction of foreign bonds held. We will treat the case of two stable roots denoted by λ_1, λ_2, and a single unstable root denoted by λ_3, as normal and impose the requirement that the system converge to its steady state, i.e.

$$\lim_{t\to\infty} e(t) = \tilde{e} \qquad \lim_{t\to\infty} p(t) = \tilde{p} \qquad \lim_{t\to\infty} b^{\mathrm{d}}(t) = 0$$

Convergence then requires that the coefficients of the unstable root are zero.[24] Thus $A_3 = 0$ and, via (2.34), $B_3 = C_3 = 0$.

In keeping with the literature on exchange rate dynmics, we assume that, while discontinuous jumps in the exchange rate are possible, the price of nontraded goods is constrained to move continuously. The fact that the exchange rate is determined by virtually continuous trading in an auction market, while the prices of nontraded goods are determined mainly by a large number of longer-term contracts, makes this assumption plausible. This constraint implies the initial condition

$$p(0) = 0 \quad \text{or} \quad B_1 + B_2 = -\bar{m} \tag{2.35}$$

Similarly, the requirement that foreign assets can be acquired only continuously over time requires that the asset disturbance cannot move b^{d} from its initial level on impact, and so

$$b^{\mathrm{d}}(0) = 0 \quad \text{or} \quad C_1 + C_2 = 0 \tag{2.36}$$

Equations (2.35) and (2.36), together with the four equations contained in (2.34) for $i = 1, 2$, determine the six coefficients of the stable roots, namely A_i, B_i, C_i, $i = 1, 2$.

Assuming stability, consider now the value of the exchange rate immediately after the increase in the supplies of money and bonds takes place at $t = 0$. This value, denoted by $e(0+)$, is given by $A_1 + A_2 + \bar{m}$. Thus the exchange rate overshoots its new steady state level as the values of A_1 and A_2, derived from (2.34)–(2.36), yield $A_1 + A_2 \gtrless 0$.

Solving these equations for A_1 and A_2 we find that the criterion for the exchange rate to overshoot initially can be written in the form

$$A_1 + A_2 \equiv \frac{\{c_2(a_3c_2 - a_2c_3) + a_2(a_1c_2 - a_2c_1)\}\bar{m}}{c_2\lambda_1\lambda_2 + (a_1 - \lambda_1 - \lambda_2)(a_1c_2 - a_2c_1) + c_1(a_3c_2 - a_2c_3)} \gtrless 0 \tag{2.37}$$

For the case in which there is no output response ($\rho = 0$), the denominator of (2.37) is unambiguously positive. Whether or not overshooting occurs then depends upon the sign of the numerator, namely whether

$$\sigma_1\delta^2 D\left(\sigma_1 - \frac{1}{\gamma} + \frac{1-\alpha_2}{\alpha_1}\right) \lesseqgtr 0 \tag{2.38}$$

where

$$D \equiv \frac{1-\mu_2}{\gamma} + \frac{\mu_2}{\alpha_1} > 0 \tag{2.39}$$

A necessary and sufficient condition for overshooting to occur is therefore that

$$\sigma_1 + \frac{1-\alpha_2}{\alpha_1} > \frac{1}{\gamma} \tag{2.40}$$

Thus overshooting inevitably occurs when $\gamma \rightarrow \infty$, as is the case in the Dornbusch model, or when $\sigma_1 \rightarrow \infty$ and asset adjustment is infinitely fast. Dornbusch also considers the case in which income in endogenous and shows how the income effect in the demand for money can lead to undershoot. However, even when income is fixed ($\rho = 0$), the presence of imperfectly elastic speculation ($\gamma < \infty$) can lead to a reversal of inequality (2.40) and therefore to exchange rate undershoot. This is more likely to occur when speculation is inelastic (γ is small), money demand is interest and wealth elastic (a_1 and α_2 are large), and savings is unresponsive to wealth (σ_1 is low).

The phenomenon of overshooting has been cited as a reason for the observed volatility of exchange rates: changes in asset supplies create movements in exchange rates that exaggerate the implications of these changes for steady state. According to this interpretation, speculation acts to 'destabilize' the foreign exchange market. As risk aversion on the part of speculators falls, making the supply of speculative funds more elastic, the exchange rate reacts more sharply to changes in asset supplies.

To understand this result observe that, since the price of nontraded goods are sticky, changes in nominal asset supplies constitute, on impact, changes in real asset supplies. The exchange rate and interest rate must adjust to restore asset market equilibrium. An increase in the nominal supplies of money and domestic bonds increases both the supply of and demand for money, the second via a wealth effect. Taking the likely case $\alpha_2 < 1$, the net impact on the money market is to create an excess supply. To maintain equilibrium in the money market during the adjustment period requires a lower domestic interest rate, which in turn requires a lower forward premium f on foreign exchange.

When speculation is perfectly elastic, $f = \dot{e}$. In this case a lower domestic interest rate requires a continuous appreciation ($\dot{e} < 0$) during the adjustment period. If the exchange rate is to appreciate to its new higher steady state value, it must initially depreciate to a value above $\bar{e}$, i.e. the exchange rate must overshoot.

When speculation is less than perfectly elastic ($\gamma < \infty$), however, an exchange rate depreciation also impinges on forward market equilibrium by revaluing domestic holdings on foreign bonds. This revaluation creates an excess supply of foreign exchange forward which acts to bid down the forward premium f on foreign exchange. If the drop in f required to restore forward market equilibrium exceeds the drop required to restore money market equilibrium, then a continuous depreciation ($\dot{e} > 0$) is needed to maintain equilibrium in both markets. For this continuous depreciation to converge to the new steady state exchange rate, the depreciation on impact must be less than the steady state depreciation, i.e. exchange rate undershoot must occur.

As asset adjustment becomes more rapid the increase in domestic asset supplies soon leads to a decrease in the real value of foreign bonds held by the public. The forward exchange premium f must consequently fall. In this case maintaining forward market equilibrium enhances the case for overshoot.[25]

To illustrate the complete dynamic response to an increase in domestic asset supplies we focus on two special cases, one in which asset accumulation proceeds very slowly and the other in which assets adjust very rapidly.

4.1 Slow asset adjustments

The first case we consider is one where the savings adjustment to the shock is very slow relative to the price level adjustment. This can be approximated by considering the limiting case $\sigma_1 \to 0$, $\sigma_2 \to 0$. Using equations (2.34) and (2.37) we obtain the following solutions for the exchange rate and price of nontraded goods:

$$e(t) = \left\{1 + \frac{a_2}{a_1 - \lambda_1} \exp(\lambda_1 t)\right\}\bar{m} \tag{2.41a}$$

$$p(t) = \{1 - \exp(\lambda_1 t)\}\bar{m} \tag{2.41b}$$

Consider now the value of the exchange rate immediately after the increase in the money and bond supplies at $t = 0$. This value, denoted by $e(0+)$, is given by

$$e(0+) = \left(1 + \frac{a_2}{a_1 - \lambda_1}\right)\bar{m} \tag{2.42}$$

It can be established that, with $\lambda_2 = 0$, the smaller root λ_1 satisfies

$$\lambda_1 < a_1 - \theta < a_1$$

so that $e(0+) \lesseqgtr \tilde{e}(=\bar{m})$ as $a_2 \gtreqless 0$ and the overshooting criterion (2.37) simplifies to

$$\gamma\{(1 - \alpha_2)\delta - \alpha_3\rho\} - \alpha_1\delta \gtreqless 0 \tag{2.37$'$}$$

Note that since $e(0+)$ is always positive while $p(0) = 0$, the real exchange rate always overshoots. Differentiating $e(0+)$ with respect to γ indicates that, as long as $\alpha_2 < 1$, $de(0+)/d\gamma > 0$; an increase in the elasticity of speculation raises the impact effect on the exchange rate of a change in nominal asset supplies.[26]

4.2 Rapid asset adjustment

The second case we consider is one in which wealth adjusts very fast relative to the price level. Analogously, this can be approximated by considering the limiting case in which $\sigma_1 \to \infty$, so that b^{d} adjusts virtually instantaneously to keep wealth constant at its desired level. Letting $\sigma_1 \to \infty$, we find that the solutions for the exchange rate and price level tend to

$$e(t) \to \left\{1 + \frac{a_2'}{a'_1 - \lambda_1} \exp(\lambda_1 t)\right\}\bar{m} \tag{2.43a}$$

$$p(t) \to \{1 - \exp(\lambda_1 t)\}\bar{m} \tag{2.43b}$$

where $a_1' \equiv a_1 + a_3(1 - \delta - \mu_2)/\mu_2$ and $a_2' \equiv a_2 + a_3\delta/\mu_2$.

Immediately following the increase in the supplies of money and bonds, the exchange rate is given by

$$\mathrm{e}(0+) \to \left(1 + \frac{a_2'}{a_1' - \lambda_1}\right)\bar{m} \tag{2.44}$$

As before, $\mathrm{a}_1' - \lambda_1$ is positive so that $e(0+) \gtreqless \tilde{e}$ as $a_2' \gtreqless 0$, i.e. as

$$\gamma\mu_2(\delta - \alpha_3\rho) + \alpha_1(1 - \mu_2)\,\delta \gtreqless 0. \tag{2.45}$$

Again, when $\rho = 0$ and $\gamma = \infty$, overshooting necessarily occurs. When wealth is maintained as a constant level, however, the result can be reversed only by an income effect ($\rho > 0$). In addition, differentiating (2.44) with respect to γ yields an expression ambiguous in sign; increasing elastic speculation may raise or lower the impact effect on the exchange rate of the change in nominal asset supplies. When δ is near unity, so that nontraded goods are the major component of the price index, then increasingly elastic speculation will, as before, increase the degree of overshoot. The opposite occurs as δ approaches zero.

The effect of the increase in domestic asset supplies on the real value of foreign bonds held by the public is

$$b^{\mathrm{d}}(0+) + \delta e(0+) \rightarrow \frac{1-\mu_2}{\mu_2}\left\{\frac{a_1'}{a_1'-\lambda_1}(1-\delta) - \delta\right\}\bar{m} \qquad (2.46)$$

which is always negative. Since $e(0+) > 0$, while (2.46) is negative, $b^{\mathrm{d}}(0+) < 0$. Thus the effect of a proportional increase in domestic nominal assets is to create an initial balance-of-payments deficit, which is then offset by a surplus as the nominal foreign bond supply is restored to its initial level. The rate of change of foreign bond holdings, and hence the current account, during the return to steady state is given by

$$\dot{b}^{\mathrm{d}}(t) \rightarrow \frac{\lambda_1}{\mu_2(a_1'-\lambda_1)}\left\{(\mu_2-1)\left(\frac{\alpha_3\rho}{\alpha_1}+\frac{\delta}{\lambda}\right) - \frac{\mu_2\delta}{\alpha_1} + \delta\lambda_1\right\}\exp(-\lambda_1 t)$$

which is always positive. Thus there will be a simultaneous exchange rate appreciation ($\dot{e} < 0$) and balance-of-payments surplus if overshoot occurs on impact, and simultaneous depreciation ($\dot{e} > 0$) and surplus in the event of undershoot.

5 EXCHANGE RATE DYNAMICS: OPEN MARKET OPERATION

In section 4 we analysed a change in nominal asset supplies that was neutral in the sense that it generated proportional changes in the steady state domestic price level and exchange rate with no change in the steady state domestic interest rate. We now consider a once-and-for-all increase of $\bar{m}$ percent in the domestic money supply that is achieved by a purchase of domestic bonds. The percentage change in bond supplies required is given by

$$\bar{a} = \frac{-(1-\mu_1-\mu_2)}{\mu_1}\bar{m} \qquad (2.47)$$

Starting from initial levels of zero, the percentage changes in the steady state exchange rate, price level, and forward premium are

$$\tilde{e} = \tilde{p} = \frac{\mu_2\gamma\bar{m}}{\mu_2\gamma + (1 - \mu_2)\alpha_1} \leqslant \bar{m} \tag{2.48b}$$

and

$$\tilde{f} = \frac{-(1 - \mu_2)\bar{m}}{\mu_2\gamma + (1 - \mu_2)\,\alpha_1} \leqslant 0 \tag{2.48b}$$

respectively, while domestic holdings of foreign bonds change by

$$\tilde{b}^{\mathrm{d}} = \frac{(1 - \mu_2)\gamma\bar{m}}{\mu_2\gamma + (1 - \mu_2)\,\alpha_1} > 0 \tag{2.48c}$$

As our analysis in section 3 indicated, only when speculators are risk-neutral ($\gamma \to \infty$) do the exchange rate and price level change in proportion to $\bar{m}$ and the interest rate remain unchanged. Otherwise, there is a less than proportional increase in $\tilde{e}$ and $\tilde{p}$, while $\tilde{f}$ falls. Note that, as γ rises, so does the steady state response of b^{d} to the open-market expansion.

The transition to the new steady state can again be described by the system (2.31), the only difference being that a_0 and c_0 are replaced by $a_0'' = -\bar{m}/\alpha_1$ and $c_0'' = 0$ respectively. The same boundary conditions on p, e and b^{d} apply.

In the first case considered in section 4 in which asset adjustment is infinitely slow ($\sigma_1 \to \sigma_2 \to 0$), the new steady state is never reached. Hence we consider only the polar case of very rapid asset adjustment ($\sigma_1 \to \infty$). The analysis proceeds as in section 4.2.

Our criterion for the overshooting of the exchange rate in section 4.2 continues to apply. However, an interesting question emerges concerning the effect on impact of the operation on the domestic holdings of foreign bonds, which is given by

$$b^{\mathrm{d}}(0+) \to \frac{1 - \delta - \mu_2}{\mu}\, e(0+) \tag{2.49}$$

This expression is ambiguous in sign. The open-market operation can, on impact, create a current account surplus or deficit depending upon whether the share of traded goods in consumption exceeds or is exceeded by the same of foreign bonds in wealth. The expression may also be smaller or larger than $\tilde{b}^{\mathrm{d}}$. Foreign bond holdings may overshoot their new steady state level, requiring a subsequent deficit. Conversely, they may undershoot, so that a surplus will always be maintained. Which takes place is independent of whether exchange rate overshooting occurs. Consequently, the variety of simultaneous dynamic adjustments of e and b^{d} is large.

We can also consider an open-market operation in the form of a purchase of foreign bonds in exchange for domestic money. For the case in which asset adjustment is very rapid ($\sigma_1 \to \infty$), the dynamic analysis of section 4.2 again applies. In the absence of income effects, exchange rate overshooting necessarily occurs. Since e is greater, while a_1', a_2', and λ_1 are as before, $e(0+)$ is increased. Because the monetary authority has purchased foreign bonds from the public and the exchange rate depreciation on impact is greater, so is the initial current account surplus induced by the operation.

6 CONCLUSION

The assumption that speculative foreign exchange positions require a risk premium has implications for a number of propositions about open economies with flexible exchange rates. In particular, propositions about the impotence of fiscal policy and the equality in steady state between domestic and foreign interest rates based on the assumption of perfect capital mobility require the strong version of this assumption – uncovered interest rate parity – to hold. They do not obtain if only the weaker assumption of covered interest rate parity holds.

Furthermore, introducing risk aversion along with wealth effects in the demand for money has implications for exchange rate dynamics. It tends to reduce the presumption of exchange rate overshooting in response to monetary disturbances, both the likelihood that it happens at all and the amount by which it occurs if it does occur. To the extent that the major sources of disturbances are changes in nominal asset supplies, factors encouraging currency speculation, such as an increase in the number of speculators, are likely to reduce the overall risk aversion exhibited by the market and increase the volatility of the exchange rates. In this sense speculators destabilize the market.

NOTES

1 Other authors draw the distinction between perfect capital mobility between countries and perfect substitutability between domestic and foreign bonds. The former term corresponds to the weaker definition of CIP, while the latter describes the strong definition of UIP (see Frankel, 1982). Elsewhere (Eaton and Turnovsky 1983), we explore the implications of this distinction for the efficacy of policy and the international transmission of disturbances.

2 The usual procedure adopted in the empirical literature testing these hypotheses is to use the *ex post* realization of $\Delta E_t/E_{t-1}$ as a proxy for the expected rate of exchange depreciation.

3 This result points to a deficiency with the assumption, at least as a basis for analysing behavior in steady state. As the size of a country's debt grows, so does its incentive to depreciate its currency (if debt is denominated in domestic currency) or to default. Either will lead to departures from UIP or CIP. Credit rationing could eliminate capital mobility at the margin altogether. An additional problem, of course, is that a small country running a perpetual deficit will eventually develop a debt that looms large in

international capital markets if its debt grows faster than the world economy. In this case its debt will have an impact on world interest rates.

4 Steady states possessing varying degrees of stationarity are familiar from the literature (see for example Dornbusch, 1976; Turnovsky 1977).

5 This proposition is of course based on the presumption that the world is not characterized by conditions of secular inflation, an assumption made throughout this analysis. Under secularly inflationary conditions, the steady state relationship between the domestic and foreign interest rates under UIP is $R = R^* + e$, where e is the secular rate of exchange depreciation. It is clear that, through e, domestic policies are able to influence the domestic nominal rate of interest even if UIP obtains.

6 This result has also been obtained by Harris and Purvis (1982).

7 We stress that this statement refers to models based on similar assumptions to those we shall introduce. A good deal of attention has been devoted to the literature establishing the robustness of the overshooting phenomenon and many models in which it does not occur now exist. Dornbusch (1976) shows that introducing variable output can eliminate overshooting. Turnovsky (1981) shows that introducing imperfect substitutability between bonds and wealth effects can also eliminate the phenomenon in a model in which prices are assumed to be perfectly flexible. His analysis does not distinguish between imperfect substitutability arising from exchange risk (leading to departures from UIP) and from political risk (leading to departures from CIP). Elsewhere (Eaton and Turnovsky 1983) we show that each has potentially different implications for the response of the economy to a monetary shock.

8 Note also that we include real output, rather than real income, in the money demand function. This allows us to ignore the effects of change in real income from foreign bonds on money demand. In the absence of any strong theoretical argument in favor of using real income rather than real output as a proxy for transaction demand, and, in view of the simplicity that obtains when the latter is used, we have adopted this specification. See Dornbusch and Fischer (1980) for an alternative approach, although their analysis treats real income as fixed.

9 We find it analytically convenient to separate forward market participation into pure speculation and pure arbitrage. We implicitly treat the acquisition of an amount of uncovered foreign bonds as combining a covered investment of x in foreign bonds and a speculative purchase of foreign currency forward in amount x. In a portfolio model of foreign investment we identify a third motive for participating in the forward market as hedging against domestic inflation. Forward positions for hedging purposes depend upon the relative variability of the domestic and foreign price levels and do not respond to the variables that we are concerned with here. Thus we can treat the forward position due to hedging as a constant absorbed in J (see Eaton and Turnovsky, 1981).

10 The notion of a "risk premium" on forward exchange in a nonstochastic model is somewhat awkward, although no more so than having different rates of return on different securities as is commonplace in conventional

deterministic macroeconomics. Our main reason for doing this is to preserve analytical tractability and also to enable us to preserve comparability with the existing literature, which is also deterministic. One interpretation of our approach is that, while expectations are on average realized, nevertheless the returns are subject to risk, the magnitude of which will affect the function J (see Eaton and Turnovsky, 1981).

11 This form of price adjustment rule is specified by $\dot{P} = \omega(Y - \widetilde{Y})$. Equation (2.11) is then obtained by combining this equation with (2.10) to yield $\dot{P} = \omega Z(E/P) = G(E/P)$. The theory of staggered contracts, as developed, for example, by Gray (1976), Fischer (1977), and Phelps and Taylor (1977), provides a justification for this specification of the supply of nontraded goods and the determination of their prices given in equations (2.10) and (2.11). Recently, Calvo (1981) has derived output and price response functions of precisely the forms we assume here from a macroeconomic utility-maximizing model with staggered fixed-price contracts that expire stochastically. Firms meet demands at the contracted price. When $Y \leqslant \widetilde{Y}$ this assumption is compatible with voluntary exchange. When $Y > \widetilde{Y}$ we can assume the firms meet demand to maintain customer relationships. Otherwise, we must assume $Z(E/P) = 0$ for all $E/P > 1$.

12 To see this, observe that with bond financing the dynamics of E, P involve only equations (2.7), (2.3), (2.8), (2.10) and (2.11). With a money-financed deficit, equation (2.12), with $A \equiv 0$, must be considered as well. The fact that bond accumulation may continue in steady state in the absence of wealth effects in relevant demand functions is familiar from the simple IS–LM model (see for example Turnovsky, 1977 ch. 4).

13 Another policy worth noting is the balanced budget. As long as H enters the money demand function, steady state always requires $g = b = 0$, irrespective of the elasticity of the speculative demand for forward exchange with respect to the risk premium. The same applies if L is independent of H, as long as J' is finite. In the limiting case of infinitely elastic speculation, steady state requires only that $g = 0$.

14 This type of specification is used, for example, by Tobin and Buiter (1976) for a closed economy.

15 Given (2.10) and (2.17), the steady state real stock of wealth is $\bar{H}(\widetilde{Y}, R^*)$. Note that we have chosen the simplest form of this type of savings function for our purposes. Other variants are also possible. For example, we could replace Y by $Y - T/P + RA/P + R^*EB^{\mathrm{d}}/P$ as a measure of disposable income.

16 Even in this limiting case, propositions 3 and 4 do not necessarily hold under alternative plausible specifications of asset supply and asset accumulation behavior. Consider the case in which taxes are maintained at a constant level in real terms. If the government deficit is bond financed and if the demand for money is independent of H propositions 3 and 4 do still hold. However, if the deficit is money financed an increase in the stock of domestic bonds causes a proportionate change in E, which through the deficit leads to an eventual proportionate change in M. This contradicts proposition 4, while the causality of 3 is reversed. With a balanced budget the exchange rate is

homogeneous of degree 1 in money and domestic bonds.

17 More precisely fiscal policy changes the flow of A.

18 For the case in which the country we are considering is a net *debtor* in terms of foreign currency denominated bonds, b^d should be interpreted as the logarithm deviation of this country's *debt* from its steady state level. The term μ_2 will then be a negative number, where $-\mu_2$ is the logarithm of the net foreign currency denominated debt.

19 When the country we are considering is a net debtor in foreign currency denominated bonds, then b^d should be interpreted as in note 18. The right-hand side of (2.28) should then be reversed in sign.

20 This specification deviates slightly from that adopted by Dornbusch and other authors in which prices are assumed to adjust in proportion to excess demand, as a result of which the domestic interest rate also appears in (2.29). We have chosen our specification not only for reasons of its simplicity, but also because it follows directly from a model based on long-term contracts.

21 In interpreting this initial steady state in which all variables are zero it should be recalled that all variables are measured in deviation form.

22 Buiter and Miller (1981) also develop a third-order system to model exchange rate dynamics. However, they can obtain explicit solutions only for numerical examples.

23 This statement applies whether the country is a net creditor or a net debtor.

24 Convergence may follow by appealing to transversality conditions from appropriate optimizing models which, provided that the underlying utility function satisfies suitable restrictions, ensure that price movements remain bounded.

25 If we consider a net debtor, the role of speculation in determining the impact response of the exchange rate is much more complicated. Its analysis is left as an exercise for the interested reader.

26 On the other hand, $\mathrm{d}|\lambda_1|/\mathrm{d}\gamma > 0$ as well; a reduction in the risk aversion of speculators increases the speed with which the exchange rate and domestic level attain their new equilibrium values.

REFERENCES

Adler, M. and Dumas, B. (1977) The microeconomics of the firm in an open economy. *American Economic Review, Papers and Proceedings*, 67, 180–9.

Aliber, R. Z. (1973) The interest rate parity theorem: a reinterpretation. *Journal of Political Economy*, 81, 1451–9.

Bilson, J. F. O. (1978) Rational expectations and the exchange rate. In *The Economics of Exchange Rates* (eds. J. A. Frenkel and H. G. Johnson). Reading, MA: Addison-Wesley.

Buiter, W. H. and Miller, M. (1981) Real exchange rate overshooting and the output cost of bringing down inflation. NBER Working Paper 749.

Calvo, G. A. (1981) Staggered contracts in a utility-maximizing framework. Columbia University, Department of Economic Discussion Paper 127.

Dornbusch, R. (1976) Exchange rate expectations and monetary policy. *Journal of Political Economy* 84, 1161–76.

—— and Fischer, S. (1980) Exchange rates and the current account. *American Economic Review*, 70, 960–71.

Driskill, R. (1980) Exchange rate dynamics, portfolio balance, and relative prices. *American Economic Review* 70, 776–83.

Eaton, J. and Turnovsky, S. J. (1981) Exchange risk, political risk and macroeconomic equilibrium. Economic Growth Center Discussion Paper 388.

—— and —— (1983) Exchange risk, political risk and microeconomic equilibrium. *American Economic Review* 73, 183–9.

Fischer, S. (1977) Wage indexation and macroeconomic stability. In *Stabilization of the Domestic and International Economy* (eds K. Brunner and A. Meltzer). Amsterdam: North-Holland.

Fleming, J. M. (1962) Domestic financial policies under fixed and floating exchange rates. *IMF Staff Papers* 9, 369–79.

Frankel, J. A. (1979) Monetray and portfolio-balance models of exchange rate determination. In *The International Transmission of Economic Disturbances under Flexible Exchange Rates* (eds J. Bhandari and B. Putnam). Cambridge, MA: MIT Press.

—— (1982) The diversifiability of exchange risk. *Journal of International Economics*, 9, 379–93.

—— and Levich, R. M. (1975) Covered interest arbitrage: exploited profits? *Journal of Political Economy* 83, 325–38.

—— and —— (1977) Transactions costs and interest arbitrage: tranquil versus turbulent periods. *Journal of Political Economy* 85.

Gray, J. A. (1976) Wage indexation: a macroeconomic approach. *Journal of Monetary Economics*, 2, 221–35.

Gray, M. R. and Turnovsky, S. J. (1979) The stability of exchange rate dynamics under perfect myopic foresight. *International Economic Review*, 20, 643–60. Reprinted in this volume as chapter 1.

Hansen, L. P. and Hodrick, R. J. (1980) Forward exchange rates as optimal predictors of future spot rates. *Journal of Political Economy*, 88, 829–53.

Harris, R. G. and Purvis, D. D. (1982) Incomplete information and equilibrium determination of the forward exchange rate. *Journal of International Money and Finance*, 1, 241–53.

Kouri, P. J. K. (1976) The determinants of the forward premium. Institute for International Economic Studies Paper 62. University of Stockholm.

Levich R. (1978) Tests of forecasting models and market efficiency in the international money market. In *The Economics Exchange Rates* (eds J. A. Frenkel and H. G. Johnson). Reading, MA: Addison-Wesley.

Mundell, R. A. (1963) Capital mobility and stabilization policy under fixed and flexible exchange rates. *Candian Journal of Economics and Political Science*, 29, 475–85.

Phelps, E. S. and Taylor, J. B. (1977) Stabilizing powers of monetary policy under rational expectations. *Journal of Political Economy*, 85, 163–90.

Solnik, B. (1973) *European Capital Markets*. Lexington, MA: D. C. Heath.

Tobin, J. and Buiter, W. (1976) Long-run effects of fiscal and monetary policy on aggregate demand. In *Monetarism* (ed. J. L. Stein). Amsterdam: North-Holland.

Turnovsky, S. J. (1977) *Macroeconomic Analysis and Stabilization Policy*. Cambridge: Cambridge University Press.

—— (1981) The asset market approach to exchange rate determination: some short-run stability, and steady state properties. *Journal of Macroeconomics*, 3, 1–32.

Wilson, C. (1979) Anticipated shocks and exchange rate dynamics *Journal of Political Economy*, 87, 639–47.

3 Short-term and Long-term Interest Rates in a Monetary Model of a Small Open Economy

1 INTRODUCTION

Most economists would subscribe to the view that portfolio decisions are generally more flexible than real expenditure decisions. Consequently, it seems reasonable to assume that the former are based on short-term rates of interest, while the latter are more likely to depend upon long-term rates. Nevertheless, most existing macroeconomic models treat assets as being of common maturity in these two sets of decisions. Typically, this is assumed to be either extremely short (a short-term bill) or infinitely long (a perpetuity). Recently, several authors have recognized the fact that different agents in the economy are concerned with rates of return over different time horizons. Using standard domestic macroeconomic models they have shown how arbitrage between the long-term and short-term rates in efficient financial markets provides important linkages between the present and the future. The forward-looking information contained in the long rates turns out to have important implications for the effects of monetary and fiscal policy (see Blanchard, 1981, 1984; Turnovsky and Miller, 1984).

In this chapter we introduce the distinction between short-term and long-term interest rates in a standard monetary model of an open economy.[1] Much of the current literature in this area emphasizes the informational content of the exchange rate. It is clear that a similar informational role is played by the long-term interest rate. In this chapter, we analyse the effects of a variety of disturbances, both

Originally published in *Journal of International Economics*, 20, 1986, 291–311.

unanticipated and anticipated, and discuss the time paths followed by the short-term and long-term interest rates in response to these disturbances. In particular, the divergence in the adjustment between the short-term and long-term rates in anticipation of such disturbances, is highlighted.

The chapter is structured as follows. In section 2 the model (which for the most part is familiar), together with its solution, is outlined. Sections 3 and 4 analyse two alternative disturbances, namely (a) domestic monetary expansion and (b) domestic fiscal expansion. The conclusions are summarized in section 5, and some of the technical details of the analysis are contained in an appendix.

2 THE MODEL

The model we employ is a variant of the standard Dornbusch (1976) model, embodying perfect foresight (see Gray and Turnovsky, 1979, this volume ch. 1). It consists of the following equations:

$$Z = \beta_1\bar{Y} - \beta_2 R + \beta_3(E - P) + G \qquad 0 < \beta_1 < 1,\ \beta_2 > 0,\ \beta_3 > 0 \tag{3.1a}$$

$$M - P = \alpha_1\bar{Y} - \alpha_2 i \qquad \alpha_1 > 0,\ \alpha_2 > 0 \tag{3.1b}$$

$$i = i^* + \dot{E} \tag{3.1c}$$

$$r = i - \dot{P} \tag{3.1d}$$

$$r = R - \dot{R}/R \tag{3.1e}$$

$$\dot{P} = \gamma(Z - \bar{Y}) \qquad \gamma > 0 \tag{3.1f}$$

where Z is the real aggregate demand for domestic output, $\bar{Y}$ is the supply of domestic output, assumed to be fixed at full employment, G is the real domestic government expenditure, R is the domestic long-term real rate of interest, r is the domestic short-term real rate of interest, i is the domestic short-term nominal interest rate, i^* is the foreign nominal (and real) interest rate, taken to be fixed, E is the exchange rate (expressed in terms of units of foreign currency per unit of domestic currency), expressed in logarithms, P is the domestic price level, expressed in logarithms, and M is the domestic nominal money supply, expressed in logarithms.

Equation (3.1a) specifies the aggregate demand for domestic output to be a negative function of the domestic long-term real interest rate and a positive function of the relative price $E - P$, where we assume that the foreign price level remains fixed at unity. It also depends positively upon the fixed level of output and upon real government expenditure.

The introduction of the long-term interest rate R into the real expenditure function Z is a key part of the model. While this specification has by now been adopted by several authors, it nevertheless merits further comment (see also Blanchard, 1981, 1984; Turnovsky and Miller, 1984; Sachs and Wyplosz, 1984). Several justifications for this can be given. First, to the extent that Z includes expenditures on investment goods, it depends upon "Tobin's q," which in turn is inversely related to the long-term real interest rate. Secondly, it reflects asset values and their impact through the wealth effect on current consumption (see Blanchard, 1981). Finally, Buiter and Miller (1983) suggest that, for the United Kingdom, most government debt is held by institutional investors with long-term horizons, such as pension funds, so that some notion of permanent real interest income based on a long-term rate provides a better approximation of the actual flow of disposable interest income to the ultimate wealth-owning and spending units. This leads them to argue for the plausibility of the long-term rate as a determinant of private expenditure. It is also possible for consumption to depend upon the short-term real rate of interest r as well. The inclusion of this variable, in addition to R, does not alter the substance of our analysis in any essential way.

Domestic money market equilibrium is specified by (3.1b), with the demand for money depending upon the short-term nominal interest rate. Note that we follow Dornbusch and do not introduce the distinction between the price of domestic output and the overall domestic cost of living. To introduce this distinction adds little insight and merely complicates the analysis.[2] Domestic and foreign bonds are assumed to be perfect substitutes on an uncovered basis, so that the uncovered interest parity condition (3.1c) applies, while the short-term real rate of interest is defined in (3.1d).

The long-term real rate of interest is defined to be the yield on a consol paying a constant (real) coupon flow of unity. If we denote such a yield by R, the price of the consol is $1/R$. The instantaneous rate of return on consols is therefore

$$R + \frac{\mathrm{d}(1/R)/\mathrm{d}t}{1/R} = R - \frac{\dot{R}}{R}$$

We assume that the long-term and short-term bonds are perfect substitutes, so that their instantaneous real rates of return are equal as in (3.1e).[3] Integrating this equation, we obtain

$$R(t) = \frac{1}{\int_t^\infty \exp\{-\int_t^x r(t')\,\mathrm{d}t'\}\,\mathrm{d}x} \qquad (3.1e')$$

This relationship shows explicitly how the current long-term rate embodies information about the future (expected) short rates.[4] Finally, equation (3.1f) describes the rate of price adjustment in terms of a simple Phillips curve relationship.

The steady state of the economy is attained when $\dot{R} = \dot{P} = \dot{E} = 0$ and is described by

$$(1-\beta)\bar{Y} = -\beta_2\widetilde{R} + \beta_3(\widetilde{E} - \widetilde{P}) + G \tag{3.2a}$$

$$M - \widetilde{P} = \alpha_1\bar{Y} - \alpha_2\widetilde{R} \tag{3.2b}$$

$$\widetilde{R} = \widetilde{r} = \widetilde{i} = i^* \tag{3.2c}$$

where the tildes denote steady state values. In equilibrium, the product market clears and the short-term and long-term real and nominal rates are all equal to the exogenously given world interest rate i^*. The following long-run equilibrium effects are immediately deduced:

$$\frac{d\widetilde{E}}{dM} = \frac{d\widetilde{P}}{dM} = 1 \qquad \frac{d\widetilde{R}}{dM} = 0 \tag{3.3a}$$

$$\frac{d\widetilde{P}}{dG} = \frac{d\widetilde{R}}{dG} = 0 \qquad \frac{d\widetilde{E}}{dG} = -\frac{1}{\beta_3} < 0 \tag{3.3b}$$

An expansion in the domestic nominal money supply leads to long-run proportional changes in the exchange rate and domestic price level, leaving the long-run interest rates unchanged. An expansion in domestic government expenditure leaves the domestic price level and interest rate(s) unchanged. The exchange rate must appreciate, thereby lowering private demand and accommodating the increased government expenditure, given the fixed output.

Linearizing the system about the stationary equilibrium and substituting, the dynamics can be reduced to the following matrix equation in R, E, and P:

$$\begin{bmatrix} \dot{R} \\ \dot{E} \\ \dot{P} \end{bmatrix} = \begin{bmatrix} \widetilde{R}(1-\gamma\beta_2) & \widetilde{R}\gamma\beta_3 & -\widetilde{R}(1/\alpha_2 + \gamma\beta_3) \\ 0 & 0 & 1/\alpha_2 \\ -\gamma\beta_2 & \gamma\beta_3 & -\gamma\beta_3 \end{bmatrix} \begin{bmatrix} R - \widetilde{R} \\ E - \widetilde{E} \\ P - \widetilde{P} \end{bmatrix} \tag{3.4}$$

It can be shown that the three eigenvalues λ_1, λ_2, and λ_3 of this system have the following properties:

$$\lambda_1\lambda_2\lambda_3 = -\frac{\gamma\beta_3}{\alpha_2}\widetilde{R} < 0$$

$$\lambda_1\lambda_2 + \lambda_2\lambda_3 + \lambda_3\lambda_1 = -\gamma\left(\widetilde{R}\beta_3 + \frac{\beta_3}{\alpha_2} + \widetilde{R}\frac{\beta_3}{\alpha_2}\right) < 0$$

It then follows from these two relationships that there must be one negative and two positive roots, say $\lambda_1 < 0$, $\lambda_2 > 0$, and $\lambda_3 > 0$. The system therefore possesses saddlepoint behavior. We assume that while the price level P always evolves continuously in accordance with the Phillips curve, both the exchange rate and the long-term real rate can jump discontinuously in response to unanticipated disturbances. They are therefore 'news' variables.

In sections 3.4 and 3.5 we consider once-and-for-all unit increases in (a) domestic nominal money supply and (b) domestic government expenditure.[5] These changes are assumed to be announced at time zero for time $T \geqslant 0$, with the limiting case $T = 0$ describing an unanticipated shock.

In the appendix we derive the general solution to (3.4) on the assumption that the economy begins in an initial steady state. Given the assumptions that we have made about the nature of the dynamic variables, these solutions are unique. They form the basis for our subsequent descriptions of the response of the economy to the various disturbances. Because the dynamics is third order, we are unable to give a simple two-dimensional illustration of the phase diagram in the three state variables R, P, and E. However, we do see from the solutions (3.A.3a′)–(3.A.3c′) that, when $t \geqslant T$, i.e. after the announced disturbance has occurred, R, E, and P follow the pairs of linear relationships which ensure stable adjustment of the economy:

$$E - \widetilde{E} = \frac{h_{23}}{\lambda_1}(P - \widetilde{P}) \tag{3.5a}$$

$$R - \widetilde{R} = \frac{-(\lambda_1 h_{13} + h_{12}h_{23})}{(h_{11} - \lambda_1)\lambda_1}(P - \widetilde{P}) \tag{3.5b}$$

where $\lambda_1 < 0$ and the h_{ij} are the elements of the matrix of coefficients appearing in (3.4). It is seen that $h_{13} < 0$, $h_{12} > 0$, and $h_{23} > 0$, and adding the restriction $1 > \gamma\beta_2$ ensures $h_{11} > 0$. Equation (3.5a) is indeed the locus of the stable arm of the saddlepoint in terms of the exchange rate and the domestic price level, familiar from the Dornbusch model, and is *negatively* sloped. Equation (3.5b) is an analogous relationship between the long-term real rate and the domestic price level. Under the conditions stated above, it is *positively* sloped.

3 DOMESTIC MONETARY EXPANSION

Insofar as possible, our treatment will be graphical. Formal solutions for the time paths for this (and other) disturbances can be obtained from the general solution given in the appendix. After the monetary expansion, the economy follows a stable first-order locus (the stable arm of the saddlepoint) and is easily illustrated. In the case of an announced increase, however, during the period after the announcement, but prior to the change, the economy follows an unstable third-order locus. In this case it is difficult to illustrate the time paths precisely, and the paths we have illustrated in a few instances are based on a consideration of plausible limiting cases.[6]

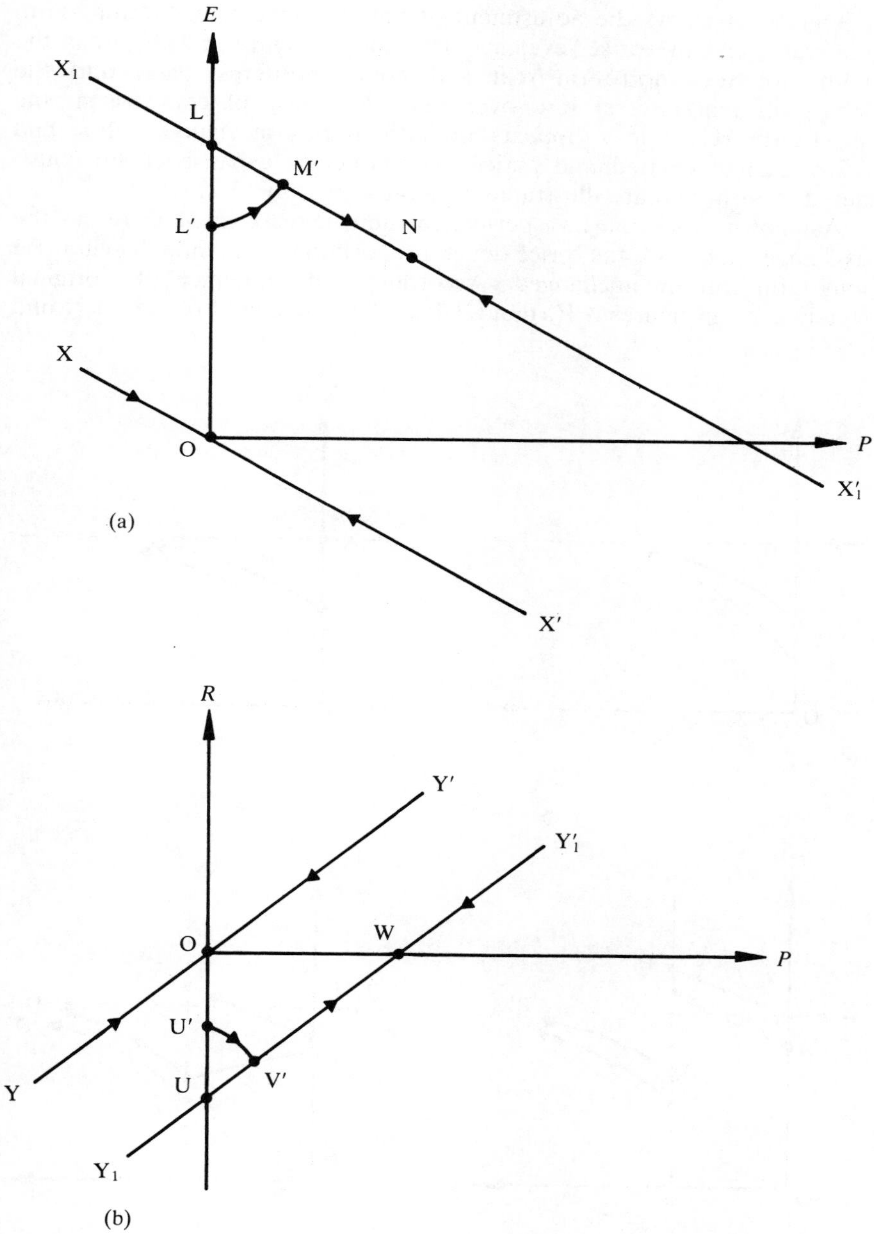

Figure 3.1 Response to domestic monetary expansion: (a) adjustment of E and P; (b) adjustment of R and P.

Figure 3.1 shows the adjustment of the exchange rate, the long-term real rate, and the price level in phase space. Figure 3.2 illustrates the paths for the short-term real and nominal interest rates and the long-term real interest rate over time. For ease of comparison, the short-term real rate r appears in both graphs in figures 3.2(a) and 3.2(b). Unanticipated and anticipated monetary expansions are considered in turn, and are illustrated separately in figure 3.2.

As shown in section 2, a permanent unit increase in M increases the exchange rate and the price level proportionately, while leaving the long-term rate R unchanged. Accordingly, if O depicts the original steady state in figures 3.1(a) and 3.1(b) the new equilibria are at N and

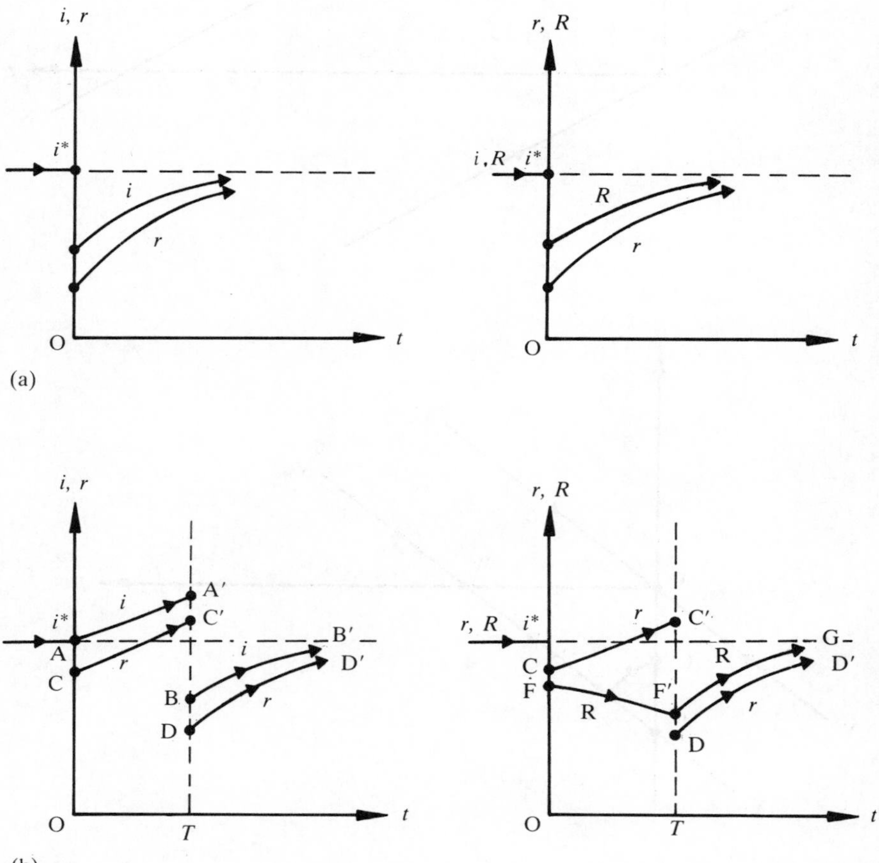

Figure 3.2 Response of interest rates to domestic monetary increase: (a) unanticipated monetary disturbance; (b) anticipated monetary disturbance.

W respectively. Thus the monetary expansion causes the stable loci corresponding to (3.5a) and (3.5b), and illustrated by XX′ and YY′, to move to X_1X_1' and Y_1Y_1' respectively.

3.1 Unanticipated domestic monetary expansion

An unanticipated increase in the domestic money supply causes the exchange rate to jump instantaneously from O to L on X_1X_1'. Thereafter, the exchange rate begins to appreciate gradually, while the price level begins to increase, taking the system toward N. This figure illustrates the well-known 'overshooting' of the exchange rate in the Dornbusch (1976) model.[7] At the same time, the monetary expansion causes the long-term real rate to fall instantaneously from O to U. It then begins to climb gradually back towards its original level, as the price begins to increase.

The time paths for the interest rates i, r, and R are illustrated in figure 3.2(a). The fact that, following the initial depreciation, the exchange rate begins to appreciate immediately at $A(\dot{E} < 0)$ means that

$$i(0) < i^*$$

so that the domestic short-term nominal interest rate is immediately driven below the world rate. With the price level rising and the nominal money stock now fixed at its new (higher) level, the real money stock begins to fall and the domestic short-term nominal rate rises back up toward the equilibrium world rate.

A further consequence of the steadily rising price subsequent to the monetary expansion ($\dot{P} > 0$) is that $r < i$, so that the short-term real rate lies below the short-term nominal rate. At the same time, since the short-term rate is rising over time and the long-term real rate R is discounting the expected future time path of r, it follows that the current long-term real rate must always exceed the current short-term real rate. Another way of seeing this is from the arbitrage relationship (3.1e), which we can write as

$$\dot{R}/R = R - r \tag{3.1e''}$$

Since the long-term real rate rises continuously following the initial drop, for the short-term and long-term rates of return to be equal, $R > r$ as illustrated.

3.2 Anticipated monetary expansion

Suppose that at time zero the domestic monetary authorities announce an expansion in the money supply to take effect at time T say. The announcement of this event causes the exchange rate to depreciate to L′, while the long-term real rate of interest falls to U′. The combination of the fall in the long-term real rate coupled with the devaluation of the exchange rate, leads to an increase in real demand Z, causing the domestic price level to begin rising.

Given that the money supply remains fixed prior to time T and that the price level is constrained to move continuously, the real money stock remains fixed at the time of announcement ($t = 0$). Hence the short-term nominal interest rate i also remains fixed at time zero. The interest rate parity condition (3.1c) therefore implies that, following the initial jump in the exchange rate, the rate of exchange depreciation is immediately zero ($\dot{E} = 0$). However, as the price level begins to rise in anticipation of the monetary expansion, the domestic real money stock begins to fall and the exchange rate starts to increase again to equilibrate the money market: in E–P space, the economy moves along the locus L′M′ in figure 3.1(a). At time T, when the anticipated monetary expansion takes place, E and P begin to move along the stable locus X_1X_1'.

The behavior of the long-term real rate is given in figure 3.1(b) and is more difficult to establish. The arbitrage condition indicates that the behavior of R depends upon the difference between the short-term and long-term real rates of interest. The announcement of the monetary expansion causes the long-term real rate to fall. However, at the same time the short-term real rate also falls, by virtue of the short-run rise in the rate of inflation and the fact that the nominal interest rate remains fixed. A linear approximation to the difference $R - r$, and therefore to the initial rate of change $\dot{R}$, expressed in terms of the initial discrete change in R and E is given by

$$\mathrm{d}\dot{R}(0) = \widetilde{R}(1 - \gamma\beta_2)\,\mathrm{d}R(0) + \widetilde{R}\gamma\beta_3\,\mathrm{d}E(0) \tag{3.6}$$

In principle, it appears that either the long-term real rate effect or the short-term real rate effect (which operates via the inflation rate) may dominate, in which case $R(0)$ may either begin to rise or begin to fall ($\dot{R}(0) \gtrless 0$). Much depends upon the flexibility of the domestic price level, as described by γ. However, if we assume that the price level moves sufficiently slowly for the fall in the long-term real rate to dominate, then R will continue to fall following its initial fall. Thus the real rate follows a time path such as that illustrated by U′V′ in figure 3.1(b). Following the monetary expansion at time T, the long-term real rate begins to rise, along with the price level, as R and P move along the locus Y_1Y_1'.

We turn now to the time paths of interest rates illustrated in figure 3.2(b). As noted, at the time of announcement the real money supply remains fixed, so that, for money market equilibrium to prevail, the demand for money and hence the short-term nominal interest rate remain fixed instantaneously. As the price level rises during the period prior to the monetary expansion (the interval $(0, T)$), the real money stock falls and the short-term nominal interest rate rises along AA′. At the time of the monetary expansion, the real money stock $M - P$ rises, so that the short-term nominal interest rate falls. Thereafter, with the nominal money supply fixed at the new level and the price level continuing to rise, the real money stock falls continuously and the short-term nominal interest rate must again be rising. The short-term nominal rate must have fallen to a point such as B, which lies below the equilibrium level i^*, which it then approaches along the path BB′.

The initial positive inflation rate, generated by the announcement, means that on impact the short-term real rate of interest falls, as already noted. With prices rising throughout the adjustment, this also means that the short-term real rate is always less than the short-term nominal rate (see figure 3.2(b)). The adjustment of the short-term rate during the period $(0, T)$ depends upon whether the exchange rate increases faster than the price level. We have drawn the time path on the assumption that this is the case, so that r rises along with the nominal rate i. However, we cannot rule out the opposite behavior.

At the time of the monetary expansion (time T) the inflation rate moves continuously. This is seen from equations (3.1a) and (3.1f), where the E, P, and R constrained to adjustment continuously everywhere (other than for possible jumps in the latter two at the announcement date), the same must apply to the rate of inflation $\dot{P}$. It then follows that the fall in the short-term real rate at time T must equal that of the short-term nominal rate at that time, i.e. the distances A′B and C′D in figure 3.2(b) must be equal.

In the second part of figure 3.2(b) we have plotted the short-term and long-term real rates. We have commented how at time zero the long-term rate drops by an amount which is likely to exceed the fall in the short-term real rate. This means that, for the arbitrage condition to hold, the long-term real rate must continue to fall (at least initially). If the short-term real rate r, which is primarily driven by the rise in the short-term nominal rate, begins to rise, then the long-term rate will lie below it and will continue to fall in order to generate the capital gains to ensure the equality between the real rates of return on the short-term and long-term securities.

The long-term real rate falls along FF′ and therefore is less than the short-term real rate until F′, when the monetary expansion takes place. At that time, the stable locus is reached and R begins to rise. At the same instant, the downward jump in the short-term rate occurs, so that DD′ lies below F′G as R and r approach their common equilibrium level i^*.

Looking at the two parts of figure 3.2(b) together, we see that the various interest rates being considered exhibit diverse behavior during the various phases of adjustment. The short-run monetary contraction generated by the rising price level, which immediately follows the announcement, causes the nominal interest rate to begin rising in the short run. The short-term real rate will initially fall, but will likely then begin rising and follow the nominal rate. The long-term rate, however, also falls initially, but, in contrast with the short-term real rate, will likely continue falling as it discounts the expected future downward jump in the short-term real rate which will take place at time T. Prior to the monetary expansion at time T, the long-term real rate lies below the short-term real rate; after the policy change is introduced, this relationship is reversed.

4 DOMESTIC FISCAL EXPANSION

A permanent unit increase in domestic government expenditure leads to a long-run appreciation of the exchange rate, while the steady state domestic price level and real rate of interest remains unchanged. This means that the stable locus in $E-P$ space shifts down from XX′ to X_1X_1', while YY′ remains fixed in $R-P$ space.

4.1 Unanticipated increase in government expenditure

The effect on the economy of an unanticipated fiscal expansion is very simple. All it does is to cause the exchange rate to appreciate instantaneously to its new steady state level at N in figure 3.3(a), with the domestic price level and real (and nominal) interest rates remaining unchanged. The transitional dynamics degenerates.

4.2 Anticipated increase in government expenditure

The response of the economy to an announced fiscal expansion is very different. At the time of the announcement, the exchange rate immediately appreciates to L in figure 3.3(a). However, the immediate response in the long-term real rate $R(0)$ is not clear. It is shown in the appendix that, in the short run, the long-term real rate of interest will rise if the interest elasticity of the demand for money, η say, evaluated at the long-run equilibrium is greater than unity (in magnitude); otherwise, it will fall.

An intuitive explanation for this behavior runs as follows. A large value of the equilibrium rate of interest $\tilde{R}$, and hence, for a given value of α_2 a large value of the interest elasticity η of the demand for money, will tend to generate a low level of real private expenditure. This in turn generates a high rate of deflation, thereby leading to a high level of the short-term real rate. Now, the long-term real interest rate at any moment in time is a discounted average of all the expected future short-term real rates. As we will see below, following an announced

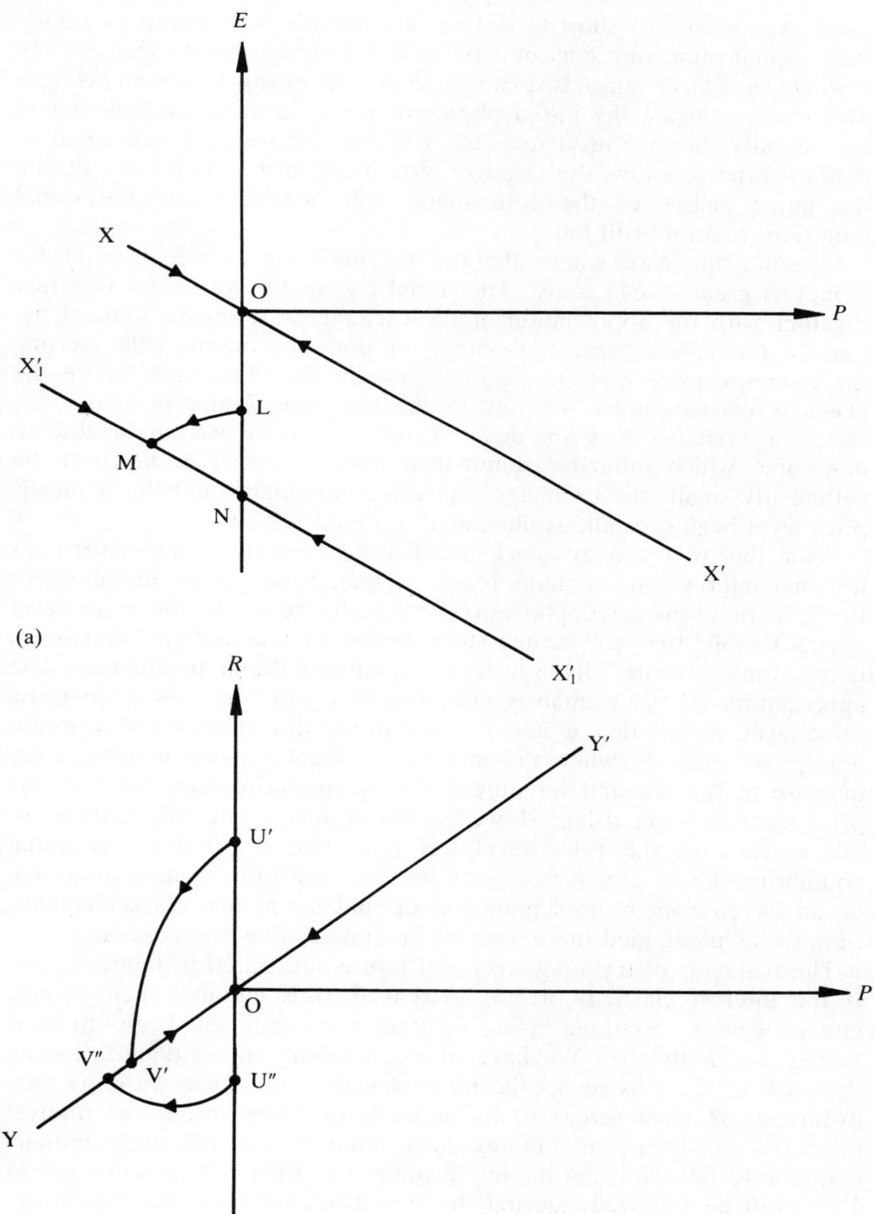

Figure 3.3 Response to anticipated domestic fiscal expansion: (a) adjustment of *E* and *P*; (b) adjustment of *R* and *P*.

fiscal expansion, the short-term real rate initially rises above its steady state equilibrium and subsequently falls below this level. Thus, if the elasticity η is large and r is relatively large, the positive movements in r, which occur during the initial phases of the adjustment, will dominate and initially the long-term real rate will rise. However, if η is small so that r is relatively low, the negative movements in r, which occur during the latter phases of the adjustment, will dominate and the initial long-term real rate will fall.

Consider the case where the interest elasticity of the demand for money is greater than unity. The initial rise in the long-term real rate together with the appreciation of the exchange rate means that, at the time of the announcement, demand for domestic output falls, causing the domestic price level to begin falling. In the other case where the elasticity exceeds unity, the fall in the long-term real rate offsets the effect of exchange rate on demand and in general we are unable to determine which influence dominates. However, if T is taken to be sufficiently small, the exchange rate effect dominates and the domestic price level begins to fall, as illustrated in figure 3.3(b).

With the real money stock fixed instantaneously, the short-term nominal interest rate remains fixed, so that, following its initial jump, the rate of exchange depreciation is initially zero. As the price level begins to fall, the real money stock begins to rise and the short-term nominal interest rate falls in order to equilibrate the money market. The appreciation of the exchange rate, together with the falling domestic price level, means that E and P move in the direction of LM in figure 3.3(a). At time T, when the anticipated fiscal expansion occurs, the increase in the demand for output thus generated causes the domestic price level to begin rising. However, the exchange rate will continue to fall as long as the price level has not been restored to its initial equilibrium level. This is necessary because, until this occurs, there will be an increase in the real money stock and for money market equilibrium to be maintained there must be an appreciating exchange rate.

The behavior of the long-term real rate is illustrated in figure 3.3(b). If the interest elasticity $\eta > 1$, so that R rises initially, then R may either begin to continue rising or it may immediately begin to start falling, i.e. $\dot{R}(0) \gtreqless 0$.[8] We have drawn it falling and initially following the path U′V′. This seems the most plausible case since we know that eventually R must return to its initial level. However, if the interest elasticity $\eta < 1$ and R initially falls, then it will definitely initially continue to fall following the initial jump, i.e. $\dot{R}(0) < 0$. A path such as U″V″ will be followed. During the transition, following the announcement but prior to the fiscal expansion, the long-term real rate will have fallen below its equilibrium. At time T, when the expansion occurs, the knowledge that the short-term real rate of interest is below its equilibrium and will therefore rise in the future causes the long-term real rate to begin rising at time T.[9]

We now consider the time paths of the interest rates shown in figure 3.4. The short-term nominal rate remains fixed at the time of announcement. With the price level falling during the period prior to the expansion $(0, T)$, the real money stock rises and the short-term nominal interest rate falls along the path AA′. At the time of the fiscal expansion, the real domestic money stock remains unchanged, so that the path for the nominal interest is continuous at that point. However,

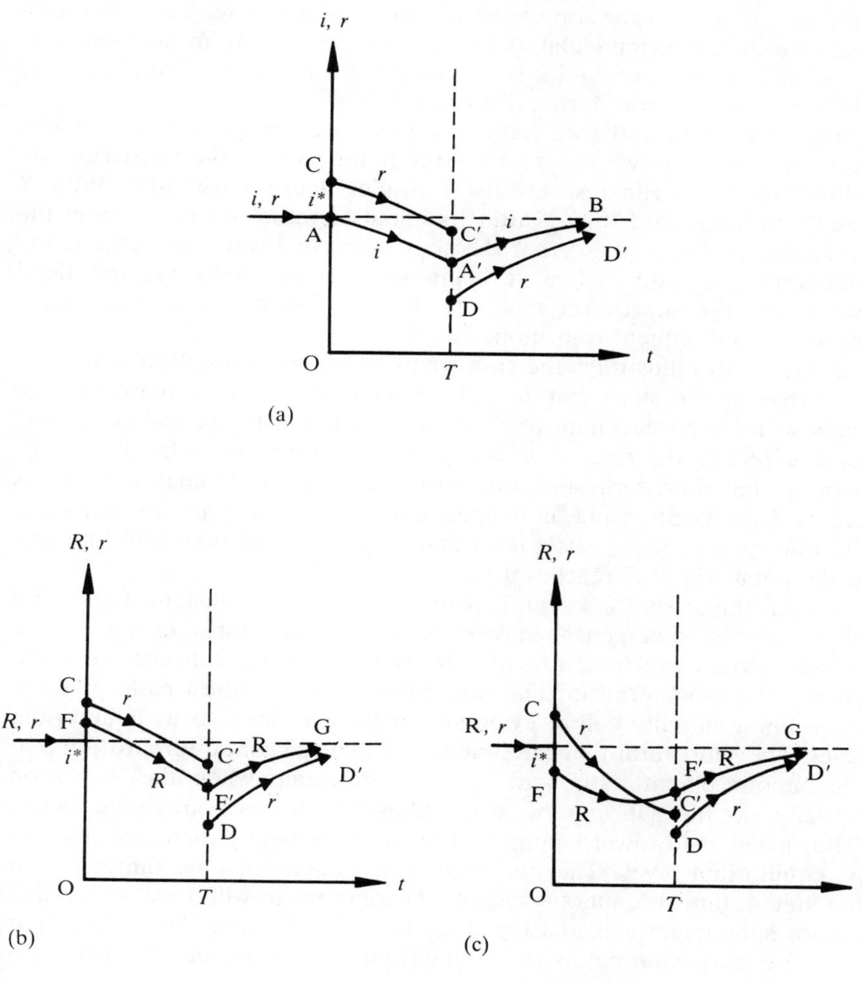

Figure 3.4 Response of interest rates to anticipated domestic fiscal expansion.

with the price level now beginning to rise, the real money stock now begins to fall and the nominal interest rate begins to rise back toward the equilibrium world rate.

The initial deflation at time zero generated by the announcement means that the short-term real rate immediately rises above the short-term nominal rate. With prices falling throughout the entire period $(0, T)$, this means that r always lies above i during that phase. Whether the short-term rate is actually rising or falling depends upon whether the exchange rate falls faster than the price level. We have drawn the time path on the assumption that this is the case, so that r falls with i. At the time of the fiscal expansion the price level begins to rise. The short-term real rate therefore immediately falls below the short-term nominal rate. It remains there during its subsequent adjustment to equilibrium as prices continue to rise during this phase.

The short-term and long-term real rates are drawn in figures 3.4(b) and 3.4(c) for the two cases where the latter rises in the short run and falls in the short run respectively. Consider figure 3.4(b) first. With R falling during period $(0, T)$, after its initial increase, it follows from the arbitrage condition (3.1e) that the short-term real rate must exceed the long-term real rate. When R begins to increase following the fiscal expansion, the short-term real rate drops below it and remains there during the subsequent transition.

Figure 3.4(c) illustrates the case where R initially falls. While we have seen that in the short run R will continue to fall, it is reasonable to suppose that the declining price level, together with the falling R, will tend to reduce the rate of deflation. As a consequence, the divergence between the short-term and long-term real rates is eliminated, and this causes R to begin rising as it approaches the locus YY′. In that case, the time paths for the short-term and long-term real rates will intersect at the point where R reaches it minimum level.

As in the case of an anticipated monetary expansion, figure 3.4 illustrates the divergent behavior of the various rates of interest in response to an anticipated fiscal expansion, particularly during the initial phase. The short-term nominal rate follows the smoothest path, gradually declining initially before eventually increasing back to its equilibrium level. The short-term real rate undergoes two jumps: an upward jump at the announcement date, and a downward jump when the expansion actually occurs. During the early phase it declines gradually, while following the downward jump at time T it gradually increases towards its equilibrium level. The long-term rate undergoes only jump, i.e. at the initial time of announcement. Thereafter, it will tend to decline before subsequently increasing back to its equilibrium level. Like i it may also always lie below the equilibrium world rate, but this need not be the case.

5 CONCLUSIONS

In this chapter we have analysed the effects of monetary and fiscal disturbances, both unanticipated and anticipated, on the dynamic behavior of a monetary model of a small open economy. Attention has focused on the adjustment of the short-term and long-term interest rates and the divergence of their transitional time paths, particularly in anticipation of these disturbances. We have shown how the anticipation of a future policy change can generate perverse short-run behavior. Thus, for example, the announcement of a future fiscal expansion may cause the long-term rate to rise initially. In this case, initial contractionary effects in the economy are generated, though these are eventually reversed when the fiscal expansion occurs. It is also possible for the initial responses of the short-term and long-term rates to be in opposite directions, thereby twisting the yield curve in the short run. The essential reason for the difference in behavior of the short-term and long-term rates is the fact that the latter is dominated by anticipated future events, while the former is primarily determined by current influences.

APPENDIX

General solution to the model

We will write the dynamic system (3.4) as

$$\begin{bmatrix} \dot{R} \\ \dot{E} \\ \dot{P} \end{bmatrix} = \begin{bmatrix} h_{11} & h_{12} & h_{13} \\ 0 & 0 & h_{23} \\ h_{31} & h_{32} & h_{33} \end{bmatrix} \begin{bmatrix} R - \widetilde{R} \\ E - \widetilde{E} \\ P - \widetilde{P} \end{bmatrix} \tag{3A.1}$$

where the h_{ij} are identified by the corresponding elements in the matrix in (3.4). We assume that at time zero the system is in the steady state with $R = \widetilde{R}_1$, $E = \widetilde{E}_1$, and $P = \widetilde{P}_1$. At time zero a change is anticipated to take effect at time T. The new steady state is given by $\widetilde{R}_2$, $\widetilde{E}_2$, and $\widetilde{P}_2$.

The solution to (3A.1) is as follows. For $0 < t \leq T$

$$R - \widetilde{R}_1 = -\sum_{i=1}^{3} \left\{ \frac{\lambda_i h_{13} + h_{12} h_{23}}{(h_{11} - \lambda_i)\lambda_i} \right\} C_i \exp(\lambda_i t) \tag{3A.2a}$$

$$E - \widetilde{E}_1 = h_{23} \sum_{i=1}^{3} \frac{C_i}{\lambda_i} \exp(\lambda_i t) \tag{3A.2b}$$

$$P - \widetilde{P}_1 = \sum_{i=1}^{3} C_i \exp(\lambda_i t) \tag{3A.2c}$$

and for $t \geqslant T$

$$R - \widetilde{R}_2 = -\sum_{i=1}^{3} \left\{ \frac{\lambda_i h_{13} + h_{12} h_{23}}{(h_{11} - \lambda_i)\lambda_i} \right\} C_i' \exp(\lambda_i t) \qquad \text{(3A.3a)}$$

$$E - \widetilde{E}_2 = h_{23} \sum_{i=1}^{3} \frac{C_i'}{\lambda_i} \exp(\lambda_i t) \qquad \text{(3A.3b)}$$

$$P - \widetilde{P}_2 = \sum_{i=1}^{3} C_i' \exp(\lambda_i t) \qquad \text{(3A.3c)}$$

$\lambda_1 < 0$, $\lambda_2 > 0$, and $\lambda_3 > 0$ are the eigenvalues. There are six arbitrary constants to be determined: C_i, C_i', $i = 1, 2, 3$. They are determined as follows.

1 In order for the system to remain bounded as $t \to \infty$, we require

$$C_2' = C_3' = 0 \qquad \text{(3A.4a)}$$

2 We assume that P evolves continuously from its initial given condition, so that

$$C_1 + C_2 + C_3 = 0 \qquad \text{(3A.4b)}$$

3 The time paths for R, E, and P are assumed to be continuous for $t > 0$.

In particular, at $t = T$ the solutions for (3A.2) and (3A.3) must coincide. Thus,

$$(C_1 - C_1')\exp(\lambda_1 T) + C_2 \exp(\lambda_2 T) + C_3 \exp(\lambda_3 T) = \widetilde{P}_2 - \widetilde{P}_1 \qquad \text{(3A.4c)}$$

$$\frac{h_{23}}{\lambda_1}(C_1 - C_1')\exp(\lambda_1 T) + \frac{h_{23}}{\lambda_2} C_2 \exp(\lambda_2 T) + \frac{h_{23}}{\lambda_3} C_3 \exp(\lambda_3 T)$$

$$= \widetilde{E}_2 - \widetilde{E}_1 - \frac{(\lambda_1 h_{13} + h_{12} h_{23})(C_1 - C_1')\exp(\lambda_1 T)}{(h_{11} - \lambda_1)\lambda_1}$$

$$- \frac{(\lambda_2 h_{13} + h_{12} h_{23}) C_2 \exp(\lambda_2 T)}{(h_{11} - \lambda_2)\lambda_2} \qquad \text{(3A.4d)}$$

$$\frac{-(\lambda_3 h_{13} + h_{12} h_{23}) C_3 \exp(\lambda_3 T)}{(h_{11} - \lambda_3)\lambda_3} = \widetilde{R}_2 - \widetilde{R}_1 \qquad \text{(3A.4e)}$$

Thus the general solution for the system is as follows. For $0 < t \leqslant T$

$$R - \widetilde{R}_1 = -\sum_{i=1}^{3} \left\{ \frac{\lambda_i h_{13} + h_{12} h_{23}}{(h_{11} - \lambda_i)\lambda_i} \right\} C_i \exp(\lambda_i t) \qquad \text{(3A.2a)}$$

$$E - \widetilde{E}_1 = h_{23} \sum_{i=1}^{3} \frac{C_i}{\lambda_i} \exp(\lambda_i t) \qquad \text{(3A.2b)}$$

$$P - \widetilde{P}_1 = \sum_{i=1}^{3} C_i \exp(\lambda_i t) \tag{3A.2c}$$

and for $t \geqslant T$

$$R - \widetilde{R}_2 = \frac{-(\lambda_1 h_{13} + h_{12}h_{23})}{(h_{11} - \lambda_1)\lambda_1} C_1' \exp(\lambda_1 t) \tag{3A.3a$'$}$$

$$E - \widetilde{E}_2 = \frac{h_{23}C_1'}{\lambda_1} \exp(\lambda_1 t) \tag{3A.3b$'$}$$

$$P - \widetilde{P}_2 = C_1' \exp(\lambda_1 t) \tag{3A.3c$'$}$$

where C_1, C_2, C_3, and C_1' are determined by (3A.4a)–(3A.4d). The values of these constants depend upon the change in the steady state. This in turn depends upon the particular disturbance to the system and in each case can be obtained from equations (3.3a) and (3.3b).

Determination of sgn R(0) following the announcement of fiscal expansion

To begin, note that since λ_1, λ_2, and λ_3 are eigenvalues, they satisfy the characteristic equation of the dynamic system (3.4), i.e.

$$\lambda^3 = \{\widetilde{R}(1 - \gamma\beta_2) - \gamma\beta_3\}\lambda^2 - \gamma\left\{\widetilde{R}\beta_3 + \frac{\beta_3}{\alpha_2} + \frac{\widetilde{R}\beta_2}{\alpha_2}\right\}\lambda + \frac{\gamma\beta_3\widetilde{R}}{\alpha_2} = 0, \tag{3A.5}$$

Using the standard properties of roots of polynomials, we have

$$\lambda_1\lambda_2\lambda_3 = -\frac{\gamma\beta_3\widetilde{R}}{\alpha_2} \tag{3A.6a}$$

$$\lambda_1\lambda_2 + \lambda_2\lambda_3 + \lambda_3\lambda_1 = \gamma\left(\widetilde{R}\beta_3 + \frac{\beta_3}{\alpha_2} + \frac{\widetilde{R}\beta_2}{\alpha_2}\right) \tag{3A.6b}$$

$$\lambda_1 + \lambda_2 + \lambda_3 = \widetilde{R}(1 - \gamma\beta_2) - \gamma\beta_3 \tag{3A.6c}$$

These relationships can easily be expressed in terms of the h_{ij}. We define the quantity

$$\phi(\lambda) \equiv -\lambda^2 - \gamma\lambda(\widetilde{R}\beta_2 + \beta_3) + \frac{\gamma\beta_3}{\alpha_2} \tag{3A.7}$$

so that (3A.5) can be written as

$$(\widetilde{R} - \lambda)\phi(\lambda) + \widetilde{R}\gamma\beta_2\lambda\left(\widetilde{R} - \frac{1}{\alpha_2}\right) = 0 \tag{3A.8}$$

In the case of a fiscal expansion,

$$\widetilde{R}_2 = \widetilde{R}_1 (= \widetilde{R} \text{ say}) \qquad \widetilde{P}_2 - \widetilde{P}_1 = 0 \qquad \widetilde{E}_2 - \widetilde{E}_1 = -1/\beta_3$$

Solving equations (3A.4b)–(3A.4e) for C_1, C_2, C_3, and C_1', and substituting back into (3A.2a), we can express the solution as

$$R(0) - \widetilde{R} = \frac{(h_{23}h_{32} + \lambda_1\lambda_3)(h_{23}h_{32} + \lambda_1\lambda_2)}{\beta_2 h_{23}h_{31}\lambda_1} \times \left\{\frac{\exp(-\lambda_3 T) - \exp(-\lambda_2 T)}{\lambda_2 - \lambda_3}\right\} \tag{3A.9}$$

where $\lambda_1 < 0$, $\lambda_2 > 0$, and $\lambda_3 > 0$. The term in braces on the right-hand side is greater than zero, and thus

$$\operatorname{sgn}\{R(0) - \widetilde{R}\} = \operatorname{sgn}\{(h_{23}h_{32} + \lambda_1\lambda_3)(h_{23}h_{32} + \lambda_1\lambda_2)\} \tag{3A.10}$$

Multiplying out the expression on the right-hand side of (3A.10) and using (3A.6a)–(3A.6c), we find

$$(h_{23}h_{32} + \lambda_1\lambda_3)(h_{23}h_{32} + \lambda_1\lambda_2) = \frac{\gamma\beta_3}{\alpha_2}\phi_1$$

where

$$\phi_1 \equiv \phi(\lambda_1)$$

Thus

$$\operatorname{sgn}\{R(0) - \widetilde{R}\} = \operatorname{sgn}\phi_1 \tag{3A.11}$$

Now setting $\lambda = \lambda_1$ in (3A.8) yields

$$\phi_1 = \frac{\widetilde{R}\gamma\beta_2\lambda_1(1 - \alpha_2\widetilde{R})}{\alpha_2(\widetilde{R} - \lambda_1)} \tag{3A.12}$$

so that

$$\operatorname{sgn}\phi_1 = \operatorname{sgn}(\alpha_2\widetilde{R} - 1) \tag{3A.13}$$

Since the money supply is measured in logarthims, $-\alpha_2$ is the semi-elasticity of demand so that $-\alpha_2$R measures the interest elasticity of demand evaluated at steady state equilibrium. Letting $\gamma = \alpha_2\widetilde{R}$ and combining (3A.11) and (3A.12), we obtain

$$\operatorname{sgn}\{R(0) - \widetilde{R}\} = \operatorname{sgn}(\gamma - 1) \tag{3A.14}$$

NOTES

1 The distinction between short-term and long-term interest rates in the context of an open economy is briefly considered by Sachs and Wyplosz (1984) in their simulation model.

2 Most importantly, this would introduce the distinction between alternative measures of real interest rates.

3 This relationship is based on the assumption of risk neutrality. To take adequate account of risk-averse agents would require a full stochastic model going beyond the scope of this chapter.

4 Equation (1.1e) assumes that the future short-term rates are known exactly. If this is not the case, $r(t')$ would be replaced by $r^*(t', t)$, the prediction of the future short-term rate for time t' formed at time t. We can define an analogous relationship between the short-term and the long-term nominal rates. However, since the latter does not play any role in the model, this is not required.

5 In an expanded version of this analysis, we also examine the effects of a once-and-for-all unit increase in the foreign interest rate.

6 For example, the limiting cases $\beta_3 \to \infty$ (purchasing power parity) and $\beta_3 \to 0$ (zero substitutability between domestic and foreign goods in demand) provide some insight into the behavior of the economy in these special cases.

7 From equation (3.5a) we see that

$$\frac{\mathrm{d}E(0)}{\mathrm{d}M} = 1 - \frac{1}{\alpha_2\lambda_1} > 1$$

This is identical with the expression obtained by Gray and Turnovsky (1979, this volume, ch. 1) for the amount of exchange rate overshoot in the Dornbusch model.

8 The behavior of $\dot{R}(0)$ can be seen from equation (3.6) and it should be noted that, while $R(0)$ may either rise or fall, $E(0)$ definitely falls.

9 In considering the partial phase diagrams illustrated in figure 3.3, it is interesting to note that, if the fiscal expansion is unannounced, the adjustment is instantaneous. However, the adjustment to an anticipated disturbance takes an *infinite* time, even if the lead time T is small but strictly positive. In this case, the adjustments in R and P would be small, while E would jump close to its new equilibrium level. However, in a strict formal sense, it would still take an infinite time to reach the new equilibrium.

REFERENCES

Blanchard, O. (1981) Output, the stock market, and interest rates, *American Economic Review*, 71, 132–43.

—— (1984) Current and anticipated deficits, interest rates and economic activity, *European Economic Review*, 25, 7–27.

Buiter, W. H. and Miller, M. H. (1983) Changing the rules: economic consequences of the Thatcher regime. *Brookings Papers on Economic Activity*, 2, 305–65.

Dornbusch, R. (1976) Exchange rate expectations and monetary policy. *Journal of Political Economy*, 84, 1161–76.

Gray, M. R. and Turnovsky, S. J. (1979) The stability of exchange rate dynamics under perfect myopic foresight. *International Economic Review*, 20, 643–60. Reprinted in this volume as chapter 1.

Sachs, J. and Wyplosz, C. (1984) Real exchange rate effects of fiscal policy. NBER Working Paper 1255.

Turnovsky, S. J. and Miller, M. H. (1984) The effects of government expenditure on the term structure of interest rates. *Journal of Money, Credit and Banking*, 16, 16–33.

4 Monetary and Fiscal Policy under Perfect Foresight: A Symmetric Two-country Analysis

1 INTRODUCTION

The last decade has witnessed an explosion of literature analysing exchange rate dynamics under rational expectations and efficient markets. This work focuses almost exclusively on small open economies, with virtually no attention being devoted to large two-country models.[1] Presumably, the main reason for this neglect is the technical difficulty of computing and analysing rational expectations equilibria in these more complex models.

In this chapter we analyse the effect of monetry and fiscal policies in a two country macromodel of two symmetric economies. The assumption of symmetry is not unreasonable as a first approximation, since there is no a priori reason for, say, the United States and Europe to differ in terms of their aggregate behavior in any systematic way. Further, this assumption is being adopted extensively in the current literature when game theory is applied to problems of international policy coordination.[2] It has the enormous advantage of allowing a method introduced by Aoki (1981) to be exploited. This procedure enables the dynamics of the system to be decoupled into (a) averages and (b) differences of the relevant variables. Not only does this render the analysis tractable, but it also helps to provide insight into the analysis.

Originally published in *Economica*, 53, 1986, 139–57. This research was supported in part by Grant no. SES-8409886 from the National Science Foundation.

The main focus of the analysis will be on the impact of monetary and fiscal expansions in one economy, say the domestic, on both the domestic and foreign economies. The decomposition of the dynamics into averages and differences makes it clear how anticipations of future policy changes, which operate through their impact on the current exchange rate, affect the two economies in offsetting ways in the short run. Thus, for example, we will demonstrate how the anticipation of a future domestic monetary expansion will, in the short run, generate increased output and inflation domestically, while causing a recession and deflation abroad. The anticipation of a fiscal expansion has the opposite effects in the two economies during the initial phase of the adjustment.

The remainder of the chapter is organized as follows. The model is described in section 2. The steady state and the solution to the dynamics are discussed in the following two sections. The effects of both unanticipated and anticipated domestic monetary expansions are analysed in section 5, and section 6 deals with fiscal expansion. The conclusions are contained in section 7. The formal details are contained in the appendix.

2 A TWO-COUNTRY MACROECONOMIC MODEL

We consider the following two-country macroeconomic model, which is a direct extension of the standard Dornbusch (1976) framework (see for example Gray and Turnovsky, 1979; this volume, chapter 1). It describes two economies, each specializing in the production of a distinct good and trading a single common bond:

$$Y = d_1 Y^* - d_2(I - \dot{C}) + d_3(P^* + E - P) + G \qquad (4.1)$$

$$Y^* = d_1 Y - d_2(I^* - \dot{C}^*) - d_3(P^* + E - P) + G^*$$

$$0 < d_1 < 1,\ d_2 > 0,\ d_3 > 0 \qquad (4.1')$$

$$M - C = \alpha_1 Y - \alpha_2 I \qquad \alpha_1 > 0,\ \alpha_2 > 0 \qquad (4.2)$$

$$M^* - C^* = \alpha_1 Y^* - \alpha_2 I^* \qquad (4.2')$$

$$I = I^* + \dot{E} \qquad (4.3)$$

$$C = \delta P + (1 - \delta)(P^* + E) = P + (1 - \delta)(P^* + E - P) \qquad (4.4)$$

$$C^* = \delta P^* + (1 - \delta)(P - E)$$

$$= P^* - (1 - \delta)(P^* + E - P) \qquad \tfrac{1}{2} < \delta < 1 \qquad (4.4')$$

$$\dot{P} = \gamma Y \qquad \gamma > 0 \qquad (4.5)$$

$$\dot{P}^* = \gamma Y^* \qquad (4.5')$$

where Y is the real output, measured as a deviation about its natural rate level, P is the price of output, expressed in logarithms, C is the consumer price index, expressed in logarithms, E is the exchange rate (measured in terms of units of foreign currency per unit of domestic currency), expressed in logarithms, I is the nominal interest rate, M is the nominal money supply, expressed in logarithms, and G is the government expenditure. Domestic variables are unstarred; foreign variables are denoted with an asterisk.

Equations (4.1) and (4.1′) describe goods market equilibrium in the two economies. Private demand depends upon the real interest rate, the output in the other country, and the relative price.[3] The corresponding effects across the two economies are identical, with the relative price influencing demand in exactly offsetting ways. The money market equilibrium in the economies is standard and is described by (4.2) and (4.2′).[4] The perfect substitutability of domestic and foreign bonds is described by the interest parity condition (4.3). Equations (4.4) and (4.4′) describe the consumer price index (CPI) at home and abroad. The assumption is made that the proportion of consumption δ spent on the respective home good is the same in the two economies. We assume $\delta > \frac{1}{2}$, so that residents in both countries have a preference for their own good. Finally, equations (4.5) and (4.5′) define the price adjustment in the two economies in terms of simple Phillips curves.

The complete world system described by equations (4.1)–(4.5) consists of a third-order dynamic system in the prices P, P^* of the two outputs and the exchange rate E. We assume that the prices P, P^* adjust continuously everywhere, while the exchange rate is free to jump in response to new information. The analysis can be simplified by defining the averages and differences for any variable X say:

$$X^{a} \equiv \tfrac{1}{2}(X + X^*)$$

$$X^{d} \equiv X - X^*$$

Eliminating C and C^* we can write the dynamics in terms of the following decoupled system.

Averages:

$$(1 - d_1 - d_2\gamma)Y^{a} = -d_2 I^{a} + G^{a} \tag{4.6a}$$

$$M^{a} - P^{a} = \alpha_2 I^{a} \tag{4.6b}$$

$$\dot{P}^{a} = \gamma Y^{a} \tag{4.6c}$$

Differences:

$$(1 + d_1)Y^{d} = d_2(1 - 2\delta)(\dot{E} - \dot{P}^{d}) + 2d_3(E - P^{d}) + G^{d} \tag{4.7a}$$

$$M^{d} - 2(1 - \delta)E + (1 - 2\delta)P^{d} = \alpha_1 Y^{d} - \alpha_2 \dot{E} \tag{4.7b}$$

$$\dot{P}^{d} = \gamma Y^{d} \tag{4.7c}$$

Equations (4.6a)–(4.6c) describe the aggregate world economy. The aggregate IS and LM curves (4.6a) and (4.6b) determine the average output level and average nominal interest rate in terms of the average price level, the evolution of which is described by the Phillips curve (4.6c). We assume that

$$1 - d_1 - \gamma d_2 > 0$$

so that the IS curve in Y^a–I^a space is downward sloping. Equations (4.7) describe the differences in the two economies, together with the exchange rate. It is shown below that the dynamics of P^d and E is of the saddlepoint type.

3 STEADY STATE

Since the analysis is based on perfect foresight, the dynamics, which is our prime concern, is determined in part by the steady state. It is therefore convenient to begin with a characterization of this equilibrium. It is attained when $\dot{P} = \dot{P}^* = \dot{E} = 0$, so that $\bar{Y} = 0$, $\bar{I} = \bar{I}^*$, where the bars denote the steady state. Thus the equilibrium in the goods and money markets of the two economies is

$$d_2\bar{I} - d_3(\bar{P}^* + \bar{E} - \bar{P}) = G \tag{4.8a}$$

$$d_2\bar{I} + d_3(\bar{P}^* + \bar{E} - \bar{P}) = G^* \tag{4.8b}$$

$$M - \bar{P} - (1 - \delta)(\bar{P}^* + \bar{E} - \bar{P}) = -\alpha_2\bar{I} \tag{4.9a}$$

$$M^* - \bar{P}^* + (1 - \delta)(\bar{P}^* + \bar{E} - \bar{P}) = -\alpha_2\bar{I} \tag{4.9b}$$

The solutions to these equations are

$$\bar{I} = \frac{1}{2d_2}(G + G^*) \tag{4.10a}$$

$$\bar{\sigma} \equiv \bar{P}^* + \bar{E} - \bar{P} = \frac{1}{2d_3}(G^* - G) \tag{4.10b}$$

$$\bar{P} = M + \left(\frac{\alpha_2}{2d_2} + \frac{1-\delta}{2d_3}\right)G + \left(\frac{\alpha_2}{2d_2} - \frac{1-\delta}{2d_3}\right)G^* \tag{4.10c}$$

$$\bar{P}^* = M^* + \left(\frac{\alpha_2}{2d_2} - \frac{1-\delta}{2d_3}\right)G + \left(\frac{\alpha_2}{2d_2} + \frac{1-\delta}{2d_3}\right)G^* \tag{4.10d}$$

$$\bar{E} = M - M^* + \left(\frac{1-2\delta}{2d_3}\right)(G - G^*) \tag{4.10e}$$

It can be seen that, in the long run, an increase in government expenditure at home or abroad will raise the equilibrium interest rate equally. An increase in domestic government expenditure will raise the relative price of domestic goods, while an increase in foreign government expenditure will have the reverse effect. The increase in the world interest rate lowers the demand for money in both countries. The rise in the relative price of domestic goods increases the real stock of domestic money. Given that the nominal stock remains fixed, the price $\bar{P}$ of domestic output must increase in order to reduce the real supply of money and maintain money market equilibrium. However, the rise in the relative price of foreign goods causes the real stock of foreign money to decrease. This requires the foreign price level to increase less than the domestic price level, and in extreme cases it may even fall. The effects of an increase in foreign government expenditure on the two price levels are symmetric. The nominal exchange rate depends upon the differential government expenditure in the two economies. With $\delta > \frac{1}{2}$, the increase in domestic government expenditure causes a nominal appreciation of the domestic currency, while the opposite applies with respect to an increse in G^*.

An increase in the domestic money supply increases the domestic price level proportionately, causing the domestic nominal exchange rate to depreciate proportionately. The foreign price level, and also the real exchange rate and world interest rate, remain unchanged. The effects of an increase in the foreign money supply are analogous.

4 SOLUTIONS TO DYNAMICS

The solution to the dynamic adjustment of the economy is obtained in two parts: first for the average variables, and then for the differences. These solutions are then transformed to the original variables. We assume that at time zero the world economy is in steady state with $P = \bar{P}_1$, $P^* = \bar{P}_1^*$, $E = \bar{E}_1$. At time zero a policy change is anticipated to take effect at time T. The new steady state corresponding to the disturbed system is $P = \bar{P}_2 = \bar{P}_1 + \mathrm{d}\bar{P}$, $P^* = \bar{P}_2^* = \bar{P}_1^* + \mathrm{d}\bar{P}^*$, $E = \bar{E}_2 = \bar{E}_1 + \mathrm{d}\bar{E}$.

By substitution, equations (4.6a)–(4.6c) describing the behavior of the average world economy can be expressed by the following equation in the average price level:

$$\dot{P}^{\mathrm{a}} = \frac{-\gamma d_2}{D}(P^{\mathrm{a}} - \bar{P}^{\mathrm{a}}) \equiv \lambda_1(P^{\mathrm{a}} - \bar{P}^{\mathrm{a}}) \tag{4.11}$$

where

$$D \equiv \alpha_2(1 - d_1 - d_2\gamma) + \alpha_1 d_2 > 0$$

$$\bar{P}^{\mathrm{a}} = \tfrac{1}{2}(\bar{P}_1 + \bar{P}_1^*) = \text{steady state value of } P^{\mathrm{a}}$$

Integrating equations (4.11), we obtain the solution to the average economy as follows: for $0 < t < T$

$$P^a = \bar{P}^a_1 \tag{4.12a}$$

$$Y^a = 0 \tag{4.12b}$$

$$I^a = \bar{I}^a_1 \tag{4.12c}$$

and for $t \geqslant T$

$$P^a = \bar{P}^a_2 + (\bar{P}^a_1 - \bar{P}^a_2)\exp\{\lambda_1(t - T)\} \tag{4.13a}$$

$$Y^a = \frac{d_2}{D}(\bar{P}^a_1 - \bar{P}^a_2)\exp\{\lambda_1(T - T)\} \tag{4.13b}$$

$$I^a = \bar{I}^a_2 + \frac{1 - d_1 - d_2\gamma}{D}(\bar{P}^a_1 - \bar{P}^a_2)\exp\{\lambda_1(t - T)\} \tag{4.13c}$$

where $\bar{I}^a_1$, $\bar{I}^a_2$ denote steady state values with $\bar{I}^a_2 = \bar{I}^a_1 + \bar{I}^a$. Since the dynamics of the average economy is determined by the average price level, which is sluggish, these variables do not respond in anticipation of a future disturbance, but instead remain stationary until the moment it actually occurs. This simple fact turns out to be important in our subsequent discussion of the transition of policy changes. After the disturbance, the world economy converges monotonically to its new steady state.

By substitution, equations (4.7a)–(4.7c) can be written to express the dynamics of price differentials and the exchange rate by the following equation:

$$\begin{bmatrix} \dot{E} \\ \dot{P}^d \end{bmatrix} = \begin{bmatrix} h_{11} & h_{12} \\ h_{21} & h_{22} \end{bmatrix} \begin{bmatrix} E - \bar{E} \\ P^d - \bar{P}^d \end{bmatrix} \tag{4.14}$$

where[5]

$$h_{11} \equiv \frac{2d_3\alpha_1 + 2(1 - \delta)\{(1 + d_1) + d_2\gamma(1 - 2\delta)\}}{\Delta} > 0$$

$$h_{12} \equiv \frac{-2d_3\alpha_1 - (1 - 2\delta)\{(1 + d_1) + d_2\gamma(1 - 2\delta)\}}{\Delta}$$

$$h_{21} \equiv \frac{2d_3\gamma\alpha_2 + 2\gamma d_2(1 - \delta)(1 - 2\delta)}{\Delta}$$

$$h_{22} \equiv \frac{-\{2d_3\gamma\alpha_2 + \gamma d_2(1 - 2\delta)^2\}}{\Delta} < 0$$

$$\Delta \equiv -\alpha_1 d_2(1 - 2\delta) + \alpha_2\{d_2\gamma(1 - 2\delta) + 1 + d_1\} > 0$$

It can be verified that $h_{11}h_{22} - h_{12}h_{21} < 0$, so that (4.14) describes saddlepoint behavior of E and P^d.

We will focus on the bounded solution to (4.14). This is as follows:

for $0 < t < T$

$$P^{\mathrm{d}} = \bar{P}_1^{\mathrm{d}} + A_2 \exp(\lambda_2 t) + A_3 \exp(\lambda_3 t) \tag{4.15a}$$

$$E = \bar{E}_1 + \frac{h_{12} A_2 \exp(\lambda_2 t)}{\lambda_2 - h_{11}} + \frac{h_{12} A_3 \exp(\lambda_3 t)}{\lambda_3 - h_{11}} \tag{4.15b}$$

and for $t \geqslant T$

$$P^{\mathrm{d}} = \bar{P}_2^{\mathrm{d}} + A_2' \exp(\lambda_2 t) \tag{4.16a}$$

$$E = \bar{E}_2 + \frac{h_{12} A_2'}{\lambda_2 - h_{11}} \exp(\lambda_2 t) \tag{4.16b}$$

where $\lambda_2 < 0$, $\lambda_3 > 0$ are the (real) eigenvalues of the system. The arbitrary constants A_2, A_3, A_2' are determined by

$$A_2 + A_3 = 0 \tag{4.17a}$$

$$(A_2 - A_2') \exp(\lambda_2 T) + A_3 \exp(\lambda_3 T) = \mathrm{d}\bar{P}^{\mathrm{d}} = \mathrm{d}\bar{P} - \mathrm{d}\bar{P}^* \tag{4.17b}$$

$$\frac{h_{11}}{\lambda_2 - h_{11}} (A_2 - A_2') \exp(\lambda_2 T) + \frac{h_{12}}{\lambda_3 - h_{11}} A_3 \exp(\lambda_3 T) = \mathrm{d}\bar{E} \tag{4.17c}$$

where the changes in the steady state equilibrium are dependent upon the specific disturbance. Equation (4.17a) is obtained from the initial condition on the price level and the assumption that P_1 and P_2 move continuously everywhere. The latter two equations are obtained by assuming that prices and the exchange rate move continuously at time T. By contrast, we allow the exchange rate to undergo an initial jump at the announcement date $t = 0$ in response to the new information impinging on the economy at that time. It is this jump that brings about the eventual stability of the system. After the change occurs at time T, P^{d} and E converge monotonically to their new equilibrium values at a rate λ_2.

It is seen from the solutions (4.15), (4.16b) that the nature of the time path of the nominal exchange rate, and in particular whether at any stage it overshoots or undershoots its equilibrium response to an anticipated monetary disturbance, depends upon the sign of h_{12}. If output is fixed, $h_{12} > 0$, but with output endogeneous, in general $h_{12} \gtreqless 0$. To be specific, we shall base our exposition on the assumption

$$h_{12} > 0$$

Loosely speaking, this condition will be met if the income effect in demand for money is sufficiently small.[6] We will also assume

$$h_{21} > 0$$

A sufficient condition for this to be met is $d_3 > d_2/8\alpha_2$, which for plausible parameter values will surely be met.[7] The economic explanation of the results will require minor modification if either of these inequalities is reversed, as in principle they may be.

Combining (4.12), (4.13), (4.15), and (4.16), we obtain the solution of the system in terms of the original variables P, P^*, and E as follows: for $0 \leqslant t < T$

$$P = \bar{P}_1 + \tfrac{1}{2}\{A_2 \exp(\lambda_2 t) + A_3 \exp(\lambda_3 t)\} \tag{4.18a}$$

$$P^* = \bar{P}_1^* - \tfrac{1}{2}\{A_2 \exp(\lambda_2 t) + A_3 \exp(\lambda_3 t)\} \tag{4.18b}$$

$$E = \bar{E}_1 + \frac{h_{12}}{\lambda_2 - h_{11}} A_2 \exp(\lambda_2 t) + \frac{h_{12}}{\lambda_3 - h_{11}} A_3 \exp(\lambda_3 t) \tag{4.18c}$$

and for $t \geqslant T$

$$P = \bar{P}_2 - \tfrac{1}{2}(\mathrm{d}\bar{P} + \mathrm{d}\bar{P}^*) \exp\{\lambda_1(t - T)\} + \tfrac{1}{2}A_2' \exp(\lambda_2 t) \tag{4.19a}$$

$$P^* = \bar{P}_2' - \tfrac{1}{2}(\mathrm{d}\bar{P} + \mathrm{d}\bar{P}^*) \exp\{\lambda_1(t - T)\} - \tfrac{1}{2}A_2' \exp(\lambda_2 t) \tag{4.19b}$$

$$E = \bar{E}_2 + \frac{h_{12}A_2'}{\lambda_2 - h_{11}} \exp(\lambda_2 t) \tag{4.19c}$$

where the constants A_2, A_3, and A_2' satisfy (4.17).

The solutions (4.18) and (4.19) form the basis for our anlysis. The solutions for Y, Y^*, I, and I^*, as well as the real exchange rate and real interest rates, can be derived from these solutions.

5 DOMESTIC MONETARY EXPANSION

Consider a unit increase in the domestic money supply, with the foreign money supply held constant, i.e. $\mathrm{d}M = 1$, $\mathrm{d}M^* = 0$. It follows from (4.10) that $\mathrm{d}\bar{P} = \mathrm{d}\bar{E} = 1$, $\mathrm{d}\bar{P}^* = 0$.

5.1 Unanticipated monetary expansion

The formal solution to the model in the case of an unanticipated monetary distrbance is given in equation (4A.1) and is illustrated in figure 4.1, on the assumption that $h_{12} > 0$. In this case, the exchange rate overshoots its long-run response, on impact, thereafter appreciating toward its new steady state level. The price of domestic output gradually increases, while domestic output initially increases, thereafter falling monotonically towards its natural rate level. The monetary expansion causes an immediate fall in the domestic interest rate, which thereafter rises monotonically toward its equilibrium. All these effects are familiar from the Dornbusch model or its immediate variants.

The effects of the domestic monetary expansion on the foreign economy are less clear cut. The rate of inflation $\dot{P}^*$ of foreign goods and the level of output abroad will rise or fall on impact, depending upon whether λ_2 is greater or less than λ_1. The monetary expansion in

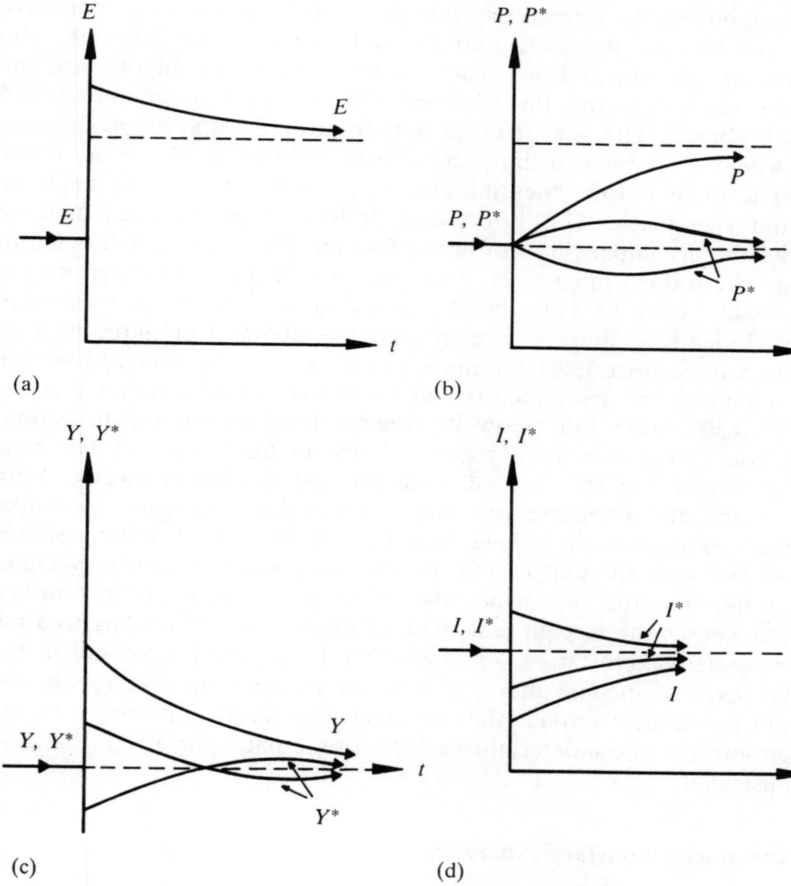

Figure 4.1 Unanticipated monetary expansion: (a) exchange rate; (b) prices; (c) outputs; (d) interest rates.

the domestic economy increases both the average world output, Y^a and the difference Y^d. While this obviously implies a rise in the domestic level of output, foreign output will rise if and only if the increase in average output exceeds half the increase in the difference.

More intuitively, the appreciation of the foreign currency *vis-à-vis* the domestic currency, following the domestic monetary expansion, leads to an increase in the relative price of foreign goods, leading to a fall in demand, and hence in output and in inflation abroad. However, the fact that the foreign currency immediately begins to depreciate following its initial (discrete) appreciation increases the rate of inflation abroad, thereby reducing the foreign real rate of interest. This leads to a positive effect on foreign demand, output, and inflation. In addition, the increase in domestic output leads to an increase in imports by the domestic economy, and this also leads to an increase in output and inflation abroad. The net effect on output and inflation abroad depends upon which of these two opposing effects dominates. However, if the foreign level of output does initially rise, it will immediately begin to fall, and vice versa. This is because, if foreign output does increase initially, the accompanying rise in the foreign inflation rate will begin to increase the foreign price level. Thus the level of the real foreign money supply will begin to fall, thereby inducing a contraction in foreign output. Indeed, as long as foreign output is above it equilibrium level and the foreign price level continues to rise, the contractionary force on foreign output will continue. It can be shown from equation (4A.1e) that Y^* will always fall below its original level during the transition, giving rise to the overshoot pattern shown in figure 4.2(c).[8] The time path is reversed in the case of an initial fall in foreign output. With $h_{12} > 0$ and the domestic currency appreciating following the initial monetary expansion, it follows that the fall in the domestic nominal interest rate exceeds that of the foreign rate, which in fact may either rise or fall. On the one hand, the initial appreciation of the foreign currency causes the foreign real stock of money to rise, leading to a fall in the foreign interest rate. On the other hand, the rise or fall in the foreign level of income may generate an increase or decrease in the demand for money abroad, thereby rendering the overall effect on the foreign interest rate indeterminate.[9] Both time paths for Y^*, P^*, and I^* are illustrated.[10]

5.2 Announced monetary expansion

Consider now the behavior of the economy in response to a monetary expansion which the authorities announce at time zero to take place at some further time $T > 0$. The formal solution is given in (4A.3) and (4A.3′), while the time paths for the relevant domestic and foreign variables are illustrated in figure 4.2.

At the time of announcement ($t = 0$) the domestic currency immediately depreciates in anticipation of the future monetary expansion. Whether the initial jump involves overshooting of the exchange rate depends upon the lead time T. Following the announcement, the domestic currency continues to depreciate until time T, when it reaches a point above the new long-run equilibrium. Thereafter, it appreciates steadily until the new steady state equilibrium is reached. This behavior is identical with that in the Gray–Turnovsky (1979) model.

The anticipation of the future monetary expansion causes the domestic price level to begin rising at time zero. The inflation rate increases

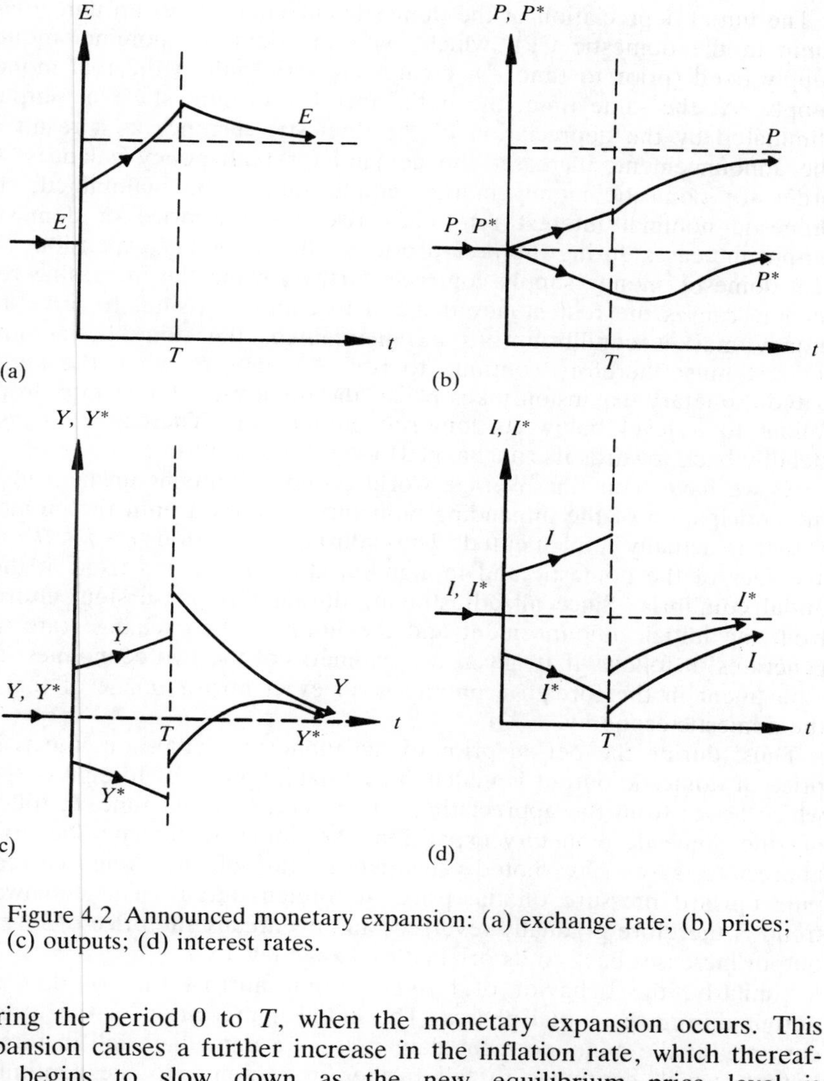

Figure 4.2 Announced monetary expansion: (a) exchange rate; (b) prices; (c) outputs; (d) interest rates.

during the period 0 to T, when the monetary expansion occurs. This expansion causes a further increase in the inflation rate, which thereafter begins to slow down as the new equilibrium price level is approached. The behavior of the inflation rate is mirrored in the level of output. The positive inflation rate generated by the announcement is accompanied by an immediate increase in output, which increases continuously until the monetary expansion occurs at time T. At that time a further discrete increase in output occurs. Thereafter, as a domestic currency appreciates, the relative price of domestic goods rises and demand and domestic output gradually decline to the equilibrium level.

The initial depreciation of the domestic currency causes an immediate jump in the domestic CPI, which, with the domestic nominal money supply fixed (prior to time T), creates an initial fall in the real money supply. At the same time, the initial increase in domestic real output, stimulated by the depreciation of the domestic currency as a result of the announcement, increases the demand for real money balances. In order for domestic money market equilibrium to be maintained, the domestic nominal interest rate must rise. As the price of domestic output increases during the period prior to the monetary expansion, the real domestic money supply contracts further, while the increasing real income causes the real money demand to continue rising. In order for money market equilibrium to be maintained, the domestic nominal interest must therefore continue to rise. At time T, when the anticipated monetary expansion takes place, the domestic interest rate drops, falling to a level below its long-run equilibrium. Thereafter, it rises steadily back towards its (unchanged) long-run equilibrium.

As we have seen, the average world economy remains unchanged by the anticipation of the impending monetary expansion until the moment that it is actually implemented. Thus, during the period $0 \leq t < T$, the averages of the domestic and foreign variables all remain fixed at their initial equilibria. Since all adjustments during this phase stem entirely from the initial announcement and the jump in the exchange rate this generates, it follows that, given the symmetry of the two economies, the adjustment in the foreign economy is an exact mirror image of that in the domestic economy.

Thus, during the period prior to the monetary expansion, the rising price of domestic output is matched by a falling price of foreign output, which arises from the appreciating foreign currency. At time T, following the domestic monetary expansion, the domestic currency begins to appreciate, as we have noted. This depreciation of the foreign currency puts upward pressure on the price of foreign output. The downward trend is therefore gradually reversed, and eventually the price of foreign output increases back to its original exchange level.

Similarly, the behavior of foreign output mirrors that of domestic output during the initial phases. The initial appreciation of the foreign currency at the announcement date causes an immediate fall in foreign output, which continues to fall further in response to the continuing appreciation of the foreign currency. The increase in the foreign inflation rate occurring at time T causes the real interest rate abroad to decline, thereby stimulating foreign demand and foreign output at that time. During the subsequent transition, the depreciating foreign currency stimulates foreign output sufficiently to cause it to rise above its national rate level, after which it declines monotonically.[11]

The appreciation of the foreign currency at the time of announcement causes the real money supply abroad to increase, while the fall in foreign output leads to a decline in the foreign demand for money. These two effects together ensure an immediate reduction in the foreign interest rate. This continues to be the case with the appreciating foreign currency, the declining foreign output, and its price level during this initial phase. At time T, when the domestic monetary expansion occurs, the foreign interest rate increases to a level above the domestic rate but below its long-run equilibrium. Thereafter, I^* increases steadily toward its equilibrium. The reason is that the increase in foreign output at time T, stimulated by the domestic monetary expansion, increases the demand-for-money balances abroad. Since the foreign nominal money balances remain fixed, and since prices and the exchange rate move continuously at time T, the real stock of foreign money balances remains fixed at time T. Thus, in order for foreign money market equilibrium to hold, the foreign nominal interest rate must rise in order to offset the increased money demand resulting from the higher level of income. With the continuous appreciation of the domestic currency following the monetary expansion, the fact that I^* must lie above I during the subsequent transition back to equilibrium is an immediate consequence of the interest rate parity condition.

Finally, we should note that it is possible to analyse the effects of the monetary disturbance upon other variables such as the real exchange rate $E + P^* - P$, the domestic and foreign CPIs C and C^* and the domestic and foreign real interest rates $I - \dot{C}$ and $I^* - \dot{C}^*$. Their responses are essentially composites of those that we have been discussing.

Taking an overview of figure 4.2, it is seen that the anticipation of a future domestic monetary expansion has markedly different effects on the two economies, particularly during the initial phases. Domestically, it gererates an increase in output, together with rising prices, although the boom is reversed after the expansion occurs. Abroad, it initially generates a recession with falling prices, although this is also reversed after the expansion.

6 DOMESTIC FISCAL EXPANSION

We now turn to a consideration of a unit increase in domestic government expenditure, i.e. $\mathrm{d}G = 1$. The corresponding changes in the equilibrium exchange rate and price levels are

$$\mathrm{d}\bar{E} = \frac{1 - 2\delta}{2d_3} < 0$$

$$\mathrm{d}\bar{P} = \frac{\alpha_2}{2d_2} + \frac{1 - \delta}{2d_3} > 0$$

$$\mathrm{d}\bar{P}^* = \frac{\alpha_2}{2d_2} - \frac{1-\delta}{2d_3}$$

where we shall assume that $\mathrm{d}\bar{P}^* > 0$.

6.1 Unanticipated fiscal expansion

The solutions for the relevant variables are given in (4A.4), and the time paths are illustrated in figure 4.3.

The increase in demand resulting from the increase in government expenditure leads to an increase in the relative price of the domestic good. With the prices of domestic and foreign goods fixed instantaneously, this is brought about by an appreciation of the domestic currency.[12] At the same time, the fiscal expansion leads to an increase

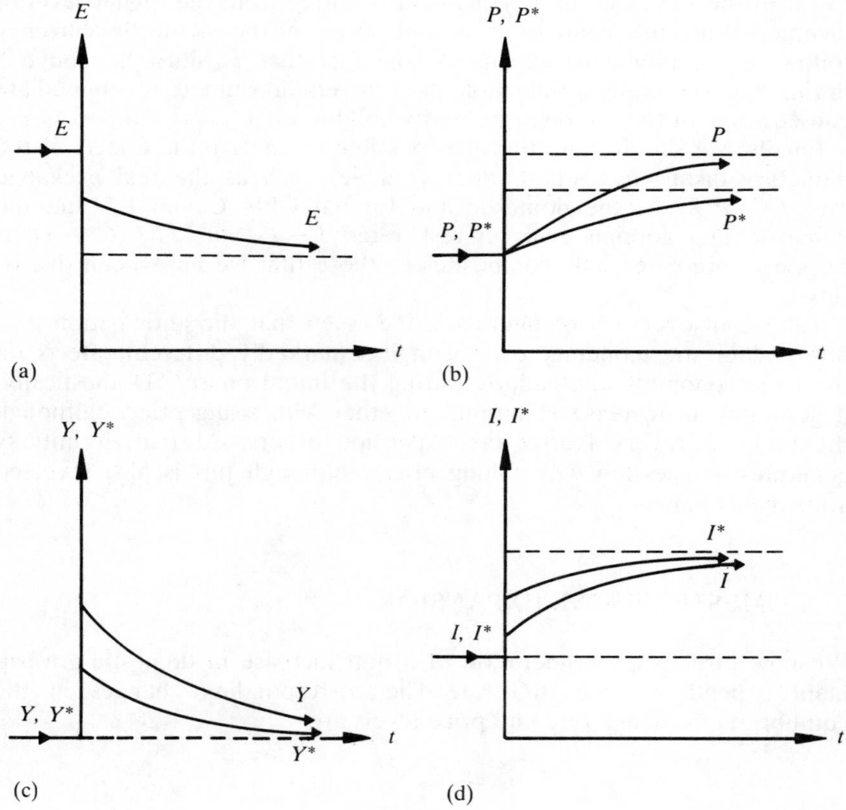

Figure 4.3 Unanticipated fiscal expansion: (a) exchange rate; (b) prices; (c) outputs; (d) interest rates.

in domestic output, thereby causing the rate of inflation of domestic output to increase. With the domestic nominal money supply fixed, the initial appreciation of the domestic currency causes the real domestic money supply to increase, while the expansion in output stimulates the demand for real money balances. The response of the domestic interest rate depends upon which of these two effects dominates. We have illustrated the more usual response, where the latter is dominant, in which case the domestic interest rate rises.

The initial appreciation for the domestic currency is only partial. Thereafter, it continues to appreciate gradually toward its new equilibrium level. As a result of this, the fall in the relative price of foreign goods continues, causing the demand for domestic goods to decline. This in turn moderates the rate of inflation of domestic goods. The combination of the appreciating domestic currency and the rising real money supply, together with the falling output, causes the domestic interest rate to continue rising.

The impact of the domestic fiscal expansion of the foreign economy is slightly less clear cut, although the effects are probably as indicated.[13] The initial depreciation of the foreign currency stimulates the demand for the foreign good and its output. At the same time, the upward pressure on interest rates (without the accompanying increase in government expenditure abroad) has a contractionary effect abroad. We assume that, on balance, the expansionary effect dominates and foreign output rises, although by a lesser amount than does the domestic. As a consequence, the inflation rate abroad rises, although again less than in the domestic economy. The combination of the depreciating foreign currency and increase in foreign output drives the foreign interest rate up.

The continued depreciation of the foreign currency following its initial depreciation causes real money balances abroad to continue declining. This is contractionary, so that output begins to fall steadily. While the depreciating foreign currency puts upward pressure on the foreign price level, these contractionary effects cause the foreign inflation rate to decline, with the price of foreign output ultimately leveling off at its new equilibrium level, which as we have noted is below that in the domestic economy. Finally, the rising domestic interest rate and the depreciating foreign currency means that the foreign interest rate must keep rising, remaining above the domestic rate during the transition.

6.2 Announced fiscal expansion

The solution for an announced fiscal expansion is given in (4A.5) and the time paths are illustrated in figure 4.4.

The anticipation of the future fiscal expansion and the long-run appreciation of the domestic currency leads to an immediate partial

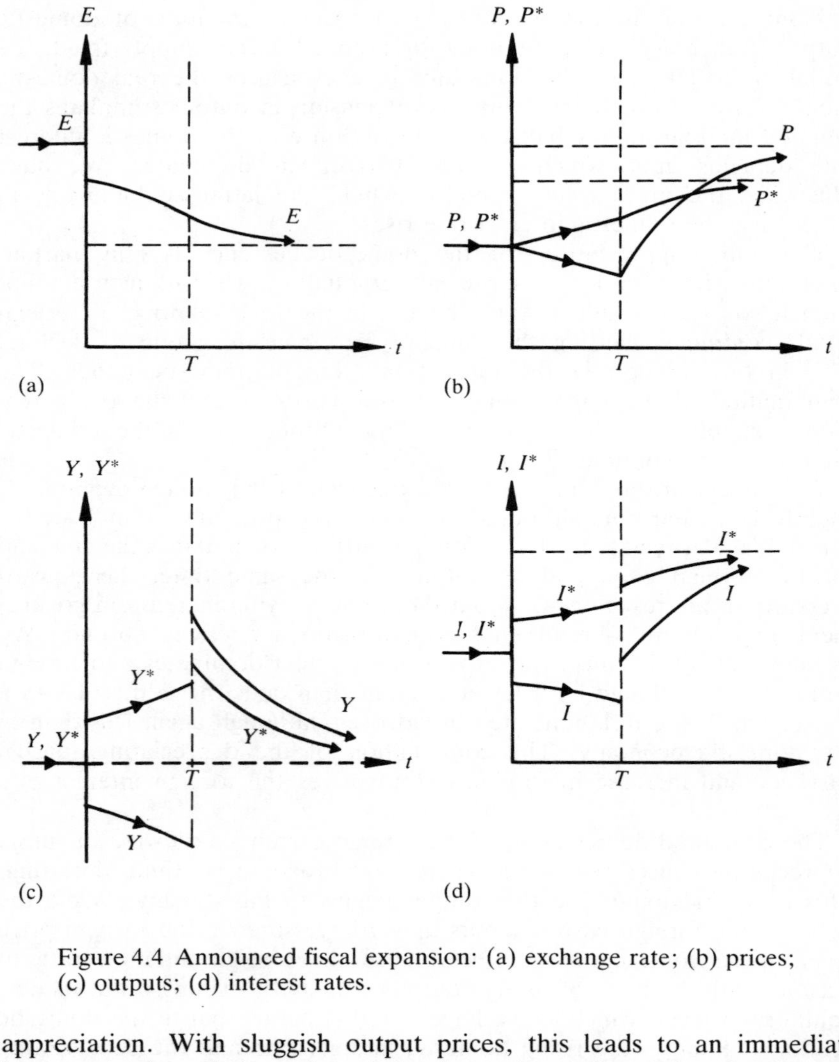

Figure 4.4 Announced fiscal expansion: (a) exchange rate; (b) prices; (c) outputs; (d) interest rates.

appreciation. With sluggish output prices, this leads to an immediate increase in the relative price of the domestic good, causing the demand for domestic output, and hence domestic output itself, to decline. This fall in activity causes the price of domestic output to begin falling. The appreciation of the domestic currency, given the fixed nominal money supply, raises the domestic real money supply, while the fall in output leads to a decline in real money demand. For domestic money market equilibrium to prevail, the domestic nominal interest rate must fall.

The domestic currency continues to appreciate following the announcement. This further reduces demand for the domestic good, thereby continuing to reduce domestic output and the domestic rate of inflation. The combination of the continuously appreciating exchange rate and falling domestic price level, together with falling real output, generates a continuously downward pressure in the domestic nominal interest rate.

The pattern continues until time T, when the anticipated fiscal expansion occurs. This expansion stimulates domestic ouput to a level above its long-run equilibrium. The deflation is reversed, and the price of domestic output begins to rise. This in turn means that the real stock of domestic money starts to fall, thereby providing an offset contractionary effect to output, which then gradually falls to its equilibrium level. As this occurs, the inflation rate is moderated and the price of domestic output gradually approaches its new higher equilibrium level. The expansion in output at time T, generated by the additional government expenditure, also increases the demand for money. With real money balances fixed at that point, this causes the domestic interest rate to undergo a discrete jump at time T, after which it continues to rise toward its new equilibrium level. The fiscal expansion at time T impacts most directly on domestic output. As a consequence, the domestic demand for money rises relative to the foreign demand. If it is assumed that the respective real money stocks in the two economies are given at time T (since they adjust continuously at that time), this means that the domestic interest rate must rise more than the foreign, so that the real rate of appreciation of the domestic currency is reduced at time T. Thereafter, the domestic currency continues appreciating, gradually approaching its new equilibrium level.

We now turn to the foreign economy. As in the case of an anticipated monetary expansion, the aggregate world economy remains stationary until time T, when the fiscal expansion actually takes place. Since the appreciation of the domestic currency during the initial phase $0 < t \leqslant T$ is, *ipso facto*, a depreciation of the foreign currency, during this period the foreign economy behaves as an exact mirror image of the domestic. Again, this is an immediate consequence of the symmetry being assumed.

Thus, during the period following the announcement, but prior to the fiscal expansion, the initial fall in domestic output, together with the subsequent continuous fall, is matched by an equivalent initial increase and continued rise abroad stemming from the depreciation of the foreign currency. The rising foreign output causes the price of foreign output to begin rising at an increasing rate. The initial depreciation of the foreign currency, together with the increase in foreign output, forces an immediate increase in the foreign interest rate, which continues to rise during the initial phase.

At the time of the fiscal expansion, the increase in domestic activity thus stimulated generates some spillover effects onto demand and output in the foreign economy. Output abroad therefore undergoes a modest increase at time T, increasing the foreign rate of inflation at that time. With the foreign money supply fixed throughout, the increase in the real demand for money abroad resulting from the increase in output causes the foreign interest rate to rise at that point. The rising foreign price level causes the relative price of foreign goods to increase, causing foreign output to fall and thereby moderating the inflation. The fiscal expansion in the domestic economy drives up the long-run world rate of interest, and the foreign rate continues to converge to this new equilibrium level.

7 CONCLUDING REMARKS

In this chapter we have analysed the effects of anticipated and unanticipated domestic monetary and fiscl expansions on both domestic and foreign economies. The analysis is based on symmetric behavior, enabling it to be carried out in terms of the sums and differences of the two economies. The properties of the dynamic time paths following these disturbances have been discussed in the text and the details need not be repeated here. However, one striking aspect that is worth highlighting is that the domestic and foreign economies are affected in precisely offsetting ways during the initial phase of the adjustment, following the announcement of the future policy change. This behavior is a direct consequence of the symmetry underlying the analysis.

The analysis has considered the effects stemming from unilateral policy actions by the domestic government on the level of economic performance at home and abroad. By symmetry, analogous policy changes abroad will have similar effects on the domestic economy. It is easy to establish that, if both governments undertake parallel expansions simultaneously, of either the monetary or the fiscal type, so that either $\mathrm{d}M = \mathrm{d}M^*$ or $\mathrm{d}G = \mathrm{d}G^*$, the exchange rate will remain fixed.[14] As a consequence, neither economy responds to the announcement of a future policy change of this type. Instead, the adjustment begins only when the policy change is actually implemented.

Finally, we should note that the framework that we have adopted in this chapter is well suited to considering questions of strategic behavior behavior by domestic and foreign governments with respect to monetary and fiscal policy. We plan to pursue this topical issue in subsequent work.

APPENDIX

In this appendix we present the formal solutions for the system in the case of the specific disturbances analysed in the text.

Unanticipated monetary expansion

The arbitary constants in the solution for the case of an unanticipated monetary expansion are obtained by setting $T = 0$, $d\bar{E} = d\bar{P} = 1$, $d\bar{P}^* = 0$ in (4.17a)–(4.17c). The relevant constant is $A_2' = -1$. Substituting into (4.19), the solutions for P, P^*, and E are given by (for $t \geqslant 0$)

$$P = \bar{P}_2 - \tfrac{1}{2}\exp(\lambda_1 t) - \tfrac{1}{2}\exp(\lambda_2 t) \tag{4A.1a}$$

$$P^* = \bar{P}_2^* - \tfrac{1}{2}\exp(\lambda_1 t) + \tfrac{1}{2}\exp(\lambda_2 t) \tag{4A.1b}$$

$$E = \bar{E}_2 - \frac{h_{12}}{\lambda_2 - h_{11}}\exp(\lambda_2 t) \tag{4A.1c}$$

From these equations and the basic model, we obtain

$$Y = -\frac{\lambda_1}{2\gamma}\exp(\lambda_1 t) - \frac{\lambda_2}{2\gamma}\exp(\lambda_2 t) \tag{4A.1d}$$

$$Y^* = -\frac{\lambda_1}{2\gamma}\exp(\lambda_1 t) + \frac{\lambda_2}{2\gamma}\exp(\lambda_2 t) \tag{4A.1e}$$

$$I = \bar{I} - \frac{1 - d_1 - d_2\gamma}{2D}\exp(\lambda_1 t) - \frac{h_{12}\lambda_2}{2(\lambda_2 - h_{11})}\exp(\lambda_2 t) \tag{4A.1f}$$

$$I^* = \bar{I} - \frac{1 - d_1 - d_2\gamma}{2D}\exp(\lambda_1 t) + \frac{h_{12}\lambda_2}{2(\lambda_2 - h_{11})}\exp(\lambda_2 t) \tag{4A.1g}$$

Announced monetary expansion

The solutions for the arbitrary constants in the case of an announced monetary expansion are

$$-A_2 = A_3 = \frac{h_{22} + h_{21} - \lambda_2}{\lambda_3 - \lambda_2}\exp(-\lambda_3 T) \tag{4A.2a}$$

$$A_2' = \frac{h_{22} + h_{21} - \lambda_3}{\lambda_3 - \lambda_2}\exp(-\lambda_2 T) - \frac{h_{22} + h_{21} - \lambda_2}{\lambda_3 - \lambda_2}\exp(-\lambda_3 T) \tag{4A.2b}$$

where $\lambda_2 < 0$, $\lambda_3 > 0$ are the solutions to the characteristic equation

$$\lambda_2 - (h_{11} + h_{22})\lambda + (h_{11}h_{22} - h_{12}h_{21}) = 0$$

Using the elementary properties of the roots of the quadratic equation, it is easy to show that, given $h_{11} > 0$, $h_{22} < 0$, $h_{12} > 0$, and $h_{21} > 0$, then $A_3 > 0$.

The solutions for the relevant variables are as follows. For $0 \leqslant t < T$

$$P = \bar{P}_1 + \tfrac{1}{2}A_3\{\exp(\lambda_3 t) - \exp(\lambda_2 t)\} \tag{4A.3a}$$

$$P^* = \bar{P}_1^* - \tfrac{1}{2}A_3\{\exp(\lambda_3 t) - \exp(\lambda_2 t)\} \tag{4A.3b}$$

$$E = \bar{E}_1 + h_{12}A_3\left\{\frac{\exp(\lambda_3 t)}{\lambda_3 - h_{11}} - \frac{\exp(\lambda_2 t)}{\lambda_2 - h_{11}}\right\} \tag{4A.3c}$$

$$Y = \tfrac{1}{2}A_3\{\lambda_3 \exp(\lambda_3 t) - \lambda_2 \exp(\lambda_2 t)\} \tag{4A.3d}$$

$$Y^* = -\tfrac{1}{2}A_3\{\lambda_3 \exp(\lambda_3 t) - \lambda_2 \exp(\lambda_2 t)\} \tag{4A.3e}$$

$$I = \bar{I}_1 + \tfrac{1}{2}h_{12}A_3\left\{\frac{\lambda_3 \exp(\lambda_2 t)}{\lambda_3 - h_{11}} - \frac{\lambda_2 \exp(\lambda_2 t)}{\lambda_2 - h_{11}}\right\} \tag{4A.3f}$$

$$I^* = \bar{I}_1 - \tfrac{1}{2}h_{12}A_3\left\{\frac{\lambda_3 \exp(\lambda_3 t)}{\lambda_3 - h_{11}} - \frac{\lambda_2 \exp(\lambda_2 t)}{\lambda_2 - h_{11}}\right\} \tag{4A.3g}$$

where A_3 is given by (4A.2a)

For $t \geqslant T$

$$P = \bar{P}_2 - \tfrac{1}{2}\exp\{\lambda_1(t - T)\} + \tfrac{1}{2}A_2' \exp(\lambda_2 t) \tag{4A.3a'}$$

$$P^* = \bar{P}_2^* - \tfrac{1}{2}\exp\{\lambda_1(t - T)\} - \tfrac{1}{2}A_2' \exp(\lambda_2 t) \tag{4A.3b'}$$

$$E = \bar{E}_2 + \frac{h_{12}A_2'}{\lambda_2 - h_{11}}\exp(\lambda_2 t) \tag{4A.3c'}$$

$$Y = -\tfrac{1}{2}\lambda_1 \exp\{\lambda_1(t - T)\} + \tfrac{1}{2}A_2'\lambda_2 \exp(\lambda_2 t) \tag{4A.3d'}$$

$$Y^* = -\tfrac{1}{2}\lambda_1 \exp\{\lambda_1(t - T)\} - \tfrac{1}{2}A_2'\lambda_2 \exp(\lambda_2 t) \tag{4A.3e'}$$

$$I = \bar{I} - \frac{1 - d_1 - d_2\gamma}{2D}\exp\{\lambda_1(t - T) + \frac{1}{2}\frac{h_{12}A_2'\lambda_2}{\lambda_2 - h_{11}}\exp(\lambda_2 t) \tag{4A.3f'}$$

$$I^* = \bar{I}^* - \frac{1 - d_1 - d_2\gamma}{2D}\exp\{\lambda_1(t - T) - \frac{1}{2}\frac{h_{12}A_2'\lambda_2}{\lambda_2 - h_{11}}\exp(\lambda_2 t) \tag{4A.3g'}$$

where A_2' is given by (4A.2b).

Unanticipated fiscal expansion

The arbitrary constants in this case are obtained by setting $T = 0$, $\mathrm{d}\bar{E} = (1 - 2\delta)/2d_3$, $\mathrm{d}\bar{P} = \alpha_2/2d_2 + (1 - \delta)/2d_3$, and $\mathrm{d}\bar{P}^* = \alpha_2/2d_2 - (1 - \delta)/2d_3$ in (4.17a)–(4.17c). This implies that $A_2' = -(1 - \delta)/d_3$, and, substituting into (4.19), the solution for P, P^*, E, and other variables is as follows:

$$P = \bar{P}_2 - \frac{\alpha_2}{2d_2}\exp(\lambda_1 t) - \frac{1 - \delta}{2d_3}\exp(\lambda_2 t) \tag{4A.4a}$$

$$P^* = \bar{P}_2^* - \frac{\alpha_2}{2d_2}\exp(\lambda_1 t) + \frac{1-\delta}{2d_3}\exp(\lambda_2 t) \qquad (4A.4b)$$

$$E = \bar{E}_2 - \frac{h_{12}(1-\delta)}{(\lambda_2 - h_{11})d_3}\exp(\lambda_2 t) \qquad (4A.4c)$$

$$Y = -\frac{-\alpha_2\lambda_1}{2d_2}\exp(\lambda_1 t) - \frac{(1-\delta)\lambda_2}{2d_3}\exp(\lambda_2 t) \qquad (4A.4d)$$

$$Y^* = -\frac{-\alpha_2\lambda_1}{2d_2}\exp(\lambda_1 t) + \frac{(1-\delta)\lambda_2}{2d_3}\exp(\lambda_2 t) \qquad (4A.4e)$$

$$I = \bar{I} - \frac{(1-d_1-d_2\gamma)\alpha_2}{2Dd_2}\exp(\lambda_1 t) - \frac{h_{12}\lambda_2(1-\delta)}{2(\lambda_2 - h_{11})d_3}\exp(\lambda_2 t) \qquad (4A.4f)$$

$$I^* = \bar{I}^* - \frac{(1-d_1-d_2\gamma)\alpha_2}{2Dd_2}\exp(\lambda_1 t) + \frac{h_{12}\lambda_2(1-\delta)}{2(\lambda_2 - h_{11})d_3}\exp(\lambda_2 t) \qquad (4A.4g)$$

Announced fiscal expansion

The solutions for the arbitary constants are

$$-A_2 = A_3 = -\frac{2(1-\delta)(\lambda_3 - h_{11}) + (1-2\delta)h_{21}}{2d_3(\lambda_2 - \lambda_3)}\exp(-\lambda_3 T) \qquad (4A.5a)$$

$$A_2' = \frac{2(1-\delta)(\lambda_3 - h_{11}) + (1-2\delta)h_{21}}{2d_3(\lambda_2 - \lambda_3)}\exp(-\lambda_3 T) - \frac{2(1-\delta)(\lambda_2 - h_{11}) + (1-2\delta)h_{21}}{2d_3(\lambda_2 - \lambda_3)}\exp(-\lambda_2 T) \qquad (4A.5b)$$

the solution to the system for $0 \leqslant t < T$ is again given by (4A.3a)–(4A.3g), with the constant A_3 now given by (4A.5a). For $t \geqslant T$

$$P = \bar{P}_2 - \frac{\alpha_2}{2d_2}\exp\{\lambda_1(t-T) + \frac{1}{2}A_2'\exp(\lambda_2 t) \qquad (4A.6a)$$

$$P^* = \bar{P}_2^* - \frac{\alpha_2}{2d_2}\exp\{\lambda_1(t-T)\} - \frac{1}{2}A_2'\exp(\lambda_2 t) \qquad (4A.6b)$$

$$E = \bar{E}_2 + \frac{h_{12}A_2'}{\lambda_2 - h_{11}}\exp(\lambda_2 t) \qquad (4A.6c)$$

$$Y = -\frac{\alpha_2\lambda_1}{2d_2}\exp\{\lambda_1(t-T)\} + \frac{1}{2}A_2'\lambda_2\exp(\lambda_2 t) \qquad (4A.6d)$$

$$Y^* = -\frac{\alpha_2\lambda_1}{2d_2}\exp\{\lambda_1(t-T)\} - \frac{1}{2}A_2'\lambda_2\exp(\lambda_2 t) \qquad (4A.6e)$$

$$I = \bar{I}_2 - \frac{(1-d_1-d_2\gamma)\alpha_2}{2Dd_2}\exp\{\lambda_1(t-T) + \frac{h_{12}A_2'\lambda_2}{2(\lambda_2-h_{11})}\exp(\lambda_2 t) \qquad (4A.6f)$$

$$I^* = \bar{I}_2^* - \frac{(1-d_1-d_2\gamma)\alpha_2}{2Dd_2}\exp\{\lambda_1(t-T) - \frac{h_{12}A_2'\lambda_2}{2(\lambda_2-h_{11})}\exp(\lambda_2 t) \qquad (4A.6g)$$

where A_2' is now given by (4A.5b).

NOTES

1 See for example the comprehensive survey of exchange rate dynamics by Obstfeld and Stockman (1984). Several of the early Mundell–Fleming-type models do of course analyse monetary and fiscal policy for two countries, but in a static context. In addition, some of the more recent work on transmission mechanisms uses two-country models, although these also are typically static, or perhaps assume some kind of backward-looking dynamics (see for example Hamada and Sakurai, 1978; Corden and Tunovsky, 1983).

2 See for example Canzoneri and Gray (1985), Miller and Salmon (1985), and Oudiz and Sachs (1985).

3 It is assumed that a unit increase in foreign output has a less than equivalent increase on the demand for the domestic good, i.e. $d_1 < 1$.

4 As in most of the literature, it is assumed that the residents of each country do not hold the money of the other country. We should also note that the analysis remains unchanged if the money demand functions are modified to $M - C = \alpha_1(P + Y - C) - \alpha_2 I$, and analogously for the foreign demand function, with $\alpha_1 < 1$.

5 In signing h_{11}, h_{22}, we are assuming $\delta > 1/2$. In addition, to establish $\Delta > 0$, use is being made of the assumption that $1 - d_1 - \gamma d_2 > 0$.

6 $h_{12} > 0$ implies the following upper bound on α_1: $\alpha_1 < (2\delta - 1)\{(1 + d_1) + d_2\gamma(1 - 2\delta)\}/2d_3$.

7 The numerator of the expression of h_{21} is $4\gamma d_2\delta^2 - 6\gamma d_2\delta + 2\gamma(d_2 + d_3\alpha_2)$. This will be positive everywhere in the range $0 < \delta < 1$, and hence $h_{21} > 0$ if and only if $d_3 > d_2/8\alpha_2$.

8 I am grateful to a referee for drawing this to my attention. From (4.1e), we see that $Y^* = \bar{Y}$ at $t^* = \ln(\lambda_1/\lambda_2)/(\lambda_2 - \lambda_1)$. With $\lambda_1 < 0$ and $\lambda_2 < 0$, this quantity is necessarily positive.

9 In the case that $h_{12} < 0$, the exchange rate does not overshoot, and so $\dot{E} > 0$ throughout the adjustment. The interest parity condition then implies that $I > I^*$.

10 The time path of I^* may or may not overshoot its long-run adjustment during the transition. We have drawn monotonic adjustment paths.

11 This occurs at the point where the foreign price level begins to rise. If the spillover of the domestic monetary expansion is sufficiently great to cause the foreign price level to begin rising immediately at time T, then Y^* will be driven above its equilibrium level at that time.

12 If $\delta = 1$, as in the Dornbusch model, then the exchange rate completes its adjustment instantaneously in response to an unanticipated fiscal expansion.

13 If $\delta \approx 1$, for example, the adjustment will be as illustrated.

14 In either of these cases it follows from (4.10c)–(4.10e) that the long-run exchange rate remains fixed, while the price of domestic and foreign goods increases proportionately. It then follows from (4.17a)–(4.17c) that $A_2 = A_3 = A'_2 = 0$, so that the exchange rate remains fixed at all times. Since anticipations of future policy changes impinge on the current system through the exchange rate, it follows that these are nonoperative in the case of such balanced policy changes.

REFERENCES

Aoki, M. (1981) *Dynamic Analysis of Open Economics*. New York: Academic Press.

Canzoneri, M. and Gray, J. A. (1985) Monetary policy and the consequences of non-cooprative behavior. *International Economic Review*, 26, 547–64.

Corden, W. M. and Turnovsky, S. J. (1983) Negative transmission of economic expansion. *European Economic Review*, 20, 289–310.

Dornbusch, R. (1976). Expectations and exchange rate dynamics. *Journal of Political Economy*, 84, 1161–76.

Gray, M. R. and Turnovsky, S. J. (1979) The stability of exchange rate dynamics under perfect myopic foresight. *International Economic Review*, 20, 643–60. Reprinted in this volume as chapter 1.

Hamada, K. and Sakurai, M. (1978) International transmission of stagflation under fixed and flexible exchange rates. *Journal of Political Economy*, 86, 877–95.

Miller, M. H. and Salmon, M. (1985) Policy coordination and dynamic games. In *International Economic Policy Coordination* (eds W. H. Buiter and R. C. Marston). Cambridge: Cambridge University Press.

Obstfeld, M. and Stockman, A. C. (1984) Exchange rate dynamics. In *Handbook in International Economics* (eds R. W. Jones and P. B. Kenen). Amsterdam: North-Holland.

Oudiz, G. and Sachs, J. (1985) International policy coordination in dynamic macroeconomic models. In *International Economic Policy Coordination* (eds W. H. Buiter and R. C. Marston). Cambridge: Cambridge University Press.

Part II

Stochastic Models

5 Monetary Policy and Foreign Price Disturbances under Flexible Exchange Rates

1 INTRODUCTION

The analysis of monetary policy under flexible exchange rates has received extensive treatment during recent years. Particular attention has been devoted to the role of exchange rate expectations, with a general conclusion being that many of the propositions of the traditional static Fleming–Mundell model (Fleming, 1962, Mundell, 1968) require substantial modification once such expectations are taken into account (see Niehans, 1975; Dornbusch, 1976; Turnovsky, 1977). With few exceptions, the analysis has been carried out in a deterministic framework. The usual assumption made is that any monetary expansion that is introduced is initially (*ex ante*) unanticipated, but, having taken place, it is then (*ex post*) expected to be permanent. This assumption underlies, for example, the recent contribution by Dornbusch (1976) and much of the subsequent work that stems from it.[1]

This assumption, while very natural, is also polar. In pratice, agents in the economy may attempt to anticipate monetary policy and the policies themselves may, and may be expected to, vary in their permanency. It is intuitively clear that the effects of monetary policy – and for that matter any other policy – will vary substantially, depending upon the extent to which it is predicted and the permanence with which it is expected to continue. This view would seem to be one of the central messages to emerge from the current rational expectations literature.

The prime objective of the present chapter is to analyse the effects of monetary policy under flexible exchange rates, allowing for more general assumptions regarding these kinds of expectational issues. To do

Originally published in *Journal of Money, Credit, and Banking*, 13 (2), May 1981, 156–76.

I am grateful for helpful comments received from members of seminars at the University of Minnesota, Virginia Polytechnic Institute, and Duke University.

this, it is desirable to develop the analysis within a stochastic framework. However, having constructed the framework, it is then straightforward to use it to investigate similar kinds of issues with respect to other exogenous disturbances. One of the more interesting of these concerns foreign price disturbances. This has also been receiving increased attention recently, with economists investigating the extent to which flexible exchange rates insulate the domestic economy against such disturbances (see Kouri, 1976; Laidler, 1977; Floyd, 1978; Turnovsky, 1979). However precisely the same limitation characterizes the existing literature in this area; it deals with *ex ante* unanticipated, but *ex post* expected permanent, changes in the foreign price level. Thus a secondary objective of this chapter is to generalize these kinds of assumptions about foreign price changes.

Like much of the current work on exchange rate determination, expectations play a central role in our analysis. The expectations of the endogenous variables appearing in the model (the one-period expectations of the exchange rate and the cost of living) are assumed to be consistent with the structure of the model and conditional on the perdiction of the exogenous variables (the money supply and foreign price level). Through this process the predictions of all future exogenous variables impinge on the current state of the economy. Such a rational expectations framework is attractive and natural for analysing the kinds of expectational issues we have noted, enabling us to distinguish explicitly between actual and anticipated changes on the one hand, and permanent and temporary changes on the other. Indeed, the application to exchange rate determination is not new. This framework has been employed recently by Frenkel (1976), Mussa (1976), Barro (1978) and Cox (1980), among others, and the present chapter can be viewed as an extension of this work. In particular, more attention is devoted to analysing the response of the complete system to alternative forms of monetary disturbances.[2]

The rest of the chapter proceeds as follows. In section 2 the model is detailed and reduced to a form convenient for further analysis. In order to determine the short-run equilibrium, it is first necessary to solve the system for the endogenously determined rational expectations, and this is undertaken in section 3. The short-run equilibrium is summarized in section 4, and the following section analyses the effects of a variety of anticipated and actual monetary disturbances. Section 6 briefly deals with the effects of foreign price disturbances, while our main conclusions are summarized in the final section.

2 STOCHASTIC MODEL OF AN OPEN ECONOMY UNDER FLEXIBLE EXCHANGE RATES

The model we will develop shares much in common with the recent models emphasizing the monetary approach to exchange rate determination (see Dornbusch, 1976; Barro, 1978; Parkin, 1978; Gray and Turnovsky, 1979, this volume, ch. 1).[3] Two general features that we wish to stress at the outset are the following. First the country is assumed to produce a single (composite) commodity of which part is consumed domestically and the remainder is exported. The price of this commodity is determined in the market for domestic output, so that the price of exports is endogenously determined. However, we assume that the country is sufficiently competitive in the market for its imports to take the (foreign) price of imports as given. Second, the domestic bond market is assumed to be perfectly integrated with that in the rest of the world. Thus the model is described by the following five equations:

$$Y_t = d_1 Y_t - d_2\{r_t - (C^*_{t+1,t} - C_t)\} + d_3(Q_t + E_t - P_t)$$
$$0 < d_1 < 1,\ d_2 > 0,\ d_3 > 0 \qquad (5.1a)$$

$$C_t = \delta P_t + (1 - \delta)(Q_t + E_t) \qquad (5.1b)$$

$$M_t - C_t = \alpha_1 Y_t - \alpha_2 r_t, \qquad \alpha_1 > 0, \alpha_2 > 0 \qquad (5.1c)$$

$$r_t = \rho + E^*_{t-1,t} - E_t \qquad (5.1d)$$

$$Y_t = \alpha + \gamma_1(P_t - C^*_{t,t-1}) + \gamma_2(P_t - P^*_{t,t-1}) \quad \gamma_1 > 0, \gamma_2 > 0 \qquad (5.1e)$$

where Y is the real domestic output at time t, expressed in logarithms, r_t is the domestic nominal interest rate at time t, ρ is the foreign nominal interest rate, taken to be exogenous and fixed, P_t is the price of the domestically produced good (in terms of domestic currency), expressed in logarithms, Q_t is the price of imported good (in terms of foreign currency), expressed in logarithms, E_t is the logarithm of the current exchange rate (measured in units of the domestic currency per unit of foreign currency), C_t is the domestic cost of living (measured in domestic currency), expressed in logarithms, M_t is the domestic nominal supply expressed in logarithms, $E^*_{t+s,t}$ are the expectations of E for time $t + s$ held at time t, $s = 1, 2, \ldots$, all t, $C^*_{t+s,t}$ is the expectation of C for time $t + s$, held at time t, $s = 1, 2, \ldots$, all t, and $P^*_{t+s,i}$ is the expectation of P for time $t + s$, held at time t, $s = 1, 2, \ldots$, all t.

Before proceeding further, the following points regarding the formulation should be noted. First, the specification of some variables in terms of logarithms is purely for convenience, enabling us to avoid the problems of linearization, which would otherwise be necessary. Second, as our concern is with the distinction between actual and anticipated components of the money supply and foreign price level, the only random disturbances we need consider are embodied in these variables. Additive random variables could be appended to each of these relationships, but these would be of no relevance for the issues that we wish to discuss.

Equation (5.1a) describes the domestic economy's IS curve. The demand for domestic output varies positively with domestic income and the relative price of foreign to domestic goods.[4] It varies inversely with the real rate of interest, which is defined to be the domestic nominal rate, less the expected rate of inflation of the domestic consumer price index (CPI). Equation (5.1b) defines the domestic CPI to be a multiplicatively weighted average of the price of domestic goods and the domestic price of foreign goods. While we choose this form primarily for convenience, it does have some theoretical merit. It is the "true" cost-of-living index if the domestic residents' utility function, defined with domestic goods and foreign goods as arguments, is Cobb–Douglas (see Samuelson and Swamy, 1974). The relative weight δ can be used to parameterize the degree of openness of the economy: the larger δ, the less open the economy, and vice versa.

The monetary sector is summarized in equations (5.1c) and (5.1d). The first of these equations describes the domestic LM curve, and makes the usual assumption that all domestic money is held by domestic residents who also hold no foreign currency.[5] Note that the domestic stock of money is deflated by the overall CPI, reflecting the fact that part of the transactions demand for money is for imports. The specification of the real transactions variable by Y follows convention, though it is at best only a proxy. A more accurate measure of real transactions would involve some weighted average of the consumption of imports plus domestic goods. However, this would be intractable, since these components of aggregate consumption are themselves endogenous.[6] The assumption of perfect capital integration is embodied in the interest rate parity condition (equation (5.1d)). The domestic nominal interest rate r_t equals the exogenous world rate ρ plus the expected rate of exchange depreciation.

Finally, the supply of domestic output is governed by equation (5.1e). This resembles a Lucas (1973) supply function, although, as Flood (1979) has argued, with both international and international trading, this rationale is inappropriate. Rather, it may be justified in terms of the wage determination model of Gray (1976) and Fischer (1977). We assume that the nominal wage contract (the logarithm of the money wage) is set with the goal of equating the expected supply of labor to the expected demand. If we assume that workers are concerned with their real wage in terms of the CPI, their expected supply of labor $N^{s*}_{t,t-1}$ is described by

$$N^{s*}_{t,t-1} = a + b(W_t - C^*_{t,t-1}) \qquad a > 0,\ b > 0 \tag{5.2a}$$

If we assume further a production function linking the logarithm of output and employment of the form

$$Y_t = \varepsilon N_t \qquad 0 < \varepsilon < 1 \tag{5.2b}$$

it follows that the expected demand for labor is determined by the marginal product condition

$$\ln \varepsilon + (\varepsilon - 1)N^{d*}_{t,t-1} = W_t - P^*_{t,t-1} \tag{5.2c}$$

where firms evaluate real wages in terms of the price of their product (domestic output). In order to ensure that the labor market is expected to clear, W_t must be set to equate the expected demands and supply appearing in equations (5.2a) and (5.2c), i.e.

$$W_t = \frac{\ln \varepsilon + (\varepsilon - 1)a + (1 - \varepsilon)bC^*_{t,t-1} + P^*_{t,t-1}}{1 + b(1 - \varepsilon)} \tag{5.2d}$$

so that W_t increases with the respective price expectations of both workers and firms. However, actual employment is assumed to depend inversely upon the realized real wage in accordance with the firm's marginal product schedule:

$$\ln \varepsilon + (\varepsilon - 1)N_t = W_t - P_t \tag{5.2c$'$}$$

Combining equations (5.2b), (5.2c′), and (5.2d) yields

$$Y_t = \frac{\varepsilon(a + b \ln \varepsilon)}{1 + b(1 - \varepsilon)} + \frac{\varepsilon}{1 - \varepsilon}\left\{\frac{(1 - \varepsilon)b(P - C^*_{t,t-1}) + (P_t - P^*_{t,t-1})}{1 + b(1 - \varepsilon)}\right\} \tag{5.2e}$$

which is of the form (5.1e).[7]

The two key exogenous variables in the model upon which we wish to focus are M_t and Q_t. The endogenous variables to be determined by the system include Y_t, r_t, E_t, P_t and C_t. These are determined on the assumption that expectations are rational in the sense that expectations of the endogenous variables $C^*_{t,t-1}$ etc. are equal to the predictions yielded by the model, conditional upon the expectations of the exogenous variables held at the same time. These latter expectations, since they pertain to variables exogenous to the model, can themselves be taken to be exogenous.

In order to simplify notation, it is convenient to define initial base levels $\bar{M}$ and $\bar{Q}$ of the exogenous variables and to consider subsequent changes in the system relative to the base level so defined. Thus we can express the system in deviation form about an initial equilibrium as

$$(1 - d_1)y_t = -d_2\{(e^*_{t+1,t} - e_t) - (c^*_{t+1,t} - c_t)\} + d_3(e_t + q_t - p_t) \tag{5.3a}$$

$$c_t = \delta p_t + (1 - \delta)(q_t + e_t) \tag{5.3b}$$

$$m_t - c_t = \alpha_1 y_t - \alpha_2(e^*_{t+1,t} - e_t) \tag{5.3c}$$

$$r_t - p = e^*_{t+1,t} - e_t \tag{5.3d}$$

$$y_t = \gamma(p_t - c^*_{t,t-1}) + \gamma_2(p_t - p^*_{t,t-1}) \tag{5.3e}$$

where lower-case letters denote deviations, i.e. $m_t = M_t - \bar{M}$ etc. The advantage of defining the system about its initial equilibrium is that it enables us to incorporate the constants and exogenous parameters of the system (such as ρ) in the initial equilibrium solution.

The basic scenario we will analyse is a situation in which, prior to some initial time period $t = 0$ say, the economy is in stationary equilibrium. Then at time zero, for a variety of reasons, individuals may begin to expect the exogenous variables to change over subsequent periods. These changes in expectations may come about through announcements, "leaks in information," observation of events taking place or expected to take place at home and abroad, etc. The details of what generate the changes in these expectations of exogenous variables are themselves exogenous to the model and need not concern us. Our task is to trace through the effects of changes in these expectations, as well as the effects of change in the actual variable (when and if they actually occur), on the endogenous variables of the economy.

To solve the model it is further convenient to eliminate $(r_t - p)$, c_t, $c^*_{t,t+1}$, and $c^*_{t+1,t-1}$ from equations (5.3a), (5.3c), and (5.3d). This can be done by first taking conditional expectations of (5.3b) at time $t - 1$:

$$c^*_{t,t-1} = \delta p^*_{t,t-1} + (1 - \delta)(q^*_{t,t-1} + e^*_{t,t-1}). \tag{5.4}$$

Then substituting from (5.3b), (5.3d), and (5.4), we obtain

$$\begin{aligned}(1 - d_1)y_t = -d_2\{\delta(e^*_{t+1,t} - e_t) - \delta(p^*_{t+1,t} - p_t) \\ - (1 - \delta)(q^*_{t+1,t} - q_t)\} \\ + d_3(e_t + q_t - p_t)\end{aligned} \tag{5.5a}$$

$$\begin{aligned}y_t = \gamma_1\{p_t - \delta p^*_{t,t+1} - (1 - \delta)(q^*_{t,t+1} + e^*_{t,t+1})\} \\ + \gamma_2(p_t - p^*_{t,t-1})\end{aligned} \tag{5.5b}$$

$$m_t = \delta p_t + (1 - \delta)(q_t + e_t) + \alpha_1 y_1 - \alpha_2(e^*_{t+1,t} - e_t) \tag{5.5c}$$

Equations (5.5a), (5.5b), and (5.5c) yield three stochastic difference equations in domestic output y_t, the price p_t of the domestic good and its expectations, the exchange rate e_t and its expectations, and the exogenous variables m_t and q_t and their expectations.

3 SOLUTION FOR EXPECTATIONS

In order to determine the solutions for y_t, p_t, and e_t, it is first necessary to solve for the expectations of the endogenous variables appearing in equations (5.5a)–(5.5c). To do this, we take conditional expectations of (5.5a)–(5.5c) for an arbitrary date i, held at the initial time zero:

$$(1 - d_1)y^*_{i,0} = -d_2\{\delta(e^*_{i+1,0} - e^*_{i,0}) - \delta(p^*_{i+1,0} - p^*_{i,0}) - (1 - \delta)(q^*_{i+1,0} - q^*_{i,0})\} + d_3\{e^*_{i,0} + q^*_{i,0} - p^*_{i,0} \tag{5.6a}$$

$$y^*_{i,0} = \gamma_1(1 - \delta)(p^*_{i,0} - e^*_{i,0} - q^*_{i,0}) \tag{5.6b}$$

$$m^*_{i,0} = \delta p^*_{i,0} + (1 - \delta)(e^*_{i,0} + q^*_{i,0}) + \alpha_1 y^*_{i,0} - \alpha_2(e^*_{i+1,0} - e^*_{i,0}) \tag{5.6c}$$

where for any variable X, say $X^*_{i+1,t}$ denotes the prediction formed at time t $(t = 0, 1, \ldots)$ for time $t + i (i = 0, 1, \ldots)$. In forming these expectations, we are using the familiar property of conditional expectations operators

$$\mathscr{E}_{t-1}\{\mathscr{E}_t(X_{t+i})\} = \mathscr{E}_{t-1}(X_{t+i}) = X^*_{t+1,t-1} \tag{5.7}$$

and we define $X^*_{t,t} = X_t$. This last assumption merely asserts that the prediction of the current value of a variable is the actual current value and is another way of saying that the variable is instantly observable.

The most convenient procedure for solving for the expectations of the endogenous variable is a follows. First, let us define the relative price of domestic to foreign goods at time zero, say:

$$z_0 \equiv p_0 - q_0 - e_0 \tag{5.8}$$

Therefore the expectation of the relative price formed at time zero for time i, say, is

$$z^*_{i,0} = p^*_{i,0} - q^*_{i,0} - e^*_{i,0} \tag{5.8$'$}$$

Substituting for $y^*_{i,0}$ from equation (5.6b) into (5.6a) and using the definition (5.8′) yields the following first-order difference equation in $z^*_{i,0}$:

$$d_2\delta z^*_{i+1,0} - \{d_2\delta + \gamma_1(1 - d_1)(1 - \delta) + d_3\}z^*_{i,0} = -d_2(q^*_{i+1,0} - q^*_{i,0}) \tag{5.9}$$

The general solution to this equation is

$$z^*_{i,0} = A(1/\mu)^i + \frac{\mu}{\delta}\sum_{j=0}^{\infty}(q^*_{i+j,0} - q^*_{i+j-1,0})\mu^{j-1} \tag{5.10}$$

where A is an arbitrary constant and

$$\mu = \frac{d_2\delta}{d_2\delta + \gamma_1(1 - d_1)(1 - \delta) + d_3} < 1$$

Since $1/\mu > 1$, as long as $A \neq 0$, the expectations of the relative price held at time zero over lengthening forecast horizons (i.e. as $i \to \infty$) will diverge. In order to rule out such behavior and thus ensure that $z^*_{i,0}$ remains bounded we set $A = 0$. This procedure, typical of rational expectations models, is often justified on the grounds that the instability that would otherwise occur would be inconsistent with observed behavior. Alternatively, it may be justified more formally by appealing to transversality conditions from appropriate optimizing models, which provided that the underlying utility function satisfies suitable restrictions, ensure that the expected price movements remain bounded (see Brock, 1974). Thus setting $A = 0$, the solution reduces to

$$z^*_{i,0} = \frac{1}{\delta} \sum_{j=1}^{\infty} (\Delta q^*_{i+j,0})\mu^j \tag{5.11}$$

where

$$\Delta q^*_{i+j,0} \equiv q^*_{i+j,0} - q^*_{i+j,-1,0}$$

On substituting the solution for $z^*_{i,0}$ into equation (5.6b), the corresponding solution for the expected value of real output $y^*_{i,0}$ is given by

$$y^*_{i,0} = \frac{\gamma_1(1-\delta)}{\delta} \sum_{j=1}^{\infty} (\Delta q^*_{i+j,0})\mu^j \tag{5.12}$$

From equations (5.11) and (5.12) it is observed that the expectations $z^*_{i,0}$ and $y^*_{i,0}$ of the *real* variables are independent of expectations about the nominal money supply $m^*_{j,0}$. They are also incependent of any sustained uniform increase in the foreign price level that is expected to occur at or before time i. However, any increase in the foreign price level that is expected to occur after period i will influence these expectations. For example, a once-and-for-all increase in the foreign price level that is expected to occur in period $i + J$ will generate a reduction in the expected real rate of interest for period $i + J$, thereby stimulating the expected demand and expected output for that period and forcing up the expected relative price of domestic output. These effects taper off as $J \to \infty$.

To determine the solutions for the expectations of the nominal variables $e^*_{i,0}$ and $p^*_{i,0}$, we note equation (5.8′) and substitute for $z^*_{i,0}$ and $y^*_{i,0}$ into equation (5.6c). This yields the following equation in $e^*_{i,0}$:

$$\alpha_2 e^*_{i+1,0} - (1+\alpha_2)e^*_{i,0} = \left\{1 + \frac{\alpha_1\gamma_1(1-\delta)}{\delta}\right\} \sum_{j=1}^{\infty} (\Delta q^*_{i+j,0})\mu^j + q^*_{i,0} - m^*_{i,0} \tag{5.13}$$

With $\alpha_2 > 0$, the complementary function for this equation implies an unbounded solution for $e^*_{i,0}$. Thus, in order to ensure stability, its coefficient in the general solution for solution must be set to zero, yielding the following solution for $e^*_{i,0}$:

$$e^*_{i,0} = \frac{1}{1+\alpha_2}\left\{\sum_{k=0}^{\infty} m^*_{i+k,0} - q^*_{i+k,0})\lambda^k\right\} - \frac{1}{1+\alpha_2}\left\{1 + \frac{\alpha_1\gamma_1(1-\delta)}{\delta}\right\}\left\{\sum_{k=0}^{\infty} \lambda^k \sum_{j=1}^{\infty} (\Delta q^*_{i+j+k,0})\mu^j\right\} \tag{5.14}$$

where

$$\lambda = \frac{\alpha_2}{1 + \alpha_2} < 1$$

The expectation of the exchange rate held at time zero for time i, say, depends upon the time profile of the expectations of the money supply and foreign price level for all time periods beginning at time i and extending indefinitely into the future. For example, if the money supply is expected to undergo an increase dm^* beginning at time $i + J$, say, and if this increase is expected to continue permanently, the exchange rate at time i will be expected to devalue by an amount

$$\frac{\partial e^*_{i,0}}{\partial m^*} = \lambda^j \tag{5.15}$$

If $J = 0$ and the increase is expected to occur immediately, the expected percentage devaluation will be equal to the expected percentage increase in the money supply. Otherwise, the expected devaluation will be less than proportional and, indeed as $J \rightarrow \infty$, the effect will dampen out. The effects of an expected future increase in the foreign price level on currently held expectations of the exchange rate can be similarly analysed, though the expression is somewhat more complex owing to the expected real interest rate effect that it generates.

Finally, substituting the solution for $e^*_{i,0}$ into equation (5.11), and using (5.8′), we obtain the following solution for the expected price of domestic output:

$$p^*_{i,0} = q^*_{i,0} + \frac{1}{1 + \alpha_2} \sum_{k=0}^{\infty} (m^*_{i+k,0} - q^*_{i+k,0})\lambda^k + \frac{1}{\delta} \sum_{j=1}^{\infty} (\Delta q^*_{i+j,0})\mu^j$$
$$- \frac{1}{1 + \alpha_2} \left\{1 + \frac{\alpha_1 \gamma_1 (1 - \delta)}{\delta}\right\} \left\{ \sum_{k=0}^{\infty} \lambda^k \sum_{j=1}^{\infty} (\Delta q^*_{i+j+k,0})\mu^j \right\} \tag{5.16}$$

The effects of expected future increases in the domestic money supply and foreign price level on currently held expectations of the price level can be calculated from this equation.

4 SHORT-RUN EQUILIBRIUM OF THE SYSTEM

The short-run solutions for the endogenous variables y_t, p_t, and e_t obtained from equations (5.5a), (5.5b), and (5.5c) can be expressed in terms of the conditional expectations $e^*_{t+1,t}$, $e^*_{t,t-1}$, $z^*_{t+1,t}$, $z^*_{t,t-1,t}$. It is clear that the choice of conditioning date zero in section 3 was made for notational convenience, and that analogous expressions to equations (5.11), (5.12), (5.14), and (5.16) hold with respect to expectations formed at any arbitrary time t for any arbitrary time $t + i$. Specifically,

$$z^*_{t+i,t} = \frac{1}{\delta}\sum_{j=1}^{\infty}(\Delta q^*_{t+i+j,t})\mu^j \tag{5.12'}$$

$$\begin{aligned} e^*_{t+i,t} = {} & \frac{1}{1+\alpha_2}\sum_{k=0}^{\infty}(m^*_{t+i+k,t} - q^*_{t+i+k,t})\lambda^k \\ & - \frac{1}{1+\alpha_2}\left\{1 + \frac{\alpha_1\gamma_1(1-\delta)}{\delta}\right\}\left\{\sum_{k=0}^{\infty}\lambda^k\sum_{j=1}^{\infty}\Delta q^*_{t+i+j+k,t}\mu^j\right\} \end{aligned} \tag{5.14'}$$

Thus the solutions for y_t, p_t, and e_t can be expressed most conveniently by writing equations (5.5a)–(5.5c) as the matrix equation

$$\begin{bmatrix} 1-d_1 & d_3 + d_2\delta & -(d_3 + d_2\delta) \\ -1 & \gamma & 0 \\ \alpha_1 & \delta & 1 - \delta + \alpha_2 \end{bmatrix}\begin{bmatrix} y_t \\ p_t \\ e_t \end{bmatrix} = \begin{bmatrix} d_2\delta z^*_{t+1,t} + d_2(q^*_{t+1,t} - q_t) \\ (\gamma_1\delta + \delta_2)z^*_{t,t-1} + \gamma(q^*_{t,t-1} + e^*_{t,t-1}) \\ m_t + \alpha_2 e^*_{t+1,t} - (1-\delta)q_t \end{bmatrix} \tag{5.17}$$

where $\gamma \equiv \gamma_1 + \gamma_2$, $q^*_{t+1,t}$ and $q^*_{t,t-1}$ are exogenous, and $z^*_{t+1,t}$, $z^*_{t,t-1}$, and $e^*_{t+1,t}$ are obtained by setting $i = 1$ in equations (5.12′) and (5.14′). Through these latter variables, the solutions for y_t, p_t, and e_t depend upon the expectations of all future values of the exogenous variables (as formed at times $t-1$ and t), an aspect that is a central feature of rational expectations models.

Our concern will be to analyse the effects of actual and anticipated changes in the money supply and the level of foreign prices on the endogenous variables of the system. We will interpret such changes in m as reflecting actual and anticipated autonomous policy changes. However, we could also postulate the money supply to be generated by some feedback control law, in which case it would follow some stochastic process. In this case, the anticipated change would be derived by calculating conditional expectations of the stochastic process embodied in the control law.[8] This approach constrains the possible range of policy changes, and for our purposes it is more convenient to leave the specification of the domestic monetary process rather general. Finally, we could allow q to be generated by some specific stochastic process, but here too we find it useful to keep the specification of actual and foreign price changes quite open.

5 DOMESTIC MONETARY EXPANSION

It will be recalled that all variables in equation (5.17) have been measured as deviations about an initial deterministic equilibrium. To analyse the effects of actual and anticipated monetary expansions it is convenient to assume that the foreign price level remains fixed, and is expected to remain fixed, at its initial level, $\bar{Q}$. Hence we can set $q^*_{t+i,t} = \bar{q}_t = 0$. The solutions for the (deviations of) domestic output, price level, and the exchange rate can be expressed in a variety of equivalent ways, of which the following are probably the simplest and most easily interpreted:

$$y_t = \frac{\gamma(d_3 + d_2\delta)}{J}\left\{(m_t - m^*_{t,t-1}) + \sum_{k=1}^{\infty}(m^*_{t+k,t} - m^*_{t+k,t-1})\lambda^k\right\} \tag{5.18a}$$

$$p_t = \frac{d_3 + d_2\delta}{J}\left\{(m_t - m^*_{t,t-1}) + \sum_{k=1}^{\infty}(m^*_{t+k,t} - m^*_{t+k,t-1})\lambda^k\right\} + \frac{1}{1+\alpha_2}\sum_{k=0}^{\infty} m^*_{t+k,t-1}\lambda^k \tag{5.18b}$$

$$e_t = \frac{(1-d_1)\gamma + (d_3 + d_2\delta)}{J}\left\{(m_t - m^*_{t,t-1}) + \sum_{k=1}^{\infty}(m^*_{t+k,t} - m^*_{t+k,t-1})\lambda^k\right\} + \frac{1}{1+\alpha_2}\sum_{k=0}^{\infty} m^*_{t+k,t-1}\lambda^k \tag{5.18c}$$

where

$$J = \gamma(1 - d_1)(1 - \delta + d_2) + (d_3 + d_2\delta)(1 + \alpha_2 + \alpha_1\delta) > 0 \tag{5.19}$$

Two critical factors appearing throughout these expressions are $m_t - m^*_{t,t-1}$ and $m^*_{t+k,t} - m^*_{t+k,t-1}$, $k = 1, 2, \ldots$. The first of these is simply the unanticipated component of the actual money supply at time t, relative to what was anticipated at time $t - 1$. The second term measures the amount by which the forecast of the money supply for time $t + k$ is revised between times $t - 1$ and t, presumably on the basis of new information acquired during period t.

From equations (5.18) we can draw the following general conclusions. The level of domestic output, its price, and the rate of exchange all vary positively with the unanticipated component of the money supply at time t. They also vary positively with the discounted sum of the amounts by which the forecasts for all future periods are revised between time $t - 1$ and time t. In addition, the monetary variables p_t and e_t depend upon the discounted sum (weighted average) of the expected money supplies for all future periods (as perceived at time $t - 1$), with the weights summing to unity.

Using equations (5.18) enables us to determine the effects of a multitude of types of actual and anticipated monetary disturbances on the economy. For obvious reasons, we restrict ourselves to just a few examples that are convenient to categorize as follows: (a) partial expectations effects, (b) actual monetary expansions, and (c) announcement effects.

5.1 Partial expectations effects

(1) The anticipation at time $t-1$ of an increase in the money supply for the *single* period $t+K$, which *ex post* at time t is no longer expected to occur (i.e. $\mathrm{d}m^*_{t+K,t-1} > 0$, $\mathrm{d}m^*_{t+k,t-1} = 0$, $k \neq K$; $\mathrm{d}m^*_{t+k,t} = 0$, all k), will cause the price of domestic output to rise and the level of domestic output to fall. The reason is that the expectation of the increase in the money supply will increase the expected price of domestic goods (equation (5.16)). This leads to an upward shift in the domestic supply function for period t, forcing the actual price of domestic goods to increase during the period, and thereby reducing the demand for these goods and causing domestic output to fall. Both responses are proportional to λ^K, and so tend to zero as $K \to \infty$.

The effect on the exchange rate is indeterminate, and is given by the expression

$$\frac{\partial e_t}{\partial m^*_{t+K,t-1}} = \frac{\gamma\{\alpha_1(d_3 + d_2\delta) - (1-d_1)\delta\}\lambda^K}{J(1+\alpha_2)} \tag{5.10}$$

On the one hand, the endogenous increase in p_t will raise the demand for money; on the other hand, the decrease in y_t will reduce the demand for money. The net effect of these two offsetting influences can be shown to *decrease* the demand for by an amount proportional to $\alpha_1(d_3 + d_2\delta) - (1-d_1)\delta$.[9] Thus, in the event that this term is positive, the demand for money will decrease. At the same time, the net effect of an increase in e_t, taking into account both its effect on the cost of living and its effect on the domestic interest rate, is to raise the demand for money.[10] Hence if $\alpha_1(d_3 + d_2\delta) - (1-d_1)\delta > 0$, the domestic exchange rate must increase (depreciate) in order to increase the demand for money and maintain equilibrium with the exogenously given fixed nominal supply. The opposite argument applies if the sign of this term is reversed.

The changes in the variables y_t, p_t, and e_t are only transitory. In period $t+1$, when expectations are revised back down, these variables will return to their original levels. We can also observe that essentially the same adjustment applies if the initial increase in expectations occurring in period $t-1$ is expected to apply uniformly to all periods beyond $t+K$. The responses are simply scaled by a factor $1/(1-\lambda) = 1 + \alpha_2$.

(2) The anticipation of an expansion in the money supply, initially expected in period t to take place in the single period $t+K$ ($\mathrm{d}m^*_{t+k,t-1} = 0$, all k; $\mathrm{d}m^*_{t+K,t} > 0$, $\mathrm{d}m^*_{t+k,t} = 0$, $k \neq K$), will raise all

three variables – the real domestic output, the price of domestic goods and the exchange rate – during period t. The reason is that the immediate effect of the increase in $m^*_{t+K,t}$ is to raise both $p^*_{t+1,t}$ and $e^*_{t+1,t}$ proportionately. The domestic nominal interest rate will rise, reducing the demand for money, though the domestic real interest rate will remain unchanged. With the nominal money supply fixed, the demand for money will have to be increased, and this can occur through increases in y_t, e_t, or p_t. Assuming that the most rapid adjustment is in e_t, this will put an upward pressure on domestic prices, stimulating output. If in period $t + 1$ expectations are revised back down to their original levels, y_{t+1}, p_{t+1}, and e_{t+1} will respond as in case 1. In period $t + 2$, they will be back to their original levels.

(3) Combining cases 1 and 2 we see that an anticipation of an expansion in the money supply for the single priod $t + K$ initially formed at time $t - 1$ and maintained at time t ($\mathrm{d}m^*_{t+K,t-1} = \mathrm{d}m^*_{t+K,t} > 0$) will have no effect on real income during period t, which we noted above responds to the rate of forecast revision. The current price of domestic output and the exchange rate will both rise by the same amount, leaving the relative price of domestic output unaffected.

5.2 Actual monetary expansions

(1) A purely unanticipated random increase in the level of the domestic money supply, which is not expected to continue beyond the current period ($\mathrm{d}m^*_{t+k,t-1}=\mathrm{d}m^*_{t+k,t} = 0$, all k, $\mathrm{d}m_t > 0$), has no expansionary effect on domestic output and leads to an increase in the domestic price level coupled with a depreciation of the domestic currency. With expectations unchanged, the adjustment is quite conventional and accords with traditional analyses of monetary policy for flexible rate systems under perfect capital mobility and static expectations (see Fleming, 1962; Mundell, 1968).

(2) One of the most interesting disturbances to consider is that of an increase in the domestic money supply that is initially unanticipated, but, having occurred, is then expected to continue permanently ($\mathrm{d}m^*_{t+k,t-1} = 0$, for all k; $\mathrm{d}m_t = \mathrm{d}m^*_{t+k,t}>0$, for $k = 1, 2, \ldots$). This is precisely the monetary disturbance analysed by Dornbusch (1976) and subsequent authors, and it has been shown in some cases to be associated with "overshooting" of the short-run exchange rate in relation to its long-run equilibrium proportionate response. In the present context such a disturbance leads to an unambiguous increase in the three variables – the domestic output, the price of domestic output, and the exchange rate. The short-run percentage increase in the price of domestic output is less than that of the money supply, so that p_t undershoots its long-run proportionate response, just as it does in these

other models.[11] Rewriting equation (5.18c) we can show

$$\frac{de_t}{dm_t} = 1 + \frac{\gamma\{\delta(1 - d_1) - \alpha_1(d_3 + d_2\delta)\}}{J} \tag{5.21}$$

Hence, whether or not the exchange rate overshoots its ultimate proportionate response depends upon $\delta(1 - d_1) - \alpha_1(d_3 + d_2\delta)$. If $\delta(1 - d_1) - \alpha_1(d_3 + d_2\delta) > 0$, it is clear from equation (5.21) that $de_t/dm_t > 1$ and that short-run overshooting occurs; if $\delta(1 - d_1) - \alpha_1(d_3 + d_2\delta) < 0$, $de_t/dm_t < 1$, the short-run exchange rate adjusts only partially toward its equilibrium.

To understand the response of the exchange rate further, it is convenient to write the third equation appearing in (5.17) in the form

$$\alpha_1 y_t + \delta z_t = (1 + \alpha_2)(m_t - e_t) \tag{5.22}$$

To derive equation (5.22) we have set $q_t = 0$; in addition, equation (5.14′) in conjunction with the expectational assumption enables us to set $e^*_{t+1,t} = m_t$. The expression on the left-hand side is the net effect of the demand for money resulting from changes in the real variables income y_t and the relative price z_t. Given the increase in y_t associated with this monetary disturbance, the relative pice z_t must fall in order to stimulate demand and maintain product market equilibrium. Thus the net effect of these two changes on the demand for money is ambiguous and turns out to be proportional to $\alpha_1(d_3 + d_2\delta) - \delta(1 - d_1)$.[12] If this term is negative, say, then these two components generate a net fall in the demand for money. In this case it follows from equation (5.22) that in order to generate sufficient additional demand to absorb the increased supply, $de_t/dm_t > 1$.

Hence the likelihood of overshooting decreases with d_1, d_2, d_3, and α_1, and will increase or decrease with δ accordingly as $\alpha_1 d_2 - (1 - d_1) \lesseqgtr 0$. This is perfectly consistent with Dornbusch (1976), who takes $\delta = 1$ and throughout most of his analysis assumes that output is fixed, which is equivalent to setting $\alpha_1 = 0$. Overshooting is then inevitable. With endogenous income and $\alpha_1 > 0$ the possibility of undershoot arises. In effect, the larger is α_1, the more the burden of adjustment to an increase in the money supply is undertaken by income and the less need be borne by the exchange rate, reducing the likelihood of overshoot. In the limiting case when $\delta = 0$, undershooting will always occur.

To conclude this case, two further points should be made. First, our propositions regarding overshooting or undershooting, while developed for an initially totally unexpected increase in the money supply, continue to hold as long as the initial disturbance is underpredicted ($dm_t > dm^*_{t,t-1}$). Second, assuming that the increase in the money supply undertaken at time t is still expected at time $t + 1$ to continue permanently (i.e. $dm^*_{t+k,t+1} = dm_t$), we immediately see that

$dy_{t+1} = de_{t+1} = dm_t$. The economy adjusts to its new equilibrium in just *one* period. The contrast with Dornbusch in this respect arises simply because of our different choice of supply function, which is the source of the gradual adjustment in his analysis.

We now turn briefly to three other disturbances.

(3) An anticipated increase in the money supply, which *ex ante* is expected to be permanent but which *ex post* is expected to be only transitory ($dm^*_{t+k,t-1} = dm_t$, $k = 0, 1, \ldots$; $dm^*_{t+k,t} = 0$, $k = 1, \ldots$), has a contractionary effect on income. It also leads to short-run increases in both p_t and e_t, though in both cases the percentage increase will be less than that of the money supply. This is because the contractionary effect of a given expected increase in the money supply more than outweighs the expansionary effect resulting from the actual increase. The fall in output must be met by a rise in the relative price z_t in order to maintain product market equilibrium. Thus p_t must rise by more that e_t, and since with $dm^*_{t+k,t}$ the response of p_t is necessarily less than that of m_t (this can be shown from equation (5.18b)) the same must be true of e_t.

(4) A fully anticipated increase in the money supply, which both *ex ante* and *ex post* is expected to be only transitory ($dm^*_{t,t-1} = dm_t$; $dm^*_{t+k,t-1} = dm^*_{t+k,t} = 0$, $k = 1, \ldots$), will have *no* effect on real output, and as in case 3 will lead to partial increases in both p_t and e_t.

(5) Finally, a fully anticipated increase in the money supply, which both *ex ante* and *ex post* is expected to be permanent ($dm^*_{t+k,t-1} = dm^*_{t+k,t} = dm$, all k), will have no effect on real output. Both the price of domestic output and the exchange rate will rise immediately by the full amount of the monetary increase.

5.3 Announcement effects

The effect of an announcement of a future monetary expansion on the current exchange rate has been investigated in the context of the Dornbusch model in two recent papers by Gray and Turnovsky (1979, this volume, ch. 1) and Wilson (1979). These authors demonstrate that the announcement at time zero, say, of a monetary expansion to take effect at a future time T will lead to an upward jump in the exchange rate at time zero. Thereafter, the exchange rate will continue to rise in a continuous exponential manner until the stable arm of the saddle is reached, which is then followed toward the new equilibrium.[13] The announcement moderates the initial jump, and indeed, with sufficient lead time, the initial overshoot may no longer occur. In this case a lesser degree of overshoot will take place at some point before the monetary expansion actually takes effect.

The solution we have given in equation (5.18) can easily be used to analyse announcement effects in the present context. Suppose that the monetary authority announces at time zero a monetary expansion of dm to be introduced at time T. Assuming that this is believed by the public, we can write

$$\begin{aligned} dm^*_{t',t} &= 0 \qquad t' = 1, \ldots, T-1, \text{ all } t < t' \\ &= dm \qquad t' = T, T+1, \ldots \\ dm_t &= 0 \qquad t = 1, \ldots, T-1 \\ &= dm \qquad t = T, T+1, \ldots \end{aligned} \tag{5.23}$$

Now substituting these values into equations (5.18a)–(5.18c) we obtain the following solutions for the changes in the three endogenous variables:

$$\begin{aligned} dy_t &= 0 \qquad t = 1, \ldots, T-1 \\ &= 0 \qquad t = T, \ldots \end{aligned} \tag{5.24a}$$

$$\begin{aligned} dp_t &= \lambda^{T-t} dm \qquad t = 1, \ldots, T-1 \\ &= dm \qquad t = T, \ldots \end{aligned} \tag{5.24b}$$

$$\begin{aligned} de_t &= \lambda^{T-t} dm \qquad t = 1, \ldots, T-1 \\ &= dm \qquad t = T, \ldots \end{aligned} \tag{5.24c}$$

The behavior of the economy is very simple. In the period following the announcement both the price of domestic output and the exchange rate will rise by an amount λ^{T-1}. Thereafter, they will both increase monotonically at the rate (per period) $1/\alpha_2$ until time T when the monetary expansion takes place, when they will have risen by the full amount of the monetary expansion dm.[14] In contrast with the analyses by Gray and Turnovsky (1979, this volume, ch. 1) and Wilson (1979) there is no overshooting of the exchange rate. The reason for the difference is that we do not take the price level to be fixed in the short-run, thereby allowing it to bear some of the necessary adjustment. Note that if $T = 1$, the adjustment is completed within one period; the present analysis essentially reduces to case 5 in section 5.2.

The other feature to observe is that real output remains fixed throughout the entire adjustment process. The reason for this is evident from equation (5.18a), where we have commented that real output responds to forecast errors and to the revision of forecasts for further periods. However, with the future monetary expansion announced, neither of these phenomena occur. The monetary expansion at time T is perfectly foreseen. Also, during the transition (i.e. before time T) there is no reason to update forecasts. Thus while the announcement of the monetary expansion leads to immediate responses in the nominal variables p_t and e_t, these adjustments turn out to be identical, leaving the *real* variables, such as the relative price and the level of output, unaffected. The only instant at which the real variables will be affected is at time zero, the announcement date itself, when previously held expectations are revised. These effects prevail for only one period, with output immediately returning to its equilibrium level and the nominal variables following the transitional paths described above.

6 CHANGES IN FOREIGN PRICE LEVEL

With $e^*_{t+1,t}$ in particular being a rather complex function of the expected foreign price level for all future periods (see equation (5.14′)), a detailed analysis of the effects of future expected price disturbances on the current behavior of the system becomes rather tedious. We will therefore restrict our attention to the case where these expectations formed at time t are held uniformly for all future periods, i.e.

$$q^*_{t+k,t} = q^*_t \qquad k = 1, \ldots, \text{all } t \tag{5.25}$$

where q^*_t denotes the uniformly held expectations at time t. It is also convenient to assume that the money supply remains, and is expected to remain, at its original equilibrium level $\bar{M}$, enabling us to set $m_t = m^*_{t+k,t} = 0$. With these assumptions, the two critical expectations (equations (5.12′) and (5.14′), simplify drastically to

$$z^*_{t+1,t} = 0 \tag{5.12″}$$

$$e^*_{t+1,t} = -q^*_t \tag{5.14″}$$

Substituting equations (5.12″) and (5.14″) into the matrix equation (5.17) we obtain the following solutions for y_t, p_t, and e_t:

$$y_t = \frac{\gamma}{J}\{d_3\alpha_2 - d_2(1 - \delta)(1 + d_2)\}(q_t - q^*_t) \tag{5.26a}$$

$$p_t = \frac{1}{J}\{d_3\alpha_2 - d_2(1 - \delta)(1 + d_2)\}(q_t - q^*_t) \tag{5.26b}$$

$$e_t = -q_t + \eta(q_t - q^*_t) \tag{5.26c}$$

where

$$\eta = \frac{1}{J}\,[\{(1 - d_1)\gamma + d_3 + d_2\delta\}\alpha_2 + (\delta + \alpha_1\gamma)d_2] > 0$$

With the assumption of uniformity of expectations, the initially held expectations of q (i.e. those formed at time $t - 1$) play no role. The reason is that any increase in q^*_{t-1} that would influence the system through the domestic supply function is exactly offset by a decrease in $e^*_{t,t-1}$ (see equation (5.14″)), leaving the supply function and the system unaffected. Indeed, the critical factor determining the behavior of the system is the term $q_t - q_t^*$. This measures the extent to which q_t is expected to change uniformly during subsequent periods. It therefore describes the *expected transitory* component of the current foreign price level (relative to the future). If the current foreign price level is expected to continue permanently, then $q_t = q_t^*$; if the current level is expected to be a purely transitory positive deviation from Q, then $q_t > 0$, $q_t^* = 0$.

From equations (5.26a)–(5.26c) we find that any increase in the foreign price level q_t, which at time t is expected to be permanent ($dq_t^* = dq_t$), will have no effect on either real domestic output or its price.[15] The exchange rate will appreciate equally, leaving the relative price z_t unchanged. By contrast, an increase in q_t that is expected to be at least partly temporary ($dq_t - dq_t^*$) will have an impact on both y_t and p_t. However, these effects are ambiguous and depend upon the sign of the expression $d_3\alpha_2 - d_2(1 - \delta)(1 + \alpha_2)$. The sources of the indeterminacy are primarily the real and nominal interest rates $r_{e,t}$ and r_t, which using equations (5.14″) can be written as

$$r_{e,t} = \delta z_t + (q_t - q_t^*)$$

$$r_t = z_t - p_t + (q_t - q_t^*)$$

For given values of z_t and p_t, an increase in $(q_t - q_t^*)$ will lead to corresponding increases in both the real and nominal rate. The first of these will tend to reduce the demand for domestic goods, causing its price and hence supply to fall. This is reflected in the term $-d_2(1 - \delta + \alpha_2)$. At the same time the increase in the nominal rate will reduce the demand for money. With the supply of money fixed, output and the price level will have to increase in order to restore demand and maintain money market equilibrium. This is reflected in the term $(d_3 + d_2\delta)\alpha_2$. Finally, the response of the exchange rate given in equation (5.26c) implies that $de_t/dq_t > -1$, i.e. the exchange rate will appreciate by less than the amount of the foreign price increase.

7 CONCLUSIONS

In this chapter we have developed a stochastic model of a small open economy operating under a flexible exchange rate and we have considered its response to two types of exogenous disturbances: a domestic monetary expansion and a foreign price increase. With respect to the former, we have shown that the level of domestic output, its price, and the exchange rate at a given time all vary positively with (a) the unanticipated component of money supply during that period, and (b) the discounted sum of the amounts by which the forecasts for all future money supplies are revised during that period from what they were in the previous period. In addition, the latter two variables depend upon the discounted sum (with weights adding to unity) of the expected money supplies for all future periods, as perceived at the end of the previous period.[16] When these factors are all taken into account, any given monetary disturbance can generate a variety of short-run effects, depending upon the accuracy with which it is predicted and how it causes expectations to be revised. It may be associated with overshooting or undershooting of the exchange rate, depending in part upon how accurately it is predicted, and may even have perverse short-run effects on output.[17] Such will be the case if the monetary expansion is initially perceived as being permanent, but, having taken place, is than expected to be only temporary.

In equilibrium, the model possesses the usual monetary neutrality properties in that a 1 percent increase in the money supply will have no effect on real output and will raise the price level and exchange rate proportionately. The transitional dynamics to a given monetary disturbance can take various forms, depending particularly upon how rapidly expectations of future money supplies adjust and the time period between the announcement (if any) of the policy and its implementation. In contrast with previous analyses, the announcement of a future monetary expansion eliminates the overshooting of the exchange rate. While it will give rise to immediate adjustments in the nominal variables, with the exception of the instant at which the announcement is made, it will leave the real behavior of the system unaffected.

The responses to a foreign price change can be most usefully summarized by relating them to the discussion concerning the insulation properties of flexible exchange rates against such disturbances, as mentioned in section 1. As noted there, this literature is conducted in a deterministic framework and has focused on initially unanticipated permanent increases in the foreign price level. Much of the emphasis has been on the role of the wealth of domestic residents held in domestic and foreign denominated currencies. A principal conclusion is that flexible rates will provide only partial insulation against a foreign price increase as long as domestic residents hold some foreign securities in their portfolios. Unfortunately, to include wealth effects in a log-linear framework such as this is not easily accomplished, so that our analysis does not incorporate this aspect. Under the assumptions of the present model, the existing literature draws the conclusion that flexible exchange rates will provide complete insulation against foreign price disturbances.

The analysis of section 6 has shown that in the absence of wealth effects in the asset demand functions, flexible exchange rates will provide perfect insulation against increases in the foreign price level that are *expected* to be permanent (however, thay need not actually be permanent). Moreover, this proposition is true irrespective of the accuracy with which the foreign price level is initially anticipated. The latter proposition depends upon the uniformity assumption upon which section 6 is based and need not hold if expectations vary between the various future periods. However, even abstracting from wealth effects, a flexible rate does not provide complete insulation against a foreign price disturbance that *ex post* is expected to be only transitory. Indeed the more transitory it is expected to be, the less the insulation will be. This raises the question of what the optimal exchange rate regime – or the optimal intervention policy in the face of such disturbances – ought to be. However, this is a subject for future research.

NOTES

1 This statement refers to the bulk of the literature that deals with *unannounced* monetary expansions. Recently, some authors have analysed the effects of a *preannounced* monetary expansion (Gray and Turnovsky, 1979, this volume, ch. 1; Wilson, 1979). Obviously this is anticipated by the time it actually takes place.

2 In some respects our analysis parallels Fischer's (1979) recent paper analysing the neutrality of monetary disturbances in a closed economy.

3 It is worth noting that these models vary considerably with respect to their detailed specification. Some (e.g. Dornbusch, 1976) assume sticky prices with goods market disequilibrium; others, including the present analysis, assume that the domestic goods market clears each period; still others (e.g. Barro, 1978) assume that the domestic goods market is perfectly integrated with that in the rest of the world. Not surprisingly, these differences in assumptions account to some extent for the differences in implications, particularly with respect to exchange rate overshooting.

4 We abstract from wealth effects, which are difficult to incorporate adequately in a log-linear framework, because wealth is an *arithmetic* sum of separate components.

5 This means that we are abstracting from the possibility of "currency subsitution," an issue that is receiving increasing attention in the international monetary literature (Girton and Roper, 1981; Miles, 1978; Bilson, 1979).

6 In any event, our general conclusions are reasonably robust with respect to alternative specifications of the money demand function.

7 Note that equation (5.1e) reduces to an exact analog of the Lucas function when $\delta = 1$. The general conclusions of our analysis continue to hold if equation (5.1e) is replaced by an expectations augmented Phillips curve, though in this case the lags embodied in the price adjustment will introduce additional lags into the system.

8 For example, if the money supply is generated by the feedback rule

$$m_t = \rho_1 m_{t-1} + \rho_2 y_{t-1} + \rho_3 p_{t-1} + \rho_4 e_{t-1}$$

then the expectation of the money supply must satisfy

$$m^*_{t+i+1,t-1} = \rho_1 m^*_{t+i,t-1} + \rho_2 y^*_{t+i,t-1} + \rho_3 p^*_{t+i,t-1} + \rho_4 e^*_{t+i,t-1}$$

In order to determine the conditional expectations $y^*_{t+i,t-1}$, the procedure outlined in section 3 must now take into account conditional expectations of the control law itself.

9 The net effect on the demand for money m^{d} resulting from the changes in p_t and y_t is

$$\frac{\partial m_t^{\mathrm{d}}}{\partial m^*_{t+K,t-1}} = \frac{\delta \partial p_t}{\partial m^*_{t+K,t-1}} + \frac{\alpha_1 \partial y_t}{\partial m^*_{t+K,t-1}}$$

Calculating the appropriate partial derivatives from equation (5.18a) and (5.18b), and substituting, yields

$$\frac{\partial m_t^d}{\partial m^*_{t+K,t-1}} = \frac{-\gamma(1-\delta+\alpha_2)\{\alpha_1(d_3+d_2\delta)-(1-d_1)\delta\}}{J(1+\alpha_2)}$$

10 The net effect of an increase in e_t on the demand for money is $\partial m_t^{\mathrm{d}}/\partial e_t = 1 - \delta + \alpha_2 > 0$.

11 In other words, an unanticipated permanent change in the money supply is not neutral. The same conclusion, arising for the same reason, is obtained in the Fischer model when supply is assumed to be generated by a Lucas supply function (see Fischer, 1979, p.246).

12 In this case we have

$$\delta \frac{\partial z_t}{\partial m_t} + \alpha_1 \frac{\partial y_t}{\partial m_t} = \frac{-\delta\gamma(1-\alpha_1)(1+\alpha_2) + \gamma\alpha_1(d_3+d_2\delta)(1+\alpha_2)}{J}$$

$$= \frac{\gamma(1+\alpha_2)\{\alpha_1(d_3+d_2\delta)-(1-d_1)\delta\}}{J}$$

13 Because of the lagged price adjustment embodied in the Phillips curve, the dynamics of the systems considered by these authors is second order, having one stable and one unstable root, thus exhibiting saddlepoint-type instability.

14 The rate of change per unit period is $(1-\lambda)/\lambda = 1/\alpha_2$.

15 Strictly speaking, our analysis of foreign price disturbances is incomplete. In practice q_t is an endogenous variable in the rest of the world, as is the foreign interest rate ρ. Thus any stochastic shift in q_t is likely to be accompanied by a stochastic change in ρ, as both variables respond to the common random influence. The degree of correlation between these two foreign variables will vary, depending upon the source of the foreign disturbance. By ignoring accompanying changes in the interest rate, we are making a special assumption about the nature of the underlying disturbance.

16 We have restricted our attention to the price of domestic output. The response of the overall domestic CPI can easily be derived from that of the price of domestic output and the exchange rate using equation (5.3b). Indeed it is just an average of that p_t and $q_t + e_t$ and for that reason is not discussed separately.

17 The reason for the possible perverse short-run effect of a monetary expansion on output in the present analysis is quite different from the reason for the similar result obtained by Niehans (1975). In our case it results from expectational errors: a monetary expansion that is initially perceived as being

permanent turns out only to be transitory. Niehans's result, however, arises if an increase in the exchange rate leads to a substantial deterioration in the balance of trade; in effect it occurs if the Marshall–Lerner conditions are strongly violated.

REFERENCES

Barro, R. J. (1978) A stochastic equilibrium model of an open economy under flexible exchange rates. *Quarterly Journal of Economics*, 92, 149–64.

Bilson, J. F. O. (1979) Recent developments in monetary models of exchange rate determination. *IMF Staff Papers*, 26, 201–23.

Brock, W. A. (1974) Money and growth: the case of long-run perfect foresight. *International Economics Review*, 15, 750–77.

Cox, W. M. (1980) Unanticipated money, output, and prices in the small economy. *Journal of Monetary Economics*, 6, 359–84.

Dornbusch, R. (1976) Exchange rate expectations and monetary policy. *Journal of Political Economy,* 84, 1161–76.

Fischer, S. (1977) Wage indexation and macroeconomic stability. In *Stabilization of the Domestic and International Economy* (eds K. Brunner and A. Meltzer), 107–47. Amsterdam: North-Holland.

—— (1979) Anticipations and the nonneutrality of money. *Journal of Political Economy*, 87, 225–52.

Fleming, J. M. (1962) Domestic financial policies under fixed and floating exchange rates. *IMF Staff Papers*, 9, 369–79.

Flood, R. (1979) Capital mobility and the choice of exchange rate system, *International Economic Review,* 20, 405–16.

Floyd, J. E. (1978) The asset market theory of the exchange rate: a comment, *Scandinavian Journal of Economics*, 80, 100–3.

Frenkel, J. A. (1976) A monetary approach to the exchange rate: doctrinal aspects and empirical evidence. *Scandinavian Journal of Economics*, 78, 200–24.

Girton, L. and Roper, D. (1981) Theory and implications of currency substitution. *Journal of Money, Credit, and Banking,* 13, 12–30.

Gray, J. A. (1976) Wage indexation: a macroeconomic approach. *Journal of Monetary Economics*. 2, 221–35.

Gray, M. R. and Turnovsky, S. J. (1979) The stability of exchange rate dynamics under perfect myopic foresight. *International Economic Review*, 20, 643–60. Reprinted in this volume as chapter 1.

Kouri, P. J. K. (1976) The exchange rate and the balance of payments in the short run and in the long run: a monetary approach. *Scandinavian Journal of Economics* 78, 280–304.

Laidler, D. (1977) Expectations and the behaviour of prices and output under flexible exchange rates. *Economica*, 44, 327–36.

Lucas, R. E., Jr. (1973) Some international evidence on output-inflation tradeoffs. *American Economic Review*, 63, 326–34.

Miles, M. A. (1978) Currency substitution, flexible exchange rates and monetary independence. *American Economic Review*. 68, 428–36.

Mundell, R. A. (1968) *International Economics*. New York: Macmillan.

Mussa, M. (1976) The exchange rate, the balance of payments and monetary and fiscal policy under a regime of controlled floating. *Scandinavian Journal of Economics*, 78, 229–48.

Niehans, J. (1975) Some doubts about the efficancy of monetary policy under flexible exchange rates. *Journal of International Economics*, 5, 275–81.

Parkin, J. M. (1978) A comparison of alternative techniques of monetary control under rational expectations. *Manchester School* 46, 252–87.

Samuelson, P. A. and Swamy, S. (1974) Invariant economis index numbers and canonical duality: survey and synthesis. *American Economic Review*, 64, 566–93.

Turnovsky, S. J. (1977) *Macroeconomic Analysis and Stabilization Policy*. Cambridge: Cambridge University Press.

—— (1979) On the insulation properties of flexible exchange rates. *Revue Economique*, 30, 719–46.

Wilson, C. A. (1979) Anticipated shocks and exchange rate dynamics. *Journal of Political Economy*, 87, 639–47.

6 Effects of Monetary Disturbances on Exchange Rates with Risk-averse Speculation

(WITH J. EATON)

1 INTRODUCTION

With the general increase in exchange rate flexibility, the analysis of the determination of exchange rates has become a major area of research. An important aspect of the modeling of this process is the degree of capital mobility, with the polar assumption of perfect mobility being most widely adopted. This assumption, which is justified in terms of the observed mobility among the major currencies of the world, is usually specified in terms of uncovered interest parity, meaning that speculation brings the forward exchange rate in line with the expectations of the future spot rate (see for example Argy and Porter, 1972; Bilson, 1978). Furthermore, the recent literature on rational expectations and exchange rate dynamics in particular, has been built on this assumption (see for example Dornbusch, 1976; Turnovsky and Kingston, 1977; Flood, 1979; Gray and Turnovsky, 1979, this volume, ch. 1; Wilson, 1979).

However, as several authors have shown, even if domestic and foreign bonds are perfect substitutes on a covered basis, the assumption of uncovered interest parity follows only if the strong assumption that investors are risk-neutral is added. If, more reasonably, investors are taken to be risk-averse, the forward rate is not in general an unbiased predictor of the spot rate expected to prevail when the forward contract matures. The bias depends upon, among other things, asset supplies, the variability of exchange rates, and the degree of risk aversion (see for example Solnik 1973; Grauer et al., 1976; Kouri, 1976; Adler and

Originally published in *Journal of International Money and Finance*, 1, 1982, 21–37.

Dumas, 1977; Roll and Solnik, 1977; Eaton, 1978; Fama and Farber, 1979 Frankel, 1979; Stein, 1980). Furthermore, the theoretical existence of this bias is generally supported by available empirical evidence (see Levich, 1978, 1979; Hansen and Hodrick, 1980).

The relationship between the forward and expected future spot rates is crucial in determining the domestic interest rate, and hence in determining the current spot rate, the domestic price level, and domestic income. It is therefore important to analyze the determination of the exchange rate under the more general assumption of risk-averse speculative behavior.[1]

Therefore this chapter has two objectives. The first is to develop a stochastic model of exchange rate determination which allows for risk-averse speculative behavior. The second is to analyse the effects of a variety of disturbances consisting of (a) changes in the supplies of money and bonds, (b) forward market intervention, and (c) certain relevant foreign variables. In particular, we shall contrast the effects of transitory and permanent changes in these variables on the domestic economy and show how an increase in the elasticity of speculation with respect to the forward premium (reflecting a reduction in the degree of risk aversion) may influence the effects of the two types of disturbances in opposite ways. For example, we will show that an increase in the degree of speculation is likely to *reduce* the expansionary effects of a *transitory* monetary disturbance, on the one hand, but to *increase* the expansionary effects of a *permanent* monetary disturbance, on the other. This result can also be looked at another way. It means that if in fact investors are risk averse, then the prevalent procedure of equating the forward rate to the expected future spot rate (and hence assuming risk neutrality) may *understate* the effects on income and the spot rate of temporary changes in the money supply and necessarily overstates the corresponding effects of *permanent* changes.

We will also show that less risk-averse speculation increases the sensitivity of income to announcements of *future* changes in money supply. As speculators become less risk-averse, forward intervention policy and changes in the domestic supply of bonds have less effect on income and exchange rates regardless of whether these policies are temporary or permanent. Domestic income becomes more sensitive to changes in foreign variables, however, as speculation becomes more risk-neutral.

The remainder of the chapter proceeds as follows. In section 2 we outline the model underlying our analysis; the solution is provided in section 3. The effects of changes in the money supply, bond supply and forward market intervention, and foreign variables are discussed in section 4, 5, and 6 respectively. Some concluding remarks are provided in section 7.

2 THE FORWARD EXCHANGE MARKET IN A SIMPLE MACROMODEL

The model we will consider is kept as simple as possible to enable us to focus on the main issues without undue complication. Specifically, we will assume that there is a single traded commodity, whose price in terms of foreign currency is given. Also, we will assume that the domestic bond is a perfect substitute for a traded world bond when fully covered against exchange risk. Thus purchasing power parity (PPP) and covered interest parity (CIP) are assumed to hold:

$$p_t = e_t^{\mathrm{s}} + p_t^* \tag{6.1}$$

$$i_t = i_t^* + e_t^{\mathrm{f}} - e_t^{\mathrm{s}} \tag{6.2}$$

where p_t is the domestic price of the traded good at time t, expressed in logarithms, p_t^* is the foreign price of the traded good at time t, expressed in logarithms, e_t^s is the current *spot* exchange rate (measured in units of domestic currency per unit of foreign currency), expressed in logarithms, e_t^{f} is the forward exchange rate at time t for delivery at time $t+1$ (measured in terms of units of domestic currency per unit of foreign currency), expressed in logarithms, i_t is the domestic nominal interest rate at time t, and i_t^* is the foreign nominal interest rate at time t. The domestic economy is assumed to be small so that p_t^* and i_t^* are exogenous; foreign bonds and goods are supplied perfectly elastically at the world interest rate i_t^* and foreign price level p_t^* respectively.

Domestic money market equilibrium is described by the relationship

$$m_t - p_t = \alpha_1 y_t - \alpha_2 i_t \tag{6.3}$$

where m_t is the domestic nominal money supply, expressed in logarithms, and y_t is the domestic real output at time t, expressed in logarithms. This specification is of the usual form. In particular, we make the conventional assumption that all domestic money is held by domestic residents, who in turn hold no foreign money.

The specification of the forward market requires rather more discussion. Private participation in the forward market may take place for two reasons, speculation or arbitrage.[2] The net *supply* of foreign exchange forward for *arbitrage* purposes in real terms equals the net real holdings of foreign bonds by the domestic, private sector. Forward market equilibrium requires that this quantity equal the net *speculative demand* for foreign exchange forward plus net government purchases of foreign exchange forward, both in real terms. The condition for forward market equilibrium at time t is therefore

$$\frac{E_t D_t^{\mathrm{F}}}{P_t} = \frac{D_t^{\mathrm{F}}}{P_t^*} = S_t + \frac{G_t}{P_t^*} \tag{6.4}$$

where E_t, P_t, and P_t^* denote the exchange rate, the domestic price level, and the foreign price level, all measured in natural units, D_t^F is the nominal stock of foreign bonds (denominated in foreign currency) held by domestic residents, S_t is the real speculative demand for foreign exchange forward, and G_t is net nominal holdings by the government of foreign exchange forward. (The first part of (6.4) follows from the purchasing power parity condition $P_t = E_t P_t^*$.)

The real demand for foreign exchange for speculation is a function of the expected rate of return on the forward purchase of foreign currency. We approximate this relationship by the expression

$$S_t = \gamma(e_{t+1,t}^{\mathrm{s}} - e_t^{\mathrm{f}}) \tag{6.5}$$

where $e_{t+1,t}^{\mathrm{s}}$ denotes the expectation of the spot for time $t + 1$ as of time t. The parameter γ is a decreasing function of the degree of relative risk aversion. As the degree of relative risk aversion tends to zero, so that risk neutrality is approached, $\gamma \to \infty$, implying $e_{t+1}^{\mathrm{s}} = e_t^{\mathrm{f}}$, i.e. the forward rate becomes an unbiased predictor of the spot rate.

Since, by assumption, covered foreign bonds are perfect substitutes for domestic bonds, the real demand for foreign bonds is simply the real demand D_t for *all* bonds less the real supply B_t/P_t of domestic bonds, where B_t is the nominal stock of domestic bonds denominated in domestic currency, i.e.

$$\frac{D_t^{\mathrm{F}}}{P_t^*} = D_t - \frac{B_t}{P_t} \tag{6.6}$$

The total real demand D_t for bonds is specified by the relationship

$$D_t = \omega_1 y_t + \omega_2 i_t \qquad \omega_2 > 0 \tag{6.7}$$

Elsewhere (Eaton and Turnovsky, 1981) we have derived asset demand equations of a form consistent with equations (6.3), (6.5) and (6.7) from a representative individual's two-period expected-utility maximization problem where real money balances provide transactions services. Note that since money and bonds are the only available assets, and since we assume that domestic bonds and money *are* net wealth, equations (6.3) and (6.7) implicitly define a savings function.[3] Since savings as well as the demand for real money balances rises with income, our theory provides no presumption about the sign of ω_1.

The presence of the term B_t/P_t in (6.6) causes the demand for foreign bonds to remain nonlinear. If we denote $\ln B_t$ by b_t, a linear approximation to D_t^{F}/P_t^* is given by[4]

$$\frac{D_t^{\mathrm{F}}}{P_t^*} = D_t - \omega_4 - \omega_3(b_t - p_t) \tag{6.8}$$

where $\omega_3 \approx \bar{B}_{\mathrm{t}}/\bar{P}_{\mathrm{t}}$, the average stock of domestic bonds divided by the average price level, and $\omega_4 \approx \omega_3(1 - \ln \omega_3)$. We will normalize units so that $\ln \omega_3 = 1$ and $\omega_4 = 0$, in which case, substituting (6.7) into (6.8), we obtain

$$\frac{D_t^{\mathrm{F}}}{P_t^*} = \omega_1 y_t + \omega_2 i_t - \omega_3(b_t - p_t) \tag{6.8$'$}$$

Likewise, the real government intervention G_t/P_t^* is also nonlinear and, by a similar process, a linear approximation is given by[5]

$$\frac{G_t}{P_t^*} = \lambda(g_t - p_t^*) \tag{6.9}$$

where $\lambda \approx (\bar{G}_t/\bar{P}_t^*)$, the average real stock of forward exchange held by the government, and $g_t \equiv \ln G_t$. Units are chosen so that $\ln \lambda = 1$. Substituting equations (6.5), (6.8′) and (6.9) into (6.4), we obtain the following condition for forward market equilibrium:

$$\omega_1 y_t + \omega_2 i_t - \omega_3(b_t - p_t) = \gamma(e_{t+1,t}^{\mathrm{s}} - e_t^{\mathrm{f}}) + \lambda(g_t - p_t^*) \tag{6.10}$$

Finally, we assume that deviations in output from its natural level $\bar{y}$ are determined by the unanticipated component of the domestic price level, i.e.

$$y_t = \theta(p_t - p_{t,t-1}) \tag{6.11}$$

where we normalize units by setting $\bar{y} = 0$, and $p_{t,t-1}$ denotes the expectation of the price level for time t formed at time $t - 1$. Such a specification follows from the contract theory of wage determination of Gray (1976), Fischer (1977), and Phelps and Taylor (1977).

This completes the specification of the model. Together, equations (6.1), (6.2), (6.3), (6.10), and (6.11) determine the equilibrium values of five endogenous variables p_t, i_t, e_t^{s}, e_t^{f}, and y_t in terms of the expectations $e_{t+1,t}^{\mathrm{s}}$, $p_{t,t-1}$ and the exogenous variables i_t^*, p_t^*, m_t, b_t, g_t as well as the structural parameters of the system. The only thing that remains before solving the model is the description of expectations, which we take to be formed rationally, i.e. price and exchange rate expectations are optimally generated forecasts based on a solution of the model itself using all available information.

3 DETERMINATION OF SOLUTION

Substituting equations (6.1), (6.2) and (6.11) into equations (6.3) and (6.10) we obtain two equations, one a condition for money market equilibrium and the other a condition for forward market equilibrium. Together these equations determine the spot and forward rates of exchange. In matrix form, the two equilibrium equations are

$$\begin{bmatrix} 1 + \alpha_1\theta + \alpha_2 & -\alpha_2 \\ \omega_2 - \omega_1\theta - \omega_3 & -\omega_2 - \gamma \end{bmatrix} \begin{bmatrix} e_t^{\mathrm{s}} \\ e_t^{\mathrm{f}} \end{bmatrix} = \begin{bmatrix} v_t^{\mathrm{m}} \\ v_t^{\mathrm{f}} \end{bmatrix} \tag{6.12}$$

where

$$v_t^m \equiv m_t - (1 + \alpha_1\theta)p_t^* + \alpha_2 i_t^* + \alpha_1\theta p_{t,t-1}$$

$$v_t^{\mathrm{f}} \equiv -\omega_3 b_t - \lambda g_t + (\omega_1\theta + \omega_3 + \lambda)p_t^* + \omega_2 i_t^* - \omega_1\theta p_{t,t-1} - \gamma e_{t+1,t}^{\mathrm{s}}$$

Given current expectations about the future and past expectations about the present, the first line of (6.12) determines a relationship between e_t^{s} and e_t^{f} that equilibrates the money market and which we label the MM curve. It appears in figure 6.1 and has slope $(1 + \alpha_1\theta + \alpha_2)/\alpha_2 > 1$. The second line of (6.12) determines a relationship between e_t^{s} and e_t^{f} that equilibrates the forward exchange market and which we label the FF curve. It has slope $(\omega_2 - \omega_1\theta - \omega_3)/(\omega_2 + \gamma)$ which can be of either sign. We will assume, however, that it is less steep than the MM curve. This will certainly be so if the income elasticity ω_1 of the demand for bonds is not strongly negative.

The ambiguity in the slope of the FF curve arises for the following

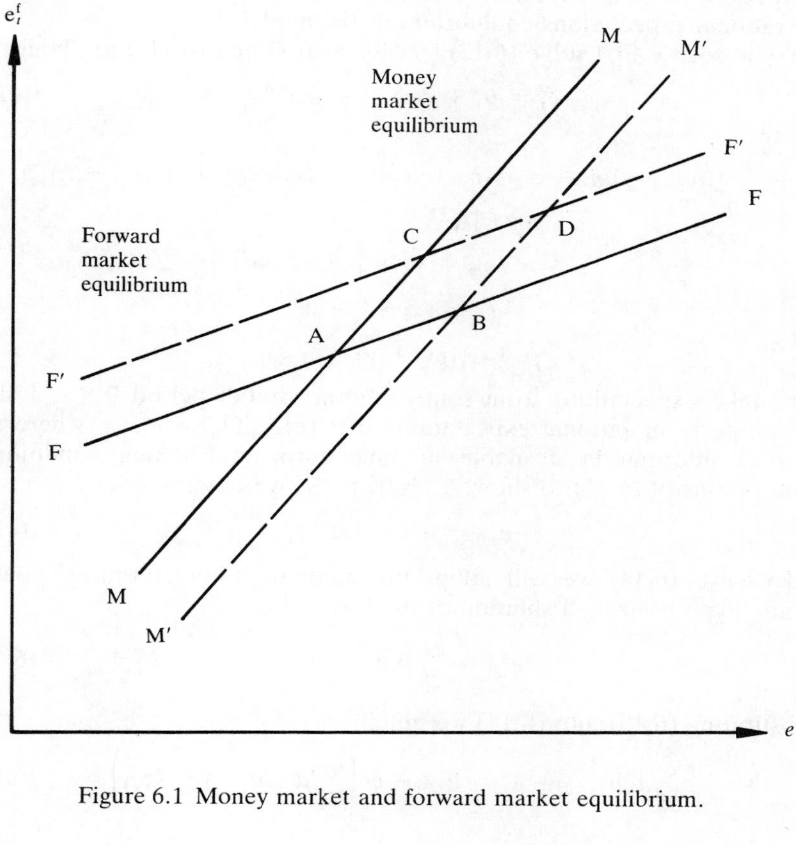

Figure 6.1 Money market and forward market equilibrium.

reason. An increase in e_t^s causes p_t to rise, reducing the real supply of domestic bonds. This raises the demand for foreign bonds and hence the supply of foreign exchange forward. To generate an offsetting speculative demand for foreign exchange forward requires a lower value of e_t^f. However, an increase in e_t^s also lowers i_t and hence the demand for bonds. This has the opposite effect on e_t^f. The first effect dominates where domestic bonds are a large share of total bond holdings and the demand for bonds is relatively interest-inelastic ($\omega_3 > \omega_2$). Conversely, the second effect dominates when $\omega_2 > \omega_3$.

For the case in which speculators are risk-neutral ($\gamma \to \infty$) and FF curve becomes horizontal. The forward rate is determined solely in the forward market by speculative behavior, which ensures that $e_t^f = e_{t+1,t}^s$. When the demand for money is interest-inelastic, $\alpha_2 = 0$ and the MM curve becomes vertical. The spot rate is determined solely by money market equilibrium. Otherwise, equilibrium values of the two rates are determined simultaneously in the two markets.

In drawing the MM and FF curves, the expectations $e_{t+1,t}^s$, $p_{t,t-1}$ have been taken as given. We now endogenize these variables by solving for the rational expectations equilibrium of the model.

To do so, we first solve (6.12) (recalling (6.1) and (6.11)) to obtain

$$e_t^s = u_t^s + \phi e_{t+1,t}^s - \rho \Delta^{-1} y_t \tag{6.13}$$

where

$$u_t^s \equiv [(\omega_2 + \gamma)m_t + \alpha_2\omega_3 b_t + \alpha_2\lambda g_t - \{\omega_2 + \gamma + \alpha_2(\omega_3 + \lambda)\}p_t + \alpha_2\gamma i_t^*]\Delta^{-1}$$

$$\Delta \equiv (\omega_2 + \gamma) + \alpha_2(\gamma + \omega_3)$$

$$\phi \equiv \alpha_2\gamma\Delta^{-1} < 1$$

$$\rho \equiv \alpha_1(\omega_2 + \gamma) + \alpha_2\omega_1$$

Now take expectations from some arbitrary initial period $0 < t$. Using the property of rational expectations that $(e_{t+1,t}^s | \Omega_0) = e_{t+1,0}^s$, where Ω_0 denotes information available at time zero, and taking conditional expectations of (6.11) to show $y_{t,\tau} = 0$, $\tau < t$, we obtain

$$e_{t,0}^s = u_{t,0}^s + \phi e_{t+1,0}^s \tag{6.14}$$

To solve (6.14) we will adopt the method of undetermined coefficients, hypothesizing a solution of the form

$$e_{t,0}^s = \sum_{i=0}^{\infty} \mu_i u_{t+i,0}^s + k_t \tag{6.15}$$

Substituting (6.15) into (6.14) we obtain

$$\sum_{i=1}^{\infty} \mu_i u_{t+i,0}^s + k_t = u_{t,0}^s + \phi\left(\sum_{i=1}^{\infty} \mu_{i-1} u_{t+i,0}^s + k_{t+1}\right) \tag{6.16}$$

Equating coefficients, we find

$$k_t = \phi k_{t+1} \tag{6.17a}$$

$$\mu_i = \phi \mu_{i-1} \tag{6.17b}$$

$$\mu_0 = 1 \tag{6.17c}$$

The general solution to (6.14) is thus of the form

$$e^{\mathrm{s}}_{t,0} = \sum_{i=0}^{\infty} \phi^i u^{\mathrm{s}}_{t+i,0} + k_0 \phi^{-i} \tag{6.18}$$

where k_0 is an arbitrary constant. Since $\phi < 1$, to ensure that $e^{\mathrm{s}}_{t,0}$ remains bounded as $t \to \infty$, we impose the restriction that $k_0 = 0$.[6] Thus it follows from (6.18) that

$$e^{\mathrm{s}}_{t+1,t} = \sum_{i=0}^{\infty} \phi^i u^{\mathrm{s}}_{t+i+1,t} \tag{6.19}$$

The solution e^{s}_t for the actual spot rate is obtained by substituting (6.19) into (6.13), recalling that $u^{\mathrm{s}}_{t,t} = u^{\mathrm{s}}_t$. Thus we obtain

$$e^{\mathrm{s}}_t = \sum_{i=0}^{\infty} \phi^i u^{\mathrm{s}}_{t+i,t} - \rho \Delta^{-1} y_t \tag{6.20}$$

To solve for the current output y_t we substitute the purchasing power relationship (6.1) into the supply function (6.11). Using (6.19) at time $t-1$, together with (6.20), we can write the solution for y_t in the form

$$y_t = \frac{\theta \Delta}{\Delta + \rho \theta} \{(u^{\mathrm{s}}_t - u^{\mathrm{s}}_{t,t-1}) + \sum_{i=1}^{\infty} \phi^i (u^{\mathrm{s}}_{t+i,t} - u^{\mathrm{s}}_{t+i,t-1}) + p^*_t - p^*_{t,t-1}\} \tag{6.21}$$

From (6.21) we observe that y_t depends upon the unanticipated components of changes in the foreign price level $p^*_t - p^*_{t,t-1}$ and the composite disturbance term $u^{\mathrm{s}}_t - u^{\mathrm{s}}_{t,t-1}$. In addition, it depends upon an infinite discounted sum of terms $u^{\mathrm{s}}_{t+i,t} - u^{\mathrm{s}}_{t+i,t-1}$ which measure the extent to which forecasts of u^{s}_{t+i} are updated between periods $t-1$ and t as information at time t becomes available.

An expression for e^{f}_t can be obtained by solving (6.12) and substituting (6.19), yielding

$$\begin{aligned} e^{\mathrm{f}}_t = u^{\mathrm{f}}_t &+ (1 + \alpha_2)\gamma \Delta^{-1} \sum_{i=0}^{\infty} \phi^i u^{\mathrm{s}}_{t+i+1,t} \\ &+ \{\alpha_1(\omega_2 - \omega_3) - (1 + \alpha_2)\omega_2\} \Delta^{-1} y_t \end{aligned} \tag{6.22}$$

where

$$\begin{aligned} u^{\mathrm{f}}_t \equiv \{&(\omega_2 - \omega_3) m_t + (1 + \alpha_2)\omega_3 b_t + \lambda(1 + \alpha_2)(g_t - p^*_t) \\ &- (\omega_2 + \alpha_2 \omega_3)(i^*_t + p^*_t)\} \Delta^{-1} \end{aligned}$$

Through the terms $e^{s}_{t+i,t}$ the current values of income and the spot and forward exchange rates depend upon the entire time profile of expectations of all future money supplies, bond supplies, government position in the forward market, and the relevant foreign disturbances. Equations (6.20)–(6.22) form the basis for our subsequent analysis. Reduced-form expressions for e^{s}_{t} and e^{f}_{t} can be obtained by substituting (6.21), the solution for y_t into (6.20) and (6.22), but it is not necessary to report these explicitly. In subsequent sections below we consider the effects of three types of disturbances on the economy:

1 various forms of domestic monetary expansion;
2 various forms of bond market or forward market intervention by the domestic monetary authorities;
3 international disturbances taking the form of changes in the foreign price level and foreign interest rate.

These three topics are addressed in sections 4, 5, and 6 respectively.

4 DOMESTIC MONETARY EXPANSION

The effects of an infinite range of monetary disturbances can in principle be analysed from the solution (6.20)–(6.22). These disturbances can most usefully be distinguished in terms of (a) the extent to which they are anticipated or unanticipated, (b) their expected permanence or transience; and (c) whether they occur immediately or are announced. Any specific monetary disturbance can be parameterized quite explicitly by imposing the appropriate changes on the relevant terms appearing in the expressions $u^{s}_{t+i,t}$, $u^{f}_{t+i,t}$. Obviously we can discuss just a limited number of disturbances, although others can be considered along similar lines. In all cases, the monetary disturbance will take the form of an increase dm_t in the money supply, which is effected by a transfer. An open-market operation can, however, be readily treated in a similar way (see note 9 below).

4.1 An unanticipated temporary increase in the money supply

We will consider an initial disturbance in the money supply which is (a) unanticipated as of period $t-1$ and (b) expected to last only during period t. It is therefore a purely random one-period shock. Accordingly, $du^{s}_{t+i,t} = du^{s}_{t+i,t-1} = 0$, $i \neq 0$.

This disturbance can be treated quite conveniently by means of the MM and FF curves given in figure 6.1. Since $u^{s}_{t+i,t}$ remains fixed, the spot rate expected to prevail in period $t+1$ and given by expression (6.19) is also unaffected by the changes being considered, i.e.

$de^{s}_{t+1,t} = 0$. Thus the assumption of constant expectations incorporated in the MM and FF curves is consistent with rational expectations when disturbances are perceived as temporary.

The effect of a random transfer in the money supply dm is to shift the MM curve to the right. At any given forward rate, a higher spot rate is required to restore money market equilibrium. The FF curve is unaffected by the change. Since, by assumption, the MM curve is steeper than the FF curve, the spot rate rises, as does the forward rate if FF is upward sloping. In terms of figure 6.1, the equilibrium moves from A to B say. As long as the slope of the FF curve is less than unity (which will be the case unless ω_3 is highly negative), e^{s}_{t} rises by more than e^{f}_{t} and the domestic interest rate falls. Thus a temporary increase in the money supply is reflected more in the current spot rate than it is in the forward rate. Given that we would expect the spot rate to be more sensitive to current random disturbances, while forward rates will tend to reflect more permanent changes, this result makes good intuitive sense.

The effect of an increase in m_t on income y_t is given by

$$\left(\frac{\mathrm{d}y_t}{\mathrm{d}m_t}\right)_{\mathrm{tr}} = \frac{\theta(\omega_2 + \gamma)}{\Delta + \rho\theta} \tag{6.23}$$

where the subscript tr denotes "transitory." Thus an unanticipated increase in the money supply that is not expected to persist has an expansionary effect. Differentiating (6.23) with respect to γ reveals that an increase in the elasticity of speculation has an ambiguous effect on the size of the income response. If the FF curve slopes up, more elastic speculation diminishes the effect, and conversely. The same comments apply to the effects of increased speculation on the spot rate.

An increase in γ ties the forward rate more closely to the expected future spot rate: whatever its slope, the FF curve becomes more horizontal. When the FF curve slopes up an increase in the money supply raises the forward rate while monetary expansion lowers the forward rate when the FF curve slopes down. Either way, increased speculation reduces the absolute magnitude of the response. If the FF curve slopes up, increased speculation reduces the rise in the forward rate accompanying monetary expansion. Through the CIP condition (equation (6.2)), the drop in the domestic interest rate caused by monetary expansion is thereby larger. Since as a result of increased speculation a given monetary expansion induces a larger fall in i_t, the rise in y_t compatible with monetary market equilibrium (equation (6.3)) is consequently smaller.

The opposite occurs when the FF curve slopes down. Monetary expansion then generates a fall in the forward rate, but increased speculation reduces its size. The consequent drop in i_t is therefore smaller. A larger rise in y_t is thus consistent with money market equilibrium.

4.2 The effects of changes in expectations

Any change in the money supply that is expected to be permanent also has effects on expectations. In order to consider these we analyse the effects of an increase in $e^s_{t+1,t}$ on e^s_t and e^f_t.

An increase in $e^s_{t+1,t}$ shifts the FF curve upward by an amount $\gamma/(\omega_2 + \gamma)$, leaving the MM curve unchanged and thereby shifting the equilibrium from A to C in figure 6.1. Both the spot and forward rates rise, the forward rate by proportionately more. As the elasticity of speculation increases, so does the response of both rates to changes in expectations, with the increased responsiveness of the spot rate increasing that of income.

4.3 The effects of an unanticipated permanent change

We now consider the effects of a monetary expansion that initially is unanticipated, but, having occurred, is expected to be permanent. This form of monetary disturbance has recently been discussed extensively in the literature, and has been shown to give rise to the possibility of "overshooting" of the spot exchange rate in response to a monetary disturbance (see Dornbusch, 1976).

Any monetary expansion that is expected to be permanent influences the system in two ways. It operates first through the channels discussed in section 4.1 and second through its effects on expectations noted in section 4.2. These changes are illustrated in figure 6.1 as a change from A to D. In the extreme case in which speculators are infinitely risk-averse ($\gamma = 0$), expectations have no effect on the present and it is therefore irrelevant whether a particular change is perceived as permanent or temporary. Otherwise, both channels must be considered.

The impact effect of an unanticipated change in the money supply that *ex post* is expected to be permanent is given by

$$\left(\frac{dy_t}{dm_t}\right)_p = \frac{\theta(\omega_2 + \gamma)}{(1 - \phi)(\Delta + \rho\theta)} \tag{6.24}$$

where subscript p denotes "permanent." Comparing (6.24) with (6.23), note that the response of income is larger when the change in the money supply is perceived as being permanent. In this case $e^s_{t+1,t}$ becomes greater, thereby reinforcing the expansionary effect resulting from the increased money supply.

The effects on the spot and forward rates are given by

$$\left(\frac{de^s_t}{dm_t}\right)_p = \frac{\omega_2 + \gamma}{(1 - \phi)(\Delta + \rho\theta)} \tag{6.25a}$$

$$\left(\frac{de^f_t}{dm_t}\right)_p = \frac{\omega_2 - \theta\omega_1 - \omega_3 + (1 + \rho\theta/\Delta)\gamma}{(1 - \phi)(\Delta + \rho\theta)} \tag{6.25b}$$

From (6.25a) it can be seen that a 1 percent increase in the money supply leads to a devaluation of the spot rate of less than 1 percent. Provided that the FF curve is upward sloping, the monetary expansion will increase the forward rate, although again less than proportionately. The ratio of the effects of a permanent increase in the money supply upon the forward and spot rates is given by the expression

$$\frac{\omega_2 - \theta\omega_1 - \omega_3 + (1 + \rho\theta/\Delta)\gamma}{\omega_2 + \gamma} \tag{6.26}$$

while the corresponding ratio with respect to temporary disturbances is

$$\frac{\omega_2 - \theta\omega_1 - \omega_3}{\omega_2 + \gamma} \tag{6.27}$$

Comparing these two ratios we can infer that, unless ω_1 is very negative, an increase in the money supply will have a relatively greater effect on the forward rate when it is expected to be permanent than when it is expected to be transitory. This result makes perfectly good intuitive sense for the reasons noted in section 4.1.

An increase in the elasticity of speculation increases the extent to which income and the two exchange rates respond to a permanent increase in the money supply. This result contrasts with the ambiguous effects of increasingly elastic speculation on the response to a temporary increase. Since elastic speculation ties the current spot rate and income more closely to the future, it may dampen the effects of temporary changes, but it amplifies the effects of permanent ones. As the elasticity of speculation tends to infinity, we obtain

$$\left(\frac{\mathrm{d}e_t^{\mathrm{s}}}{\mathrm{d}m_t}\right)_{\mathrm{P}} = \frac{1 + \alpha_2}{1 + \alpha_1\theta + \alpha_2} < 1 \tag{6.28a}$$

$$\left(\frac{\mathrm{d}e_t^{\mathrm{f}}}{\mathrm{d}m_t}\right)_{\mathrm{P}} = 1 \tag{6.28b}$$

Thus far we have considered only the impact effects of a permanent change in the money supply. These short-run responses in the exchange rates e_t^{s} and e_t^{f} include an income effect, which operates through the last term in equations (6.20) and (6.22). For $\tau > t$, income reverts to its steady state level of zero. The permanent changes in the spot and forward rates are respectively

$$\left(\frac{\mathrm{d}e_\tau^{\mathrm{s}}}{\mathrm{d}m_t}\right)_{\mathrm{P}} = \frac{\omega_2 + \gamma}{\omega_2 + \gamma + \alpha_2\omega_3} \qquad \tau > t \tag{6.29a}$$

and

$$\left(\frac{\mathrm{d}e_\tau^{\mathrm{f}}}{\mathrm{d}m_t}\right)_{\mathrm{P}} = \frac{\omega_2 - \omega_3 + \gamma}{\omega_2 + \gamma + \alpha_2\omega_3} \qquad \tau > t \tag{6.29b}$$

When $\omega_3 > 0$ and $\alpha_2 > 0$ the permanent change in the spot rate is less than the permanent change in the money supply while the permanent change in the forward rate is even lower. The reason is that the initial increase in the price level reduces the real supply of bonds, increasing the demand for foreign bonds and lowering e_t^f. The consequent decline in the domestic interest rate raises the demand for money, so that a proportional change in the price level is not required.

Comparing (6.29a) and (6.25a) we see that the steady state response of the spot exchange rate to an unanticipated permanent increase in the money supply exceeds its reponse on impact, i.e. the exchange rate undershoots its long-run response. While this result is in contrast with the overshooting obtained by Dornbusch, the difference is due to differences in assumptions and accords with similar results in the literature. The critical factors in our model are (a) that the domestic price level is not only flexible, but is also tied to the world price via PPP, and (b) the endogeneity of income. As a consequence, any nominal expansion in the money supply is accommodated partly by income changes and partly by price changes, thereby requiring less adjustment in the exchange rate.[7]

4.4 Announcement effects

Thus far we have considered temporary and permanent increases in the money supply that were unanticipated as of the period before which they actually occurred. If, instead, we consider changes in period t that are announced in period $t - k$, our analysis is subject to several modifications.

First, there are real effects only during period $t - k$, when the announcement is made. In all subsequent periods prices are correctly anticipated. The effects of one-period changes in period t, the time the policy is put into effect, on e_t^s and e_t^f can be obtained as before, only with the income effects removed. Algebraically, these results can be obtained by setting $\theta = 0$ in the analysis in section 4.1. No qualitative differences in the responses of e_t^s and e_t^f arise when temporary changes are anticipated. When permanent changes are anticipated, e_t^s and e_t^f assume their new steady state values as income effects are now absent.

Exchange rates from periods $t - k$ until t are affected solely by the effect of the announcement on expectations. Having computed the effect on e_t^s of either temporary or permanent changes in policy, the effects on e_{t-1}^s and e_{t-1}^f can be derived via the analysis in section 4.2, again with the income effects suppressed (unless $k - 1$). The effects on e_{t-1}^s $k > i > 1$ can be solved similarly via backward iteration. In the announcement period $t - k$ the income effect is no longer suppressed.

The effect of an announcement of a change in policy to occur in period t on income durng the announcement period y_{t-k} is given by the expression

$$\frac{\mathrm{d}y_{t-k}}{\mathrm{d}x_t} = \frac{\Delta\theta\phi^k}{\Delta + \rho\theta} \frac{\mathrm{d}e_t^s}{\mathrm{d}x_t} \tag{6.30}$$

where $\mathrm{d}x_t$ denotes the (temporary or permanent) policy change in period t. Thus the effect on y_{t-k} is qualitatively independent of the lag, but since $0 \leq \phi < 1$, it declines quantitatively as the lag becomes longer and speculation and money demand become less elastic. In particular, if the demand for money is interest-inelastic or speculation-inelastic, then $\phi = 0$ so that changes announced in advance have no effects on real activity at any stage. Thus less risk-averse speculation raises the sensitivity of income to preannounced monetary changes.

5 FORWARD MARKET INTERVENTION AND CHANGES IN DOMESTIC BOND SUPPLY

The effects of forward market intervention by the domestic government and changes in the supply of domestic bonds can be described by considering various changes in g_t and b_t. Note that g_t and b_t appear in (6.12) additively. Thus changes in these policy variables have parallel effects.[8] An increase in b_t reduces the demand for foreign bonds and hence the supply of foreign exchange forward for arbitrage. The private speculative demand for foreign exchange forward required to equilibrate the forward market is thereby reduced. A government purchase of foreign exchange forward does the same thing directly. In either case a higher value of e_t^f is compatible with forward market equilibrium. As with a monetary disturbance, these two changes can take various forms (anticipated versus unanticipated, temporary versus permanent, etc.) and can be analysed in a similar fashion to that used in section 4. For this reason our comments can be brief.

Consider the effects of an unanticipated one-period increase in the supply of domestic bonds or, equivalently, a one-time central bank purchase of foreign exchange in the forward market. Either will bid up e_t^f, given any value of e_t^s: the FF curve in figure 6.1 shifts up. Both spot and forward rates will therefore rise. Since the slope of the MM curve exceeds unity, the forward rate rises by more than the spot rate, so that the domestic interest rate rises. Since e_t^s rises, so does the domestic price level, and with it domestic output. Thus these effects are qualitatively similar to those of a temporary monetary expansion, except that direct intervention in the forward market has a relatively greater effect on the forward rate. Consequently expansion is accompanied by an increase rather than a decrease in the interest rate.

As the elasticity of speculation increases, the forward rate becomes increasingly tied to the expected future rate and the upward shift in the FF curve diminishes, reducing the overall impact of the intervention on the endogenous variables e_t^s, e_t^f, and y_t. In the limit, as speculation becomes perfectly elastic, all these effects vanish.

Turning now to an unannounced increase in b_t that *ex post* is expected to be permanent or, equivalently, a central bank purchase of foreign exchange forward that is expected to be maintained each period, we can show that, as with a temporary change in g_t, or b_t, the forward rate responds more than the spot rate. This is true both on impact and in steady state. Thus an increase in g_t or b_t will raise the domestic interest rate permanently, unless the elasticity γ is infinite, in which case all effects tends to zero.[9]

Finally, we note that steady state values of e^s, e^f and p are homogeneous of degree 1 in b and m, while i and y are homogeneous of degree 0. Hence permanent proportional increases in b and m have no effect on the covered interest differential Δc.

6 INTERNATIONAL DISTURBANCES

The effects of disturbances in the two foreign variables p^* and i^* can be analysed similarly. In general, these two variables will move simultaneously as they respond to common influences abroad. For example, an increase in demand abroad will cause both p^* and i^* to rise, while a monetary expansion abroad will cause i^* to fall but p^* to rise. For simplicity, we will focus on the two disturbances separately, recognizing that any real world disturbance will be some composite of the two effects.

6.1 Foreign price level disturbance

An unanticipated temporary increase in p_t^* will shift the MM curve to the left while the FF curve falls vertically, causing both e_t^s and e_t^f to fall. As speculation becomes more elastic the size of the shift in the FF curve diminishes and in the limit, as $\gamma \rightarrow \infty$, the FF curve remains fixed. Thus as γ rises the effects of a foreign price increase on the exchange rate diminishes.

The effect of the foreign price disturbance on domestic income is

$$\left(\frac{\mathrm{d}y_t}{\mathrm{d}p_t^*}\right)_{\mathrm{tr}} = \frac{\theta\alpha_2(\gamma - \lambda)}{\Delta + \rho\theta} \tag{6.31}$$

Provided that the average of level intervention in the forward market is less than the elasticity of speculation ($\lambda < \gamma$), an increase in the foreign price level generates a less than proportional fall in the spot rate so that the domestic price level rises, causing income to rise as well. The existence of a positive government position in the forward market ($\lambda > 0$) causes e_t^s and e_t^f to fall further in response to an increase in p_t^*, providing an offsetting contractionary effect. Indeed, if the net government position is sufficiently large, income may actually fall. Only when $\alpha_2 = 0$ or $\gamma = \lambda$ is the response of the exchange rate proportional, so that income is unaffected. As speculation becomes more elastic, exchange rates are influenced more by future expectations and respond less to current foreign price changes. The effect of a change in the foreign price level is consequently more fully reflected in the domestic price level, so that the response of income is increased.

In the absence of a government net position in the forward exchange market, the effect of an unanticipated permanent change in p_t^* on y_t is zero. The spot rate appreciates by the amount of the foreign price increase. Thus there is no effect on the domestic price level. The forward rate also changes by the same amount. Therefore, even on impact, changes in the foreign price level that are perceived as permanent have no real effects (see Harris and Purvis (1979) for a similar result). With $\lambda < 0$, however, an unanticipated permanent increase in p_t^* generates a more than proportional appreciation of the spot rate, causing domestic income to fall.

6.2 Foreign interest rate disturbance

An unanticipated one-period increase in i_t^* leads to downward shifts in both the MM and FF curves. The fall in the former exceeds that of the latter so that the spot rate rises, while the response of the forward rate is ambiguous. Because of the rise in the spot rate, the domestic price level and output also rise. As speculation becomes more elastic the shift of the FF curve declines in absolute magnitude and the increases in the spot rate and income become greater.

The effect on income of an unanticipated change in the foreign interest rate that is perceived as being permanent is

$$\left(\frac{\mathrm{d}y_t}{\mathrm{d}i_t^*}\right)_{\mathrm{P}} = \frac{\alpha_2\gamma\theta}{(1-\phi)(\Delta+\rho\theta)} \tag{6.32}$$

with an increase in the elasticity of speculation increasing the magnitude of this impact. It is interesting to note that, in steady state, the change in the domestic interest rate resulting from a permanent change in the foreign rate is

$$\left(\frac{\mathrm{d}i_t}{\mathrm{d}i_t^*}\right)_{\mathrm{P}} = 1 + \left(\frac{\mathrm{d}e_t^{\mathrm{f}}}{\mathrm{d}i_t^*}\right)_{\mathrm{P}} - \left(\frac{\mathrm{d}e_t^{\mathrm{s}}}{\mathrm{d}i_t^*}\right)_{\mathrm{P}} = \frac{\gamma}{\omega_1+\gamma+\alpha_2\omega_3} \tag{6.33}$$

In general a permanent rise in the foreign interest rate leads to a less than proportional rise in the domestic interest rate. If speculation is perfectly inelastic there is no effect, while as speculation becomes perfectly elastic the effect tends toward exact proportionality.

7 CONCLUSIONS

In this chapter we have developed a macroeconomic model in which domestic and foreign bonds are perfect substitutes on a covered basis, but in which speculators are assumed to be risk-averse. Under such conditions, previous portfolio investment models have shown that a risk premium on forward exchange is likely to be established. We have analysed the effects of various transitory and permanent disturbances on the economy and shown how the existence of the risk premium has important implications for macroeconomic behavior.

Perhaps, of greatest interest is the proposition that an increase in the degree of speculation, reflecting a reduction in the degree of risk aversion, may diminish the expansionary effects of a transitory increase in the money supply on the one hand, while it amplifies the expansionary effects of a permanent increase on the other. From this it follows that the assumption of perfectly elastic speculation (under which the risk premium is eliminated) is likely to overstate the difference between permanent and temporary changes. This assumption also tends to exaggerate the announcement effects of changes to occur in the future.

Because our model explicitly incorporates a forward market, it suggests some interesting implications as to how spot and forward rates reveal information about expectations. Typically, changes that are perceived as being permanent are reflected relatively more in the forward rate, while the spot rate responds more to changes that are seen as being only temporary.

Our analysis has focused primarily on how the economy responds to temporary and permanent changes in the money and bond supplies and in the central bank's forward market position. A natural extension of this is the design of money supply and forward market intervention rules that stabilize the domestic economy in the face of stochastic disturbances. This issue is taken up elsewhere (see Eaton and Turnovsky, 1984).

NOTES

1 Two other macroeconomic models which incorporate a more general specification of speculation in the determination of forward market equilibrium are those of Eaton (1978) and of Harris and Purvis (1979). Both models assume full employment so that the income effects of various disturbances cannot be analysed. Both also focus on situations in which current information is not fully available, and consider the information revealed by spot and forward exchange rates.

2 There is no loss of generality in separating forward market participation into

pure speculation and pure arbitrage. We implicitly treat the acquisition of an amount x of *uncovered* foreign bonds as combining a *covered* investment of x in foreign bonds and a *speculative purchase* of foreign currency forward in amount x. In a portfolio model of foreign investement we identify a third motive for participating in the forward market as hedging against domestic inflation. Forward positions for hedging purposes depend upon the relative variability of the domestic and foreign price levels and do not respond to the variables we are concerned with here. We can thus treat the forward position due to hedging as a constant absorbed in S_t (Eaton and Turnovsky, 1981). Note that any given individual may be speculating *and* arbitraging simultaneously.

3 See, for example, Lucas (1975) who follows an equivalent procedure, i.e. specifying *all* asset demand functions and thereby defining a savings function residually.

4 The approximation in (6.8) is obtained as follows

$$\frac{B_t}{P_t} \approx \frac{\bar{B}}{\bar{P}} + \frac{\bar{B}}{\bar{P}}\left(\frac{B_t - \bar{B}}{\bar{B}}\right) - \frac{\bar{B}}{\bar{P}}\left(\frac{P_t - \bar{P}}{\bar{P}}\right) = \omega_3\left(1 + \frac{B_t - \bar{B}}{\bar{B}} - \frac{P_t - \bar{P}}{\bar{P}}\right)$$

Now

$$\frac{B_t - \bar{B}}{\bar{B}} \approx \ln\left(1 + \frac{B_t - \bar{B}}{\bar{B}}\right) = \ln\left(\frac{B_t}{\bar{B}}\right) = b_t - \ln \bar{B}$$

Similarly

$$\frac{P_t - \bar{P}}{\bar{P}} \approx p_t - \ln \bar{P}$$

so that

$$\frac{B_t}{P_t} \approx \omega_3\{1 + (b_t - \ln \bar{B}) - (p_t - \ln \bar{P})\}$$

$$= \omega_3(1 - \ln \omega_3) + \omega_3(b_t - p_t)$$

5 The argument is similar to that in note 4, with G_t/P_t^* in place of B_t/P_t.

6 One rationale for this procedure is obtained by imposing a transversality condition on a corresponding infinite-horizon optimization problem.

7 See Turnovsky (1981, this volume, ch. 5) for further discussion of this issue. Elsewhere (Eaton and Turnovsky, 1983, this volume, ch. 2) we consider the implication of risk-averse speculation for exchange rate dynamics in a model that incorporates short-run price inflexibility (see also Driskill 1980; Driskill and McCafferty, 1980).

8 This result does *not* carry over to situations in which bonds are subject to default risk as well as exchange risk (see Eaton and Turnovsky, 1981).

9 A monetary expansion taking the form of an open-market operation is described by $\mathrm{d}M + \mathrm{d}B = 0$, which in terms of logarithms is $\mathrm{d}m + (B/M)\,\mathrm{d}b = 0$. In effect this is a combination of the policies discussed in section 6.4 and 6.5, and the various cases can be considered as an extension of these results. It is worth noting that in the absence of wealth effects ($\omega_3 = 0$) an open-market operation is equivalent to the monetary expansion discussed in the text.

REFERENCES

Adler, M. and Dumas, B. (1977) The microeconomics of the firm in an open economy. *American Economic Review, Papers and Proceedings*, 67, 180–9.

Argy, V. and Porter, M. G. (1972) The forward market and the effects of domestic and external disturbances under alternative exchange rate system. *IMF Staff Papers*, 19, 503–32.

Bilson, J. F. O. (1978) Rational expectations and the exchange rate. In *The Economics of Exchange Rates* (eds J. A. Frenkel and H. G. Johnson). Reading, MA: Addison-Wesley.

Dornbusch, R. (1976) Exchange rate expectations and monetary policy. *Journal of Political Economy*, 84, 1161–76.

Driskill, R. (1980) Exchange rate overshooting, the trade balance and rational expectations, mimeo.

—— and McCafferty, S. (1980) Exchange-rate variability, real and monetary shocks, and the degree of capital mobility under rational expectations. *Quarterly Journal of Economics*, 95, 577–86.

Eaton, J. (1978) A stochastic equilibrium model of exchange rate determination and monetary policy with rational expectations, mimeo, Princeton University.

—— and Turnovsky, S. J. (1984) The forward exchange rate market, speculation, and exchange market intervention. *Quarterly Journal of Economics,* 99, 45–69.

—— and —— (1981) Exchange risk, political risk and macroeconomic equilibrium. Discussion Paper 388, Economic Growth Center, Yale University, September.

—— and —— (1983) Covered interest parity, uncovered interest parity and exchange rate dynamics. *Economic Journal*, 93, 555–75. Reprinted in this volume as chapter 2.

Fama, E. and Farber, A. (1979) Money, bonds, and foreign exchange. *American Economic Review*, 69, 639–49.

Fischer, S. (1977) Wage indexation and macroeconomic stability. In *Stabilization of the Domestic and International Economy* (eds K. Brunner and A. Meltzer). Amsterdam: North-Holland.

Flood, R. (1979) Capital mobility and the choice of exchange rate system. *International Economic Review*, 20, 405–16.

Frankel, J. A. (1979) The diversifiability of exchange risk. *Journal of International Economics*, 9, 378–93.

Grauer, F. L. A., Litzenberger, R. H. and Stehle, R. E. (1976) Sharing rules and equilibrium in an international capital market under uncertainty. *Journal of Finance and Economics*, 3, 233–56.

Gray, J. A. (1976) Wage indexation: a macroeconomic approach. *Journal of Monetary Economics*, 2, 221–35.

Gray, M. R. and Turnovsky, S. J. (1979) The stability of exchange rate dynamics under perfect myopic foresight. *International Economic Review*, 20, 643–60. Reprinted in this volume as chapter 1.

Hansen, L. P. and Hodrick, R. J. (1980) Forward exchange rates as optimal

predictors of future spot prices. *Journal of Political Economy*, 88, 829–53.
Harris, R. G. and Purvis, D. D. (1979) Equilibrium theories of the forward exchange rates. Institute for Economic Research Discussion Paper 354, Queen's University.
Kouri, P. J. K. (1976) The determinants of the forward premium. Institute for International Economic Studies Paper 62, University of Stockholm.
Levich, R. (1978) Tests of forecasting models and market efficiency in the international money market. In *The Economics of Exchange Rates* (eds J. A. Frenkel and H. G. Johnson). Reading, MA: Addison-Wesley.
—— (1979) The efficiency of markets for foreign exchange: a survey. In *International Economic Policy: An Assessment of Theory and Evidence* (eds R. Dornbusch and J. A. Frenkel), Baltimore, MD: Johns Hopkins University Press.
Lucas, R. E., Jr. (1975) An equilibrium model of the business cycle. *Journal of Political Economy*, 83, 1113–44.
Phelps, E. S. and Taylor, J. B. (1977) Stabilizing powers of monetary policy under rational expectations. *Journal of Political Economy*, 85, 963–1190.
Roll, R. and Solnik, B. (1977) A pure foreign exchange asset pricing model. *Journal of International Economics*, 7, 161–179.
Solnik, B (1973) *European Capital Markets*. Lexington, MA: D. C. Heath.
Stein, J. L. (1980) The dynamics of spot and forward prices in an efficient foreign exchange market. *American Economic Review*, 70, 565–83.
Turnovsky, S. J. (1981) Monetary policy and foreign price disturbances under flexible exchange rates: a stochastic approach. *Journal of Money, Credit and Banking*, 13, 156–76. Reprinted in this volume as chapter 5.
—— and Kingston, G. H. (1977) Monetary and fiscal policies under flexible exchange rates and perfect myopic foresight in an inflationary world. *Scandinavian Journal of Economics*, 79, 424–41.
Wilson, C. A. (1979) Anticipated shocks and exchange rate dynamics. *Journal of Political Economy*, 87, 639–47.

Part III

Exchange Market Intervention and Wage Indexation

7 Exchange Market Intervention Policies in a Small Open Economy

1 INTRODUCTION

Traditionally, the international macroeconomic literature has been concerned almost exclusively with analysing perfectly fixed or perfectly flexible exchange rate systems. Yet both these regimes represent polar forms of intervention policy. In the former, the domestic monetary authorities continually intervene in the foreign exchange market so as to maintain the exchange rate at some given target level. In the latter case, the domestic monetary authorities abstain from any active intervention, allowing the exchange rate to fluctuate freely in response to market forces. Intermediate between these two extremes is that of a "managed float" in which the monetary authorities intervene partly to offset movements in the exchange rate, so that the adjustment to changes in market pressure are met by a combination of both movements in the exchange rate and the accumulation or decumulation of foreign reserves. The intensity with which the domestic monetary authorities intervene in the foreign exchange market can be treated as a policy parameter, subject to their choice. Accordingly, it is natural to address the question of the optimal degree of intervention. This issue is the topic of the present chapter.

The question of optimal exchange market intervention has begun to receive attention in the literature. Boyer (1979) and Roper and Turnovsky (1980) analyse the problem by extending the framework developed by Poole (1970) in his well-known analysis of the monetary instrument problem. These analyses are based on the assumption that

Originally published in J. S. Bhandari and B. Putnam (eds), *Economic Interdependence and Flexible Exchange Rates*, Cambridge, MA: MIT Press, 1983. I wish to thank Bill Branson, Don Hanson and Don Roper for helpful comments on a previous version of this chapter.

the price of domestic output remains fixed. While this assumption may be convenient for pedagogic purposes, it obviously needs to be relaxed if the analysis is to be at all relevant for current conditions in which the price mechanism is one key channel through which the international transmission of disturbances takes place. In another recent paper Buiter (1979) analyses intervention policy in terms of discrete time control theory. Casting the intervention rule in the form of a feedback control law is restrictive, however, because current intervention is related only to past rather than present market data.[1] Some market data, such as the exchange rate and the quantity of central liabilities outstanding, are observable on a fairly current basis. As Kareken et al. (1973) have shown in their work on optimal monetary strategy for a closed economy, currently observable data provide information about the sources of random shocks to the economy, the exploitation of which allows a greater degree of economic stability to be achieved.[2]

In this chapter we analyse optimal intervention policy in a small open economy in which the domestic price level, as well as the domestic real output, is endogenously determined, with the policy-maker's objective being to stabilize a function involving both these variables. Particular attention is devoted to exchange rate expectations and price expectations, both of which are assumed to be formed rationally. Also, the analysis in this chapter follows the strategy of Kareken et al. in considering an intervention policy designed to exploit the information contained in observable market data.

2 A SMALL OPEN ECONOMY

In order to keep the technical details to a minimum, we will base our analysis on the simplest model, Specifically we will assume that there is one traded commodity whose price in terms of foreign currency is given. Also, there is a single traded bond, with the domestic bond market perfectly integrated with that in the rest of the world. Thus purchasing power parity and interest rate parity hold throughout.

The model can be summarized as follows:[3]

$$P_t = Q_t + E_t \tag{7.1a}$$

$$M_t - P_t = \alpha_1 Y_t - \alpha_2 r_t + u_{1t} \tag{7.1b}$$

$$r_t + \Omega_t + E^*_{t+1,t} - E_t \tag{7.1c}$$

$$M_t = \bar{M} - \mu(E_t - \bar{E}) \tag{7.1d}$$

$$Y_t - \hat{Y} = \gamma(P_t - P^*_{t,t-1}) + u_{2t} \tag{7.1e}$$

while for any variable, X say

$$X^*_{s,t} = \mathcal{E}_t(X_s) \tag{7.1f}$$

where $\mathcal{E}_t$ is the conditional expectations operator, conditional on information at time t, P_t is the domestic price of the traded good at time t, expressed in logarithms, Q_t is the world price of the traded good at time t, expressed in logarithms, E_t is the current exchange rate (measured in units of the domestic currency per unit of foreign currency), expressed in logarithms, $\bar{E}$ is the equilibrium (steady-state) level of E, endogenously determined, M_t is the domestic nominal money supply, expressed in logarithms, Y_t is the real domestic output at time t, expressed in logarithms, $\hat{Y}$ is the full employment level of Y, r_t is the domestic nominal interest rate at time t, Ω_t is the foreign exogenous component of the domestic nominal supply, $E^*_{t+s,t}$ is the expectation of E for time $t+s$, held at time t ($s = 1, 2, \ldots$, all t), $P^*_{t+s,t}$ is the expectation of P for time $t+s$, held at time t ($s = 1, 2, \ldots$, all t), u_{1t} is the stochastic disturbance in demand for domestic money, and u_{2t} is the stochastic disturbance in domestic output supply.

The equations of the model are in the main fairly standard. Given purchasing power parity, the domestic price of a freely traded commodity equals the price abroad multiplied by the exchange rate. Equation (7.1a) is just the logarthmic version of this relation. The domestic monetary sector is summarized by equations (7.1b)–(7.1d). The first of these equations describes the domestic LM curve, making the usual assumption that all domestic money is held by domestic residents who also hold no foreign currency.[4] The assumption of perfect capital market integration is embodied in the interest rate parity condition (7.1c). The intervention policy is specified by (7.1d), which describes the degree of intervention by the authority as a function of the observed deviation of the exchange rate from its long-run equilibrium level and which the authorities are assumed to know. The limiting cases $\mu = \infty$, $\mu = 0$ correspond to fixed and flexible regimes respectively, while any finite nonzero value of μ describes a managed float. A policy of setting $\mu > 0$ implies that, if the current exchange rate is above its long-run level, the monetary authorities should introduce a monetary contraction (set M below $\bar{M}$), thereby reducing the pressure on the exchage rate. Differentiating (7.1d) with respect to t implies $\dot{M} = -\mu\dot{E}$, i.e. the domestic money supply is decreased at a rate which is proportional to the rate of exchange depreciation. Such a policy is often described as "leaning against the wind." If $\mu < 0$, the monetary authorities react to a devaluing exchange rate by adopting an expansionary policy, thereby adding to the pressure on the exchange rate. This can be referred to as "leaning with the wind." The optimal intervention policy is to choose μ to optimize an objective yet to be specified, and, as we will demonstrate, an optimal policy may involve either $\mu > 0$ or $\mu < 0$ depending upon the primary source of the stochastic disturbances. Note that the reaction function (7.1d) is expressed in terms of current values of M and E, which are therefore assumed to be instantly observable.[5]

The supply of domestic output is specified by (7.1e). This relation postulates the deviation in output from its full employment level to depend upon the unanticipated component of the current domestic price of output. This formulation resembles a Lucas (1973) supply function, although as Flood (1979) has argued this rationale is inappropriate for both international and intranational, trading. Rather, it may be justified in terms of the wage determination model of Gray (1976) and Fischer (1977a). Finally, equation (7.1f) describes the rationality of expectations.

The two domestic stochastic disturbances u_{1t}, u_{2t} are assumed to have zero means and finite second moments satisfying

$$\mathcal{E}(u_{1t}) = \mathcal{E}(u_{2t}) = 0 \tag{7.2a}$$

$$\mathcal{E}(u_{1t}^2) = \sigma_1^2 \qquad \mathcal{E}(u_{2t}^2) = \sigma_2^2 \qquad \mathcal{E}(u_{1t}u_{2t}) = \sigma_1\sigma_2\rho \tag{7.2b}$$

where ρ is the correlation coefficient between the two variables. Although we have written u_{1t} as reflecting a stochastic disturbance in demand, it can equally well be interpreted (with sign change) as being a stochastic disturbance in supply. The two foreign variables in the system, Ω_t and Q_t, are also assumed to be random and are described by

$$Q_t = \bar{Q} + q_q \tag{7.3a}$$

$$\Omega_t = \bar{\Omega} + \omega_t \tag{7.3b}$$

where $\bar{Q}$ and $\bar{\Omega}$ are constant (see appendix) and

$$\mathcal{E}(q_t) = \mathcal{E}(\omega_t) = 0 \tag{7.4a}$$

$$\mathcal{E}(q_1^2) = \sigma_q^2 \qquad \mathcal{E}(\omega_t^2) = \sigma_\omega^2 \qquad \mathcal{E}(q_t\omega_t) = \sigma_q\sigma_\omega\eta \tag{7.4b}$$

where η denotes the corresponding correlation coefficient. In addition, all random variables are assumed to be independently distributed over time and for simplicity we assume that domestic and foreign variables are uncorrelated. This enables us to distinguish quite clearly between domestic and foreign stochastic influences.

However, whereas q_t, ω_t are exogenous to the small country, they are themselves endogenously determined in the rest of the world, reflecting the various disturbances occurring there. It is important to recognize this endogeneity when it comes to determining the optimal degree of intervention. This is because the sign of the correlation coefficient η which appears in the expression for the optimal degree of intervention, depends crucially upon the origin of the random fluctuations in the foreign price level and interest rate.

To determine q_t and ω_t it is reasonable, given the small-country assumption of the domestic economy, to treat the rest of the world as effectively a closed economy. As such, we will assume that its structure is described by

$$Z_t = d_1'Z_t - d_2'\{\Omega_t - (Q^*_{t+1,t} - Q_t)\} + v_{0t} \tag{7.5a}$$

$$\bar{M}' - Q_t = \alpha_1'Z_t - \alpha_2'\Omega_t + v_{1t} \tag{7.5b}$$

$$Z_t - \hat{Z} = \gamma'(Q_t - Q^*_{t,t-1}) + v_{2t} \tag{7.5c}$$

where Z_t denotes output in the rest of the world, with $\hat{Z}$ its full employment level, and $\bar{M}'$ denotes the nominal money supply in the rest of the world, taken to be fixed exogenously. These three equations describe output market equilibrium, money market equilibrium, and output supply function respectively in the rest of the world, with v_{0t}, v_{1t}, v_{2t} denoting the corresponding random disturbances assumed to have zero means and finite variances $\sigma_0'^2$, $\sigma_1'^2$, $\sigma_2'^2$ respectively. Although v_{1t} has been introduced in the form of a random disturbance in the foreign demand for money, it can equally well (with sign change) be interpreted as a random disturbance in the foreign supply of money. We shall refer to v_{1t} quite neutrally as being a disturbance in the monetary sector. As shown in the appendix, the solutions for the two foreign variables q_t, ω_t which impinge on the domestic economy are

$$q_t = \frac{\alpha_2'v_{0t} - d_2'v_{1t} - \{(1 - d_t')\alpha_2' + \alpha_1'd_2'\}v_{2t}}{\gamma'\{\alpha_2'(1 - d_1') + \alpha_1'd_2'\} + d_2'(1 + \alpha_2')} \tag{7.6a}$$

$$\omega_t = \frac{(1 + \alpha_1'\gamma')v_{0t} + \{\gamma'(1 - d_1') + d_2'\}\,v_{1t} + \{d_2'\alpha_1' - (1 - d_1')\}\,v_{2t}}{\gamma'\{\alpha_2'(1 - d_1') + \alpha_1'd_2'\} + d_2'(1 + \alpha_2')} \tag{7.6b}$$

From (7.6a) and (7.6b) it is immediately apparent that the sign of the correlation between q_t and ω_t depends critically upon the source of the random disturbances abroad.[6] For example, if the only foreign random disturbances are in output demand, then an increase in v_{0t} will raise both q_t and ω_t proportionately, so that $\eta = 1$. However, for random fluctuations in the monetary sector, $\eta = -1$, while for disturbances originating on the supply side $\eta = \pm 1$, depending upon whether $d_2'\alpha_1' - (1 - d_1')$ is greater or less than zero.

The steady state or stationary equilibrium of the small open economy being considered is defined by setting all disturbances in (7.1a)–(7.1e) to zero and assuming that expectations are realized. Denote the steady state by bars; then this can be summarized by

$$\bar{P} = \bar{Q} + \bar{E} \tag{7.7a}$$

$$\bar{M} - \bar{P} = \alpha_1\bar{Y} - \alpha_1\bar{r} \tag{7.7b}$$

$$\bar{r} = \bar{\Omega} \tag{7.7c}$$

$$\bar{Y} = \hat{Y} \tag{7.7d}$$

These four equations determine the steady state equilibrium values of the four endogenous variables $\bar{r}$, $\bar{Y}$, $\bar{E}$ and $\bar{P}$. It should be noted that these equilibrium values relate to the means of the long-run distributions of the random variabls r_t, Y_t, E_t, P_t, not conditional on any knowledge of disturbances.

Differentiating these equations with respect to $\bar{M}$ and $\bar{Q}$, we deduce the following familiar neutrality properties:

$$\frac{\mathrm{d}\bar{P}}{\mathrm{d}\bar{M}} = \frac{\mathrm{d}\bar{E}}{\mathrm{d}\bar{M}} = 1 \qquad \frac{\mathrm{d}\bar{Y}}{\mathrm{d}\bar{M}} = \frac{\mathrm{d}\bar{r}}{\mathrm{d}\bar{M}} = 0 \tag{7.8}$$

$$\frac{\mathrm{d}\bar{E}}{\mathrm{d}\bar{Q}} = -1 \qquad \frac{\mathrm{d}\bar{Y}}{\mathrm{d}\bar{Q}} = \frac{\mathrm{d}\bar{r}}{\mathrm{d}\bar{Q}} = \frac{\mathrm{d}\bar{P}}{\mathrm{d}\bar{Q}} = 0 \tag{7.9}$$

A 1 percent increase in the exogenous component of the domestic money supply will raise the domestic level and exchange rate by 1 percent. It will have no effect on domestic output or interest rate, which are determined by the real phenomena. A 1 percent increase in the equilibrium foreign price level will lead to a 1 percent revaluation of the domestic exchange rate, insulating the remaining domestic variables fully from this disturbance.

Subtracting (7.7) from (7.1), we can express the behavior of the system in the following deviation form:

$$p_t = q_t + e_t \tag{7.10a}$$

$$-\mu e_t - p_t = \alpha_1 y_t - \alpha_2\{e^*_{t+1,t} - e_t\} + u_{1t} - \alpha_2 \omega_t \tag{7.10b}$$

$$y_t = \gamma(p_t - p^*_{t,t+1}) + u_{2t} \tag{7.10c}$$

where lower case letters denote deviations, i.e. $p_t \equiv p_t - \bar{P}$ and so forth and for convenience r_t and m_t have been eliminated. Equations (7.10a)–(7.10c) yield three stochastic difference equations in domestic output y_t, the domestic price of output p_t and its expectations, together with the exchange rate e_t and its expectation.

3 SOLUTION OF THE SYSTEM

There are various procedures for solving system (7.10). The most convenient in the present context is the original method proposed by Muth (1961) because this approach highlights certain nonuniqueness problems which may characterize rational expectations systems (see Taylor, 1977).

We begin by writing (7.10a)–(7.10c) in the following matrix form:

$$\begin{bmatrix} 0 & 1 & -1 \\ \alpha_1 & 1 & \mu + \alpha_2 \\ 1 & -\gamma & 0 \end{bmatrix} \begin{bmatrix} y_t \\ p_t \\ e_t \end{bmatrix} = \begin{bmatrix} q_t \\ \alpha_2 e^*_{t+1,t} - u_{1t} + \alpha_2 \omega_t \\ -\gamma p^*_{t,t-1} + u_{2t} \end{bmatrix} \tag{7.11}$$

Taking conditional expectations of (7.10a) at time $t - 1$ and noting that q_t is assumed to be independently distributed over time, we have

$$p^*_{t,t-1} = e^*_{t,t-1} \tag{7.12}$$

Solving (7.11) for e_t and using (7.12), we derive the following equation involving e_t and its conditional expectations:

$$(1 + \alpha_2 + \mu + \alpha_1\gamma)e_t = \alpha_2 e^*_{t+1,t} + \alpha_1\gamma e^*_{t,t-1} + \xi_t \tag{7.13}$$

where

$$\xi_t \equiv -u_{1t} - \alpha_1 u_{2t} + \alpha_2\omega_t - (1 + \alpha_1\gamma)q_t \tag{7.14}$$

We now propose a solution for e_t of the form

$$e_t = \delta_0\xi_t + \delta_1\xi_{t-1} + \delta_2\xi_{t-2} + \dots \tag{7.15}$$

where the δ_t are parameters to be determined and the ξ_{t-i} are defined by (7.14). Taking conditional expectations of (7.15) at time $t - 1$, we have

$$e^*_{t,t-1} = \delta_1\xi_{t-1} + \delta_2\xi_{t-2} + \dots. \tag{7.16}$$

Calculating $e^*_{t+1,t}$ from (7.16) and substituting this expression with $e^*_{t,t-1}$, e_t back into (7.13) yields

$$\begin{aligned}(1 + \alpha_2 + \mu + \alpha_1\gamma)&(\delta_0\xi_t + \delta_1\xi_{t-1} + \delta_2\xi_{t-2} \dots)\\ &= \alpha_2(\delta_1\xi_t + \delta_2\xi_{t-1} + \dots) + \alpha_1\gamma(\delta_1\xi_{t-1} + \delta_2\xi_{t-2} + \dots) + \xi_t\end{aligned} \tag{7.17}$$

which is a set of identities in the parameters δ_i. Equating coefficients of ξ_{t-i} we obtain the following relations:

$$\delta_0 = \frac{1 + \alpha_2\delta_1}{1 + \alpha_2 + \mu + \alpha_1\gamma} \tag{7.18a}$$

$$\delta_{i+1} = \left(\frac{1 + \alpha_2 + \mu}{\alpha_2}\right)^i \delta_1 \tag{7.18b}$$

where δ_1 is a constant yet to be determined.

Substitute from (7.18a) and (7.18b) into (7.15); then the solution for e_t is

$$e_t = \left(\frac{1 + \alpha_2\delta_1}{1 + \alpha_2 + \mu + \alpha_1\gamma}\right)\xi_t + \delta_1(\xi_{t-1} + \theta\xi_{t-2} + \theta^2\xi_{t-3} \dots) \tag{7.19a}$$

where

$$\theta \equiv \frac{1 + \alpha_2 + \mu}{\alpha_2} \tag{7.20}$$

Moreover, taking conditional expectations of (7.19a), which yields $e^*_{t,t-1}$, and using (7.12), we can substitute for e_t, $p^*_{t,t-1}$ back into (7.10a) and (7.10c) to obtain the following solutions for p_t and y_t:

$$y_t = \gamma\left(\frac{1 + \alpha_2\delta_1}{1 + \alpha_2 + \mu + \alpha_1\gamma}\right)\xi_t + \gamma q_t + u_{2t} \tag{7.19b}$$

$$p_t = \left(\frac{1 + \alpha_2\delta_1}{1 + \alpha_2 + \mu + \alpha_1\gamma}\right)\xi_t + \delta_1(\xi_{t-1} + \theta\xi_{t-2} + \theta^2\xi_{t-3} \ldots) + q_t \tag{7.19c}$$

It is evident from (7.19a) and (7.19c) that whether the asymptotic variances of e_t and p_t, σ_e^2 and σ_p^2, respectively, are infinite or finite depends critically upon whether θ lies outside or inside the unit circle. This in turn depends upon the intervention parameter μ, and two cases $|\theta| > 1$, $|\theta| < 0$ need to be treated separately. We will refer to these two cases as characterizing unstable intervention and stable intervention respectively.

3.1 Unstable intervention

A necessary and sufficient condition for θ to lie outside the unit circle and for the intervention to imply instability is that[7]

$$\mu > -1 \quad \text{or } \mu < -(1 + 2\alpha_2) \tag{7.21a}$$

In this case, as long as $\delta_1 \neq 0$, the asymptotic variances σ_e^2, σ_p^2 will both be infinite. Let us impose the requirement that these asymptotic variances remain finite. It then follows that $\delta_1 = 0$, and the solutions for domestic output and the associated price level are

$$y_t = \frac{\gamma(\alpha_2 + \mu)q_t + (1 + \alpha_2 + \mu)u_{2t} + \gamma(\alpha_2\omega_t - u_{1t})}{1 + \alpha_2 + \mu + \alpha_1\gamma} \tag{7.22a}$$

$$p_t = \frac{(\alpha_2 + \mu)q_t - \alpha_1 u_{2t} + \alpha_{2t}\omega_t - u_{1t}}{1 + \alpha_2 + \mu + \alpha_1\gamma} \tag{7.22b}$$

This is, both y_t and p_t fluctuate in response to the domestic to the domestic random variables (u_{1t}, u_{2t}) as well as the foreign random variables (q_t, ω_t), which themselves are generated by (7.6a) and (7.6b). Note that the intervention parameter affects how both variables respond to all the random variables.

The notion that an intervention rule satisfying (7.21a) will lead to infinite asymptotic variances σ_e^2, σ_p^2 unless the exchange rate fluctuates independently over time (i.e. $\delta_1 = 0$) is not as surprising as may at first appear. Consider, for example, the case of a perfectly flexible exchange rate (no intervention, $\mu = 0$), which is consistent with this condition. It is known that under rational expectations such a system is inherently unstable in the sense that unless initial conitions are chosen appropriately, expectations of future exchange rates will diverge. Moreover, a policy of leaning against the wind ($\mu > 0$) will increase the tendency to diverge. This is because, for given exchange rate expectations $e^*_{t,t-1}$, such policy reduces the expected money supply, thereby forcing up the expected rate of interest, and hence the expected rate of exchange $e^*_{t+1,t-1}$ for the next period, thereby accentuating the instability.

Indeed, the requirement that σ_e^2 remain finite is equivalent to the requirement that the time path of the conditional exchange rate expectations $e^*_{t+i,t-1}$ be stable as the forecast horizon $i \to \infty$. To see this consider the difference equation (7.13). Taking conditional expectations at time $t-1$ for time $t+i$ yields

$$(1 + \alpha_2 + \mu)e^*_{t+i,t-1} = \alpha_2 e^*_{t+i+1,t-1} \tag{7.13'}$$

The solution to this is

$$e^*_{t+i,t-1} = A\theta^i \qquad i = 1, 2, \ldots$$

where A is an arbitrary constant and θ is as defined above. If θ lies outside the unit circle, $e^*_{t+i,t-1}$ will diverge unless the arbitrary constant A is set to zero. Indeed, setting $A = 0$ is precisely equivalent to setting $\delta_1 = 0$ in (7.19a). The rationale for this former procedure is usually given by appealing to transversality conditions for corresponding models based on optimizing behavior, which under appropriate conditions impose boundedness on expectations. Thus setting $A = 0$ and using (7.12), we have $e^*_{t,t-1} = p^*_{t,t-1} = 0$, i.e. exchange rate expectations and price expectations must be static. The same conclusions can be obtained by setting $\delta_1 = 0$ in (7.19a) and taking conditional expectations at time $t-1$.

Thus, while we refer to the present case as being one of "unstable intervention", this term is something of a convenient shorthand. The system is more appropriately characterized as being "inherently" unstable in the sense that if it were to start from some arbitrary initial condition, it would diverge. However, by appropriate choice of initial condition the instability is eliminated, so that in fact the system remains stable.

3.2 Stable intervention

Suppose now that

$$-(1 + 2\alpha_2) < \mu < -1 \tag{7.21b}$$

implying that $|\theta| < 1$. In this case, the requirement that the asymptotic variances σ_e^2, σ_p^2 remain finite imposes no restriction on δ_1. For any arbitrary value δ_1, we can calculate the finite asymptotic variance

$$\sigma_e^2 = \left\{\left(\frac{1 + \alpha_2\delta_1}{1 + \alpha_2 + \mu + \alpha_1\gamma}\right)^2 + \frac{\delta_1^2}{1 - \theta^2}\right\}\sigma_\xi^2 \tag{7.23}$$

and a corresponding expression can be determined for σ_p^2. The rational expectations solution to the system is accordingly nonunique.

One procedure for determining all the weights δ_1 uniquely is to appeal to the stronger requirement that the asymptotic variance, σ_e^2 say, be minimized. The value of δ_1 can thus be obtained by differentiating (7.23) with respect to δ_1 and setting $\partial\sigma_e^2/\partial\delta_1 = 0$. However, this procedure is essentially arbitrary. There is no obvious market mechanism which ensures that σ_e^2 will be minimized in this way. Furthermore, the value of δ_1 which minimizes σ_e^2 is not the same as that which minimizes σ_p^2, and the question of what variances (if any) rational expectations do actually minimize is not at all clear. Indeed, the same objection might be raised to the requirement adopted in section 3.1 that relevant asymptotic variances be finite, although, as we have noted, in this case some justification may be provided by appealing to appropriate transversality conditions. In fact, in the present instance, choosing δ_1 to minimize σ_e^2 (or σ_p^2) turns out to be extremely cumbersome. It yields a complicated solution for y_t and p_t, rendering the subsequent determination of the optimal intevention policy too complicated to be of much interest.

However, in the absence of any fully developed theory of rational expectations in disequilibrium, some arbitrary procedure such as the above must be followed in order to determine the weights uniquely. Accordingly, we will choose a modification to the Taylor procedure, which at least is analytically simple yet able to illustrate the main issues involved. Specifically, we will assume that δ_1 is chosen to minimize the conditional variance $\mathscr{E}_{t-1}\{e_t - \mathscr{E}_{e-1}(e_t)\}^2$ of e_t. From (7.19a) we obtain

$$\mathscr{E}_{t-1}\{e_t - \mathscr{E}_{t-1}(e_t)\}^2 = \left(\frac{1 + \alpha\delta_1}{1 + \alpha_2 + \mu + \alpha_1\gamma}\right)^2 \sigma_\xi^2 \tag{7.24}$$

which is minimized by setting

$$\delta_1 = -1/\alpha_2 \tag{7.25}$$

Substituting (7.25) into (7.19b) and (7.19c) gives these solutions for y_t and p_t:

$$y_t = \gamma q_t + u_{2t} \tag{7.26a}$$

$$p_t = \frac{-1}{\alpha_2}(\xi_{t-1} + \theta\xi_{t-2} + \theta^2\xi_{t-3} + \ldots) + q_t \tag{7.26b}$$

From (7.26a) it is seen that in this case y_t is independent of u_{1t} and ω_t and, more significantly in *invariant* with respect to the intervention parameter μ. The time path of prices is now generated by a distributed lag of all the past disturbances, the coefficient of which depends critically upon the intervention parameter.

The invariance of y_t with respect to μ is not a robust proposition. It depends critically upon the fact that we have chosen δ_1 to minimize (7.24) rather that (7.23).[8] While we readily acknowledge the arbitrariness of this choice, the interim justification for the whole approach provoded by Taylor would seem to be at least as applicable to minimizing (7.25) as it is to minimizing (7.23). Taylor suggests that in the absence of a theory of transitional expectations, the procedure can be justified by appealing to the notion that since people have a preference for price stability, "collective rationality" will lead them to choose their expectations to generate the most stable system for the exchange rate. However, since the expectations in the model pertain to a single-period forecast horizon, it seems reasonable for the associated stability to relate to the single-period variances as well.

4 DETERMINATION OF OPTIMAL INTERVENTION: GENERAL ANALYSIS

We now turn to the question of the optimal degree of intervention. In choosing the optimal μ, we will assume that the policy-maker's objective is to minimize the asymptotic variance[9]

$$C(\mu) \equiv \lambda\sigma_y^2 + (1-\lambda)\sigma_p^2 \qquad 0 \leqslant \lambda \leqslant 1 \tag{7.27}$$

That is, the objective is assumed to be to stabilize a weighted average of domestic real income and the domestic price level, with λ denoting the relative weight assigned to each of these objectives in the overall objective function. A value of $\lambda = 1$ means that the objective involves only income stability; if $\lambda = 0$, the sole concern is with price stability.

To determine the optimal μ, the cases of both unstable and stable intervention must be considered. Furthermore, the optimal μ which emerges from the optimization must be consistent with the initial restriction imposed on μ by the stability consideration. The eventual choice of the optimal μ is obtained by comparing the asymptotic variance (7.27) in the two cases.

4.1 Unstable intervention

As demonstrated in section 3, the solutions for y_t and p_t in this case are given by (7.22a) and (7.22b) respectively, with the intervention parameter μ satisfying (equation (7.21a))

$$\mu > -1 \text{ or } \mu < -(1 + 2\alpha_2)$$

To calculate the objective function (7.27) prior to optimization, we introduce the following notation:

$$a_t \equiv \gamma q_t + u_{2t} \tag{7.28a}$$

$$b_t \equiv u_{2t} + \gamma(\alpha_2 \omega_t - u_{1t}) \tag{7.28b}$$

$$c_t \equiv q_t \tag{7.28c}$$

$$d_t \equiv -\alpha_1 u_{2t} + \alpha_2 \omega_t - u_{1t} \tag{7.28d}$$

We then have

$$y_t = \frac{(\alpha_2 + \mu)\, a_t + b_t}{1 + \alpha_2 + \mu + \alpha_1 \gamma} \tag{7.29a}$$

$$p_t = \frac{(\alpha_2 + \mu)\, c_t + d_t}{1 + \alpha_2 + \mu + \alpha_1 \gamma} \tag{7.29b}$$

so that the objective function (7.27) becomes

$$C(\mu) = \frac{(\alpha_2 + \mu)^2 \{\lambda \sigma_a^2 + (1 - \lambda)\sigma_c^2\} + \{\lambda \sigma_b^2 + (1 - \lambda)\sigma_d^2\}}{(1 + \alpha_2 + \mu + \alpha_1 \gamma)^2} + \frac{2(\alpha_2 + \mu)\{\lambda \sigma_{ab} + (1 - \lambda)\sigma_{cd}\}}{(1 + \alpha_2 + \mu + \alpha_1 \gamma)^2} \tag{7.30}$$

where σ_a^2 etc. are the variances of the composite disturbance defined in (7.28) and σ_{ab} and σ_{cd} are the corresponding covariances. Using the definitions (7.28), we can express these parameters in terms of the variances and covariances of the underlying random variables in the system.

The optimal intervention policy is obtained by differentiating (7.30) with respect to μ and setting $\partial C/\partial \mu = 0$, yielding[10]

$$\mu = \hat{\mu}_1 = -\alpha_2 + \frac{\lambda \sigma_b^2 + (1 - \lambda)\sigma_d^2}{(1 + \alpha_1 \gamma)\{\lambda \sigma_a^2 + (1 - \lambda)\sigma_c^2\} - \{\lambda \sigma_{ab} + (1 - \lambda)\sigma_{cd}\}} - \frac{(1 + \alpha_1 \gamma)\{\lambda \sigma_{ab} + (1 - \lambda)\sigma_{cd}\}}{(1 + \alpha_1 \gamma)\{\lambda \sigma_a^2 + (1 - \lambda)\sigma_c^2\} - \{\lambda \sigma_{ab} + (1 - \lambda)\sigma_{cd}\}} \tag{7.31}$$

However, the value $\hat{\mu}_1$ given by (7.31) must be consistent with unstable intervention, since that is the assumption underlying the solutions (7.22a) and (7.22b), from which the objective function (7.30) is derived. In other words, $\hat{\mu}_1$ implied by (7.31) must satisfy either $\hat{\mu}_1 > -1$ or $\hat{\mu}_1 < -1 - 2\alpha_2$. If $\hat{\mu}_1$ as given by (7.31) lies in the range $-(1 + 2\alpha_2) < \hat{\mu}_1 < -1$, then we must set $\mu = -1$ or $\mu = 1 - 2\alpha_2$ (strictly letting μ tend to these values from above and below respectively) and choose that value which yields the lower variance.[11]

4.2 Stable intervention

The optimization in this case is much more straightforward. Output and the domestic price level are now given by (7.26a), (7.26b), with y_t independent of the intervention parameter μ. Accordingly, the optimization of (7.27) simply reduces to minimizing σ_p^2. Since p_t is generated by (7.26b), the asymptotic variance of p_t is

$$\sigma_p^2 = \sigma_q^2 + \frac{\sigma_\xi^2}{\alpha_2^2 - (1 + \alpha_2 + \mu)^2}$$

where σ_ξ^2 denotes the variance of ξ_t. This is minimized by setting

$$\mu = \hat{\mu}_2 \equiv -(1 + \alpha_2) \tag{7.32}$$

which obviously lies within the stable region and is therefore consistent with those values of μ for which p_t is generated by (7.26b). Hence, if μ is to be chosen in the range $(-1 - 2\alpha_2, -1)$, then the solution is always (7.32). This expression is much simpler than the policy in the unstable case (7.31) and, in contrast with it, is independent of the variances and covariances of the underlying random disturbances. The corresponding minimized value of the objective function in this case is

$$\lambda(\sigma_\xi^2 + \gamma^2\sigma_q^2) + (1 - \lambda)\left(\sigma_q^2 + \frac{\sigma_\xi^2}{\alpha_2^2}\right). \tag{7.33}$$

The overall optimal degree of intervention μ^o can now be obtained by considering the various cases in turn. First, the asymptotic variance (7.30) corresponding to $\hat{\mu}_1$ is calculated; second, if $\hat{\mu}_1$ lies within the range $-(1 + 2\alpha_2) < \hat{\mu}_1 < -1$, the variances corresponding to the limiting values $\mu = -1$, $\mu = -1 - 2\alpha_2$, are also calculated; third, the variance (7.33) corresponding to the stable intervention is calculated. The optimal policy is then determined as being the one which yields the lowest variance.

In general, the properties of the optimal intervention policy, insofar as it given by (7.31), are complex. Thus, in order to obtain more insight, it is important to focus on the separate stochastic disturbances in turn. This will be undertaken in section 5. In concluding the present discussion, we wish to make two observations. First, since μ is not a general infinity or zero, fixed or flexible rates that correspond to these extreme values are not generally optimal. Second, the optimal policy may involve either leaning against the wind ($\mu > 0$) or leaning with the wind ($\mu < 0$).

5 OPTIMAL INTERVENTION POLICY: SPECIFIC CASES

Because of the intractablility of the general expression (7.31), we now focus on the optimal intervention policy corresponding to the separate individual random disturbances, taken one at a time. We will deal with the domestic and foreign disturbances in turn. In most cases it is convenient to focus directly on the solutions (7.22) and (7.24) for y_t and p_t.

5.1 Domestic disturbances

Domestic monetary disturbance $\mathbf{u}_{1t}$ If the only stochastic disturbance in the economy occurs in the domestic monetary sector (i.e. $u_{2t} \equiv q_t \equiv \omega_t \equiv 0$), the optimal intervention policy (7.31) is $\hat{\mu}_1 = \infty$. Setting $\hat{\mu} = \infty$ in the solutions for y_t and p_t corresponding to unstable intervention ((7.22a) and (7.22b)), we see that this implies

$$y_t \equiv p_t \equiv 0$$

and hence

$$\sigma_y^2 = \sigma_p^2 = 0$$

The optimal policy corresponding to stable intervention, i.e. $\hat{\mu}_2 = -(1 + \alpha_2)$, yields

$$\sigma_y^2 = 0 \qquad \sigma_p^2 = \sigma_1^2/\alpha_2^2.$$

Thus setting $\mu^\circ = \infty$, so that the exchange rate is fixed, is the global optimum, stabilizing both prices and income perfectly.

The economic reasoning behind this result is straightforward. Given that the domestic price level is determined by the purchasing power parity condition (7.10a), it follows that if e is fixed and there are no disturbances in q_t, then p_t must also be fixed. It then follows from the domestic output supply function (7.10c) that, if p_t is fixed and if in addition (a) price expectations are static, as the stability condition requires, and (b) there are no disturbances in domestic supply, then domestic output itself must also remain fixed.

The perfect stability of y_t and p_t can also be viewed as an example of the following general characteristic. As noted at the beginning of this chapter, the current observability of certain market variables implies information on the sources of the random shocks in the economy. More specifically, the observability of m_t and e_t can be shown to be equivalent to the observability of a known linear combination of the random variables in the system.[12] With only *one* random variable present, it follows that its actual value can be inferred and be appropriately offset, thereby maintaining perfect stability of the system.

Domestic output supply disturbance $\mathbf{u}_{2t}$ In this case, the optimal policy (7.31) corresponding to unstable intervention is

$$\hat{\mu}_1 = \frac{(1 - \lambda)\alpha_1 - \gamma\lambda(1 + \alpha_2)}{\gamma\lambda}$$

provided that $\hat{\mu}_1 > -1$ or $\hat{\mu}_1 < -1 - 2\alpha_2$. It can also be shown that the value of the asymptotic variance corresponding to the two limiting values $C(\mu = -1)$, $C(\mu = -1 - 2\alpha_2)$ satisfies $C(\mu = -1) < C(\mu = -1 - 2\alpha_2)$, so that if $\hat{\mu}_1$ lies the range $-1 - 2\alpha_2 < \mu_1 < -1$, the policy $\hat{\mu}_1 = -1$ will be superior. The optimal policy corresponding to stable intervention is as before: $\hat{\mu}_2 = -(1 + \alpha_2)$. A comparison of (7.30) for $\mu = -1$ with (7.33) shows that the stable intervention policy yields a larger asymptotic variance. Hence, the optimal intervention policy is[13]

$$\frac{\alpha_1}{\gamma\alpha_2} \begin{cases} > \dfrac{\lambda}{1 - \lambda} & \text{then } \mu^{\circ} = \dfrac{\alpha_1(1 - \lambda)}{\gamma\lambda} - (1 + \alpha_2) \qquad (7.34a) \\ < \dfrac{\lambda}{1 - \lambda} & \text{then } \mu^{\circ} = 1. \qquad (7.34b) \end{cases}$$

The optimal policy in this case depends critically upon the relative weight λ given to the two components of the overall objective function, and through this the target of price stability and output stability involve a conflict of policy. If $\lambda = 0$, so that the policy-maker is concerned entirely with price stability, the optimal intervention policy is one of a perfectly fixed exchange rate ($\mu = \infty$). If λ is small, i.e. the objective function is weighted primarily towards price stability, then the optimal policy will be one of leaning against the wind. However, for the very specific relative weight $\lambda = \alpha_1/\{\alpha_1 + \lambda(1 + \alpha_2)\} < 1$, a perfectly flexible rate will be optimal, while as the objective function becomes more heavily weighted toward output stability, the output policy will move toward being one of leaning with the wind.

Most discussions of intervention policy limit their attention to parameters which characterize leaning against the wind. The intuitive idea is that such a policy will alleviate fluctuations in the exchange rate, thereby increasing the stability within the economy. The fact that an optimal policy may involve exacerbating swings in the exchange rate is therefore of interest and merits further comment. Suppose that (7.34a) holds, so that intervention is unstable. It follows from (7.12) and (7.19a), together with the requirement that $\delta_1 = 0$, that $e^*_{t+1,t} = p^*_{t,t-1} = 0$. With the only stochastic disturbance being in u_{2t}, the system (7.10a)–(7.10c) reduces to[14]

$$-\mu e_t = (1 + \alpha_2)e_t + \alpha_1 y_t \qquad (7.10b')$$

$$y_t = \gamma e_t + u_{2t} \qquad (7.10c')$$

It is evident from (7.10b′) that a policy of leaning with the wind ($\mu < 0$) will tend to provide greater insulation for y_t from the random disturbance u_{2t}, forcing it to be absorbed more fully by the exchange rate. Thus if, for instance, the exchange rate tends to appreciate, the domestic interest rate must take on higher values and m_t must be contracted to keep y_t from rising. If the objective function puts most of the weight on the stabilization of output, this strategy is clearly appropriate.

5.2 Foreign disturbances

We now consider the various foreign disturbances. While these impinge on the domestic economy through the foreign variables q_t and ω_t, as discussed insection 7.1, these variables are themselves endogenous, reflecting more fundamental random disturbances abroad. These sources are indicated in equations (7.6a) and (7.6b) and will be considered in turn.

Foreign output demand disturbance v_{0t} In this case the solution for y_t and p_t corresponding to unstable expectations, expressed in terms of the basic foreign random variable v_{0t}, is

$$y_t = \frac{\gamma\{(\alpha_2 + \mu)\,\alpha_2' + \alpha_2(1 + \alpha_1'\gamma')\}v_{0t}}{(1 + \alpha_2 + \mu + \alpha_1\gamma)\Delta'} \tag{7.35a}$$

$$p_t = \frac{\{(\alpha_2 + \mu)\alpha_2' + \alpha_2(1 + \alpha_1'\gamma')\}v_{0t}}{(1 + \alpha_2 + \mu + \alpha_1\gamma)\Delta'} \tag{7.35b}$$

where

$$\Delta' \equiv \gamma'\{\alpha_2'(1 - d_1') + \alpha_1' d_2'\} + d_2'(1 + \alpha_2') > 0$$

The optimal policy (7.23) is

$$\hat{\mu}_1 = -\frac{\alpha_2}{\alpha_2'}(1 + \alpha_1'\gamma') - \alpha_2 < 0 \tag{7.36}$$

which, when implemented, yields $y_t \equiv p_t \equiv 0$. The policy (7.36) is consistent with instability as long as

$$\frac{\alpha_2}{\alpha_2'}(1 + \alpha_1'\gamma') < 1 - \alpha_2 \quad \text{or} \quad \frac{\alpha_2}{\alpha_2'}(1 + \alpha_1'\gamma') > 1 + \alpha_2 \tag{7.37a}$$

If, in contrast, $\hat{\mu}_1$ lies in the stable range so that

$$1 - \alpha_2 < \frac{\alpha_2}{\alpha_2'}(1 + \alpha_1'\gamma') < 1 + \alpha_2 \tag{7.37b}$$

we must consider the limiting cases $\mu = -1$, $\mu = -(1 + 2\alpha_2)$ as well as the policy corresponding to stable expectations $\hat{\mu}_2 = -(1 + \alpha_2)$. It can be shown that of the two polar cases $C(\mu = -1) < C(\mu = -1 - 2\alpha_2)$, so that $\mu = -(1 + 2\alpha_2)$ is never optimal. However, whether $C(\mu = -1)$ is less or greater than (7.33) depends in a rather complicated way upon the various parameter values, and either $\mu = -1$ or $\hat{\mu}_2 = -(1 + \alpha_2)$ may be optimal. The precise conditions favoring one or the other turn out to be cumbersome and not worth reporting. It is sufficient to note that, whether (7.37a) or (7.37b) holds, the optimal policy will always be one of leaning with the wind.

Foreign monetary disturbance v_{1t} While the foreign monetary disturbances have been introduced as occurring in demand, they may equally well be interpreted (with appropriate sign change) as representing stochastic disturbances in foreign money supply.[15] Whichever interpretation is chosen, the solution for y_t and p_t corresponding to unstable expectations is

$$y_t = \frac{\gamma\{-\mu d_2' + \alpha_2\gamma'(1 - d_1')\}v_{1t}}{(1 + \alpha_2 + \mu + \alpha_1\gamma)\Delta'} \tag{7.38a}$$

$$p_t = \frac{\{-\mu d_2' + \alpha_2\gamma'(1 - d_1')\}v_{1t}}{(1 + \alpha_2 + \mu + \alpha_1\gamma)\Delta'} \tag{7.38b}$$

It is clear that the optimal policy is

$$\hat{\mu}_1 = \frac{\alpha_2\gamma'(1 - d_1')}{d_2'} > 0 \tag{7.39}$$

This policy, which is one of leaning against the wind (and therefore consistent with $\mu > -1$ as required for instability of expectations), ensures that $y_t \equiv p_t \equiv 0$ and hence $\sigma_y^2 = \sigma_p^2 = 0$. It is therefore clearly the overall optimum.

Foreign output supply disturbance v_{2t} This case is similar to the case involving v_{0t}. The solutions for y_t and p_t corresponding to unstable expectations are

$$y_t = \frac{-\gamma\{\mu[(1 - d_1')\alpha_2' + \alpha_1' d_2'\} + \alpha_2(1 - d_1')(1 + \alpha_2')\}v_{2t}}{(1 + \alpha_2 + \mu + \alpha_1\gamma)\Delta'} \tag{7.40a}$$

$$p_t = \frac{-[\mu\{(1 - d_1')\alpha_2' + \alpha_1' d_2'\} + \alpha_2(1 - d_1')(1 + \alpha_2')]v_{2t}}{(1 + \alpha_2 + \mu + \alpha_1\gamma)\Delta'} \tag{7.40b}$$

The optimal policy corresponding to (7.31) is

$$\hat{\mu}_1 = \frac{-\alpha_2(1 - d_1')(1 + \alpha_2')}{(1 - d_1')\alpha_2' + \alpha_1' d_2'} \tag{7.41}$$

which when implemented yields perfect stabilization: $y_t \equiv p_t \equiv 0$. For the solution to be consistent, we require that (7.41) satisfy (7.21a). If instead it satisfies (7.21b), we must consider the limiting cases $\mu = -1$, $\mu = -(1 + 2\alpha_2)$, as well as the optimal policy for stable expectations $\hat{\mu}_2 = (1 + \alpha_2)$. As for the case involving v_{0t}, it can be shown that $\mu = -(1 + 2\alpha_2)$ is never optimal and that the choice between $\mu = -1$

and $\hat{\mu}_2 = -(1 + \alpha_2)$ depends in a rather complicated way upon the parameters of both the domestic and foreign economies. In any event, however, the optimal policy is one of leaning with the wind.

Taken together, these expressions for optimal intervention policies in the face of foreign random disturbances yield interesting conclusions. First, provided that the random fluctuations in the foreign price level and foreign nominal interest rate originate in a *single* sector abroad, it may be possible to achieve perfect insulation of the domestic output and price level (in the sence $\sigma_y^2 = \sigma_p^2 = 0$) against such random fluctuations. This will generally require the domestic monetary authorities to engage in some form of active intervention policy, and except for very special cases a perfectly flexible rate will never be optimal. Perfect insulation can never be achieved by the simple intervention rule that we are considering if the random fluctuations in q_t and ω_t reflect more than a single foreign disturbance.[16] In this case, however, the nonoptimality of perfectly flexible rates remains ture.

Second, a comparison of the optimal policies for the three cases shows that the appropriate policy can vary dramatically, depending upon what factors the random fluctuations in the foreign price level and nominal interest rate are reflecting. In the cases involving v_{0t} and v_{2t} the appropriate policy is to lean with the wind, whereas in the case involving v_{1t} it is to lean against the wind. The reason for the difference involves the covariance between q_t and ω_t, which varies depending upon the source of the foreign random disturbances. In all cases, the critical expression determining y_t and p_t (for unstable intervention) is

$$\alpha_2(q_t + \omega_t) + \mu q_t$$

and in all these cases μ must be chosen to ensure that this expression is zero, thereby ensuring $y_t = p_t = 0$. In the cases involving v_{0t} and v_{2t} the covariance between q_t and ω_t is such as to make $\text{cov}(q_t + \omega_t, q_t) > 0$, while in the case involving v_{1t} we have $\text{cov}(q_t + \omega_t, q_t) < 0$. It is this change in the sign of the covariance which is the essential feature giving rise to the qualitative difference in the optimal policies.

6 FIXED VERSUS FLEXIBLE EXCHANGE RATES

One of the most extensively debated topics in international macroeconomics, going back to Friedman (1953) and Meade (1955), concerns the relative advantage of fixed versus flexible exchange rates. While these early discussions were conducted at a fairly general level, recently the issue has been reconsidered by a number of authors at a more formal level, but from the narrower perspective of the relative stability of the two regimes (see Turnovsky, 1976; Fischer, 1977b; Flood, 1979). Within the present context, the debate can be viewed as comparing the relative stability properties (in the sense of appropriate variances) of the two specific intervention policies corresponding to $\mu = 0$ (flexible rates) and $\mu = \infty$ (fixed rates). Just as in the earlier models, a general comparison in which all random variables appear simultaneously is quite impractical, and we will focus on the separate random variables individually, in turn. We consider their effects on the variances of prices and income under the two regimes and summarize the results in table 7.1.[17]

Since the topic has been discussed at length elsewhere in the literature, our discussion can be brief. The superiority of a fixed exchange rate in the face of domestic monetary disturbances follows immediately from the result obtained previously that the fixed rate is in fact optimal. The choice of regime when the disturbances originate on the domestic supply side gives rise to a conflict. A fixed exchange rate provides a greater degree of price stability, but a lesser degree of income stability than does a flexible rate. The choice therefore depends critically upon how these two goals are weighted in the overall objective function. The reason for the conflict can easily be explained as follows. Under a fixed-rate regime and with no foreign disturbances, given purchasing power parity, the domestic price level remains fixed (see (7.10a)). With the expected price $p^*_{t,t-1} = 0$ (obtained by talking conditional expectations of (7.22b)) and the actual price level fixed, it follows from the domestic supply function (7.10c) that any random fluctuation is fully met by a corresponding fluctuation in output. However, under a flexible rate, the domestic price level is no longer fixed. Accordingly, any random disturbance in u_{2t} is shared between fluctuations in domestic output and fluctuations in the domestic price level. The amount of random fluctuation in output therefore declines, while the variations in the domestic price level is increased.

The choice between the two regimes in the face of foreign disturbances is in all cases ambiguous, depending upon the various parameters at home and abroad. No definitive conclusions can be drawn, and either regime may prove to provide greater stability. One case worth noting arises when the domestic economy is "similar" to the rest of the world in the sense that corresponding parameters are equal, i.e. $\alpha_1 = \alpha'_1$ and so forth. Under this assumption, fixed and flexible rates yield equal stability in the case involving v_{0t}, while the flexible rate will be superior in the case involving v_{2t}. The relative stability where the disturbances originate in the foreign monetary sector remains indeterminate.

7 CONCLUDING COMMENTS

In this chapter we have investigated the question of the optimal degree of exchange market intervention. To illustrate the procedure, the model

TABLE 7.1 *Fixed versus flexible exchange rates*

	σ_y^2	σ_p^2
Domestic disturbances		
Domestic monetary sector		
$\mu = 0$	$\left(\dfrac{\gamma}{1 + \alpha_2 + \alpha_1\gamma}\right)^2 \sigma_1^2$	$\dfrac{\sigma_1^2}{(1 + \alpha_2 + \alpha_1\gamma)^2}$
$\mu = \infty$	0	0
Fixed rate is superior (optimal)		
Domestic supply of output		
$\mu = 0$	$\left(\dfrac{1 + \alpha_2}{1 + \alpha_2 + \alpha_1\gamma}\right)^2 \sigma_2^2$	$\dfrac{\alpha_1}{1 + \alpha_2 + \alpha_2\gamma}\,\sigma_2^2$
$\mu = 0$	σ_2^2	0
There is a conflict: flexible rates favor income stability; fixed rates favor price stability		
Foreign disturbances		
Foreign output demand		
$\mu = 0$	$\left\{\dfrac{\gamma\alpha_2(1 + \alpha_2' + \alpha_1'\gamma')}{(1 + \alpha_2 + \alpha_1\gamma)\Delta'}\right\}^2 \sigma_0'^2$	$\left\{\dfrac{\alpha_2(1 + \alpha_2' + \alpha_1'\gamma')}{(1 + \alpha_2 + \alpha_1\gamma)\Delta'}\right\}^2 \sigma_0'^2$
$\mu = \infty$	$\left(\dfrac{\gamma\alpha_2'}{\Delta'}\right)^2 \sigma_0'^2$	$\left(\dfrac{\alpha_2'}{\Delta'}\right)^2 \sigma_0'^2$
Fixed rate is superior if $\alpha_2(1 + \alpha_1'\gamma') - \alpha_2'(1 + \alpha_1\gamma) > 0$ Flexible rate is superior if $\alpha_2(1 + \alpha_1'\gamma') - \alpha_2'(1 + \alpha_1\gamma) < 0$		
Foreign monetary sector		
$\mu = 0$	$\left\{\dfrac{\gamma\gamma'\alpha_2(1 - d_1')}{(1 + \alpha_2 + \alpha_1\gamma)\Delta'}\right\}^2 \sigma_1'^2$	$\left\{\dfrac{\gamma'\alpha_2(1 - d_1')}{(1 + \alpha_2 + \alpha_1\gamma)\Delta'}\right\}^2 \sigma_1'^2$
$\mu = \infty$	$\left(\dfrac{\gamma d_2'}{\Delta'}\right)^2 \sigma_1'^2$	$\left(\dfrac{d_2'}{\Delta'}\right)^2 \sigma_1'^2$
Fixed rate is superior if $\gamma'\alpha_2(1 - d_1') - d_2'(1 + \alpha_2 + \alpha_1\gamma) > 0$ Flexible rate is superior if $\gamma'\alpha_2(1 - d_1') - d_2'(1 + \alpha_2 + \alpha_1\gamma) < 0$		
Foreign output supply		
$\mu = 0$	$\left\{\dfrac{\gamma\alpha_2(1 - d_1')(1 + \alpha_2')}{(1 + \alpha_2 + \alpha_1\gamma)\Delta'}\right\}^2 \sigma_2'^2$	$\left\{\dfrac{\alpha_2(1 - d_1')(1 + \alpha_2')}{(1 + \alpha_2 + \alpha_1\gamma)\Delta'}\right\}^2 \sigma_2'^2$
$\mu = \infty$	$\left[\dfrac{\gamma\{(1 - d_1')\alpha_2' + \alpha_1' d_2'\}}{\Delta'}\right]^2 \sigma_2'^2$	$\left\{\dfrac{(1 - d_1')\alpha_2' + \alpha_1' d_2'}{\Delta'}\right\}^2 \sigma_2'^2$
Fixed rate is superior if $\alpha_2\{(1 - d_1') - \alpha_1' d_2'\} - \{(1 - d_1')\alpha_2' + \alpha_1' d_2'\}(1 + \alpha_1\gamma) > 0$ Flexible rate is superior if $\alpha_2\{(1 - d_1') - \alpha_1' d_2'\} - \{(1 - d_1')\alpha_2' + \alpha_1' d_2'\}(1 + \alpha_1\gamma) < 0$		

has been kept as simple as possible. However, even for such a simple model, no strong conclusions emerge. In general, it is seen that the optimal policy may require the monetary authorities to lean with or against the wind, depending upon the source of the random disturbances impinging on the domestic economy. Most policy discussions of intervention policy have been expressed in terms of the monetary authorities responding to downward market pressure by adopting a contractionary policy. The fact that quite the opposite may in fact be appropriate for maximizing domestic stability is quite significant.

The second general conclusion to be drawn is that the case for a perfectly flexible exchange rate is not very great, at least not from the viewpoint of domestic stability. Whereas, under appropriate circumstances – for example, when the disturbances originate in the domestic monetary sector – a fixed rate may be optimal, this is not the case for flexible rates, unless appropriate coefficients take on extreme values.[18] Furthermore, a fixed rate may provide greater stability in circumstances in which a traditionally flexible rate may be thought to be superior. For example, abstracting from capital gains resulting from the effects of exchange rate changes on the components of wealth denominated in different currencies – an issue not addressed in the present analysis – it is sometimes argued that flexible exchange rates will provide perfect insulation in the face of foreign monetary disturbances. The present analysis shows that this is not so. On the contrary, a conclusion of the comparison in section 6 is that a fixed rate may be superior, even in this case. This will be so if, for example, the domestic interest elasticity of the demand for money is sufficiently large.

Obviously it is difficult to extrapolate the implications of a simple model such as this to provide reliable guidance to real world intervention policies. However, the conclusions of our analysis do suggest that the appropriate choice of policy is extremely difficult as it is highly sensitive to relevant parameters in the domestic economy and the rest of the world as well as to the relative importance of the various sources of the random disturbances impinging on the economy. Clearly, reliable information on these empirical issues is a necessary ingredient for the implementation of appropriate intervention policies.

APPENDIX DETERMINATION OF THE SHORT-RUN SOLUTION IN THE REST OF THE WORLD

This appendix derives the expressions given in (7.6a) and (7.6b) in the text for q_t and ω_t in terms of the stochastic disturbances in the rest of the world.

We begin by recalling the specification of the behavioral relation in the rest of the world ((7.5a)–(7.5c)):

$$Z_t = d'_1 Z_t - d'_2\{\Omega_t - (Q^*_{t+1,t} - Q_t)\} + v_{0t} \tag{7A.1a}$$

$$\bar{M}' - Q_t = \alpha'_1 Z_t - \alpha'_2 \Omega_t + v_{1t} \tag{7A.1b}$$

$$Z_t - \hat{Z}_t = \gamma'(Q_t - Q^*_{t,t-1}) + v_{2t} \tag{7A.1c}$$

where all variables are as defined in the text. The deterministic steady state equilibrium solution to this system, obtained by setting all stochastic disturbances to zero and assuming that expectations are realized, is

$$(1 - d'_1)\bar{Z} = -d'_2\bar{\Omega} \tag{7A.2a}$$

$$\bar{M}' - \bar{Q} = \alpha'_1\bar{Z} - \alpha'_2\bar{\Omega} \tag{7A.2b}$$

$$\bar{Z} = \hat{Z} \tag{7A.2c}$$

Subtracting (7A.1) from (7A.2) and noting (7.3a) and (7.3b), we can express the system in deviation form as

$$z_t = d'_1 z_t - d'_2\{\omega_t - (q^*_{t+1,t} - q_t)\} + v_{0t} \tag{7A.3a}$$

$$-q_t = \alpha'_1 z_t - \alpha'_2\omega_t - v_{1t} \tag{7A.3b}$$

$$z_t = \gamma'(q_t - q^*_{t,t-1}) + v_{2t} \tag{7A.3c}$$

Solving (7A.3) for q_t yields the equation

$$\begin{aligned}\{H + \gamma' d'_2(1 + \alpha'_2)\}q_t - Hq^*_{t,t-1} - \gamma'\alpha'_2 d'_2 q^*_{t+1,t}\\ = \gamma'\alpha'_2 v_{0t} - \gamma' d'_2 v_{1t} + Hv_{2t}\end{aligned} \tag{7A.4}$$

where

$$H \equiv \alpha'_2(1 - d'_2) + \alpha'_1 d'_2 > 0$$

Taking expectations of (7A.4) at time $t - 1$ for time $t + i$, we obtain the following difference equation in $q^*_{t+i,t-1}$:

$$(1 + \alpha'_2)q^*_{t+i,t-1} - \alpha'_2 q^*_{t+i+1,t-1} = 0 \qquad i = 0, 1, \ldots \tag{7A.5}$$

In order for this solution to be stable, we require

$$q^*_{t+i,t-1} = 0 \qquad i = 0, 1, \ldots, \text{all } t \tag{7A.6}$$

On substituting (7A.6) into (7A.3), the three endogenous variables satisfy the matrix equation

$$\begin{bmatrix} 1 - d'_1 & d'_2 & d'_2 \\ \alpha'_1 & -\alpha'_2 & 1 \\ 1 & 0 & -\gamma' \end{bmatrix}\begin{bmatrix} z_t \\ \omega_t \\ q_t \end{bmatrix} = \begin{bmatrix} v_{0t} \\ -v_{1t} \\ v_{2t} \end{bmatrix} \tag{7A.7}$$

The solution to this equation is

$$q_t = \frac{1}{\Delta'}[\alpha_2' v_{0t} - d_2' v_{1t} - \{(1 - d_2')\alpha_2' + \alpha_2' d_2'\} v_{2t}] \qquad (7A.8a)$$

$$\omega_t = \frac{1}{\Delta'}\{(1 + \alpha_1'\gamma')v_{0t} + \gamma'(1 - d_1') + d_2'\} v_{1t}$$
$$+ \{d_2'\alpha_1' - (1 - d_1')\} v_{2t}] \qquad (7A.8b)$$

where Δ' is defined in section 5.2, thus yielding (7.6a) and (7.6b) of the text, together with

$$z_t = \frac{1}{\Delta'}\{\gamma'\alpha_2' v_{0t} - \gamma' d_2' v_{1t} + d_2'(1 + \alpha_2')v_{2t}\} \qquad (7A.8c)$$

which is not required.

NOTES

1 It is, of course, possible to formulate control laws in terms of current data, as well as past data, provided that the current data are immediately observable. Indeed, this is what is proposed here.

2 Other recent contributions to intervention policy that should be mentioned include those by Henderson (1979) and Cox (1980).

3 For simplicity we abstract from all issues pertaining to wealth accumulation.

4 We therefore abstract from the possibility of "current substitution", an issue which is receiving increasing attention in the international monetary literature.

5 In deriving the optimal intervention policy, it is important to distinguish between those variables which the authority can in effect currently observe and those that are, at least in the short run, unobservable. Given that data on exchange rates and the money supply are available with much greater frequency than income figures, we will assume that E_t and M_t are observable and that Y_t is unobservable (at time t). This is one of the reasons why in general policy-makers cannot stabilize income perfectly. The period of time for which this assumption is most applicable would be something like a month, since income is usually observed only quarterly and weekly money figures have considerable noise.

6 The foreign stochastic demand disturbances satisfy the "adding up condition"

$$v_{0t} + v_{1t} + v_{3t} = 0$$

where v_{3t} is the random disturbance in the foreign bond market, which has been eliminated by virtue of the overall foreign budget constraint. Thus the disturbances to v_{0t}, v_{1t} discussed in the text are in both cases offset by corresponding changes in v_{3t}.

7 It is interesting to note that if $\alpha_2 = 0$, so that the LM curve is vertical, only the unstable case exists.

8 When δ_1 is chosen to minimize (7.23) the resulting expression for y_t is a

rather complicated function of μ. However, it is possible for the value of δ_1 which provides a finite asymptotic variance in the unstable case to be identical with that which yields the minimized variance in the stable case. If this is so, the solutions for y_t and p_t in the two cases will be given by the same expression. This phenomenon occurs if (following Flood, for example) we were to modify the interest rate parity condition (7.1c) to $r_t = \Omega_t + E^*_{t+1,t-1} - E^*_{t,t-1}$, conditioning the expectations at time $t-1$. This specification, however, has the disadvantage of rendering the domestic interest rate as predetermined at time t.

9 The specification of the objective function in terms of the asymptotic variance is the standard approach in stabilization problems of this type. However, in the present context we might consider whether some short run variance conditional on current information is more appropriate. This issue only arises in the stable case; in the case of unstable intervention, the system is always fluctuating around steady state, and so the conditional variances and the steady state variance coincide.

10 The equation $\partial C/\partial\mu = 0$ has multiple roots, namely (7.31) and $\mu = -(1 + \alpha_2 + \alpha_1\gamma)$. Of these (7.31) is consistent with the second-order condition $\partial^2 C/\partial\mu^2 > 0$. The second root yields a maximum rather than a minimum; indeed, when the value of μ is inserted into (7.30), the asymptotic variance becomes infinite.

11 In other words, we should consider $\mu = -1 + \varepsilon$, $\mu = -1 - 2\alpha_2 - \varepsilon$, where $\varepsilon > 0$ tends to zero. In the limit we have $\mu = -1 +$, $\mu = -1 - 2\alpha_2 -$.

12 For example setting $e^*_{t+1,t} = p^*_{t,t-1} = 0$ (as instability of the intervention rule implies) in (7.10a)–(7.10c), writing $m_t = -\mu e_t$, and eliminating y_t reduces these three equations to a single relation between m_t and e_t:

$$m_t = (1 + \alpha_2 + \alpha_1\gamma)e_t + u_{1t} + \alpha_1 u_{2t} + (1 + \alpha_1\gamma)q_t - \alpha_2\omega_t$$

The observability of m_t and e_t, together with the fact that the coefficients are assumed to be known, implies that the composite disturbance $u_{1t} + \alpha_1 u_{2t} + (1 + \alpha_1\alpha_1\gamma)q_t - \alpha_2\omega_t$ is in effect observed. Roper and Turnovsky (1980) describe the above relation between m_t and e_t as measuring exchange market pressure.

13 Strictly speaking, the optimum in (7.34b) should by $\mu = -1 + \varepsilon$, where $\varepsilon > 0$ is infinitesimally small.

14 Perfect insulation of y_t would require $\mu = -(1 + \alpha_2)$. However, this is not feasible as it is inconsistent with the requirement that intervention be unstable.

15 This is the form of foreign stochastic disturbance considered by Cox (1980).

16 This is because the correlation between q_t and ω_t is less than perfect, making it impossible to offset the disturbance exactly.

17 It is worth noting that the choice of exchange rate system under perfect capital mobility is equivalent to the familiar monetary instrument problem. The fixed exchange rate is equivalent to pegging the interest rate; the flexible rate corresponds to pegging the money supply.

18 For example, a flexible rate will be optimal in the face of foreign disturbances (from all sources) if $\alpha_2 = 0$.

REFERENCES

Boyer, R. (1978) Optimal foreign exchange market intervention. *Journal of Political Economy*, 86, 1045–56.

Buiter, W. (1979) Optimal foreign exchange market intervention with rational expectations. In *Trade and Payments Adjustment under Flexible Exchange Rates* (eds J. Martin and A. Smith). London: Macmillan.

Cox, W. M. (1980) Unanticipated money output, and prices in the small economy. *Journal of Monetary Economcs*, 6, 359–384.

Fischer, S. (1977a) Wage indexation and Macroecomomic Stability. In *Stabilization of the Domestic and International Economy* (eds K. Brunner and A Meltzer). Amsterdam: North-Holland.

—— (1977b) Stability and exchange rate systems in a monetarist model of the balance of payments. In *The Political Economy of Monetary Reform*. (ed. R. Aliber) Montclair, NJ: Allanheld, Osmun and Co.

Flood, R. (1979) Capital mobility and the choice of exchange rate system. *International Economy Review*. 20, 405–16.

Friedman, M. (1953) The case for flexible exchange rates. In *Essays in Positive Economics* (ed. M. Friedman). Chicago, IL: University of Chicago Press.

Gray, J. (1976) Wage indexation: a macroeconomic approach. *Journal of Monetary Economics*, 2, 221–35.

Henderson, D. W. (1979) Financial policies in open economics. *American Economic Review, Papers and Proceedings*, 69, 232–9.

Kareken, J. H., Muench, T., and Wallace, N. (1973) Optimal open market strategy: the use of information variables. *American Economic Review*, 63. 156–72.

Lucas, R. E., Jr. (1973) Some international evidence on output inflation trade-offs. *American Economic Review*, 63, 326–34.

Meade, J. (1955) The case for variable exchange rates. *Three Banks Review* 3–27.

Muth, J. F. (1961) Rational expectations and the theory of price movements *Econometrica*, 29, 315–35.

Poole, W. (1970) Optimal choice of monetary policy instruments in a simple stochastic macro model. *Quarterly Journal of Economics*, 84. 197–216.

Roper, D. E. and Turnovsky, S. J. (1980) Optimal exchange market intervention in a simple stochastic macro model. *Canadian Journal of Economics*, 13, 296–309.

Taylor, J. (1977) Conditions for unique solutions in stochastic macroeconomic models with rational expectations. *Econometrica*, 45, 1377–85.

Turnovsky, S. J. (1976) The relative stability of alternative exchange rate systems in the presence of random disturbances. *Journal of Money, Credit and Banking*, 8, 29–50.

8 Wage Indexation and Exchange Market Intervention in a Small Open Economy

1 INTRODUCTION

Recently, the issues of exchange market intervention on the one hand and wage indexation on the other have become topical in the international macroeconomic literature. To date, these questions have been analysed virtually independently. The intervention literature has focused exclusively on nonindexed economies. That is, the models typically assume that nominal wages are fixed by a one-period contract throughout the current period and therefore do not respond to current stochastic influences (see for example Boyer, 1978; Buiter, 1979; Henderson, 1979; Cox, 1980; Roper and Turnovsky, 1980; Turnovsky, 1983, this volume, ch. 7). This literature examines the extent to which alternative intervention policies – usually specified in terms of rules relating the current money supply and the current exchange rate – insulate the domestic economy from stochastic disturbances of varying origins. The issue of optimal intervention has also been discussed, although even for the simplest models the derivation of optimal policies proves to be quite tedious. By contrast, the indexation models typically deal with the extreme regimes of perfectly fixed and perfectly flexible rates and study the extent to which alternative forms of wage indexation insulate the economy from various stochastic disturbances under these two regimes. Optimal indexation schemes have also been discussed (see Flood and Marion, 1982; Marston, 1982, 1984).[1]

Originally published in *Canadian Journal of Economics*, 16 (4), November 1983, 574–92.

I wish to thank Joshua Aizenman, Richard Marston, two anonymous referees, and the editor, Michael Parkin, for helpful comments on an earlier draft of this paper.

In fact, exchange market intervention and wage indexation are highly interdependent policy instruments. Both are intended to reduce the effects of current stochastic disturbances on the economy. The indexation scheme does so by adjusting the current nominal wage to these disturbances insofar as they are reflected by the price index governing the indexation scheme. The indexation rule therefore impinges directly on the supply function of the economy; hence it can be viewed as being a *real* form of policy intervention. By contrast, the intervention rule adjusts the money supply to the random disturbances insofar as they are reflected by the current exchange rate. Since it is a monetary rule, it is a *nominal* form of policy intervention.

In this chapter we analyse the effectiveness of exchange market intervention and wage indexation as joint policy instruments. It is evident that by changing the slope of the supply function, the degree of wage indexation must influence the effectiveness of exchange market intervention and in turn the optimal degree of intervention. The converse is also true.

Within the indexation literature there is a debate concerning not only the appropriate degree of indexation but also the appropriate price against which to index. While traditionally the consumer price index (CPI) is the chosen measure, it has been proposed that wage indexation schemes should be based on the movement of the domestic price index (the GNP deflator). It has been argued that this form of indexation will shield the domestic economy from increases in the prices of imported goods.[2] In our analysis we will allow for differential degrees of indexation to domestic and foreign prices. We therefore consider three policy instruments: the two indexation parameters together with the degree of exchange market intervention.

The framework we employ is a standard stochastic model of a small open economy under rational expectations (see for example Cox, 1980; Turnovsky, 1981, this volume, ch. 5; Marston, 1982). Our strategy is to solve the system for the relevant endogenous variables in terms of the stochastic disturbances and the three policy parameters. In principle, we could postulate an objective function and optimize simultaneously for the three policy parameters. This turns out to be intractable, and we prefer to focus on the various disturbances individually and collectively and to consider how the degree of intervention and indexation interact in neutralizing the influence of these disturbances on the economy.

While the detailed results are discussed below, one conclusion is worth highlighting at the outset. First, if the current wage is fully adjusted to current price changes, in the sense that the sum of the degree of indexation to the domestic price change plus the foreign price change is unity, then irrespective of the relative weights assigned to these two prices in the indexation scheme, exchange market intervention becomes totally ineffective in insulating the real part of the domestic economy from any stochastic disturbance. However, if the monetary authority intervenes in the exchange market so as to render the excess demand for nominal money balances dependent only upon real variables, then wage indexation becomes impotent in influencing real behavior. In either case, the respective policy will still retain influence over the nominal part of the system.

The remainder of the chapter is structured as follows. The description of the model and its solution is outlined in section 2. The interdependence between the two types of policy variables is discussed in section 3. In sections 4 and 5 we analyse the stabilization of domestic and foreign disturbances in turn, while in section 6 we summarize our main findings. Finally, certain computational details are given in the appendix.

2 THE MODEL

The country we consider is fully specialized in the production of a single (composite) commodity, of which part is consumed domestically and the remainder is exported. Domestic residents consume two goods, the domestic good and an imported good, the foreign price of which they take as given. There are two financial assets held in the portfolios of domestic residents. These include domestic money, which is nontraded, and a single bond, which is traded internationally in a perfect bond market. The model is described by the following set of equations:

$$Y_t = d_1 Y_t - d_2\{r_t - (C^*_{t+1,t} - C_t)\} + d_3(Q_t + E_t - P_t) + u_{1t} \qquad 0 < d_1 < 1,\ d_2 > 0,\ d_3 > 0 \quad (8.1a)$$

$$C_t = \delta P_t + (1 - \delta)(Q_t + E_t) \qquad 0 < \delta < 1 \quad (8.1b)$$

$$M_t - C_t = \alpha_1(Y_t + P_t - C_t) - \alpha_2 r_t + u_{2t} \qquad 0 < \alpha_1 < 1,\ \alpha_2 > 0 \quad (8.1c)$$

$$r_t = \Omega_t + E^*_{t+1,t} - E_t \quad (8.1d)$$

$$M_t - \bar{M} = -\mu(E_t - \bar{E}) \quad (8.1e)$$

$$Y_t = \gamma_0 + \gamma(P_t - W_t) + u_{3t} \qquad \gamma > 0 \quad (8.1f)$$

$$W_t = W^c_{t,t-1} + T_1(P_t - P^*_{t,t-1}) + T_2(Q_t + E_t - Q^*_{t,t-1} - E^*_{t,t-1}) \quad (8.1g)$$

while for any variable X, say,

$$X^*_{s,t} = \mathcal{E}_t(X_s)$$

where Y_t is the real domestic output at time t, measured in logarithms, r_t is the domestic nominal interest rate at time t, Ω_t is the foreign nominal interest rate at time t, P_t is the price of domestically produced good (in terms of domestic currency), expressed in logarithms, Q_t is the price of imported good (in terms of foreign currency), expressed in logarithms, E_t is the current exchange rate (measured in units of the domestic currency per unit of foreign currency), expressed in logarithms, $\bar{E}$ is the equilibrium (steady state) level of E, endogenously determined, C_t is the domestic cost of living (measured in domestic currency), expressed in logarithms, M_t is the domestic nominal money supply, expressed in logarithms, $\bar{M}$ is the fixed exogenous component of the domestic nominal money supply, $E^*_{t+s,t}$ is the expectation of E for time $t+s$, held at time t_1 ($s = 1, 2, \ldots$, all t), $P^*_{t+s,t}$ is the expectation of P for time $t+s$, held at time t ($s = 1, 2, \ldots$, all t), $Q^*_{t+s,t}$ is the expectation of Q for time $t+s$, held at time t ($s = 1, 2, \ldots$, all t), $C^*_{t+s,t}$ is the expectation of C for time $t+s$, held at time t ($s = 1, 2, \ldots$, all t), $W^c_{t,t-1}$ is the contracted wage negotiated at time $t-1$ for time t, expressed in logarithms, W_t is the nominal wage at time t, expressed in logarithms, $\mathcal{E}_t$ is the conditional expectations operator, conditional on information at time t, u_{1t} is the stochastic disturbance in the demand for domestic output, u_{2t} is the stochastic disturbance in the demand for domestic money, u_{3t} is the stochastic disturbance in the supply of domestic output.

The first four equations are standard. Equation (8.1a) describes the domestic economy's IS curve. Equation (8.1b) defines the domestic cost of living to be a log-linear weighted average of the price of the domestic good and the domestic price of the imported good. The third equation specifies the domestic LM curve, while the assumption of perfect capital mobility is embodied in the uncovered interest parity condition (8.1d), which equates the expected rate of return on domestic and foreign bonds.[3]

The intervention policy is described by (8.1e). This describes the degree of intervention by the authority as a function of the observed deviation from its long-run equilibrium level, which the authority is assumed to know. The limiting cases of $\mu = \infty$, $\mu = 0$, correspond to fixed and flexible regimes respectively, while any finite nonzero value of μ describes a managed float. The optimal intervention policy is to choose μ to optimize some specified objective and as has been shown previously, an optimal policy may involve either $\mu > 0$ or $\mu < 0$, depending upon the primary source of the stochastic disturbances. Note that the reaction function (8.1e) is expressed in terms of current values of M and E which are assumed to be instantly observable.[4]

The supply side of the economy is described by equations (8.1f) and (8.1g). The first is the short-run supply function, where γ_0 and γ are related to the underlying production function (see (8.3) below). The latter equation describes the current wage and the wage indexation scheme.[5] At time $t-1$ a nominal wage rate $W^c_{t,t-1}$ is contracted for time

t, based on information available up to time $t-1$, i.e. before the realizations of the stochastic disturbances at time t are known. The critical information components include the expectations $P^*_{t,t-1}$ and $C^*_{t,t-1}$ of the prices of domestic output and the domestic CPI. At time t, when the actual prices become known, the current wage rate is adjusted in proportion to the difference between the actual and expected prices. The coefficient T_1 describes the extent to which the wage rate is indexed to the current domestic price, and T_2 is the degree of indexation to the foreign price. Typically, T_1 and T_2 are constrained to lie in the range 0 to 1, although this need not be optimal (see note 14 below). In short, the contract wage imposes a nominal short-run rigidity on the system, which the indexation scheme is intended to offset as far as possible.

A number of special indexation schemes merit mention. If $T_1 > 0$, $T_2 = 0$, the wage is indexed solely to the domestic price level, with $T_1 = 1$ being full indexation. The case $T_1 = 0$, $T_2 > 0$ describes indexation to the foreign price level, with $T_2 = 1$ being full indexation. Thirdly, if $T_1 = T\delta$, $T_2 = T(1-\delta)$, then noting (8.1b), equation (8.1g) becomes

$$W_t = W^c_{t,t-1} + T(C_t - C^*_{t,t-1}) \tag{8.1g'}$$

which describes indexation to the CPI. Full indexation occurs when $T = 1$, i.e. $T_1 = \delta$, $T_2 = 1 - \delta$. More generally, we will say that the current wage is *fully indexed* if $T_1 + T_2 = 1$. In this case (8.1g) becomes

$$\begin{aligned} W_t = W^c_{t,t-1} &+ T_1(P_t - P^*_{t,t-1}) \\ &+ (1 - T_1)(Q_t + E_t - Q^*_{t,t-1} - E^*_{t,t-1}) \end{aligned} \tag{8.1g''}$$

This is equivalent to the wage being fully indexed to a weighted average of the domestic and foreign prices, with the weights being T_1 and $1 - T_1$ respectively. The first three schemes noted are merely special cases of this general notion.

The next step in the specification of the model is the determination of the wage contract $W^c_{t,t-1}$. Specifically, we will assume that this wage is set so that, given the expectations of firms and workers, the labor market is expected to clear. If it is assumed that workers are concerned with their real wages in terms of the expected CPI, the expected supply of labor at the contract wage is

$$N^s_{t,t-1} = a + b(W^c_{t,t-1} - C^*_{t,t-1}) \tag{8.2a}$$

If it is assumed further that there is a production function linking the logarithm of output to the logarithm of employment N_t by

$$Y_t = \varepsilon_t + \beta N_t \tag{8.2b}$$

where ε_t is a stochastic disturbance reflecting technological uncertainty and having mean zero, it follows that the expected demand for labor $N^{d}_{t,t-1}$ (based on expected profit maximization) is determined by the marginal product condition

$$\ln\beta + (\beta - 1)N^{d}_{t,t-1} = W^{c}_{t,t-1} - P^{*}_{t,t-1} \tag{8.2c}$$

where firms value real wages in terms of their expected product price. The contract wage is determined by equating the expected demand and supply of labor appearing in (8.2a) and (8.2c), yielding

$$W^{c}_{t,t-1} = \frac{\ln\beta + (\beta - 1)a + (1 - \beta)bC^{*}_{t,t-1} + P^{*}_{t,t-1}}{1 + b(1 - \beta)} \tag{8.1h}$$

Short-run actual employment is assumed to be determined by the short-run marginal productivity condition for firms after the stochastic variables ε_t, W_t, and P_t are realized, namely

$$\varepsilon_t + \ln\beta + (\beta - 1)N_t = W_t - P_t \tag{8.2c$'$}$$

Combining (8.2b) and (8.2c′), we obtain the supply function

$$Y_t = \frac{\beta\ln\beta}{1 - \beta} + \frac{\beta}{1 - \beta}(P_t - W_t) + \frac{\varepsilon_t}{1 - \beta} \tag{8.3}$$

which is of the form (8.1f), with

$$\gamma_0 \equiv \frac{\beta\ln\beta}{1 - \beta} \qquad \gamma \equiv \frac{\beta}{1 - \beta}, \qquad u_{3t} \equiv \frac{\varepsilon_t}{1 - \beta}$$

The three domestic stochastic variables u_{1t}, u_{2t}, and u_{3t} are assumed to have zero means and finite variances:

$$\mathcal{E}(u_{it}) = 0 \qquad i = 1, 2, 3 \tag{8.4a}$$

$$\mathcal{E}(u_{it}^2) = \sigma_i^2 \qquad i = 1, 2, 3 \tag{8.4b}$$

The two foreign variables in the system (Ω_t and Q_t) are also assumed to be random, and are described by

$$Q_t = \bar{Q} + q_t \tag{8.5a}$$

$$\Omega_t = \bar{\Omega} + \omega_t \tag{8.5b}$$

where $\bar{Q}$ and $\bar{\Omega}$ are constant and

$$\mathcal{E}(q_t) = \mathcal{E}(\omega_t) = 0 \tag{8.6a}$$

$$\mathcal{E}(q_t^2) = \sigma_q^2 \qquad \mathcal{E}(\omega_t^2) = \sigma_\omega^2 \tag{8.6b}$$

In addition, all random variables are assumed to be independently distributed over time, which means that $Q^{*}_{t+s,t} = \bar{Q}$. Also, for simplicity, we assume that domestic and foreign variables are uncorrelated, thereby enabling us to distinguish quite clearly between domestic and foreign stochastic influences.[6]

The model thus contains the eight equations (8.1a)–(8.1h), which jointly determine the eight endogenous variables Y_t, r_t, E_t, M_t, P_t, C_t, W_t, and $W^c_{t,t-1}$. These are determined on the assumption that the expectations appearing in the model are formed rationally. In order to analyse the model it is desirable to make several transformations.

1 To reduce the dimensionality of the system we substitute from (8.1b), (8.1d), (8.1g), and (8.1h) to eliminate r_t, C_t, W_t, and $W^c_{t,t-1}$.
2 It is convenient to consider an initial equilibrium defined by assessing that all expectations are realized and setting all random variables to zero, thereby enabling us to incorporate all constants in the initial equilibrium.
3 We define the relative price of foreign to domestic goods (the inverse of the terms of trade) by

$$S_t = Q_t + E_t - P_t$$

Following these procedures, we can reduce the system to the four stochastic difference equations in the two real variables y_t and s_t and the two nominal variables p_t and m_t, where lower case letters are used to denote deviations from the equilibrium, i.e. $e_t \equiv E_t - \bar{E}$ etc. These calculations are straightforward and details are relegated to the appendix.

These equations involve the expectations of the relative price $s^*_{t+1,t}$ and the nominal price level $p^*_{t+1,t}$. The solution procedures for determining these expectations are familiar and are omitted. First, it can be shown that the only solution for the forecast of the relative price consistent with stability is $s^*_{t+1,t} = 0$, for all t.[7] In the case of nominal price expectations it can be shown that the nature of the stable solution depends upon the intervention parameter μ. If $\mu > -1$ or $\mu < -(1 + 2\alpha_2)$, the only solution consistent with stability is $p^*_{t+1,t} = 0$. However, for $-(1 + 2\alpha_2) < \mu < -1$ the stable solution for $p^*_{t+1,t}$ turns out to be indeterminate. We resolve this indeterminacy by choosing the solution $p^*_{t+1,t} = 0$. While this choice is arbitrary, it is simple and has the virtue of yielding a solution with a form which is independent of the choice of intervention parameter μ.[8]

Thus, setting all expectations to zero and substituting for the intervention rule, the system can be expressed in the following form:

$$(1 - d_1)y_t - (d_2\delta + d_3)s_t = u_{1t} - d_2(\omega_t + q_t) \tag{8.7a}$$

$$\alpha_1 y_1 + \{(1 - \delta)(1 - \alpha_1) + \alpha_2 + \mu\}s_t + (1 + \alpha_2 + \mu)p_t$$
$$= -u_{2t} + \alpha_2(\omega_t + q_t) + \mu q_t \tag{8.7b}$$

$$y_t + \gamma T_2 s_t - \gamma(1 - T_1 - T_2)p_t = u_{3t} \tag{8.7c}$$

which can readily be solved for y_t, s_t, and p_t.

3 INTERDEPENDENCE BETWEEN EXCHANGE MARKET INTERVENTION AND WAGE INDEXATION

The solutions for the endogenous variables of the small open economy are summarized in table 8.1. It is clear that these variables are linear functions of the random disturbances, and in the table we list the coefficient attached to each disturbance. In the first part of the table we report the impact effects of the domestic disturbances, while the foreign disturbances are given in the second part. Notice that under a perfectly flexible rate regime ($\mu = 0$) the two foreign variables ω_t and q_t have identical effects on the domestic variables. We therefore find it convenient to break down the foreign effects into $\omega_t + q_t$ and μq_t, where the latter is an additional effect due to exchange market intervention.[9] Thus, if we denote the two elements in the first row of the second part by θ_1 and θ_2, the effect of a unit increase in the foreign interest rate on y_t is θ_1, while that of a unit increase in the foreign price level q_t is $\theta_1 + \mu\theta_2$.

It is clear from table 8.1 that y_t, s_t, and p_t all fluctuate statically in response to the three domestic random variables (u_{1t}, u_{2t}, u_{3t}) as well as the two foreign variables (q_t, ω_t). The three policy parameters μ, T_1, and T_2 influence the responses of all these endogenous variables to the exogenous random shocks in an interdependent way. The degrees of wage indexation T_1 and T_2 influence the effectiveness of exchange market intervention μ, and vice versa. In particular, the structure of the reduced form of the system (equation (8.7)) enables us to derive the following important propositions.

1 If the domestic wage rate is fully indexed in the sense that $T_1 + T_2 = 1$, then, irrespective of the relative magnitudes of T_1 and T_2, exchange market intervention becomes ineffective in insulating the real part of the domestic economy (summarized by y_t and s_t) from any stochastic disturbances. Intervention policy will still, however, be effective in influencing the nominal part of the domestic economy (summarized by p_t).
2 If the monetary authority intervenes in the foreign exchange market so as to render the excess demand for nominal money balances dependent upon only the real variables, then wage indexation becomes totally ineffective in influencing the real part of the system. However, it will still be able to influence the nominal variables.

These two propositions can immediately be established as follows. If the domestic nominal wage rate is fully indexed, i.e. $T_1 + T_2 = 1$, the domestic supply curve becomes independent of the domestic price level p_t. Rather, the two real variables y_t and s_t become jointly determined by the IS curve together with the supply function. Therefore they are

TABLE 8.1 *Impact of unanticipated disturbances*

Domestic origin	*Real demand* u_{1t}	*Monetary* u_{2t}	*Supply* u_{3t}
Real output y_t	$[\gamma(1 - T_1)\{(1 - \delta)(1 - \alpha_1) + \mu + \alpha_2\} + \gamma T_2\{\alpha_1 + \delta(1 - \alpha_1)\}]/D$	$-\gamma(d_2\delta + d_3)(1 - T_1 - T_2)/D$	$(1 + \alpha_2 + \mu)(d_2\delta + d_3)/D$
Relative price s_t	$-\{(1 + \alpha_2 + \mu) + \alpha_1\gamma(1 - T_1 - T_2)\}/D$	$-\gamma(1 - d_1)(1 - T_1 - T_2)/D$	$(1 + \alpha_2 + \mu)(1 - d_1)/D$
Price of domestic output p_t	$\{(1 - \delta)(1 - \alpha_1) + \mu + \alpha_2 - \alpha_1\gamma T_2\}/D$	$-\{d_2\delta + d_3 + \gamma T_2(1 - d_1)\}/D$	$-1/D[(d_2\delta + d_3)\alpha_1 + (1 - d_1) \times \{(1 - \delta)(1 - \alpha_1) + \mu + \alpha_2\}]$

$$D \equiv \gamma[(1 - d_1)\{(1 - \delta)(1 - \alpha_1) + \mu + \alpha_2\} + \alpha_1(d_2\delta + d_3)](1 - T_1 - T_2) + (1 + \alpha_2 + \mu)\{(d_2\delta + d_3) + \gamma T_2(1 - d_1)\} > 0$$

Foreign origin	$\omega_t + q_t$	μq_t
Real output y_t	$\gamma([(d_2\delta + d_3)\alpha_2 - d_2\{(1 - \delta)(1 - \alpha_1) + \mu + \alpha_2\}](1 - T_1) - [d_2\{\alpha_1 + \delta(1 - \alpha_1)\} + (d_2\delta + d_3)\alpha_2]T_2)/D$	$\gamma(d_2\delta + d_3)(1 - T_1 - T_2)/D$
Relative price s_t	$[\gamma\{(1 - d_1)\alpha_2 + d_2\alpha_1\}(1 - T_1 - T_2) + d_2(1 + \alpha_2 + \mu)]/D$	$\gamma(1 - d_1)(1 - T_1 - T_2)/D$
Price of domestic output p_t	$-[\{d_2(1 - \delta)(1 - \alpha_1) + d_2(\mu + \alpha_2) - (d_3 + d_2\delta)\alpha_2\} + \{(1 - d_1)\alpha_2 + d_2\alpha_1\}\gamma T_2]/D$	$\{d_2\delta + d_3 + \gamma(1 - d_1)T_2\}/D$

independent of the intervention parameter μ, which impinges through shifts in the LM curve. However, given y_t and s_t so determined, the domestic price level is determined in the domestic money market and therefore is a function of intervention.

However, if the monetary authority follows a policy of leaning with the wind and sets $\mu = -(1 + \alpha_2)$, the excess demand for nominal money balances becomes independent of the price level and depends upon only the real variables y_t and s_t. These variables become jointly determined by the IS curve together with the LM curve and are therefore independent of the degree of wage indexation, which impinges through the supply curve. Given y_t and s_t, the price level is now determined by the supply function and is therefore dependent upon the degree of wage indexation. Note that any full wage indexation policy coupled with intervention in accordance with $\mu = -(1 + \alpha_2)$ are mutually inconsistent and therefore infeasible.

The comparative static analysis with respect to various policy parameters is tedious and is not pursued. Of greater interest is the question of the optimal choice of the policy parameters μ, T_1, and T_2. The typical approach to optimal policy questions in models such as this is to specify some objective function – frequently a weighted average of the variances of income and prices – and to choose the policy parameters to minimize this objective.[10] While in principle this derivation is straightforward, in a model such as this it turns out to be complicated and not very illuminating.[11] More insight can be gained by focusing attention on the separate disturbances, taken both individually and in groups, and examining the extent to which they can be eliminated by an appropriate package of policies. We proceed to consider the domestic and foreign disturbances in turn.

In general, it is not possible to stabilize exactly for all stochastic disturbances simultaneously through indexation and/or exchange market intervention. The reason is that the number of stochastic disturbances (u_{1t}, u_{2t}, u_{3t}, ω_t, and q_t) exceeds the maximum number of contemporaneous pieces of information that may form part of the indexation of intervention rules. These include the exchange rate, the price of domestic output, the price of imported goods, and the domestic interest rate, although the latter has not been introduced into either of the rules that we are considering. Thus our problem is closely related to the early work of Gray (1976). In her analysis she introduces two stochastic disturbances a real one and a monetary one, and just one piece of contemporaneous information, the price of output, in her stabilization rule. Therefore she is also generally only able to achieve partial stabilization with respect to the two disturbances she considers. In a recent paper Karni (1983) achieves full stabilization in the Gray model by indexing wages to output as well as to price. But the fact that output quantities are typically less precisely observable than prices in the time frame envisaged by this type of analysis makes this form of indexation less appealing (see note 4).

Finally, we should note that we have restricted our analysis to only three policy parameters: μ, T_1, and T_2. Of course, it would be possible to make the money supply rule depend upon other contemporaneous variables such as the domestic interest rate and the prices of domestic and foreign goods. This in turn raises the number of policy parameters, thereby increasing the range of possible ways of stabilizing for any given set of disturbances. However, the additional insight so obtained is insufficient to compensate for the added complications, and accordingly this aspect is not pursued.

4 STABILIZATION OF DOMESTIC DISTURBANCES

Suppose first that the only stochastic disturbance is in the demand for domestic output u_{1t}. It is evident that output can be stabilized against this form of stochastic disturbance – as indeed it can against other stochastic disturbances – in an infinite number of ways. Any combination of the policy parameters T_1, T_2, and μ satisfying the condition

$$\{(1-\delta)(1-\alpha_1)+\mu+\alpha_2\}(1-T_1)+\{\alpha_1+\delta(1-\alpha_1)\}T_2=0 \tag{8.8}$$

is acceptable as long as they do not violate the condition that the Jacobian D of (8.7) is not zero.[12] If, for example, the wage rate is fully indexed to the price of domestic output alone ($T_1=1, T_2=0$), then y_t is independent of u_{1t} irrespective of the degree of intervention. Alternatively, if the wage is indexed to the extent T to the CPI ($T_1=\delta T$, $T_2=(1-\delta)T$), then the required degree of intervention is

$$\mu=-(1-\delta)(1-\alpha_1)-\alpha_2-\frac{\{\alpha_1+\delta(1-\alpha_1)\}(1-\delta)T}{1-\delta T} \tag{8.9}$$

This equation highlights the tradeoff that exists between this form of wage indexation, on the one hand, and exchange market intervention, on the other. Any degree of indexation $T \geqslant 0$ calls for an intervention policy of leaning with the wind, and the greater the degree of indexation the more intensive must this intervention be.[13]

The economic intuition for these policy responses can be seen from the basic equations (8.7) which, when only stochastic disturbances u_{1t} are present and with partial indexation to the CPI, become

$$(1-d_1)y_t-(d_2\delta+d_3)s_t=u_{1t} \tag{8.10a}$$

$$\alpha_1 y_t+\{(1-\delta)(1-\alpha_1)+\alpha_2\}s_t+(1+\alpha_2)p_t=-\mu(s_t+p_t)=-\mu e_t \tag{8.10b}$$

$$y_t=-\gamma(1-\delta)Ts_t+\gamma(1-T)p_t \tag{8.10c}$$

Suppose initially that there is no indexation and the exchange rate is perfectly flexible ($T = 0, \mu = 0$). Then a positive disturbance in u_{1t} will cause both output y_t and the price p_t of domestic output to rise, the relative price s_t will fall, and the exchange rate e_t will appreciate (see table 8.1, first part). If the monetary authority responds to the appreciating exchange rate by decreasing the money supply, more of the fluctuations generated by u_{1t} are borne by the relative price and less by y_t and p_t. In the case where the intervention follows the rule $\mu = -(1 - \delta)(1 - \alpha_1) - \alpha_2$, y_t and p_t are jointly determined by the money market and supply function which are free from stochastic fluctuations. This means that the relative price s_t is determined by the IS curve and absorbs all the fluctuations in domestic output demand. If now the wage is partially indexed ($T > 0$), then given the above intervention, the fall in s_t will be transmitted to a rise in output via the indexation rule. To avoid this, the fall in s_t must be offset by a fall in p_t and this requires the monetary contraction to be increased, i.e. the degree of intervention must be intensified.

Full indexation to the domestic CPI ($T = 1$) cannot achieve the perfect insulation of y_t. From (8.9) this would require the intervention $\mu = -(1 + \alpha_2)$ and, as already noted, this is infeasible for any full indexation scheme. However, it has been noted that the perfect insulation of both domestic output and its price can be attained by setting $T = 0$ and intervening in accordance with the rule $\mu = -(1 - \delta)(1 - \alpha_1) - \alpha_2$. Indeed, given this intervention rule, the same objective can be attained by setting $T_2 = 0$, i.e. not indexing the wage to foreign price increases, regardless of the choice of T_1. In this case all the fluctuations are absorbed by the relative price s_t. However, since none of the policy parameters impinges directly on aggregate demand, s_t is independent of them. It is therefore impossible to stabilize all three variables y_t, p_t, and s_t simultaneously, despite the fact that three policy instruments are available.[14]

In the case of the monetary disturbance u_{2t} there is no such tradeoff between intervention and indexation insofar as the stabilization of output is concerned. One of two options is possible. First, y_t can be stabilized by any full wage indexation rule $T_1 + T_2 = 1$, when s_t is also stabilized because in this case the two variables become jointly determined by the IS curve and the supply function, both of which are independent of the monetary disturbance. However, the full indexation rule renders exchange market intervention ineffective, and intervention would be required to ensure the stability of p_t. The second and superior alternative for eliminating the monetary disturbance is simply to peg the exchange rate ($\mu = \infty$). All the fluctuations in demand for money are accommodated by the supply, and y_t, p_t, and s_t are stabilized perfectly; wage indexation is unnecessary.

By contrast, complete stabilization for the supply disturbance u_{3t} is impossible. The only way that y_t and s_t can be stabilized is by the intervention rule $\mu = -(1 + \alpha_2)$, but this renders wage indexation ineffective.[15] All the stochastic disturbances originating with domestic supply are absorbed by the domestic price level. In short, wage indexation is essentially ineffective as a policy rule for the purpose of stabilizing for domestic supply disturbances.

We now shift our focus slightly and consider the extent to which domestic income can be stabilized against the three domestic disturbances u_{1t}, u_{2t}, and u_{3t} when they occur simultaneously. Clearly, perfect stabilization against all three disturbances is impossible. To stabilize for u_{3t} would require intervention $\mu = -(1 + \alpha_2)$, which renders wage indexation infeasible, and this intervention would obviously be required to stabilize for either of the other disturbances. Hence, if the policy-makers choose to stabilize for u_{3t}, then they cannot stabilize for either of the other two disturbances.

By contrast, it is possible to stabilize y_t for the two demand disturbances u_{1t} and u_{2t} simultaneously, and indeed this can be done in two ways. One possibility is to index the wage fully to only the domestic price ($T_1 = 1$, $T_2 = 0$), allowing the degree of exchange market intervention to be arbitrary; another is to peg the exchange rate and fully index the wage to the price of domestic output ($\mu = \infty$, $T_1 = 1$), allowing the degree of indexation to the foreign price level to be arbitrary.

To pursue this issue a little further, suppose that the only disturbances are on the domestic demand side, namely u_{1t} and u_{2t}, and that the primary objective is to stabilize output exactly; given that that goal is achieved, a secondary objective is to minimize the variance of the price p_t of domestic output. If we assume that the stabilization of output is attained by the indexation scheme $T_1 = 1$, $T_2 = 0$, then the solution for p_t is

$$p_t = \frac{\{(1-\delta)(1-\alpha_1) + \mu + \alpha_2\}u_{1t} - (d_2\delta + d_3)u_{2t}}{(1 + \alpha_2 + \mu)(d_2\delta + d_3)}$$

If we assume for simplicity that the two disturbances u_{1t} and u_{2t} are uncorrelated, then

$$\sigma_p^2 = \frac{\{(1-\delta)(1-\alpha_1) + \mu + \alpha_2\}^2\sigma_1^2 + (d_2\delta + d_3)^2\sigma_2^2}{(1 + \alpha_2 + \mu)^2(d_2\delta + d_3)^2} \qquad (8.11)$$

Given that output is fully stabilized by fully indexing the wage to the domestic price, the optimal degree of exchange market intervention is obtained by minimizing (8.11) with respect to μ, yielding the optimal policy

$$\mu = -\{(1-\delta)(1-\alpha_1) + \alpha_2\} + \frac{(d_2\delta + d_3)^2}{\{\delta(1-\alpha_1) + \alpha_1\}^2}\,\frac{\sigma_2^2}{\sigma_1^2}$$

Thus the optimal degree of exchange market intervention from the viewpoint of price stability as a secondary objective depends in part upon the relative variances of the two domestic disturbances. As polar cases, if $\sigma_2^2 = 0$ (i.e. there are only real demand disturbances), the optimal policy is to lean with the wind in accordance with $\mu = -\{(1-\delta)(1-\alpha_1)+\alpha_2\}$, while if $\sigma_1^2 = 0$ (i.e. there are only monetary disturbances), the optimum is to peg the exchange rate. Between these two extremes the optimal intervention will involve leaning against the wind or leaning with the wind, depending in part upon the relative magnitudes of the two variances.

Finally, it should be noted that the ability of either intervention policy or indexation policy to stabilize at least one endogenous variable perfectly for any single disturbance is a consequence of the following general characteristic. The current observation of certain market variables implies information as to the sources of the random shocks in the economy. For example, eliminating y_t, p_t, and s_t from (8.7) and noting that $m_t = -\mu e_t$ yields a linear relationship between m_t and e_t of the form

$$m_t = \psi e_t + \xi_t$$

where ψ is a function of the known coefficients of the model and ξ_t is a linear function of the unknown stochastic disturbances. The fact that m_t and e_t are observable to the monetary authority, who are also assumed to know ψ, means that they also observe the linear combination of random variables contained in ξ_t. When only one random variable is present, it follows that the observability of this linear combination reduces to the observability of the random variable itself. This may be appropriately offset, thereby maintaining perfect stability of at least one of the endogenous variables of the system.[16] A similar argument applies in the case of the information assumed in the implementation of the indexation policy.

5 STABILIZATION OF FOREIGN DISTURBANCES

We now turn our attention to the foreign disturbances that impinge on the domestic economy through q_t and ω_t. Initially, we will treat both of them separately although, as noted earlier, they are in fact jointly determined, reflecting more fundamental disturbances occurring abroad.

Domestic output can be stabilized against foreign price disturbances q_t in a number of ways, the most direct being by fully indexing the wage rate to only the price of domestic output ($T_1 = 1$, $T_2 = 0$).[17] This rule means that producers face a fixed real wage, and in the absence of domestic supply disturbances, output is thereby fixed. Having indexed in this way, the domestic price level can then be stabilized for foreign price fluctuations by adopting the exchange market intervention policy

$$\mu = \frac{d_2(1-\delta)(1-\alpha_1+\alpha_2) - \alpha_2 d_3}{d_3 - d_2(1-\delta)} \tag{8.12}$$

This may involve leaning against the wind or leaning with the wind, depending upon parameter values. The intuition underlying this response can be seen from the basic equation (8.7), which with this full wage indexation scheme reduces to

$$(d_2\delta + d_3)s_t = d_2 q_t \tag{8.13a}$$

$$(1-\delta)(1-\alpha_1)s_t + \alpha_2 e_t + p_t = -\mu e_t = m_t \tag{8.13b}$$

An increase in q_t leads to an increase in the relative price s_t and an appreciation of the exchange rate e_t. Given that expectations are static, the appreciation in the exchange rate is equivalent to an increase in the domestic interest rate. The rise in the relative price s_t leads to an increase in the demand for money, whereas the rise in the interest rate leads to a decrease. If the positive relative price effect dominates, then in order to stabilize the price level (i.e. prevent it from sharing some of the random fluctuations) the monetary authority should accommodate to the increase in the demand for money by increasing the supply. With the exchange rate appreciating, such a policy is one of leaning against the wind. Conversely, if the negative interest rate effects dominate, then the net fall in the demand for money should be met with a net reduction, i.e. a policy of leaning with the wind.

The response required to eliminate fluctuations in the foreign interest rate ω_t is similar. Output can again be stabilized by the full indexation rule $T_1 = 1$, $T_2 = 0$, while given this form of intervention the price of domestic output can be stabilized by the intervention rule

$$\mu = \frac{\alpha_2 d_3 - d_2(1-\delta)(1-\alpha_1+\alpha_2)}{d_2}$$

The explanations are virtually identical with those just given for the foreign price disturbance and can be omitted.

In general, q_t and ω_t are jointly stochastic. Irrespective of their source of variation abroad, and therefore their degree of correlation, domestic output can continue to be perfectly stabilized by fully indexing the wage to the price of domestic output ($T_1 = 1$, $T_2 = 0$). With output stabilized in this way, the solution for p_t is

$$p_t = \frac{-\{a + d_2(\mu + \alpha_2)\}(\omega_t + q_t) + (d_2\delta + d_3)\mu q_t}{(1 + \alpha_2 + \mu)(d_2\delta + d_3)}$$

where $a \equiv d_2(1-\delta)(1-\alpha_1) - \alpha_2(d_3 + d_2\delta)$. Suppose now that, as a secondary objective, the monetary authority chooses to intervene so as to minimize $\sigma_p{}^2$. If we let $z_t \equiv \omega_t + q_t$, the optimum degree of intervention is given by

$$\mu = [(a + d_2\alpha_2\}\{(1 + \alpha_2)(d_2\delta + d_3)\sigma_{qz} - (d_2 - a)\sigma_z^{\,2}\}] \times \{d_2(d_2 - a)\sigma_z^{\,2} + (d_3 + d_2\delta)^2(1 + \alpha_2)\sigma_q^{\,2} + (d_3 + d_2\delta)(a - 2d_2 - d_2\alpha_2)\sigma_{qz}\}^{-1} \tag{8.14}$$

where

$$\sigma_z^{\,2} = \sigma_\omega^{\,2} + \sigma_q^{\,2} + 2\sigma_{\omega q}; \qquad \sigma_{qz}^{\,2} = \sigma_q^{\,2} + \sigma_{\omega q}$$

The optimal degree of indexation therefore depends not only upon the variances $\sigma_\omega^{\,2}$ and $\sigma_q^{\,2}$, but also upon the covariance $\sigma_{\omega q}$, which in turn reflects the source of the disturbances abroad. A special case of interest arises if (a) the only foreign stochastic disturbances are monetary and (b) the foreign wage rate is fully indexed to the foreign price level. In that case it can be shown that

$$z_t \equiv \omega_t + q_t = 0$$

and the optimal policy is therefore to set $\mu = 0$, i.e. allow the exchange rate to float.[18] Indeed, in this circumstance a perfectly flexible rate will stabilize both domestic output and the price of domestic output, irrespective of the degree of wage indexation domestically (see also Marston, 1982).

6 CONCLUSIONS

The analysis presented in this chapter has stressed the interdependence between wage indexation, on the one hand, and exchange market intervention, on the other, as tools of macroeconomic stabilization policy in a small open economy subject to stochastic disturbances. We have shown how the choice of either policy instrument impinges on the effectiveness of the other. In particular, if the domestic money wage is fully indexed to some weighted average of the domestic and foreign price levels, then irrespective of what that chosen weight may be, exchange market intervention is rendered totally ineffective insofar as the stabilization of the real part of the domestic economy is concerned. Likewise, if the monetary authority intervenes in the exchange market so as to accommodate exactly for nominal movements in the demand for money, thereby rendering the excess demand for money dependent upon only real variables, then any form of wage indexation is totally ineffective for the stabilization of the real part of the system. In either polar case the respective instrument can stabilize the domestic price level.

The following more specific conclusions have been obtained for the stabilization of domestic and foreign disturbances.

1 There are an infinite number of combinations of wage indexation and

exchange market intervention that will fully stabilize domestic output against domestic demand disturbances. Of these the most satisfactory is to index the wage fully to (and only to) the price of domestic output. Exchange market intervention can then stabilize the price of domestic output, so that in fact the nominal and real wages are fixed.

2 Domestic output can be stabilized against domestic monetary disturbances either by fully indexing the wage to the price of domestic output or by pegging the exchange rate. Of these alternatives the latter is optimal, since it will stabilize all other variables including the price of domestic output.

3 The stabilization for domestic supply disturbances is more difficult. Since wage indexation becomes totally ineffective, stabilization must be achieved through exchange market intervention, which can stabilize either domestic output or the domestic price level, but not both.

4 Domestic output can be stabilized for either foreign interest rate disturbances or foreign price disturbances separately by a combination of intervention and indexation policies. It can be stabilized for both disturbances simultaneously by fully indexing the wage rate to the price of domestic output. The domestic price can then be stabilized by exchange market intervention, the degree of which will depend upon the nature of the shock.

While limitations imposed by considerations of analytical tractability have precluded the derivation of a complete optimal stabilization package, these results are suggestive of an intuitively appealing policy assignment rule. With the exception of domestic supply disturbances, they suggest that indexation policy should be directed towards the stabilization of output, while exchange market intervention should be directed towards the attainment of price stability.

APPENDIX DERIVATION OF EQUATIONS (8.7a)–(8.7c)

We begin by substituting from (8.1b), (8.1d), (8.1g), and (8.1h) to eliminate r_t, C_t, W_t, and $W^c_{t,t-1}$. This yields the following four equations in the remaining variables Y_t, E_t, P_t, and M_t and their relevant expectations:

$$(1-d_1)Y_t = -d_2[\Omega_t + \delta\{(E^*_{t+1,t} - E_t) - (P^*_{t+1,t} - P_t)\} \\ -(1-\delta)(Q^*_{t+1,t} - Q_t)] + d_3(Q_t - E_t - P_t) + u_{1t} \quad \text{(8A.1a)}$$

$$Y_t = \frac{\beta(a + b\ln\beta) + \beta b(1-\delta)(P^*_{t,t-1} - Q^*_{t,t-1} - E^*_{t,t-1})}{1 + b(1-\beta)} \\ + \frac{\beta}{1-\beta}(1 - T_1)(P_t - P^*_{t,t+1})$$

$$- \frac{\beta}{1 - \beta} T_2(Q_t + E_t - Q^*_{t,t-1} - E^*_{t,t-1}) + u_{3t} \quad \text{(8A.1b)}$$

$$M_t = \alpha_1 Y_t + \{\delta + \alpha_1(1 - \delta)\}P_t + (1 - \alpha_1)(1 - \delta)(Q_t + E_t)$$
$$-\alpha_2(\Omega_t + E^*_{t+1,t} - E_t) + u_{2t} \quad \text{(8A.1c)}$$

$$M_t - \bar{M} = -\mu(E_t - \bar{E}) \quad \text{(8A.1d)}$$

We now define an initial equilibrium (denoted by bars) by assuming that all expectations are realized and setting all random variables at their means:

$$(1 - d_1)\bar{Y} = -d_2\bar{\Omega} + d_3(\bar{Q} + \bar{E} - \bar{P}) \quad \text{(8A.2a)}$$

$$\bar{Y} = \frac{\beta(a + b \ln \beta) + \beta b(1 - \delta)(\bar{P} - \bar{Q} - \bar{E})}{1 + b(1 - \beta)} \quad \text{(8A.2b)}$$

$$\bar{M} = \alpha_1 \bar{Y} + \{\delta + \alpha_1(1 - \delta)\}\bar{P} + (1 - \alpha_1)(1 - \delta)(\bar{Q} + \bar{E}) - \alpha_2\bar{\Omega} \quad \text{(8A.2c)}$$

Subtracting (8A.2) from (8A.1) and using the definition

$$s_t \equiv q_t + e_t - p_t$$

together with the corresponding relationship in terms of expectations

$$s^*_{t+1,t} = q^*_{t+1,t} + e^*_{t+1,t} - p^*_{t+1,t}$$

yields

$$(1 - d_1)y_t = -d_2\delta(s^*_{t+1,t} - s_t) + d_3 s_t + u_{1t} - d_2(q_t + \omega_t) \quad \text{(8A.3a)}$$

$$y_t = -\frac{b\beta(1 - \delta)}{1 + b(1 - \beta)} s^*_{t,t-1} + \gamma(1 - T_1 - T_2)(p_t - p^*_{t,t-1})$$
$$- \gamma T_2(s_t - s^*_{t,t-1}) + u_{3t} \quad \text{(8A.3b)}$$

$$m_t = \alpha_1 y_t + (1 + \alpha_2)p_t + \{(1 - \alpha_1)(1 - \delta) + \alpha_2\}s_t$$
$$- \alpha_2(s^*_{t+1,t} + p^*_{t+1,t}) + u_{2t} - \alpha_2(q_t + \omega_t) \quad \text{(8A.3c)}$$

$$m_t = -\mu(s_t + p_t - q_t) \quad (= -\mu e_t) \quad \text{(8A.3d)}$$

Equations (8.7a)–(8.7c) of the text are obtained by setting all expectations to zero (the rational expectations solution) and substituting for the intervention rule (8A.3d).

NOTES

1 This literature in turn is an extension of the familiar closed economy model developed by Gray (1976) and Fischer (1977).

2 For a brief discussion see Marston (1982), who cites various countries where such proposals have been considered.

3 For expositional convenience we assume that the income elasticity α_1 of the demand for money is less than unity.

4 In discussing intervention policy it is important to distinguish between those variables that the authority can in effect currently observe and those that are unobservable, at least in the short run. Given that data on exchange rates and the money supply are available with much greater frequency than income figures, we will assume that E_t and M_t are observable and that Y_t is unobservable (at time t). This is one of the reasons why in general policy-makers cannot perfectly stabilize output. The period of time for which this assumption is most applicable would be something like a month, since income is usually observed only quarterly, and weekly money figures have considerable noise.

5 The wage indexation scheme assumes that the relevant prices are observable, at least to the indexation authority, within the time period of observation.

6 Although q_t and ω_t are exogenous to the small country, they themselves are endogenously determined in the rest of the world, reflecting the various stochastic influences occurring abroad. It is thus evident that these variables will almost certainly be correlated, with the sign of the correlation depending upon the sources of the disturbances abroad (see Turnovsky, 1983, this volume, ch. 7).

7 This procedure of picking the stable root is typical of rational expectations models and is often justified on the grounds that the instability that would otherwise occur would be inconsistent with observed behavior. Alternatively, it is sometimes justified more formally by appealing to transversality conditions from appropriate optimizing models, which, provided that the underlying utility function satisfies suitable restrictions, ensure that the expected price movements remain bounded (see for example Brock, 1974).

8 This result is proved by Turnovsky (1983, this volume, ch. 7).

9 The fact that shocks in the foreign nominal price level and foreign interest rate impinge identically on the domestic economy under a flexible exchange rate is of some interest. It operates through the domestic interest rate and stems from the fact that, given the stationarity of exchange rate expectations, the interest rate parity condition simplifies to $r_t = \omega_t - e_t = (\omega_t + q_t) - (s_t + p_t)$.

10 Implicit in much of our discussion is the minimization of the variance of output as being the prime policy objective. Some authors (e.g. Marston, 1984) treat the minimization of the deviations from output which would result in the absence of contact lags as being the policy objective. There is also a new developing literature that models fluctuations as an equilibrium process derived from utility-maximizing behavior. Such fluctuations should not be confused with the welfare-reducing deviations from some ideal path. See, for example, Long and Plosser (1983) for further discussion of these issues.

11 For an analysis that follows this approach see Turnovsky (1983, this volume, ch. 7). The model considered is simpler than the present one in that it assumes perfect goods mobility (purchasing power parity). Even for that simple model the general expression for the optimal intervention turns out to

be extremely complicated.

12 The expression for D is given in table 8.1. We will assume $D > 0$.

13 Most the policy discussions related to exchange market intervention are restricted to leaning against the wind, which intuitively would seem more appealing. The intuition behind why leaning with the wind may be appropriate for certain disturbances has been discussed elsewhere (see Turnovsky, 1983, this volume, ch. 7). The case of leaning with the wind is also discussed in a somewhat different type of model by Buiter and Eaton (1985).

14 Note that if the policy objective is to stabilize the price of domestic output and the monetary authority chooses not to intervene in the exchange market, the optimal indexation policy is to set

$$T_2 = \{(1 - \delta)(1 - \alpha_1) + \alpha_2\}/\alpha_1\gamma$$

i.e. the wage must be indexed to the foreign price level. Moreover, the optimal degree of indexation in this circumstance may exceed unity.

15 For expositional convenience we assume that the income elasticity α_1 of the demand for money is less than unity.

16 For some disturbances p_t and y_t move proportionately. In this case both can be stabilized simultaneously by the appropriate choice of a single policy instrument.

17 It can be shown that, as for domestic disturbances, with full indexation to the domestic CPI, it becomes impossible to stabilize domestic output perfectly in the face of either foreign price or foreign interest rate disturbances. The reason is the familiar one. To achieve stability would require intervention $\mu = -(1 + \alpha_2)$, which is infeasible given full wage indexation.

18 This result is proved by Turnovsky (1983, this volume, ch. 7).

REFERENCES

Boyer, R. (1978) Optimal foreign exchange market intervention. *Journal of Political Economy,* 86, 1045–56.

Brock, W. A. (1974) Money and growth: the case of long-run perfect foresight. *International Economic Review,* 15, 750–77.

Buiter, W. (1979) Optimal foreign exchange market intervention with rational expectations. In *Trade and Payments Adjustment under Flexible Exchange Rates* (eds J. Martin and A. Smith). London: Macmillan.

—— and Eaton, J. (1985) Policy decentralization and exchange rate management in interdependent economies. In *Exchange Rate Management under Uncertainty* (ed. J. S. Bhanderi). Cambridge MA: MIT Press.

Cox, W. M. (1980) Unanticipated money, output, and prices in the small economy. *Journal of Monetary Economics* 6, 359–84.

Fischer, S. (1977) Wage indexation and macro-economic stability. In *Stabilization of the Domestic and International Economy* (eds K. Brunner and A. Meltzer). Amsterdam: North-Holland.

Flood, R. P. and Marion, N. P. (1982) The transmission of disturbances under alternative exchange rate regimes with optimal indexing. *Quarterly Journal of Economics*, 97, 43–66.

Gray, J. A. (1976) Wage indexation: a macro-economic approach. *Journal of Monetary Economics*, 2, 221–35.

Henderson, D. W. (1979) Financial policies in open economies. *American Economic Review, Papers and Proceedings*, 69, 232–39.

Karni, E. (1983) On optimal wage indexation. *Journal of Political Economy*, 91, 282–92.

Long, J. B. and Plosser, C. I. (1983) Real business cycles. *Journal of Political Economy*, 91, 39–69.

Marston, R. C. (1982) Wages, relative prices, and the choice between fixed and flexible exchange rates. *Canadian Journal of Economics*, 15, 87–103.

—— (1984) Real wages and the terms of trade: alternative indexation rules for an open economy, *Journal of Money, Credit, and Banking,* 16, 285–301.

Roper, D. E. and Turnovsky, S. J. (1980) Optimal exchange market intervention in a simple stochastic macro model. *Canadian Journal of Economics,* 13, 296–309.

Turnovsky, S. J. (1981) Monetary policy and foreign price disturbances under flexible exchange rates. *Journal of Money, Credit, and Banking* 13, 156–76. Reprinted in this volume as chapter 5.

—— (1983) Exchange market intervention policies in a small open economy. In *Economic Interdependence and Flexible Exchange Rates* (eds J. Bhandari and B. Putnam). Cambridge, MA: MIT Press. Reprinted in this volume as chapter 7.

9 Optimal Monetary Policy and Wage Indexation under Alternative Disturbances and Information Structures

1 INTRODUCTION

Recent research in international macroeconomics has emphasized the interdependence between the degree of wage indexation and the choice of exchange rate regime from the viewpoint of optimal stabilization policy. Authors such as Flood and Marion (1982) and Marston (1982) have shown how (a) the choice between fixed and flexible exchange rate systems depends upon the degree of wage indexation, and (b) the choice of the optimal degree of wage indexation depends upon the exchange rate regime.[1]

More recently, Turnovsky (1983, this volume, ch. 8) and Aizenman and Frenkel (1985) have begun to take a more integrated approach to the question of the optimal stabilization of an open economy by analysing general rules for wage indexation and monetary policy. These authors focus on the tradeoffs between these as stabilization instruments, and their approach is directed at the design of overall integrated stabilization policy packages. Taking monetary policy to be in the form of exchange market intervention, Turnovsky showed how the degree of intervention impinges on the effectiveness of wage indexation, and vice versa. Full indexation of wages to prices renders exchange market intervention ineffective in stabilizing output. At the same time, intervention, resulting in an accommodation of the domestic money supply

Originally published in *Journal of Money, Credit and Banking*, 19, (2), May 1987, 157–80.

The constructive suggestions of two referees are gratefully acknowledged.

precisely equal to the change in the demand for money due to movements in the exchange rate, makes wage indexation become totally ineffective.[2] Aizenman and Frenkel consider the joint determination of optimal indexation and optimal monetary policy among more general forms of monetary policy rules. Their analysis stresses the relationship between the number of independent pieces of information regarding the sources of stochastic disturbances impinging on the economy and the number of independent policy parameters.

The optimal policy literature deals almost exclusively with stabilizing white noise disturbances, i.e. the stochastic shocks impinging on the economy are unanticipated, transitory, and independently distributed over time.[3] In practice, the distinction between permanent and transitory disturbances, on the one hand, and anticipated and unanticipated disturbances, on the other, is extremely important. Different types of disturbances are reflected differently in the economy and require different policy responses. Some of these have been considered for monetary rules by Turnovsky (1984).

In this chapter we address the interdependence between optimal monetary policy and optimal wage indexation in which the exogenous disturbances may be of a quite general type. The situation we envisage is an economy in which one-period wage contracts are signed in each period. These contracts introduce rigidities into the economy, and the purpose of the monetary and wage indexation rules is to attempt to eliminate these rigidities and to replicate the behavior of a frictionless economy.

We assume that there are two types of random disturbances impinging on the economy. An important element in our analysis concerns the availability of information on these variables. First, there are price and financial variables, information on which is available to all agents instantaneously. Secondly, there are real and monetary shocks, which may or may not be observed contemporaneously. Indeed, we will show how both of the optimal rules and, in some cases, the ability to replicate the frictionless economy depend critically upon the availability of information to agents in the economy.

2 THE FRAMEWORK

In this section we outline the analytical framework. To minimize details, a simple model will be employed. We consider a small open economy which produces and consumes a single traded good. We also assume a single traded bond, with the domestic bond market being perfectly integrated with that in the rest of the world. Thus purchasing power parity (PPP) and uncovered interest parity (UIP) are assumed to hold.

2.1 Availability of information

A key feature of our analysis concerns the availability of information. Our characterization of this is illustrated in figure 9.1, considered from the viewpoint of time t, which we partition into the infinitesimally short subperiod $(t, t+)$.

At time $t-1$, a contract is signed for the wage at time t, which is determined on the basis of expectations formed at time $t-1$. Prices and financial variables are assumed to be observed instantaneously by all agents, so that everyone has complete current information on these variables when they make their respective decisions. More specifically, these instantaneously observed variables include (a) the domestic and foreign interest rates, (b) the exchange rate, and (c) the domestic price level. Given PPP, (b) and (c) imply the observability of the foreign price level as well.

At time t, two sets of decisions are made. First, there are policy decisions, i.e. the implementation of the wage indexation and monetary policy rules. Here we assume, largely for expositional simplicity, that wage indexation is conducted by a public authority, as indeed is the case

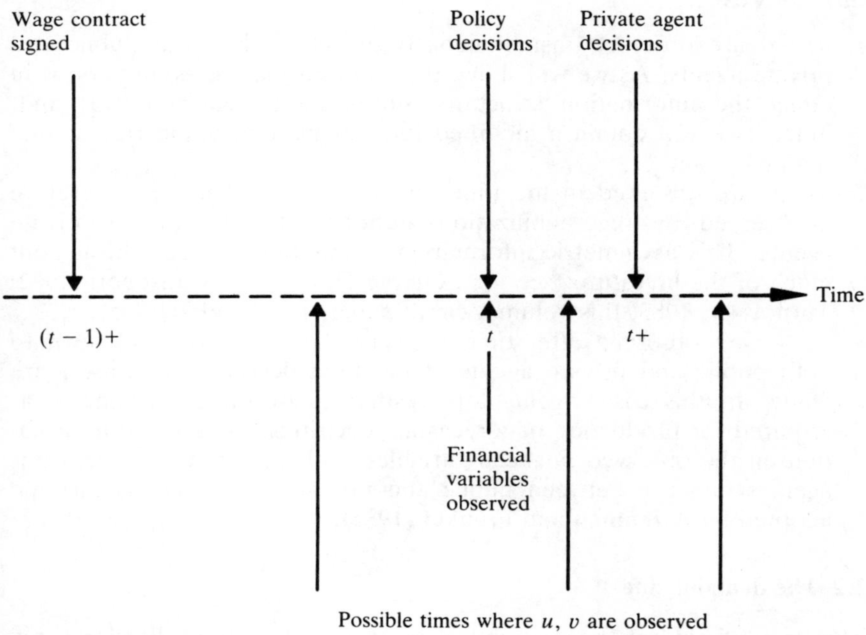

Figure 9.1 Timing of information and decisions.

in countries such as Israel and Australia. This has the advantage of enabling us to identify all stabilization activities as being conducted by a public authority. Secondly, there are the decisions of the private agents in the economy, which include the production, portfolio, and consumption decisions, as well as the formation of forecasts for the next period. We assume that these two sets of decisons are made in the above order, at instances we denote by t, $t+$ respectively. This means that the actual indexed wage, which is determined at time t, is known by the time that the production is made at the next instant of time $t+$.

This distinction in effect differentiates the information available to the public and private agents in the economy. It is possible to make further distinctions among the various private agents along the lines of Canzoneri et al. (1983). For example, we can allow investors, who form predictions of the future exchange rate, to have different information from individuals concerned with predicting prices in the determination of the wage contract whose information, in turn, may differ from that of producers. We do not pursue these refinements here.

The key informational issue concerns the observability of the domestic monetary disturbance, u_t say, and the domestic productivity disturbance, v_t say. Under our assumptions, three different informational situations exist.

1. u_t, v_t are observed instantaneously at time t by both public and private agents. As we will show, this full information assumption is in effect the information structure considered by Karni (1983) and, indeed we will obtain a modified form of his indexation rule as one optimal policy.[4]
2. u_t, v_t are observed in the time interval $(t, t+)$. They are therefore unobserved by the stabilization authority, but known to private agents. This asymmetric information assumption is made throughout much of the literature (see for example Gray, 1976; Canzoneri, 1982; Turnovsky, 1983, this volume, ch. 8; papers in Bhandari 1985).
3. u_t, v_t are observed after time $t+$. They are therefore unknown to both public and private agents at the time decisions for time t are made. In this case, agents form estimates of u_t, v_t at time t, as required for production of forecasting decisions, by utilizing information on the observed financial variables. This information structure is again symmetric between public and private agents and is the one adopted by Aizenman and Frenkel (1985).

2.2 The demand side

The demand side of the economy is summarized by the following three equations:

$$P_t = Q_t + E_t \tag{9.1}$$

$$R_t = \Omega_t + E^*_{t+1,t} - E_t \tag{9.2}$$

$$M_t - P_t = \alpha_1 Y_t - \alpha_2 R_t + u_t, \tag{9.3}$$

where P_t is the price of domestic output, expressed in logarithms, Q_t is the price of foreign output, expressed in logarithms, E_t is the exchange rate, expressed in logarithms, $E^*_{t+1,t}$ is the forecast of E_{t+1}, formed at time t, Ω_t is the foreign nominal interest rate, Y_t is the domestic output, expressed in logarithms, and u_t is the stochastic disturbance in the demand of money. These equations are standard: equation (9.1) describes PPP, equation (9.2) specifies UIP, and equation (9.3) describes equilibrium in the domestic monetary sector.

2.3 The supply side

The supply function is based on the one-period wage contract model. We assume that the contract wage for time t is determined at time $t - 1$ such that, given expectations of firms and workers, the labor market is expected to clear. The information set upon which that contract is based includes all financial and price variables up to and including time $t - 1$, i.e. all past stochastic disturbances. It may, or may not, include actual disturbances occurring at that time. In terms of our timing scheme, the contract for time t is signed at time $(t - 1)+$.

The expected supply of labor at the contract wage is

$$N^{\mathrm{s}}_{t,t-1} = n(W^{\mathrm{c}}_{t,t-1} - P^*_{t,t-1}) \qquad n > 0 \tag{9.4}$$

where $N^{\mathrm{s}}_{t,t-1}$ is the expected supply of labor formed at time $t - 1$, for time t, expressed in logarithms, $W^{\mathrm{c}}_{t,t-1}$ is the contract wage determined at time $t - 1$ for time t, expressed in logarithms, and $P^*_{t,t-1}$ is the forecast of P_t formed at time $t - 1$.

Output is produced by means of a Cobb–Douglas production function

$$Y_t = (1 - \theta)N_t + v_t \qquad 0 < \theta < 1 \tag{9.5}$$

where N_t is the employment of labor, expressed in logarithms, and v_t is the stochastic disturbance in productivity. The expected demand for labor $N^{\mathrm{d}}_{t,t-1}$ (based on expected profit maximization) is determined by the marginal productivity condition

$$\ln(1 - \theta) - \theta N^{\mathrm{d}}_{t,t-1} + v^*_{t,t-1} = W^{\mathrm{c}}_{t,t-1} - P^*_{t,t-1} \tag{9.6}$$

The contract wage is determined by equating the expected demand and supply of labor in (9.1) and (9.5), yielding

$$W^{\mathrm{c}}_{t,t-1} = P^*_{t,t-1} + \frac{\ln(1 - \theta)}{1 + n\theta} + \frac{v^*_{t,t-1}}{1 + n\theta} \tag{9.7}$$

The contract wage therefore depends upon the expected productivity disturbance as well as the expected price level.

Actual employment is assumed to be determined by the short-term marginal productivity condition after the actual wage and price are known. This is expressed by

$$\ln(1-\theta) - \theta N_t + E_t(v_t) = W_t - P_t \tag{9.8}$$

Note that we have introduced the instantaneous forecast of the productivity disturbance, denoted by $E_t(v_t)$ into the optimality condition (9.8). This allows for the possibility that firms do not observe this disturbance instantaneously.[5] If it is observed, then $E_t(v_t) = v_t$; otherwise, they must infer it from available information on current observable variables, using a forecasting technique we discuss below. Combining (9.5) and (9.8), we obtain current output as

$$Y_t = \frac{1-\theta}{\theta}\ln(1-\theta) + \frac{1-\theta}{\theta}(P_t - W_t) + \frac{1-\theta}{\theta}E_t(v_t) + v_t \tag{9.9}$$

which depends upon both the firm's estimate of v_t and v_t itself. In the event that v_t is observed, (9.9) simplifies to

$$Y_t = \frac{1-\theta}{\theta}\ln(1-\theta) + \frac{1-\theta}{\theta}(P_t - W_t) + \frac{v_t}{\theta} \tag{9.9'}$$

2.4 Wage indexation

In the situation that the productivity disturbance is observed instantaneously, the optimal form of the wage indexation rule will immediately become apparent; it will be discussed later. Otherwise, we assume that wages are indexed in accordance with the simple rule

$$W_t = W^c_{t,t-1} + \tau(P_t - P^*_{t,t-1}) \tag{9.10}$$

where τ is the indexation parameter to be determined. Combining (9.10) and (9.7) with (9.9) or (9.9′) yields the following alternative forms of supply functions, which correspond to the observability (or otherwise) of the productivity disturbance:

$$Y_t = \frac{(1-\theta)n\ln(1-\theta)}{1+n\theta} + (1-\tau)\frac{1-\theta}{\theta}(P_t - P^*_{t,t-1}) + \frac{1-\theta}{\theta}\left(E_t(v_t) - \frac{v^*_{t,t-1}}{1+n\theta}\right) + v_t \tag{9.11}$$

$$Y_t = \frac{(1-\theta)n\ln(1-\theta)}{1+n\theta} + (1-\tau)\frac{1-\theta}{\theta}(P_t - P^*_{t,t-1}) + \frac{v_t}{\theta} - \frac{1-\theta}{\theta}\frac{v^*_{t,t-1}}{1+n\theta} \tag{9.11'}$$

2.5 Monetary policy rule

In the case that the monetary authorities observe all disturbances instantaneously, the optimal rule becomes self-evident. Otherwise, we assume that the monetary authorities adjust the money supply in accordance with observed movements in the financial and price variables:

$$M_t = \nu_1 E_t + \nu_2 R_t + \nu_3 \Omega_1 + \nu_4 P_t \tag{9.12}$$

Using the PPP condition (9.1) and the UIP condition (9.2), we can express this equation in the form

$$M_t = \mu_1 E_t + \mu_2 E^*_{t+1,t} + \mu_3 \Omega_t + \mu_4 Q_t \tag{9.12'}$$

where $\mu_1 = \nu_1 - \nu_2 + \nu_4$, $\mu_2 = \nu_2$, $\mu_3 = \nu_2 + \nu_3$, and $\mu_4 = \nu_4$.

Note that the money supply is assumed to be adjusted to a wider range of pieces of information than are wages. This reflects the prevailing practice of restricting wage indexation to price movements. If, in addition, wages are assumed to be indexed to the foreign price level, nothing additional is gained as long as the money supply is adjusted to the foreign price level as well. There is a tradeoff between μ_4 and the corresponding coefficient in the wage indexation rule.

We will argue below that wage indexation is inessential. The optimum that we achieve can always be obtained by monetary policy alone. In some cases, it can also be achieved by a comprehensively based wage indexation scheme. However, this is not always so. In one important case, monetary policy is always required to achieve the optimal degree of stability.

2.6 The frictionless economy

Wage contracts introduce rigidities into the economy, leading to welfare losses relative to frictionless economy in which wages are fully flexible. The purpose of stabilization policy is to attempt to "undo" these, thereby replicating as closely as possible the output of a frictionless economy and minimizing these resulting welfare losses. It is well known that the supply of output in such an economy is given by

$$Y^{\mathrm{f}}_t = \frac{n(1-\theta)}{1+n\theta}\ln(1-\theta) + \frac{n(1-\theta)}{1+n\theta)} E_t(v_t) + v_t \tag{9.13}$$

In the case that firms observe v_t instantaneously, (9.13) reduces to

$$Y^{\mathrm{f}}_t = \frac{n(1-\theta)}{1+n\theta}\ln(1-\theta) + \frac{1+n}{1+n\theta} v_t \tag{9.13'}$$

The output level of the frictionless economy thus serves as a benchmark, with the stabailization objective being to minimize the variance of Y_t about Y^{f}_t.[6]

2.7 The complete model

The above components can now be combined to yield the following summary of the economy. It is expressed in the form of deviation about an initial equilibrium, and these deviations are denoted by lower-case letters. Thus we obtain

$$p_t = q_t + e_t \tag{9.14a}$$

$$m_t - p_t = \alpha_1 y_t - \alpha_2(\omega_t + e^*_{t+1,t} - e_t) + u_t \tag{9.14b}$$

$$m_t = \mu_1 e_t + \mu_2 e^*_{t+1,t} + \mu_3 \omega_t + \mu_4 q_t \tag{9.14c}$$

$$y_t = \frac{1-\theta}{\theta}\left[(1-\tau)\{(e_t - e^*_{t,t-1}) + (q_t - q^*_{t,t-1})\} + E_t(v_t) - \frac{v^*_{t,t-1}}{1+n\theta}\right] + v_t \tag{9.14d}$$

$$y^{\mathrm{f}}_t = \frac{n(1-\theta)}{1+n\theta}E_t(v_t) + v_t \tag{9.14e}$$

All expectations are assumed to be rational:

$$x^*_{s,t} = E_t(x_s) \qquad s > t$$

where E_t is the expectations operator, conditional on information available at time t. Note that in the case that v_t is observed instantaneously to private agents, $E_t(v_t) = v_t$, and (9.14d) and (9.14e) are amended appropriately. Also, in writing the supply function as in (9.14d), the one-period conditional expectation of (9.14a) has been taken and substituted. Finally, we should emphasize that our notation $(t, t+)$ introduced above is to parameterize the information sets available to the agents in the economy. All variables in the infinitesimal time interval $(t, t+)$ are determined simultaneously.

3 GENERAL SOLUTION

The reduced-form system (9.14) is a standard rational expectations macromodel. The solution procedures are familiar, enabling our description to be brief.

First, we consider the observability of the stochastic disturbances implied by the observability of the financial variables and prices. With m_t being adjusted in accordance with a known rule in response to observed variables, $m_t - p_t$ is observed at time t. Substituting for output from (9.14d) into (9.14b), we have

$$m_t - p_t = \alpha_1 \frac{1-\theta}{\theta}\left\{(1-\tau)\{(e_t - e^*_{t,t-1}) + (q_t - q^*_{t,t-1})\} + E_t(v_t) - \frac{v^*_{t,t-1}}{1+n\theta}\right\} - \alpha_2 r_t + (u_t + \alpha_1 v_t) \tag{9.15}$$

The quantities e_t, $e^*_{t,t-1}$, q_t, $q^*_{t,t-1}$, $E_t(v_t)$, $v^*_{t,t-1}$, and r_t are all observed at time t, enabling us to deduce the values of the composite disturbance $(u_t + \alpha_1 v_t)$. Thus if we assume that u_t, v_t are uncorrelated, the optimal estimates of u_t, v_t obtained from the observed composite disturbance are given by the least-squares predictors

$$E_t(u_t) = \frac{\sigma_u^2}{\sigma_u^2 + \alpha_1^2\sigma_v^2}(u_t + \alpha_1 v_t) \tag{9.16a}$$

$$E_t(v_t) = \frac{\alpha_1\sigma_v^2}{\sigma_u^2 + \alpha_1^2\sigma_v^2}(u_t + \alpha_1 v_t) \tag{9.16b}$$

where σ_u^2 and σ_v^2 are the variances of u_t and v_t respectively.

For notational convenience we define

$$z_t \equiv u_t + \frac{\alpha_1(1+n)}{1+n\theta}v_t + (1-\mu_4)q_t - (\alpha_2+\mu_3)\omega_t \tag{9.17}$$

The conditional expectations for time $t + j$, formed at time t, are

$$z^*_{t+j,t} = u^*_{t+j,t} + \frac{\alpha_1(1+n)}{1+n\theta}v^*_{t+j,t} + (1-\mu_4)q^*_{t+j,t} - (\alpha_2+\mu_3)\omega^*_{t+j,t} \qquad j = 0, 1, 2, \ldots \tag{9.18}$$

The instantaneous forecast $z^*_{t,t}$ depends upon the observability of u_t and v_t. In general, we have

$$\begin{aligned} E_t(z_t) \equiv z^*_{t,t} &= E_t(u_t) + \frac{\alpha_1(1+n)}{1+n\theta}E_t(v_t) + (1-\mu_4)q_t - (\alpha_2+\mu_3)\omega_t \\ &= z_t + \frac{\alpha_1(1-\theta)}{1+n\theta}\{E_t(v_t) - v_t\} \end{aligned} \tag{9.18$'$}$$

with $z^*_{t,t} = z_t$, when v_t is observed.

Substituting (9.14a), (9.14c), and (9.14d) into (9.14b) and taking conditional expectations yields the following difference equation in exchange rate expectations:

$$(\alpha_2+\mu_2)e^*_{t+i+1,t} - (1-\mu_1+\alpha_2)e^*_{t+i,t} = z^*_{t+i,t} \qquad i = 1, 2, \ldots \tag{9.19}$$

Thus, with this notation, we can show that the deviation $y_t - y_t^{\mathrm{f}}$ of output from its frictionless level is given by

$$\begin{aligned} y_t - y_t^{\mathrm{f}} = \frac{1}{\Delta}\frac{1-\theta}{\theta}\Bigg((1+\alpha_2-\mu_1) & \\ \times\left[(1-\tau)\{-e^*_{t,t-1} + (q_t - q^*_{t,t-1})\} + \frac{E_t(v_t) - v^*_{t,t-1}}{1+n\theta}\right] & \\ + (1-\tau)\left[-z_t + (\mu_2+\alpha_2)e^*_{t+1,t} + \frac{\alpha_1(1-\theta)n}{1+n\theta}\{v_t - E_t(v_t)\}\right]\Bigg) & \end{aligned} \tag{9.20}$$

where $\Delta \equiv 1 - \mu_1 + \alpha_2 + \alpha_1[(1-\theta)/\theta](1-\tau)$. The exchange rate expectations $e^*_{t+1,t}$ and $e^*_{t,t-1}$ are obtained by solving (9.19) and are given by[7]

$$e^*_{t+1,t} = -\frac{1}{1-\mu_1+\alpha_2}\left\{\sum_{j=0}^{\infty} z^*_{t+1+j,t}\left(\frac{\alpha_2+\mu_2}{1-\mu_1+\alpha_2}\right)^j\right\}$$

$$\text{if } \left|\frac{1-\mu_1+\alpha_2}{\alpha_2+\mu_2}\right| > 1 \tag{9.21a}$$

$$= \frac{1}{\alpha_2+\mu_2}\left\{\sum_{j=0}^{\infty} z^*_{t-j,t}\left(\frac{1-\mu_1+\alpha_2}{\alpha_2+\mu_2}\right)^j\right\}$$

$$\text{if } \left|\frac{1-\mu_1+\alpha_2}{\alpha_2+\mu_2}\right| < 1 \text{ for all } t \tag{9.21b}$$

where $z^*_{t+j,t}$ is defined by (9.18) and (9.18′).[8] Furthermore, setting $i = 1$ in (9.19) (at time $t-1$), using (9.18′), and substituting into (9.20), the deviation in output can be written equivalently as

$$y_t - y^{\mathrm{f}}_t = \frac{1}{\Delta}\left(\frac{1-\theta}{\theta}\right)\Bigg((1-\tau)[(\mu_2+\alpha_2)(e^*_{t+1,t} - e^*_{t+1,t-1}) - \{E_t(z_t) - z^*_{t,t-1}\}] + (1+\alpha_2-\mu_1) \times \left\{(1-\tau)(q_t - q^*_{t,t-1}) + \frac{E_t(v_t) - v^*_{t,t-1}}{1+n\theta}\right\}\Bigg) \tag{9.20′}$$

This equation indicates that the deviation in output from the frictionless level depends upon revisions to forecasts made between time $t-1$ and time t in response to new information. In the case of observed variables, such as q_t, this is the unanticipated change in that variable. In the case of exchange rate expectations, it is the update in the forecast for time $t+1$ between time $t-1$ and time t.

Our analysis below includes two important cases. The first is where all disturbances are unanticipated and transitory, so that

$$e^*_{t+1,t} = 0 \qquad \text{for all } t \tag{9.22}$$

The second is where the expectations of the composite variable z formed at time t are uniform throughout all future periods. Formally, this is described by

$$z^*_{t+i,t} = z^*_t \text{ say} \qquad i = 1, 2, \ldots \text{ for all } t \tag{9.23}$$

In particular, we consider the important case where the current disturbance in z_t is expected to be permanent so that $z^*_t = E_t(z_t)$. In this case, the stable solutions for exchange rate expectations both simplify to

$$e^*_{i+1,t} = \frac{-E_t(z_t)}{1 - \mu_1 - \mu_2} \qquad i = 1, 2, \ldots \text{ for all } t \tag{9.24}$$

4 FULL INFORMATION

Stabilization when both private agents and the stabilization authority have complete information on all random disturbances, including u_t, v_t, is straightforward, either by means of wage indexation or monetary policy.

Substracting (9.13′) from (9.9′), using (9.7), and writing the resulting expression in deviation form about the initial equilibrium, yields

$$y_t - y^{\mathrm{f}}_t = \frac{1-\theta}{\theta}\left\{p_t - p^*_{t,t-1}) - (w_t - w^{\mathrm{c}}_{t,t-1}) + \frac{v_t - v^*_{t,t-1}}{1 + n\theta}\right\} \tag{9.25}$$

so that $y_t = y^{\mathrm{f}}_t$, the frictionless level, provided that wages are indexed in accordance with

$$w_t = w^{\mathrm{c}}_{t,t-1} + (p_t - p^*_{t,t-1}) + \frac{1}{1+n\theta}(v_t - v^*_{t,t-1}) \tag{9.26}$$

That is, wages should be fully indexed to the unanticipated change in price and partially indexed to the unanticipated component of the productivity shock. Full indexation to the price change alone yields perfect stabilization if and only if the productivity disturbance is fully anticipated. Equation (9.26) can be rewritten as

$$w_t = w^{\mathrm{c}}_t + (p_t - p^*_{t,t-1}) + \frac{1}{1+n}(y_t - y^*_{t,t-1}) \tag{9.27}$$

with the rule now being expressed in terms of unanticipated movements in output. This rule is essentially equivalent to the Karni (1983) stabilization rule, which dealt with unanticipated disturbances.

Alternatively, subtractiong (9.13′) from the money market equilibrium condition, we obtain

$$y_t - y^{\mathrm{f}}_t = \frac{1}{\alpha_1}\left(m_t - p_t - u_t + \alpha_2 r_t - \alpha_1 \frac{1+n}{1+n\theta} v_t\right)$$

so that for perfect stabilization, $y_t = y^{\mathrm{f}}_t$ we require

$$m_t = p_t - \alpha_2 r_t + u_t + \alpha_1 \frac{1+n}{1+n\theta} v_t \tag{9.28}$$

Equations (9.26) and (9.28) provide alternative methods for replicating the output of the frictionless economy. Each of these offers advantages. The wage indexation scheme involves monitoring fewer pieces of information, although it does involve formulating forecasts of the productivity disturbance. In contrast, the monetary rule requires more information, but observation on only *current* disturbances. Moreover, the authority need not attempt to determine whether a disturbance is permanent of transitory. Its nature will be reflected by movements in the (observed) interest rate. Finally, eliminating p_t between (9.26) and (9.28) yields a tradeoff between the adjustment in money supply and the wage rate.

5 UNANTICIPATED DISTURBANCES

We now return to equation (9.20) and determine the optimal monetary policy and wage indexation schemes in situations where there is incomplete information. The optimal policy rules are summarized in table 9.1. The first row of the table deals with case 2 where private agents, but nor the stabilization authority, observe the demand and productivity disturbances u_t, v_t; the second row describes case 3 where neither the

TABLE 9.1 *Unanticipated disturbances*

	White noise	*Perceived permanent shifts*
Private agents observe u_t, v_t	μ_2 arbitrary $\mu_3 = -\alpha_2$ $\mu_4 = -\alpha_2 + \mu_1$ $\dfrac{(1 + \alpha_2 - \mu_1)\phi}{1 + n\theta} = (1 - \tau) \times \left\{\theta + \alpha_1\phi(1 - \theta) + \dfrac{\alpha_1 n(1 - \theta)\phi}{1 + n\theta}\right\}$ $\mu_1 \neq 1 + \alpha_2, \quad \tau \neq 1$ Imperfect stabilization	$\mu_1 = 1 + \alpha_2$ μ_2, μ_3, μ_4 arbitrary τ arbitrary but $\tau \neq 1$ Perfect stabilization
Private agents do not observe u_t, v_t	μ_2 arbitrary $\mu_3 = -\alpha_2$ $\mu_4 = -\alpha_2 + \mu_1$ $\dfrac{(1 + \alpha_2 - \mu_1)\phi}{1 + n\theta} = (1 - \tau) \times \left\{1 + \dfrac{\alpha_1 n(1 - \theta)\phi}{1 + n\theta}\right\}$ $\mu_1 \neq 1 + \alpha_2, \tau \neq 1$ Perfect stabilization	(a) $\mu_1 = 1 + \alpha_2$ μ_2, μ_3, μ_4 arbitrary τ arbitrary but $\tau \neq 1$ (b) μ_2 arbitrary $\mu_3 = -\alpha_2$ $\mu_4 = \mu_1 + \mu_2$ $\dfrac{(1 - \mu_1 - \mu_2)\phi}{1 + n\theta} = (1 - \tau) \times \left\{1 + \dfrac{\alpha_1 n(1 - \theta)\phi}{1 + n\theta}\right\}$ Perfect stabilization

private agents not the stabilization authority observe u_t, v_t. The two columns of the table pertain respectively to white noise disturbances and to disturbances which, having occurred, are then perceived as being permanent.

These optimal policies are determined as follows. Depending upon the disturbance, $e^*_{t+1,t}$, $e^*_{t,t-1}$ are calculated from (9.21) and substituted into (9.20). The policy parameters, μ_i and τ are chosen to minimize $\text{var}(y_t - y^f_t)$.

5.1 White noise disturbances

For white noise disturbances all expectations are zero, and so from (9.22)

$$e^*_{t+1,t} = e^*_{t,t-1} = 0$$

Thus, substituting into (9.20′), we obtain

$$\begin{aligned} y_t - y^f &= \frac{1}{\Delta}\frac{1-\theta}{\theta}\left[-(1-\tau)E_t(z_t) + (1+\alpha_2-\mu_1)\right. \\ &\quad \left.\times \left\{(1-\tau)q_t + \frac{E_t(v_t)}{1+n\theta}\right\}\right] \\ &= \frac{1}{\Delta}\frac{1-\theta}{\theta}\left\{-(1-\tau)(u_t+\alpha_1 v_t)\right. \\ &\quad + \frac{(1+\alpha_2-\mu_1)-(1-\tau)\alpha_1(1-\theta)n}{1+n\theta}E_t(v_t) \\ &\quad \left. + (1-\tau)(\alpha_2-\mu_1+\mu_4)q_t + (1-\tau)(\alpha_2+\mu_3)\omega_t\right\} \end{aligned} \tag{9.29}$$

Note that the solution is independent of the monetary policy parameter μ_2. This is because, for white noise disturbances, $e^*_{t+1,t} = 0$. It is evident from (9.29) that the values of the optimal policy parameters which minimize $\text{var}(y_t - y^f_t)$ can be obtained recursively. First, the effects of the foreign variables q_t, ω_t can be neutralized by setting their respective coefficients in (9.29) to zero; then the remaining variance due to the domestic variables u_t, v_t can be minimized.

Full wage indexation is nonoptimal since, when $\tau = 1$, (9.29) reduces to

$$y_t - y^f_t = \frac{1-\theta}{\theta}\frac{v_t}{1+n\theta}$$

rendering monetary policy ineffective for further variance reduction. Instead, the effects of the foreign variables can be eliminated by setting the optimal monetary policy parameters (denoted by $\wedge$)

$$\hat{\mu}_3 = -\alpha_2 \tag{9.30a}$$

$$\hat{\mu}_4 = -\alpha_2 + \hat{\mu}_1 \tag{9.30b}$$

With the foreign variables eliminated, (9.29) simplifies to

$$y_t - y_t^{\mathrm{f}} = \frac{1}{\Delta}\left(\frac{1-\theta}{\theta}\right)\Bigg[-(1-\tau)(u_t + \alpha_1 v_t) + \left\{\frac{(1+\alpha_2-\mu_1)-(1-\tau)\alpha_1(1-\theta)\mathrm{n}}{1+\mathrm{n}\theta}\right\}E_t(v_t)\Bigg\} \tag{9.29'}$$

The remaining choice is that of τ, μ_1 and this depends critically upon whether or not v_t is observed.

If v_t is observed, then $E_t(v_t) = v_t$, and it is easy to show that only one of the remaining policy parameters $\hat{\tau}$, $\hat{\mu}_1$ can be chosen independently. The optimal choice is constrained by the relationship

$$\left(\frac{1+\alpha_2-\hat{\mu}_1}{1+n\theta}\right)\phi = (1-\hat{\tau})\left\{\theta + \alpha_1\phi(1-\theta) + \frac{\alpha_1 n(1-\theta)\phi}{1+n\theta}\right\} \tag{9.31}$$

where

$$\phi \equiv \frac{\alpha_1\sigma_v^2}{\sigma_u^2 + \alpha_1^2\sigma_v^2}$$

Equation (9.31) implies a tradeoff between the degree of wage indexation and the extent to which monetary policy should respond to exchange rate movements. Either τ or μ_1 can be chosen arbitrarily, with the other being determined by this relationship. The values $\tau = 1$, $\mu_1 = 1 + \alpha_1$ are ruled out for reasons established previously by Turnovsky (1983, this volume, ch. 8) and noted above in the introduction. From (9.31) we see $d\hat{\mu}_1/d\hat{\tau} > 0$ so that if wages are more fully indexed to prices, the money supply should be expanded more (or contracted less) to a depreciation in the exchange rate.

Substituting (9.30a) and (9.30b) into (9.14c) and using the PPP and UIP relationships, the optimal policies can be specified very simply by

$$m_t = (\hat{\mu}_1 - \alpha_2)p_t - \alpha_2 r_t \tag{9.32a}$$

$$w_t = \hat{\tau}p_t \tag{9.32b}$$

where $\hat{\mu}_1$ and $\hat{\tau}$ are linked by (9.31). Written in this way, both optimal policy rules have the convenience of enabling the domestic policy-makers to monitor only domestic variables. In particular, one component of the optimal monetary rule requires accommodation to movements in the demand for money rising from changes in the interest rate. If $\hat{\tau} = 0$, the optimal can be reached through monetary policy alone, with $\hat{\mu}_1$ being set in accordance with (9.31).[9]

Turning now to the case where m_t and v_t are not observed by private agents, we have from (9.16b)

$$E_t(v_t) = \phi(u_t + \alpha_1 v_t) \tag{9.33}$$

in which case (9.29′) becomes

$$y_t - y_t^{\mathrm{f}} = \frac{1}{\Delta}\left(\frac{1-\theta}{\theta}\right)\left[-(1-\tau) + \left\{\frac{(1+\alpha_2-\mu_1)-(1-\tau)\alpha_1(1-\theta)n}{1+n\theta}\right\}\phi\right](u_t + \alpha_1 v_t) \tag{9.29″}$$

The optimal policy parameters $\hat{\mu}_1$ and $\hat{\tau}$ obtained by setting the coefficient of the composite disturbance $u_t + \alpha_1 v_t$ to zero in (9.29) now satisfy

$$\frac{1+\alpha_2-\hat{\mu}_1}{1+n\theta}\phi = (1-\hat{\tau})\left\{1 + \frac{\alpha_1(1-\theta)n\phi}{1+n\theta}\right\} \tag{9.34}$$

which again implies a positive tradeoff between them. In this case the slope is steeper than before, implying that, for a given degree of indexation, a greater monetary expansion (smaller monetary contraction) is required in response to a given depreciation in the exchange rate. On substituting (9.30a) and (9.30b) into (9.14c) and using the PPP and UIP conditions, the optimal policy rules are given by (9.32a), (9.32b), except that the tradeoff between $\hat{\mu}_1$ and $\hat{\tau}$ is now given by (9.34).

There is, however, a critical difference between these two cases. When private agents observe u_t and v_t, the optimal stabilization rule, based on incomplete information, is unable to replicate the output of the frictionless economy. In effect, the inferior information available to the stabilization authority prevents it from being able to track the behavior of a private frictionless economy perfectly. There is therefore some residual positive $\operatorname{var}(y_t - y_t^{\mathrm{f}})$. In contrast, when the disturbances are not observed by private agents, the optimal rules, with $\hat{\mu}_1$ and $\hat{\tau}$ satisfying (9.34), imply $y_t = y_t^{\mathrm{f}}$. With equal (imperfect) information to that of the private sector, the stabilization authority is able to replicate exactly the behavior of a frictionless economy. The latter is precisely the result obtained by Aizenman and Frenkel (1985).

5.2 Perceived permanent disturbances

Suppose now that the disturbances occurring at each point time t have been previously unanticipated, but, having occurred, are now preceived as being permanent. Thus $q^*_{t,t-1} = q_{t-1}$, $v^*_{t,t-1} = E_{t-1}(v_{t-1})$, and $z^*_{t+j,t} = E_t(z_t)$ for all j and t. Thus exchange rate expectations are generated by

$$e^*_{t+1,t} = -\frac{E_t(z_t)}{1-\mu_1-\mu_2} \tag{9.35a}$$

$$e^*_{t+1,t-1} = -\frac{E_{t-1}(z_{t-1})}{1 - \mu_1 - \mu_2} \tag{9.35b}$$

where $E_t(z_t)$ is given by (9.18′).

Substituting these expressions for expectations into (9.20′), the solution for $y_t - y^{\mathrm{f}}_t$ is given by

$$y_t - y^{\mathrm{f}}_t = (1 + \alpha_2 - \mu_1)\left[(1 - \tau)(q_t - q_{t-1}) + \frac{E_t(v_t) - E_{t-1}(v_{t-1})}{1 + n\theta} - \frac{(1 - \tau)\{E_t(z_t) - E_{t-1}(z_{t-1})\}}{1 - \mu_1 - \mu_2}\right] \tag{9.36}$$

From (9.36) we can obtain the expressions for the optimal policies reported in the second column of table 9.1.

In the case where the private agents, but not the stabilization authority, observe u_t, and v_t, we see by inspection that y_t is stabilized perfectly at the frictionless level y^{f}_t for all t by setting $\mu_1 = 1 + \alpha_2$. The optimal policy rules are therefore

$$m_t = (1 + \alpha_2)e_t + \mu_2 e^*_{t+1,t} + \mu_3\omega_t + \mu_4 q_t \tag{9.37a}$$

$$w_t = w^{\mathrm{c}}_{t,t-1} + \tau(p_t - p^*_{t,t-1}) \tag{9.37b}$$

where μ_2, μ_3, μ_4 and τ are all arbitrary, the only restriction being $\tau \neq 1$. This is a generalization of the result obtained by Turnovsky (1984) in the absence of wage indexation.

To understand the economic reasoning underlying this result, consider the domestic money market. Combining equations, (9.14a) and (9.14b) yields

$$m_t = q_t + e_t + \alpha_1 y_t - \alpha_2(\omega_t + e^*_{t+1,t} - e_t) + u_t \tag{9.38}$$

If the domestic monetary authority intervenes in accordance with (9.37a), it follows from (9.35a) (and assumption that u_t and v_t are observed by private agents) that

$$e^*_{t+1,t} = \frac{1}{\alpha_1 + \mu_2}\left\{u_t + \frac{\alpha_1(1 + n)}{1 + n\theta}v_t - (\alpha_2 + \mu_3)\omega_t + (1 - \mu_4)q_t\right\} \tag{9.39}$$

Exchange rate expectations adjust in response to the disturbances in u_t, v_t, ω_t, and q_t. The resulting adjustment in the domestic interest rate is precisely such as to eliminate the effects of the disturbances u_t, ω_t, and q_t from the excess demand for nominal money balances. This can be seen by substituting (9.39) and (9.37a) into (9.38):

$$(1 + \alpha_2)e_t + \mu_3\omega_t + \mu_4 q_t$$
$$= q_t + e_t + \alpha_1 y_t$$

$$- \left\{u_t + \frac{\alpha_1(1+n)}{1+n\theta}v_t + (1-\mu_4)q_t - (\alpha_2+\mu_3)\omega_t\right\}$$

$$- \alpha_2(\omega_t - e_t) + u_t \tag{9.40}$$

It is clear from this equation that whatever arbitrary values of μ_2, μ_3, and μ_4 are chosen, the expected exchange rate, given by the term in parentheses, simply adjusts to offset these stochastic effects. Upon simplification, (9.40) reduces to

$$y_t = \frac{1+n}{1+n\theta}v_t = y_t^{\text{f}} \tag{9.41}$$

thereby verifying that income is stabilized at its frictionless level.

It is interesting to note that, in contrast with the white noise disturbances discussed above, the stabilization authority, having incomplete information, can nevertheless replicate the equilibrium of a frictionless economy in response to this type of disturbance. It can dispense with wage indexation, and, in fact, in the light of the PPP and UIP conditions, the optimal monetary rule can be expressed in a number of equivalent ways, for example

$$m = (1+\alpha_2)e \qquad m = (1+\alpha_2)p \qquad m = (1+\alpha_2)r$$

The most convenient form will presumably depend upon the availability and reliability of the necessary information.

The situation where private agents do not observe u_t, and v_t leads to *two* sets of optimal policy rules, both of which yield perfect stabilization at the frictionless output level for all t. Since (9.36) does not depend upon the observability of u_t and v_t, one optimal policy is obviously $\mu_1 = 1 + \alpha_2$, again giving rise to (9.37a) and (9.37b).

The term in parentheses in (9.36) can be written in terms of the difference Δq_t, $\Delta\omega_t$, and $\Delta(u_t + \alpha_1 v_t)$. The second set of policy rules is obtained by setting the coefficients of these random variables to zero, thereby setting the right-hand side of (9.36) to zero. The resulting optimum is similar to, but not identical with, that obtained previously. Specifically, $\hat{\mu}_3 = -\alpha_2$ and $\hat{\mu}_4 = \hat{\mu}_1 + \hat{\mu}_2$, with $\hat{\mu}_1$, $\hat{\mu}_2$ and $\hat{\tau}$ being arbitrary but subject to the constraint

$$\frac{(1-\hat{\mu}_1-\hat{\mu}_2)\phi}{1+n\theta} = (1-\hat{\tau})\left\{1+\frac{\alpha_1(1-\theta)n\theta}{1+n\theta}\right\}$$

If further, we choose $\hat{\mu}_2 = -\alpha_2$, then this second set of policy rules reduces to (9.32a) and (9.32b), with the tradeoff between $\hat{\mu}_1$ and $\hat{\tau}$ again given by (9.34). This is identical with the optimal policy white noise disturbances.

5.3 Uncertain perceptions

Thus far, we have assumed that private agents are clear in their perceptions of whether the observed disturbances are permanent shifts or only transitory shocks. Of course, in time they may turn out to be wrong, but our assumption is that agents can form a subjective characterization of them. Suppose instead that agents are unable to decide whether a disturbance which has occurred represents a permanent shift or only a transitory shock. Assume that they formalize their uncertainty by assigning probabilities θ and $1 - \theta$ say to those two outcomes respectively.[10] In the case where private agents observe u_t and v_t, the expected exchange rate is

$$e^*_{t+1,t} = -\frac{\theta z_t}{1 - \mu_1 - \mu_2}$$

and the analysis can be carried out by substituting this expression into (9.20). In this case it can be shown that if $\theta < 1$, perfect stabilization about the frictionless level of output is not possible. However, if private agents do not observe u_t and v_t, we have seen that the rules (9.32a) and (9.32b) together with (9.34) replicate the frictionless economy perfectly for both white noise and permanent shifts. This rule will therefore yield perfect stability regardless of the private agents' perceptions of the nature of the shock (i.e. for *all* values of θ).

6 ANTICIPATED DISTURBANCES

As another example, suppose that at time $t - 1$ agents perfectly anticipate all disturbances for time t (but not necessarily beyond). In the case of the instantaneously observed variables, this means, for example, $q^*_{t,t-1} = q_t$, while for the potentially unobserved variables $v^*_{t,t-1} = E_t(v_t)$. That is, no new information on v_t is forthcoming between time $t - 1$ and t, so that the one-period prediction equals the future (noisy) observation. It then follows that $z^*_{t,t-1} = E_t(z_t)$ so that (9.20′) reduces to

$$y_t - y^{\mathrm{f}}_t = \frac{1}{\Delta}\left(\frac{1-\theta}{\theta}\right)(1-\tau)(\mu_2 + \alpha_2)(e^*_{t+1,t} - e^*_{t+1,t-1}) \qquad (9.20'')$$

In this case, perfect stabilization about the frictionless economy can easily be accomplished in either of two ways: (a) full wage indexation, $\tau = 1$; (b) a monetary policy rule with $\mu_2 = -\alpha_2$.

The operation of the indexation rule can be seen by comparing (9.14d) with (9.14e). Full indexation eliminates the dependence of output of price movements, so that

$$y_t = \frac{1-\theta}{\theta}\left\{E_t(v_t) - \frac{v^*_{t,t-1}}{1+n\theta}\right\} + v_t.$$

That is, employment and output depend primarily upon the change in the forecast of the supply shock between time $t-1$ and t. If $v^*_{t,t-1} = E_t(v_t)$, then

$$y_t = \frac{n(1-\theta)}{1+n\theta} E_t(v_t) + v_t = y^{\mathrm{f}}_t$$

implying perfect stabilization about the frictionless level of output.

Alternatively, the monetary policy rule

$$m_t = \mu_1 e_t - \alpha_2 e^*_{t+1,t} + \mu_3 \omega_t + \mu_4 q_t$$

also leads to perfect stabilization of output about y^{f}_t. The reason for this is that, with $E_t(v_t) = v^*_{t,t-1}$,

$$y_t - y^{\mathrm{f}}_t = \frac{1-\theta}{\theta}(1-\tau)(e_t - e^*_{t,t-1})$$

The deviation in output about the frictionless level therefore depends upon the unanticipated change in the current exchange rate. In general, $e_t - e^*_{t,t-1}$ depends upon (a) the unanticipated components of the exogenous disturbances, and (b) any revisions to exchange rate expectations formed at time t. The assumption that the disturbances are correctly anticipated eliminates the former effect, while by adopting an intervention rule with $\mu_2 = -\alpha_2$ the monetary authority eliminates the effects of the latter, which would otherwise impact through the money market. Hence setting $\mu_2 = -\alpha_2$ ensures that exchange rate expectations will be correct, which in turn implies perfect stabilization of output about its frictionless level. Further, setting the arbitrary parameters $\mu_1 = \mu_3 = \alpha_2$, $\mu_4 = 0$, the money supply rule can be written in the particulary simple form

$$m_t = -\alpha_2 r_t$$

in which the domestic monetary authorities accommodate movements in the demand for money resulting from movements in the domestic interest rate.

An important aspect of these results is that in both cases the rule yields perfect stabilization irrespective of change in exchange rate expectations between time $t-1$ and time t. Since such changes, if they occur, reflect private agents' perceptions of disturbances occurring at the time, perfect stabilization of output is obtained regardless of whether the shocks occurring at time t are perceived at that time as being permanent or transitory.

7 WAGE INDEXATION

It is seen from the analysis of sections 4–6 that wage indexation is inessential for the adopted policy specifications. All of the optima can be reached by the adoption of monetary policy alone. This is hardly surprising, given the asymmetry of information embodied in the monetary policy and wage indexation rules. At the same time we have shown that wage indexation alone can yield perfect stabilization in the cases of full information and perfectly anticipated disturbances. We now consider whether in the case of unanticipated disturbances, wage indexation rules, based on the same information as the above monetary rules, can achieve the same equilibria. Specifically, we consider the wage indexation rule

$$w_t = w^{c}_{t,t-1} + \tau_1(p_t - p^*_{t,t-1}) + \tau_2(q_t - q^*_{t,t-1}) + \tau_3(\omega_t - \omega^*_{t,t-1}) + \tau_4(e^*_{t+1,t} - e^*_{t+1,t-1}) \qquad (9.42)$$

That is, wages are indexed to unanticipated changes in the foreign price level, the foreign interest rate, and the expected exchange rate, in addition to the domestic price level. Given PPP, this rule is clearly an indexation analog to the money supply rule (9.14c).

Repeating the previous analysis, we can show that, with white noise disturbances, the choice of intervention parameter τ_1, τ_2, τ_3, and τ_4 enables the replication of the equilibria of the previous equilibria to be obtained. The reason is that τ_2 and τ_3 can eliminate the foreign variables q_t and ω_t; τ_4 is irrelevant and τ_1 can be chosen by setting $\mu_1 = 0$ in (9.31) or (9.34). In the case where private agents observe u_t and v_t, only partial stabilization is obtained, while when neither private agents nor the stabilization authority observe these disturbances, perfect stabilization results.

In the case of initially unanticipated but perceived permanent disturbances, we cannot obtain perfect stabilization about the frictionless economy with this more general wage indexation scheme alone, as long as private agents observe u_t and v_t. While indexation can stabilize for u_t, q_t and ω_t the elimination of the supply shock requires monetary policy. However, the generalized wage indexation scheme can achieve perfect stabilization when u_t and v_t are not observed by private agents.

The reason why wage indexation may or may not yield perfect stabilization can be seen from the supply function. For this purpose, we can set expectations at time $t - 1$ to zero. In this case, the deviation in output about the frictionless level is

$$y_t - y^{f}_t = \frac{1-\theta}{\theta}\left\{p_t - w_t + \frac{1}{1+n\theta}E_t(v_t)\right\}$$

which in the case that v_t is observed is modified to

$$y_t - y^{f}_t = \frac{1-\theta}{\theta}\left(p_t - w_t + \frac{v_t}{1+n\theta}\right)$$

In general, p_t is a function of more random variables than just v_t. When v_t is observed, the wage indexation rule (9.42) contains insufficient independent parameters to stabilize for both p_t and v_t exactly. With disturbances which are preceived to be permanent, the effect of the optimal monetary rule (9.37a) is essentially to eliminate, through the adjustment of exchange rate expectations, the effects of all random variables other than v_t on the price level. Indeed, the rule ensures that the real wage adjusts by precisely the amount $v_t/(1+n\theta)$, thereby leading to the perfect stabilization of output about its frictionless level. However, with transitory shocks, exchange rate expectations do not adjust and monetary policy is also unable to achieve perfect stabilization.

In contrast, when v_t is not known, $E_t(v_t)$ inferred from the least-squares prediction (9.16b) is essentially a linear function of the observed disturbances p_t, ω_t, q_t and r_t upon which the wage indexation rule is based. It is not an independent variable and the rule includes sufficient parameters to neutralize all these random shocks.

8 CONCLUSIONS

In this chapter we have analysed the interdependence between the optimal degree of wage indexation and the optimal monetary policy for a small open economy. We have investigated this relationship under a variety of assumptions regarding (a) the relative information available to private agents and the (public) stabilization authority, and (b) the perceived nature of the disturbances impinging on the economy. Several conclusions are worth highlighting.

First, if all agents have perfect information, then perfect stabilization can be achieved either by modifying the Karni indexation rule by adjusting wages to the unanticipated change in output, or by an appropriate but very simply specified monetary rule.

Most of our attention has dealt with incomplete information. Where disturbances are unanticipated, we have drawn the distinction between those that are perceived as being transitory (white noise) and those that are perceived as being permanent shifts. In the case of the former, we find that the distortions due to the wage contract can be fully eliminated, thereby replicating the output of the frictionless economy, as long as private agents and the stabilization authority have the same (imperfect) information. However, for perceived permanent shifts, perfect stabilization is achieved whether or not private agents and the stabilization authority have identical information. In the case where the information sets are identical, two sets of policy rules achieve perfect stabilization. We have also considered the situation in which private agents are unable to decide whether or not a disturbance which has occurred is permanent or transitory, and we show that with identical information between private and public agents, perect stabilization can be achieved.

However, this is not so where private agents have an informational advantage.

Finally, we have determined the optimal policies when disturbances are anticipated. We have shown how perfect stabilization can be achieved either by fully indexing wages to prices or by a simple rule accommodating the money supply to changes in the demand for money arising from movements in the domestic interest rate. In both cases, perfect stabilization obtains irrespective of whether the disturbances are expected to be temporary or permanent.

Our analysis emphasizes the policy redundancy issue. That is, some of the policy coefficient can be set arbitrarily, enabling the policy rules to be specified in many equivalent ways. In all cases wage indexation is inessential, in the sense that the quilibrium can be achieved through monetary policy alone. While this is largely a consequence of a relatively rich specification of the monetary policy rule, this is not entirely so. In one important case, where private agents have perfect information and perceive all shocks as being permanent, perfect stabilization, which can be achieved through a very simple monetary policy rule, cannot be accomplished through wage indexation based on equivalent information.

NOTES

1 See for example Aizenman, 1985; Marston, 1984. There is also an extensive literature dealing with optimal exchange rate management (optimal exchange market intervention) in nonindexed economics (see for example papers in Bhandari (1985) and the references cited therein).

2 Suppose that the nominal demand for money (specified in logarithms) is $m = \phi e + z$, where e is the exchange rate (in logarithms) and z denotes all other variables. Wage indexation becomes ineffective if the money supply m is adjusted by a rule of the form $m = \phi e$.

3 We should note that some authors, (e.g. Flood and Marion, 1982) assume that the money supply follows a random walk. However, they do not address issues of optimal stabilization plicy.

4 Note that our analysis abstracts from input and input price shocks. These are considered by several authors. A recent paper by Aizenman and Frenkel (1986) considers wage indexation and monetary rules in response to productivity and input shocks under perfect information. Marston and Turnovsky (1985a) analyse alternative wage indexation rules in response to import price shocks, again under the assumption of perfect information. By contrast, Marson and Turnovsky (1985b) analyse the case where the productivity disturbances are firm-specific. They show that if these are observed by the firm alone, perfect stabilization of the economy can be attained by the combination of a wage indexation rule and a rather complicated taxation scheme.

5 This means that instantaneously the firm may not know its own output. Of course, once v_t is observed, its output can be inferred, but the point is that this information may become available only after the current production decision is made.

6 Note that our welfare criterion is precisely the same as that introduced by Aizenman and Frenkel (1985) under their information assumptions (our case 3). Subtracting (9.13) from (9.9) yields

$$Y_t - Y_t^{\mathrm{f}} = \frac{1-\theta}{\theta}\left\{\frac{\ln(1-\theta)}{1+n\theta} + P_t - W_t + \frac{E_t(v_t)}{1+n\theta}\right\}$$

which in deviation form is

$$y_t - y_t^{\mathrm{f}} = \frac{1-\theta}{\theta}\left\{p_t - w_t + \frac{E_t(v_t)}{1+n\theta}\right\}$$

Minimizing $\operatorname{var}(y_t - y_t^{\mathrm{f}})$ is equivalent to minimizing loss function (9.31) of Aizenman and Frenkel (1985).

7 In addition the general solutions for expectations $e^*_{t+1,t}$ include a term containing an arbitrary constant, A_t say. This reflect the nonuniqueness of rational expectations solutions. In the case of (9.21a) A_t must be set to zero to ensure that the solution is stable. In the case of (9.21b) however, stability considerations alone do not suffice to determine A_t. This can be determined by invoking some additional restriction. Here we adopt the "minimal state representation" procedure proposed by McCallum (1983) and widely used (for some time) by others. This involves picking the rational expectations solution based on the simplest solution and means that $A_t = 0$, independent of stability considerations. The notion that solutions are based on minimum information is appealing in that it embodies the idea that forecasters use scarce information efficiently.

8 In (9.21b) $z^*_{t-j,t} = z_{t-j}$ for $j \geqslant 1$, meaning that past values of z are known at time t. The case where expectations are backward-looking while consistent with rational expectations, is of less economic interest. In the cases we discuss, the expectations are always forward-looking.

9 The fact that $\hat{\tau} \neq 1$ supports the claim made previously that full wage indexation is nonoptimal. It can be shown that the minimized (positive) variance obtained under this optimal rule is less than what would be obtained under full wage indexation.

10 Since the disturbances that we are considering are exogenous to the model, this procedure is perfectly consistent with agents having rational expectations.

REFERENCES

Aizenman, J. (1983) Wage flexibility and openness. *Quarterly Journal of Economics*, 100, 539–50.

Aizenman, J. and Frenkel, J. A. (1985) Optimal wage indexation, foreign exchange market intervention, and monetary policy. *American Economic Review*, 75, 402–23.

—— and —— (1986) Supply shocks, wage indexation and monetary accommodation. *Journal of Money, Credit, and Banking*, 18, 304–22.

Bhandari, J. S. (ed.) (1985) *Exchange Rate Management under Uncertainty*. Cambridge, MA: MIT Press.

Canzoneri, M. B. (1982) Exchange intervention policy in a multiple country world. *Journal of International Economics*, 13, 267–89.

——, Henderson, D. W. and Rogoff, K. S. (1983) The information content of the interest rate and optimal monetary policy. *Quarterly Journal of Economics*, 98, 545–66.

Flood, R. P. and Marion, N. P. (1982) The transmission of disturbances under alternative exchange rate regimes with optimal indexing. *Quarterly Journal of Economics*, 97, 43–66.

Gray, J. A. (1976) Wage indexation: a macroeconomic approach. *Journal of Monetary Economics*, 2, 221–35.

Karni, E. (1983) On optimal wage indexation. *Journal of Political Economy*, 91, 282–92.

McCallum, B. T. (1983) On non-uniqueness in rational expectations models: an attempt at perspective. *Journal of Monetary Economics*, 11, 139–68.

Marston, R. C. (1982) Wages, relative prices and the choice between fixed and flexible exchange rates. *Canadian Journal of Economics*, 15, 87–103.

—— (1984) Real wages and the terms of trade: alternative indexation rules for an open economy. *Journal of Money, Credit, and Banking*, 16, 285–301.

—— and Turnovsky, S. J. (1985a) Imported material prices, wage policy and macroeconomic stabilization. *Canadian Journal of Economics*, 18, 273–84.

—— and —— (1985b) Macroeconomic stabilization through taxation and indexation. *Journal of Monetary Economics*, 16, 375–95.

Turnovsky, S. J. (1983) Wage indexation and exchange market intervention in a small open economy. *Canadian Journal of Economics*, 16, 574–92. Reprinted in this volume as chapter 8.

—— (1984) Exchange market intervention under alternative forms of exogenous disturbances. *Journal of International Economics*, 17, 279–97.

10 Risk, Exchange Market Intervention, and Private Speculative Behavior in a Small Open Economy

1 INTRODUCTION

The increased fluctuations in exchange markets during the past decade or so have stimulated interest in exchange rate management and exchange market intervention (see for example Boyer, 1978; Roper and Turnovsky, 1980; Frenkel and Aizenman, 1982; papers in Bhandari, 1985). Most of the analyses have considered official intervention in the spot market and have derived optimal intervention rules under a variety of assumptions regarding such things as (a) the types of disturbances and (b) the information sets available to the agents in the economy.[1]

From time to time, however, economists have advocated that intervention in the forward exchange market may serve as an important instrument of monetary policy. This view was put forward by Keynes (1930) and later by Spraos (1959) who argued that "the forward rate should not only be supported, as a defense against speculative attack, but should be actually pegged." One of the advantages of forward market intervention is that it does not entail any tightening of domestic credit conditions and may therefore eliminate certain sources of fluctuations that may be generated by a contractionary monetary policy. More recently, Niehans (1984) has expressed a more skeptical view of forward market intervention as an instrument of stabilization policy.

In contrast with the extensive literature on spot market intervention, little work has been devoted to studying the merits of forward market intervention. One recent study of this issue is by Eaton and Turnovsky

Originally published in C. L. Stone (ed.), *Financial Risk: Theory Evidence and Implications,* Boston, MA: Kluwer, 1989.

(1984), but their analysis abstracts from one important aspect.[2] Specifically, they assume that the coefficient of speculation, which determines the demand for forward exchange, is a given parameter. However, as several authors have shown, when this demand is derived from the underlying optimization of risk-averse agents in the economy, this coefficient is not fixed. Rather, under reasonable conditions it varies inversely with the one-period variance of the spot exchange rate and thereby becomes endogenously determined, along with this variance. Moreover, since the spot exchange rate is a function of government intervention policy, this coefficient becomes dependent upon the policy regime. However, the Eaton–Turnovsky analysis ignores this channel whereby government policy impacts on private behavior.

In effect, what is at issue here is the Lucas critique. As a result of Lucas's important insights, it has become accepted that reduced-form parameters are not invariant with respect to government policy, so that a correct assessment of the effects of government policy needs to take account of these induced changes. In the present context, we have a somewhat stronger version of this proposition, namely that certain *structural parameters*, which in this case describe some aspect of private behavior, are also not invariant with respect to government policy.

This structural aspect of the Lucas critique, while receiving much less attention, particularly in the policy-related literature, has not gone unnoticed. It was first incorporated into a model of the foreign exchange market, based on mean–variance utility maximization by Driskill and McCafferty (1980). More recently, Kawai (1984) has used a similar framework to develop a model of spot and formal exchange rate determination, although his treatment of intervention is very brief. Some discussion of spot market intervention in this type of model is given by Black (1985), but he does not address issues pertaining to intervention in the forward exchange market.

This chapter analyses the effects of both spot and forward market intervention, taking account of the endogeneity of private speculation and how it is influenced by government policy. The model we employ is a slightly simplified version of the Eaton–Turnovsky model. This model has the advantage of expositional simplicity, which enables most of the analysis to be conducted graphically. By dispensing with much of the formal analytics, we are able to see more clearly the issues that are involved.

As many authors have noted, once the degree of private speculation is endogenized, the rational expectations equilibrium becomes nonlinear. This immediately raises questions of (a) the existence and (b) the nonuniqueness of equilibrium.[3] These are not simply esoteric issues, but are of relevance for policy. For example, is it the case that government intervention will succeed in helping resolve these problems? Or may what may seems to be a perfectly reasonable form of intervention generate structural imbalances in the market and thereby preclude the existence of an equilibrium? Our analysis highlights the way in which government policy exercises an influence through its impact on the behavior of private speculators. We show how in some cases this channel may dominate any direct effects, so that neglecting it can be seriously misleading.

The chapter is structured as follows. The model is outlined in setion 2 and then the equilibrium under perfectly flexible exchange rates is discussed in section 3. The effects of increased risk are analysed in section 4. Spot market and forward market intervention rules are discussed in sections 5 and 6. In section 7 we briefly compare the perfectly flexible rate not only with the fixed spot rate but with a fixed forward rate as well. The main conclusions are reviewed in the final section.

2 THE ANALYTICAL FRAMEWORK

We will consider a slightly simplified version of the Eaton–Turnovsky (1984) model by taking output to be fixed at its full employment level. Specifically, we assume that there is a single traded commodity, the price of which in terms of foreign currency is given, set a unity say. Also, we assume that the domestic bond is a perfect substitute for a traded world bond when fully covered against exchange risk. Thus purchasing power parity (PPP) and covered interest parity (CIP) are assumed to hold.

The model is summarized by the following equations

$$m_t - e_t = -\alpha r_t + u_t \qquad \alpha > 0 \tag{10.1a}$$

$$r_t = \omega_t + f_t - e_t \tag{10.1b}$$

$$h_t = \beta r_t + v_{1t} \qquad \beta > 0 \tag{10.1c}$$

$$s_t = \gamma(e^*_{t+1,t} - f_t) + v_{2t} \qquad \gamma > 0 \tag{10.1d}$$

$$h_t = (1 - \mu)(b_t + g_t - p_t) + \mu s_t \qquad 0 \leqslant \mu \leqslant 1 \tag{10.1e}$$

where e_t is the current spot exchange rate (measured in terms of units of domestic currency per unit of foreign currency), $e^*_{t+1,t}$ is the expectation of the spot exchange rate at time $t + 1$, conditional on information at time t, f_t is the forward exchange rate (measured in terms of units of domestic currency per unit of foreign currency), m_t is the domestic nominal money supply, b_t is the domestic nominal supply of bonds, h_t is the domestic demand for real bonds, s_t is the speculative demand for forward exchange, g_t is the nominal value in domestic currency units of official purchases of forward exchange, expressed as a share of outstanding bonds, r_t is the domestic nominal interest rate, ω_t is the world nominal interest rate, u_t is the stochastic disturbance in demand for money, v_{1t} is the stochastic disturbance in demand for bonds, and v_{2t} is the stochastic disturbance in speculators' demand for forward exchange. All variables except r_t, ω_t, and g_t are expressed as logarithmic deviations from steady state levels; r_t and ω_t are deviations in natural units and g_t is defined below. Given PPP and the normalization of the foreign price level, the domestic price level is simply e_t.

Equation (10.1a) describes domestic money market equilibrium in which, with output fixed, the demand for money depends only upon the domestic interest rate. All domestic money is held by domestic residents, who in turn hold no foreign money. Equation (10.1b) specifies covered interest parity and embodies the assumption that domestic bonds and foreign bonds are perfect substitutes on a covered basis.

Equation (10.1c) specifies the domestic demand for bonds. Because the bond market interacts in a crucial way with the forward exchange market, we depart from the standard practice of specifying a commodity market equilibrium or a savings or absorption equation, and suppressing the bond market equilibrium condition. Instead, we explicitly include the bond market and leave savings to be defined residually from conditions for money market and bond market equilibrium. This specification is also the most convenient in a log-linear framework and is frequently invoked in such models (see for example Lucas, 1975). We postulate a simple demand for bonds function which depends positively upon the domestic interest rate.

The specification of the forward market is given in equations (10.1d) and (10.1e) and can be derived from intertemporal portfolio maximization (see for example Solnik, 1973; Kouri, 1976; Fama and Farber, 1979; Eaton and Turnovsky, 1981). In our model, this market has two functions. First, it provides holders of foreign bonds with a means of eliminating exchange risk by selling the foreign currency proceeds of their bonds forward. Such sales constitute *arbitrage* activity on this market. Second, the forward market provides a means of *speculating* on exchange rate movements.[4] A first-order approximation to the rate of return on the forward purchase of a unit of foreign currency is $e_{t+1} - f_t$. In (10.1d) we postulate that the demand of foreign exchange for speculation s_t is an increasing function of the expected difference $e^*_{t+1,1} - f_t$.

Equilibrium in the forward exchange market is described by (10.1e). This equation asserts that the demand for forward exchange consisting of (a) demand for speculation and (b) demand by intervention authorities for stabilization purposes equals the supply for arbitrage. This equation is perhaps the least familiar aspect of the model and requires further explanation. Because of the assumption that domestic and foreign bonds are perfect substitutes, there is in fact only a single demand function for total bonds h_t; the demand for foreign bonds is simply the difference between the aggregate national demand and the supply from domestic sources, i.e.[5]

$$H_t - \frac{B_t}{P_t} = H_t^f$$

where H is the total real bond demand, B is the domestic nominal bond supply, P is the domestic price level, and H^f is the real demand for foreign bonds. All these quantities are expressed in levels.

Since foreign bonds are covered, forward market equilibrium requires that

$$H_t - \frac{B_t}{P_t} = S_t + \frac{E_t G_t}{P_t}$$

where G_t denotes government purchases of forward exchange and E_t is the level of the current spot exchange rate. The net private supply of forward exchange to cover foreign bonds equals the net private speculative demand plus net government purchases of forward exchange. Defining the quantity g_t to be the nominal value in domestic current units of these government purchases, expressed as a share of outstanding bonds

$$g_t = \frac{E_t G_t}{B_t}$$

we obtain

$$H_t - (1 + g_t)\frac{B_t}{P_t} = S_t$$

Equation (10.1e) is obtained as a log-linear approximation to this relationship, where the parameter $\mu \equiv \bar{H}^f/\bar{H}$ is the average holdings of foreign bonds, as a share of total bond demand, and arbitrary constants are deleted.[6]

An important consequence of (10.1e) is that variations in the stock of domestic government bonds and in the government's forward market position are not linearly independent. Forward market intervention is equivalent to sterilized intervention in the spot market.

Finally, the stochastic disturbances u_t, v_{1t}, and v_{2t} are assumed to have zero means and finite second moments, and to be identically and independently distributed over time. The foreign interest rate ω_t is also assumed to be stochastic and to have these same properties.

The key parameter in the model is γ, which describes the elasticity of speculation. Eaton and Turnovsky (1984) take this to be a given constant. However, when the basic model (10.1a)–(10.1e) is derived from underlying optimization of the private agents, γ becomes an endogenously determined parameter. Specifically, Eaton and Turnovsky (1981) and others have shown that optimizing a mean–variance utility function over two periods leads to a speculative demand for forward exchange in which

$$\gamma \approx \frac{1}{R\sigma_e^2(1)} \tag{10.2}$$

where $\sigma_e^2(1)$ is the one-period variance of the spot exchange rate and R is the coefficient of absolute risk aversion.[7]

It is clear from equation (10.2) that γ is jointly determined with the one-period variance of the spot rate, and is therefore endogenous. It is this nonlinearity between these variables that is the source of the possible nonexistence and nonuniqueness problems mentioned earlier. In the limiting case when investors are risk-neutral ($R \to 0$), $\gamma \to \infty$. Speculation is infinitely elastic, and the forward market equilibrium condition reduces to $f_t = e^*_{t+1,t}$, so that uncovered interest parity prevails. This is the assumption made in much of the intervention literature, when infinitely elastic speculation renders the forward market redundant.

3 EQUILIBRIUM UNDER FLEXIBLE EXCHANGE RATES

We begin by solving the model outlined in section 2 under perfectly flexible exchange rates when there is no government intervention in either the spot or forward exchange market. We therefore set $m_t = b_t = g_t = 0$ for all t, so that domestic nominal money, bonds, and forward market positions remain fixed at their constant steady state levels. Taking conditional expectations of the system (10.1) at time t for time $t + i$, we can show that expectations of future spot rates satisfy a difference equation of the form

$$e^*_{t+i,t} = \phi e^*_{t+i-1,t} \qquad i = 1, 2, \ldots \tag{10.3}$$

where $\phi > 1$ is a function of the underlying parameters. Thus, if exchange rate expectations are to remain bounded as $i \to \infty$, we require

$$e^*_{t+i,t} = 0 \qquad i = 1, 2, \ldots \tag{10.4}$$

Otherwise, expectations become unbounded and this in turn implies that the asymptotic variances of the spot and forward exchange rates will become infinite. To rule this out, we therefore focus on the bounded solution given by (10.4).[8] Setting expectations to zero in (10.1), we can reduce the system to the following three relationships:

money market $\qquad -e_t + \alpha r_t = u_t \qquad$ (10.5a)

covered interest parity $\qquad r_t - f_t + e_t = \omega_t \qquad$ (10.5b) forward market $\beta r_t + (1 - \mu)e_t + \gamma\mu f_t = v_t \qquad v_t \equiv -v_{1t} + \mu v_{2t}$ (10.5c)

Writing the relationships in this way highlights how the three disturbances impact on the domestic economy. The domestic monetary shock is introduced via the money market; the foreign interest rate shock occurs through the CIP relationship. The disturbance v_t is composite and can reflect a stochastic shift either in the demand for bonds or in speculation. It can also be interpreted as reflecting a stochastic disturbance in the supply of bonds and to this extent can be identified as being a domestic fiscal disturbance. The three relationships (10.5a)–(10.5c) determine simultaneously the equilibrium levels of the spot rate e_t, the forward rate f_t, and the domestic interest rate r_t.

The solutions to these equations are given by the expressions

$$e_t = \frac{1}{D}\{-(\beta + \mu\gamma)u_t + \alpha v_t + \alpha\mu\gamma\omega_t\} \tag{10.6a}$$

$$f_t = \frac{1}{D}[(1 - \mu - \beta)u_t + (1 + \alpha)v_t - \{\alpha(1 - \mu) + \beta\}\omega_t] \tag{10.6b}$$

$$r_t = \frac{1}{D}\{(1 - \mu + \mu\gamma)u_t + v_t + \mu\gamma\omega_t\} \tag{10.6c}$$

where

$$D \equiv \beta + \mu\gamma + \alpha(\mu\gamma + 1 - \mu) > 0$$

These solutions are expressed in terms of the elasticity of speculation γ which, we have argued, depends upon the one-period variance of the spot rate. Since white noise disturbances and future expectations are therefore all zero, the model is in fact static; the one-period variance of the spot rate (and also the asymptotic variance) is simply given by the variance of (10.6a). If we assume, for simplicity, that u_t, v_t, and ω_t are uncorrelated, this is given by

$$\sigma_e^2 = \frac{1}{D^2}\{(\beta + \mu\gamma)^2\sigma_u^2 + \alpha^2\sigma_v^2 + \alpha^2\mu^2\gamma^2\sigma_\omega^2\} \tag{10.7a}$$

The solutions for σ_e^2, σ_f^2, and σ_r^2 are therefore (10.7a), together with

$$\sigma_f^2 = \frac{1}{D^2}[(1 - \mu - \beta)^2\sigma_u^2 + (1 + \alpha)^2\sigma_v^2 + [\alpha(1 - \mu) + \beta\}^2\sigma_\omega^2] \tag{10.7b}$$

$$\sigma_r^2 = \frac{1}{D^2}\{(1 - \mu + \mu\gamma)^2\sigma_u^2 + \sigma_v^2 + \mu^2\gamma^2\sigma_\omega^2\} \tag{10.7c}$$

where

$$\gamma = \frac{1}{R\sigma_e^2} \tag{10.7d}$$

In particular, equations (10.7a) and (10.7d) highlight the joint determination of the variance of the spot rate and the elasticity of speculation. The nonlinearity of the relationship raises the question of (a) the existence and (b) the possible multiplicity of equilibria. This issue can be studied by substituting (10.7d) into (10.7a) to yield the following cubic equation in the variance σ_e^2:

$$\{\beta + \alpha(1 - \mu)\}^2 R^2(\sigma_e^2)^3 + [2\omega(1 + \alpha)\{\beta + \alpha(1 - \mu)\}R - \beta^2 R^2 \sigma_u^2 - \alpha^2 R^2 \sigma_v^2](\sigma_e^2)^2 + \{\mu^2(1 + \alpha)^2 - 2\beta R\mu\sigma_u^2\}\sigma_e^2 - \mu^2(\sigma_u^2 + \alpha^2\sigma_\omega^2) = 0 \quad (10.8)$$

The existence question revolves around whether or not there is a solution to (10.8) with $\sigma_e^2 > 0$, so that the variance of the spot rate is indeed positive.

The answer to this question depends upon the sources of shocks. If either $\sigma_u^2 > 0$ or $\sigma_\omega^2 > 0$, the constant term in this cubic equation is strictly positive, implying that the product of the three roots is positive. This means that there are either one or three positive solutions to σ_e^2. At least one equilibrium therefore exists. The conditions for a unique equilibrium are complicated and not very illuminating. However, the characterization of the equilibria simplifies when we focus on one disturbance at a time.

(1) If the only disturbance is in the domestic monetary sector ($\sigma_u^2 > 0$, $\sigma_v^2 = \sigma_\omega^2 = 0$), then we can show that there may be either one or three equilibrium solutions. For plausible parameter values it seem likely that a unique solution will prevail. For example, a sufficient, but not necessary, condition for a unique solution is

$$\beta < 1 - \mu \quad (10.9)$$

Inequality (10.9) is the condition for a positive disturbance in the demand for money to impact positively on the forward exchange rate (see (10.6b)). A positive shock in u_t tends to raise the interest rate while simultaneously leading to an appreciation of the domestic currency. The net effect on the forward rate f_t depends upon which of these two effects is dominant.

(2) If the only disturbance is in the foreign interest rate ($\sigma_\omega^2 > 0$, $\sigma_u^2 = \sigma_v^2 = 0$), then we can show that equation (10.8) has a unique solution for $\sigma_e^2 > 0$.

(3) If the only disturbance is in the bond market ($\sigma_v^2 > 0$, $\sigma_u^2 = \sigma_\omega^2 = 0$), then (10.8) reduces to

$$\sigma_e^2(\{\beta + \alpha(1 - \mu)\}^2 R^2(\sigma_e^2)^2 + [2\mu(1 + \alpha)\{\beta + \alpha(1 - \mu)\}R - \alpha^2 R^2 \sigma_v^2]\sigma_e^2$$

$$+ \mu^2(1 + \alpha)^2) = 0 \tag{10.8'}$$

Ruling out $\sigma_e^2 = 0$, leaves a quadratic equation in σ_e^2, the product of the roots of which is positive. The condition for (10.8′) to have real roots is

$$\alpha^2 R\sigma_v^2 > 4\mu(1 + \alpha)\{\beta + \alpha(1 - \mu)\} \tag{10.10}$$

Hence, with the only disturbances occurring in the bond market, the solution will have either *two* equilibria or *no* equilibrium depending on whether (10.10) is or is not met. In particular, it is of interest, and rather counter-intuitive, to observe that a larger variance in bond disturbances is more conducive to the existence of an equilibrium.

The reason for this can be seen by substituting from (10.5a) and (10.5b) into the forward market equilibrium condition (10.5c):

$$\left\{\frac{1}{\alpha}(\beta + \mu\gamma) + \mu\gamma + 1 - \mu\right\}e_t = -\frac{1}{\alpha}(\beta + \mu\gamma)u_t + v_t + \mu\gamma\omega_t \tag{10.11}$$

The left-hand side reflects the endogenous variation in the excess demand for forward exchange owing to fluctuations in the exchange rate; the right-hand side represents the fluctuations due to the exogenous random disturbances.

Suppose that the exogenous fluctuations in the bond market v_t are small, so that σ_v^2 is small. These small fluctuations in v_t will, for a given degree of speculation γ and other parameters, lead to small fluctuations in the spot exchange rate, i.e. σ_e^2 will be small. However, this will encourage private speculation, thereby increasing γ. This in turn will exacerbate the endogenous fluctuations in the demand for forward exchange. However, the variations due to the exogenous fluctuations on the right-hand side of (10.11) remain fixed. Indeed, if σ_v^2 is sufficiently small so that γ is large, it is possible for the induced fluctuations in excess demand to exceed the exogenous fluctuations given by the right-hand side so that no equilibrium exists. In contrast, for fluctuations in either u_t or ω_t, as γ increases, the exogenous fluctuations on the right-hand side and endogenous fluctuations on the left-hand side both increase together, and the problem of imbalance and disequilibrium does not arise.

Equations (10.7a)–(10.7d) determine simultaneously the solutions for σ_e^2, σ_f^2, σ_r^2, and γ. The possible nonuniqueness of equilibrium was discussed originally by McCafferty and Driskill (1980). This condition raises the question of how to choose among the various equilibria. One possibility is to choose the one having the minimum (or smaller) variance. However, as McCafferty and Driskill note, this may or may not yield the maximum (or higher) level of utility. A more appropriate criterion is to select the equilibrium having the highest expected welfare.

In the present context, the only function derived from explicit welfare considerations is the speculation function (10.1d). The profits of speculators are given by the expression

$$\pi_{t+1} = (e_{t+1} - f_t)s_t \tag{10.12}$$

Suppose that speculators wish to maximize the one-period mean–variance objective function

$$W_{t+1,t} = \pi^*_{t+1,t} - \tfrac{1}{2}RE_t[\pi_{t+1} - \pi^*_{t+1,t}]^2 \tag{10.13}$$

where E_{t-1} denotes expectations, conditional on information at time $t-1$. Calculating the expected value and one-period variance of (10.12) yields

$$\pi^*_{t+1,t} = (e^*_{t+1,t} - f_t)s_t$$

$$E_t(\pi_{t+1} - \pi^*_{t+1,t})^2 = \sigma_e^2 s_t^2 \tag{10.14}$$

and optimizing (10.13) subject to (10.14) with respect to s_t leads to (10.1d) of the model, with γ defined by (10.7d).

Now substituting for s_t into $W_{t+1,t}$, we find that with $e^*_{t+1,t} = 0$ the optimized value of $W_{t+1,t}$, denoted by $\overline{W}$, is[9]

$$\overline{W} = \frac{f_t^2}{2R\sigma_e^2}$$

so that

$$E(W) = \frac{\sigma_f^2}{2R\sigma_e^2}$$

and substituting for σ_e^2 and σ_f^2 from (10.7a) and (10.7b) leads to

$$E(\overline{W}) = \frac{(1-\mu-\beta)^2\sigma_u^2 + (1+\alpha)^2\sigma_v^2 + \{\alpha(1-\mu)+\beta\}^2\sigma_\omega^2}{(\beta+\mu\gamma)^2\sigma_u^2 + \alpha^2\sigma_v^2 + \alpha^2\mu^2\gamma^2\sigma_\omega^2}$$

This is a decreasing function of γ. Faced with the choice of (a) a high-variance σ_e^2–low-speculative elasticity γ, and (b) a low-variance σ_e^2–high-speculative elasticity γ equilibrium, speculators will prefer the former. They will choose a point such as A, rather than A″ in figure 10.1(b). Accordingly, this is the equilibrium point on which we will focus. While our welfare justification is obviously seriously incomplete, as will become evident below, the comparative statics around A as equilibrium are much more plausible than those around A″.

4 INCREASED RISK

In this section we consider the effects of increased risk, as measured by increases in the exogenous variances σ_u^2, σ_v^2, σ_ω^2 on the variances σ_e^2, σ_f^2, σ_r^2. We maintain our assumption of a perfectly flexible exchange rate with no intervention. We consider one disturbance at a time, thereby enabling us to conduct our analysis graphically. The qualitative results are summarized in table 10.1, part (a).

4.1 Domestic monetary shocks

Figure 10.1 illustrates the equilibrium for the case of monetary shocks ($\sigma_u^2 > 0$, with $\sigma_v^2 = \sigma_\omega^2 = 0$). This and all subsequent figures are constructed in the following manner. On the right-hand side of the first panel we have drawn two graphs in $\gamma - \sigma_e^2$ space. The first of these, illustrated by the locus WW, is (10.7d), which is a retangular hyperbola. The second, described by XX, is the solution for σ_e^2 given in (10.7a), setting $\sigma_v^2 = \sigma_\omega^2 = 0$. For given σ_u^2 and other parameters, this also defines a relationship between γ and σ_e^2. It can easily be verified that the slope of XX is positive or negative, depending upon whether $\beta < 1 - \mu$ or $\beta > 1 - \mu$. Accordingly, these two cases are illustrated separately in parts (a) and (b) of the figure. The lines can also be shown to have the curvature indicated.

In the case where $\beta < 1 - \mu$ (figure 10.1(a)), XX is upward sloping so that it intersects WW at a unique point A which defines the equilibrium

TABLE 10.1 *Summary of qualitative effects*

	Source		
Effect on	σ_u^2	σ_v^2	σ_ω^2
(a) Increased risk			
σ_e^2	+	+	+
σ_f^2	+	+	+
σ_r^s	+ if $\beta < 1 - \mu$? if $\beta > 1 - \mu$	+	+
(b) Spot market intervention			
σ_e^2	−	−	−
σ_f^2	−	? if $\beta < 1 - \mu$ − if $\beta > 1 - \mu$	− if $\beta < 1 - \mu$? if $\beta > 1 - \mu$
σ_r^2	− if $\beta < 1 - \mu$? if $\beta > 1 - \mu$	?	+
(c) Forward market intervention			
σ_e^2	+ if $\beta < 1 - \mu$ − if $\beta > 1 - \mu$	−	+
σ_f^2	−	−	−
σ_r^2	− if $\beta < 1 - \mu$ + if $\beta > 1 - \mu$	−	+

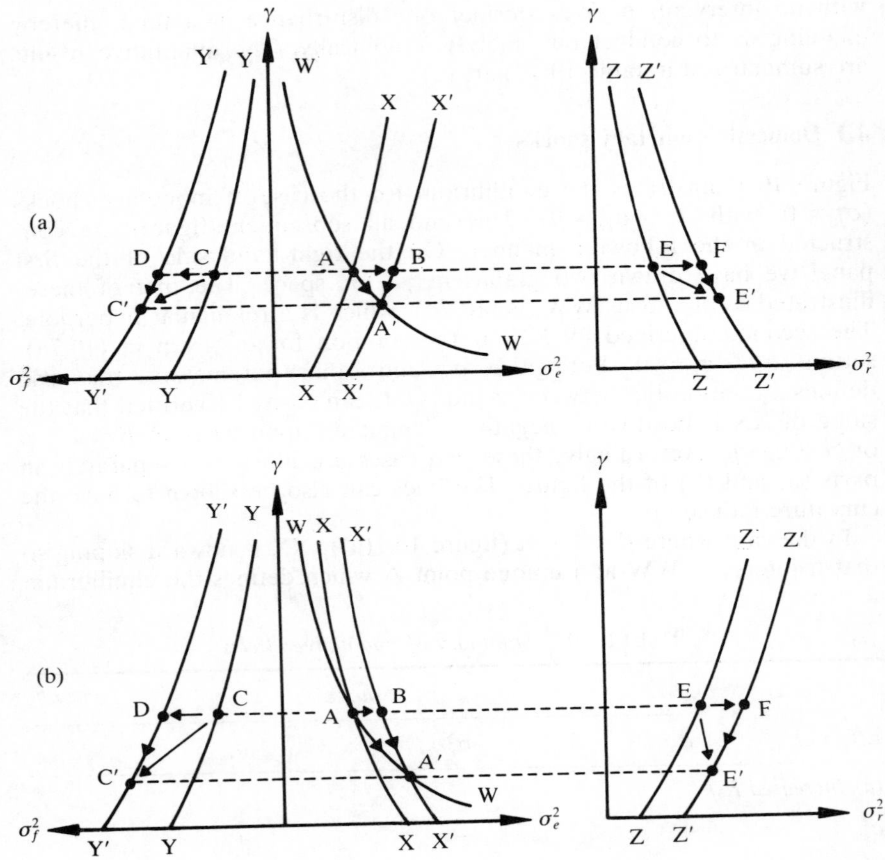

Figure 10.1 Increased risk due to domestic monetary disturbances: (a) $\beta < 1 - \mu$; (b) $\beta > 1 - \mu$.

solutions for the variance of the spot rate σ_e^2 and the implied elasticity of speculation γ. When $\beta > 1 - \mu$ (figure 10.1(b)), XX is downward sloping and may intersect WW at either one or three points. Only the case of a unique equilibrium is illustrated.

The line YY on the left-hand side of the first panel graphs the relationship between σ_f^2 and γ implied by (10.7b). Since an increase in γ raises D, it lowers σ_f^2 and the locus is therefore negatively sloped. Also, the curvature is as indicated. Corresponding to the equilibrium value of γ obtained from the point of intersection A of the WW and XX loci is point C on the YY locus, which in turn yields the equilibrium value for the variance of the forward rate σ_f^2.

Similarly, the locus ZZ in the second panel defines the relationship between γ and σ_r^2 implied by (10.7c). Like YY, its slope depends upon $\beta - (1 - \mu)$. In figure 10.1(a) it is downward sloping and in figure 10.1(b) it is upward sloping with the indicated curvature. The equilibrium variance of the interest rate σ_r^2 is at the point E, which corresponds to the solution for γ on ZZ curve.

Consider now an increase in monetary risk σ_u^2. What this does is to shift the XX, YY and ZZ curves out; the WW curve remains unchanged, because the position of this curve is independent of σ_u^2. The upshot of these shifts is that the equilibria move from points A, C, and E to A′, C′, and E′ respectively. In particular, the increase in monetary risk σ_u^2 increases the variance of the spot rate σ_e^2, thereby lowering the elasticity of speculation γ. The variance of the forward rate σ_f^2 also increases. The variance of the interest rate certainly increases when ZZ is downward sloping. It may or may not rise when ZZ is upward sloping as in figure 2.1(a).

The changes in the variances σ_e^2, σ_f^2, and σ_r^2 can be broken down into two components. The first are the increases due to the outward shifts in the XX, YY, and ZZ curves and are given by the movements AB, CD, and ED in figure 10.1. These effects assume that γ remains constant. They neglect the fact that the increase in the variance of the spot rate σ_e^2 lowers γ, thereby reducing private speculation. The second components, the effects induced by changes in the behavior of private speculators, are given by movements BA′, DC′ and FE′. These may either reinforce or counteract the first effect.

In the case of the spot exchange rate, the reduction in private speculation is stabilizing or destabilizing depending on whether β is larger or smaller than $1 - \mu$. However, the reduction in γ always destabilizes the forward rate. Both of these effects are consistent with propositions 1 and 2 of Eaton and Turnovsky (1984). The effect of a reduction in private speculation on the interest rate is also ambiguous; it is destabilizing if $\beta < 1 - \mu$, and stabilizing otherwise.

As far as the variance of the spot and forward exchange rates are concerned, the net effect of an increase in monetary risk is that it is unambiguously destabilizing. This is hardly surprising, but it is interesting to see that neglecting the response of the private sector due to the change in γ can seriously understate or overstate the true effect. While it is also probably the case that the instability of the interest rate will increase, we cannot rule out the possibility that when $\beta > 1 - \mu$, the fall in γ may be sufficiently large to shift more of the adjustment to the spot rate and actually to reduce the instability of the interest rate.

4.2 Bond (forward market) shocks

As indicated, v_t may reflect shocks in either the bond market or the forward market. The interesting feature about this disturbance is that the XX locus is downward sloping and intersects the WW locus either in zero points, when there is no equilibrium, or in two points, when multiple equilibria exist. The latter case is illustrated in figure 10.2. On the basis of the welfare analysis given in section 10.3, we assume that the equilibrium is initially at point A on the right-hand side of the first panel, rather than at A″. The YY and ZZ curves are basically the same as before, except that now they correspond to given values of σ_v^2 rather than σ_u^2.

An increase in the variance of bond shocks shifts the XX, YY, ZZ curves outward as indicated. The equilibrium variance of the spot rate

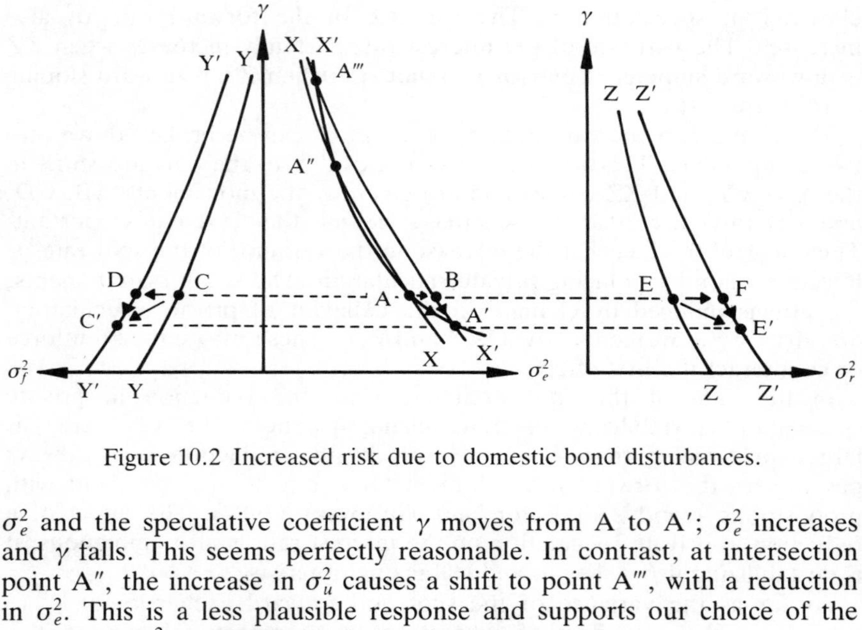

Figure 10.2 Increased risk due to domestic bond disturbances.

σ_e^2 and the speculative coefficient γ moves from A to A′; σ_e^2 increases and γ falls. This seems perfectly reasonable. In contrast, at intersection point A″, the increase in σ_u^2 causes a shift to point A‴, with a reduction in σ_e^2. This is a less plausible response and supports our choice of the low-γ–high-σ_e^2 equilibrium as being the appropriate one.

The increase in the variance of bond shocks increases the three variances σ_e^2, σ_f^2, and σ_r^2. In all cases, the reduction in private speculation, resulting from the higher variability in the spot rate, reinforces the destabilizing effects of the shift, which is again consistent with propositions 1 and 2 of Eaton and Turnovsky (1984).

4.3 Foreign interest rate shocks

Foreign interest rate shocks are illustrated in figure 10.3. In this case the XX and ZZ curves are upward sloping and pass through the origin. The increase in the foreign interest rate therefore generates rotations in these curves through the origin. Again, an increase in the variance of

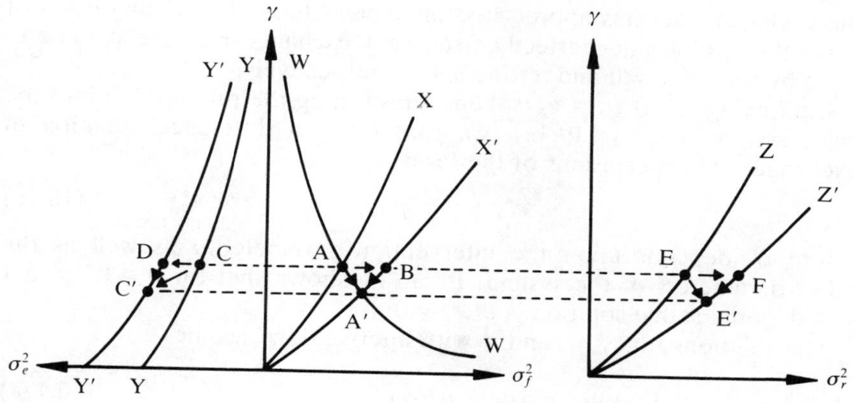

Figure 10.3 Increased risk due to foreign interest rate disturbances.

the foreign interest rate leads to higher variances in σ_e^2, σ_f^2, and σ_r^2. The increases in the variances of the spot and forward rates is apparent from the figure. The increase in σ_r^2 is not obvious, but follows from (10.7a) and (10.7c), which in the presence of only interest rate shocks yields

$$\frac{\sigma_r^2}{\sigma_e^2} = \alpha^2$$

Since this ratio is independent of γ, we see that the increase in the variance of the spot rate leads to a proportional increase in the variance of the interest rate as well. As in previous cases, the shift in equilibria from A, C, and E to A′, C′, and E′ respectively can be broken down into a direct shift and the induced response through γ. In particular, the reduction in private speculation has stabilizing effects on the spot rate and the interest rate, but a destabilizing effect on the forward rate.

5 SPOT MARKET INTERVENTION

We now consider the effects of official intervention in exchange markets. This section deals with intervention in the spot market; forward market intervention is discussed in section 6.[10]

The intervention is hypothesized to take the form

$$m_t = -ae_t \qquad a > 0 \tag{10.15}$$

This describes a policy of "leaning against the wind" and has been widely discussed in the exchange rate management literature.[11] Equation 10.15 specifies that the monetary authority expands or contracts the money supply by an amount that is proportional to the extent to which the exchange rate has appreciated or depreciated. The limiting cases of perfectly flexible and perfectly fixed spot exchange rate are parameterized by setting $a = 0$ and letting $a \to \infty$ respectively.

Continuing to set $b_t = g_t = 0$ and substituting the rule (10.15) into the basic system (10.1a)–(10.1e), we can derive a difference equation in exchange rate expectations of the form

$$e^*_{t+i+1,t} = \phi' e^*_{t+i,t} \tag{10.16}$$

where ϕ' depends upon the intervention parameter a as well as the other parameters of the system. It can be shown that for $a > 0$, $\phi' > 1$ and the only stable solution is $e^*_{t+i,t} = 0$.

The solutions for e_t, f_t, and r_t with intervention become

$$e_t = \frac{1}{D_a}\{-(\beta + \mu\gamma)u_t + \alpha v_t + \alpha\mu\gamma\omega_t\} \tag{10.17a}$$

$$f_t = \frac{1}{D_a}[(1 - \mu - \beta)u_t + (1 + \alpha + a)v_t - \{\alpha(1 - \mu) + \beta(1 + a)\}\omega_t] \tag{10.17b}$$

$$r_t = \frac{1}{D_a}\{(1 - \mu + \mu\gamma)u_t + (1 + a)v_t + (1 + a)\mu\gamma\omega_t\} \tag{10.17c}$$

where

$$D_a \equiv (1 + a)(\beta + \mu\gamma) + \alpha(\mu\gamma + 1 - \mu)$$

the variances of which are

$$\sigma_e^2 = \frac{1}{D_a^2}\{(\beta + \mu\gamma)^2\sigma_u^2 + \alpha^2\sigma_v^2 + \alpha^2\mu^2\gamma^2\sigma_\omega^2\} \tag{10.18a}$$

$$\sigma_f^2 = \frac{1}{D_a^2}[(1 - \mu - \beta)^2\sigma_u^2 + (1 + \alpha + a)^2\sigma_v^2 + \{\alpha(1 - \mu) + \beta(1 + a)\}^2\sigma_\omega^2] \tag{10.18b}$$

$$\sigma_r^2 = \frac{1}{D_a^2}\{(1 - \mu + \mu\gamma)^2\sigma_u^2 + \sigma_v^2 + (1 + a)^2\mu^2\gamma^2\sigma_\omega^2\} \tag{10.18c}$$

where

$$\gamma = \frac{1}{R\sigma_e^2} \tag{10.18d}$$

Questions of the existence and uniqueness of equilibrium again arise. In fact, the same general characterization exists as before, namely with monetary shocks there may be either one or three equilibria, with bond shocks zero or two equilibria, and with foreign interest rate shocks a unique equilibrium exists. Furthermore, it is possible for spot market intervention actually to exacerbate problems with respect to the existence of equilibrium. For example, in the case of bond shocks, $\sigma_v^2 > 0$, it was seen that existence problems arise if σ_v^2 is "too small." Since intervention taking the form of leaning against the wind typically leads to smaller variances, it will tend to increase private speculation γ, thereby increasing endogenous fluctuations in the demand for foreign exchange and unfavorably affecting the possible imbalance in equation (10.11), which was shown to be the cause of potential nonexistence of equilibrium. In other words, it is possible for the equilibrium to exist under perfectly flexible rates but to cease to exist when the monetary authority attempts to stabilize the spot exchange rate in accordance with a rule such as (10.15).[12]

We consider the qualitative effects of an increase in intervention. This can be viewed as being either a move from a perfectly flexible regime to a managed float, or alternatively as an increase in the degree of intervention a. The qualitative effects are summarized in table 10.1, part (b), and are illustrated in figures 10.4–10.6. Again, each disturbance is considered sequentially.

5.1 Domestic monetary shocks

Figure 10.4 illustrates the effects of an increase in spot market intervention in the face of monetary shocks ($\sigma_u^2 > 0$, $\sigma_v^2 = \sigma_\omega^2 = 0$). As before, WW is the rectangular hyperbola defined by (10.18d). The XX, YY and ZZ curves define the solutions for σ_e^2, σ_f^2, and σ_r^2 respectively given by (10.18a), (10.18b), and (10.18c), in terms of γ, for $\sigma_u^2 > 0$ with $\sigma_v^2 = \sigma_\omega^2 = 0$. These curves have the same properties as before. In particular, if $\beta < 1 - \mu$, XX is upward sloping, giving rise to a unique intersection point with WW. Otherwise, although figure 10.4(b) considers only a unique equilibrium, the possible of multiple equilibria exist in that case as well.

As the curves are drawn, the initial equilibria are at points A, C and E, as before. We consider now an increase in the degree of intervention a. This leaves the WW curve unchanged. By increasing the quantity D_a, it lowers σ_e^2 and σ_f^2 for any given value of γ, thereby leading to inward shifts in the XX, YY, and ZZ curves to X′X′, Y′Y′, and Z′Z′ respectively.

The new equilibria are at points A′, C′, and E′. The spot and forward rates are stabilized unambiguously, while the domestic interest rate is stabilized if $\beta < 1 - \mu$ and the ZZ curve is negatively sloping. The effects on the interest rate are less clear cut when ZZ is positively sloped.

The effects of intervention can be decomposed into two components. The first, measured by the movements AB, CD, and EF, is due to the direct shifts in the curves. The second, measured by the movements BA′, DC′, and FE′, represents the effects of increased private speculation resulting from the lower variance in the spot rate. In the case where

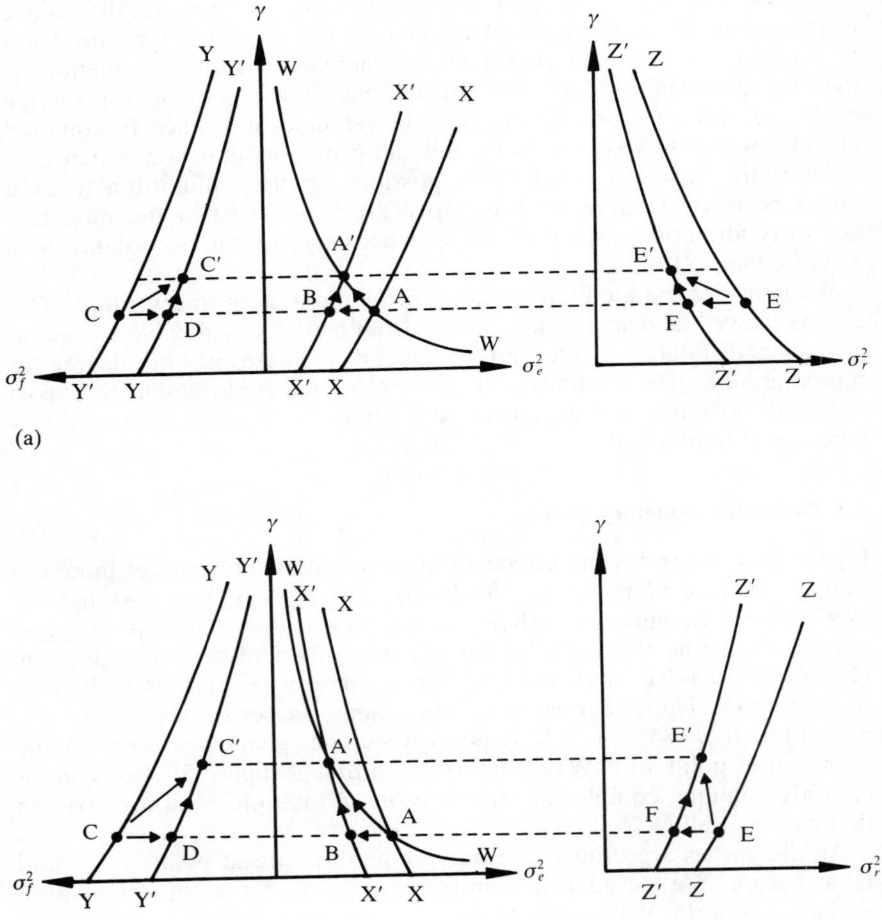

Figure 10.4 Spot market intervention – domestic monetary disturbances: (a) $\beta < 1 - \mu$; (b) $\beta > 1 - \mu$.

$\beta < 1 - \mu$, this latter effect tends to destabilize the spot rate while stabilizing the interest rate; when $\beta > 1 - \mu$, these two responses are reversed. While spot market intervention will always lead to a lower variance of the spot rate, it is possible when $\beta > 1 - \mu$ for the destabilizing effects of increased speculative activity to dominate, so that overall the interest rate is actually destabilized. This occurs when the leftward shift in ZZ to Z′Z′ in figure 10.4(b) is small and E′ lies to the right of E. By contrast, the increased private speculation always provides an additional stabilizing influence on the forward rate.

Setting $\sigma_v^2 = \sigma_\omega^2 = 0$ and dividing (10.7a) by (10.7b), we can also show

$$\frac{\sigma_e^2}{\sigma_f^2} = \frac{(\beta + \mu\gamma)^2}{(1 - \mu - \beta)^2}$$

From this relationship we obtain the rather paradoxical result that intervention in the spot market, by raising the speculative elasticity γ, in fact stabilizes the forward rate relatively more than it does the spot rate; the ratio σ_f^2/σ_e^2 falls.

5.2 Bond shocks

In considering this case we focus on only one of the two possible equilibria. As drawn, the other intersection point of the WW and XX curves would be beyond the figure. Leaning against the wind stabilizes the spot rate against all disturbances, including in this case bond disturbances v_t. The XX curve shifts to the left. However, in so doing, more of the adjustments to v_t are shifted to the interest rate and the forward rate. In fact, an increase in the degree of intervention causes the direct impact of v_t on r_t to increase, thereby resulting in a right shift of the ZZ curve. An increase in a will also cause the direct effect of v_t to impact more heavily on the forward rate if $\beta < 1 - \mu$, but less so if $\beta > 1 - \mu$. In the former case, the YY curve shifts outward; in the latter case it shifts inward.

The reduction in the spot rate stimulates private speculation. This increase in γ has a stabilizing effect on the spot rate, measured by BA′, which reinforces the direct stabilizing shift AB. The increase in γ also has a stabilizing influence on the forward rate, which is therefore definitely stabilized by the intervention rule (10.15) as long as YY is shifted inward, as it is in figure 10.5(b). However, if, as in figure 10.5(a), the YY curve is shifted out, it is quite likely that the destabilizing outward shift CD dominates the stabilizing effects of increased private speculation DC′, so that, on balance, the variance in the forward rate σ_f^2 is increased. Finally, the net effects on the interest rate are unclear. On the one hand, the outward shift in ZZ is destabilizing. On the other hand, increased private speculation is stabilizing. Either effect may dominate, and spot market intervention may either increase or decrease the variance σ_r^2.

5.3 Foreign interest rate shocks

The effects of spot market intervention in the face of foreign interest rate disturbances are illustrated in figure 10.6. An increase in a causes the XX curve to rotate inward and the ZZ curve to rotate outward. The YY curve shifts inward if $\beta < 1 - \mu$ and outward otherwise. By now the

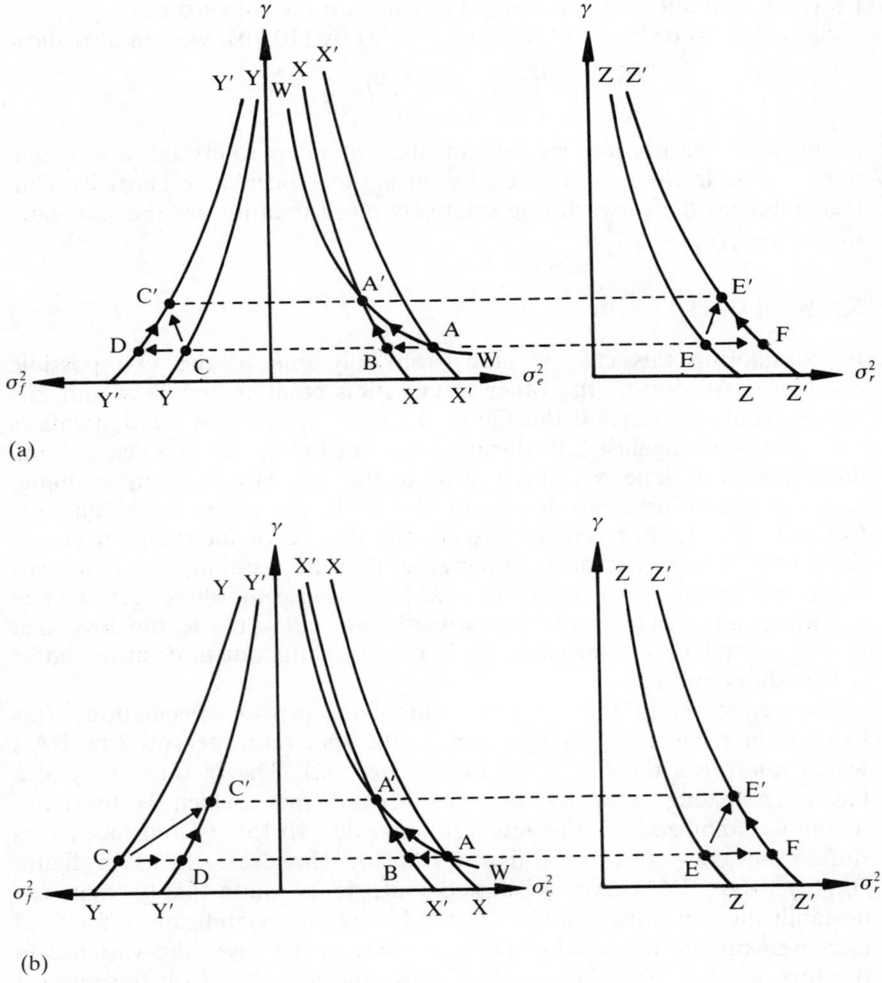

Figure 10.5 Spot market intervention – bond disturbances: (a) $\beta < 1 - \mu$; (b) $\beta > 1 - \mu$.

reasons for these shifts are clear. The direct effects of the increased intervention are given by AB, CD, and EF respectively, which measure the shifts in the XX, YY, and ZZ curves. For given γ, it is seen that more intensive speculation stabilizes the spot rate, while destabilizing the interest rate. The forward rate is stabilized as long as $\beta < 1 - \mu$, and is destabilized otherwise. However, the reduction in σ_e^2 raises γ, thereby increasing private speculation. This has a destabilizing effect on the spot

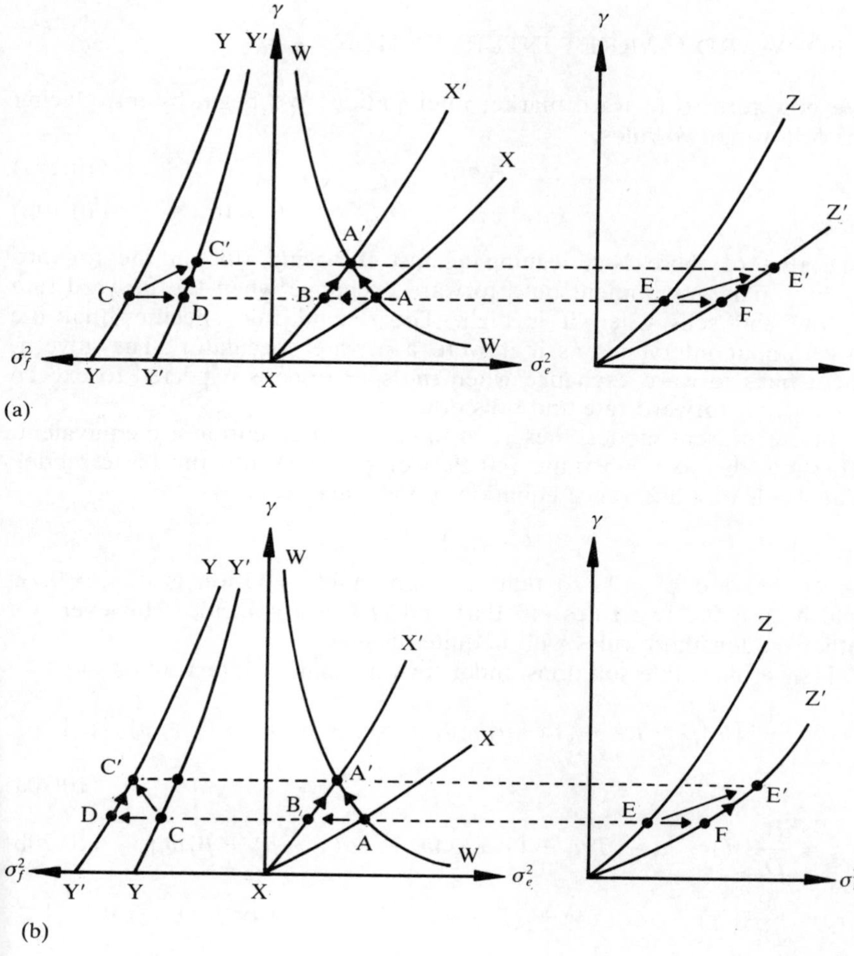

Figure 10.6 Foreign interest rate disturbances: (a) $\beta < 1 - \mu$; (b) $\beta > 1 - \mu$.

rate, which, however, is stabilized overall. This is evident from the move A to A′ along the WW curve. The increased private speculation has a stabilizing effect on the forward rate, which in figure 10.6(a), when the YY is shifted in, leads to an unambiguous reduction in the variance σ_f^2. However, in figure 10.6(b), when the YY curve shifts out, σ_f^2 may either rise or fall depending upon which effect dominates. Finally, the increase in private speculation tends to destabilize the domestic interest rate, thereby exacerbating the destabilizing effects of the outward rotation in the ZZ curve.

6 FORWARD MARKET INTERVENTION

We now turn to forward market intervention. We begin by introducing the following two rules:

$$g_t = -bf_t \tag{10.19a}$$

$$g_t = b(e^*_{t+1,t} - f_t) \qquad b > 0 \tag{10.19b}$$

The first of these is a leaning against the wind rule in the forward market. The government buys forward exchange when the forward rate is low and sells when it is high. The second rule specifies that the government intervenes as if it were a private speculator. The government buys forward exchange when the spot price is expected to exceed the current forward rate and sells otherwise.

In our present model, these two modes of intervention are equivalent. To show this, we substitute (10.19a) or (10.19b) into the basic model. This leads to a difference equation of the usual form

$$e^*_{t+i+1,t} = \phi'' e^*_{t+i,t}$$

In either case $\phi'' > 1$, so that the only stable solution is $e^*_{t+i,t} = 0$, in which case the two rules (10.19a) and (10.19b) coincide. However, for other models these rules will be quite distinct.

Hence the stable solutions under forward market intervention are

$$e_t = \frac{1}{D_b}[-\{\beta + \mu\gamma + (1-\mu)b\}u_t + \alpha v_t + \alpha\{\mu\gamma + (1-\mu)b\}\omega_t] \tag{10.20a}$$

$$f_t = \frac{1}{D_b}[(1-\mu-\beta)u_t + (1+\alpha)v_t - \{\alpha(1-\mu) + \beta\}\omega_t] \tag{10.20b}$$

$$r_t = \frac{1}{D_b}[\{(1-\mu+\mu\gamma) + (1-\mu)b\}u_t + v_t + \{\mu\gamma + (1-\mu)b\}\omega_t] \tag{10.20c}$$

where

$$D_b \equiv (\beta + \mu\gamma) + \alpha(\mu\gamma + 1 - \mu) + (1-\mu)(1+\alpha)b$$

the variances of which are

$$\sigma_e^2 = \frac{1}{D_b^2}[\{\beta + \mu\gamma + (1-\mu)b\}^2\sigma_u^2 + \alpha^2\sigma_v^2 + \alpha^2\{\mu\gamma + (1-\mu)b\}^2\sigma_\omega^2] \tag{10.21a}$$

$$\sigma_f^2 = \frac{1}{D_b^2}[(1-\mu-\beta)^2\sigma_u^2 + (1+\alpha)^2\sigma_v^2 + \{\alpha(1-\mu) + \beta\}^2\sigma_\omega^2] \tag{10.21b}$$

$$\sigma_r^2 = \frac{1}{D_b^2} [\{1 - \mu + \mu\gamma + (1 - \mu)b\}^2\sigma_u^2 + \sigma_v^2 + \{\mu\gamma + (1 - \mu)b\}^2\sigma_\omega^2] \tag{10.21c}$$

with

$$\gamma = \frac{1}{R\sigma_e^2} \tag{10.21d}$$

The same characteristics of existence and possible multiplicity of equilibria apply as before. Intervention in the forward market is shown to stabilize the spot rate against domestic bond disturbances and this can exacerbate existence problems, as it did before.

We now discuss the effects of an increase in forward market intervention. The qualitative effects are summarized in table 10.1, part (c) and are illustrated in figures 10.7, 10.8, and 10.9. Since the reasons are analogous to those given previously, our discussion can be brief.

6.1 Domestic monetary shocks

In figure 10.7 the WW, XX, YY, and ZZ curves are defined as before with the initial equilibria being at points A, C, and E. Consider now an increase in forward market intervention. This leaves the WW curve unaffected. If $\beta < 1 - \mu$, an increase in intervention shifts the XX curve to the right and the ZZ curve to the left; if $\beta > 1 - \mu$, these shifts are reversed. In all cases, the YY curve shifts inward.[13]

An increase in forward market intervention in accordance with (10.19) shifts the equilibria to A′, C′, and E′. The forward rate is always stabilized. In the case that $\beta < 1 - \mu$, such a rule destabilizes the spot rate, although the interest rate is probably, but not necessarily, stabilized. In contrast, if $\beta > 1 - \mu$, then intervention stabilizes the spot rate but destabilizes the interest rate.

The reasons for these effects can be seen by considering the two components of the shifts. In the first case, when forward market intervention destabilizes the spot price, the decrease in the elasticity of speculation γ is stabilizing. This is represented by the movement BA′, which partially, but not totally, offsets the destabilization resulting from the outward shift in the XX curve. In the case of the forward rate and the domestic interest rate, the decrease in γ is destabilizing. With respect to the former, it only partially offsets the stabilizing inward shift of the YY curve. In the case of the latter, it may dominate the inward movement of the ZZ curve and lead to a larger variance σ_r^2. However, when $\beta > 1 - \mu$, the increase in γ tends to stabilize σ_e^2 and σ_f^2 but to destabilize σ_r^2, in both cases accentuating the direct effects stemming from the shifts in the respective curves.

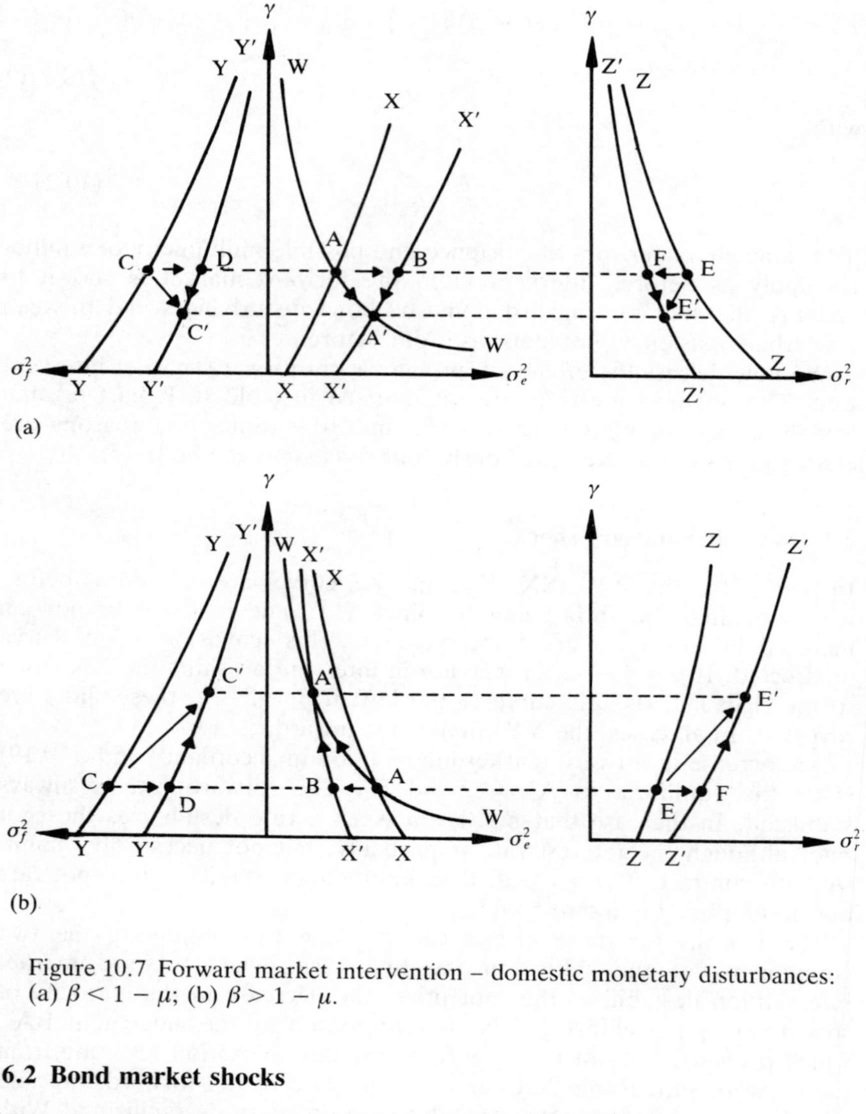

Figure 10.7 Forward market intervention – domestic monetary disturbances: (a) $\beta < 1 - \mu$; (b) $\beta > 1 - \mu$.

6.2 Bond market shocks

The effects of forward market intervention in the face of bond market shocks are clear cut. The increased intervention shifts all three curves XX, YY, and ZZ inward (figure 10.8). The direct effects resulting from the shifts, namely the movements AB, CD, and EF, are stabilizing. Moreover, the increase in γ resulting from the reduced variance of the spot rate is a further stabilizing influence in all cases.

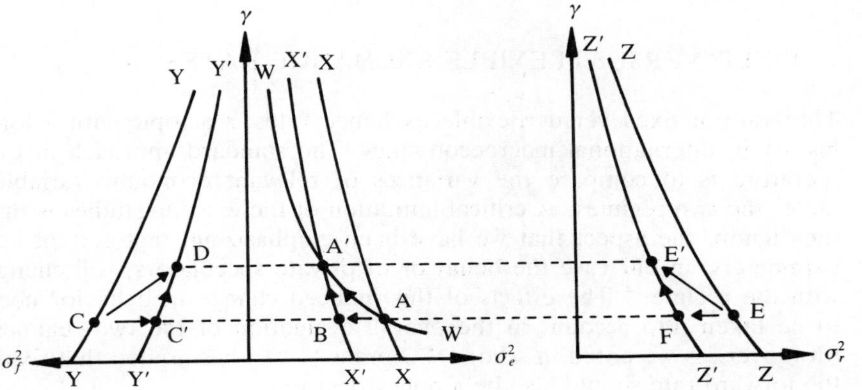

Figure 10.8 Forward market intervention – bond disturbances.

6.3 Foreign interest rate shocks

In this case an increase in forward market intervention leads not only to outward shifts in the XX and ZZ curves, but also to an inward shift in the YY curve (figure 10.9). The spot exchange rate and the interest rate are destabilized, while the forward rate is stabilized. In all cases, the reduction in γ partially, but not totally, offsets the direct effects resulting from the shifts in the curves.

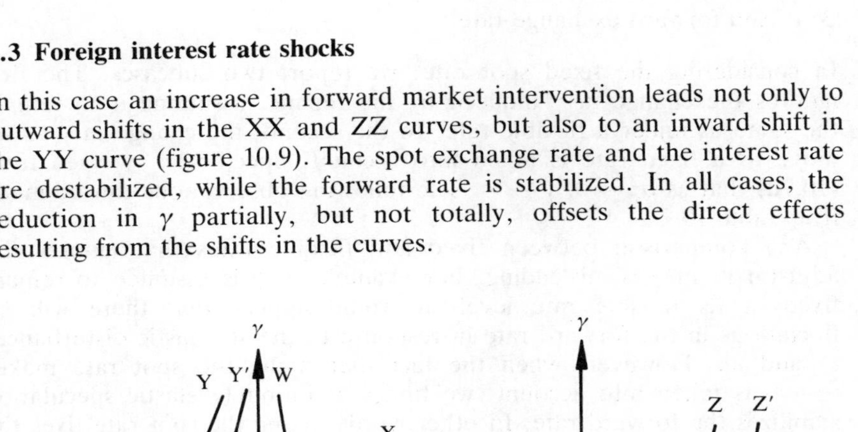

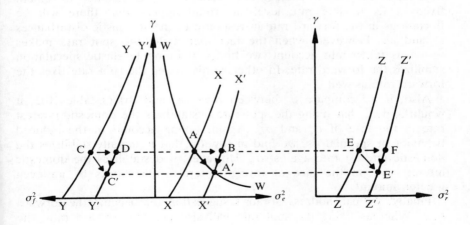

Figure 10.9 Forward market intervention – foreign market rate disturbances.

7 FIXED VERSUS FLEXIBLE EXCHANGE RATES

The issue of fixed versus flexible exchange rates is a topic with a long history in international macroeconomics. The standard approach in this literature is to compare the variances of relevant economic variables under the two regimes. A critical limitation of the existing studies is that they ignore the aspect that we have been emphasizing, that certain key parameters, in our case the behavior of private speculators, will change with the regime.[14] The effects of this induced change in behavior need to be taken into account in the overall evaluation of the two regimes. Moreover, as we noted in section 1, Spraos (1959) has argued that fixing the forward rate should also be a policy decision.

Table 10.2 compares the variances σ_e^2, σ_f^2 and σ_r^2 under three regimes:

1 a perfectly flexible exchange rate;
2 a fixed spot exchange rate;
3 a fixed forward exchange rate.

In considering the fixed spot rate, we report two subcases. The first ignores the change in γ induced by the regime, assuming it to remain the same as under a flexible rate. In the second, the change in γ as we move to a fixed rate is taken into account. Specifically, we see from (10.7d) that as $\sigma_e^2 \to 0$, $\gamma \to \infty$. The following observations can be made from table 10.2.

Any comparison between fixed and flexible rates that ignores the adjustment in γ is misleading. For example, if γ is assumed to remain fixed at its flexible rate level, it would appear that there will be fluctuations in the forward rate in response to the stochastic disturbances v_t and ω_t. However, when the fact that fixing the spot rate makes $\gamma \to \infty$ is taken into account, we find that infinitely elastic speculation stabilizes the forward rate. In other words, fixing the spot rate fixes the forward rate as well.

Also, if we compare σ_r^2 between rows (a) and (b) of table 10.2, it would appear that fixing the spot rate destabilizes the domestic interest rate in the face of σ_v^2 and σ_ω^2. Again, taking account of the induced behavior of speculators, we find in row (c) that it actually stabilizes the domestic interest rate against σ_v^2. However, it destabilizes the domestic interest rate in the face of foreign interest rate shocks by an even greater amount.

Finally, we can address Spraos's suggestion for pegging the forward rate. Whereas fixing the spot rate will also peg the forward rate, the reverse is not true. Pegging the forward rate completely stabilizes the spot rate for σ_v^2 and partially stabilizes it for σ_ω^2, but it may actually destabilize it against σ_v^2. Also, fixing the forward rate may be better or

TABLE 10.2 *Fixed versus flexible exchange rates*

Rate	σ_e^2	σ_f^2	σ_r^2
(a) Flexible rates	$\frac{(\beta+\mu\gamma)^2\sigma_u^2+\alpha^2\sigma_v^2+\alpha^2\mu^2\gamma^2\sigma_\omega^2}{\{\beta+\mu\gamma+\alpha(\mu\gamma+1-\mu)\}^2}$	$\frac{(1-\mu-\beta)^2\sigma_u^2+(1+\alpha)^2\sigma_v^2+\{\alpha(1-\mu)+\beta\}^2\sigma_\omega^2}{\{\beta+\mu\gamma+\alpha(\mu\gamma+1-\mu)\}^2}$	$\frac{(1-\mu+\mu\gamma)^2\sigma_u^2+\sigma_v^2+\mu^2\gamma^2\sigma_\omega^2}{\{\beta+\mu\gamma+\alpha(\mu\gamma+1-\mu)\}^2}$
(b) Fixed spot rate γ constant	0	$\frac{\sigma_v^2+\beta^2\sigma_\omega^2}{(\beta+\mu\gamma)^2}$	$\frac{\sigma_v^2+\mu^2\gamma^2\sigma_\omega^2}{(\beta+\mu\gamma)^2}$
(c) Fixed spot rate $\gamma \to \infty$	0	0	σ_ω^2
(d) Fixed forward rate	$\frac{\sigma_u^2+\alpha^2\sigma_\omega^2}{(1+\alpha)^2}$	0	$\frac{\sigma_u^2+\sigma_\omega^2}{(1+\alpha)^2}$

worse than fixing the spot rate from the viewpoint of interest rate stability, depending upon the sources of the disturbances. Thus the desirability of Spraos's suggestion of fixing the forward rate would appear to be questionable.

8 CONCLUSIONS

In this chapter we have emphasized the fact that private speculative behavior is endogenous. The consequences of this for the effects of (a) increased risk and (b) exchange market intervention policies have been analysed at some length using a simple model. Space limitations preclude any detailed review of specific results. The main general conclusion is that any structural change to the economy, whether exogenous or due to a changing policy regime, has two effects: (a) the direct effects of the change itself; (b) effects induced through changes in private speculative behavior. In some cases these two partial effects may reinforce one another; in other cases they are offsetting. However, both need to be taken into account, and any analysis that ignores the latter effect may be seriously misleading. Indeed, the analysis suggests the possibility that the private effects can quite plausibly be sufficiently strong to dominate and reverse the direct effects.

The policy rules that we have analysed are of the leaning against the wind type. The effects of such rules are not always clear cut and depend upon the source of the disturbances impinging on the economy. For example, stabilizing the spot rate may destabilize the forward rate, and vice versa. In fact, it is even possible under certain circumstances for leaning against the wind in the spot market to generate such an increase in private speculative behavior that the spot rate itself is destabilized rather than stabilized.

By introducing risk-averse speculators, the model introduces a second instrument of exchange rate management, namely forward market intervention. In fact, in the latter part of the chapter we have used the model to address the desirability of actually fixing the forward rate, as has been suggested in the past. Our results suggest that the desirability of such a policy is very much open to question.

Of course, we should not lose sight of the fact that the specific results pertain to a special model. We have chosen a specification that is purely static and disturbances that are purely random, so that exchange rate expectations play no role. This choice has been made intentionally because it enables much of the analysis to proceed graphically and exposes the issues that are involved. However, the principles, if not the specific details, will apply to more general models.

NOTES

1 Most of the existing studies deal with white noise disturbances arising from different sources of domestic and foreign origin. More recent work has investigated the dichotomy between transitory and permanent shocks, and unanticipated and anticipated disturbances as well as information differentials between public and private agents (see for example Aizenman and Frenkel, 1985; Turnovsky, 1987, this volume, ch. 9).

2 Reference should be made to two earlier papers by Tsiang (1959) and Day (1976, 1977). Both authors discuss intervention in the partial equilibrium context of the foreign exchange market. They do not discuss intervention as a more general instrument of macroeconomic stabilization policy.

3 These issues were first identified and discussed by McCafferty and Driskill (1980) in the context of speculation in commodities markets (see also Kawai, 1983; Turnovsky, 1983). They were also analysed at about the same time in the context of foreign exchange markets by Driskill and McCafferty (1980), who encountered the problem of nonuniqueness but not nonexistence of equilibrium. These issues were also noted by Kawai (1984) as well as Black (1985) although in his model neither problem arises.

4 We find it analytically convenient to separate forward market participation into pure speculation and pure arbitrage. We implicitly treat the acquisition of an amount x of uncovered bonds as combining a covered investment of x in foreign bonds and a speculative purchase of foreign currency forward in amount x. In a portfolio model of foreign investment, we identify a third motive for participating in the forward market as hedging against domestic inflation. Forward positions for hedging purposes depend upon the relative variability of the domestic and foreign price levels and do not respond to the variables we are concerned with here. We can thus treat the forward position due to hedging as a constant absorbed in s_t (see Eaton and Turnovsky, 1981).

5 The domestic bond market equilibrium condition is based on the assumption that foreigners hold zero stocks of domestic bonds. Eaton and Turnovsky (1981) show that this is more likely to arise when the domestic price level is more sensitive than the foreign price level to the exchange rate.

6 The approximation is obtained as follows:

$$\frac{H_t - \bar{H}}{\bar{H}} = \left\{ \frac{(1 + g_t)(B_t/P_t) - \bar{B}/\bar{P}}{\bar{B}/\bar{P}} \right\} \frac{\bar{B}/\bar{P}}{\bar{H}} + \left(\frac{S_t - \bar{S}}{\bar{S}} \right) \frac{\bar{S}}{\bar{H}}$$

If we assume that g_t is small,

$$(1 + g_t) \frac{B_t}{P_t} \approx \frac{\bar{B}}{\bar{P}} + \frac{\bar{B}}{\bar{P}} \left(g_t + \frac{B_t - \bar{B}}{\bar{B}} - \frac{P_t - \bar{P}}{P} \right)$$

Now, for any variable X,

$$\frac{X_t - \bar{X}}{\bar{X}} \approx \ln\left(1 + \frac{X_t - \bar{X}}{\bar{X}}\right) = \ln\left(\frac{X_t}{\bar{X}}\right) = x_t - \bar{x}$$

where $x = \ln X$. Assuming that in equilibrium $\bar{S} \approx \bar{H}^{\mathrm{f}}$, we can write

$$h_t = (1 - \mu)(b_t + g_t - p_t) + \mu s_t$$

7 The microeconomics underlying our model is contained in Eaton and Turnovsky (1981). In that model, the speculative coefficient γ is the only one to be endogenized in this way (see also Black, 1985).

8 This requirement that the asymptotic variance is finite can be justified by appealing to some appropriate transversality condition for a corresponding model derived from optimizing behavior. Under appropriate conditions this requirement also imposes boundedness on price expectations.

9 This analysis is ignoring v_{2t}, so that v_t must be attributed totally to fluctuations v_{1t} in the bond market.

10 The consequences of forward market intervention for the consolidated balance sheet of the fiscal authority and central bank are discussed in the appendix to Eaton and Turnovsky (1984).

11 See, for example, the papers in Bhandari (1985).

12 As discussed below, leaning against the wind in the spot market moves the XX curve to the left. In the case of bond shocks it is possible for this curve to move sufficiently far to the left that there is no intersection point such as A′ with the WW curve.

13 Alternatively, if we interpret our specification of intervention as being equivalent to increased private speculation, it can be represented graphically as an outward shift in the WW curve, with all other curves remaining fixed. This representation yields precisely the same qualitative implications to those presented.

14 To the extent that this literature assumes uncovered interest parity ($\gamma \to \infty$), it is, of course, immune to this criticism.

REFERENCES

Aizenman, J. and Frenkel, J. A. (1985) Optimal wage indexation, foreign exchange market intervention and monetary policy. *American Economic Review,* 75, 402–23.

Bhandari, J. S. (ed.) (1985) *Exchange Rate Management under Uncertainty.* Cambridge, MA: MIT Press.

Black, S. W. (1985) The effect of alternative policies on the variability of exchange rates: the Harrod effect. In *Exchange Rate Management under Uncertainty* (ed. J. S. Bhandari). Cambridge, MA: MIT Press.

Boyer, R. (1978) Optimal foreign exchange market intervention. *Journal of Political Economy,* 86, 1045–56.

Day, W. H. L. (1976) The advantages of exclusive forward exchange rate support. *IMF Staff Papers,* 23, 137–63.

—— (1977) Flexible exchange rates: a case for official intervention. *IMF Staff Papers,* 24, 330–43.

Driskill, R. and McCafferty, S. (1980) Speculation, rational expectations, and stability of the foreign exchange market. *Journal of International Economy,* 10, 91–102.

Eaton, J. and Turnovsky, S. J. (1981) Exchange risk political risk and macroeconomic equilibrium. Discussion Paper 388, Economic Growth Center, Yale University, New Haven, CT.

—— and —— (1984) The forward exchange market, speculation and exchange market intervention. *Quarterly Journal of Economics,* 99, 45–69.

Fama, E. and Farber, A. (1979) Money, bonds and foreign exchange. *American Economic Review,* 69, 639–49.

Frenkel, J. A. and Aizenman, J. (1982) Aspects of the optimal management of exchange rates. *Journal of International Economics,* 13, 231–56.

Kawai, M. (1983) Price volatility of storable commodities under rational expectations in spot and futures market. *International Economic Review,* 24, 435–59.

—— (1984) The effect of forward exchange on spot-rate-volatility under risk and rational expectations. *Journal of International Economics,* 19, 155–72.

Keynes, J. M. (1930) *A Treatise on Money,* vol. 2. London: Macmillan.

Kouri, P. J. K. (1976) The determinants of the forward premium. Institute for International Economic Studies, Paper 62.

Lucas, R. E., Jr. (1975) An equilibrium model of the business cycle. *Journal of Political Economy,* 83, 1113–44.

McCafferty, S. and Driskill, R. (1980) Problems of existence and uniqueness in nonlinear rational expectations models. *Econometrica,* 48, 1313–17.

Niehans, J. (1984) *International Monetary Economics.* Baltimore, MD: Johns Hopkins University Press.

Roper, D. E. and Turnovsky, S. J. (1980) Optimal exchange market intervention in a simple stochastic macro model. *Canadian Journal of Economics,* 13, 296–309.

Solnik, B. (1973) *European Capital Markets.* Lexington, MA: Heath.

Spraos, J. (1959) Speculation, arbitrage and sterling. *Economic Journal,* 69, 1–21.

Tsiang, S. C. (1959) The theory of forward exchange and the effects of government intervention on the forward exchange market. *IMF Staff Papers,* 6, 75–106.

Turnovsky, S. J. (1983) The determination of spot and futures prices with storable commodities. *Econometrica,* 51, 1363–87.

—— (1987) Optimal monetary policy and wage indexation under alternative disturbances and information structures. *Journal of Money, Credit, and Banking,* 19, 157–80. Reprinted in this volume as chapter 9.

Part IV

Intertemporal Optimizing Models

11 Domestic and Foreign Disturbances in an Optimizing Model of Exchange Rate Determination

1 INTRODUCTION

Much has been written recently on analysing exchange rate determination in small open economies under flexible exchange rates. The models developed typically consider the effects of different disturbances on the behavior of the economy both in the short run and over time. The disturbances usually analysed are domestic monetary and fiscal policy changes on the one hand, and foreign interest rate and price changes on the other. Two issues which have received a lot of attention include the adjustment of the exchange rate to monetary disturbances, and the degree to which flexible rates insulate the domestic economy against foreign disturbances. The overwhelming bulk of the existing literature employs *ad hoc* models of an essentially arbitrary nature. As a consequence, many of the conclusions with respect to these and other issues depend upon the chosen specification of the model. Indeed, much of the thrust of the existing literature is to investigate the sensitivity of various propositions to specific assumptions.[1]

Two exceptions to the above characterization of the literature are papers by Obstfeld (1981) and Hodrick (1982), in which the impacts of various domestic policy disturbances are analysed in a model in which the behavioral functions are derived from explicit optimization on the

Originally published in *Journal of International Money and Finance,* 1, 1985, 151–71. This chapter was originally presented at the Midwest International Economics Conference held at the University of Illinois at Urbana-Champaign in April 1984. I am grateful to the discussants of the paper, Jagdeep Bhandari and Jonathan Eaton, for their comments. The suggestions of the referees are also gratefully acknowledged.

part of agents in the economy.[2] Both studies are based on the assumptions of purchasing power parity (PPP) and uncovered interest parity (UIP). In the Hodrick analysis, which is based on the assumption of a constant rate of consumer time preference, the disturbances lead to instantaneous jumps in the economy from one steady state to another. There are no transitional dynamics as is typically the case in *ad hoc* models based on similar assumptions. By contrast, the Obstfeld analysis endogenizes the rate of time preference in a manner suggested by Uzawa (1968) and finds the optimizing system to exhibit saddlepoint behavior.

In this chapter we analyse the effects of both domestic and foreign disturbances using an optimizing approach under the more plausible empirical assumption that capital is only imperfectly mobile internationally, in the sense that UIP does not hold.[3] The framework that we employ is an adaptation of the Brock and Turnovsky (1981) perfect foresight equilibrium. This is characterized as follows: (a) all relationships are derived from optimizing behavior; (b) all expectations are realized; (c) all markets clear. We retain the assumption of PPP, as the degree of substitutability between domestic and foreign goods is inessential to the results that we obtain.

The remainder of the chapter proceeds as follows. In section 2 we outline the framework, spelling out the optimization and deriving the perfect foresign equilibrium. The steady state equilibrium is discussed in section 3, while the transitional dynamics are considered in the following section. The short-run effects on the domestic economy of the various domestic and foreign disturbances are analysed in section 5. The main findings of the study are reviewed in the final section, where some generalizations of the analysis are also discussed.

2 THE FRAMEWORK

The model contains three sectors: (a) consumers, (b) firms, and (c) the government. To preserve analytical tractability we assume that all consumers and firms are identical, enabling us to focus on the representative individual in each group.

2.1 Structure of the economy

We assume that the domestic economy is small. It produces a single traded good, the foreign price of which is given on the world market. In percentage change terms, the PPP relationship implies

$$p = q + e$$

where p is the rate of inflation of the good in domestic currency, q is the rate of inflation of the good in foreign currency, and e is the rate of exchange depreciation.

We assume that domestic residents may hold three assets. The first is domestic money, which is not held by foreigners. Secondly, they may hold a nontraded bond, issued by the domestic government, which is denominated in terms of domestic currency and pays a nominal interest rate r. Thirdly, they may hold (or issue) a traded bond denominated in foreign currency and paying an exogenous world interest rate r^*.

The representative consumer's plans are obtained by solving the following intertemporal optimization problem[4]

$$\max \int_0^\infty \exp(-\beta t)\{U(c, l) + V(m)\}\, dt \qquad U_c > 0,\ U_l < 0,\ V' > 0 \tag{11.1a}$$

$$U_{cc} < 0,\ U_{ll} < 0,\ U_{cl} < 0,\ V'' < 0$$

subject to

$$c + \dot{m} + \dot{b} + \dot{a} = wl + \pi + (r^* - q)b + (r - q - e)a - (q + e)m - \tfrac{1}{2}\alpha b^2 - \tau \tag{11.1b}$$

and initial conditions

$$m(0) = \frac{M_0}{P(0)} \qquad a(0) = \frac{A_0}{P(0)} \qquad b(0) = \frac{B_0}{Q_0} \tag{11.1c}$$

where c is the real consumption, m are real money balances, M are nominal money balances, b is the real stock of traded bonds, B is the nominal stock of traded bonds, a is the real stock of nontraded bonds, A is the nominal stock of nontraded bonds, l is labor, w is the real wage rate, taken as parametrically given, π is the real profit, taken as parametrically given, r is the domestic nominal interest rate, r^* is the foreign nominal interest rate, e is the anticipated rate of exchange depreciation, which is equal to the actual rate of exchange depreciation, τ is the lump-sum tax, β is the rate of time preference, taken to be constant, P is the domestic price level, and Q is the foreign price level.

The budget constraint is straightforward, although several features merit comment. First, since the analysis is based on perfect foresight, the anticipated rate of exchange depreciation is assumed to be equal to the actual rate of exchange depreciation. Second, since the domestic assets are denominated in domestic currency, they are subject to the unit rate of capital loss of $p = q + e$. By contrast, since the traded bond is denominated in foreign currency, the corresponding rate of capital loss is q. Third, the budget constraint includes a cost item $\frac{1}{2}\alpha b^2$. This term is meant to capture, in a certainty equivalent framework, the imperfect substitutability between domestic and foreign bonds. In a stochastic model the cost parameter α would be a function of the degree of exchange risk and the degree of risk aversion of domestic investors. While our representation of imperfect capital mobility is restrictive, it will be seen below that it is perfectly sensible in the sense that the demand function it yields for traded bonds is precisely equivalent to those derived from standard stochastic optimization models.

The utility function is assumed to be concave in its arguments c, l, and m. The assumption $U_{cl} < 0$ that the marginal utility of consumption decreases with labor (increases with leisure) is plausible and renders the results more determinate. The separability of utility into a function of c and l on the one hand and m on the other is made primarily for expositional simplicity. It leads to a separation of the real part of the system from the nominal. In the concluding section we note how relaxing this assumption changes our results in a minimal way.

In determining his optimal plans for c, l, m, b, and a, the consumer is assumed to take e, g, π, τ, w, r, r^*, the price level P, and the exchange rate E as parametrically given. The initial conditions in (11.1c) relate to the initial stocks of real bonds and real stock of money balances held by consumers. By definition these are the corresponding initial nominal stocks divided by the initial price level.

Firms are assumed to produce output by hiring labor to maximize real profit

$$\pi = f(l) - wl \tag{11.2}$$

where $f(l)$ is the firm's production function, assumed to possess the usual neoclassical property of positive, but diminishing, marginal product of labor.

The domestic government's budget constraint, expressed in real terms, is

$$\dot{m} + \dot{a} = g + ra - \tau - (q + e)(m + a) \tag{11.3}$$

where g denotes real government expenditure and all other variables are defined above. This equation asserts that total real expenditures, including interest payments, less the lump-sum tax and 'inflation tax' revenues, must be financed either through printing money or by issuing bonds.

The rate of accumulation of traded bonds is by definition equal to the balance of payments on current account, which in turn equals the balance of trade plus the real interest payments on the net holdings of foreign debt. With a single traded commodity the balance of trade is simply the excess of domestic production over domestic absorption by the domestic private and government sector. In real terms the relationship is given by

$$\dot{b} = f(l) - c - g + (r^* - q)b \tag{11.4}$$

Ignoring the term $\frac{1}{2}\alpha b^2$, which is an attempt to express the consumer budget constraint in certainty equivalent terms, we can see that the constraints (11.1b), (11.2), (11.3), and (11.4) are linearly dependent. One can therefore be ignored.

2.2 Determination of perfect foresight equilibrium

We consider a perfect foresight equilibrium to the model to be one in which the planned demand and supply functions that solve the optimization problems, consistent with the accumulation equations, clear all markets at all points of time. We now proceed to develop these conditions for the economy.

Beginning with consumers, we write the optimization problem (11.1a) and (11.1b) in the Lagrangian form

$$\begin{aligned} H \equiv\ & \exp(-\beta t)\{U(c, l) + V(m)\} \\ & + \mu \exp(-\beta t)\{wl + \pi + (r^* - q)b + (r - q - e)a \\ & - (q + e)m - \dot{m} - \dot{b} - \dot{a} - c - \tfrac{1}{2}\alpha b^2 - \tau\} \end{aligned} \tag{11.5}$$

where $\exp(-\beta t)$ is the associated discounted Lagrange multiplier. The optimality conditions for consumers are

$$U_c(c, l) - \mu = 0 \tag{11.6a}$$

$$U_l(c, l) + w\mu = 0 \tag{11.6b}$$

$$V'(m) - \mu(q + e) = -\dot{\mu} + \mu\beta \tag{11.6c}$$

$$\mu(r^* - \alpha b - q) = -\dot{\mu} + \mu\beta \tag{11.6d}$$

$$\mu\{r - (q + e)\} = -\dot{\mu} + \mu\beta \tag{11.6e}$$

together with the budget constraint (11.1b) and initial conditions (11.1c). In addition there are transversality conditions at infinity:

$$\lim_{t\to\infty} \mu m \exp(-\beta t) = \lim_{t\to\infty} \mu b \exp(-\beta t) = \lim_{t\to\infty} \mu a \exp(-\beta t) = 0 \tag{11.6f}$$

Equations (11.6a)–(11.6e) are the Euler equations corresponding to the optimization with respect to *c, l, m, b,* and *a* respectively. Combining equations (11.6d) and (11.6e), we derive

$$b = \frac{1}{\alpha}(r^* + e - r) \tag{11.7}$$

This equation expresses the net demand for foreign bonds by domestic residents as being proportional to the uncovered interest differential on foreign and domestic bonds. This form of demand function has been postulated by Driskill and McCafferty (1980) and Turnovsky and Bhandari (1982), among others. It is essentially analogous to that derived in a two-period mean–variance stochastic framework by Eaton and Turnovsky (1981) and Dornbusch (1980). In terms of that framework, $\alpha \approx A\sigma_e^2$, where A is a measure of absolute risk aversion and σ_e^2 is the one-period variance of the exchange rate. Since $R = Az$, where R denotes the coefficient of relative risk aversion and z is real wealth, and assuming that R is constant, we can express the demand function derived using the mean–variance approach in terms of a portfolio fraction.[5]

Taking α to be constant, as we shall throughout our analysis, our formulation is essentially a certainty-equivalent specification of constant absolute risk aversion. However, postulating α to be inversely proportional to wealth is analogous to assuming constant relative risk aversion. In either case, the coefficient α can be used to parameterize the degree of capital mobility. In the case of perfect capital mobility (no exchange risk or risk neutrality), $\alpha = 0$ and (11.7) reduces to the UIP condition

$$r = r^* + e \tag{11.7$'$}$$

In the case of zero capital mobility, $\alpha \rightarrow \infty$, so that $b = 0$, i.e. domestic residents hold no traded bonds. Thus the specification of the cost term in the budget constraint gives rise to a demand for foreign bonds which is entirely reasonable and accords with previous specifications, both derived theoretically or simply postulated.

The equilibrium conditions for the representative firm are simply the usual marginal condition

$$f'(l) = w \tag{11.8a}$$

together with the definition of profit

$$\pi = f(l) - wl \tag{11.8b}$$

To complete the specification, government policy needs to be spelled out. We assume that the government sets its real expenditure g exogenously. It also sets a constant rate of nominal monetary growth θ so that the rate of growth of the real money stock is

$$\dot{m} = (\theta - q - e)m \tag{11.9}$$

It then sets the lump-sum tax τ so as to balance its budget, so that the real stock of government bonds outstanding remains fixed at $a = \bar{a}$, with $\dot{a} = 0$.[6]

Combining the optimality conditions (11.6a)–(11.6e), (11.8a), and (11.8b), together with the accumulation equations (11.3) and (11.4), and the policy specification (11.9), we can express the perfect foresight equilibrium by the following independent equations:

$$U_c(c, l) = \mu \tag{11.10a}$$

$$U_l(c, l) = -f'(l)\mu \tag{11.10b}$$

$$V'(m) = r\mu \tag{11.10c}$$

$$\alpha b = r^* + e - r \tag{11.10d}$$

$$\dot{m} = (\theta - q - e)m \tag{11.10e}$$

$$\dot{b} = f(l) - c - g + (r^* - q)b \tag{11.10f}$$

$$\dot{\mu} = \mu\{\beta - (r - q - e)\} \tag{11.10g}$$

together with the balanced budget condition

$$g + r\bar{a} - \theta m - (q + e)\bar{a} - \tau = 0 \tag{11.10h}$$

Taken in pairs, the first three equations describe the marginal rate of substitution conditions necessary for consumer optimality. The marginal rate of substitution between consumption and labor must equal the real wage, and the marginal rate of substitution between consumption and money balances must equal the nominal rate of interest. Equations (11.10d)–(11.10g) are unchanged from before. Of these, the first three have already been discussed. The last equation, which we can write as

$$r - (q + e) = \beta - \dot{U}_c/U_c$$

is the usual arbitrage condition for the rate of return on consumption.[7]

In general, the evolution of the system proceeds as follows. Equations (11.10a)–(11.10d) determine the short-run solutions for c, l, r, and e in terms of the marginal utility of consumption μ, the real stock of money m, and the real stock of foreign bonds b, as well as the exogenous parameters g, θ, q, r^*. Substituting these solutions into (11.10e)–(11.10g) determines the evolution of the state variables m, b, and μ. In addition there is the government budget constraint (11.10h). Under our assumption that a is fixed and that the budget is balanced by the imposition of the lump-sum tax, the required level of τ is determined residually, enabling this equation to be ignored.

One further requirement that we will impose is the intertemporal budget constraint on the economy, ruling out the possibility that the country can run up an indefinite credit or debt with the rest of the world. This is expressed by

$$\lim_{t\to\infty} \exp\{-(r^* - q)t\}\, b(t) = 0 \tag{11.11}$$

Integrating (11.10f) we obtain

$$b(t) = \exp(r^* - q)\left[b_0 + \int_0^t \exp\{-(r^* - q)t'\}\{f(l) - c - g\}\,\mathrm{d}t'\right]$$

so that the constraint reduces to

$$b_0 + \int_0^\infty \exp\{-(r^* - q)t'\}\{f(l) - c - g\}\,\mathrm{d}t' = 0 \tag{11.11'}$$

With imperfect capital mobility this condition is automatically met. However, in the limiting case of perfect capital mobility it does impose an additional constraint which needs to be taken into account.

The system of equations (11.10a)–(11.10g) provides the basis for the short-run and long-run analysis of the system and its response to the various disturbances undertaken in the following sections.

3 STEADY STATE EQUILIBRIUM

Since the analysis is based on the assumption of perfect foresight, the transitional dynamic adjustment path of the system is determined in part by the expectations of the long-run steady state. It is therefore convenient to begin with a consideration of the steady state and the long-run effects of the various disturbances.

The steady state equilibrium is attained when $\dot{m} = \dot{b} = \dot{\mu} = 0$, implying that

$$e = \theta - q, \qquad p = \theta \tag{11.12a}$$

$$f(l) + (r^* - q)b = c + g \tag{11.12b}$$

$$b = \frac{1}{\alpha}(r^* - q - \beta) \tag{11.12c}$$

That is, in steady state equilibrium, the rate of exchange depreciation equals the difference between the domestic monetary growth rate (equal to the long-run domestic rate of inflation) and the foreign rate of inflation. Total domestic absorption $c + g$ is constrained by output augmented by net interest earned on domestic residents' holdings of foreign bonds. The net demand for foreign bonds is proportional to the difference between the real rate of return on foreign bonds and the rate of time preference. Combining (11.12a), (11.12c), and (11.10d) yields

$$r = \beta + \theta \tag{11.12d}$$

The domestic nominal rate of interest is fixed by $\beta + \theta$; the real rate of interest is therefore equal to the rate of time preference.

Except in the total absence of capital mobility, the real rate of interest in a small open economy is dependent upon the real rate of interest abroad. The same therefore applies to the rate of time preference. Indeed, in the limiting case of perfect capital mobility (UIP), previous authors have demonstrated that for a well-defined steady state equilibrium to exist, the two must be equal (see for example Hodrick, 1982). More generally, the relationship will depend largely upon the degree of capital mobility. Given our parameterization of this in terms of α, it seems reasonable to postulate that β is given by the weighted average

$$\beta = \frac{1}{1+\alpha}(r^* - q) + \frac{\alpha}{1+\alpha}\bar{\beta} \tag{11.13}$$

where $\bar{\beta}$ is taken to be a constant, independent of the foreign real interest rate.[8] In the limiting case of perfect capital mobility, $\alpha = 0$, implying $\beta = r^* - q$. In this case (11.12d) implies the long-run real interest parity relationship

$$r - \theta = r^* - q \tag{11.14}$$

At the other extreme of perfect capital immobility $\alpha \to \infty$ and $\beta \to \bar{\beta}$, and the domestic interest rate becomes independent of the rate abroad. Our representation of the case of imperfect capital mobility is as a weighted average of those two extremes, with the weight reflecting the assumed degree of capital mobility.

Using equations (11.12) and (11.13), we can reduce the steady state equilibrium to

$$U_l(c, l) = f'(l)U_c(c, l) = 0 \tag{11.15a}$$

$$V'(m) - \left(\frac{r^* - q}{1+\alpha} + \frac{\alpha\bar{\beta}}{1+\alpha} + \theta\right) U_c(c, l) = 0 \tag{11.15b}$$

$$f(l) = c + g - (r^* - q)b \tag{11.15c}$$

$$(1+\alpha)b = r^* - q - \bar{\beta} \tag{11.15d}$$

which determines the four variables c, l, m, and b in terms of the exogenous policy parameters and disturbances. The equilibrium is obtained in the following recursive manner. First, the equilibrium stock of traded bonds is determined from the uncovered real interest differential (11.15d). This determines net real interest income to the economy. Given this, (11.15a) and (11.15c) together determine real activity, namely employment (and output) and consumption. The real money supply is then obtained residually from the marginal rate of substitution condition (11.15b).

Our objective is to analyse the effects of changes in (a) the domestic monetary growth rate θ, (b) the domestic government expenditure g, (c) the foreign nominal interest rate r^*, and (d) the foreign rate of inflation q. These are summarized in tables 11.1 and 11.2.

In the steady state an expansion in the monetary growth rate has the usual neutrality properties. All real activity, as described by output, employment, consumption, and the trade balance, as well as the marginal utility of consumption, remains unchanged. The real interest rate and the real stock of traded bonds also do no change, while the real stock of money falls. The domestic nominal after-tax interest rate, the domestic rate of inflation, and rate of exchange depreciation all rise proportionately.[9]

TABLE 11.1 *Steady state effects of changes in domestic monetary growth rate and domestic government expenditure*

	Change in	
Effect on	*Domestic monetary growth rate* θ	*Domestic government expenditure* g
Traded bonds b	0	0
Employment l	0	$-\dfrac{U_{lc} + f' U_{cc}}{\Delta} > 0$
Consumption c	0	$\dfrac{U_{ll} + (f'' U_c + f' U_{cl})}{\Delta} < 0$
Trade balance T	0	0
Marginal utility of consumption U_c	0	$\Omega/\Delta > 0$
Real money stock m	$\dfrac{U_c}{V''} < 0$	$\dfrac{\beta + \theta}{V''} \dfrac{\Omega}{\Delta} < 0$
Nominal interest rate	1	0
Real interest rate	0	0

$\Omega \equiv U_{cc}(U_{ll} + f'' U_c) - U_{lc}^2 > 0$

$\Delta \equiv -\{U_{ll} + (f'' U_c + f' U_{cl})\} - f'(U_{cl} + f' U_{cc}) > 0$

An increase in government expenditure has no effect on the demand for traded bonds, or on the real or nominal interest rates. Employment increases, while consumption falls, implying that the output expenditure multiplier is less than unity. The reason for this result is simply that the higher equilibrium marginal utility of wealth ($= U_c$) causes consumers to substitute more employment for less consumption. Domestic output rises, the balance of trade of the private sector goes into surplus, while the country's net trade balance, inclusive of government purchases, remains unchanged.

The steady state *ceteris paribus* effects of changes in the foreign interest rate and foreign inflation rate are qualitatively equal and opposite to one another, so that only the former need be discussed. In both cases, the changes incorporate the induced changes in the domestic rate of time preference β, as indicated by (11.13). The effect of an increase in the foreign nominal interest rate r^* is to raise the after-tax domestic nominal and real interest rates by a factor $1/(1 + \alpha)$ and the real holdings of foreign bonds by the same amount.[10] In the case of perfect capital mobility, the effect on the interest rates is proportional. A one percentage point increase in r^* leads to a one percentage point

TABLE 11.2 *Steady state effects of unit increase in foreign nominal interest rate or unit decrease in foreign inflation rate q*

Bonds b	$\frac{1}{1+\alpha} > 0$
Employment l	$\psi \frac{dl}{dg}$ (<0)
Consumption c	$\psi \frac{dc}{dg}$ (>0)
Trade balance T	$\psi\left(f' \frac{dl}{dg} - \frac{dc}{dg}\right)$ (<0)
Marginal utility of consumption U_c	$\psi \frac{\Omega}{\Delta}$ (<0)
Real money stock m	$\frac{1}{V''}\left\{\frac{\mu}{1+\alpha} + (\beta+\theta)\,\psi \frac{\Omega}{\Delta}\right\} \gtrless 0$
Nominal interest rate	$\frac{1}{1+\alpha} > 0$
Real interest rate	$\frac{1}{1+\alpha} > 0$

$$\psi \equiv -\left\{b + \frac{(r^* - q)}{1+\alpha}\right\} \ (<0)$$

increase in the domestic (real and nominal) interest rates. Otherwise, the degree of responsiveness declines with the degree of capital mobility and in the limiting case there is no effect.

A change in r^* impinges on the real part of the system through the real interest income term $-(r^* - q)b$. Provided that b is not too negative, so that the domestic economy is not too great a debtor to the rest of the world, then the impact effect through the real interest income term is negative and operates qualitatively like a decrease in government expenditure. We consider this to be the more likely case, with the signs in parentheses therefore being "probable" signs. The higher interest earnings leads to increased consumption, while output and employment fall. Since government expenditure is assumed to be fixed, the balance of trade therefore falls. The domestic steady state rate of inflation and exchange depreciation are obviously unaffected by the change.

The effects that we have been discussing are reversed in the case of an increase in the rate of inflation abroad. Furthermore, the rate of exchange depreciation falls proportionately, while the domestic rate of inflation remains unchanged.

These results on foreign disturbances shed some light on the issue of the degree of insulation provided by flexible exchange rates against foreign inflationary disturbances. It is evident that flexible rates do not provide complete insulation against foreign inflationary pressures alone. This is because a change in the foreign inflation rate alone constitutes a real disturbance. However, a change in the foreign inflation rate is likely to be accompanied by a change in the foreign nominal interest rate, as these two variables respond to the common influences abroad. A necessary and sufficient condition for a flexible exchange rate to insulate the domestic economy completely against disturbances in the foreign inflation is that the rest of the world be "Fisherian" in the sense that the nominal interest rate abroad fully adjusts to the foreign inflation rate, namely

$$\frac{\mathrm{d}r^*}{\mathrm{d}q} = 1$$

In essence, the Fisherian condition ensures that the foreign price disturbance is purely nominal.[11] Thus, the condition for perfect insulation originally obtained by Turnovsky (1977) continues to apply in the present optimizing model.

Finally, we wish to make the following observation. A key difference between the domestic and foreign disturbances is that the equilibrium real stock of traded bonds is *independent* of the former, but is *responsive* to changes in the latter.[12] This difference turns out to be crucial in contrasting the dynamic response of the economy to these two sets of disturbances.

4 TRANSITIONAL DYNAMICS: GENERAL CHARACTERISTICS

To analyze the transitional dynamics of the economy we must consider the short-run equilibrium conditions (11.10). These yield solutions for the short-run variables c, l, e, and r of the form[13]

$$l = l(\mu) \qquad l_\mu > 0 \tag{11.16a}$$

$$c = c(\mu) \qquad c_\mu < 0 \tag{11.16b}$$

$$r = r(\mu, m) \qquad r_\mu < 0,\ r_m < 0 \tag{11.16c}$$

$$e = e(\mu, m, b) \qquad e_\mu < 0,\ e_m < 0,\ e_b > 0 \tag{11.16d}$$

The signs of the partial derivatives are as indicated and are derived in the appendix.

Intuitively, a *ceteris paribus* increase in the marginal utility of consumption μ means that consumption is reduced and the supply of labor rises. With the real stock of money fixed, the marginal rate of substitution condition implies that the nominal interest rate must fall. Given the real stock of traded bonds, the uncovered interest differential remains unchanged. The rate of return on domestic bonds must fall, i.e. the rate of exchange depreciation must fall. An increase in the money stock leaves c and l unchanged. The marginal utility of money falls, implying that the domestic interest rate declines and hence the rate of exchange depreciation falls as well. An increase in b leaves c, l, and r unaffected. The rate of return on foreign bonds must rise, i.e. the rate of exchange depreciation must increase.

Linearizing the differential equations (11.10e)–(11.10g) about the steady state equilibrium, we can write the dynamics in the form

$$\begin{bmatrix} \dot{m} \\ \dot{b} \\ \dot{\mu} \end{bmatrix} = \begin{bmatrix} -e_m\tilde{m} & -e_b\tilde{m} & -e_\mu\tilde{m} \\ 0 & r^* - q & f'l_\mu - c_\mu \\ 0 & \tilde{\mu}\alpha & 0 \end{bmatrix} \begin{bmatrix} m - \tilde{m} \\ b - \tilde{b} \\ \mu - \tilde{\mu} \end{bmatrix} \tag{11.17}$$

where $\tilde{m}$, $\tilde{b}$, and $\tilde{\mu}$ denote the steady state equilibrium determined in section 11.4 and the partial derivatives in (11.17) are evaluated at steady state. From the matrix in (11.17) we see that the three eigenvalues λ_1, λ_2, and λ_3 have the properties

$$\lambda_1 + \lambda_2 + \lambda_3 = r^* - e_m\tilde{m} > 0 \tag{11.18a}$$

$$\lambda_1\lambda_2\lambda_3 = e_m\tilde{m}\,\tilde{\mu}\,\alpha(f'l_\mu - c_\mu) < 0 \tag{11.18b}$$

From this pair of inequalities we deduce that there is *one* negative (stable) root and two positive (unstable) roots, implying a unique convergent path. Focusing on this path, stable solutions for m, b, and μ are of the form[14]

$$m(t) = \{m(0) - \tilde{m}\}\exp(\lambda_1 t) + \tilde{m} \tag{11.19a}$$

$$b(t) = (b_0 - \tilde{b})\exp(\lambda_1 t) + \tilde{b} \tag{11.19b}$$

$$\mu(t) = \{\mu(0) - \tilde{\mu}\}\exp(\lambda_1 t) + \tilde{\mu} \tag{11.19c}$$

where $\lambda_1 < 0$ is the stable root.[15] We assume that the real stock of foreign bonds evolves continuously from its initial level b_0, while the initial values of $m(0)$ and $\mu(0)$ are determined endogenously. Since the nominal stock of money is determined by the monetary growth rule, the initial nominal stock M_0 is predetermined, so that the initial real stock $m(0)$ is determined by some appropriate initial jump in the domestic price level (exchange rate). The initial jump in $\mu(0)$ takes place through initial jumps in consumption and employment.

Differentiating (11.19) with respect to t and substituting into (11.17) yields

$$\begin{bmatrix} -e_m\tilde{m} - \lambda_1 & -e_b\tilde{m} & -e_\mu\tilde{m} \\ 0 & r^* - q - \lambda_1 & f'l_\mu - c_\mu \\ 0 & \alpha\tilde{\mu} & -\lambda_1 \end{bmatrix} \begin{bmatrix} m - \tilde{m} \\ b - \tilde{b} \\ \mu - \tilde{\mu} \end{bmatrix} = 0 \tag{11.20}$$

confirming that λ_1 is an eigenvalue of (11.16) with $(m - \tilde{m}, b - b,$

$\mu - \tilde{\mu}$) being the corresponding eigenvector. Equation (11.20) which holds for all t, involves three linearly dependent relationships between the three elements of the eigenvector. Assume that the system starts out in steady state equilibrium so that $b_0 = \bar{b}$ say. Then, the first and third equations of (11.20) considered at time zero, but immediately following a disturbance, imply

$$\mu(0) - \tilde{\mu} = \frac{\alpha \tilde{\mu}}{\lambda_1}(\bar{b} - \tilde{b}) \tag{11.21a}$$

$$m(0) - \tilde{m} = \frac{-\alpha\, \tilde{\mu}\, \tilde{m}\{1 - (\beta + \theta)/\lambda_1\}(\bar{b} - \tilde{b})}{\tilde{m} V'' + \tilde{\mu} \lambda_2} \tag{11.21b}$$

where in deriving (11.21b) we substitute for the partial derivatives e_i, $i = m, b, \mu$, from the expressions given in the appendix, and μ and m are evaluated at steady state.

Our objective is to analyse the effects of the various disturbances on the adjustment path of the economy. The most critical determinant of this is how the initial jumps in $\mu(0)$, $m(0)$ respond to these disturbances. This is because these initial jumps transmit the impacts of these shocks to the other short-run variables via the short-run equilibrium relationships (11.16).

Differentiating equations (11.21a) and (11.21b) with respect to some arbitrary variable x, say, yields to the first order of approximation

$$\frac{d\mu(0)}{dx} = \frac{d\tilde{\mu}}{dx} - \frac{\alpha \tilde{\mu}}{\lambda_1}\frac{d\tilde{b}}{dx} \tag{11.22a}$$

$$\frac{dm(0)}{dx} = \frac{d\tilde{m}}{dx} + \frac{\alpha\, \tilde{\mu}\, \tilde{m}\{1 - (\beta + \theta)/\lambda_1\}}{\tilde{m} V'' + \tilde{\mu} \lambda_1}\frac{d\tilde{b}}{dx} \tag{11.22b}$$

where henceforth the tilde on the equilibrium values μ and m is omitted. Equations (11.22a) and (11.22b) can be used to determine the short-run impact effects of the various disturbances, to which we now turn.

5 ANALYSIS OF DISTURBANCES

In this section we discuss in turn the dynamic adjustment following disturbances of domestic and foreign origin.

5.1 Domestic monetary expansion

Consider an increase in the monetary growth rate θ. From Table 11.1 we see that

$$\frac{d\tilde{b}}{d\theta} = \frac{d\tilde{\mu}}{d\theta} = 0$$

which, using (11.22a) and (11.22b), implies

$$\frac{d\mu(0)}{d\theta} = 0 \tag{11.23a}$$

$$\frac{dm(0)}{d\theta} = \frac{d\tilde{m}}{d\theta} = \frac{\mu}{V''} < 0 \tag{11.23b}$$

Equation (11.23a), together with the short-run solutions (11.16a) and (11.16b), yield

$$\frac{dl(0)}{d\theta} = \frac{dc(0)}{d\theta} = \frac{dT(0)}{d\theta} = 0 \tag{11.24}$$

The initial responses of the financial variables are obtained by taking the derivatives of (11.10c) and (11.10d) at time zero to yield

$$\frac{V''dm(0)}{d\theta} = \mu\frac{dr(0)}{d\theta} = \mu\frac{de(0)}{d\theta} \tag{11.25}$$

Combining (11.23b) and (11.25) we obtain

$$\frac{de(0)}{d\theta} = \frac{dr(0)}{d\theta} = 1 \tag{11.26a}$$

The implied instantaneous jump in the level $E(0)$ of the exchange rate is

$$\frac{dE(0)/d\theta}{E(0)} = \frac{-dm(0)/d\theta}{m(0)} = \frac{-d\tilde{m}/d\theta}{m} = \frac{-\mu}{mV''} > 0 \tag{11.26b}$$

A change in the monetary growth rate causes the economy to jump instantaneously to its new steady state. In this new equilibrium all real variables such as employment, output, consumption, and the trade balance remain unchanged. The jump is brought about by a discrete depreciation of the exchange rate, causing the real stock of money balances in the economy to fall by an amount which is precisely equal to its long-run decline. As a result of this, the rate of exchange depreciation, and hence the domestic rate of inflation, increases instantaneously by the amount of the increase in the monetary growth rate. The exchange rate neither overshoots or undershoots, in the sense that the real money balance immediately adjusts to its new equilibrium level.

5.2 Increase in domestic government expenditure

Referring to table 11.1, it is recalled that an increase in government expenditure leaves the long-run position in traded bonds unchanged, while leading to an increase in the marginal utility of consumption and a decrease in the real stock of money. Consequently, equations (11.22) imply

$$\frac{d\mu(0)}{dg} = \frac{d\tilde{\mu}}{dg} = \frac{\Omega}{\Delta} > 0 \tag{11.27a}$$

$$\frac{dm(0)}{dg} = \frac{d\tilde{m}}{dg} = \frac{\beta + \theta}{V''}\frac{\Omega}{\Delta} < 0 \tag{11.27b}$$

which, together with the short-run solutions (11.16a) and (11.16b), yield

$$\frac{dl(0)}{dg} = \frac{d\tilde{l}}{dg} > 0 \tag{11.28a}$$

$$\frac{dc(0)}{dg} = \frac{d\tilde{c}}{dg} < 0 \tag{11.28b}$$

$$\frac{dT(0)}{dg} = f'\frac{d\tilde{l}}{dg} - \frac{d\tilde{c}}{dg} - 1 = 0 \tag{11.28c}$$

Turning to the financial variables and differentiating (11.10c) and (11.10d) with respect to g and noting the above relationships, we find

$$\frac{de(0)}{dg} = \frac{dr(0)}{dg} = 0 \tag{11.29a}$$

Thus, as in the case of the domestic monetary expansion, there is no transitional dynamics. The expansion in government expenditure causes the exchange rate to depreciate instantaneously by an amount

$$\frac{dE(0)/dg}{E(0)} = \frac{-dm(0)/dg}{m(0)} > 0 \tag{11.29b}$$

Output expands and consumption falls. The private balance of trade increases by an amount equal to the increase in government expenditures, so that the country's net balance of trade is unchanged. The rate of exchange depreciation and the domestic rate of interest also both remain unchanged. Again, the reason for the complete instantaneous adjustment is the fact that the long-run equilibrium stock $\tilde{b}$ of traded bonds, which in an important sense drives the short-run dynamics, is unaffected by the change in government expenditure.

These findings regarding the instantaneous adjustment of the system to changes in the domestic policy variables θ and g are sensitive to certain aspects of the specification of the model. Under alternative assumptions they cease to hold. For example, if we assume that all forms of income, including interest income, are taxed at a fixed rate, that the budget is balanced through changing the tax rate, rather than through lump-sum taxation, then the equilibrium stock of traded bonds will be responsive to changes in θ and g, and the adjustment to the new steady state will be gradual. Alternatively, if we assume that the cost parameter α varies inversely with the stock of wealth (as it would with constant relative risk aversion), then the equilibrium stock of traded bonds is given by the expression

$$\tilde{b} = \frac{1}{\alpha'}(r^* - q - \beta)(\tilde{m} + \bar{a} + \tilde{b}) \tag{11.30}$$

In this case $\widetilde{b}$ is affected by θ and g through the wealth effect, thereby again rendering the adjustment gradual.

5.3 Foreign interest rate disturbances

Consider now a foreign monetary disturbance, taking the form of an increase in the foreign nominal interest rate r^*. From table 11.2 we see that this leads to an increase in the equilibrium real stock of traded bonds, namely

$$\frac{\mathrm{d}\widetilde{b}}{\mathrm{d}r^*} = \frac{1}{1+\alpha} > 0 \tag{11.31}$$

Accordingly, the short-run responses $\mu(0)$ and $m(0)$ are given by

$$\frac{\mathrm{d}\mu(0)}{\mathrm{d}r^*} = \frac{\mathrm{d}\widetilde{\mu}}{\mathrm{d}r^*} - \frac{\alpha\mu}{\lambda_1(1+\alpha)} > \frac{\mathrm{d}\widetilde{\mu}}{\mathrm{d}r^*} \tag{11.32a}$$

$$\frac{\mathrm{d}m(0)}{\mathrm{d}r^*} = \frac{\mathrm{d}\widetilde{m}}{\mathrm{d}r^*} + \frac{\alpha\mu m\{1-(\beta+\theta)/\lambda_1\}}{mV'' + \mu\lambda_1}\frac{1}{1+\alpha} < \frac{\mathrm{d}\widetilde{m}}{\mathrm{d}r^*} \tag{11.32b}$$

where the corresponding steady state responses are reported in table 11.2. These effects imply the following short-run responses of the real part of the economy:

$$\frac{\mathrm{d}l(0)}{\mathrm{d}r^*} = l_\mu \frac{\mathrm{d}\mu(0)}{\mathrm{d}r^*} = \frac{\mathrm{d}\widetilde{l}}{\mathrm{d}r^*} - \frac{l_\mu\alpha\mu}{\lambda_1(1+\alpha)} > \frac{\mathrm{d}\widetilde{l}}{\mathrm{d}r^*} \tag{11.33a}$$

and similarly

$$\frac{\mathrm{d}c(0)}{\mathrm{d}r^*} = \frac{\mathrm{d}\widetilde{c}}{\mathrm{d}r^*} - \frac{c_\mu\alpha\mu}{\lambda_1(1+\alpha)} < \frac{\mathrm{d}\widetilde{c}}{\mathrm{d}r^*} \tag{11.33b}$$

$$\frac{\mathrm{d}T(0)}{\mathrm{d}r^*} = \frac{\mathrm{d}\widetilde{T}}{\mathrm{d}r^*} - \frac{(f'l_\mu - c_\mu)\alpha\mu}{\lambda_1(1+\alpha)} > \frac{\mathrm{d}\widetilde{T}}{\mathrm{d}r^*} \tag{11.33c}$$

An increase in the foreign nominal interest rate raises the equilibrium stock $\widetilde{b}$ of traded bonds. Hence, the marginal utility of consumption (wealth), falls less on impact than it does in the steady state (see (11.22a)). As a consequence, the fall in domestic employment, the rise in consumption, and the deterioration in the balance of trade are all less than they are in steady state. Indeed, it is possible for all these impact effects to reverse the long-run effects qualitatively. This occurs if and only if the positive effect of an increase in r^* on steady state bonds outweighs the negative effect on the steady state marginal utility of consumption.

The effects on the financial variables are obtained by first differentiating (11.10c) and (11.10d) to yield

$$V''\frac{\mathrm{d}m(0)}{\mathrm{d}r^*} = \mu\frac{\mathrm{d}r(0)}{\mathrm{d}r^*} + r\frac{\mathrm{d}\mu(0)}{\mathrm{d}r^*}$$

$$1 + \frac{de(0)}{dr^*} = \frac{dr(0)}{dr^*}$$

and then utilizing (11.32a) and (11.32b). This result is

$$\frac{dr(0)}{dr^*} = \frac{1}{(1 + \alpha)(V''m + \mu\lambda_1)} \{\mu\lambda_1 + mV''(1 + \alpha) + \alpha V'\} \gtrless 0 \tag{11.34a}$$

$$\frac{de(0)}{dr^*} = \frac{V' - \mu\lambda_1}{V''m + \mu\lambda_1}\left(\frac{\alpha}{1 + \alpha}\right) < 0 \tag{11.34b}$$

In addition, the effect on the nominal exchange rate $E(0)$ is given by

$$\frac{dE(0)/dr^*}{E(0)} = -\frac{dm(0)/dr^*}{m(0)} \gtrless 0 \tag{11.34c}$$

where the initial jump in the real money stock, derived from (11.32b), is

$$\frac{dm(0)}{dr^*} = \frac{(\beta + \theta)\psi\Omega}{V''\Delta} + \frac{\mu}{1 + \alpha}\left[\frac{1}{V''} + \frac{\alpha m\{1 - (\beta + \theta)/\lambda_1\}}{mV'' + \mu\lambda_1}\right] \tag{11.34d}$$

It is evident that as long as $\alpha \neq 0$, so that traded and domestic bonds are less than perfect substitutes, the impact effect of an increase in the foreign interest rate is to move the domestic economy to a point which does not coincide with the new steady state. Thereafter the economy approaches its new equilibrium asymptotically; there is therefore a gradual dynamic adjustment. With perfect capital mobility ($\alpha = 0$), however, the economy jumps immediately to steady state.

Strictly speaking, the immediate response of the domestic interest rate is indeterminate, although intuitively we would expect it to rise. A sufficient condition for this to be so is

$$\eta < -\frac{\alpha}{1 + \alpha} \tag{11.35}$$

where $\eta = mV''/V'$ is the elasticity of the marginal utility of money. Clearly, the higher the degree of capital mobility, the more likely this condition is to be met and the more likely the domestic rate of interest is to rise. In the other limiting case, where there is zero substitutability ($\alpha \to \infty$), it can be shown that $dr(0)/dr^* \to 0$.[16] In general, comparing (11.34a) with the steady state, we see

$$\frac{dr(0)}{dr^*} - \frac{d\tilde{r}}{dr^*} = \frac{\alpha(mV'' + V')}{(1 + \alpha)(mV'' + \mu\lambda_1)} \tag{11.36}$$

implying that as long as $\eta < 1$ and capital is imperfectly mobile, the interest rate undershoots its steady state adjustment on impact.

A more intuitive explanation of the initial phases of the dynamic adjustment is the following. Suppose that there is an exogenous increase in the foreign interest rate. Generally this gives rise to an instantaneous fall in the trade balance which is offset by an increase in the flow of interest income if the country is a net creditor. The net effect on the current account balance is therefore ambiguous and the domestic economy may initially either accumulate or decumulate traded bonds. At the same time, the fall in the rate of exchange depreciation e implies that the real money stock starts to rise, while the rise in the foreign interest rate means that, through the consumer arbitrage condition, the marginal utility of consumption starts to fall. This latter effect implies a decrease in output, accompanied by an increase in consumption, leading to a decrease in the trade balance. The fall in μ, together with the increase in m and the change in b, has offsetting effects on the rate of exchange depreciation, although on balance e will rise. The decrease in the trade balance means that the rate of accumulation of foreign bonds will fall. The adjustment so described is stable and eventually the economy converges to the steady state described in section 4.

5.4 Foreign inflationary disturbance

Given the symmetry with which the foreign variables impinge on the domestic economy, the effects of a unit increase in the foreign inflation rate q alone are identical with those of an equivalent decrease in the foreign interest rate r^*. The effects on the real and financial variables therefore follow immediately from (11.32)–(11.34) in section 5.3. In addition we can establish

$$\frac{\mathrm{d}p(0)}{\mathrm{d}q} = \frac{\mathrm{d}e(0)}{\mathrm{d}q} + 1 = \frac{\alpha(\mu\lambda_1 - V')}{(1+\alpha)(mV'' + \mu\lambda_1)} > 0$$

so that the domestic inflation rate rises. As long as domestic and foreign bonds are less than perfect substitutes, an increase in the foreign inflation rate imposes an initial jump on the domestic economy followed by a gradual adjustment toward the new steady state equilibrium. The economic explanation for this behavior is identical with that which would stem from a decrease in the foreign interest rate.

It is evident from these results that the flexible exchange rate does not in general insulate the domestic economy in the short run against once-and-for-all increases in the foreign inflation rate. However, it will provide perfect short-run insulation against disturbances in the foreign inflation rate if and only if the Fisherian condition noted in section 3 applies, i.e. the flexible exchange rate will provide perfect insulation against disturbances in the foreign inflation rate in the short run as well as the long run if and only if the foreign nominal interest rate fully adjusts to the foreign inflation rate.

6 CONCLUSIONS

In this chapter we have analysed the effects of various disturbances of domestic and foreign origin in a model of a small open economy in which the behavioral relationships are derived from optimization by the private sector. The main conclusion of the analysis is a simple one. In this model, the domestic economy jumps instantaneously to its new equilibrium steady state following a change in either the domestic monetary growth rate or domestic fiscal policy. In response to a disturbance in either the foreign interest rate or inflation rate, however, undergoes an initial jump taking it part way toward its new equilibrium, which it thereafter approaches gradually. The critical driving force in determining the nature of the adjustment to a specific disturbance is the response of the steady state equilibrium stock of traded bonds to this disturbance. When the demand for these assets is derived from intertemporal utility maximization, as we have done, this equilibrium stock turns out to be independent of the domestic policy variables we consider, but it is dependent upon both the foreign interest and inflation rates. The magnitude of the initial jump and the speed of adjustment following disturbances in these latter variables depends critically upon the degree of capital mobility. In the limiting case where domestic and foreign bonds are perfect substitutes, the economy adjusts instantaneously to foreign as well as domestic disturbances.

The results that we have obtained are relevant to the issues of exchange rate adjustment and the insulation properties of flexible exchange rates noted previously. The fact that the economy adjusts fully on impact to a change in the monetary growth rate means that the exchange rate neither overshoots nor undershoots its long-run response. Moreover, *ad hoc* equilibrium models of asset accumulation and imperfect substitutability which involve gradual adjustments to domestic policy changes may in fact be somewhat misleading, since the adjustments may occur instantaneously. Secondly, the Fisherian condition obtained previously as being necessary and sufficient for perfect insulation holds in the present optimizing framework.

Of course, the analysis is based on a number of specific assumptions and, in concluding, the effects of relaxing a number of these should be noted. First, the separability of the consumer utility function into consumption and labor on the one hand and real money balances on the other is made for expositional convenience. If, instead, we assume a nonseparable function $U(c, l, m)$ say, then the only difference is that the recursive nature of the solution breaks down. As a consequence, the monetary growth rate will have effects on the real variables such as employment, consumption, and output. In all other respects the nature of the solution remains unchanged.

Second, it is straightforward to relax the assumption of PPP and to introduce a domestic good which is an imperfect substitute for the traded commodity. The relative price is introduced as an additional variable, but again this does not alter the character of our analysis in any essential way.

Third, as Turnovsky and Brock (1980) argued, it is reasonable to introduce government expenditure as a direct argument of the utility function to reflect the fact that consumers derive direct utility from public expenditure. Again this does not affect the character of our analysis, although it does change the specific responses to change in g, r^*, and q. In the limiting case where consumers view private and public goods as being perfect substitutes it can easily be established that fiscal policy has no real effects; there is "direct" crowding out.

Finally, and most importantly, the instantaneous adjustment of the economy in response to the domestic policy shocks does depend upon our specification of the cost parameter α as being constant. If instead, we postulate this to vary inversely with wealth, then the domestic policy variables will influence the equilibrium stock of traded bonds through the wealth effect. As a consequence of this dependence, a change in domestic monetary or fiscal policy will generate a true dynamic adjustment in the domestic economy.

Thus while models based on *ad hoc* relationships are often criticized as being arbitrary, models based on optimizing behavior are not entirely immune from this criticism either. As our results here indicate, their implications are also dependent upon specification of the optimization which to some degree is also arbitrary.

APPENDIX DERIVATION OF PARTIAL DERIVATIVES OF SHORT-RUN SOLUTIONS

Consider equations (11.10a) and (11.10b). The differentials of this pair of equations are given by

$$\begin{bmatrix} U_{cc} & U_{cl} \\ U_{lc} & U_{ll} + \mu f'' \end{bmatrix} \begin{bmatrix} \mathrm{d}c \\ \mathrm{d}l \end{bmatrix} = \begin{bmatrix} \mathrm{d}\mu \\ -f'\mathrm{d}\mu \end{bmatrix} \tag{11A.1}$$

the solution of which is

$$\frac{\partial l}{\partial \mu} = -\frac{f' U_{cc} + U_{lc}}{\Omega} > 0 \tag{11A.2a}$$

$$\frac{\partial c}{\partial \mu} = \frac{U_{ll} + f''\mu + U_{cl} f'}{\Omega} < 0 \tag{11A.2b}$$

where

$$\Omega \equiv U_{cc}(U_{ll} + \mu f'') - U_{lc}^2 > 0$$

Differentiating (11.10c) yields

$$V'' \, \mathrm{d}m = r \, \mathrm{d}\mu + \mu \, \mathrm{d}r$$

so that

$$\frac{\partial r}{\partial m} = \frac{V''}{\mu} < 0 \tag{11A.3a}$$

$$\frac{\partial r}{\partial \mu} = \frac{-r}{\mu} < 0 \tag{11A.3b}$$

Finally, taking the differential of (11.10d),

$$\mathrm{d}e = \alpha \, \mathrm{d}b + \mathrm{d}r$$

implying

$$\frac{\partial e}{\partial m} = \frac{V''}{\mu} < 0 \tag{11A.4a}$$

$$\frac{\partial e}{\partial \mu} = -\frac{r}{\mu} < 0 \tag{11A.4b}$$

$$\frac{\partial e}{\partial b} = \alpha > 0 \tag{11A.4c}$$

NOTES

1 The exchange rate overshooting question in particular has generated a voluminous literature, too extensive to document here. The robustness of the phenomenon to changes in assumptions about (a) the degree of capital mobility, (b) output flexibility, and (c) price flexibility has been considered by a number of authors.

2 More recently, Obstfeld has applied the intertemporal optimizing model to a number of issues in international macroeconomics. Some of these are summarized in the survey paper by Obstfeld and Stockman (1984).

3 The term "perfect capital mobility" is often used quite loosely. Even if UIP does not hold, capital may still be perfectly mobile in the weaker sense of covered interest parity (CIP) (see for example Eaton and Turnovsky, 1983, this volume, ch. 2). The empirical evidence supporting the stronger definition of UIP is not particularly strong. Bilson (1978), Levich (1978) and Hansen and Hodrick (1980) report systematic deviations from UIP for several exchange rates over long periods, reflecting risk-averse behavior by speculators. Obstfeld (1982) also briefly considers the case of imperfect capital mobility. However, he does so by arbitrarily postulating some relationship between the stock of bonds and the interest rate, rather than deriving such a relationship as an equilibrium condition from the optimizing framework.

4 We adopt the following notational convention. Except where noted, partial

derivatives are denoted by corresponding lower case letters, while total derivatives of a function of a single argument are denoted by primes.

5 More specifically, the two-period mean–variance optimization yields a demand function for foreign bonds of the form

$$b = \frac{1}{A\sigma_e^2}(r^* + e - r) = \frac{z}{R\sigma_e^2}(r^* + e - r)$$

where $z = m + a + b$.

6 The same results as those derived in this chapter are obtained if we assume instead that the government (a) finances its budget by issuing bonds and (b) engages in an initial open-market operation to ensure that the stock of bonds generated by the government budget constraint is consistent with the consumers' transversality conditions.

7 For example, this relationship is equivalent to the optimality condition in Yaari (1964).

8 This scheme is admittedly a simple one. It is meant to capture the notion that the more closely the domestic economy is tied financially to the rest of the world, the less independent the domestic rate of time preference can be. Alternatively, we could endogenize β along the lines of Obstfeld (1981).

9 The neutrality breaks down if we postulate the cost parameter α to be inversely dependent upon wealth, so that the alternative bond demand function of note 5 applies. By means of the wealth effect, m, b, l, and c are all dependent upon the monetary growth rate and domestic government expenditure.

10 These propositions are established by considering (11.12d) and (11.13), and (11.15d), respectively.

11 If we assume that interest income is taxed by the domestic government, then certain mild asymmetries between changes in the foreign inflation and interest rate are introduced. In particular, even if the after-tax foreign nominal interest rate fully adjusts to the foreign inflation rate, the effects of a unit increase in the latter are non-neutral. This is because the taxes provide a real transfer from the foreign to the domestic economy. Neutrality is restored if the taxes on foreign bonds are collected by the foreign government. These issues are discussed in an earlier version of this paper.

12 The comment regarding the independence of the equilibrium stock of traded bonds with respect to domestic disturbances applies to θ and g. If interest income is taxed, the equilibrium stock of traded bonds *does* depend upon the income tax rate.

13 We prefer to depart from our notational convention and denote $\mathrm{d}l/\mathrm{d}\mu$ by l_μ rather than by l'.

14 The two unstable roots may be either real or complex, while the single stable root is necessarily real. Thus the stable adjustment path to equilibrium is necessarily monotonic.

15 Given the recursivity of the model, the roots are $\lambda_3 = -e_m/m$ (unstable), while λ_1 and λ_2 ($\lambda_1 < 0, \lambda_2 > 0$) are the roots of the quadratic equation $\lambda^2 - (r^* - q)\lambda - (f'l_\mu - c_\mu)\mu\alpha = 0$, and we assume that $r^* - q > 0$.

16 As $\alpha \to \infty$, it can be seen from the solution to the characteristic equation

given in note 15 that $\lambda_1 \to 0(\alpha^{1/2})$. Thus, letting $\alpha \to \infty$ in (11.34a) and noting this fact, we can easily see that $\mathrm{d}r(0)/\mathrm{d}r^* \to 0$.

REFERENCES

Bilson, J. F. O. (1978) Rational expectations and the exchange rate. In *The Economics of Exchange Rates* (eds J. A. Frenkel and H. G Johnson). Reading, MA: Addison-Wesley.

Brock, W. A., and Turnovsky, S. J. (1981) The analysis of macroeconomic policies in perfect foresight equilibrium *International Economic Review*, 22, 179–209.

Dornbusch, R. (1980) Exchange rate risk and the macroeconomics of exchange rate determination, Working Paper 493, National Bureau of Economic Research.

Driskill, R., and McCafferty, S. A. (1980) Exchange rate variability, real and monetary shocks, and the degree of capital mobility under rational expectations *Quarterly Journal of Economics*, 95, 577–86.

Eaton, J. and Turnovsky, S. J. (1981) Exchange risk, political risk, and macroeconomic equilibrium. Discussion Paper 388, Economic Growth Center, Yale University.

—— and —— (1983) Covered interest parity, uncovered interest parity and exchange rate dynamics. *Economic Journal*, 93, 555–75. Reprinted in this volume as chapter 2.

Hansen, L. P. and Hodrick, R. J. Forward exchange rates as optimal predictors of future spot rates. *Journal of Political Economy*, 88, 829–53.

Hodrick, R. J. (1982) On the effects of macroeconomic policy in a maximizing model of a small open economy. *Journal of Macroeconomics*, 4, 195–213.

Levich, R. (1978) Tests of forecasting models and market efficiency in the international money market. In *The Economics of Exchange Rates* (eds J. A. Frenkel and H. G. Johnson). Reading, MA: Addison-Wesley.

Obstfeld, M. (1981) Macroeconomic policy, exchange rate dynamics and optimal asset accumulation. *Journal of Political Economy*, 89, 1142–61.

—— (1982) Aggregate spending and the terms of trade: is there a Laursen-Meltzer effect? *Quarterly Journal of Economics*, 97, 251–70.

—— and Stockman, A. C. (1984) Exchange rate dynamics. In *Handbook of International Economics* (eds R. W. Jones and P. B. Kenen). Amsterdam: North-Holland.

Turnovsky, S. J. (1977) *Macroeconomic Analysis and Stabilization Policy*. Cambridge: Cambridge University Press.

—— and Brock, W. A. (1980) Time consistency and optimal government policies in perfect foresight equilibrium. *Journal of Public Economics*, 13, 183–212.

—— and Bhandari, J. S. (1982) The degree of capital mobility and the stability of an open economy under rational expectations. *Journal of Money, Credit, and Banking*, 14, 303–26.

Uzawa, H. (1968) Time preference, the consumption function, and optimum asset holdings. In *Value, Capital and Growth: Papers in Honor of Sir John Hicks* (ed. J. N. Wolfe). Chicago, IL: Aldine.
Yaari, M. (1964) On the consumer's lifetime allocation process. *International Economic Review*, 5, 304–317.

12 Tariffs, Capital Accumulation, and the Current Account in a Small Open Economy

(WITH P. SEN)

1 INTRODUCTION

Recently, there has been a revival of interest in the macroeconomic effects of commercial policies under flexible exchange rates. Discredited after the 1930s, they have returned to playing a much more central role in policy discussions. Theoretical models have been slow to appear, but by now a substantial literature has developed. This literature has addressed the two issues which are at the forefront of the policy discussions, namely the effects of commercial policies on employment, on the one hand, and on the current account, on the other. Most of the attention has focused on tariffs, but unlike the analysis of tariffs in pure trade theory, no retaliatory action is assumed to occur.

The modern theoretical literature analysing the macroeconomic effects of tariffs originated with Mundell (1961), who established the proposition that a tariff is contractionary. The essential steps of the argument were that a tariff will raise the terms of trade, thereby increasing savings, reducing aggregate demand, and necessitating a fall in aggregate supply in order for the goods market to clear. While the result was based on a very simple model, relying on the Laursen–Metzler effects, subsequent work by Chan (1978), and more recently by Krugman (1982), suggests that the result is in fact quite robust with respect to

Originally published in *International Economic Review*, 30, 1989 811–31. This chapter has benefited from seminar presentations at the University of Washington and the University of Toronto, as well as from the constructive comments of two referees.

various extensions of the basic IS–LM model.[1] Krugman also demonstrated that by reducing income more than expenditure, the tariff will lead to a deterioration of the current account balance.

The basic Mundell model is static. The first analysis of tariffs in a macrodynamic setting was that by Eichengreen (1981) who, using a currency substitution model, emphasized the intertemporal tradeoffs involved in a tariff. Whereas the contractionary effects suggested by Mundell were found to hold in the long run, the short-run effects of a tariff are likely to be expansionary.[2] However, this is gradually reversed over time through savings and the current account surplus which occurs. Kimbrough (1982) introduced a nontraded good and showed how the effect of the tariff on the current account balance depends critically upon the complementarity or substitutability of the imported good and the nontraded good in consumption demand.

Optimizing models analysing the effect of tariffs are fewer, unless the contributions studying the Laursen–Metzler effects are included.[3] Van Wijnbergen (1987) lays out a two-country–two-period model, and the effects of a tariff are analysed in both a full employment and real wage rigidity (in the tariff-imposing country) setting. In the full employment case, a permanent tariff has no effect on the current account because permanent income and permanent consumption both fall by the same amount. However, a temporary tariff leads to a current account surplus. In contrast, with rigid real wages these results are subject to substantial modification; for example, a permanent tariff may now plausibly lead to a current account deficit.[4] Engel and Kletzer (1987) analyse the effects of a tariff in a two-sector model (with labor mobile between the sectors) and capital employed in the import-competing sector. Two alternatives are postulated for the consumers: the first where they have a variable rate of time preference as in Uzawa (1968), and the second where they face a constant probability of death as in Yaari (1965). In the former case it is demonstrated that current account surpluses characterize the adjustment path; in the uncertain lifetime case, deficits are possible, but not inevitable. Brock (1986) discusses trade liberalization in a model which resembles ours in some respects. However, he has the small open economy facing given terms of trade, importing all its capital from abroad, and with employment fixed.

In this chapter we analyse the effects of an increase on the tariff rate within an infinite-horizon utility-maximizing framework. The key feature of the model is that it incorporates capital accumulation by means of a q-theoretic investment function as in Hayashi (1982) and Abel and Blanchard (1983). For reasons which will become evident in due course, in introducing capital it is important to endogenize the employment of labor, and we do so by introducing the labor–leisure choice as an integral part of the intertemporal optimization. We also allow the terms of trade to be determined endogenously. Our analysis therefore focuses on the dynamics of employment, capital accumulation, the terms of trade, and output, all of which are important aspects of the macrodynamics of tariffs.

By contrast, most of the existing literature abstracts from investment, in which case the current account surplus is identical with savings. To the extent that capital accumulation is considered, it is introduced in restrictive ways. Engel and Kletzer (1987), for instance, do have capital, but in order to maintain equality between the return to capital and the given foreign interest rate, the stock of capital jumps at the moment that the tariff is imposed. (This is brought about by a swap of foreign bonds with capital.) In Brock (1986) all the capital stock is imported but there are installation costs in the various domestic sectors (i.e. the allocation is not costless). In an extension to his basic model, van Wijnbergen (1987) discusses endogenous investment which depends upon the ratio of the value of future output relative to the cost of producing capital.[5]

Three types of tariff changes are analysed: an unanticipated permanent increase, an unanticipated temporary increase and a future anticipated permanent increase. Using this framework we show how a tariff reduces output and employment in both the short run and the long run. At the same time, we show that a tariff reduces the rate of investment, while generating a current account surplus along the adjustment path.

These findings represent something of a combination of the Mundell–Krugman and Eichengreen results. The contractionary effect of the tariff is as in Mundell, but is contrary to the short-run expansionary effect discussed by Eichengreen. However, the current account surplus is consistent with Eichengreen, although the mechanism is entirely different. In our analysis it is the result of reduced investment, rather than additional savings, and the latter may or may not increase.

This chapter is organized as follows. The model is set out in section 2 and the dynamics is considered in the following section. The long-run and dynamics effects of the tariff are analyzed in section 4 and 5 respectively. Some concluding remarks are provided in section 6.

2 THE MODEL

We consider an economy which is specialized in the production of a single commodity. However, households in this economy also consume another good which is imported from abroad. The economy is large enough to affect the terms of trade. It can borrow or lend as much as it wants at a given world interest rate, though subject to an intertemporal budget constraint. However, by being able to influence the terms of trade, the real interest rate relevant for the economy is endogenously determined.

2.1 Structure of the economy

Consider first the representative consumer. His decisions are made by solving the following intertemporal optimization problem:

$$\max \int_0^\infty \{U(x,y) + V(l)\} \exp(-\delta t)\, \mathrm{d}t \tag{12.1a}$$

subject to

$$\dot{b} = \frac{1}{\sigma}(\pi + wl - x) - \gamma y + i^* b + T \tag{12.1b}$$

and the initial condition

$$b(0) = b_0 \tag{12.1c}$$

where x is the consumption of the domestic good, y is the consumption of the imported good, σ is the relative price of the foreign good in terms of the domestic good (i.e. the real exchange rate), l is the labor supplied by the representative household, b is the stock of foreign bonds held by the household (in units of foreign output), w is the real wage rate, mesured in terms of the domestic good, π are the real profits distributed to the household, γ is one plus the tariff rate, i^* is the world rate of interest, taken as given, δ is the consumer's discount rate, taken to be constant, and T are lump-sum transfers from the government.

The instantaneous utility function is assumed to be additively separable in goods and labor. We also assume that the utility function is increasing in the consumption of goods, but decreasing in labor, and that it is strictly concave. Finally, the two goods are taken to be Edgeworth complementary, so that $U_{xy} > 0$.[6]

In determining his optimal plans for x, y, l, and b, the representative consumer is assumed to take σ, π, w, and i^* as given. These decisions are made subject to the budget constraint (12.1b), which is expressed for convenience in units of the foreign good. Note that the tariff rate, τ say, which is the focus of our analysis, is absorbed in the term $\gamma = 1 + \tau$.

The current-value Hamiltonian for the household maximization problem is given by

$$H_h \equiv U(x, y) + V(l) + \lambda\left\{\frac{1}{\sigma}(\pi + wl - x) - \gamma y + i^* b + T\right\} \tag{12.2}$$

where λ is the co-state variable associated with (12.1b). The first-order optimality conditions, with respect to the decision variables x, y, and l are respectively[7]

$$U_x(x, y) = \frac{\lambda}{\sigma} \tag{12.3a}$$

$$U_y(x, y) = \lambda\gamma \tag{12.3b}$$

$$V'(l) = -\frac{\lambda}{\sigma}w \tag{12.3c}$$

In addition, the co-state variable evolves according to

$$\dot{\lambda} = \lambda(\delta - i^*) \tag{12.3d}$$

Since δ and i^* are both fixed, the ultimate attainment of a steady state is possible if and only if $\delta = i^*$. Henceforth we assume this to be the case. This implies $\dot{\lambda} = 0$ everywhere, so that λ is always at its steady-state value $\bar{\lambda}$ (to be determined below).

To rule out Ponzi-type situations we need to impose the transversality condition

$$\lim_{t\to\infty} b(t) \exp(-i^* t) = 0 \tag{12.3e}$$

The representative firm produces domestic output z by means of a production function with capital k and labor as inputs. This function is assumed to have the usual neoclassical properties of positive, but diminishing, marginal products and constant returns to scale, i.e.

$$z = F(k, l) \qquad F_k > 0, F_l > 0$$

$$F_{kk} < 0, F_u < 0, F_{kk}F_{ll} - F_{kl}^2 = 0 \tag{12.4}$$

Profit net of investment expenditure at time t, say, is defined to be

$$\pi(t) = F(k, l) - wl - C(I) \tag{12.5}$$

where I is the rate of investment. The function $C(I)$ represents the installation costs associated with the purchase of I units of new capital. It is assumed to be an increasing convex function of I: $C' > 0$, $C'' > 0$. In addition, we assume

$$C(0) = 0 \qquad C'(0) = 1$$

so that the total cost of zero investment is zero, and the marginal cost of the initial installation in unity. This formulation of the installation function follows the original specification of adjustment costs introduced by Lucas (1967), Gould (1968), and Treadway (1969). More recent work by Hayashi (1982) and Abel and Blanchard (1983) postulates an installation function which depends upon k as well as I. This modification makes little difference to our analysis and for simplicity we retain the simpler formulation. The specification implies that in the case that disinvestment occurs (for example, as we shall show, following a tariff increase), $C(I) < 0$ for low rates of disinvestment. This can be interpreted as reflecting the revenue as capital is sold off. The possibility that all changes in capital are costly can be incorporated by introducing sufficiently large fixed costs, so that $C(0) > 0$. This does not alter our analysis in any substantive way.[8]

Thus the firm's optimization problem is to

$$\max \int_0^\infty \pi(t) \exp\left\{-\int_0^t i(s)\,\mathrm{d}s\right\} \mathrm{d}t$$

$$= \int_0^\infty \{F(k, l) - wl - C(I)\} \exp\left\{-\int_0^t i(s)\,\mathrm{d}s\right\} \mathrm{d}t \tag{12.6a}$$

subject to

$$\dot{k} = I \tag{12.6b}$$

and the initial condition

$$k(0) - k_0 \tag{12.6c}$$

and where $i(t)$ denotes the domestic real interest rate. Given the assumption of interest rate parity, this is related to the world rate i^* by

$$i(t) = i^* + \dot{\sigma}/\sigma$$

where $\dot{\sigma}/\sigma$ is the (expected) peercentage change in the terms of trade. Three further points should be noted about the formulation of the firm's problem. First, equation (12.6b) abstracts from depreciation. This simplifies the dynamics considerably, without much loss of generality. Second, for expositional simplicity, we assume that the firm finances investment through retained earnings. This assumption is unimportant, since, as is well known, in a model such as this, which abstracts from taxation, all forms of financing yield the same optimality conditions.[9] Third, the real interest rate appropriate to firms is $i = i^* + \dot{\sigma}/\sigma$, while that relevant to households is i^*. The difference arises from the fact that it is convenient to express the real accumulation equation for households (equation (12.1b)) in terms of the unit of the traded bond, namely foreign output, while profit for domestic firms is expressed in terms of domestic output. If we were to transform (12.1b) to domestic good units, then i would become the relevant interest rate for households.[10]

The current-value Hamiltonian for the firm maximization problem is

$$H_\mathrm{f} \equiv F(k, l) - wl - C(I) + ql$$

where q is the co-state variable associated with (12.6b). The relevant optimality conditions for firms with respect to l and I are

$$F_l(k, l) = w \tag{12.7a}$$

$$C'(I) = q \tag{12.7b}$$

while q evolves according to

$$\dot{q} = i(t)q - F_k \tag{12.7c}$$

In addition there is the accumulation equation (12.6b) and the initial condition (12.6c), as well as the transversality condition

$$\lim_{t\to\infty} qk \exp\left\{-\int_0^t i(\tau)\,\mathrm{d}\tau\right\} = 0 \tag{12.7d}$$

The government's role in this economy is a simple one. It just collects the tariff revenue from the public and redistributes it in a lump-sum fashion, so that

$$(\gamma - 1)y = T \tag{12.8}$$

Finally, adding the household's budget constraint (12.1b) and the government's budget constraint (12.8), and noting the definition of $\pi(t)$ in (12.5), we find that the current account surplus of the economy is given by

$$\dot{b} = \frac{1}{\sigma}\{F(k, l) - x - C(I)\} - y + i^*b \tag{12.9}$$

i.e. income less absorption.

2.2 Macroeconomic equilibrium

The macroeconomic equilibrium we consider is defined to be one where the planned demand and supply functions derived from the optimizations, consistent with the accumulation equations, clear all markets at all points of time. Combining the optimality conditions for households ((12.3a)–(12.3e)) and for firms ((12.7a)–(12.7d)) together with the accumulation equations (12.1b), (12.5), and (12.6b), the following equilibrium conditions are obtained:

$$U_x(x, y) = \bar{\lambda}/\sigma \tag{12.10a}$$

$$U_y(x, y) = \bar{\lambda}\gamma \tag{12.10b}$$

$$V'(l) = \frac{\bar{\lambda}}{\sigma} F_l(k, l) \tag{12.10c}$$

$$C'(I) = q \tag{12.10d}$$

$$F(k, l) = x + Z(\sigma) + C(I) \tag{12.10e}$$

$$\dot{q} = (i^* + \dot{\sigma}/\sigma)q - F_k(k, l) \tag{12.10f}$$

$$\dot{k} = I(q) \tag{12.10g}$$

$$\dot{b} = \frac{1}{\sigma}\{F(k, l) - C(I) - x\} - y + i^*b \tag{12.10h}$$

where $Z(\cdot)$ is the amount of domestic good exported, with $Z'(\sigma) > 0$. As noted, the co-state variable λ remains constant over time at its steady state value $\bar{\lambda}$, determined below. In addition, the transversality conditions (12.3c) and (12.7d) must also hold.

Equations (12.10a)–(12.10c) define the short-run equilibrium. Pairwise, (12.10a)–(12.10c) define the usual rate of substitution for consumers. Note that the distortionary effect of the tariff is included in γ. Equation (12.10d) equates the marginal cost of capital to the shadow price of investment, which is essentially a Tobin q theory of investment.[11] Finally, equation (12.10e) describes market clearing in the domestic goods market.

These five equations can be solved for x, y, l, I and σ in terms of $\bar{\lambda}$, k, q, and γ:

$$x = x(\bar{\lambda}, k, q, \gamma) \qquad x_{\bar{\lambda}} < 0,\ x_k > 0,\ x_q < 0,\ x_\gamma < 0 \qquad (12.11a)$$

$$y = y(\bar{\lambda}, k, q, \gamma) \qquad y_{\bar{\lambda}} < 0,\ y_k > 0,\ y_q < 0,\ y_\gamma < 0 \qquad (12.11b)$$

$$l = l(\bar{\lambda}, k, q, \gamma) \qquad l_{\bar{\lambda}} \gtreqless 0,\ l_k \gtreqless 0,\ l_q < 0,\ l_\gamma < 0 \qquad (12.11c)$$

$$\sigma = \sigma(\bar{\lambda}, k, q, \gamma) \qquad \sigma_{\bar{\lambda}} > 0,\ \sigma_k > 0,\ \sigma_q > 0,\ \sigma_\gamma < 0 \qquad (12.11d)$$

$$I = I(q) \qquad I' > 0 \qquad (12.11e)$$

An increase in the marginal utility of wealth $\bar{\lambda}$ leads to a reduction in the domestic consumption of both goods. The reduction in demand for the domestic good causes its relative price to fall, i.e. σ rises, thereby stimulating exports. The overall effect on the demand for domestic output depends upon whether or not this exceeds the reduction in x. If so, domestic output and employment rise; if not, employment falls. An increase in the stock of capital raises output and the real wage. The higher domestic income stimulates the consumption of x, though by a lesser amount, and the relative price σ rises, i.e. $\sigma_k > 0$. Since the two goods are complementary in utility ($U_{xy} > 0$), the increase in the demand for the domestic good increases the demand for the import good. While the rise in the real wage rate tends to decrease V', thereby stimulating employment, the rise in σ has the opposite effect; the net effect on employment depends upon which influence dominates. An increase in q stimulates investment. This generates an increase in the demand for domestic goods and the relative price σ falls, i.e. $\sigma_q < 0$. This raises the marginal utility of the domestic good, implying that the consumption of x must fall, and with $U_{xy} > 0$, y falls as well. On balance, the increase in investment exceeds the fall in demand stemming from the reduction in x and lower exports, so that domestic output and employment rises. Finally, an increase in the tariff rate reduces the demand for the import good and, with $U_{xy} > 0$, the demand for x as well. This lowers the relative price of the domestic good, thereby reducing domestic output and employment. However, this describes only the partial effect of a short-run change in the tariff rate. In addition, it generates jumps in $\bar{\lambda}$ and q, thereby inducing further responses. The complete short-run responses consists of a combination of these two effects and will be discussed in section 5.

One further observation regarding the short-run solution is appropriate at this stage. Even though both the increase in $\bar{\lambda}$ and the partial effect of an increase in the tariff γ lead to an increase in the relative price σ, thereby stimulating exports, only in the case of the former is the effect sufficiently large to give rise to the possibility that employment may increase. To see the difference it is convenient to take the differential of (12.10e):

$$\left(V'' + \frac{\bar{\lambda}}{\sigma}F_{ll}\right)\mathrm{d}l = -\, F_l\,\mathrm{d}\left(\frac{\bar{\lambda}}{\sigma}\right)$$

The increase in σ resulting from a tariff lowers the marginal utility of the domestic consumption good, there is substitution in favor of leisure, and labor falls. However, although an increase in $\bar{\lambda}$ raises σ, the net effect on the marginal utility $\bar{\lambda}/\sigma$ is indeterminate, in which case employment may either rise or fall.

The three final equations describe the dynamics. The first two equations can be reduced to a pair of autonomous differential equations in q and k, and these constitute the core of the dynamics. To see this, we first note that the path of the relative price σ must be consistent (from (12.11d)) with the dynamic paths of k and q, as well as the constant value of $\bar{\lambda}$ determined by the steady state equilibrium. As a consequence, differentiating (12.11d) with respect to t yields

$$\dot{\sigma} = \sigma_k \dot{k} + \sigma_q \dot{q} \tag{12.11d'}$$

where, as already shown, $\sigma_k > 0$ and $\sigma_q < 0$. Substituting this equation, together with (12.11c) and (12.11d), into (12.10f) and (12.10g) leads to a pair of dynamic equations in q and k. Note that since this pair of equations is determined in part by the constant steady state value of the marginal utility $\bar{\lambda}$, the steady state in part determines the entire dynamic adjustment path. Finally, (12.10h) equates the accumulation of foreign assets by the economy to its current account surplus. Using the domestic goods market-clearing condition (12.10e), we can express this equivalently in terms of exports minus imports:

$$\dot{b} = \frac{1}{\sigma}\{Z(\sigma) - \sigma y + \sigma i^* b\} \tag{12.10h'}$$

This equation in turn can be reduced to an autonomous differential equation in b after substituting the solutions for q and k.

3 EQUILIBRIUM DYNAMICS

Carrying out the procedure outlined above, we can express (12.10f) and (12.10g) as the following pairs of linearized differential equations around the steady state:

$$\begin{bmatrix} \dot{q} \\ \dot{k} \end{bmatrix} = \begin{bmatrix} \theta(i^* + \sigma_k I' q/\sigma - F_{kl} l_q) & -\theta(F_{kk} + F_{kl} l_k) \\ I/C'' & 0 \end{bmatrix} \begin{bmatrix} q - \tilde{q} \\ k - \tilde{k} \end{bmatrix} \tag{12.12}$$

where $\theta \equiv \sigma/(\sigma - \sigma_q q) > 0$ and $\sim$ denotes steady state values.

The determinant of the coefficient matrix in (12.12) is negative and therefore the long-run equilibrium is a saddlepoint with eigenvalues $\mu_1 < 0$ and $\mu_2 > 0$. It is clear that, while the capital stock always evolves continuously, the shaodw price q of capital may jump instantaneously in response to new information. Therefore along the stable arm k and q follows the paths

$$k = \tilde{k} + (k_0 - \tilde{k}) \exp(\mu_1 t) \tag{12.13a}$$

$$q = \tilde{q} + \frac{\mu_1}{I'}(k - \tilde{k}) \tag{12.13b}$$

To determine the dynamics of the current account, we consider (12.10h′) in the form

$$\dot{b} = \frac{Z\{\sigma(\bar{\lambda}, k, q)\}}{\sigma(\bar{\lambda}, k, q)} - y(\bar{\lambda}, k, q) + i^* b \tag{12.14}$$

Linearizing this equation around the steady state yields

$$\dot{b} = \frac{1}{\tilde{\sigma}}\{(\beta\sigma_k - \sigma y_k)(k - \tilde{k}) + (\beta\sigma_q - \sigma y_q)(q - \tilde{q})\} + i^*(b - \tilde{b})$$

where $\beta \equiv Z' + i^* b - y$. Using (12.13a) and (12.13b), we can write this equation as

$$\dot{b} = \Omega(k_0 - \tilde{k}) \exp(\mu_1 t) + i^*(b - \tilde{b}) \tag{12.15}$$

where

$$\Omega \equiv \frac{1}{\tilde{\sigma}}\left\{(\beta\sigma_k - \sigma y_k) + (\beta\sigma_q - \sigma y_q)\frac{\mu_1}{I'}\right\}$$

If we assume that the economy starts out with an initial stock traded bonds $b(0) = b_0$, the solution to (12.15) is

$$b(t) = \tilde{b} + \frac{\Omega(k_0 - \tilde{k})}{\mu_1 - i^*} \exp(\mu_1 t) + \left\{b_0 - \tilde{b} - \frac{\Omega}{\mu_1 - i^*}(k_0 - \tilde{k})\right\} \exp(i^* t)$$

Invoking the intertemporal budget constraint for the economy (equation (12.3e)) implies

$$b_0 = \tilde{b} + \frac{\Omega}{\mu_1 - i^*}(k_0 - \tilde{k}) \tag{12.16}$$

so that the solution for $b(t)$ consistent with long-run solvency is

$$b(t) = \tilde{b} + \frac{\Omega}{\mu_1 - i^*}(k_0 - \tilde{k})\exp(\mu_1 t) \tag{12.17}$$

Equation (12.17) describes the relationship between the accumulation of capital and the accumulation of traded bonds. Of particular significance is the sign of this relationship. Writing Ω as

$$\Omega \equiv \frac{1}{\tilde{\sigma}}\left\{\beta\left(\sigma_k + \sigma_q \frac{\mu_1}{I'}\right) - \sigma\left(y_k + y_q \frac{\mu_1}{I'}\right)\right\}$$

emphasizes that Ω measures the effects of two channels of influence of capital on the current account. First, an increase in k raises the relative price σ_k both directly and also through the accompanying fall in q, as seen in (12.13b). What this does to the trade balance depends upon β. Evaluating β at steady state, we can show that[12]

$$\beta = Z' + i^* b - y = Z' - \frac{Z}{\sigma}$$

so that $\beta > 0$ if and only if the relative price elasticity of the foreign demand for exports exceeds unity. At the same time, the increase in k increases imports both directly and again through the fall in q, and this reduces the trade balance. While either case is possible, we will assume that the relative price effect dominates, so that $\Omega > 0$.

The steady state of the economy is obtained when $\dot{k} = \dot{q} = \dot{b} = 0$ and is given by the following set of equations:

$$U_x(\tilde{x}, \tilde{y}) = \frac{\bar{\lambda}}{\tilde{\sigma}} \tag{12.18a}$$

$$U_y(\tilde{x}, \tilde{y}) = \bar{\lambda}\gamma \tag{12.18b}$$

$$V'(\tilde{l}) = -F_l(\tilde{k}, \tilde{l})\frac{\bar{\lambda}}{\tilde{\sigma}} \tag{12.18c}$$

$$\tilde{q} = 1 \tag{12.18d}$$

$$F(\tilde{k}, \tilde{l}) = \tilde{x} + Z(\tilde{\sigma}) \tag{12.18e}$$

$$F_k(\tilde{k}, \tilde{l}) = i^* \tag{12.18f}$$

$$F(\tilde{k}, \tilde{l}) = \tilde{x} + \tilde{\sigma}\tilde{y} - \tilde{\sigma} i^* \tilde{b} \tag{12.18g}$$

$$\tilde{b} - b_0 = -\frac{\Omega}{i^* - \mu_1}(\tilde{k} - k_0) \tag{12.18h}$$

These equations jointly determine the steady state equilibrium values of $\tilde{x}$, $\tilde{y}$, $\tilde{l}$, $\tilde{k}$, $\tilde{\lambda}$, $\tilde{\sigma}$, $\tilde{q}$, and $\tilde{b}$.

This long-run equilibrium is straightforward, although several aspects merit comment. Note that the steady state value of q is unity, consistent with the Tobin q theory of investment. The steady state marginal physical product of capital is equated to the foreign interest rate. Equations (12.18e) and (12.18g) together imply that in steady state equilibrium the balance of payments on current account must be zero; the trade balance must offset net interest earnings on the traded bonds. Equation (12.18h) describes the equilibrium relationship between the change in the equilibrium stock of capital and the change in the equilibrium net credit of the economy. Note further that the steady state depends upon the initial stocks k_0 and b_0. As we will show below, this has important consequences for the effects of temporary changes in the tariff rate.

4 LONG-RUN EFFECTS OF AN INCREASE IN THE TARIFF RATE

The long-run effects of an increase in the tariff rate, obtained by differentiating the steady state relationships (12.18), are reported in table 12.1.

Since the world interest rate i^* is assumed to remain fixed, the marginal product condition (12.18f) implies that the capital–labor ratio is a constant, independent of γ. Capital and labor therefore change in the same proportions, so that the marginal product of labor, and hence the real wage rate, also remain constant. From table 12.1 it is seen that the increase in the tariff leads to a long-run reduction in both employment and capital, and therefore in output. Intuitively, the imposition of a tax, in the form of a tariff, on the imported good leads to a substitution away from that good toward the two other goods favored by consumers, namely the domestic good and leisure. Consumers are willing to supply less labor so that equilibrium employment falls. This reduces the marginal physical product of capital, so that the equilibrium capital stock, and hence output, fall as well. The long-run effects of the tariff are therefore contractionary, consistent with the long-run results of Eichengreen (1981). The decline in output raises the relative price of the domestic good, i.e. σ falls. In contrast, the relative price $\gamma\sigma$ of good y facing the consumer is higher than before. The decline in the stock of capital leads to a long-run increase in the stock of traded bonds held by the economy. Also, the decline in employment, coupled with the fall in σ, means that the (constant) marginal utility of wealth $\bar{\lambda}$ must also decline.

Combining (12.18e) and (12.18g) in the form

$$Z(\tilde{\sigma}) - \tilde{\sigma}\,\tilde{y} = -i^*\,\tilde{\sigma}\,\tilde{b}$$

we see that the imposition of the tariff certainly causes the steady state trade balance, when measured in term of the foreign currency $(-i^*\,\tilde{b})$ to fall. When measured in terms of domestic currency, however, it will

TABLE 12.1 *Long-run effects of increase in tariffs*

1 Capital–labor ratio:

$$\frac{\mathrm{d}(\widetilde{k/l})}{\mathrm{d}\gamma} = 0$$

2 Capital, employment, and output:

$$\frac{\mathrm{d}\,\tilde{k}/\mathrm{d}\gamma}{k} = \frac{\mathrm{d}\,\tilde{l}/\mathrm{d}\gamma}{l} = \frac{\mathrm{d}\,\tilde{z}/\mathrm{d}\gamma}{z} = -\frac{\lambda}{D}\frac{F_l}{l\sigma}(-U_{xx}\sigma Z' - \beta U_{xy}) < 0$$

3 Relative price:

$$\frac{\mathrm{d}\,\tilde{\sigma}}{\mathrm{d}\gamma} = \frac{\bar{\lambda}}{\sigma D}\left(V''\sigma + \frac{\sigma}{l}FF_lU_{xx} + \psi U_{xy}F_l\right) < 0$$

4 Domestic good:

$$\frac{\mathrm{d}\,\tilde{x}}{\mathrm{d}\gamma} = -\frac{\bar{\lambda}}{D}\left\{U_{xy}\frac{F_l}{\sigma}\left(\frac{F\beta}{l} + Z'\psi\right) + V''Z'\right\} \gtrless 0$$

5 Import good:

$$\frac{\mathrm{d}\,\tilde{y}}{\mathrm{d}\gamma} = \frac{\bar{\lambda}}{D}\left\{U_{xx}\frac{F_l}{\sigma}\left(\frac{F\beta}{l} + Z'\psi\right) + V''\frac{\beta}{\sigma}\right\} \gtrless 0$$

6 Marginal utility

$$\frac{\mathrm{d}\bar{\lambda}}{\mathrm{d}\gamma} = \frac{\bar{\lambda}}{D}\left\{V''\left(-\sigma Z'U_{xx} + \frac{\bar{\lambda}}{\sigma} + \beta U_{xy}\right) + \frac{\bar{\lambda}F_l}{\sigma^2}\left(\frac{\sigma FU_{xx}}{l} + \psi U_{xy}\right)\right\} < 0$$

where

$$\psi \equiv -\frac{\sigma i^*\Omega}{i^* - \mu_1}\left(\frac{k}{l}\right) < 0 \qquad \beta \equiv Z' - y + i^*b > 0$$

$$D \equiv -V''\left(U_{xy}Z' + \gamma\frac{\bar{\lambda}}{\sigma} - Z'\gamma U_{xx}\sigma\right) - V''\beta\left(U_{xy}\gamma - \frac{1}{\sigma}U_{yy}\right) +$$

$$+\Delta\frac{Fe}{\sigma}\left(\frac{F\beta}{l} + \psi Z'\right) - F_l\psi U_{xy}\gamma\frac{\bar{\lambda}}{\sigma^2} - F_lFU_{xx}\gamma\frac{\bar{\lambda}}{\sigma l} > 0, \text{ and}$$

$$\Delta \equiv U_{xx}U_{yy} - U_{xy}^2 > 0$$

---

also fall as long as the country is a debtor nation ($\tilde{b} < 0$). For a creditor nation, it may either rise or fall, depending upon the size of the relative price effect.

The overall impact of the higher tariff on the domestic consumptions of the two goods $\tilde{x}$ and $\tilde{y}$ is unclear. While the substitution effect is away from y in favor of x, the income effect is ambiguous. One effect of the reduction in domestic output resulting from the higher tariff is to reduce domestic income. However, at the same time, the reduction in the relative price serves to raise income as measured in terms of domestic goods. The net effect depends upon which dominates.

5 TRANSITIONAL DYMNAMICS OF AN INCREASE IN TARIFF

We now consider the dynamic adjustment path of the economy following an increase in the tariff rate. As noted previously, the dynamics of q and k are described by a saddlepoint in k–q space. The stable arm XX is given by

$$q = 1 + \frac{\mu_1}{I'}(k - \widetilde{k})$$

and is negatively sloped; the unstable arm YY is described by

$$q = 1 + \frac{\mu_2}{I'}(k - \widetilde{k})$$

and is positively sloped. The phase diagram is illustrated in figure 12.1.

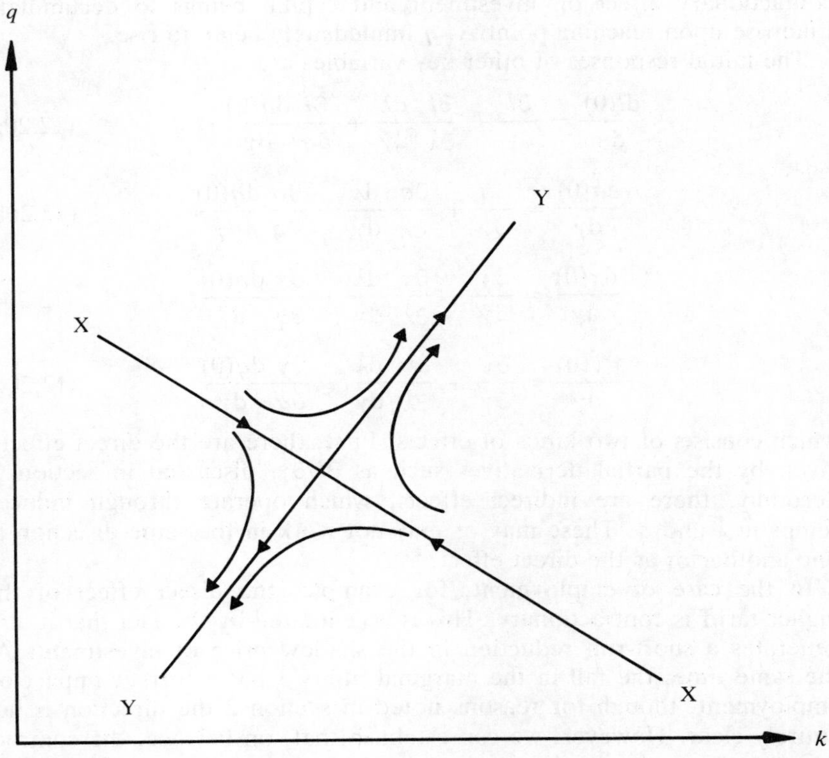

Figure 12.1 Phase diagram.

As long as no future shock is anticipated, the system must lie on the stable locus XX. The initial jump in $q(0)$, following an unanticipated permanent increase in γ, is

$$\frac{dq(0)}{d\gamma} = -\frac{\mu_1}{I'}\frac{d\widetilde{k}}{d\gamma} < 0 \tag{12.19}$$

The long-run fall in the capital stock is seen to give rise to a short-run drop in the shadow price $q(0)$.

The dynamics following an unanticipated permanent increase in the tariff rate is illustrated in figure 12.2. Figure 12.2(a) shows the dynamics of q and k, while figure 12.2(b) shows the accumulation of traded bonds. Suppose that the economy is initially in steady state equilibrium at the point P on the stable arm XX and that there is a permanent increase in γ. The new steady state is at the point Q, having a reduced equilibrium capital stock $\widetilde{k}$ with an unchanged shadow price of capital. In the short run q drops from P to A on the new stable locus X′X′. From (12.10g) it is seen that the decrease in q has an immediate contactionary effect on investment and capital beings to decumulate. Likewise upon reaching point A, q immediately begin to rise.

The initial responses of other key variables are

$$\frac{dl(0)}{d\gamma} = \frac{\partial l}{\partial \gamma} + \frac{\partial l}{\partial \bar{\lambda}}\frac{d\bar{\lambda}}{d\gamma} + \frac{\partial l}{\partial q}\frac{dq(0)}{d\gamma} < 0 \tag{12.20a}$$

$$\frac{d\sigma(0)}{d\gamma} = \frac{\partial \sigma}{\partial \gamma} + \frac{\partial \sigma}{\partial \bar{\lambda}}\frac{d\bar{\lambda}}{d\gamma} + \frac{\partial \sigma}{\partial q}\frac{dq(0)}{d\gamma} \tag{12.20b}$$

$$\frac{dx(0)}{d\gamma} = \frac{\partial x}{\partial \gamma} + \frac{\partial x}{\partial \bar{\lambda}}\frac{d\bar{\lambda}}{d\gamma} + \frac{\partial x}{\partial q}\frac{dq(0)}{d\gamma} \tag{12.20c}$$

$$\frac{dy(0)}{d\gamma} = \frac{\partial y}{\partial \gamma} + \frac{\partial y}{\partial \bar{\lambda}}\frac{d\bar{\lambda}}{d\gamma} + \frac{\partial y}{\partial q}\frac{dq(0)}{d\gamma} \tag{12.20d}$$

which consists of two kinds of effects. First, there are the direct effects, given by the partial derivatives such as $\partial l/\partial \gamma$, discussed in section 2. Secondly, there are indirect effects, which operate through induced jumps in $\bar{\lambda}$ and q. These may or may not work in the same direction as one another or as the direct effect.

In the case of employment, for example, the direct effect of the higher tariff is contractionary. This is accentuated by the fact that it also generates a short-run reduction in the shadow price of investment. At the same time, the fall in the marginal utility $\bar{\lambda}$ has a further impact on employment, though for reasons noted in section 2 the direction is not entirely clear. However, we can establish that, on balance, the contractionary effects dominate, so that the imposition of the tariff reduces employment and output in the short run. There are various ways to see why this must be so. One way is to consider what happens to (12.10f)

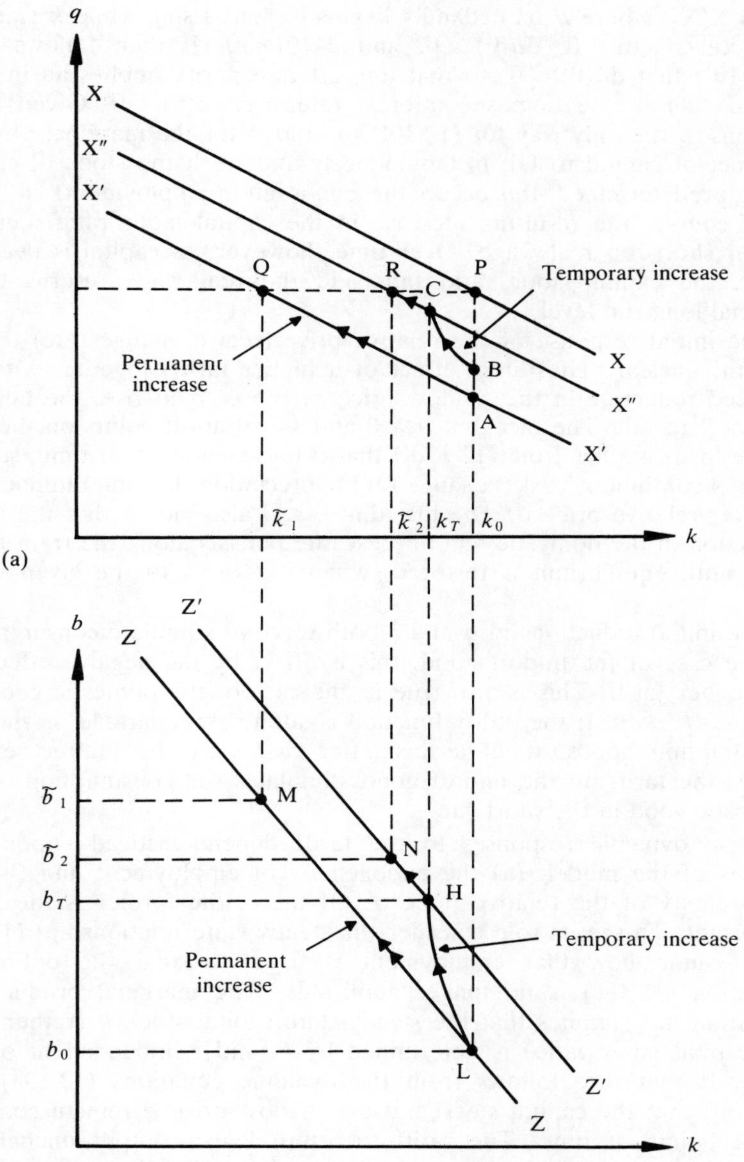

Figure 12.2 Increase in tariff.

on impact. We have already seen that the immediate effect of the tariff is to cause q to drop instantaneously to the point A on the new stable locus X′X′, where q immediately begins to start rising while k starts to fall, i.e. $dq(0) < 0$, $d\dot{q}(0) > 0$, and $d\dot{k}(0) < 0$. It then follows from (12.11d′) that $d\dot{\sigma}(0) < 0$, so that interest rate parity implies an instantaneous fall in the domestic interest rate, i.e. $di(0) < 0$. Given these responses, the only way for (12.10f) to hold is for the marginal physical product of capital to fall instantaneously and, with the stock of capital being predetermined, this occurs through a fall in employment.

Of course, the resulting increase in the capital–labor ratio means a higher short-run real wage. Over time, however, as capital is decumulated, the capital–labor ratio falls and the real wage returns to its original long-run level.

The initial response of the relative price (real exchange rate) σ is in general unclear. The direct effect of a higher tariff, together with the induced reduction in the shadow price q, causes σ to rise; the fall in $\bar{\lambda}$ causes it to fall. The fact that $\dot{q} > 0$ and $\dot{k} < 0$ at all points on the new stable locus implies from (12.11d′) that σ falls steadily over time, so that there is continuous real exchange rate appreciation. leading ultimately to a lower relative price σ. The fact that $\dot{\sigma} < 0$ also means that the initial reduction in the domestic real interest rate persists along the transitional path until equilibrium is restored, when it returns to the given world rate.

The initial reductions in q and $\bar{\lambda}$ both serve to stimulate consumption. In the case of the import good, this is offset by the negaive effects of the higher tariff. This is also true in the case of the domestic good, as long as $U_{xy} > 0$. If the utility function is additively separable on the two consumption goods, then in this latter case only the indirect effects occur; the tariff on the import good stimulates the consumption of the domestic good in the short run.

These dynamic responses to the tariff depend critically upon two aspects of the model: (a) the endogeneity of employment and (b) the endogeneity of the relative price σ. Of these, the former is the more important. To see its role consider the steady state relationships (12.18) and assume now that employment is fixed, so that the optimality condition (12.18c) is no longer applicable. The marginal productivity condition now implies that the steady-state capital stock k (rather than the capital–labor ratio) is determined by i^* and is independent of the tariff. It therefore follows from the dynamic equations (12.13a) and (12.13b) that the capital stock and the shadow price q remain constant at all points of time. The tariff therefore leaves output unchanged! There are no dynamics. The only effect of the tariff is to generate a once-and-for-all adjustment in the relative price in the comsumptions x and y. Turning to the role of the relative price, suppose that the economy is sufficiently small for this to be fixed exogenously. It is clear from (12.10a) and (12.10b) that consumptions x and y are determined by the constant values of $\bar{\lambda}$, γ, and σ, and are therefore constant over time. However, since employment is a function of the capital stock via (12.11c), it does evolve over time as capital is decumulated. In order to restore dynamics to the consumption levels x and y, the assumption of additive separability of utility in goods and labor being made in this analysis must be dropped. In that case, x and y will depend upon the dynamics of k in the same way as does employment.

Figure 12.2(b) illustrates the relationship between b and k which, combining (12.13a) and (12.17), is given by

$$b - \widetilde{b} = -\frac{\Omega}{i^* - \mu_1}(k - \widetilde{k})$$

This is a negatively sloped locus, denoted by ZZ. Since neither k nor b are jump variables, this line remains fixed over time. The movement along A to Q in figure 12.2(a) is translated to a movement along LM in figure 12.2(b). From this figure it is seen that an increase in the tariff rate causes an immediate accumulation of foreign bonds. This stems from the fact that our assumption $\Omega > 0$ implies that the net effect of the decumulation of capital is to create a current account surplus. With b being predetermined, the trade balance, as measured in terms of the foreign good, also rises. In terms of the domestic good, it will rise if the relative price σ increases, but it may fall if σ falls sufficiently. Over time, the initial accumulation of foreign bonds is reversed. This occurs through the fall in σ and k, which causes the trade balance to decline over time.

Consider now a temporary increase in the tariff. Specifically, suppose that at time zero, γ increases, but is expected to be restored to its original level at time T. The transitional adjustment is now as follows.[13] As soon as the increase in γ occurs, the stable arm XX will drop instantaneously (and temporarily) to X′X′, while the shadow price q falls to the point B which lies above X′X′. At the same time, the marginal utility of consumption $\bar{\lambda}$ will fall by precisely the same (constant) amount as if the shock were permanent. However, since the fall in the shadow price $q(0)$ is only to the point B, the fall in initial investment is moderated. The same is true of employment. As a result of the initial fall in q, captial begins to decumulate and q begins to rise, for analogous reasons to those noted in connection with the permanent shock. Moreover, the decumulation of capital is accompanied by an accumulation of traded bonds. Immediately following the initial jump, q and k follow the path BC in figure 12.2(a) while k and b follow the corresponding path LH in figure 12.2(b). At time T, when the tariff is restored to its original level, the stock of capital and traded bonds will have reached a point such as H in figure 12.2(b). The accumulated stocks of these assets, denoted by k_T and b_T respectively, will now serve as initial conditions for the dynamics beyond time T when γ reverts permanently to its original level. As noted in section 12.3, they will therefore in part determine the new steady state equilibrium. With no new information being received at time t (since the temporary nature of the shock was announced at the outset) and no further jumps, the stable locus relevant for subsequent adjustments in q and k beyond time T is the locus X″X″, parallel to XX, which passes through the point $k = k_T$. Likewise, the relevant locus linking the accumulation of capital and traded bonds is now Z′Z′.

After time T, q and k follow the stable locus CR in figure 12.2(a) to the new steady state equilibrium at R, while correspondingly k and b follow the locus HN in figure 12.2(b) to the new equilibrium point N. It can be established formally that X″X″ lies below the original stable locus XX, while Z′Z′ lies above ZZ, as these curves have been drawn. In the new steady state, the shadow price q reverts to unity, but with a lower stock of capital and a higher stock of traded bonds than originally. The striking feature of the adjustment is that the temporary tariff leads to a permanent reduction in the stock of capital, accompanied by a higher stock of traded bonds. This is because during the transitional adjustment period, when the higher tariff is in effect,the accumulation of capital and bonds will influence subsequent initial conditions, which in turn will affect the subsequent steady state.

As the figures are drawn, C lies below R and H lies below N. The complete adjustment paths BCR and LHN are therefore monotonic. We are unable to rule out the possibility of C lying above R and H lying above N, in which case the accumulation of capital and accumulation of bonds would be reversed at some point during the transition. In any event, the temporary increase in the terms of trade generates an initial current account surplus, which continues as long as capital is being decumulated.

As a third disturbance, we briefly consider a future permanent increase in the tariff which is announced at time zero, to take effect at time T. This is not illustrated in the figure. At the time of the announcement, q drops instantaneously to a point such as B which lies above A on X′X′. This reduction in q implies a smaller intial decumulation in the capital stock than when the permanent deterioration occurs instantaneously.

Since neither γ nor $\bar{\lambda}$ change until time T, when the announced increase in the tariff rate actually occurs, the initial responses of l, σ, x and y are determined solely by the initial downward jump in $q(0)$. Hence the announcement causes employment and output to fall, while the relative price and the two consumptions both rise. However, the reduction in employment is smaller than for an unanticipated increase. Consequently, the fall in the marginal physical product of capital is moderated and q continues to fall (see (12.10f)). Thus, following the announcement, both q and k decline while foreign bonds are accumulated. At time T, when the announced increase in the tariff rate occurs, the stocks k_T and b_T of capital and bonds at that time will determine the stable paths X″X″ and Z′Z′ relevant for subsequent adjustments beyond T. Because of the changed initial conditions at time T, from time zero, these paths will not coincide with the corresponding paths X′X′ and ZZ for unannounced changes. In particular, X″X″ can be shown to lie above X′X′ in figure 12.2(a). This implies that the long-run contraction in the capital stock following an increase in the tariff rate is reduced by announcing this change in advance.

6 CONCLUSIONS

In this chapter we have analysed the effects of a tariff in an intertemporal optimizing model, emphasizing the role of capital accumulation. Three types of increases in the tariff rate have been considered: (a) unanticipated permanent; (b) unanticipated temporary; (c) anticipated permanent. There are two main general conclusions to be drawn from the analysis.

The first is that the introduction (or increase) of a tariff is contractionary in both the short run and the long run. In particular, employment is reduced in both the short run and the long run, so that there is no significant intertemporal tradeoff, as obtained by Eichengreen (1981). The fall in the long-run capital stock causes an immediate reduction in the rate of investment, which in turn leads to a current account surplus. While this response of the current account is in accordnce with much (but not all) of the existing literature, the mechanism by which it is achieved, namely the decumulation of capital, has not previously been considered. Also, the fact that the declining capital stock is accompanied by an accumulation of foreign bonds means that the savings effect of the tariff are unclear, depending upon which influence dominates.[14] However, this ambiguity of savings is very different from those occurring in other studies. For example, the absence of capital accumulation in Edwards (1987) model means that the ambiguity of the current account to a tariff translates directly to an ambiguity in savings. In the Engel–Kletzer (1987) model, the response of savings is shown to depend upon the formulation of consumer behavior. The second major conclusion stems from the fact that the steady state depends upon the initial stocks of the assets. As a consequence, a temporary tariff, by altering these initial conditions for some later date when the tariff is removed, leads to a permanent effect on the economy.

The qualitative conclusions that we have obtained are based on the assumption that the two goods are complementary in the sense $U_{xy} > 0$. As noted previously (note 6), we view this as being plausible, particularly when dealing with aggregate commodities. Since the main driving force of the results are the long-run response of the capital stock, it is evident from table 12.1 that the key qualitative aspects of the results will continue even if U_{xy} is mildly negative. However, if U_{xy} is strongly negative, so that the effect of the tariff is to raise the long-run capital stock, then both the short-run and long-run effects of the tariff on employment are expansionary. The detailed analysis of this case can be carried out following the procedures of this paper. However, we should caution that this case raises the possibility that the dynamics may no longer be a saddlepoint. In this case, with capital being assumed to evolve smoothly, the perfect foresight equilibrium, which now coincides with the steady state, cannot be sustained without some active form of government intervention.[15]

The model is obviously simple and could be extended in several ways. For instance, monetary considerations could be introduced and the exchange rate regime would determine how much of a change in terms of trade would pass into domestic prices and how much into a change in the nominal exchange rate. The issue of real wage rigidity could also be discussed. Finally, we could extend the framework into a two-counrty setting and introduce game-theoretic considerations.

NOTES

1 Krugman (1982) presents a comprehensive survey of this model. His analysis includes the case of nominal and real wage rigidty, fixed and flexible prices, and immobile and mobile capital.

2 Eichengreen (1981) considers two forms of expectations, static and rational. In the former case, the short-run effect of the tariff is definitely expansionary. In the latter case, it may or may not be expansionary depending upon the extent to which the domestic currency appreciates in the short run.

3 See for example Obstfeld (1982) and Svensson and Razin (1983).

4 A recent paper by Edwards (1987) develops a two-period optimizing model to analyze the effects of changes in tariffs and shocks in the terms of trade on both the real exchange rate and the current account. In general he shows how in his model a tariff may lead to either an appreciation or depreciation of the real exchange rate, in which case the response of the current account is also ambiguous. By imposing additional restrictions, a tariff is shown to lead to a real depreciation in both periods.

5 Other papers which examine the current account with capital accumulation include Buiter (1987), Ghosh (1987), and Matsuyama (1987). However, these authors do not analyse issues related to tariffs, which are the focus of this paper.

6 While this assumption is restricitve, at the aggregate it is reasonably plausible and is met by a variety of widely used utility functions. For example, it holds if $U(x, y)$ is any utility function, homogeneous of degree 1. It also holds for more specific utility functions, such as the constant elasticity of substitution function, when these are homogeneous of any arbitrary degree less than 1. It

is also clear that our results hold if $U(x, y)$ is additively separable in the two goods.

7 Throughout the chapter we will adopt the following notational convention. Where appropriate, primes will denote derivatives, subscripts will denote partial derivatives, and a dot will denote a derivative with respect to time.

8 For an alternative interpretation of $C(I) < 0$, see Hayashi (1982).

9 More specifically, if we let gross profits $\pi'(t) = F(k, l) - wl$, the assumption that investment $C(I)$ is financed from retained earnings (RE) implies that dividends $= \pi'(t) - \mathrm{RE} = \pi(t)$, as defined in (12.6a).

10 Suppose that $b' = \sigma b$ is the stock of bonds expressed in terms of domestic output. Then $\dot{b}' = \dot{\sigma} b + \sigma \dot{b}$. Combining this with (12.1b) and using the interest arbitrage relationship, the household accumulation equation becomes $\dot{b}' = \pi + wl - x - \sigma y + ib' + T$. Alternatively (but less conveniently), if the real stock of bonds were expressed in terms of a representative consumption basket, then the relevant real interest rate would be the rate defined in terms of that basket. Since any change in unit leads to a corresponding adjustment in the shadow price λ and its evolution, the choice is arbitrary and can be dictated by convenience, as we have done.

11 In the case where the installation cost function in homogeneous of degree 1 in I and k, the investment function (12.11e) is modified to $I/k = I(q)$.

12 This can immediately be established by considering equations (12.18e) and (12.18g).

13 The formal derivations of these adjustment paths are omitted, but are available from the authors on request.

14 Savings S along the transition path is given by $S = \dot{k} + \sigma\dot{b} + \dot{\sigma} b = I + Z - \sigma y + i\sigma b$, and this may be either positive or negative during the adjustment.

15 It is well known that in order for a unique equilibrium solution to exist, the number of unstable roots must equal the number of jump variables, a condition that is met by a saddlepoint. The case $U_{xy} < 0$ raises the possibility of there being more unstable roots (two) than jump variables (one), and it is this insufficiently of the latter that requires active intervention by the government if the system is not to diverge.

REFERENCES

Abel, A. B. and Blanchard, O. J. (1983) An intertemporal model of saving and investment. *Econometrica*, 51, 673–92.

Brock, P. L. (1986) Permanent and temporary tariff reductions. Unpublished working paper.

Buiter, W. H. (1987) Does an improvement in the current account of the trade balance at full employment require a depreciation of the real exchange rate? Presented at NBER Summer Institute.

Chan, K. S. (1978) The employment effects of tariffs under a free exchange rate regime. *Journal of International Economics*, 8, 414–24.

Edwards, S. (1987) Tariffs, terms of trade, and the real exchage rate in an intertemporal optimizing model of the current account. NBER Working Paper 2175.

Eichengreen, B. J. (1981) A dynamic model of tariffs, output, and employment under flexible exchage rates. *Journal of International Economics*, 11, 341–59.

Engel, C. and Kletzer, K. (1987) Tariffs, saving and the current account. National Bureau of Economic Research, Working Paper 1869.

Ghosh, A. R. (1987) The terms of trade and the current accounts: an investment dynamics approach, Harvard University.

Gould, J. P. (1968) Adjustment costs in the theory of investment of the firm. *Review of Economic Studies*, 35, 213–24.

Hayashi, F. (1982) Tobin's *q*, rational expectations, and optimal investment plan, *Econometrica*, 50, 213–24.

Kimbrough, K. P. (1982) Read disturbances, the current account, and the real exchange rate: the case of a tariff. *Journal of International Economics*, 13, 291–300.

Krugman, P. (1987) The macroeconomics of protection with a floating exchange rate. In *Monetary Regimes and Protectionism* (eds K. Brunner and A. H. Meltzer). Carnegie-Rochester Conference Series on Public Policy, vol. 16. Amsterdam: North-Holland.

Lucas, R. E. (1967) Adjustment costs and the theory of supply. *Journal of Political Economy*, 75, 321–34.

Matsuyama, K. (1987) Current account dynamics in a finite horizon model. *Journal of International Economics*, 23, 299–313.

Mundell, R. (1961) Flexible exchange rates and employment policy. *Canadian Journal of Economics and Political Science*, 27, 509–17.

Obstfeld, M. (1982) Aggregate spending and the terms of trade: is there a Laursen–Metzler effect? *Quarterly Journal of Economics*, 97, 251–70.

Svensson, L. E. O. and Razin, A. (1983) The terms of trade and the current account: the Harberger–Laursen–Melzler effect. *Journal of Political Economy*, 91, 97–125.

Treadway, A. (1969) On rational entrepreneurial behavior and the demand for investment. *Review of Economic Studies*, 36, 227–40.

Uzawa, H. (1968) Time preferences, the consumption function, and optimum asset holdings. In *Value, Capital, and Growth: Papers in Honor of Sir John Hicks* (ed. J. H. Wolfe). Chicago, IL: Aldine.

van Wijnbergen (1987) Tariffs, employment, and the current account: real wage resistance and the macroeconomics of protection. *International Economic Review*, 32, 137–50.

Yaari, M. (1965) Uncertain lifetime, life insurance, and the theory of the consumer, *Review of Economic Studies*, 32, 137–50.

Part V

Strategic Aspects of Policy-Making

13 Monetary Policies in Interdependent Economies with Stochastic Disturbances: A Strategic Approach

(WITH V. D'OREY)

1 INTRODUCTION

Western economies have become increasingly interdependent during recent years. An important consequence of this is that the effects of macroeconomic policies within these economies have become more closely related. A policy implemented in one country will generate effects abroad, while the impacts of this policy on the domestic economy are modified by the behavior and policies of the foreign economies with which it is interacting. Thus policy-making in a multicountry context necessarily involves strategic behavior.

Analysis of strategic behavior within the context of international macroeconomic policy began with the pioneering work of Hamada (1976), who investigated this question under the assumptions of Cournot and Stackelberg behavior. His analysis is based on a fixed exchange rate regime and the objective function involves the tradeoff between inflation and the balance of payments. More recently, Canzoneri and Gray (1985) consider alternative strategic monetary policies within the context of two economies subject to a mutual oil disturbance.[1]

In this chapter we continue the analysis of strategic monetary policy. The framework it employs is a two-country stochastic macromodel in which both economies are subjected to stochastic demand and supply shocks and expectations are rational.[2] The policy-makers in the two countries seek to optimize their respective objective functions, which are

Originally published in *The Economic Journal,* 96, 696–721, September 1986. This research was supported in part by Grant SES-8409886 from the National Science Foundation. We are grateful to Tamer Basar and Pradeep Dubey for helpful comments. The criticisms of two referees encouraged substantial revision of the chapter.

taken to be functions of unanticipated movements in output and in the consumer price index (CPI). The model begins by determining the usual Cournot and Stackelberg equilibria for this model. However, these represent just two possible equilibria, and a number of alternatives are also considered. In particular, in the derivation of the Cournot equilibrium, each agent takes the behavior of his opponent as given, and therefore assumes that his rival does not react to his actions. However, each agent is shown to respond in accordance with a reaction function, so that *ex post* the assumption of no response is incorrect. By contrast, we also consider a consistent conjectural variations (CCV) equilibrium in which each policy-maker, in determining his own actions, correctly conjectures the response of his opponent. The requirement of consistency is appealing and we therefore find this equilibrium concept to be particularly interesting.[3]

These three equilibrium concepts are all noncooperative; agents behave in their own self-interest under alternative strategic assumptions. We also consider a number of cooperative solutions. The first of these is where the agents choose to maximize their joint aggregate welfare. However, as Canzoneri and Gray and others have argued, cooperative equilibria may be hard to enforce in that the individual agents my have incentives to cheat and break the rules of the game.

Finally, two alternative forms of monetary regimes are considered, namely perfectly flexible and perfectly fixed exchange rates. These represent the traditional regimes in both international macroeconomic theory and policy discussions. Although they are not usually viewed in this way, they can be regarded as representing cooperative behavior. In the first of these, the policy-makers in the two economies agree to do nothing, allowing the exchange rate to respond freely to market pressures. In the latter, they agree to intervene mutually in the exchange market to maintain a fixed rate. In fact, this rate can be pegged by coordinating their policies in an infinite number of ways, and one natural alternative is considered in this chapter.

An important objective of the analysis is to compare the relative merits of the various equilibria. In the process of doing this, we touch upon the old debate of fixed versus flexible rates, but our analysis can be viewed as embedding this discussion within a larger class of equilibrium concepts. Our analysis also addresses the more topical issue concerning the gains from cooperation over the alternative noncooperative equilibria.

The theoretical framework is outlined in section 13.2, with the four strategic equilibria being discussed in sections 13.3–13.5. Insofar as possible, our study is conducted, analytically. Because of their complexity, the formal expressions characterizing the optimal policies and equilibria provide only limited insight and to obtain further understanding we combine the formal analysis of the model with numerical simulations and sensitivity analysis.[4] These numerical procedures are outlined in section 13.7, while the numerical solutions and the sensitivity analysis are given in sections 13.8 and 13.9. The main conclusions and general comments are given in section 13.10.

2 THE THEORETICAL FRAMEWORK

The analysis is based on the following two-country macroeconomic model, which is a direct extension of the recent stochastic rational expectations open-economy framework (see for example papers in Bhandari, 1985). It describes two identical economies, each specializing in the production of a distinct good and trading a single common bond.[5] In deviation form, it is expressed by the following equations:

$$Y_t = d_1 Y_t^* - d_2[I_t - \{\mathcal{E}_t(P_{t+1}) - P_t\}] + d_3(P_t^* + E_t - P_t) + u_t \tag{13.1}$$

$$Y_t^* = d_1 Y_t - d_2[I_t^* - \{\mathcal{E}_t(P_{t+1}^*) - P_t^*\}] - d_3(P_t^* + E_t - P_t) + u_t^*$$
$$0 < d_1 < 1,\ d_2 > 0,\ d_3 > 0 \tag{13.1$'$}$$

$$M_t - P_t = \alpha_1 Y_t - \alpha_2 I_t \qquad (\alpha_1 > 0,\ \alpha_2 > 0) \tag{13.2}$$

$$M_t^* - P_t^* = \alpha_1 Y_t^* - \alpha_2 I_t^* \tag{13.2$'$}$$

$$I_t = I_t^* + \mathcal{E}_t(E_{t+1}) - E_t \tag{13.3}$$

$$Y_t = \gamma\{P_t - \mathcal{E}_{t-1}(P_t)\} + v_t \qquad \gamma > 0 \tag{13.4}$$

$$Y_t^* = \gamma\{P_t^* - \mathcal{E}_{t-1}(P_t^*)\} + v_t^* \tag{13.4$'$}$$

$$C_t = \delta P_t + (1 - \delta)(P_t^* + E_t) \qquad \tfrac{1}{2} < \delta < 1 \tag{13.5}$$

$$C_t^* = \delta P_t^* + (1 - \delta)(P_t - E_t) \tag{13.5$'$}$$

where Y is the real output, measured as a deviation about its natural rate level, P is the price of domestic output, expressed in logarithms, C is the consumer price index, expressed in logarithms, E is the exchange rate (measured in terms of units of domestic currency per unit of foreign currency), measured in logarithms, I is the nominal interest rate, expressed in natural units, M is the nominal money supply, expressed in logarithms, $\mathcal{E}_t$ is the expectation, conditioned on information at time t, u_t is the stochastic shift in demand, and v_t is the stochastic shift in supply. Domestic variables are unstarred; foreign variables are denoted with asterisks. We will also refer to these as country 1 and country 2 respectively.

Equations (13.1) and (13.1′) describe equilibrium in the two goods markets. Output depends upon the real interest rate, output in the other country, the relative price, and the stochastic shift in demand. The corresponding effects across the two economies are identical and the relative price influences demand in exactly offsetting ways. The money market equilibrium conditions in the two countries are standard and are described by (13.2) and (13.2′) respectively.[6] It is trival to modify these relationships to allow for shifts in the money demand analogous to u_t and v_t. Such shifts can simply be absorbed in the money supply M and accommodated directly in any money supply adjustment rule.[7] The perfect substitutability between domestic and foreign bonds is described by the interest rate condition (13.3). Equations (13.4) and (13.4′) describe the CPI in the two economies. They embody the assumption that in each country a proportion δ of income is spent on the respective home good. We assume that residents of each country have a preference for their own good, so that $\delta > \frac{1}{2}$. Note that the real interest rate in (13.1) and (13.1′), and the real money supplies in (13.2) and (13.2′), are deflated by the output price of the respective economies. Little would be changed, except for additional detail, if the deflators were in terms of their respective CPIs.[8] Finally, equations (13.5) and (13.5′) describe outputs in the two economies in terms of standard Lucas supply functions; the deviation in output from its natural rate is postulated to be a positive function of the unanticipated movement in the price of output, together with the stochastic shift in supply.

The stochastic variables u_t, v_t, u_t^* and v_t^* are assumed to be independently distributed with zero means. If, in addition, as in fact turns out to be the case, M_t and M_t^* depend only on these current disturbances, then, as is well known, the rational expectations solution to the system (13.1)–(13.5) implies that

$$\mathcal{E}_t(P_{t+s}) = \mathcal{E}_t(P^*_{t+s}) = \mathcal{E}_t(E_{t+s}) = 0 \quad \text{for all } t, s \tag{13.6}$$

The exchange rate and price level in all future periods are both expected to remain constant. The fact that this constant is zero is simply a consequence of specifying the system in deviation form. In particular, setting $s = 1$ in (13.6) yields

$$\mathcal{E}_t(P_{t+1}) = \mathcal{E}_t(P^*_{t+1}) = \mathcal{E}_t(E_{t+1}) = 0 \quad \text{for all } t \tag{13.6′}$$

One further important feature is that the shifts u_t, u_t^*, v_t, v_t^* are assumed to be observed at time t and therefore to determine the policy-makers' decisions at that time. Indeed, these shifts are what generate the strategic problem.

Equations (13.1)–(13.5), together with (13.6), describe the structure of the two economies. The policy-makers in these economies are assumed to minimize quadratic cost functions specified in terms of unanticipated deviations in output and the CPI from their respective expected levels. Under the assumptions on the underlying stochastic variables, these expectations are all zero. Thus the respective functions to be optimized are simply

$$\Omega \equiv aY_t^2 + (1-a)C_t^2 \tag{13.7}$$

$$\Omega^* = aY_t^{*2} + (1-a)C_t^{*2} \tag{13.7'}$$

where a and $1-a$ are the relative weights assigned to output stability on the one hand and price stability on the other.

Using (13.6′), we can solve equations (13.1)–(13.5) for Y_t, Y_t^*, and E_t as follows:

$$Y_t = \phi_1 M_t + \phi_2 M_t^* + \phi_3 u_t + \phi_4 u_t^* + \phi_5 v_t + \phi_6 v_t^* \tag{13.8a}$$

$$Y_t^* = \phi_2 M_t + \phi_1 M_t^* + \phi_4 u_t + \phi_3 u_t^* + \phi_6 v_t + \phi_5 v_t^* \tag{13.8b}$$

$$E_t = \beta_1(M_t - M_t^*) + \beta_2(u_t - u_t^*) + \beta_3(v_t - v_t^*) \tag{13.8c}$$

where

$$\phi_1 \equiv \frac{\gamma}{2}\left(\frac{d_2}{D} + \frac{d_2 + 2d_3}{D}\right) > 0 \qquad \phi_2 \equiv \frac{\gamma}{2}\left(\frac{d_2}{D} - \frac{d_2 + 2d_3}{D'}\right)$$

$$\phi_3 \equiv \frac{\alpha_2\gamma}{2}\left(\frac{1}{D} + \frac{1}{D'}\right) > 0 \qquad \phi_4 \equiv \frac{\alpha_2\gamma}{2}\left(\frac{1}{D} - \frac{1}{D'}\right) > 0$$

$$\phi_5 \equiv \frac{1+\alpha_2}{\gamma}\phi_1 > 0 \qquad \phi_6 \equiv \frac{1+\alpha_2}{\gamma}\phi_2$$

$$\beta_1 \equiv \frac{\gamma(1+d_1) + d_2 + 2d_3}{D'} > 0 \qquad \beta_2 \equiv \frac{-(\gamma\alpha_1 + 1)}{D'} < 0$$

$$\beta_3 \equiv \frac{(1+d_1) - \alpha_1(d_2 + 2d_3)}{D'}$$

$$D = \gamma\{(1-d_1)\alpha_2 + d_2\alpha_1\} + d_2(1+\alpha_2) > 0$$

$$D' = \gamma\{(1+d_1)\alpha_2 + (d_2 + 2d_3)\alpha_1\} + (d_2 + 2d_3)(1+\alpha_2) > 0$$

Equations (13.8a)–(13.8c) have several interesting features. First, the symmetry of the underlying economies is reflected in the symmetry of these reduced-form solutions. As expected, an increase in M_t, as well as positive disturbances in domestic demand u_t or supply v_t, leads to increases in domestic output. A positive foreign demand shock u_t^* also leads to an increase in domestic output, although by a lesser amount than when the demand shock is of domestic origin. The reason for the positive spillover is that an increase in u_t^* leads to an appreciation of the foreign currency (depreciation of the domestic currency), thereby stimulating demand for domestic output and domestic output itself. The effect of an increase in the foreign money supply on domestic output ϕ_2, and vice versa, is highly indeterminate. This is because an increase in M_t^* raises foreign output and demand, giving rise to the usual positive spillover onto domestic demand and output. However, at the same time, the foreign monetary expansion leads to a depreciation of the foreign currency (appreciation of the domestic currency). This leads to an increase in the relative price of domestic goods, thereby leading to a contraction in domestic demand and output. This "negative transmission" mechanism is a familiar one, dating back to early work by Mundell (1963). The direction of the net effet is given by

$$\operatorname{sgn}\phi_2 = \operatorname{sgn}[\alpha_2\{d_2d_1 - d_3(1 - d_1)\}]$$

For plausible parameter values, we find that the negative effect dominates. Indeed, the small numerical magnitude of ϕ_2 turns out to be very important for the numerical comparison of the alternative strategic equilibria. When ϕ_2 is small or negative, this turns out to reduce the quantitative degree of interaction between the policy instruments in the two economies. In this case, the strategic elements in the determination of optimal policy are minimal and the various strategic equilibria all tend to be numerically close. When the relative price effect d_3 is small, so that $\phi_2 > 0$ and larger numerically, the interaction between the policy instruments increases in importance. Also, the role of prices in market clearing decreases in importance, thereby increasing the scope for discretionary monetary policy. Greater numerical variation between the various equilibria is obtained. For this reason, it is important in our numerical work below to make the distinction between "large" and "small" values of d_3.[9]

The other interesting point to note is that the exchange rate responds purely to differentials between the domestic and foreign variables. Any shock or policy change which is common to both economies leaves the exchange rate unchanged.

Combining the solutions (13.8a)–(13.8c) with (13.4), (13.4′), (13.6), and (13.6′) and substituting into (13.5) and (13.5′), we obtain the following solutions for the CPI:

$$C_t = \eta_1 M_t + \eta_2 M_t^* + \eta_3 u_t + \eta_4 u_t^* + \eta_5 v_t + \eta_6 v_t^* \tag{13.9a}$$

$$C_t^* = \eta_2 M_t + \eta_1 M_t^* + \eta_4 u_t + \eta_3 u_t^* + \eta_6 v_t + \eta_5 v_t^* \tag{13.9b}$$

where

$$\eta_1 \equiv \frac{\delta\phi_1 + (1-\delta)\phi_2}{\gamma} + \beta_1(1 - \delta) > 0$$

$$\eta_2 \equiv \frac{\delta\phi_2 + (1-\delta)\phi_1}{\gamma} - \beta_1(1 + \delta)$$

$$\eta_3 \equiv \frac{\delta\phi_3 + (1-\delta)\phi_4}{\gamma} + \beta_2(1 - \delta)$$

$$\eta_4 \equiv \frac{\delta\phi_4 + (1-\delta)\phi_3}{\gamma} - \beta_2(1 - \delta)$$

$$\eta_5 \equiv \frac{\delta(\phi_5 - 1) + (1-\delta)\phi_6}{\gamma} + \beta_3(1 - \delta)$$

$$\eta_6 \equiv \frac{\delta\phi_6 + (1-\delta)(\phi_5 - 1)}{\gamma} - \beta_3(1-\delta)$$

By raising domestic output demand and causing the domestic currenty to depreciate, a domestic monetary expansion raises the domestic CPI. By contrast, a foreign monetary expansion causes the domestic currency to appreciate which, together with the likely negative output transmission effects, generally (but not always) causes the domestic CPI to fall.

3 OPTIMAL STRATEGIES

The optimal policy problem confronting each of the policy-makers is to choose their respective nominal money supplies to minimize their cost functions (13.7) and (13.7′) subject to the constraints (13.8a), (13.8b), (13.9a) and (13.9b). A key feature in the determination of the equilibrium concerns the strategic behavior and the following equilibria will be derived.

3.1 Cournot

Under the Cournot assumption, each policy-maker chooses his money supply so as to minimize his respective cost function, taking the behavior of this opponent as remaining fixed. Taking partial derivatives of (13.7) and (13.7′) respectively, this gives rise to the optimality conditions:[10]

$$\frac{\partial\Omega}{\partial M} \equiv aY\frac{\partial Y}{\partial M} + (1-a)C\frac{\partial C}{\partial M} = 0 \qquad (13.10a)$$

$$\frac{\partial\Omega^*}{\partial M^*} \equiv aY^*\frac{\partial Y^*}{\partial M^*} + (1-a)C^*\frac{\partial C^*}{\partial M^*} = 0 \qquad (13.10b)$$

Substituting (13.8a), (13.8b), (13.9a), and (13.9b), as well as the appropriate partial derivatives, into (13.10a) and (13.10b) yields the pair of linear equations in M and M^*:

$$\frac{\partial\Omega}{\partial M} \equiv \Psi_{11}M + \Psi_{12}M^* + \Psi_{13}u + \Psi_{14}u^* + \Psi_{15}v + \Psi_{16}v^* = 0 \qquad (13.11a)$$

$$\frac{\partial\Omega^*}{\partial M^*} \equiv \Psi_{12}M + \Psi_{11}M^* + \Psi_{14}u + \Psi_{13}u^* + \Psi_{16}v + \Psi_{15}v^* = 0 \qquad (13.11b)$$

where

$$\Psi_{1j} \equiv a\phi_1\phi_j + (1-a)\eta_1\eta_j \qquad j = 1, \ldots, 6$$

Equations (13.11a) and (13.11b) define the reaction curves for country 1 (the domestic economy) and country 2 (the foreign economy) respectively. The slopes of these curves in M–M^* space are

$$\left(\frac{\mathrm{d}M^*}{\mathrm{d}M}\right)_1 = -\frac{\Psi_{11}}{\Psi_{12}} \qquad \left(\frac{\mathrm{d}M^*}{\mathrm{d}M}\right)_2 = -\frac{\Psi_{12}}{\Psi_{11}}$$

and, with $\Psi_{11} > 0$, their signs depend upon $\operatorname{sgn}\Psi_{12} = \operatorname{sgn}\{a\phi_1\phi_2 + (1-a)\eta_1\eta_2\}$. Given ϕ_1, $\eta_1 > 0$, and with ϕ_2 and η_2 tending to be negative (the latter strongly so), $\Psi_{12} < 0$. This in fact turns out to be so for 49 of the 50 parameter sets we consider. Thus taking $\Psi_{12} < 0$, the reaction curves are positively sloped, implying that a monetary expansion in one country induces a monetary expansion in the other.

The Cournot equilibrium is attained at the intersection of the two reaction curves (13.11a) and (13.11b):

$$M = -\frac{\alpha_2}{d_2}u - \frac{1+\alpha_2}{\gamma}v - \frac{\Psi_{13} - (\alpha_2/d_2)\Psi_{11}}{\Psi_{11} - \Psi_{12}}(u - u^*) + \frac{(1-a)\eta_1}{\gamma(\Psi_{11}^2 - \Psi_{12}^2)}(\Psi_{11}v - \Psi_{12}v^*) \tag{13.12a}$$

$$M^* = -\frac{\alpha_2}{d_2}u^* - \frac{1+\alpha_2}{\gamma}v^* + \frac{\Psi_{13} - (\alpha_2/d_2)\Psi_{11}}{\Psi_{11} - \Psi_{12}}(u - u^*) + \frac{(1-a)\eta_1}{\gamma(\Psi_{11}^2 - \Psi_{12}^2)}(\Psi_{11}v^* - \Psi_{12}v) \tag{13.12b}$$

The shifts in domestic demand and supply impact directly upon domestic output through the aggregate demand function and the aggregate supply function respectively. Equations (13.12) indicate that one component of the optimal monetary policies in the two economies is to contract the money supply sufficiently to ensure that the domestic interest rate rises so as to neutralize exactly these effects on output.[11] These adjustments are described by the terms $-\alpha_2 u/d_2 - (1+\alpha_2)v/\gamma$ in (13.12a) and $-\alpha_2 u^*/d_2 - (1+\alpha_2)v^*/\gamma$ in (13.12b). We will refer to these as being the "direct shift" component of the optimal policy rules. However, in addition, the shocks are transmitted across the two economies through movements in the exchange rate (relative price movements) and the policy responses themselves. These effects are incorporated in the terms involving $u - u^*$ and $\Psi_{11}v - \Psi_{12}v^*$ for the domestic economy, and the analogous expressions for the foreign country. We will refer to these as being the "interactive" component of the optimal policy rule.

3.2 Demand shocks

It is interesting to note that these interactive components of the demand shifts require totally symmetric adjustments in the two economies. It can be verified by direct evaluation that $\{\Psi_{13} - (\alpha_2/d_2)\Psi_{11}\}/(\Psi_{11} - \Psi_{12}) < 0$, so that in response to a positive domestic demand shock, say, the domestic monetary authority should expand its money supply in response to the interactive effect, thereby offsetting (but only partially) the initial contraction in response to the direct shift effect.[12] At the same time, the foreign monetary authority should contract its money supply by an amount which exactly matches the interactive component of the domestic authority's response.

The reason for this is as follows. It is seen from the reduced-form solutions (13.8) that the net effect of the initial expansion in domestic demand, together with the direct monetary contraction, on domestic output is $\mathrm{d}Y = \phi_3 - \alpha_2\phi_1/d_2 < 0$. By neglecting the relative price effect and policy interaction, the domestic monetary authority overcontracts its money supply and domestic output falls. At the same time, both the demand expansion and the initial domestic monetary contraction cause the domestic exchange rate to appreciate, i.e. the foreign currency depreciates, thereby inducing an expansion abroad. In order to stabilize the foreign economy, the foreign monetary authority contracts its money supply thereby now causing an appreciation of the foreign currency, with positive spillovers to the domestic economy. Furthermore, by now expanding its money supply, the domestic monetary authority is able to correct for the initial overcontraction which occurred.

The second demand shock of interest is that of a worldwide expansion, shared equally by the two economies so that $u = u^*$. In this case, the optimal response is simply for each policy-maker to contract his money supply to neutralize the effects of the disturbance in his economy. There are in effect no relative price spillover effects to be taken into account.

The solutions for output and inflation in the two economies are reported in equations (13A.1) and (13A.6) of the appendix. From these equations we see that after each policy-maker has accommodated the direct disturbances in his own economy, output, inflation, and therefore welfare costs in the two economies depend upon the difference between the domestic and foreign demand shocks, i.e. $u - u^*$. Again this is a consequence of the symmetry of the two economies. Consider a domestic demand shock $u > 0$. After allowing for the contractions in the money supply which occur both at home and abroad, output in the home economy rises, while output abroad falls. At the same time, the domestic CPI falls and the CPI abroad increases. Basically, this is because of the appreciation of the domestic currency, which more than offsets the positive effects of the domestic demand expansion on the price of domestic output.

The most interesting feature of these results is the perfect symmetry of the demand effects across the two economies. A unit shift in demand in country 1, say, has precisely equal and opposite effects on output and the CPI in the two economies. The welfare effects, as measured by the quadratic objective functions, are therefore equally borne by both economies. A further consequence is that if the two economies are both subjected to identical shifts in demand, reflecting a worldwide demand shift, then the monetary authorities need simply neutralize the direct effects of these shocks in their respective economies. This will ensure that the output level and CPI in the two economies remain pegged at their respective equilibrium levels. Welfare costs are minimized at zero; both economies will attain their respective Bliss points.

3.3 Supply shocks

The adjustments to the interactive components of the supply shocks are not perfectly symmetric. A positive shock in domestic supply requires a domestic monetary expansion in order to adjust for the effects of the initial (direct) monetary contraction, namely $-(1 + \alpha_2)v/\gamma$. The reasoning for this is essentially analogous to that for demand shocks, described above. The combined effects of the positive supply shock and the direct monetary contraction on output are $\phi_5 - \phi_1(1 + \alpha_2)/\gamma = 0$, i.e. they are exactly offsetting. However, they lead to an appreciation of the domestic currency, resulting in a reduction in the domestic CPI. Given the quadratic cost function, domestic welfare is improved by now increasing the money supply, thereby moderating the reduction in the domestic CPI and requiring output to increase somewhat.

The overall effects of the domestic supply shock on the domestic money supply depends critically upon the relative cost a of output stability in the welfare function. If this is large, the expansionary component is dominated by the direct contractionary component and, on balance, the money stock in the domestic economy falls. However, if the objective function is weighted towards price stability, the expansionary effect is dominant, leading to an overall increase in the domestic money supply.

The response abroad, or equivalently the domestic response to a foreign supply shock, depends upon whether Ψ_{12} is greater or less than zero. Taking the more likely case where $\Psi_{12} < 0$, so that the reaction functions are positively sloped, we see that the increase in the domestic money supply resulting from the interactive component leads to a monetary expansion abroad.

The net effect of a positive domestic supply shock on the two economies is seen in equations (13A.4). Output at home and abroad both increase, with the domestic effect being larger. At the same time, the CPIs in the two economies will fall, with the greater effect again being in the domestic economy. Thus, in contrast with the perfectly symmetric effects of a single-country demand shock, a domestic supply shock has significantly greater effect on the output and CPI of the domestic economy than it does on the foreign economy. The welfare costs are therefore borne more heavily by the economy in which the shock is taking place.

Worldwide supply shifts, experienced equally by both economies, generate equal output and CPI effects in the two countries. The nominal exchange rate remains unchanged. The effects of the shocks in the two economies compound one another, making the attainment of the Bliss point (zero welfare costs) impossible. In this respect, worldwide supply shocks impose a much more serious stabilization policy problem than do worldwide demand shocks.

4 STACKELBERG EQUILIBRIUM

In deriving the Stackelberg equilibrium we will treat country 1 as the leader with country 2 being the follower. The procedure is familiar. Country 1 optimizes its welfare function subject to the reaction curve of the follower. The solutions for the optimal policies and the outputs and inflation rates are of the same general form as for the Cournot case. However, since the expressions turn out to be rather involved, and not particularly enlightening, we merely summarize their main qualitative aspects.

First, part of the adjustment of the policy instruments should be to accommodate to the "direct shift" terms, just as was the case in the Cournot equilibrium. Secondly, the demand shifts u and u^* enter the "interactive" component of the optimal rules symmetrically, although in contrast with the Cournot case the coefficients for the leader are different from those for the follower. Thirdly, because of this symmetry, if both economies are subject to identical shifts in demand, then the monetary authorities in each country need simply neutralize the direct effects of the demand shifts in their own economy. This will ensure the attainment of the Bliss point.

Supply shifts are more complicated. First, domestic and foreign disturbances enter asymmetrically. Moreover, they impact differently on the leader from the follower. A variety of patterns regarding the effects of the supply shifts on outputs and inflation in the two countries are found and are noted further in section 8.

5 CONSISTENT CONJECTURAL VARIATIONS

Under Cournot behavior, each policy-maker assumes that the other does not respond to his actions. In fact, however, each policy-maker will respond in accordance with his reaction curve. In the Cournot equilibrium each policy-maker is therefore consistently wrong in predicting the response of the rival. The CCV equilibrium assumes that each agent, in choosing his own strategy, takes the response of his rival into account. Furthermore, the response is correctly anticipated and hence the solution corresponds to a rational expectations equilibrium.

The optimality conditions for the two countries under the assumption of CCV are given by

$$\frac{\partial \Omega}{\partial M} + \frac{\partial \Omega}{\partial M^*}\left(\frac{\mathrm{d}M^*}{\mathrm{d}M}\right)_2 = 0 \qquad (13.13\text{a})$$

$$\frac{\partial \Omega^*}{\partial M^*} + \frac{\partial \Omega^*}{\partial M}\left(\frac{\mathrm{d}M}{\mathrm{d}M^*}\right)_1 = 0 \qquad (13.13\text{b})$$

where $(\mathrm{d}M^*/\mathrm{d}M)_2$ and $(\mathrm{d}M/\mathrm{d}M^*)_1$ denote the correctly conjectured response on the part of the opponent to each policy-maker's decisions. For notational convenience we let

$$\left(\frac{\mathrm{d}M^*}{\mathrm{d}M}\right)_2 \equiv x_2 \qquad \left(\frac{\mathrm{d}M}{\mathrm{d}M^*}\right)_1 \equiv x_1$$

Performing the partial differentiation in (13.13a) and (13.13b) gives the optimality conditions in the two countries as respectively

$$\begin{aligned}(\Psi_{11} + x_2\Psi_{12})M + (\Psi_{12} + x_2\Psi_{22})M^* \\ = -(\Psi_{13} + x_2\Psi_{23})u - (\Psi_{14} + x_2\Psi_{24})u^* \\ - (\Psi_{15} + x_2\Psi_{25})v - (\Psi_{16} + x_2\Psi_{26})v^*\end{aligned} \qquad (13.14\text{a})$$

$$\begin{aligned}(\Psi_{12} + x_1\Psi_{22})M + (\Psi_{11} + x_1\Psi_{12})M^* \\ = -(\Psi_{14} + x_1\Psi_{24})u - (\Psi_{13} + x_1\Psi_{23})u^* \\ -(\Psi_{16} + x_1\Psi_{26})v - (\Psi_{15} + x_1\Psi_{25})v^*\end{aligned} \qquad (13.14\text{b})$$

where

$$\Psi_{2j} \equiv a\phi_2\phi_j + (1 - a)\eta_2\eta_j \qquad j = 1, \ldots, 6$$

From (13.14a) and (13.14b) we obtain

$$\left(\frac{\mathrm{d}M}{\mathrm{d}M^*}\right)_1 \equiv x_1 = -\left(\frac{\Psi_{12} + x_2\Psi_{22}}{\Psi_{11} + x_2\Psi_{12}}\right) \tag{13.15a}$$

$$\left(\frac{\mathrm{d}M^*}{\mathrm{d}M}\right)_2 \equiv x_2 = -\left(\frac{\Psi_{12} + x_1\Psi_{22}}{\Psi_{11} + x_1\Psi_{12}}\right) \tag{13.15b}$$

The slope of the reaction curve of each policy-maker depends upon the slope of the reaction function of his rival. These two equations provide a pair of equations in x_1 and x_2. It is immediately seen that the solutions are

$$x_1 = x_2 = x$$

where x satisfies the quadratic equation

$$\Psi_{12}x^2 + (\Psi_{11} + \Psi_{22})x + \Psi_{12} = 0 \tag{13.16}$$

Thus the optimal monetary policies under CCV, obtained by solving (13.14a) and (13.14b) are given by

$$\begin{aligned} M = &-\frac{\alpha_2}{d_2}u - \left(\frac{1+\alpha_2}{\gamma}\right)v \\ &- \frac{\{\Psi_{13} - (\alpha_2/d_2)\Psi_{11}\} + x\{\Psi_{23} - (\alpha_2/d_2)\Psi_{12}\}}{(\Psi_{11} + x\Psi_{12}) - (\Psi_{12} + x\Psi_{22})}(u - u^*) \\ &+ \frac{(1-a)(\eta_1 + x\eta_2) \times \{(\Psi_{11} + \Psi_{12}x)v - (\Psi_{12} + \Psi_{22}x)v^*\}}{\gamma\{(\Psi_{11} + x\Psi_{12})^2 - (\Psi_{12} + x\Psi_{22})^2\}} \end{aligned} \tag{13.17a}$$

$$\begin{aligned} M^* = &-\frac{\alpha_2}{d_2}u^* - \left(\frac{1+\alpha_2}{\gamma}\right)v^* \\ &+ \frac{\{\Psi_{13} - (\alpha_2/d_2)\Psi_{11}\} + x\{\Psi_{23} - (\alpha_2/d_2)\Psi_{12}\}}{(\Psi_{11} + x\Psi_{12}) - (\Psi_{12} + x\Psi_{22})}(u - u^*) \\ &+ \frac{(1-a)(\eta_1 + x\eta_2) \times \{(\Psi_{11} + \Psi_{12}x)v^* - (\Psi_{12} + \Psi_{22}x)v\}}{\gamma\{(\Psi_{11} + x\Psi_{12})^2 - (\Psi_{12} + x\Psi_{22})^2\}} \end{aligned} \tag{13.17b}$$

where x is the solution to (13.16). The optimal policies are of the same general form as (13.12a) and (13.12b). Observe that since x is the solution to a quadratic equation, there are two roots. Denoting these two roots by x^1 and x^2, say we see that they are (a) real with (b)

$$x^1x^2 = 1 \qquad x^1 + x^2 = -\frac{\Psi_{11} + \Psi_{22}}{\Psi_{12}}$$

If $\Psi_{12} < 0$, then $x^1 > 1$ and $0 < x^2 < 1$; if $\Psi_{12} > 0$, the two roots lie in the ranges $x^1 < -1$ and $-1 < x^2 < 0$. Thus there are two equilibria which correspond to CCV. In the case of country-specific supply shocks these equilibria may give rise to conflicts in welfare for the two economies. One solution is better for one country, while the other equilibrium is preferable for the other. In this case we choose the solution having lower aggregate welfare costs as the equilibrium.

The solutions for output and CPI in the two countries are obtained by substituting (13.17a) and (13.17b) into (13.8a), (13.8b), (13.9a), and (13.9b), with the resulting expressions being reported in equations (13A.2) of the appendix. Since the qualitative properties of both the optimal rules and the behavior of the economy are similar to those under Cournot, we do not discuss these expressions further at this time.

6 COOPERATIVE EQUILIBRIA

The solutions discussed so far have all been noncooperative. We now consider alternative forms of cooperative equilibria.

6.1 Pareto optimal

Assume that the two policy-makers collude to minimize their aggregate joint cost function:

$$\Omega + \Omega^* \equiv a(Y^2 + Y^{*2}) + (1 - a)(C^2 + C^{*2}) \tag{13.18}$$

Differentiating (13.18) with respect to M and M^* yields the optimality conditions

$$a\left(Y \frac{\partial Y}{\partial M} + Y^* \frac{\partial Y^*}{\partial M}\right) + (1 - a)\left(C \frac{\partial C}{\partial M} + C^* \frac{\partial C^*}{\partial M}\right) = 0 \tag{13.19a}$$

$$a\left(Y \frac{\partial Y}{\partial M^*} + Y^* \frac{\partial Y^*}{\partial M^*}\right) + (1 - a)\left(C \frac{\partial C}{\partial M^*} + C^* \frac{\partial C^*}{\partial M^*}\right) = 0 \tag{13.19b}$$

with the optimal policies being

$$\begin{aligned} M = &- \frac{\alpha_2}{d_2} u - \frac{1 + \alpha_2}{\gamma} v \\ &- \frac{\{\Psi_{13} - (\alpha_2/d_2)\Psi_{11}\} - \{\Psi_{23} - (\alpha_2/d_2)\Psi_{12}\}}{\Psi_{11} + \Psi_{22} - 2\Psi_{12}} (u - u^*) \\ &- \frac{(1 - a)\{2\eta_2\Psi_{12} - \eta_1(\Psi_{11} + \Psi_{22})\}}{\{(\Psi_{11} + \Psi_{22})^2 - 4\Psi_{12}^2\}\gamma} v \\ &- \frac{(1 - a)\{2\eta_1\Psi_{12} - \eta_2(\Psi_{11} + \Psi_{22})\}}{\{(\Psi_{11} + \Psi_{22})^2 - 4\Psi_{12}^2\}\gamma} v^* \end{aligned} \tag{13.20a}$$

$$M^* = -\frac{\alpha_2}{d_2}u^* - \frac{1+\alpha_2}{\gamma}v^*$$
$$-\frac{\{\Psi_{13} - (\alpha_2/d_2)\Psi_{11}\} - \{\Psi_{23} - (\alpha_2/d_2)\Psi_{12}\}}{\Psi_{11} + \Psi_{22} - 2\Psi_{12}}(u^* - u)$$
$$-\frac{(1-a)\{2\eta_2\Psi_{12} - \eta_1(\Psi_{11} + \Psi_{22})\}}{\{(\Psi_{11} + \Psi_{22})^2 - 4\Psi_{12}^2\}\gamma}v^*$$
$$-\frac{(1-a)\{2\eta_1\Psi_{12} - \eta_2(\Psi_{11} + \Psi_{22})\}}{\{(\Psi_{11} + \Psi_{22})^2 - 4\Psi_{12}^2\}\gamma}v \qquad (13.20b)$$

As in the previous forms of strategic behavior, the optimal rules require the neutralization of what we have termed the direct shift terms

$$\frac{-\alpha_2 u}{d_2} - \frac{(1+\alpha_2)v}{\gamma} \qquad \frac{-\alpha_2 u^*}{d_2} - \frac{(1+\alpha_2)v^*}{\gamma}$$

In addition, the interaction components exhibit the same general characteristics as in the other equilibria, although the magnitudes of the adjustments are modified.[13]

Demand shocks The interactive components of the demand shocks are perfectly symmetrical, with the coefficient of $(u - u^*)$ in the domestic (foreign) monetary policy function being positive (negative), but smaller in magnitude than the direct effect. Thus both the domestic and foreign economies should contract their respective money supplies in response to a domestic demand shock, with the same reasoning as for the Cournot equilibrium continuing to apply. However, in contrast with the Cournot equilibrium, relatively more of the adjustment is shifted to the foreign economy.

The effects of the demand shocks on output and CPI in the two economies are given by (13A.3a) and (13A.3b). As before, the effects depend upon the difference between the domestic and foreign demand shifts. The net effect of a shift in domestic demand is to increase output and to reduce output abroad. The domestic CPI falls and the foreign CPI rises. The less balanced monetary adjustments in the two economies (relative to the Cournot equilibrium) and the fact that output is more sensitive to the domestic, rather than the foreign, money stock means the rise in domestic output and fall in foreign output are both larger than under Cournot. A further consequence of the less balanced adjustment is that appreciation of the domestic currency is reduced so that the adjustments in the domestic and foreign CPI are reduced. In short, cooperation leads to more variation in output accompanied by less variation in the CPI than in the Cournot equilibrium. The same comparison holds with respect to the CCV equilibrium. The symmetry with respect to demand shifts across the two economies, obtained in the previous equilibria, holds in the cooperative solution as well.

Supply shocks As before, the symmetry associated with demand shifts does not apply. Moreover, the appropriate response of the money supply to both domestic and foreign shocks depends critically upon the relative weight a assigned to output stability in the objective function. The reasoning is basically as for the Cournot equilibrium discussed above.

The net effect of the domestic supply shock, together with the policy responses, is to raise domestic output, with the effect on the foreign output being indeterminate. On the one hand, the expansion in the domestic economy generates positive spillovers abroad. On the other hand, the monetary contractions, typically conducted in the two economies, tend to generate contractionary effects. The supply shock always reduces the CPI in both economies, with the effect in the domestic economy being the numerically larger. Overall, the foreign adjustment to the domestic supply shock is less than that of the domestic economy, so that, under cooperation, the greater instability, and therefore the greater welfare losses, are incurred by the domestic economy. Moreover, relative to the Cournot equilibrium, we find that domestic welfare is increased while foreign welfare declines. The economy experiencing the supply shock therefore gains from cooperation, while its partner loses. This is a consequence of the fact that the shift is confined to one country; if it occurs in both, then both economies are better off under cooperation.

6.2 Flexible exchange rate

An important form of monetary cooperation arises when the policy-makers in the two countries agree to do nothing. This of course is the case of a perfectly flexible exchange rate and is specified by

$$M = M^* = 0. \tag{13.21}$$

It serves as a useful benchmark case.[14]

6.3 Fixed exchange rate

The other extreme form of cooperation is where the monetary authorities in the two countries agree to maintain a fixed exchange rate, at $E = 0$ say. From (13.8c) this is attained when

$$\beta_1(M - M^*) + \beta_2(u - u^*) + \beta_3(v - v^*) = 0$$

In general there are an infinite number of combinations of intervention which will satisfy this condition, and these in general all produce different welfare costs. Given the symmetry of the two economies, we will consider the most natural candidate,[15]

$$M = \frac{1}{2\beta_1}\{\beta_2(u^* - u) + \beta_3(v^* - v)\}$$
$$M^* = \frac{1}{2\beta_1}\{\beta_2(u - u^*) + \beta_3(v - v^*)\} \tag{13.22}$$

7 NUMERICAL PROCEDURES

The parameters appearing in the optimal policies and solutions are themselves complex functions of the underlying parameters of the model. While we have been able to characterize the various equilibria in some detail, to gain further insight into the general welfare implications of the different regimes, we resort to numerical analysis.

Table 13.1, part (a), indicates two sets of base parameter values. These are chosen on the basis of reasonable empirical evidence. The elasticity of the demand for domestic output with respect to foreign output is $d_1 = 0.3$; the semi-elasticity of the demand for output with respect to the real interest rate is $d_2 = 0.5$; the income elasticity of the demand for money is $\alpha_1 = 1$; the semi-elasticity of the demand for money with respect to the nominal interest rate is 0.5; the share of domestic output in domestic consumption is $\delta = 0.6$ for both economies; the slopes of the supply functions are $\frac{4}{3}$; the relative weight given to output stabilization in the objective function is $a = 0.75$.

The choice of the relative price elasticity d_3 is more problematical. Our initial chosen value was $d_3 = 1$, which is close to that assumed by others.[16] However, for $d_3 = 1$, we find that ϕ_2 and η_2 both turn out to be very small numerically relative to ϕ_1 and η_1, a consequence of which is that both Ψ_{12} and Ψ_{22} are small relative to Ψ_{11}. The significance of all

TABLE 13.1 *Parameter values*

(a) Base sets

$d_1 = 0.3$, $d_2 = 0.5$, $d_3 = 0.1$, or $d_3 = 1$, $\alpha_1 = 1.0$, $\alpha_2 = 0.5$
$\delta = 0.6$, $\gamma = \frac{4}{3}$, $a = 0.75$

(b) Variants: additional 48 parameter sets

d_1: 0, 0.2, 0.4, 0.6, 0.8
d_2: 0.01, 0.25, 1.0, 5
$\alpha_1 = 0, 0.5$
$\alpha_2 = 0.1, 1.0, 5$
$\delta = 0.5, 0.75, 0.99$
$\gamma = 1, 2$
$a = 0. 0.2, 0.4, 0.6, 1$

this is that the effects of policies within the economy overwhelm the effects of these policies abroad. The linkage between the economies is weak, so that the interaction between the policy-makers is small. In ths situation, the differences between the strategic equilibria are minimal. In all cases, the welfare differences between, say, the Cournot and the Pareto optimal cooperative equilibria are less than 1 percent for demand disturbances and 2 percent for supply disturbances (see tables 13.2, part (b), 13.3, part (b), and 13.5, part (b)). To a first approximation, each policy-maker can act in isolation and it does not matter very much how his rival responds.

For values of d_3 larger than unity, the strategic equilibria continue to be close and this is true for all variations of the other parameter sets. One conclusion of this is that, for $d_3 > 1$, the gains from cooperation are extremely modest, a conclusion which is also consistent with some of the simulations of Oudiz and Sachs (1984). At the same time, the gains from any form of strategic behavior over simple rules such as fixed or flexible exchange rates are significant. As d_3 declines, we find that Ψ_{12} and Ψ_{22} increase in size relative to Ψ_{11} and greater divergence between the equilibria results. Thus as our preferred values we take $d_3 = 0.1$, although we recognize that this may be somewhat low.

While these values seem reasonable, they are arbitrary. Therefore in table 13.1, part (b), we consider variants of these values allowing the parameters to range between low and high values. To consider all combinations of these parameter values would be impractical. Our approach is therefore to begin with the base parameter set and to introduce one parameter change at a time. Combining these with the two values $d_3 = 0.1$ and $d_3 = 1$ gives a total of 50 parameter sets, which can be identified from table 13.1. Introducing the parameter changes singly in this way enables a numerical form of comparative statics to be performed.

8 ALTERNATIVE EQUILIBRIA: BASE PARAMETER SET

Tables 13.2–13.5 summarize the equilibria resulting from various types of stochastic disturbances, for the base parameter sets. In addition to the four strategic equilibria, we also present the extremes of the perfectly flexible and perfectly fixed exchange rates. Results for the other parameter sets are available from the authors. These tables summarize the optimal monetary policies and the responses of the key macrovariables Y, Y^*, E, C, and C^*, as well as the implied welfare costs. In the case of the Stackelberg equilibrium country 1 is the leader and country 2 is the follower. We have already commented on how the CCV requirement gives rise to two equilibria. In the case of a single-country supply shock, these equilibria may give rise to a conflict

TABLE 13.2 *Domestic demand disturbance ($u = 10$)*

	M	M^*	Y	Y^*	E	C	C^*	Ω	Ω^*
(a) $d_3 = 0.1$									
Cournot	−4.499	−5.501	1.334	−1.334	−7.332	−2.733	2.733	3.201	3.201
Stackelberg	−4.710	−5.537	1.261	−1.349	−7.481	−2.830	2.764	3.195	3.274
CCV	−4.665	−5.335	1.279	−1.279	−7.615	−2.854	2.854	3.264	3.264
Cooperative	−3.694	−6.306	1.597	−1.597	−5.957	−2.143	2.143	3.062	3.062
Flexible	0	0	2.940	0.600	−8.187	−1.772	4.427	7.265	5.170
Fixed	4.795	−4.795	4.510	−0.970	0	1.738	0.917	16.01	0.915
(b) $d_3 = 1$									
Cournot	−5.100	−4.900	0.377	−0.377	−3.042	−1.160	1.160	0.443	0.443
Stackelberg	−5.122	−4.903	0.369	−0.378	−3.052	−1.168	1.168	0.443	0.443
CCV	−5.119	−4.881	0.369	−0.369	−3.062	−1.169	1.169	0.444	0.444
Cooperative	−4.979	−5.021	0.428	−0.428	−2.913	−1.101	1.101	0.440	0.440
Flexible	0	0	2.189	1.351	−2.935	0.216	2.439	3.606	2.855
Fixed	2.756	−2.756	3.345	0.195	0	1.564	1.091	9.002	0.326

from a welfare point of view. We have chosen the Pareto superior solution.

8.1 Demand disturbances

Table 13.2 reports the numerical solution in the case where country 1 is subject to a 10 unit positive random shock in demand.

Consider as a benchmark the case of a perfectly flexible exchange rate. In the absence of intervention, the increase in demand in country 1 leads to an increase in the output of country 1, together with an appreciation of its currency. The latter is of sufficient magnitude to lead to a reduction in the domestic CPI. At the same time, the increase in domestic output and the appreciation of the domestic currency stimulates demand and output abroad, and puts upward pressure on the foreign CPI. Overall, the accommodation in the world economy to the monetary shock in country 1 is accomplished by a relatively large quantity adjustment in country 1 together with a relatively large price adjustment in country 2.

Now suppose that each policy-maker follows Cournot behavior. In particular, both countries respond to the stimulus in demand by decreasing their respective money stocks. This will tend to moderate the increase in output in country 1 and in fact cause a decline in output in country 2. At the same time, the relatively larger monetary contraction abroad moderates the depreciation of the foreign currency, thereby moderating the increase in its CPI. By shifting the relative adjustment away from output and toward the CPI in country 1, and the reverse in country 2, the welfare costs are reduced in both cases. This is an immediate consequence of the quadratic cost function.

In reaching the Cournot equilibrium, each policy-maker assumes that his opponent will not react. In the CCV solution, each policy-maker correctly takes account of his opponent's reaction. The slope of country 2's reaction function is (for $d_3 = 0.1$) $-\Psi_{12}/\Psi_{11} = 0.172$, while the slope of the consistency conjectured reaction is $x = 0.162$, which is flatter. Thus, with consistent conjectures, country 1 correctly expects less monetary contraction on the part of country 2 in response to its own contraction, and therefore contracts more itself. The reverse applies in country 2. The slope of the consistently conjectured reaction of country 1 is steeper than country 1's reaction function. Country 2 expects a greater contraction by country 1 than indicated by the conventional reaction function, and therefore contracts less itself. The consequences of this are that the increase in output in country 1, and the decrease in country 2, are both moderated relative to the Cournot equilibrium. The appreciation of country 1's currency is increased and this leads to greater variations in the CPI. Given the quadratic cost functions, the move toward less output variation and more price variation leads to lower welfare in both economies.

The Stackelberg solution involves a degree of cooperation in that each player assumes a specific role. The leader is aware of the follower's reaction function and the fact that the latter will contract his money supply less than proportionately in response to his own monetary contract. This increases the appreciation of the domestic currency (relative to the Cournot equilibrium). Welfare in country 1 is increased. Fluctuations in both output and CPI in country 2 are increased, resulting in a welfare loss abroad.

All the Cournot, Stackelberg, and CCV equilibria involve relatively low variations in output, accompanied by relatively large fluctuations in the CPI. Given the quadratic cost function, both countries can be made better off by cooperating, with country 1 contracting less and country 2 contracting more. This arrangement leads to larger fluctuations in output, but smaller fluctuations in the exchange rate and CPI, leading to a higher overall level of welfare.

Finally, the authorities can achieve a perfectly fixed exchange rate with an appropriate monetary expansion in country 1 matched by an equivalent contraction abroad. This shifts more of the adjustment in country 1 to output and less to the CPI, which, given the relative weight in the objective function, reduces domestic welfare. However, the stable exchange rate eliminates the key mechanism whereby the domestic disturbance is transmitted abroad. Thus, from the viewpoint of the foreign economy, the fixed exchange rate is the preferred regime.

The results where the demand disturbances occur in the foreign country are symmetrical and need not be discussed. Also, the case of a worldwide shift in demand, giving rise to identical shifts in the two countries, leads to the attainment of the Bliss point (zero-cost equilibrium) as demonstrated previously.

8.2 Supply disturbances

The equilibria for positive supply disturbances are reported in tables 13.3–13.5 like the demand shocks these are assumed to have a magnitude of ten units. Turning first to the case of a domestic supply disturbance, it is clear that in all equilibria the adjustment is borne overwhelmingly by the domestic economy, with only modest effects being transmitted abroad.

To see why this is so, it is useful to begin with the benchmark case of a flexible exchange rate. The positive domestic supply shock leads to an increase in domestic output. The effect abroad can be either positive or negative, depending upon whether the positive direct spillover effect dominates the negative relative price effect. If the former dominates, foreign output rises, forcing up the foreign interest rate and causing the foreign currency to appreciate. If the latter dominates, foreign output

TABLE 13.3 *Domestic supply disturbance ($v = 10$)*

	M	M^*	Y	Y^*	E	C	C^*	Ω	Ω^*
(a) $d_3 = 0.1$									
Cournot	−4.793	1.112	2.215	0.465	−2.937	−4.539	−0.952	8.829	0.388
Stackelberg	−5.144	1.052	2.095	0.439	−3.185	−4.700	−0.900	8.812	0.347
CCV	−5.133	0.990	2.097	0.418	−3.122	−4.680	−0.934	8.774	0.349
Cooperative	−5.819	−0.971	1.838	−0.259	−2.034	−4.564	−1.751	7.741	0.817
Flexible	0	0	3.833	0.149	2.105	−1.888	−2.625	11.91	1.739
Fixed	−1.233	1.233	3.430	0.553	0	−2.791	−1.722	10.77	0.971
(b) $d_3 = 1$									
Cournot	−6.372	0.661	1.865	0.096	−5.254	−5.734	−0.296	10.83	0.0288
Stackelberg	−6.481	0.646	1.823	0.094	−5.304	−5.773	−0.289	10.82	0.0275
CCV	−6.480	0.641	1.823	0.091	−5.301	−5.773	−0.291	10.82	0.0275
Cooperative	−6.628	0.162	1.792	−0.214	−4.952	−5.738	−0.577	10.64	0.118
Flexible	0	0	4.350	−0.367	−1.509	−3.257	−1.257	16.84	0.496
Fixed	1.417	−1.417	4.944	−0.962	0	−2.564	−1.950	19.97	1.644

TABLE 13.4 *Foreign supply disturbance ($v^* = 10$)*

	M	M^*	Y	Y^*	E	C	C^*	Ω	Ω^*
(a) $d_3 = 0.1$									
Stackelberg	−4.806	1.039	0.439	2.210	2.885	−0.986	−4.528	0.388	8.787
(b) $d_3 = 0.1$									
Stackelberg	0.655	−6.372	0.094	1.864	5.252	−0.298	−5.733	0.0288	10.82

TABLE 13.5 *World supply disturbance* ($v = v^* = 10$)

	M	M^*	Y	Y^*	E	C	C^*	Ω	Ω^*
(a) $d_3 = 0.1$									
Cournot	−3.681	−3.681	2.679	2.679	0	−5.491	−5.491	12.92	12.92
Stackelberg	−4.105	−3.754	2.534	2.649	−0.300	−5.685	−5.428	12.90	12.63
CCV	−4.143	−4.143	2.516	2.516	0	−5.613	−5.613	12.62	12.62
Cooperative	−6.780	−6.789	1.579	1.579	0	−6.316	−6.316	11.84	11.84
Flexible	0	0	3.982	3.982	0	−4.513	−4.513	16.99	16.99
Fixed	0	0	3.982	3.982	0	−4.513	−4.513	16.99	16.99
(b) $d_3 = 1$									
Cournot	−5.711	−5.711	1.961	1.961	0	−6.029	6.029	11.97	11.97
Stackelberg	−5.826	−5.826	1.917	1.958	−0.053	−6.071	−6.023	11.97	11.94
CCV	−5.840	−5.840	1.915	1.915	0	−6.064	−6.064	11.94	11.94
Cooperative	−6.789	−6.789	1.579	1.579	0	−6.316	−6.316	11.84	11.84
Flexible	0	0	3.982	3.982	0	−4.513	−4.513	16.99	16.99
Fixed	0	0	3.982	3.982	0	−4.513	−4.513	16.99	16.99

falls and the foreign currency depreciates. In either case, the effect on foreign output is quantitatively small relative to the domestic effect. At the same time, the expansion in domestic output puts downward pressure on the domestic CPI, which is larger when the dominance of the relative price effect causes the domestic currency to appreciate. Likewise, the foreign CPI falls, and this is larger when the dominance of the direct spillover effect brings about an appreciation of the foreign currency.

Consider now the Cournot equilibrium. The domestic economy contracts its money supply, while the foreign economy expands. This tends to moderate the increase in output in country 1, although exacerbating the fall in the CPI. Given the weight in the objective function, this is a desirable tradeoff. The combination of a domestic monetary contraction coupled with a foreign expansion generates a depreciation of the foreign currency, stimulating output abroad, somewhat but stemming the fall in the foreign CPI substantially. This is also desirable from a welfare viewpoint.

For reasons discussed above, in the CCV equilibrium the domestic monetary contraction is increased while the expansion abroad is decreased relative to Cournot. This increases the appreciation of the domestic currency. Domestic and foreign outputs are less unstable; the fall in the domestic CPI is increased, while the foreign CPI is stabilized. Welfare is improved in both economies. The Stackelberg equilibrium is close to the CCV, with both the leader and follower being better off than under Cournot.

The cooperative equilibrium calls for less variation in output accompanied by greater variation in CPI. This can be achieved by the domestic economy's increasing its monetary contraction and the foreign economy's reducing its rate of expansion or even contracting its money supply modestly. Such an equilibrium is certainly welfare improving for the domestic economy, although the foreign economy is made worse off. Without compensation, the latter has an incentive to cheat. However, the gains to country 1 are sufficient to enable it to compensate the foreign country and still make both better off.

Finally, the fixed rate, achieved by an equivalent contraction in 1 and expansion in 2 significantly destabilizes output in both economies. Welfare costs are increased relative to all four strategic equilibria. Whether the fixed rate is worse than the flexible depends in part upon d_3.

In the situation where the supply shock occurs in the foreign economy, for all but the Stackelberg equilibrium the responses are symmetric to those arising from supply disturbances in the domestic economy and are not reported. The Stackelberg equilibrium in which the supply shock occurs in the follower economy is given in table 13.4. The appropriate policies are approximately the same as if the shock occurs in the domestic economy; the money supply in the domestic economy should be contracted, while the money supply abroad (the country experiencing the shock) should be expanded. Most of the welfare costs are then forced onto the foreign economy.

Finally, table 13.5 illustrates the case of a worldwide supply disturbance which impinges equally on the two economies. Except in the Stackelberg equilibrium, the symmetry of the shock leaves the exchange rate unchanged, so that the fixed and flexible regimes are identical. All strategic equilibria call for monetary contraction. The three noncooperative equilibria lead to insufficient monetary contraction, with too much variation in output and too little in the CPI. In the cooperative equilibrium, the increase in monetary contraction shifts the adjustment from output to inflation, resulting in welfare improvements to both economies.

9 SENSITIVITY ANALYSIS

Table 13.6 summarizes the welfare rankings of the alternative equilibria for the base parameter set. With one exception, the rankings of the four strategic equilibria, Cournot (N), Stackelberg (S), CCV and cooperative (C) hold across all parameter sets, although in some cases the differences are quantitatively negligible. The exception is the case $d_2 = 0.01$, when for domestic demand disturbances the Stackelberg leadership dominates the cooperative equilibrium. The relative rankings of the fixed and flexible regimes are more parameter sensitive. For example, for extremely large values of d_2, the fixed regime becomes the worst equilibrium for a country facing foreign demand disturbances, rather than the preferred equilibrium, as in the base case. Also, while the flexible rate generally does not perform particularly well, it is the

TABLE 13.6 *Welfare rankings of alternative equilibria (base parameter set)*

Domestic demand disturbances
Domestic economy: C > S > N > CCV > F > P
Foreign economy: P > C > N > CCV > S > F
Domestic supply disturbances
Domestic economy: C > CCV > S > N > P > F
Foreign economy: S > CCV > N C > P > F
Worldwide supply disturbance
Both economies: C > CCV > S > N > P = F

> denotes "is superior to."
C, cooperative; S, Stackelberg; N, Cournot; CCV, consistent conjectural variations; F, flexible rate; P, fixed rate.

TABLE 13.7 *Qualitative effects on welfare costs of parameter changes*

Increase in Disturbance		Ω^{N}	Ω^{S}	Ω^{CCV}	Ω^{C}	Ω^{F}	Ω^{P}	Ω^{*N}	Ω^{*S}	Ω^{*CCV}	Ω^{*C}	Ω^{*F}	Ω^{*P}
d_1	$u > 0$	−	−	−	−	−	−	−	−	−	−	−	−
	$v > 0$	−	−	−	−	−	−	+	+	+	+	+	+
	$v = v^* > 0$	+	+	+	+	+	+	+	+	+	+	+	+
d_2	$u > 0$	−	−	−	−	−	−	−	−	−	−	−	−
	$v > 0$	+	+	+	+	+	+	−	−	−	−	−	−
	$v = v^* > 0$	−	−	−	−	+	+	−	−	−	−	+	+
d_3	$u > 0$	−	−	−	−	−	−	−	−	−	−	−	−
	$v > 0$	−	−	−	−	−	−	+	+	+	+	+	+
	$v = v^* > 0$	−	−	−	0	+	+	−	−	−	0	+	+
α_1	$u > 0$	−	−	0	0	−	−	−	+	0	0	+	−
	$v > 0$	+	+	0	0	−	−	+	−	0	0	−	−
	$v = v^* > 0$	+	+	0	0	−	−	+	0	0	0	−	−
α_2	$u > 0$	+	+	0	0	+	+	+	−	0	0	−	+
	$v > 0$	−	−	0	0	−	−	−	+	0	0	−	−
	$v = v^* > 0$	−	−	0	0	−	−	−	−	0	0	−	−
δ	$u > 0$	−	−	−	−	−	+	−	−	−	−	−	−
	$v > 0$	+	+	+	+	+	+	−	−	−	−	−	−
	$v = v^* > 0$	−	−	−	0	0	0	−	−	−	0	0	0
γ	$u > 0$	+	+	+	+	+	+	+	+	+	+	−	−
	$v > 0$	−	−	−	−	−	−	−	−	−	−	−	−
	$v = v^* > 0$	−	−	−	−	−	−	−	−	−	−	−	−
a	$u > 0$	.	.	.	.	+	+	.	.	.	.	−	+
	$v > 0$	.	.	.	.	+	+	.	.	.	.	−	−
	$v = v^* > 0$	.	.	.	.	−	−	.	.	.	.	−	−

Ω^{X} and Ω^{*X} denote welfare costs at home and abroad under regime X(X ≡ N, S, CCV, C, F, P).

preferred equilibrium for an economy confronting its own supply shocks, provided that the objective is weighted primarily towards price stability.

In table 13.7 we have summarized the qualitative effects of changes in the parameter across the sample sets on the welfare costs in the two economies. These effects are straightforward and space limitations preclude any detailed discussion. However, the following general observations can be made.

1 In almost all cases, the four strategic equilibria N, S, CCV, and C in each economy all respond similarly to a given parameter change. Exceptions arise with respect to changes in the money demand parameters α_1 and α_2. Welfare in the CCV and S equilibria are independent of these parameters. However, in the case of domestic demand or supply shocks, increases in these parameters have qualitatively opposite effects on the Cournot and Stackelberg equilibria in the foreign economy.
2 The qualitative effects of parameter changes are typically dependent upon the sources of the disturbances. Consider, for example, an increase in the degree of interdependence, as measured by an increase in d_1. In the case of a domestic demand shock, an increase in d_1 reduces the welfare costs in both countries. In the case of a domestic supply shock, an increase in d_1 improves domestic welfare but lowers welfare abroad. In the case of a worldwide supply disturbance, both economies are worse off with increased interdependence.
3 With just two exceptions, increases in the parameter values have qualitatively the same welfare effects for the four strategic equilibria in the two economies, in the face of domestic demand shocks.[17] In the case of domestic supply shocks, in contrast, the welfare effects on the two economies are generally opposite. However, this is not so in the case of changes in γ; an increase in the slope of the supply curve is always welfare improving for both economies.
4 There are no entries for the qualitative effects of changes in the relative weight a in the objective function on the strategic equilibria, N, S, CCV, and C. This is because the corresponding welfare cost functions are all nonlinear functions of a, and are zero at the end-points $a = 0$ and $a = 1$ when each policy-maker has only one objective, in which case the strategic policy problem degenerates.

10 CONCLUSIONS

Several general conclusions can be drawn from the analysis.

1 Demand shocks are much less problematical than supply disturbances, from the viewpoint of macrostabilization. In all cases, a country-

specific demand disturbance of a given magnitude gives rise to less aggregate welfare costs (as measured by the sum $\Omega + \Omega^*$) than does a supply disturbance of equal magnitude. Moreover, worldwide demand shocks pose no problem whatsoever. Their effects can be eliminated entirely, provided that each country simply adjusts its respective money supply so as to ensure that the interest rate in its economy rises sufficiently so as to neutralize the effects of the shocks on aggregate demand exactly. Worldwide supply shocks, however, are mutually compounding and their effects can never be eliminated.[18]

2 The superiority of the (Pareto optimal) cooperative equilibrium over the various noncooperative equilibria (as measured by the aggregate welfare costs $\Omega + \Omega^*$) is small. Indeed, if the relative price elasticity of demand exceeds unity, say, it is almost negligible. However, even for smaller values of this parameter it is never large. The reason for this is the old Mundell negative transmission mechanism which operates under flexible exchange rates and perfect capital mobility. Under these conditions, the effects of monetary policies on output and CPI abroad, as measured by ϕ_2 and η_2, are dominated by their domestic effects ϕ_1 and η_1, so that the interactions between the policy-makers are small.

3 The strategic equilibria all show substantial margins of superiority over the traditional equilibria of fixed or flexible exchange rates. While fixed rates may be superior for one country in specific situations (such as when it faces foreign demand shocks), this is at the substantial cost of the other country, so that aggregate welfare is low.

4 One result of interest is the fact that, despite its use of superior knowledge, the CCV equilibrium may be dominated by the Cournot equilibrium from a welfare viewpoint. In the present analysis, this occurs with domestic demand shocks. The tendency for more contraction by the domestic economy and less abroad leads to too much variation in the CPI and too little adjustment in output relative to the Cournot equilibrium.

In conclusion, we should note some of the limitations of the analysis and some directions for future work. First, the analysis is based on two identical economies and it would clearly be of interest to relax this assumption. More importantly, the model is purely static, with the disturbances being transitory white noise. Finally, it is clearly desirable to extend this type of analysis to a dynamic framework. To analyse intertemporal strategic behavior involves dynamic game theory. Some initial work along these lines has been undertaken using somewhat different models by Miller and Salmon (1985), Oudiz and Sachs (1985), and Currie and Levine (1985). In particular, an interesting issue is whether or not the small gains from cooperation obtained in this static analysis become larger over time.

APPENDIX SOLUTIONS FOR OUTPUT AND THE CONSUMER PRICE INDEX

Given the symmetry of the underlying economies, the solutions for output and the CPI for the domestic and foreign economies in the Cournot, CCV, and cooperative equilibria are symmetric; the domestic and foreign shocks are simply reversed. Thus only the solutions for the domestic economy need be reported.

Cournot equilibrium:

$$Y = \frac{\gamma(1-a)\eta_1(1-\delta)}{(\Psi_{11}-\Psi_{12})D'}(u-u^*) + \frac{(1-a)^2\eta_1^2\Theta}{(\Psi_{11}^2-\Psi_{12}^2)\gamma}(v+v^*) + \frac{(1-a)\eta_1(\phi_1-\phi_2)}{(\Psi_{11}-\Psi_{12})\gamma}v \tag{13A.1a}$$

$$C = \frac{-\gamma a\phi_1(1-\delta)}{(\Psi_{11}-\Psi_{12})D'}(u-u^*) - \frac{a(1-a)\phi_1\eta_1\Theta}{(\Psi_{11}^2-\Psi_{12}^2)\gamma}(v+v^*) - \frac{a\phi_1(\phi_1-\phi_2)}{(\Psi_{11}-\Psi_{12})\gamma}v \tag{13A.1b}$$

where

$$\Theta \equiv \phi_2\eta_1 - \phi_1\eta_2 = \frac{\gamma^2(1-\delta)(1+d_1)d_2}{DD'} > 0$$

Consistent conjectural variations equilibrium:

$$Y = \frac{\gamma(1-a)(\eta_1+x\eta_2)(1-\delta)}{\{(\Psi_{11}+x\Psi_{12})-(\Psi_{12}+x\Psi_{22})\}D'}(u-u^*) + \frac{(1-a)^2(\eta_1+x\eta_2)^2\Theta}{\{(\Psi_{11}+x\Psi_{12})^2-(\Psi_{12}+x\Psi_{22})^2\}\gamma}(v+v^*) + \frac{(1-a)(\eta_1+x\eta_2)(\phi_1-\phi_2)}{\{(\Psi_{11}+x\Psi_{12})-(\Psi_{12}+x\Psi_{22})\}\gamma}v \tag{13A.2a}$$

$$C = -\frac{\gamma a(\phi_1+x\phi_2)(1-\delta)}{\{(\Psi_{11}+x\Psi_{12})-(\Psi_{12}+x\Psi_{22})\}D'}(u-u^*) - \frac{a(1-a)(\phi_1+x\phi_2)(\eta_1+x\eta_2)\Theta}{\{(\Psi_{11}+x\Psi_{12})^2-(\Psi_{12}+x\Psi_{22})^2\}\gamma}(v+v^*) - \frac{a(\phi_1+x\phi_2)(\phi_1-\phi_2)}{\{(\Psi_{11}+x\Psi_{12})-(\Psi_{12}+x\Psi_{22})\}\gamma}v \tag{13A.2b}$$

where x is a solution of

$$\Psi_{12}x^2 + (\Psi_{11} + \Psi_{22})x + \Psi_{12} = 0$$

Cooperative equilibrium:

$$Y = \frac{\gamma(1-a)(\eta_1 - \eta_2)(1-\delta)}{(\Psi_{11} + \Psi_{22} - 2\Psi_{12})D'}(u - u^*) + \frac{(\Psi_{11} - \Psi_{22})\Delta(1-a)}{\{(\Psi_{11} + \Psi_{22})^2 - 4\Psi_{12}^2\}\gamma}v$$
$$+ \frac{(1-a)\Omega\{(1-a)(\eta_1^2 - \eta_2^2) - a(\phi_1^2 - \phi_2^2)\}}{\{(\Psi_{11} + \Psi_{22})^2 - 4\Psi_{12}^2\}\gamma}v^* \quad (13A.3a)$$

$$C = \frac{-\gamma a(\phi_1 - \phi_2)(1-\delta)}{(\Psi_{11} + \Psi_{22} - 2\Psi_{12})D'}(u - u^*) - \frac{2a\Delta\Theta}{\{(\Psi_{11} + \Psi_{22})^2 - 4\Psi_{12}^2\}\gamma}v^*$$
$$- \frac{a[(\Psi_{11} + \Psi_{22})(\phi_1 - \phi_2)^2 + 2\phi_1\phi_2\{\Psi_{11} + \Psi_{22} - 2\Psi_{12}\}]}{\{(\Psi_{11} + \Psi_{22})^2 - 4\Psi_{12}^2\}\gamma}v, \quad (13A.3b)$$

where

$$\Delta \equiv \phi_1\eta_1 - \phi_2\eta_2 > 0$$

Note that qualitatively, all these solutions are of the form

$$Y = f_1(u - u^*) + f_2 v + f_3 v^* \quad (13A.4a)$$
$$C = e_1(u - u^*) - e_2 v - e_3 v^* \quad (13A.4b)$$

where for Cournot and CCV $f_1 > 0$, $f_2 > f_3 > 0$, $e_1 > 0$, $e_2 > e_3 > 0$, and for cooperative $f_1 > 0$, $f_2 > 0$, $f_2 > f_3$, $f_3 \gtreqless 0$, $e_1 > 0$, $e_2 > e_3 > 0$. If we write the above solutions as

$$Y = Y(u, u^*, v, v^*) \quad (13A.5a)$$
$$C = C(u, u^*, v, v^*) \quad (13A.5b)$$

the corresponding solutions in the foreign economy can be summarized by

$$Y^* = Y(u^*, u, v^*, v) \quad (13A.6a)$$
$$C^* = C(u^*, u, v^*, v) \quad (13A.6b)$$

NOTES

1 See also the analysis included in Bryant (1980) and Jones (1983).

2 A similar framework is employed in a recent paper by Canzoneri and Henderson (1985). However, since the purpose of their paper is primarily expositional, neither their model nor their analysis is as comprehensive as that undertaken here.

3 See Bresnahan (1981) and Perry (1982) for applications of the consistent conjectural variations equilibrium to oligopoly theory. A recent paper by Brandsma and Hughes Hallett (1984) considers conjectural variations (which are not necessarily consistent) in a dynamic policy game framework. Although some game theorists view the CCV equilibrium with some skepticism (see Friedman, 1983, ch. 5), it appears to be gaining their acceptance and interest (see Basar, 1986).

4 The use of numerical simulations as a method of analysing small macromodels has been employed by a number of authors recently (see for example Oudiz and Sachs (1984), Taylor (1985), and Carlozzi and Taylor (1985)) for policy simulations in two-country macromodels.

5 The assumption of perfectly symmetric economies being made in this chapter is made virtually uniformly throughout the two-country policy coordination literature. One empirical investigation of coordination which allows for asymmetric economies has been undertaken by Hughes Hallett (1984).

6 We maintain the usual assumption that residents of each country do not hold the currency of the other country.

7 For example, if a shift term w, say, is added to the demand for money, our analysis remains unchanged by redefining $M' = M - w$.

8 In fact we have carried out such simulations and the results are little changed.

9 This characteristic of relatively weak impact of domestic monetary policy on foreign activity (and vice versa) arises, and for precisely the same reason, in the paper by Carlozzi and Taylor (1985).

10 Since the model is static, henceforth we will delete the time subscript t.

11 To show this, first set $\mathcal{E}_t(P_{t+1}) = 0$ in (13.1) and $\mathcal{E}_{t-1}(P_t) = 0$ in (13.4), in accordance with (13.6′). Next substitute (13.4) into (13.1) to yield

$$\left(1 + \frac{d_2}{\gamma}\right) Y = d_1 Y^* - d_2 I + d_3(P^* + E - P) + u + \frac{d_2 v}{\gamma}$$

Clearly, the effects of u and v on aggregate demand are neutralized if the interest rate I is adjusted by

$$I = \frac{u}{d_2} + \frac{v}{\gamma}$$

Now substituting (13.4) into (13.2) gives

$$M = \left(\alpha_1 + \frac{1}{\gamma}\right) Y - \alpha_2 I - \frac{v}{\gamma}$$

The implied adjustment in the money stock, which holds demand and output constant, is therefore

$$M = -\frac{\alpha_2}{d_2} u - \frac{1 + \alpha_2}{\gamma} v$$

which is the first component of (13.12a).

12 First, $\Psi_{11} - \Psi_{12} = a\phi_1(\phi_1 - \phi_2) + (1 - a)\eta_1(\eta_1 - \eta_2) > 0$. Secondly,

$$\Psi_{13} - \frac{\alpha_2}{d_2}\Psi_{11} = a\phi_1\left(\phi_3 - \frac{\alpha_2}{d_2}\phi_1\right) + (1 - a)\eta_1\left(\eta_3 - \frac{\alpha_2}{d_2}\eta_1\right)$$

Substituting for ϕ_i and η_i into this expression we can show $\Psi_{13} - (\alpha_2/d_2)\Psi_{11} < 0$.

13 The symmetry of the optimal policies is a consequence of not only the symmetry of the underlying model, but also the fact that each country is weighted equally in the joint cost function. The case of equal weights is just a special case of the more general Pareto criterion, the minimization of $\beta\Omega + (1 - \beta)\Omega^*$, $0 < \beta < 1$.

14 Our flexible exchange rate regime can also be described as being one of setting monetary targets.

15 We have also considered another natural means of pegging the exchange rate

$$M = -\frac{1}{\beta_1}(\beta_2 u + \beta_3 v)$$

$$M^* = -\frac{1}{\beta_1}(\beta_2 u^* + \beta_3 v^*)$$

This requires each country to accommodate only to its own disturbances. This rule turns out to be inferior to (13.22).

16 Miller and Salmon (1985) assume $d_3 = 1$, while Oudiz and Sachs (1984) take it to be somewhat larger, around 1.5. As noted, Carlozzi and Taylor (1985) run into similar problems regarding small linkage effects and take $d_3 = 0.1$. Currie and Levine (1985) take a slightly larger value of 0.3.

17 The exceptions are the effects of changes in the monetary parameters α_1 and α_2 in the Stackelberg equilibrium.

18 The difficulty of stabilizing for supply shocks is also emphasized by Taylor (1984).

REFERENCES

Basar, T. (1986) A tutorial on dynamic and differential games. In *Dynamic Games and Applications in Economics* (ed. T. Basar). Berlin: Springer-Verlag.

Bhandari, J. S. (ed.) (1985) *Exchange Rate Management under Uncertainty*. Cambridge, MA: MIT Press.

Brandsma, J. A. and Hughes Hallett, A. J. (1984) Economic conflict and the solution of dynamic games. *European Economic Review,* 26, 13–32.

Bresnahan, T. F. (1981) Duopoly models with consistent conjectures. *American Economic Review,* 71, 934–45.

Bryant, R. (1980) *Money and Monetary Policy in Interdependent Nations*. Washington, DC: Brookings Institution.

Canzoneri, M. and Henderson, D. (1985) Strategic aspects of macroeconomic policymaking in interdependent economies: the fundamentals. Presented at USJF-SSRC Conference, Tokyo, March.

—— and Gray, J. A. (1985) Monetary policy games and the consequences of noncooperative behavior. *International Economic Review*, 26, 547–64.

Carlozzi, N. and Taylor, J. B. (1985) International capital mobility and the coordination of monetary rules. In *Exchange Rate Management under Uncertainty* (ed. J. S. Bhandari). Cambridge, MA: MIT Press.

Currie, D. and Levine, P. (1985) Macroeconomic policy design in an interdependent world. In *International Economic Policy Coordination*. (eds W. H. Buiter and R. C. Marston) Cambridge: Cambridge University Press.

Friedman, J. (1983) *Oligopoly Theory*. Cambridge: Cambridge University Press.

Hamada, K. (1976) A strategic analysis of monetary interdependence. *Journal of Political Economy,* 84, 677–700.

Hughes Hallett, A. J. (1984) Competitive or cooperative policies for interdependent economies? The case for coordinating US and EEC policies. Erasmus University.

Jones, M. (1983) International liquidity: a welfare analysis. *Quarterly Journal of Economics,* 98, 1–23.

Miller, M. H. and Salmon, M. (1985) Policy coordination and dynamic games. In *International Economic Policy Coordination* (eds W. H. Buiter and R. C. Marston) Cambridge: Cambridge University Press.

Mundell, R. A. (1963) Capital mobility and stabilization policy under fixed and flexible exchange rates. *Canadian Journal of Economics and Political Science,* 29, 475–87.

Oudiz, G. and Sachs, J. (1984) Macroeconomic policy coordination among the industrial economies. *Brookings Papers on Economic Activity,* 1, 1–64.

—— and —— (1985) International policy coordination in dynamic macroeconomic models. In *International Economic Policy Coordination* (eds W. H. Buiter and R. C. Marston). Cambridge: Cambridge University Press.

Perry, M. K. (1982) Oligopoly and consistent conjectural variations. *Bell Journal of Economics,* 13, 197–205.

Taylor, J. B. (1985) International coordination in the design of macroeconomic policy rules. *European Economic Review,* 28, 53–81.

14 Dynamic Strategic Monetary Policies and Coordination in Interdependent Economies

(WITH T. BASAR AND V. D'OREY)

1 INTRODUCTION

With the increasing interdependence between national economies, there has been a growing interest in problems of strategic policy-making and international policy coordination. Research into these issues began with the seminal work of Hamada (1976) who analysed issues of monetary policy under Cournot and Stackelberg behavior. His approach was a static one and was based on a fixed exchange rate. His contribution has recently been extended by various authors including Jones (1983), Canzoneri and Gray (1985), and Turnovsky and d'Orey (1986).

In this chapter we consider the problem of strategic monetary policy-making within a dynamic framework. The basic model we employ is a two-country version of the standard Dornbusch (1976) model in which the policy-makers in the two economies seek to optimize their respective objective functions, which are taken to be intertemporal quadratic cost functions defined in terms of deviations in output from its natural rate level, on the one hand, and the rate of inflation of the domestic consumer price index (CPI) on the other.

The consideration of these issues within a dynamic context is obviously important. Strategic policies, which are optimal from a short-run viewpoint, may however, generate intertemporal tradeoffs which over

Originally published in *American Economic Review*, 78, 1988, 341–61. Previous versions of this chapter were presented at the SEDC Conference held at Imperial College, London, June 1985, the Summer Workshop held at the University of Warwick, Coventry, 1985, and the ASSA meetings in New York, December 1985. The comments of a referee are gratefully acknowledged. This research was supported in part by grant SES-8409886 from the National Science Foundation.

time prove to be adverse. In fact, our results below will suggest this to be the case. Furthermore, the extension to a dynamic framework emphasizes new issues such as the information structure and the corresponding equilibrium concepts. The equilibria we consider are all feedback solutions in which the policies at each stage make use of current information on key economic variables such as price and exchange rates, which under our assumptions are observable at that time. Using such information we analyse and compare two noncooperative equilibria which we consider to be of interest: (a) feedback Nash, and (b) feedback Stackelberg[1].

A basic question throughout the recent policy discussion concerns the gains from policy coordination. We address this issue by deriving the Pareto optimal cooperative equilibrium where the two policy-makers agree to minimize their aggregate joint welfare costs. This equilibrium is then compared with the two noncooperative equilibria.

Any strategic policy problem must be generated by some disturbance to an initial equilibrium situation, thereby creating a conflict for the two policy-makers. In the present analysis, this is taken to be an initial misalignment in the real exchange rate. In general, this may be the result of a variety of underlying causes. Here, it most naturally reflects past differences in monetary policy, resulting in differential price movements in the two economies and leading to the inherited exchange rate misalignment. The policy problem is therefore to return to equilibrium with a minimum of welfare losses.[2]

The analysis is based on two symmetric economies. This has the advantage of simplifying the feedback rules, with the real money supply in each economy being adjusted to the real exchange rate. Our procedure is to derive analytical expressions for the optimal policies. We then use these analytical expressions to compute values for the policy rules and the welfare gains, using numerical estimates of the parameters of the model.

This is not the first study to apply dynamic game theory to problems of international macroeconomic policy-making. Indeed, the area has recently begun to receive increased attention and recent work by Hughes Hallett (1984), Currie and Levine, (1985), Miller and Salmon (1985), Oudiz and Sachs (1985), and Taylor (1984) should be noted in particular. These contributions can be generally characterized as being variants of the standard Keynesian IS–LM Phillips curve framework, and for reasons of analytical complexity employ numerical simulation methods. While the characterization is also true of the present study, it differs in many key respects.[3] One of these is in the types of strategic equilibria considered. As noted, we focus on feedback solutions, which are determined using dynamic programming methods and are known to be time consistent. By contrast, authors such as Miller and Salmon, Oudiz and Sachs, and Hughes Hallett emphasize the contrast between time-consistent and time-inconsistent solutions.

Much of the literature focuses on the gains from cooperation. In this regard, Miller and Salmon present an example in which cooperation may actually lead to welfare losses, a finding also obtained previously by Rogoff (1985), although for substantially different reasons. By contrast, this study, like those of Oudiz and Sachs (1985) and Taylor (1985), finds cooperation to yield welfare gains. These are found to be of the order of around 6–10 percent, which are similar in magnitude to those obtained by Taylor, but larger than those suggested by Oudiz and Sachs. Also, in contrast with these latter authors, who find the cooperative solution to be more inflationary than the noncooperative, we find just the reverse in fact to be the case. This result would appear to be generally consistent with Taylor whose multicountry analysis does not yield a uniform pattern in this respect. Finally, our approach differs from the previous literature in two further aspects. First, to avoid the danger of excessive reliance on specific parameter values, a much more detailed sensitivity analysis is conducted, the result of which is to suggest that our findings are in fact quite robust across parameter sets. Second, unlike previous authors, our analysis stresses the contrast between the results obtained in the present dynamic analysis with those obtained previously for the more familliar short-run (one-period) model. The differences are shown to be quite striking, highlighting the intertemporal as well as the intratemporal tradeoffs involved.

2 THE THEORETICAL FRAMEWORK

The analysis in this chapter is based on the following two-country macroeconomic model, which is a direct extension of the Dornbusch (1976) framework. It describes two identical countries, each specializing in the production of a distinct good and trading single common bond. It assumes perfect foresight and is expressed, using discrete time, by the following set of equations:

$$Y_t = d_1 Y_t^* - d_2\{I_t - (P_{t+1} - P_t)\} + d_3\,(P_t^* + E_t - P_t) \quad (14.1)$$

$$0 < d_1 < 1,\ d_2 > 0,\ d_3 > 0$$

$$Y_t^* = d_1 Y_t - d_2\{I_t^* - (P_{t+1}^* - P_t^*)\} - d_3(P_t^* + E_t - P_t) \quad (14.1')$$

$$M_t - P_t = e_1 Y_t - e_2 I_t \qquad e_1 > 0,\ e_2 > 0 \quad (14.2)$$

$$M_t^* - P_t^* = e_1 Y_t^* - e_2 I_t^* \quad (14.2')$$

$$I_t = I_t^* + E_{t+1} - E_t \quad (14.3)$$

$$C_t = \delta P_t + (1 - \delta)(P_t^* + E_t) \qquad 1 > \delta > \tfrac{1}{2} \quad (14.4)$$

$$C_t^* = \delta P_t^* + (1 - \delta)(P_t^* - E_t) \quad (14.4')$$

$$P_{t+1} - P_t = \gamma Y_t \qquad \gamma > 0 \tag{14.5}$$

$$P^*_{t+1} - P^*_t = \gamma Y^*_t \tag{14.5'}$$

where Y is the real output, expressed in logarithms, measured as a deviation about its natural rate level, P is the price of domestic output, expressed in logarithms, C is the consumer price index, expressed in logarithms, E is the exchange rate (measured in terms of units of foreign currency per unit of domestic currency), expressed in logarithms, I is the nominal interest rate, expressed in natural units, and M is the nominal money supply, expressed in logarithms. Domestic variables are unstarred; foreign variables are denoted with asterisks. We will also refer to these as country 1 and country 2 respectively.

Equations (14.1) and (14.1′) describe equilibrium in the two-goods markets. Output depends upon the real interest rate, output in the other country, and the relative price. The corresponding effects across the two economies are identical, with relative price influencing demand in exactly offestting ways. The money market equilibrium conditions in the two economies are standard and are described by (14.2) and (14.2′), respectively.[4] The perfect substitutability between domestic and foreign bonds is described by the interest rate parity condition (14.3). Equations (14.4) and (14.4′) described the consumer price index (CPI) in the two economies. They embody the assumption that the proportion of consumption δ spent on the respective home good is the same in the two economies.[5] Note that the real interest rate in (14.1) and (14.1′) and the real money supplies in (14.2) and (14.2′) are deflated by the output price of their respective economies. Little would be changed except for additional details, if the deflators were in terms of their respective CPIs. Equations (14.5) and (14.5′) define the price adjustment in the two economies in terms of Phillips curve relationships, with prices responding with a one-period lag to demand. However, the assumption of perfect foresight is embodied in future price level and future exchange rate appearing in the real interest rate parity in (14.1) and (14.9′), and in interest rate relationship (14.3).

Equations (14.1) and (14.5) describe the structure of the two economies. The policy-makers in these economies are assumed to have intertemporal objective functions

$$\sum_{t=1}^{T}\{aY_t^2 + (1-a)(C_{t+1} - C_t)^2\}\rho^{t-1} \qquad 0 < a < 1,\ 0 < \rho < 1 \tag{14.6}$$

$$\sum_{t=1}^{T}\{aY_t^{*2} + (1-a)(C^*_{t+1} - C^*_t)^2\}\rho^{t-1} \tag{14.6'}$$

which they seek to optimize, i.e. each policy-maker chooses to minimize an intertemporal cost function. The cost incurred at each point of time is quadratic, defined in terms of deviations in output from its equilibrium, natural rate, level, and the rate of inflation of the domestic cost of living. The relative weights attached to these components of the objective functions are a and $1 - a$ respectively. The total cost to be minimized is a discounted sum of the costs incurred at each period, with ρ denoting the discount rate. Equations (14.1)–(14.5) can be solved for Y_t, Y_t^*, and $E_{t+1} - E_t$ as follows:

$$Y_t = \phi_1 m_t + \phi_2 m_t^* + \phi_3 s_t \tag{14.7a}$$

$$Y_t^* = \phi_2 m_t + \phi_1 m_t^* - \phi_3 s_t \tag{14.7b}$$

$$E_{t+1} - E_t = -\beta_1 m_t + \beta_1 m_t^* + \beta_3 s_t \tag{14.7c}$$

where $s_t \equiv P_t^* + E_t - P_t$ denotes the relative price (real exchange rate) at time t, $m_t \equiv M_t - P_t$, and $m_t^* \equiv M_t^* - P_t^*$ denotes the real stocks of money at home and abroad at time t,

$$\phi_1 \equiv \frac{d_2}{2}\left(\frac{1}{\mathrm{D}} + \frac{1}{\mathrm{D}'}\right)$$

$$\phi_2 \equiv \frac{d_2}{2}\left(\frac{1}{\mathrm{D}} - \frac{1}{\mathrm{D}'}\right)$$

$$\phi_3 = \frac{e_2 d_3}{D'}$$

$$\beta_1 = \frac{1 + d_1 - d_2\gamma}{D'}$$

$$\beta_2 = \frac{2e_1 d_3}{D'}$$

$$D \equiv e_2(1 - d_1 - d_2\gamma) + e_1 d_2$$

$$D' \equiv e_2(1 + d_1 - d_2\gamma) + e_1 d_2$$

We assume that $1 - d_1 - d_2\gamma > 0$, implying that the IS curve of the aggregate world economy is downward sloping. It follows that

$$D' > D > 0$$

and hence

$$\phi_1 > \phi_2 > 0$$

If we take the differences of the cost of living equations (14.4) at two consecutive points in time, and using (14.5), (14.5′), and (14.7a)–(14.7c), the rates of inflation of the CPI become

$$C_{t+1} - C_t = \eta_1 m_t + \eta_2 m_t^* + \eta_3 s_t \tag{14.8a}$$

$$C_{t+1}^* - C_t^* = \eta_2 m_t + \pi_1 m_t^* - \eta_3 s_t \tag{14.8b}$$

where

$$\eta_1 \equiv \gamma\{\delta\phi_1 + (1 - \delta)\,\phi_2\} - \beta_1(1 - \delta)$$

$$\eta_2 \equiv \gamma\{\delta\phi_2 + (1 - \delta)\,\phi_1\} + \beta_1(1 - \delta),$$
$$\eta_3 \equiv \gamma\phi_3(2\delta - 1) + \beta_2(1 - \delta)$$

The optimal policy problem confronting each of the policy-makers is to choose their respective money supplies to minimize their cost functions (14.6) and (14.6′) subject to constraints (14.8a), (14.8b), (14.9a) and (14.9b). Given the assumption that prices move gradually at home and abroad, we assume that both P_t and P_t^* are observed at time t. Thus it is convenient to treat the monetary control variables as being the real quantities m and m^*. Second, we assume that the current nominal exchange rate E_t is observed instantaneously and can therefore be monitored by the monetary authorities.[6] Thus the relative price s_t is observable to both policy-makers at time t, and in fact the optimal monetary policies will be obtained as feedback solutions in terms of s_t. Combining equations (14.5), (14.5′), and (14.7c) we find that s_t follows the path

$$s_{t+1} = cs_t + bm_t - bm_t^* \tag{14.9}$$

where

$$c \equiv 1 + \beta_2 - 2\gamma\phi_3$$
$$b \equiv -\frac{1 + d_1}{D'}$$

In considering equation (14.9), it should be noted that m_t and m_t^* denote *real* money stocks, which, given that the price levels P_t and P_t^* are constrained to move sluggishly, can be treated as policy variables. With forward-looking variables, such as the nominal exchange rate, we normally expect the dynamics of such a system to involve a saddlepoint. This is in fact also the case here, when we make the usual assumption that the *nominal* money supplies remain fixed or follow some exogenous path. In this case, to specify the dynamics we need to combine (14.9) with the price adjustment equations (14.5) and (14.5′) together with (14.7a) and (14.7b). The result of this is the following matrix equation system

$$\begin{bmatrix} s_{t+1} \\ P_{t+1} \\ P_{t+1}^* \end{bmatrix} = \begin{bmatrix} c & -b & b \\ \phi_3 & 1 - \gamma\phi_1 & -\gamma\phi_2 \\ -\phi_3 & -\gamma\phi_2 & 1 - \gamma\phi_1 \end{bmatrix} \begin{bmatrix} s_t \\ P_t \\ P_t^* \end{bmatrix} + \begin{bmatrix} b & -b \\ \gamma\phi_1 & \gamma\phi_2 \\ \gamma\phi_2 & \gamma\phi_1 \end{bmatrix} \begin{bmatrix} M_t \\ M_t^* \end{bmatrix} \tag{14.10}$$

Under plausible conditions, for given M_t and M_t^*, this will have two stable roots and one unstable root, with the real exchange rate jumping (via the nominal rate) to ensure that the system is always following a stable path.[7] However, with endogenous feedback policy, stability can be accomplished through appropriate adjustments in the policy variables. The unstable root can be eliminated from the system, ruling out the need for the exchange rate to undergo endogenous jumps.

In order to see how the strategic problem is generated, suppose that prior to time 1 the two monetary authorities have been allowing their respective nominal money stocks to follow exogenous time paths. From equations (14.10) we see that the real exchange rate s_{t+1} is generated by

$$\begin{aligned} s_{t+1} &= cs_t - b(P_t - P_t^*) + b(M_t - M_t^*) \\ &= cs_t + b\{(M_t - P_t) - (M_t^* - P_t^*)\} \\ &= \{1 - \gamma(\phi_1 - \phi_2) + c\}s_t + [c\{1 - \gamma(\phi_1 - \phi_2)\} \\ &\quad + 2b\phi_3]s_{t-1} + b(\Delta M_t - \Delta M_t^*) \end{aligned}$$

Assume that at some distant time in the past, the world economy was in long-run equilibrium with $s = 0$. It is then evident from this equation (or more precisely from its stable solution) that the misalignment in the real exchage rate, which forms the starting point for the present strategic analysis, reflects differential monetary policies in the two economies over the entire prior period and in particular how these manifest themselves in differential real money stocks. These disturbances can be either transitory, lasting just one period, or they can be sustained differences in monetary growth rates. These will simply result in different values of the real exchange rate at time 1. Even though any stable adjustment path will ensure the ultimate re-attainment of the equilibrium exchange rate, the introduction of strategic behavior at some arbitrary point can be viewed as an attempt to accelerate this adjustment process. In a more general model, a misaligned initial exchange rate could also reflect other factors, such as differential fiscal policies or supply shocks to the two economies.

The dynamic optimization problem faced by the two policy-makers can be summarized as follows:

$$\min J_T = \sum_{t=1}^{T} \{aY_t^2 + (1 - a)(C_{t+1} - C_t)^2\}\rho^{t-1} \tag{14.11}$$

subject to

$$Y_t = \phi_1 m_t + \phi_2 m_t^* + \phi_3 s_t \tag{14.12}$$

$$C_{t+1} - C_t = \eta_1 m_t + \eta_2 m_t^* + \eta_3 s_t \tag{14.13}$$

and

$$\min J_T^* = \sum_{t=1}^{T} \{aY_t^{*2} + (1 - a)(C_{t+1}^* - C_t^*)^2\}\rho^{t-1} \tag{14.11'}$$

subject to

$$Y_t^* = \phi_2 m_t + \phi_1 m_t^* - \phi_3 s_t \tag{14.12'}$$

$$C_{t+1}^* - C_t^* = \eta_2 m_t + \eta_1 m_t^* - \eta_3 s_t \tag{14.13'}$$

where

$$s_{t+1} = cs_t + bm_t - bm_t^* \tag{14.14a}$$

$$m_t = f_t(s_t) \qquad m_t^* = f_t^*(s_t^*) \tag{14.14b}$$

and the minimizations in (14.10) and (14.10′) are performed over the policy rules f_t and f_t^* respectively under different modes of decision-making.

3 DERIVATION OF NONCOOPERATIVE EQUILIBRIA

Equations (14.11)–(14.14) specify a dynamic game, the solution to which will be considered under different behavioral assumptions for the policy-makers in each country. Specifically, we will study the equilibrium solution under the assumption of (a) Cournot–Nash and (b) Stackelberg behavior on the part of the policy-makers.

To begin, we first substitute (14.12) and (14.13) into (14.11) and (14.12′) and (14.13′) into (14.11′) enabling us to express each country's objective function in terms of only the state variable s_t and the control variables m_t and m_t^* of both countries. The resulting expressions are

$$J_T = \sum_{t=1}^{T} (Q_1 s_t^2 + 2Q_2 s_t m_t + 2Q_3 s_t m_t^* + 2Q_4 m_t m_t^* + Q_5 m_t^2 + Q_6 m_t^{*2})\rho^{t-1} \tag{14.15}$$

$$J_T^* = \sum_{e=1}^{T} (Q_1^* s_t^2 + 2Q_3^* s_t m_t + 2Q_2^* s_t m_t^* + 2Q_4^* m_t m_t^* + Q_5^* m_t^{*2} + Q_6^* m_t^2)\rho^{t-1} \tag{14.15'}$$

where

$$Q_1 \equiv a\phi_3^2 + (1-a)\eta_3^2 \equiv Q_1^*$$
$$Q_2 \equiv a\phi_1\phi_3 + (1-a)\eta_1\eta_3 \equiv -Q_2^*$$
$$Q_3 \equiv a\phi_2\phi_3 + (1-a)\eta_2\eta_3 \equiv -Q_3^*$$
$$Q_4 \equiv a\phi_1\phi_2 + (1-a)\eta_1\eta_2 \equiv Q_4^*$$
$$Q_5 \equiv a\phi_1^2 + (1-a)\eta_1^2 \equiv Q_5^*$$
$$Q_6 \equiv a\phi_2^2 + (1-a)\eta_2^2 \equiv Q_6^*$$

Together with the evolution equation for the state variable (14.14a), and the policy rules (14.14b), the expressions for the cost functionals J_T

and J_T^*, as given by (14.15) and (14.15′), provide a convenient framework for the application of the available theory on dynamic games to this two-country model,[8]

3.1 Closed-loop (feedback) Nash equilibrium solution

The first type of equilibrium we will be addressing is the noncooperative Nash equilibrium under the so-called feedback information pattern (for both countries) as dictated by (14.14a).[9] Using the recursive technique given by Basar and Olsder (1983, ch. 6), we can show that the solution of the dynamic game is unique and linear in the current value of the state, yielding the expressions given below in Proposition 14.1. It is also time consistent.[10]

Proposition 14.1. For the T-period dynamic game, the feedback Nash equilibrium solution in unique and is given by

$$m_t = f_{t,T}(s_t) = \alpha_\tau s_t \tag{14.16}$$

$$M_t^* = f_{t,T}^*(s_t) = \alpha_\tau^* s_t \tag{14.16′}$$

$$\tau \equiv T - t,\ t = 1, 2, \ldots, T$$

where

$$\alpha_\tau = \frac{q_{2,\tau}q_{5,\tau}^* - q_{2,\tau}^* q_{4,\tau}}{q_{4,\tau}q_{4,\tau}^* - q_{5,\tau}q_{5,\tau}^*} \tag{14.17}$$

$$\alpha_\tau^* = \frac{q_{2,\tau}^* q_{5,\tau} - q_{2,\tau}q_{4,\tau}^*}{q_{4,\tau}^* q_{4,\tau} - q_{5,\tau}^* q_{5,\tau}} \tag{14.17′}$$

$$\begin{aligned}
q_{1,\tau} &= \rho c^2 \varepsilon_{\tau-1} + Q_1 \\
q_{1,\tau}^* &= \rho c^2 \varepsilon_{\tau-1}^* + Q_1^* \\
q_{2,\tau} &= \rho cb \varepsilon_{\tau-1} + Q_2 \\
q_{2,\tau}^* &= -\rho cb \varepsilon_{\tau-1}^* + Q_2^* \\
q_{3,\tau} &= -\rho cb \varepsilon_{\tau-1} + Q_3 \\
q_{3,\tau}^* &= \rho cb \varepsilon_{\tau-1}^* + Q_3^* \\
q_{4,\tau} &= -\rho b^2 \varepsilon_{\tau-1} + Q_4 \\
q_{4,\tau}^* &= -\rho b^2 \varepsilon_{\tau-1}^* + Q_4^* \\
q_{5,\tau} &= \rho b^2 \varepsilon_{\tau-1} + Q_5 \\
q_{5,\tau}^* &= \rho b^2 \varepsilon_{\tau-1}^* + Q_5^* \\
q_{6,\tau} &= \rho b^2 \varepsilon_{\tau-1} + Q_6 \\
q_{6,\tau}^* &= \rho b^2 \varepsilon_{\tau-1}^* + Q_6^*
\end{aligned} \tag{14.18}$$

and

$$\varepsilon_\tau = q_{1,\tau} + 2q_{2,\tau}\alpha_\tau + 2q_{3,\tau}\alpha^*_\tau + 2q_{4,\tau}\alpha_\tau\alpha^*_\tau + q_{5,\tau}\alpha^2_\tau + q_{6,\tau}\alpha^{*2}_\tau \qquad (14.19)$$

$$\varepsilon^*_\tau = q^*_{1,\tau} + 2q^*_{2,\tau}\alpha^*_\tau + 2q^*_{3,\tau}\alpha_\tau + 2q^*_{4,\tau}\alpha_\tau\alpha^*_\tau + q^*_{5,\tau}\alpha^{*2}_\tau + q^*_{6,\tau}\alpha^2_\tau \qquad (14.19')$$

$$\tau = 0, 1, 2, \ldots, T-1$$

with the boundary conditions for the q and q^* being

$$q_{i,0} = Q_i,\ q^*_{i,0} = Q^*_i \qquad i = 1, 2, \ldots, 5$$

The corresponding Nash equilibrium values for J_T and J^*_T, denoted by $J_{T,1}$ and $J^*_{T,1}$ respectively are

$$J_{T,1} = \varepsilon_{T-1}s^2_1 \qquad J^*_{T,1} = \varepsilon^*_{t-1}s^2_1 \qquad (14.20)$$

Note that the unique Nash equilibrium optimal policy rules, characterized by the two sequences $\{\alpha_\tau\}$ and $\{\alpha^*_\tau\}$, depends only on the difference τ between the terminal time T and the current time t, which therefore represents the "time to go." Since the problem is time invariant, this implies that letting $T \rightarrow \infty$ is equivalent to letting $\tau \rightarrow \infty$ in the determination of the stationary equilibrium policy rules.

The time paths followed by the two economies are obtained by substituting (14.16) and (14.17) into (14.7)–(14.9). A question which our analysis leaves unresolved concerns the initial real exchange rate s_1. In rational expectations models this is often determined through an initial jump which takes the economy onto a stable manifold, thereby ensuring convergence. With active stabilization, however, convergence can be attained without such jumps as long as the system is controllable. This condition is obviously met for the present model, and indeed our numerical results below confirm stability for all parameter sets yielding nondegenerate optimization problems. Under these circumstances, the motivation for the initial jump is not apparent.[11]

No violation either to stability or to the rationality of expectations is incurred by treating s_1 as being determined by past monetary policies. Furthermore, other than as a scale factor, the determination of s_1 is irrelevant to either the nature of the optimal feedback policy rules, or the time profile of the dynamics, which are our main concern. However, it would be straightforward and lead to little change if we allowed s_1 to be determined by some tradeoff of the future costs contained in (14.20), with some initial adjustment costs.[12]

3.2 Feedback Stackelberg solution

The Nash equilibrium solution considered above is a symmetric equilibrium concept in terms of the roles of the players in the game. Suppose now that one of the two policy-makers (called the leader) has the power to dominate the decision process. Even in a model such as this, where the structures of the two economies are taken to be symmetric, this case is of interest. For example, country 1 can be taken to be the United States, say, and country 2 to be comprised of a large number of small countries, which together make up Europe and collectively are approximately equivalent to the United States in size and structure. Nevertheless, it does not seem unreasonable to assume that the United States, by consisting of a single decision-making unit, is able to be the dominant player. Such an asymmetry in the roles of the players leads to the Stackelberg solution, which admits two different definitions – global and feedback – depending upon whether the dominant player can enforce his policy over the entire duration of the game or only from one period to another. The latter mode of play, which corresponds to the "feedback Stackelberg solution," allows for a recursive derivation and is the equilibrium solution we will adopt.

In the derivation of the feedback Stackelberg solution, we follow the recursive technique presented by Basar and Olsder (1983, ch. 7), which is parallel to the derivation of the Nash solution, the only difference being that now a static Stackelberg game, instead of a Nash game, is solved at every stage. Taking country 1 as the leader and country 2 as the follower, the solution to the T-period dynamic game (which, like the feedback Nash solution, is time consistent) is presented as follows.

Proposition 14.2. For the T-period dynamic game, the feedback Stackelberg solution is unique and is given by

$$m_t = f_{t,T}(s_t) = \alpha_\tau s_t \tag{14.21}$$

$$M_t = f^*_{t,T}(s_t) = \alpha^*_t s_t \tag{14.21'}$$

$$\tau \equiv T - t,\ t = 1, 2, \ldots, T$$

where

$$\alpha_\tau = \frac{q_{2,\tau} - q_{3,\tau}(q^*_{4,\tau}/q^*_{5,\tau}) - q_{4,\tau}(q^*_{2,\tau}/q^*_{5,\tau}) + q_{6,\tau}(q^*_{2,\tau}/q^*_{5,\tau})(q^*_{4,\tau}/q^*_{5,\tau})}{2q_{4,\tau}q^*_{4,\tau}/q^*_{5,\tau} - q_{5,\tau} - q_{6,\tau}(q^*_{4,\tau}/q^*_{5,\tau})^2} \tag{14.22}$$

$$\alpha^*_\tau = -\frac{1}{q^*_{5,\tau}}(q^*_{2,\tau} + q^*_{4,\tau}\alpha_\tau) \tag{14.22'}$$

and $q_{i,\tau}$, $q^*_{i,\tau}$ $i = 1, 2, \ldots, 5$, ε_τ, and ε^*_τ satisfy the same equations as before, i.e. (14.18), (14.19), and (14.19′). The corresponding feedback Stackelberg equilibrium values of $J_{T,1}$ and $J^*_{t,1}$ are

$$J_{T,1} = \varepsilon_{T-1}s_1^2 \qquad J^*_{T,1} = \varepsilon^*_{T-1}s_1^2$$

4 COOPERATIVE EQUILIBRIUM

Suppose now that the two players agree to cooperate by minimizing their joint cost function $\widetilde{J}_T = J_T + J_T^*$. By substitution, this can be written as

$$\min \widetilde{J}_T = \sum_{t=1}^{T} (\widetilde{Q}_1 s_t^2 + 2Q_2 s_t m_t + 2\widetilde{Q}_3 s_t m_t^* + 2\widetilde{Q}_4 m_t m_t^* + \widetilde{Q}_5 m_t^2 + \widetilde{Q}_6 m_t^{*2})\rho^{t-1} \tag{14.23}$$

subject to (14.14a) and (14.14b), where

$$\widetilde{Q}_1 = Q_1 + Q_1^* \qquad \widetilde{Q}_4 = Q_4 + Q_4^*$$
$$\widetilde{Q}_2 = Q_2 + Q_3^* \qquad \widetilde{Q}_5 = Q_5 + Q_6^*$$
$$\widetilde{Q}_3 = Q_3 + Q_2^* \qquad \widetilde{Q}_6 = Q_6 + Q_5^*$$

and Q_i and Q_i^* are as defined previously. This is a standard problem in intertemporal optimization, the solution to which is

$$m_t = \widetilde{\alpha}_\tau s_t \tag{14.24a}$$

$$m_t^* = \widetilde{\alpha}_\tau^* s_t \tag{14.24b}$$

where

$$\widetilde{\alpha}_\tau = \frac{\widetilde{q}_{3,\tau}\widetilde{q}_{4,\tau} - \widetilde{q}_{2,\tau}\widetilde{q}_{6,\tau}}{\widetilde{q}_{5,\tau}\widetilde{q}_{6,\tau} - \widetilde{q}_{4,\tau}^{2}} \tag{14.25a}$$

$$\widetilde{\alpha}_\tau = \frac{\widetilde{q}_{2,\tau}\widetilde{q}_{4,\tau} - \widetilde{q}_{3,\tau}\widetilde{q}_{5,\tau}}{\widetilde{q}_{5,\tau}\widetilde{q}_{6,\tau} - \widetilde{q}_{4,\tau}^{2}} \tag{14.25b}$$

and the $\widetilde{q}_{i,\tau}$ are determined by equations analogous to (14.18) and (14.19). The corresponding cooperative equilibrium value for $\widetilde{J}_{T,1}$ is

$$\widetilde{J}_{T,1} = \widetilde{\varepsilon}_{T-1} s_1^2$$

with the costs being borne equally by two economies.

5 STATIONARY EQUILIBRIA

The solutions discussed in this and the previous section are based on a fintie time horizon. These games are expressed in recursive intensive form, which enables the steady state equilibrium solutions to be derived as the limit of the iterative solutions given above. This procedure is discussed in an expanded version of this chapter. Here we only refer briefly to some of the issues.

The stationary solutions are obtained by considering the limits, as $\tau \to \infty$, of the solutions given in (14.17) and (14.18), in the case of the Nash game, and the analogous equations for the other games. Defining the limits

$$\lim_{\tau \to \infty} \alpha_\tau = \bar{\alpha} \qquad \lim_{\tau \to \infty} \alpha_\tau^* = \bar{\alpha}^*$$

and likewise for $\bar{q}$, $\bar{q}^*$, $\bar{\varepsilon}$, and $\bar{\varepsilon}^*$, we obtain the steady state policy rules

$$m_t = \bar{\alpha} s_t \tag{14.26a}$$

$$m_t^* = \bar{\alpha}^* s_t \tag{14.26b}$$

where $\bar{\alpha}$, and $\bar{\alpha}^*$, are the solutions to the set of equations obtained by letting $\tau \to \infty$ in (14.18) and (14.19). These constitute highly nonlinear coupled algebraic equations in $\bar{q}$ and $\bar{\varepsilon}$, and the recursive procedure we have outlined provides a solution (which is unique) to these coupled equations.

The equilibrium steady state path obtained by substituting (14.26a) and (14.26b) into (14.9) is given by

$$s_{t+1} = \{c + b(\bar{\alpha} - \bar{\alpha}^*)\} s_t \equiv \theta s_t \qquad t = 1, 2, \ldots$$

from which stability follows if and only if

$$|c + b(\bar{\alpha} - \bar{\alpha}^*)| < 1 \tag{14.27}$$

The parameter θ is the steady state rate of convergence and governs the rate of convergence of all variables in the two economies. Our numerical simulations indicate that this condition is satisfied by our equilibrium solution candidates

$$\lim_{T \to \infty} J_{T,1} = \bar{\varepsilon} s_1^2 \qquad \lim_{T \to \infty} J_{T,1}^* = \bar{\varepsilon}^* s_1^2$$

both of which are finite.

6 NUMERICAL PROCEDURES

The parameters describing the optimal policies under the various strategic regimes are themselves complex functions of the underlying parameters of the model. Thus, apart from revealing the general nature of the optimal policies, it is difficult to gain much insight into the general welfare implications of the different regimes. We therefore use plausible numerical parameter values to evaluate the rules and their welfare differences.

Table 14.1 indicates a set of base parameter values. These are chosen on the basis of reasonable empirical evidence. The elasticity of the demand for domestic output with respect to the foreign output is $d_1 = 0.3$, the semi-elasticity of the demand for output with respect to the real interest rate is $d_2 = 0.5$, and the elasticity of the demand for output with respect to the relative price is $d_3 = 1$. The income elasticity of the demand for money is $e_1 = 1$ and the semi-elasticity of money

TABLE 14.1 *Parameter values*

(a) Base set (parameter set 1)
$d_1 = 0.3$, $d_2 = 0.5$, $d_3 = 1$, $e_1 = 1.0$, $e_2 = 0.5$
$\delta = 0.6$, $\gamma = 0.75$, $\alpha = 0.75$, $\rho = 0.9$

(b) Variants (parameter sets 2–28)
d_1: 0, 0.2, 0.4, 0.6, 0.8
d_2: 0.01, 0.25, 1.0, 10
$e_1 = 0, 0.5$
$e_2 = 0.1, 1.0, 10$
$\delta = 0.5, 0.75, 0.99$
$\gamma = 0.5, 0.1$
$\alpha = 1, 0.2, 0.4, 0.6, 1$
$\rho = 0.8, 1, 0$ (static)

Since d_3 appears as a scale variable applied to s, the results are insensitive to changes in d_3 (except for a scale factor). We therefore do not consider changes in d_3, but instead have maintained $d_3 = 1$ throughout.

demand with respect to the nominal interest rate is 0.5. The share of domestic consumption is 0.6 for the two economies; the slopes of their respective Phillips curves are 0.75. The relative weights given to output stabilization in the objective function is $\alpha = 0.75$, while the discount rate $\rho = 0.9$.

While these values seem reasonable, they are uncertain. In table 14.1, part (b), we therefore consider variants of these values, allowing the parameters to range between low values and high values. Note that since d_2 and e_2 are semi-elasticities, the values of $d_2 = 0.5$ and $e_2 = 0.5$ correspond to elasticities of around 0.03 and 0.05 respectively.[13]

To consider all combinations of these parameter values would be impractical. Therefore our approach is to begin with the base set and introduce one parameter change at a time. Performing these changes in d_1, d_2, e_1, e_2, δ, γ, α, and ρ gives a total of 28 parameter sets. Parameter set 1 is the base set; sets 2–28 are obtained by substituting the corresponding values into the base set.

7 ALTERNATIVE EQUILIBRIA: BASE PARAMETER SET

Figures 14.1–14.4 illustrate the time paths for the equilibrium solutions corresponding to the base parameter set, described in table 14.1. These have been drawn for an initial unit positive shock in the relative price s, i.e. for a given initial real depreciation of the currency of country 1. The figures are drawn for a time horizon of $T = 12$ periods. The three equilibrium solutions are discussed in turn.

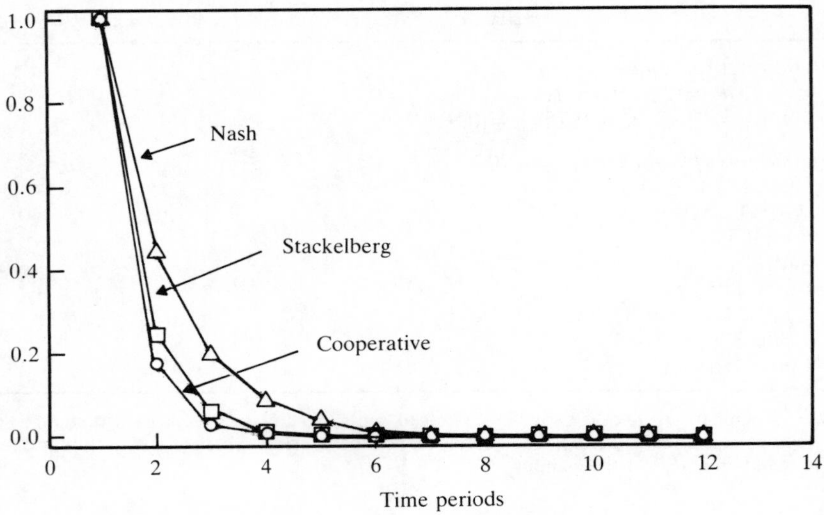

Figure 14.1 Time paths for real exchange rate.

7.1 Feedback Nash

The time paths for s_t, m_t, Y_t, and $\Delta C_{t+1} \equiv C_{t+1} - C_t$ under feedback Nash behavior are illustrated in figures 14.1, 14.2(a), 14.3(a) and 14.4(a). Given the symmetry of the model, the effects on the two economies are identical (in magnitude), so that the time paths for m^*, Y^*, ΔC^* are just mirror images of those of m, Y, and ΔC.

As a benchmark, suppose initially that in response to a unit increase in s, there is no response on the part of the two policy-makers, i.e. $m_t = m_t^* = 0$. In effect, the policy-makers agree to allow the exchange rate to float freely, so that this is a kind of cooperative equilibrium. In the first instance, the positive disturbance in s raises the demand for domestic output and reduces the demand for foreign output. This leads to an increase in domestic output Y, matched by an equivalent decrease in foreign output Y^*. With the real money stocks held constant in both economies, these changes in output will lead to an increase in the domestic interest rate, accompanied by a decrease in the foreign interest rate, the net effect of which is to cause the rate of exchange depreciation of the domestic currency to increase. The increase in domestic output. This, together with the increase in the rate of exchange depreciation, causes the rate of inflation of the overall domestic CPI to increase; the opposite occurs abroad.

Next, suppose that, as in Turnovsky and d'Orey (1986), each policy-maker follows a Nash strategy using a one-period (static) objective

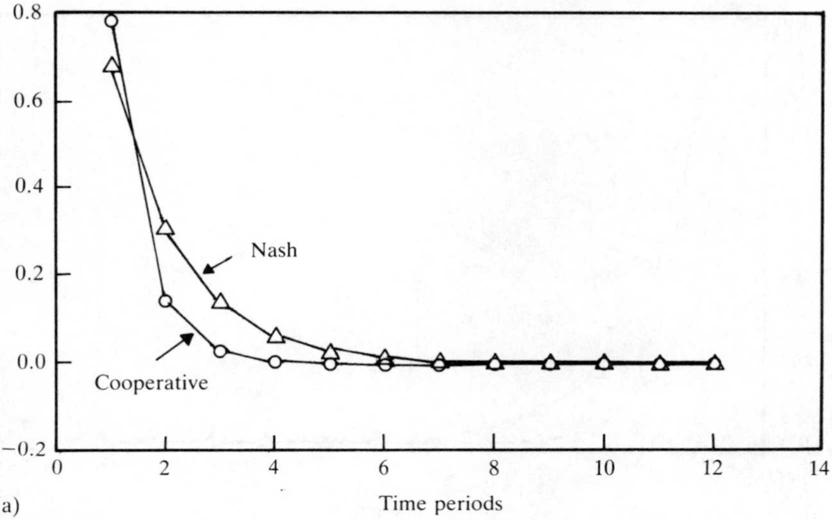

(a)

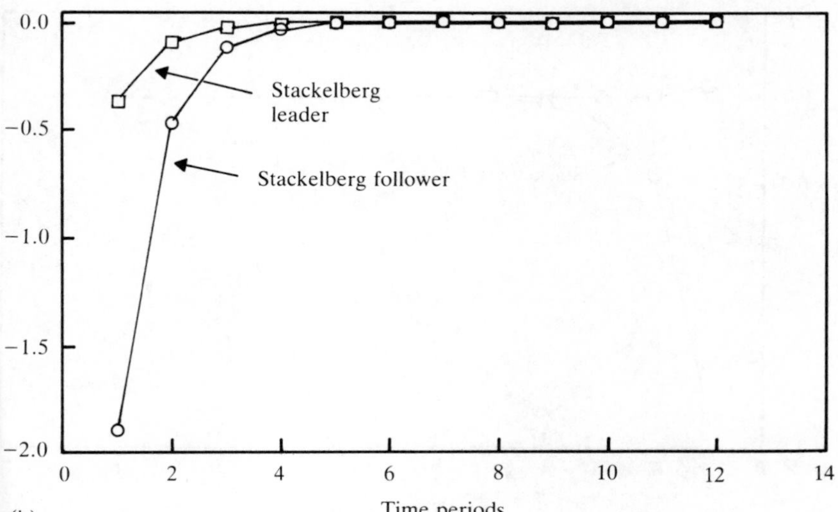

(b)

Figure 14.2 Time paths for real money supply: (a) feedback Nash and cooperative; (b) feedback Stackelberg.

function. In this case, if country 1 responds to the increase in the relative price by reducing its real money stock, this mitigates the expansion in domestic output while at the same time raising the

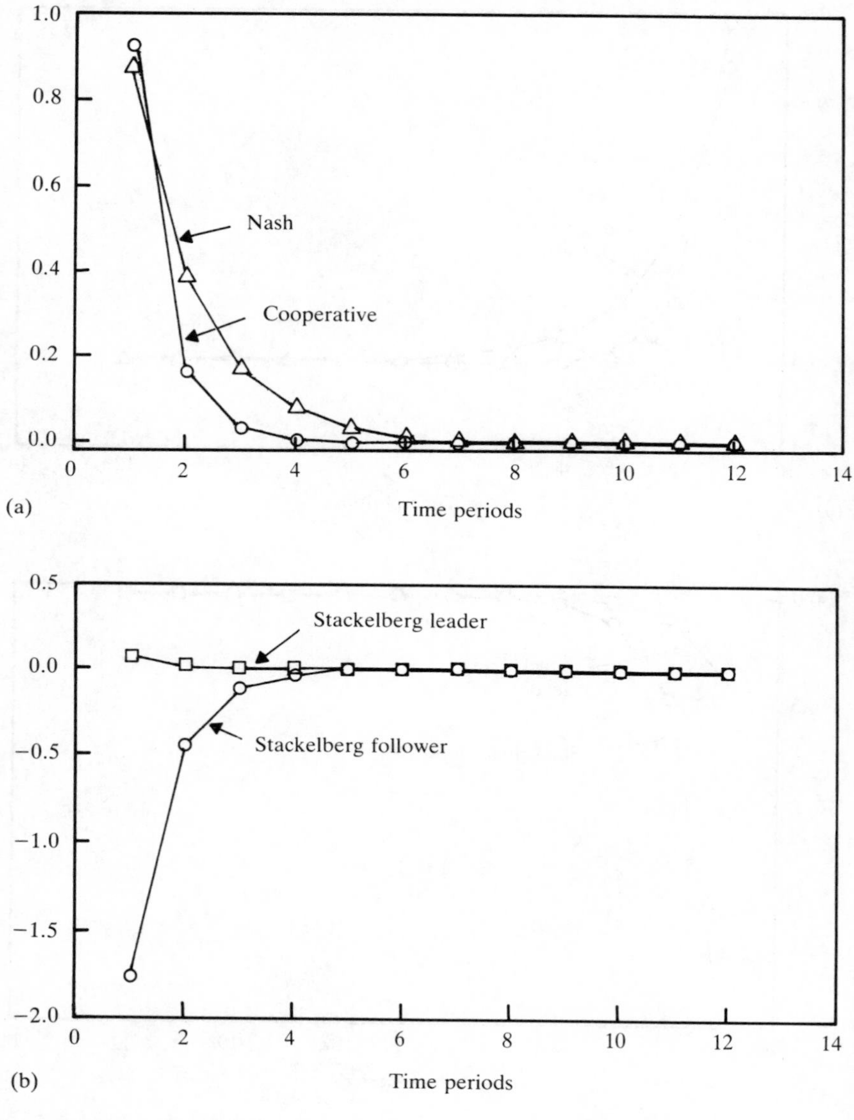

Figure 14.3 Time paths for real output: (a) feedback Nash and cooperative; (b) feedback Stackelberg.

domestic interest rate. The opposite effects occur abroad, causing the rate of exchange depreciation of the domestic economy to increase relative to the benchmark case of a perfectly flexible regime. This in

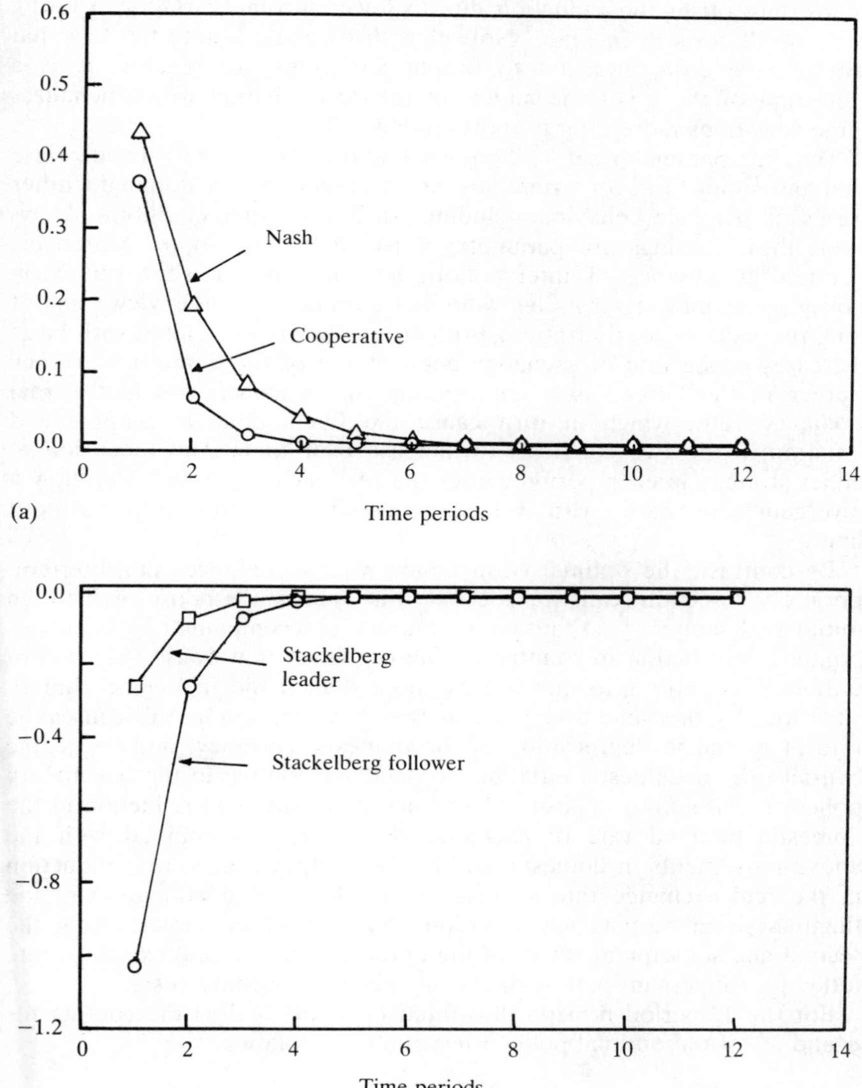

Figure 14.4 Time paths for consumer price index: (a) feedback Nash and cooperative; (b) feedback Stackelberg.

turn leads to larger short-run variations in the rate of inflation. The increases in welfare costs associated with this increased price variation more than offset the reduction due to lower income variation, causing the overall costs to increase. Note that this occurs despite the fact that the relative costs attached to output variations are greater. It is a reflection of the quadratic nature of the cost function which penalizes large variations more than proportionately.

Thus for parameter set 1, Turnovsky and d'Orey (1986) demonstrate that the simple rule of essentially no intervention can dominate other forms of strategic behavior including Nash and other equilibria. However, these findings are parameter sensitive, as they note. Moreover, neither the absence of intervention, nor the optimal short-run Nash policy of leaning against the wind is desirable from the viewpoint of long-run welfare maximization. Both strategies are associated with large increases in the rate of exchange depreciation of the domestic currency (larger in the latter case), contributing to large increases in the real exchange rate, which in turn cause the fluctuations in outputs and inflation in the two countries to increase over time. The repetition of either strategy in each period causes the real exchange rate s to follow a divergent time path, with welfare costs ultimately increasing without limit.

By contrast, the optimal Nash policy, which minimizes the intertemporal cost function, calls for precisely the *opposite* response, namely an initial real monetary expansion in country 1 accompanied by a corresponding contraction in country 2. These policies now cause the level of output in country 1 to increase by more than it did in the benchmark situation. By the same token and by the above reasoning, this causes the rate of exchange depreciation of the domestic currency, and hence the overall rate of domestic inflation, to decrease relative to the benchmark policy. Precisely the opposite effects occur abroad. The reduction in the domestic nominal rate of exchange depreciation, combined with the above movements in domestic and foreign outputs, leads to a reduction in the real exchange rate s. This in turn leads to a mitigation in the fluctuations in outputs and inflation. As a result of implementing the second and subsequent stages of the optimization, the real exchange rate follows a convergent path with steadily declining welfare costs.

For the 12-period horizon illustrated in figure 14.2(a) the coefficients α and α^* of the optimal policy rules evolve as follows:

$$\alpha_\tau = -\alpha_\tau^* = 0.6847 \qquad \tau = 11, \ldots, 4$$

$$\alpha_3 = -\alpha_3^* = 0.6856$$

$$\alpha_2 = -\alpha_2^* = 0.6873$$

$$\alpha_1 = -\alpha_1^* = 0.6439$$

$$\alpha_0 = -\alpha_0^* = -0.9036$$

The interesting point to observe is that in the last period the policy rule changes sign. This reflects the change in optimal behavior in going from a static to an intertemporal objective function. In fact, the static analysis of Turnovsky and d'Orey (1986) is identical with the one-period-to-go solution of the present dynamic analysis. It is also of interest to note that the policy rule converges to its steady state ($\bar{\alpha} = 0.6837$ and $\bar{\alpha}^* = -0.6837$) within just five periods. Finally, the speed of the adjustment of the economy along the optimal trajectory is given by $\theta = 0.446$, implying that around 55 percent of the adjustment is completed within the first period.[14]

The contrast between the optimal short-run and the optimal long-run policies is striking. We will restrict our comments to the domestic economy, although analogous reasoning applies abroad. The basic cause of the difference stems from the *intratemporal* tradeoff between output and price variations incorporated in the model, and how this is shifted over time by the chosen policies. Under our assumptions, a depreciation of the domestic real exchange rate generates an increase in the demand for domestic output, leading to an increase in domestic output itself. In effect there is an outward shift in the domestic IS curve, which also leads to an increase in the domestic interest rate while the increase in domestic output leads to increases in the inflation rates of both the price of domestic output and the domestic CPI. A domestic monetary contraction, as dictated by the short-run optimal strategy, mitigates the short-run fluctuations in output, However, at the same time this causes the domestic interest rate to increase further, leading to additional increases in the rates of depreciation of both the nominal and real domestic exchange rates in the following period. This in turn leads to a further outward shift in the domestic IS curve and to a deterioration in the next period's tradeoff between output and inflation. For a myopic government, concerned only with the present, this longer-run adverse movement is irrelevant. The short-run contractionary policy, with its dampening effects on output, is clearly desirable.

However, the long-run effects of the depreciation of the real exchange rate stemming from such a contraction are clearly destabilizing. As s_t continues to increase, longer-run fluctuations in real output are generated and variations in the inflation rate are increased. This is not in the interests of a government having a longer-run horizon. Instead, such a government will find it optimal to expand its money supply in the short-run. While this will increase the short-run fluctuations in output, it will also stabilize the fluctuation in the real exchange rate both in the short-run and over time. As a consequence of this, a stable long-run adjustment path will be followed. It is interesting to note that this switch in policy occurs within just two periods, the minimum within which the intertemporal (in addition to the intratemporal) tradeoff is introduced. Moreover, the result is robust across all parameter sets.

7.2 Feedback Stackelberg

At each stage, the follower's response to the leader's action is given by the relationship

$$m_t^* = -\frac{q_{2,\tau}^* s_t + q_{4,\tau}^* m_t}{q_{5,\tau}^*}$$

This defines the follower's reaction function the slope of which is $-q_{4,\tau}^*/q_{5,\tau}^*$. Since this is a function of τ, it changes at each stage. Using the base parameter set, Turnovsky and d'Orey (1986) show that for the one-period objective $q_4^* = 0.046$ and $q_5^* = 0.305$, so that the short-run reaction curve has a negative slope equal to -0.15. This means that the foreign (follower) economy responds to a unit expansion in the domestic (leader) real money supply with a monetary contraction of 0.15. Turnovsky and d'Orey characterize the negative slope as being a beggar thy neighbor world.[15] This less than proportionate response by the follower implies that the Stackelberg equilibrium lies at a point on the follower's reaction function away from the Nash equilibrium in the direction of the follower's Bliss point. At this equilibrium point, the leader experiences a somewhat larger increase in output accompanied by a smaller increase in inflation relative to the Nash equilibrium, while for the follower the negative fluctuations in both these variables are diminished in magnitude. Furthermore, while the welfare of the leader is higher than at the Nash equilibrium, the gains to the follower are relatively larger.

In the short-run Stackelberg equilibrium of the Turnovsky–d'Orey analysis, the real depreciation of the domestic currency leads to a monetary contraction by the leader. This action, together with the initial real appreciation of the foreign currency, has adverse effects on the level of output in the foreign economy. The foreign monetary authority (the follower) reacts to these negative effects by expanding its money supply, thereby tending to stabilize its level of output. For the same reasons as those given for the feedback Nash solution presented above, these responses lead to an increase in the relative price s_t and cause the economy to embark on an unstable time path.

As shown in figure 14.2(b), the appropriate initial responses become very different with an intertemporal objective function. Both the leader and the follower should now contract their respective real money stocks, with the contraction by the follower being significantly greater than in the Nash feedback case. The reason for the difference stems from the changed nature of the follower's short-run reaction function. In the initial period, we find $q_4^* = -4.481$ and $q_5^* = 4.883$, so that the slope of the reaction function is now 0.927 and is *positive*; this is characterized as being a locomotive world.

The leader knows that if he follows the feedback Nash strategy of expanding the money supply, the follower will tend to respond in a similar fashion. This tends to exacerbate the fluctuations in output in both economies, although the more balanced adjustment means that it is likely to be accompanied by smaller fluctuations in the rate of exchange depreciation (which responds to *differential* monetary policies), and hence in the rate of inflation of the CPI. Given that the cost function assigns greater weight to output fluctuations than to fluctuations in inflation, this is a nonoptimal situation, particularly for the leader. Accordingly, his strategy is to engage in a monetary contraction, thereby inducing an even greater contraction abroad by the follower. The fact that the contraction is relatively greater abroad causes an appreciation of the domestic currency, which in turn contributes to an appreciation of the real exchange rate so that s_t begins to fall. This pattern of responses continues at each state, thereby enabling the economy to follow a stable path toward equilibrium.

A consequence of the initial worldwide monetary contraction is that the initial stimulating effects of the positive shift in the relative price s on the leader economy is largely eliminated. Indeed, in period 1 output increases by only 0.06 units compared with around 0.7 for the Nash equilibrium. At the same time, the monetary contraction means that the inflation of 0.4 percent under Nash becomes a deflation of 0.25 percent under Stackelberg. In the follower economy, the initial reductions in output and inflation under Nash are even greater under Stackelberg. These comparisons become evident upon examination of figures 14.3(a), 14.3(b), 14.4(a), and 14.4(b).

Perhaps the most interesting feature of these results is the contrast in the welfare of the leader and the follower between the single-period and the multiperiod time horizon. We have already noted that for a one-period horizon, the follower is better off than under Nash. Now we see that over time, the leader improves his welfare vastly, through at the expense of the follower. The welfare costs under Nash to both are 0.759. Under feedback Stackelberg, however, the leader's costs are reduced to 0.020, making him much better off, while for the follower they rise to 2.758, resulting in a considerable loss in welfare.

The key to the difference between the short-run and long-run welfare costs is the switch in the follower's reaction function which occurs over time. As noted, the optimal one-period policies, involving a combination of monetary contraction in the domestic economy and a monetary expansion abroad, destabilize the real exchange rate, affecting both countries adversely over time. To a myopic policy-maker this is of no concern, but to a far-sighted policy-maker the long-run instability becomes important. The follower knows this and realizes that at each point of time it is up to him to respond in such a way to the leader's actions, to ensure that the relative price follows a stable path. To do this he responds to the real appreciation in his currency with a monetary contraction, at the same time trying to match more closely the qualitative response of the leader. The reason for this is that, since s_t depends critically upon the difference $m_t - m_t^*$ in the real money stocks, minimizing this difference will tend to reduce the instability in s_t. Thus he will tend to contract when the leader contracts, and vice versa.

For his part, the leader knows the follower's response. However, he also knows that the monetary contraction undertaken by the follower in response to his own actions will tend to have an adverse effect on his economy, and he therefore compensates by contracting less. In forcing the follower to respond at each stage to ensure that the relative price is stabilized, the leader is able to exploit his leadership more effectively over time. Basically he can act in his own self interests and is able to impose most of the burden of adjustment on the follower, forcing him to bear the bulk of the adjustment costs. This reversal of the relative welfare occurs even within a two-period horizon, although the differences increase with the length of the time horizon.

This finding raises serious questions of conflict in a multiperiod horizon. Obviously, in this situation neither country will agree to be the follower, raising serious doubts about the viability of the Stackelberg regime, unless there is some other mechanism whereby leadership is determined and enforced.

Finally, the convergence properties of the base parameter set can be summarized. For the 12-period horizon illustrated in figures 14.2(a) and 14.2(b) the coefficients α_τ and α_τ^* of the policy rules evolve as follows:

$$\alpha_\tau = -0.3717 \qquad \alpha_\tau^* = -0.1891 \qquad \tau = 11, \ldots, 5$$

$$\alpha_4 = -0.3718 \qquad \alpha_4^* = -0.1890$$

$$\alpha_3 = -0.3716 \qquad \alpha_3^* = -0.1881$$

$$\alpha_2 = -0.3493 \qquad \alpha_2^* = -0.1778$$

$$\alpha_1 = -0.1004 \qquad \alpha_1^* = -0.1130$$

$$\alpha_0 = -0.7767 \qquad \alpha_0^* = 0.8843$$

In this case, the convergence of the policy rule to its steady state form takes five periods. Note again the large jump in the size of the coefficients between the second to last and the last period. While the leader should always adopt a leaning against the wind policy, the response of the follower changes qualitatively during these two periods. The speed of the adjustment of the economy, as described by θ, is 0.247, implying that 75 percent of the adjustment occurs within one period. This is considerably faster than for the feedback Nash equilibrium.

7.3 Cooperative equilibrium

Under noncooperative Nash behavior, the monetary authorities in both countries ignore the fact that their own policy responses to the initial disturbance in the real exchange rate have stabilizing effects abroad. For example, the monetary expansion in country 1 causes both output and CPI inflation abroad to rise, thereby reducing the falls in these quantities abroad resulting from the combined effects of the initial disturbances together with the Nash response of the foreign monetary authority. The opposite applies with respect to country 2. By taking these externalities into account, the cooperative equilibrium calls for a larger initial monetary expansion in country 1, accompanied by an equivalently larger contraction in country 2, relative to the Nash equilibrium. This exacerbates the short-run movements in output in the two economies, while reducing the relative movements in the interest rates. The rate of exchange depreciation of the domestic currency is reduced further (relative to Nash), thereby generating a smaller increase in the domestic rate of inflation. Again, precisely the opposite reactions occur abroad. The increased interventions by the two monetary authorities cause a substantial drop in the real exchange rate in the next period, which causes reductions in domestic output and inflation. In fact, the rate of convergence of the cooperative equilibrium is so rapid that even though output fluctuations are increased initially (relative to Nash), by the second period the relative price has been reduced to such a degree that the fluctuations in both output and inflation are less than in the Nash equilibrium.

For the 12-period horizon, the coefficients α_τ and α_τ^* are as follows:

$$\alpha_\tau = -\alpha_\tau^* = 0.7859 \qquad \tau = 11, \ldots, 3$$

$$\alpha_2 = -\alpha_2^* = 0.7847$$

$$\alpha_1 = -\alpha_1^* = 0.7433$$

$$\alpha_0 = -\alpha_0^* = -0.1410$$

As in the other cases, the policy rule switches sign in the last period. The convergence of the control law to its steady state rule is even faster than before, occurring within just three periods. Also, as noted, the speed of adjustment of the system along the optimal trajectory is extremely fast, with around 82 percent of the adjustment occurring within the first period.

7.4 Overview

These results show that, at least in the case of parameter set 1, all three types of equilibria suggest a sharp contrast between optimal policy with a single-period objective and optimal policy within a dynamic policy within a dynamic objective function. Basically, the static analysis called for a monetary contraction for country 1 (experiencing the positive shock in s) accompanied by an equivalent monetary expansion in country 2. These responses tend to reduce output fluctuations while increasing fluctuations in inflation. Given the relative weights of these in the objective function, this is desirable for a one-period horizon. However, it is optimal over the longer run. Such policies generate increasing fluctuations in the relative price with increasing welfare costs in the future. These can be avioded by adopting policies which generate more variation in output and less variations in inflation.

Finally, we recall that figures 14.1–14.4 have been drawn for 12 periods. This means that in the last period the paths may begin to diverge owing to the myopic form of the policy rule in that period. Since, after 11 periods of optimal dynamic control s is by then small, such upturns may be imperceptible.[16] The time paths for the infinite-horizon case are similar, except that the values of α and $\alpha^*$are the same (at their steady state values) for all periods.

8 SENSITIVITY ANALYSIS

In order to determine the robustness of these results, we have recomputed the solutions across the 28 parameter sets discussed in table 14.1. The last of these (set 28) is simply the one-period horizon considered by Turovsky and d'Orey (1986), which corresponds to a discount rate of $\rho = 0$.[17] We consider the following three aspects summarizing the equilibria: (a) the steady state policy rules $\bar{\alpha}$ and $\bar{\alpha}^*$; (b) the steady state rate of convergence θ; (c) the steady state welfare costs.

8.1 Steady state policy rules

In virtually all cases, the Nash solution calls for leaning with the wind. Country 1 should expand its (real) money supply in response to the real depreciation of its currency; country 2 should contract in response to the real appreciation of its currency. By contrast, the Stackelberg leader should almost always lean against the wind, while the follower should always do so with the exception of set 25 ($\alpha = 1$), when the policy game degenerates.[18] Finally, except in polar cases, the cooperative equilibrium requires more intensive intervention than does the feedback Nash.

8.2 Steady state rate of convergence

For all but parameter sets 10, 21, 25, and 28, all optimal paths converge. Parameter set 28 is the static case, which for reasons discussed at length always leads to divergence. Parameter sets 21 and 25 are the degenerate extremes, when the targets are always attained perfectly in each period. In this case, the divergence of s_t is irrelevant. It can always be accommodated by increasing adjustments in the controls m_t and m_t^*. The only genuine dynamic game in which divergence occurs is set 10, with $d_2 = 10$. This value violates the condition for a downward sloping IS curve and hence instability is not so surprising.

With the exception of the extreme set 7, for all other sets with $\alpha = 0.75$, the values of θ under Nash, Stackelberg, and cooperative behavior, θ_N, θ_S, and θ_C respectively, satisfy

$$\theta_C < \theta_S < \theta_N$$

implying a clear ranking in the rates of convergence; the cooperative equilibrium is faster than Stackelberg, which in turn is faster then Nash.[19]

8.3 Steady state welfare costs and the gains from cooperation

The pattern of welfare costs is also remarkably stable and gives rise to a clear ranking among the equilibria. With the exception of the degenerate cases (sets 21 and 25) and the static case (set 28), the ranking of the different solutions obtained for the base parameter set extends to all other cases. The Stackelberg leadership is the best, while being a Stackelberg follower is the worst equilibrium. In between these extremes we find that the cooperative equilibrium dominates Nash. The welfare costs to the Stackelberg leader are remarkably stable across parameter sets and take him close to his Bliss point (zero costs). By contrast, the Stackelberg follower does extremely poorly, questioning the viability of this regime, relative to the alternatives.[20]

Allowing for compensation, the Nash equilibrium is the preferred noncooperative equilibrium from an overall welfare viewpoint. However, for the base parameter set it still yields welfare losses which are approximately 8 percent greater than those for the cooperative equilibrium. The gains from cooperation are generally of this order of magnitude, and are mildly parameter sensitive. Overall, the robustness of these results for the dynamic game are in sharp contrast with the rankings obtained by Turnovsky and d'Orey (1986) for the static game, which for the same parameter sets were found to be extremely parameter sensitive.

9 CONCLUSIONS

In this chapter we have developed dynamic strategic monetary policies using a standard two-country macromodel under flexible exchange rates. Two types of noncooperative equilibria have been considered, namely feedback Nash and feedback Stackelberg. In addition, these have been compared with the Pareto optimal cooperative equilibrium.

The optimal policies have been obtained as feedback rules in which the real money supplies in the respective economies are adjusted to movements in the real exchange rate. Even for the simple model such as this, the derivation of the optimal policies is highly complex, particularly in the limiting case of an infinite time horizon. For this reason, much of our work has proceeded numerically. In carrying out our simulations, we have compared the results obtained from the present dynamic analysis with those obtained previously for the same simulation sets, but using a single-period time horizon.

Many of the specific conclusions of our analysis have been noted previously. At this point, several general conclusions are worth highlighting. First, the optimal policies were found to yield convergence for all three equilibria in the case of virtually all parameter sets. A clear ranking in the rate of convergence was obtained: cooperative behavior yields the faster convergence, followed by the feedback Stackelberg, with feedback Nash being the slowest.

The results indicate a sharp contrast in both the optimal policies and welfare between the previous results obtained for the short-run time horizon and the present results for the long run, thereby suggesting the importance of intertemporal and intratemporal tradeoffs. As far as welfare is concerned, while in the short run the ranking of the equilibria is highly parameter sensitive, in the long run the rankings are remarkably robust across parameter sets. Specifically, in the long run we find the Stackelberg leader to be the preferred equilibrium among the noncooperative equilibria, followed by the feedback Nash and Stackelberg follower. The superiority of the Stackelberg leader suggests that it takes time for him to be able to exploit his position. The welfare gains from cooperation over Nash are typically of the order of 6–10 percent. Although these are modest, they are certainly not negligible.[21]

While these results are suggestive and appear promising, we should note at least two important limitations of our analysis. First, it is based on two symmetric economies, and while this is an obvious natural starting point, it clearly needs to be relaxed. Second, the model itself is simple in terms of minimizing the order of the dynamics; extensions in the direction of generating a richer model structure are also desirable before the results obtained can be maintained with confidence.

NOTES

1 In an expanded version of this chapter, the feedback consistent conjectural variations (CCV) equilibrium is also considered (see Fershtman and Kamien, 1985; Basar, 1986). This is a new equilibrium concept in dynamic game

theory and is a generalization of the static CCV equilibrium concept introduced by Bresnahan (1981), Perry (1982), and Kamien and Schwartz (1983). Hughes Hallett (1984) considers arbitrary, but not consistent, conjectural variations in a dynamic policy game framework. Unfortunately, space limitations preclude a detailed discussion of this equilibrium. However, some of our results are indicated in notes at appropriate places.

2 Viewed in this way, the problem can be regarded as being a strategic analog of the problem of the optimal reduction of inflation originally considered by Phelps (1967) and studied by several authors since.

3 While these papers belong to the same generic class, they differ in terms of their technical details. For example, Miller and Salmon use continuous time, with the interest rate being the policy variable. Oudiz and Sachs introduce more sluggish wage behavior, the result of which is that the optimal monetary rule depends upon a greater set of lagged variables. Currie and Levine have a stochastic model, but consider a set of simple, but not fully optimal, monetary feedback rules, while Taylor assumes staggered wages and prices. Finally, several of the authors consider open-loop as well as feedback rules.

4 We maintain the usual assumption that residents of one country do not hold the currency of the other country

5 We assume $1 > \delta > \frac{1}{2}$, so that residents in both countries have a preference for their own good.

6 This assumption of the instantaneous observability of the exchange rate is the standard one in the current exchange market intervention literature.

7 For the analysis of exogenous policy shocks in such a model, see Turnovsky (1986, this volume, ch. 4).

8 The details of the proofs are contained in a longer version of this chapter (see Basar et al., 1986).

9 In the one-period game, this equilibrium reduces to the usual Cournot equilibrium.

10 All solutions are time consistent as they are based on feedback rules which are determined using dynamic programming methods.

11 In effect we have the familiar indeterminacy problem arising from having "too many" stable roots. Using a higher-dimension system, Currie and Levine (1985) handle the issue of jumps by invoking the notion of controllability and considering solutions which have the saddlepoint property. Our procedure is the one-dimension analog of this.

12 An example of this for optimal monetary policy in a small open economy is given by Stemp and Turnovsky (1987).

13 These statements are based on values of $I = 0.10$ and $\dot{P} = 0.04$. Larger values are considered in the sensitivity analysis.

14 The feedback CCV results are generally similar to the feedback Nash. The main difference is that, since both policy-makers are aware of the others actions, each moderates his own adjustment relative to Nash. For parameter set 1, $\theta = 0.789$, implying a substantially slower rate of adjustment.

15 Note that this term is being used in a somewhat different way from its conventional usage. More commonly, a beggar thy neighbor world is one in

which an expansionary policy in one country causes a contraction (in activity) abroad. Here we are using the term to characterize the interdependence between the adjustments in the policy instruments in the two economies which in turn involves the slopes of the reaction functions. The same results apply to our usage of the term "locomotive" introduced below.

16 In the case of the CCV solution, however, the upturn is in fact quite marked.

17 Tables presenting the detailed results of the sensitivity analysis are available from the authors.

18 Note that set 21 ($\alpha = 0$) and set 25 ($\alpha = 1$) give rise to degenerate policy games. This is because in either case the objective function of each policy-maker reduces to just one target, and the two policy instruments m and m^* enable each to be attained perfectly. All solutions converge to the same with zero welfare costs being incurred.

19 For almost all parameter sets the slowest rate of adjustment is achieved under feedback CCV equilibrium. The reason is that since each policy-maker takes account of his rival's actions, this induces caution and gives rise to a more gradual adjustment.

20 The CCV equilibrium always leads to higher welfare costs than Nash. This reflects the fact that CCV is associated with slower adjustment, thereby contributing to larger intertemporal welfare costs.

21 These numerical estimates of the gains from cooperation are similar in magnitude to these obtained by Taylor (1985).

REFERENCES

Basar, T (1986) A tutorial on dynamic and differential games. In *Dynamic Games and Applications in Economics* (ed. T. Basar). Berlin: Springer-Verlag.

—— and Olsder, G. J. (1983) *Dynamic Noncooperative Game Theory*. New York: Academic Press.

——, Turnovsky, S. J. and d'Orey, V. (1986) Optimal strategic monetary policies in dynamic interdependent economics. In *Dynamic Games and Applications in Economics* (ed. T. Basar). Berlin: Springer-Verlag.

Bresnahan, T. F. (1981) Duopoly models with consistent conjectures. *American Economic Review* 71, 934–45.

Canzoneri, M. and Gray, J. A. (1985) Monetary policy games and the consequences of noncooperative behavior. *International Economic Review*, 26, 547–64.

Currie, D. and Levine, P. (1985) Macroeconomic policy design in an interdependent world. In *International Economic Policy Coordination* (eds W. H. Buiter and R. C. Marston). New York: Cambridge University Press.

Dornbusch, R. (1976) Expectations of exchange rate dynamics. *Journal of Political Economy*, 84, 1161–76.

Fershtman, C. and Kamien, M. I. (1985) Conjectural equilibrium and strategy spaces in differential games. In *Optimal Control Theory and Economic*

Analysis, vol. 2. (ed. G. Feichtinger). Amsterdam: North-Holland.
Hamada, K. (1976) A strategic analysis of monetary interdependence. *Journal of Political Economy*, 84, 677–700.
Hughes Hallett, A. J. (1984) Non-cooperative strategies for dynamic policy games and the problem of time inconsistency. *Oxford Economic Papers*, 56, 381–99.
Jones, M. (1983) International Liquidity: a welfare analysis. *Quarterly Journal of Economics*, 98, 1–23.
Kamien, M. I. and Schwartz, N. L. (1983) Conjectual variations. *Canadian Journal of Economics*, 16, 191–211.
Miler, M. H. and Salmon, M. (1985) Policy coordination and dynamic games. In *International Economic Policy Coordination* (eds W. H. Buiter and R. C. Marston). New York: Cambridge University Press.
Oudiz, G. and Sachs, J. (1985) International policy coordination in dynamic macroeconomic models. In *International Economic Policy Coordination* (eds W. H. Buiter and R. C. Marston). New York: Cambridge University Press.
Perry, M. K. (1982) Oligopoly and consistent conjectural variations. *Bell Journal of Economics*, 13, 197–205.
Phelps, E. S. (1967) Phillips curves, expectations of inflation, and optimal unemployment over time. *Economica*, 24, 254–81.
Rogoff, K. (1985) Can international monetary policy coordination be counter-productive? *Journal of International Economics*, 18, 199–217.
Stemp, P. J. and Turnovsky, S. J. (1987) Optimal monetary policy in an open economy. *European Economic Review*, 31, 111–35.
Taylor, J. B. (1985) International coordination in the design of macroeconomic policy rules. *European Economic Review*, 28, 53–81.
Turnovsky, S. J. (1986) Monetary and fiscal policy under perfect foresight: a symmetric two-country analysis. *Economica*, 53, 139–57. Reprinted in this volume as chapter 4.
—— and d'Orey, V. (1986) Monetary policies in interdependent economies: a strategic approach. In *Symposium on the Coordination of Economic Policies Between Japan and the United States*, *Economic Studies Quarterly*, 37, 114–33.

15 The Gains from Fiscal Cooperation in the Two-commodity Real Trade Model

1 INTRODUCTION

The increase in international economic interdependence during the past several years has stimulated increased interest in questions pertaining to economic policy interdependence and coordination. One particular aspect of this is the recognition that policy-making in such an environment necessarily involves strategic behavior. The formal analysis of such strategic behavior among international policy-makers began with the pioneering work of Hamada (1976) and has been extended more recently in various directions by several authors.[1]

This literature can be characterized by two features. First, it focuses on monetary policy and monetary interdependence. Second, the models employed are what might be characterized as Keynesian type macro-models in which the objective is the minimization of a quadratic loss function, typically involving inflation and output as tradeoffs. While the linear quadratic stabilization framework is well established and convenient, its limitations, in not focusing on any fundamental welfare objective, are well known.

Recent work in international macroeconomic policy has undergone something of a change in emphasis. First, with the large US government deficit, questions of *fiscal* interdependence have come more to the fore.[2] Secondly, this literature has tended to be cast in terms of utility-maximizing agents, with the effects of fiscal changes being evaluated in terms of some explicitly stated welfare function, typically the welfare of the representation individual (see for example Frenkel and Razin, 1985, 1986).

In the present chapter strategic fiscal policy-making is analysed within

Originally published in *Journal of International Economics*, 25, 1988, 111–27 I wish to thank Michael Devereux and the referee for helpful comments.

the context of the standard two-country–two-good real trade model. We first derive the optimal degrees of government expenditure on both the export and the import good under the assumption that each policy-maker behaves noncooperatively, taking his rival's actions as given. Expressions are obtained for the optimal degrees of government expenditure, which are directly analogous to the expressions for the optimal tariff originally due to Johnson (1954). We then determine the optimal degrees of government expenditure in a cooperative equilibrium where joint utilities are maximized. Certain welfare conclusions are drawn and comparisons between the two equilibria can be made.

As a special example, we consider the case of a logarithmic utility function, with output fixed and specialized in the two countries. Not only can this be solved explicitly very simply, but also some useful insights as to the numerical gains from cooperation can be obtained in this case. Indeed, following this line it would appear that the differences between noncooperative and cooperative equilibria may be significantly greater than the more traditional macromodels suggest. The reason for this is that fiscal policies generate large international spillovers through relative price movements and these render an important role for strategic policy-making.

Most of the literature focuses on a world consisting of two countries. In the latter part of the chapter, the logarithmic utility function is used to address an important, but neglected, question. We consider a world consisting of three countries and assess the effects of the formation of a coalition between two of them upon the welfare of the third.

Before proceeding with the formal analysis, we should relate the present chapter to other recent studies. Devereux (1986) looks at the question of the gains from fiscal coordination using a model based on logarithmic preferences. A number of authors, including Devereux (1986), Chari and Kehoe (1987), and Kehoe (1987), examine the divergence between noncooperative and cooperative fiscal policies as the number of economies in the world increase. Also, Hamada (1986) considers optimal strategic fiscal policy in a two-period single-commodity framework. Although our analysis is conducted within the context of the two-country–two-good trade model, in which the transmission occurs through the terms of trade, with little more than notational change we can interpret our results as applying to a two-period world much closer to the framework of Hamada or of Frenkel and Razin. In this case the relative price is the intertemporal interest rate, rather than the intertemporal terms of trade.

2 THE MODEL

Consider the standard two-country–two-good trade model, where both countries are competitive. The countries are indexed by A and B, and the goods by x and y, and we assume without loss of generality that country B imports x in return for y, which it exports to country A. There are no impediments to trade, so that relative prices in the two countries are equal.

The basic model is described by the following set of equations:

$$U^i = U^i(C^i_x, C^i_y, G^i_x, G^i_y) \qquad i = \mathrm{A, B} \tag{15.1}$$

$$\sigma \frac{\partial U^i}{\partial C^i_x} = \frac{\partial U^i}{\partial C^i_y} \qquad i = \mathrm{A, B} \tag{15.2}$$

$$F^i(Q^i_x, Q^i_y) = 0 \qquad i = \mathrm{A, B} \tag{15.3}$$

$$\sigma \frac{\partial F^i}{\partial Q^i_x} = \frac{\partial F^i}{\partial Q^i_y} \qquad i = \mathrm{A, B} \tag{15.4}$$

$$Q^i_j + E^i_j = C^i_j + G^i_j \qquad i = \mathrm{A, B} \quad j = x, y, \tag{15.5}$$

$$\sigma E^{\mathrm{A}}_y + E^{\mathrm{A}}_x = 0 \tag{15.6a}$$

$$\sigma E^{\mathrm{B}}_y + E^{\mathrm{B}}_x = 0 \tag{15.6b}$$

$$E^{\mathrm{A}}_x + E^{\mathrm{B}}_x = 0 \tag{15.7a}$$

$$E^{\mathrm{A}}_y + E^{\mathrm{B}}_y = 0 \tag{15.7b}$$

where C^i_j denotes the consumption of good j in country i ($i =$ A, B, $j = x, y$), Q^i_j denotes the production of good j in country i, E^i_j denotes excess demand for good j in country i, G^i_j denotes government expenditure on good j in country i, and σ denotes the relative price of good y to good x in the world economy.

Equations (15.1) define the utility functions of representative agents in countries A and B. These are functions of (a) private consumptions of the two goods and (b) government expenditures on the two goods. The utility functions are assumed to be increasing functions of their respective arguments and to be continuous, twice differentiable, and quasi-concave. Equations (15.2) specify the optimality conditions for consumers with respect to private consumption C^i_j in each country. The quantities of government expenditures are fixed, as far as private agents are concerned, but are determined by the two governments in accordance with the strategic behavioral regimes to be discussed below.

Equations (15.3) and (15.4) apply analogously to production. Equation (15.3) defines the production possibility curve, which is assumed to be concave while (15.4) specifies the usual marginal product conditions for optimality. Equations (15.5) define the excess demand for good j in country i to be production less private consumption and domestic government expenditure. For the import good $E < 0$.[3] We also assume that government expenditure in each country is financed by lump-sum taxation. The government budget is therefore balanced and there are no distortionary effects of taxes on consumption.

Equations (15.6) describe the balance of trade equilibrium for the two countries, while equations (15.7) specify market clearance in the world market for the two goods. It is clear from (15.6) and (15.7) that only one goods market is independent. Equilibrium in one implies equilibrium in the other, so that one equation, (15.7b) say, can be dropped.

3 OPTIMAL FISCAL POLICIES: NONCOOPERATIVE EQUILIBRIUM

The welfare of the respective representative agents in the two economies is given by the utility functions U^{A} and U^{B}. We assume initially that the two governments act noncooperatively to maximize the welfare of their respective citizens, taking the actions of the rival government as given. In each case, the government has two possible fiscal instruments: expenditure on the export good, and expenditure on the import good. Both instruments will be considered.

Consider first country A. Using (15.5), (15.6), and (15.7b), its utility function can be expressed as

$$U^{\mathrm{A}} = U^{\mathrm{A}}(Q_x^{\mathrm{A}} - \sigma E_y^{\mathrm{A}} - G_x^{\mathrm{A}}, Q_y^{\mathrm{A}} + E_y^{\mathrm{A}} - G_y^{\mathrm{A}}, G_x^{\mathrm{A}}, G_y^{\mathrm{A}})$$

To determine the optimal government expenditure on the export good, we differentiate U^{A} with respect to G_x^{A}. Taking the differential of (15.3) and using the optimality conditions (15.2) and (15.4) yields the optimality condition

$$\frac{\partial U^{\mathrm{A}}/\partial G_x^{\mathrm{A}}}{\partial U^{\mathrm{A}}/\partial C_x^{\mathrm{A}}} = 1 + E_y^{\mathrm{A}} \frac{\partial \sigma}{\partial G_x^{\mathrm{A}}} \tag{15.8}$$

This equation is obtained in precisely the same way as is the optimal tariff.[4] It is therefore the direct analog to the well-known optimal tariff formula (see for example Takayama, 1974; Bhagwati and Srinivasan, 1983). Equation (15.8) can be given a simple interpretation. In a single-commodity world, in which government expenditure is financed by lump-sum taxation, the optimal level of government expenditure on the export good is to equate the marginal rate of substitution between government expenditure and private expenditure on that good to the relative price, namely unity. However, in the present two-commodity world, the change in government expenditure on good x, say, induces a change in the relative price of good x to good y. This causes further substitution between the two private goods, the result of which is that the marginal rate of substitution between good x and the public good is adjusted away from unity in response to this relative price effect.

To derive the relative price effect we first note that the optimality conditions (15.2) and (15.4), together with (15.5) and (15.6), determine the excess demand functions

$$E_j^i = E_j^i(\sigma, G_x^i, G_y^i) \qquad i = \text{A, B} \qquad j = x, y$$

Substituting these expressions into the market-clearing condition (15.7a) and differentiating, we can show that under reasonable conditions[5]

$$\frac{\partial \sigma}{\partial G_x^{\text{A}}} < 0 \tag{15.9}$$

Plausibly, an increase in government expenditure on good x raises its relative price, and we refer to this as being the *normal* case. However, the opposite case where $\partial\sigma/\partial G_x^{\text{A}} > 0$ cannot be ruled out *a priori*.

The optimal government expenditure on the import good, obtained by differentiating U^{A} with respect to G_y^{A}, is derived similarly. Omitting details, it is given by the expression

$$\frac{\partial U^{\text{A}}/\partial G_y^{\text{A}}}{\partial U^{\text{A}}/\partial C_y^{\text{A}}} = \left(1 + \frac{E_y^{\text{A}}}{\sigma}\frac{\partial \sigma}{\partial G_y^{\text{A}}}\right) \tag{15.10}$$

where we can show that under normal conditions $\partial\sigma/\partial G_y^{\text{A}} > 0$. Hence an increase in government expenditure on the import good raises excess demand for that good, causing its relative price to rise. The marginal rate of substitution between private and government expenditure on the import good is equated to a quantity in excess of the relative private of unity.

Repeating these calculations for country B yields analogous conditions:

$$\frac{\partial U^{\text{B}}/\partial G_x^{\text{B}}}{\partial U^{\text{B}}/\partial C_x^{\text{B}}} = 1 - E_y^{\text{A}}\frac{\partial \sigma}{\partial G_x^{\text{B}}} \tag{15.11}$$

$$\frac{\partial U^{\text{B}}/\partial G_y^{\text{B}}}{\partial U^{\text{B}}/\partial C_y^{\text{B}}} = 1 - \frac{E_y^{\text{A}}}{\sigma}\frac{\partial \sigma}{\partial G_y^{\text{B}}} \tag{15.12}$$

where under normal conditions, $\partial\sigma/\partial G_x^{\text{B}} < 0$, $\partial\sigma/\partial G_y^{\text{B}} > 0$, and the interpretation of the optimality conditions (15.11) and (15.12) is analogous to that for country A.

The optimality conditions (15.8), (15.10), (15.11), and (15.12) are various reaction functions, some or all of which may apply, depending upon what fiscal instruments are being varied. For example, if the two countries optimize with respect to their respective export goods, then the reaction functions are (15.8) and (15.11) respectively, which jointly determine the Nash equilibrium noncooperative outcomes for G_x^{A} and G_y^{B}. It is also possible for both governments to optimize with respect to both commodities, in which case these four equations will determine the equilibrium values of the four variables G_x^{A}, G_y^{A}, G_x^{B}, and G_y^{B}.

4 COOPERATIVE EQUILIBRIUM

We now assume that the two policy-makers act cooperatively to maximize their joint welfare function:

$$W = U^{\mathrm{A}}[C_x^{\mathrm{A}}, C_y^{\mathrm{A}}, G_x^{\mathrm{A}}, G_y^{\mathrm{A}}] + U^{\mathrm{B}}[C_x^{\mathrm{B}}, C_y^{\mathrm{B}}, G_x^{\mathrm{B}}, G_y^{\mathrm{B}}] \tag{15.13}$$

The optimality conditions with respect to the four government expenditure variables, obtained by differentiating (15.13) subject to the equations of the system (15.1)–(15.10), are given by

$$\frac{\partial W}{\partial G_x^{\mathrm{A}}} = -\frac{\partial U^{\mathrm{A}}}{\partial C_x^{\mathrm{A}}}\left(1 + E_y^{\mathrm{A}}\frac{\partial \sigma}{\partial G_x^{\mathrm{A}}}\right) + \frac{\partial U^{\mathrm{A}}}{\partial G_x^{\mathrm{A}}} + \frac{\partial U^{\mathrm{B}}}{\partial C_x^{\mathrm{B}}} E_y^{\mathrm{A}} \frac{\partial \sigma}{\partial G_x^{\mathrm{A}}} = 0 \tag{15.14a}$$

$$\frac{\partial W}{\partial G_y^{\mathrm{A}}} = -\frac{\partial U^{\mathrm{A}}}{\partial C_y^{\mathrm{A}}}\left(1 + \frac{E_y^{\mathrm{A}}}{\sigma}\frac{\partial \sigma}{\partial G_y^{\mathrm{A}}}\right) + \frac{\partial U^{\mathrm{A}}}{\partial G_y^{\mathrm{A}}} + \frac{\partial U^{\mathrm{B}}}{\partial C_y^{\mathrm{B}}} \frac{E_y^{\mathrm{A}}}{\sigma} \frac{\partial \sigma}{\partial G_y^{\mathrm{A}}} = 0 \tag{15.14b}$$

$$\frac{\partial W}{\partial G_x^{\mathrm{B}}} = -\frac{\partial U^{\mathrm{B}}}{\partial C_x^{\mathrm{B}}}\left(1 - E_y^{\mathrm{A}}\frac{\partial \sigma}{\partial G_x^{\mathrm{B}}}\right) + \frac{\partial U^{\mathrm{B}}}{\partial G_x^{\mathrm{B}}} - \frac{\partial U^{\mathrm{A}}}{\partial C_x^{\mathrm{A}}} E_y^{\mathrm{A}} \frac{\partial \sigma}{\partial G_x^{\mathrm{B}}} = 0 \tag{15.14c}$$

$$\frac{\partial W}{\partial G_y^{\mathrm{B}}} = -\frac{\partial U^{\mathrm{B}}}{\partial C_x^{\mathrm{B}}}\left(1 - \frac{E_y^{\mathrm{A}}}{\sigma}\frac{\partial \sigma}{\partial G_y^{\mathrm{B}}}\right) + \frac{\partial U^{\mathrm{B}}}{\partial G_y^{\mathrm{B}}} - \frac{\partial U^{\mathrm{A}}}{\partial C_y^{\mathrm{A}}} \frac{E_y^{\mathrm{A}}}{\sigma} \frac{\partial \sigma}{\partial G_y^{\mathrm{B}}} = 0 \tag{15.14d}$$

Again, only some subset of these equations may apply, if only some subset of the fiscal variables is being optimized.

Consider, for example, equation (15.14a). It is evident by comparison with (15.8) that when government A acts noncooperatively, it fails to take account of the fact that its actions, by influencing the world relative price σ, generate an externality which affects the welfare of agents in country B. In particular, the noncooperative level of G_x^{A} is generally too large relative to the cooperative equilibrium level. To see this, we evaluate $\partial W/\partial G_x^{\mathrm{A}}$ at the noncooperative equilibrium level. At this equilibrium (denoted by subscript N), equation (15.8) applies, so that

$$\left.\frac{\partial W}{\partial G_x^{\mathrm{A}}}\right|_{\mathrm{N}} = \frac{\partial U_{\mathrm{B}}}{\partial C_x^{\mathrm{B}}} E_y^{\mathrm{A}} \frac{\partial \sigma}{\partial G_x^{\mathrm{A}}} \tag{15.15}$$

Thus, in general, in the normal case when $\partial\sigma/\partial G_x^{\mathrm{A}} < 0$, (15.15) implies $\partial W/\partial G_x^{\mathrm{A}}|_{\mathrm{N}} < 0$, i.e. aggregate welfare is increased if country A reduces its expenditure on the export good from its Nash equilibrium level. In the less likely case when $\partial\sigma/\partial G_x^{\mathrm{A}} > 0$, its expenditure on that good should be increased.[6] Similar comments apply to the other forms of government expenditure, enabling us to summarize with the following proposition.

Proposition 15.1 Provided that goods are normal in the sense defined, then a noncooperative equilibrium leads to an *overexpansion* of government expenditure on export goods and an *underexpansion* of government expenditure on import goods, relative to the cooperative equilibrium where joint utilities are being maximized.

The welfare function in (15.13) assigns equal (arbitrary) weights to the two economies. This is the criterion used throughout both the monetary and fiscal literature analysing the gains from policy coordination. As seen in (15.14), cooperative equilibrium involves the redistribution of income between the economies through terms of trade effects. However, this may not represent a world social optimum. Chari and Kehoe (1987) suggest an alternative benchmark in which the cooperative equilibrium and the social optimum coincide. As they note, this can be attained if, in addition to setting expenditure levels, the government sets lump-sum taxes to achieve the appropriate distribution.

The social optimum equilibrium can be formally derived as the solution to a planning problem in which private consumptions, outputs, and government expenditures are chosen to maximize a weighted average of utilities:

$$W^* = \lambda^A U^A + \lambda^B U^B$$

subject to the market-clearing conditions (15.5), (15.7a), and (15.7b). Performing the maximization, we can show that the optimality conditions characterizing the social optimum include

$$\frac{\partial W^*}{\partial G_j^i} = \lambda^i \left[\frac{\partial U^i}{\partial G_j^i} - \frac{\partial U^i}{\partial C_j^i} \right] = 0 \qquad i = \text{A, B}, \quad j = x, y$$

For example, evaluating $\partial W^*/\partial G_x^A$ at the noncooperative equilibrium yields

$$\left. \frac{\partial W^*}{\partial G_x^A} \right|_N = \lambda^A \frac{\partial U^A}{\partial C_x^A} E_y^A \frac{\partial \sigma}{\partial G_x^A} \tag{15.16}$$

which analogously to (15.15) implies an overexpansion of G_x^A in general. Indeed, an analogous proposition to proposition 15.1 holds with respect to the social optimum, although the degree of underexpansion is clearly different, reflecting the distortion of the cooperative equilibrium from the social optimum.

5 A LOGARITHMIC EXAMPLE

We consider the special case where (a) the two countries are each specialized in the production of a single good, (b) the government spends only on the domestic good, and (c) the respective utility functions are logarithmic:

$$U^i = \alpha_x^i \ln C_x^i + \alpha_y^i \ln C_y^i + \beta^i \ln G^i \qquad i = \text{A, B} \tag{15.17}$$

where $\alpha_x^i + \alpha_y^i = 1$, and good x is produced by country A and y by country B. The budget constraints for the respective economies are

$$C_x^A + \sigma C_y^A = \bar{Q}^A - G^A \tag{15.18a}$$

$$\frac{1}{\sigma} C_x^B + C_y^B = \bar{Q}^B - G^B \tag{15.18b}$$

where $\bar{Q}^A$ and $\bar{Q}^B$ denote the fixed levels of output. The demand functions for the two goods in the two economies, obtained by maximizing the utility functions subject to the respective budget constraints, are

$$C_x^A = \alpha_x^A(\bar{Q}^A - G^A) \qquad C_y^A = \alpha_y^A\left(\frac{\bar{Q}^A - G^A}{\sigma}\right) \tag{15.19a}$$

$$C_x^B = \alpha_x^B(\bar{Q}^B - G^B)\sigma \qquad C_y^B = \alpha_y^B(\bar{Q}^B - G^B) \tag{15.19b}$$

The relative price σ is obtained from the balance-of-trade equilibrium condition so that

$$C_x^B = \sigma C_y^A$$

$$\sigma = \left(\frac{\alpha_y^A}{\alpha_x^B}\right)\left(\frac{\bar{Q}^A - G^A}{\bar{Q}^B - G^B}\right) \tag{15.20}$$

The relative price is therefore inversely proportional to the disposable incomes in the two economies. Furthermore, substituting (15.20) into (15.19) leads to

$$C_x^A = \alpha_x^A(\bar{Q}^A - G^A) \qquad C_y^A = \alpha_x^B(\bar{Q}^B - G^B) \tag{15.21a}$$

$$C_x^B = \alpha_y^A(\bar{Q}^A - G^A) \qquad C_y^B = \alpha_y^B(\bar{Q}^B - G^B) \tag{15.21b}$$

The interesting feature is that, through the adjustment in the relative price, the equilibrium quantities of the imported good in each case depend upon the other country's disposable income. This fact gives rise to a large spillover in the effects of fiscal policy in one country on the other.

The next step is to substitute (15.21a) and (15.21b) into the utility functions (15.17a) and (15.17b), and this yields

$$U^i(G^A, G^B) = K^i + \alpha_x^i \ln(\bar{Q}^A - G^A) + \alpha_y^i \ln(\bar{Q}^B - G^B) + \beta^i \ln(G^i) \qquad i = \text{A, B} \tag{15.22}$$

where the constants K^i are functions of the parameters α_j^i. The noncooperative Nash equilibrium is obtained by calculating

$$\frac{\partial U^A}{\partial G^A} = -\frac{\alpha_x^A}{\bar{Q}^A - G^A} + \frac{\beta^A}{G^A} = 0 \tag{15.23a}$$

$$\frac{\partial U^B}{\partial G^B} = -\frac{\alpha_y^B}{\bar{Q}^B - G^B} + \frac{\beta^B}{G^B} = 0 \tag{15.23b}$$

Equations (15.23a) and (15.23b) are of course the respective reaction functions in the two economies. Observe that each is independent of the other's decision. This means that the Nash equilibrium is dominant and the assumption of a zero conjectured response is correct.[7] The reaction functions are plotted in figure 15.1 as horizontal and vertical lines respectively which intersect at the point A, where

$$G^{\mathrm{A}} = \left(\frac{\beta^{\mathrm{A}}}{\alpha_x^{\mathrm{A}} + \beta^{\mathrm{A}}}\right)\bar{Q}^{\mathrm{A}} \qquad G^{\mathrm{B}} = \left(\frac{\beta^{\mathrm{B}}}{\alpha_x^{\mathrm{B}} + \beta^{\mathrm{B}}}\right)\bar{Q}^{\mathrm{B}} \tag{15.24}$$

The implied levels of utility in the two countries are obtained by substituting these two solutions in (15.19a) and (15.19b).

Suppose now that the two policy-makers act cooperatively, and maximize their joint utility functions:

$$U^{\mathrm{A}} + U^{\mathrm{B}} = K^{\mathrm{A}} + K^{\mathrm{B}} + (\alpha_x^{\mathrm{A}} + \alpha_x^{\mathrm{B}})\ln(\bar{Q}^{\mathrm{A}} - G^{\mathrm{A}})$$
$$+ (\alpha_y^{\mathrm{A}} + \alpha_y^{\mathrm{B}})\ln(\bar{G}^{\mathrm{B}} - G^{\mathrm{B}}) + \beta^{\mathrm{A}}\ln G^{\mathrm{A}} + \beta^{\mathrm{B}}\ln G^{\mathrm{B}}.$$

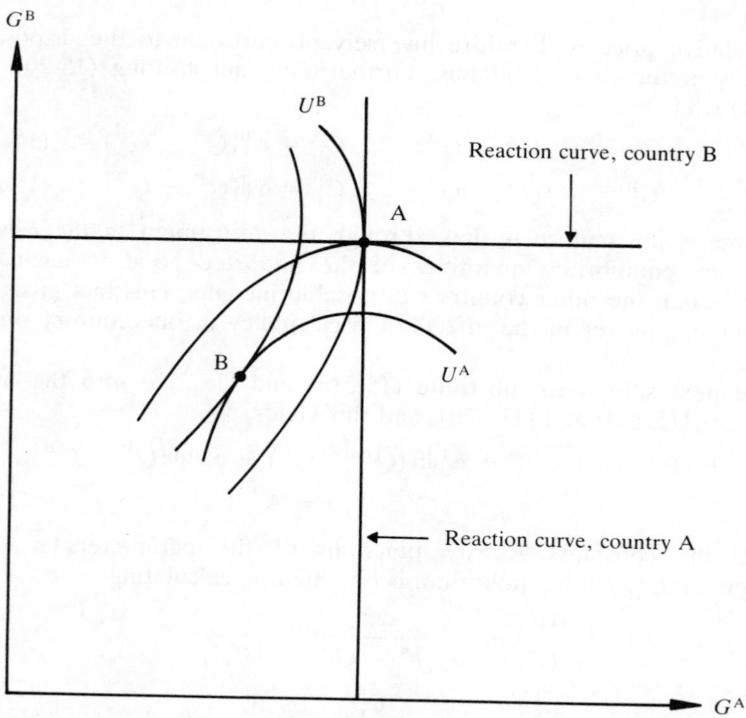

Figure 15.1 Noncooperative and cooperative equilibria: logarithmic case.

The optimality conditions are

$$-\frac{(\alpha_x^A + \alpha_x^B)}{\bar{Q}^A - G^A} + \frac{\beta^A}{G^A} = 0$$

$$-\frac{(\alpha_y^A + \alpha_y^B)}{\bar{Q}^B - G^B} + \frac{\beta^B}{G^B} = 0$$

the solutions to which are

$$G^A = \left(\frac{\beta^A}{\alpha_x^A + \alpha_x^B + \beta^A}\right)\bar{Q}^A \qquad G^B = \left(\frac{\beta^B}{\alpha_y^A + \alpha_y^B + \beta^B}\right)\bar{Q}^B \quad (15.25)$$

This is illustrated by point B in figure 15.1, which lies at the tangency points between the two indifference curves. Comparing (15.24) with (15.25) (or point A with point B), we see that cooperation leads to a reduction in the levels of government expenditure, consistent with the general result of section 5.

An interesting issue concerns the magnitude of the difference between the two equilibria. One conclusion prevalent among the macroeconomic models dealing with this question is that the noncooperative and cooperative equilibria are typically closely clustered. The numerical gains from cooperation are small. In the present example we find that the respective percentage changes in the levels of G^A and G^B (measured from the noncooperative equilibria as base) are

$$\frac{\Delta G^A}{G^A} = \frac{\alpha_x^B}{\alpha_x^A + \alpha_x^B + \beta^A} \qquad \frac{\Delta G^B}{G^B} = \frac{\alpha_y^A}{\alpha_y^A + \alpha_y^B + \beta^B}$$

Suppose, for example, that we take $\alpha_x^A = \alpha_y^B = 0.6$, $\alpha_y^A = \alpha_x^B = 0.4$, and $\beta^A = \beta^B = 0.3$, suggesting that each economy has a preference for its own good. Then from (15.24) the ratios of government expenditure to output in the noncooperative equilibrium in the two economies are $G^A/\bar{Q}^A = G^B/\bar{Q}^B = 0.333$. Moving to the cooperative equilibrium reduces these shares to around 0.231 (see (15.25)), which is a relative reduction in government expenditure of nearly 31 percent. While the ratios of consumptions to disposable income remain fixed (set by α_j^i), the absolute levels increase correspondingly by around 15 percent. Although the parameter values underlying these calculations are arbitrary, they certainly are plausible insofar as the implied shares of government expenditure in output and consumption patterns are concerned.

These differences in the equilibria are substantially larger than those typically obtained from macroeconomic models. For example, the dynamic simulations of Oudiz and Sachs (1985) find that the optimal paths followed by output and inflation under noncooperative behavior change remarkably little when a cooperative equilibrium is considered. Turnovsky and d'Orey (1986) find the changes in the optimal level of money stock between the two equilibria to be typically small (around 2–4 percent) for simulations in which the elasticity of the demand for output with respect to the relative price is around unity, although it increases to around 15 percent as this elasticity falls to 0.1. They find utility gains to be almost negligible in the former case and to increase to around 10 percent (depending upon the disturbance) in the latter case. Similarly, Taylor (1985), whose numerical analysis is also based on a relative price elasticity of 0.1, finds utility gains to be around 10 percent. Taken together, these pieces of evidence suggest that the gains from cooperation as determined by these macromodels are modest. The larger differences between the two equilibria suggested by the present analysis can be attributed to the strong international spillovers generated by relative price movements in the present framework. The utility gains, however, are arbitrary and are proportional to the choice of $\bar{Q}$.

6 THE EFFECTS OF A COALITION

Most of the formal literature deals with the gains from cooperation in a two-country world. However, in reality, cooperative arrangements are formed among groups of countries, with some countries being excluded from such coalitions. In this section we address an important issue, namely how the gains from cooperation between two countries, A and B say, impact on a third country C which produces a third good z, say.[8] For tractability, we consider the question within the logarithmic model of setion 5. In this analysis the number of economies and goods remains fixed (at three); what changes is the number of economies participating in the cooperative arrangement.

Augmented to three countries, the model contains the following relationships: the utility functions for country i

$$U^i = \alpha_x^i \ln C_x^i + \alpha_y^i \ln C_y^i + \alpha_z^i \ln C_z^i + \beta^i \ln G^i$$
$$\alpha_x^i + \alpha_y^i + \alpha_z^i = 1 \qquad i = \text{A, B, C} \tag{15.26}$$

and the corresponding budget constraints

$$C_x^{\text{A}} + C_y^{\text{A}}\sigma_y + C_z^{\text{A}}\sigma_z + G^{\text{A}} = \bar{Q}^{\text{A}}$$
$$\frac{C_x^{\text{B}}}{\sigma_y} + C_y^{\text{B}} + \frac{C_z^{\text{B}}\sigma_z}{\sigma_y} + G^{\text{B}} = \bar{Q}^{\text{B}}$$
$$\frac{C_x^{\text{C}}}{\sigma_z} + \frac{C_y^{\text{C}}\sigma_y}{\sigma_z} + C_z^{\text{C}} + G^{\text{C}} = \bar{Q}^{\text{C}} \tag{15.27}$$

where now σ_y is the relative price of good y to good x, and σ_z is the relative price of good z to good x.

There are two bilateral balance-of-trade conditions

$$C_y^A \sigma_y + C_z^A \sigma_z = C_x^B + C_x^C$$

$$\frac{C_x^B}{\sigma_y} + \frac{C_y^B \sigma_z}{\sigma_y} = C_y^A + C_y^C \tag{15.28}$$

together with three market-clearing conditions

$$C_j^A + C_j^B + C_j^C + G^i = \bar{Q}^i \qquad i = \text{A, B, C}, \quad j = x, y, z \tag{15.29}$$

although only two of these are independent.

Solving the system as before leads to

$$\sigma_y = \psi_y \frac{\bar{Q}^A - G^A}{\bar{Q}^B - G^B} \qquad \sigma_z = \psi_z \frac{\bar{Q}^A - G^A}{\bar{Q}^C - G^C}$$

where

$$\psi_y = \frac{\alpha_y^C(1 - \alpha_x^A) + \alpha_x^C \alpha_y^A}{\alpha_x^B \alpha_y^C + \alpha_x^C(1 - \alpha_y^B)} \qquad \psi_z = \frac{\alpha_z^A(1 - \alpha_y^B) + \alpha_y^A \alpha_z^B}{\alpha_x^B \alpha_y^C + \alpha_x^C(1 - \alpha_y^B)}$$

and

$$C_x^A = \alpha_x^A(\bar{Q}^A - G^A) \qquad C_y^A = \frac{\alpha_y^A(\bar{Q}^B - G^B)}{\psi_y}$$

$$C_z^A = \frac{\alpha_z^A(\bar{Q}^C - G^C)}{\psi_z} \qquad C_x^B = \alpha_x^B(\bar{Q}^A - G^A)\psi_y$$

$$C_y^B = \alpha_y^B(\bar{Q}^B - G^B) \qquad C_z^B = \frac{\alpha_z^B(\bar{Q}^C - G^C)\psi_y}{\psi_z}$$

$$C_x^C = \alpha_x^C(\bar{Q}^A - G^A)\psi_z \qquad C_y^C = \frac{\alpha_y^C(\bar{Q}^B - G^B)\psi_z}{\psi_y}$$

$$C_z^C = \alpha_z^C(\bar{Q}^C - G^C)$$

The corresponding levels of utility are therefore of the form

$$U^i = K^i + \alpha_x^i \ln(\bar{Q}^A - G^A) + \alpha_y^i \ln(\bar{Q}^B - G^B) + \alpha_z^i \ln(\bar{Q}^C - G^C) + \beta^i \ln G^i \qquad i = \text{A, B, C} \tag{15.30}$$

Suppose initially that all three countries act noncooperatively. The optimal levels of government expenditure for the three countries are of the form

$$G^A = \frac{\beta^A}{\alpha_x^A + \beta^A}\bar{Q}^A \qquad G^B = \frac{\beta^B}{\alpha_y^B + \beta^B}\bar{Q}^B \qquad G^C = \frac{\beta^C}{\alpha_x^C + \beta^C}\bar{Q}^C \tag{15.31}$$

which are analogous to (15.24), obtained previously.

Suppose now that countries A and B form a coalition and cooperate to maximize their joint welfare $U^{A} + U^{B}$. The optimality conditions are

$$G^{A} = \frac{\beta^{A}}{\alpha_x^{A} + \alpha_x^{B} + \beta^{A}} \bar{Q}^{A} \tag{15.32a}$$

$$G^{A} = \frac{\beta^{B}}{\alpha_y^{A} + \alpha_y^{B} + \beta^{B}} \bar{Q}^{B} \tag{15.32b}$$

where both G^{A} and G^{B} are reduced from their respective noncooperative levels. If these reductions are denoted by $\mathrm{d}G^{A}$ and $\mathrm{d}G^{B}$, the welfare gains for country A are

$$\mathrm{d}U^{A} = -\frac{\alpha_y^{A}}{\bar{Q}^{B} - G^{B}} \mathrm{d}G^{B} \tag{15.33}$$

where G^{B} is evaluated at the noncooperative level.

How does the formation of this coalition affect the welfare of the excluded country C? The answer is given by the expression

$$\mathrm{d}U^{C} = -\frac{\alpha_x^{C}}{\bar{Q}^{A} - G^{A}} \mathrm{d}G^{A} - \frac{\alpha_y^{C}}{\bar{Q}^{B} - G^{B}} \mathrm{d}G^{B}$$

which, with $\mathrm{d}G^{A}$ and $\mathrm{d}G^{B}$ both being negative, implies an unambiguous welfare improvement. In fact, the welfare gains to country C may quite plausibly exceed those accruing to either of the partners A and B. This is so, for example, if all countries have identical tastes and the coefficients α_j^i are equal. Essentially the reason is that the coalition reduces both G^{A} and G^{B}, and this has a favorable effect on the terms of trade for country C with respect to both its trading partners.[9] Thus we find that, at least for this logarithmic example, the formation of a coalition between two countries may yield greter benefit to an excluded country than it does to either of the partners.

Finally, suppose that country C joins the coalition, so that all three act cooperatively. Maximizing the aggregate utility $U^{A} + U^{B} + U^{C}$, we find

$$G^{i} = \frac{\beta^{i}}{\alpha_j^{A} + \alpha_j^{B} + \alpha_j^{C} + \beta^{i}} \bar{Q}^{i} \qquad i = \mathrm{A, B, C}, \qquad j = x, y, z$$

This involves a further reduction in government expenditure and the mutual gains from cooperation increase. For country A, for example,

$$\mathrm{d}U^{A} = -\frac{\alpha_y^{A}}{\bar{Q}^{B} - G^{B}} \mathrm{d}G^{B} - \frac{\alpha_z^{A}}{\bar{Q}^{C} - G^{C}} \mathrm{d}G^{C}$$

which now gains from the reduction in public expenditure in the new member country C as well as in that of G^{B}. Country C gains from joining because of the additional reductions in G^{A} and G^{B} that this induces. Thus, at least in this example, we find that the gains from cooperation increase with the number of countries cooperating.

7 CONCLUSIONS: REINTERPRETATION AS A TWO-PERIOD ANALYSIS

In this chapter we have analysed the gains from fiscal cooperation, within the context of the standard two-commodity real trade model. Using this framework, we have shown how the adjustment in the terms of trade is the critical factor in determining the effects of moving from a noncooperative equilibrium. In general, a noncooperative equilibrium leads to an overexpansion of government expenditure on the export good and an underexpansion on the import good relative to an equilibrium in which both governments act cooperatively. Aggregate world welfare will be increased by a reduction in government expenditure on the former and an increase in government expenditure on the latter. The specific example of a logarithmic economy has been considered. We have demonstrated how, at least within such an economy, the formation of a coalition among two countries may confer welfare gains on an excluded third country which exceed those accruing to either partner.

It is straightforward to reinterpret the framework in terms of a two-period single-commodity model, such as that used by Hamada (1986). The subscripts x and y can now be reinterpreted as two periods (the present and future, say), so that the utility functions (15.1) and the production possibilities curves (15.3) apply intertemporally. Furthermore, combining equations (15.5) and (15.6) yields

$$C_x^i + \sigma C_y^i = Q_x^i - G_x^i + \sigma(Q_y^i - G_y^i)$$

which can now be interpreted as being a two-period intertemporal budget constraint in which σ denotes the intertemporal price (the interest rate) rather than the intratemporal terms of trade.[10] Formally, everything else applies as before. The assumptions $E_y^{\mathrm{A}} > 0$ and $E_x^{\mathrm{B}} > 0$ can now be interpreted as follows: country A has an excess demand for future goods and is therefore a lender, while country B has an excess demand for current goods and is a borrower.

With this interpretation, the effects of fiscal cooperation depend upon the adjustment of the interest rate. In what we have called the normal case, an increase in government expenditure on the current good raises the current interest rate, while an increase in government expenditure in the future period lowers it. In general, we find that a noncooperative equilibrium leads to an overexpansion of government expenditure on present goods and an underexpansion on future goods, by the lender, relative to the cooperative equilibrium. The reverse holds true with respect to the borrower.

NOTES

1 See, for example, Canzoneri and Gray (1985), Currie and Levine (1985), Miller and Salmon (1985), Oudiz and Sachs (1985), Taylor (1985), and Turnovsky and d'Orey (1986, this volume, ch. 13).

2 This change of emphasis is apparent from the recent NBER Conference on the international aspects of fiscal policy (see Frenkel, 1987).

3 Our choice of import and export goods implies $E_y^A > 0$, $E_x^A < 0$, $E_x^B > 0$, $E_y^B < 0$.

4 Recall that the formula for the optimal tariff is independent of the utility function or marginal utility. The reason for this is that, unlike government expenditure, the tariff rate does not enter the utility function directly. If, to complete the analogy, we assume that G_x^A does not generate independent utility, then (15.13) reduces to $1 + E_y^A \partial\sigma/\partial G_x^A = 0$. This can be rewritten as

$$\frac{G_x^A}{E_x^A} = \frac{\partial\sigma}{\partial G_x^A}\frac{G_x^A}{\sigma}$$

That is, the ratio of government expenditure to the excess supply for the export good equals the elasticity of the relative price with respect to government expenditure on the export good.

5 Two conditions assumed are (a) that an increase in the relative price of good x in either country reduces the excess demand for that good, while increasing it for the other good, and (b) that the Marshall–Lerner condition holds. Condition (a) in turn requires the usual assumption that the substitution effect of a price change dominates the income effect.

We can show how invoking (a) and (b) implies

$$\operatorname{sgn}\left(\frac{\partial\sigma}{\sigma G_x^A}\right) = \operatorname{sgn}\left(\frac{\partial E_y^A}{\partial G_n^A}\right)$$
$$= \operatorname{sgn}\left\{-\frac{\mathrm{d}}{\mathrm{d}C_x^A}\left(\frac{\partial U^A/\partial C_y^A}{\partial U^A/\partial C_x^A}\right) + \frac{\mathrm{d}}{\mathrm{d}G_x^A}\left(\frac{\partial U^A/\partial C_y^A}{\partial U^A/\partial C_x^A}\right)\right\}$$

The first term in parentheses can be shown to be proportional to the effect of a decrease in income on the excess demand E_y^A and is presumably negative. This reflects the fact that an increase in G_x^A raises taxes, thereby lowering disposable income, private consumption of good y, and excess demand for that good. The second term describes how the change in government expenditure on good x affects the marginal rate of substitution between the two private goods. Under mild restrictions, including weak separability of the utility function in private and public goods, when this latter term is zero, the first term dominates, implying inequality (15.9).

6 We can also show that in the "normal" case, the reduction in G_x^A as we move from the noncooperative to the cooperative equilibrium will raise real national output in both countries and the volume of real trade, both measured in terms of good x.

7 That is, the Nash noncooperative equilibrium is also a consistent conjectural variations equilibrium.

8 My interest in analysing this issue grew out of remarks made at a conference on the international effects of monetary policy, held recently at the University of Illinois at Urbana-Champaign.

9 The terms of trade are

$$\frac{1}{\sigma_z} = \frac{1}{\psi_z}\,\frac{\bar{Q}^{\mathrm{C}} - G^{\mathrm{C}}}{\bar{Q}^{\mathrm{A}} - G^{\mathrm{A}}} \qquad \frac{\sigma_y}{\sigma_z} = \frac{\psi_y}{\psi_z}\,\frac{\bar{Q}^{\mathrm{C}} - G^{\mathrm{C}}}{\bar{Q}^{\mathrm{B}} - G^{\mathrm{B}}}$$

It is clear that these both improve through reductions in $\mathrm{d}G^{\mathrm{A}}$ and $\mathrm{d}G^{\mathrm{B}}$.

10 More precisely, we redefine $\sigma = 1/(1 + r)$, where r is the interest rate.

REFERENCES

Bhagwati, J. N. and Srinivasan, T. N. (1983) *Lectures on International Trade*. Cambridge, MA: MIT Press.

Canzoneri, M. and Gray, J. A. (1985) Monetary policy games and the consequences of noncooperative behavior. *International Economic Review,* 26, 547–64.

Chari, V. V. and Kehoe, P. J. (1987) International coordination of fiscal policy in limiting economies. Working paper 317, Federal Reserve Bank of Minneapolis.

Currie, D. and Levine, P. (1985) Macroeconomic policy design in an interdependent world. In *International Economic Policy Coordination*. (eds W. H. Buiter and R. C. Marston) Cambridge: Cambridge University Press.

Devereux, M. (1986) The international coordination of fiscal policy and the terms of trade: An example. Unpublished manuscript, University of Toronto.

Frenkel, J. A. (ed.) (1987) *International Aspects of Fiscal Policy*. Chicago, IL: NBER, University of Chicago Press.

—— and Razin, A. (1985) Government spending, debt and international economic interdependence. *Economic Journal,* 95, 619–36.

—— and —— (1986) Fiscal policies in the world economy. *Journal of Political Economy,* 94, 564–94.

Hamada, K. (1976) A strategic analysis of monetary interdependence. *Journal of Political Economy,* 84, 677–700.

—— (1986) Strategic aspects of international fiscal interdependence. *Economic Studies Quarterly,* 37, 165–80.

Johnson, H. G. (1954) Optimum tariffs and retaliation. *Review of Economic Studies,* 21, 142–53.

Kehoe, P. J. (1987) Coordination of fiscal policies in a world economy. *Journal of Monetary Economics,* 19, 349–76.

Miller, M. H, and Salmon M. (1985) Policy coordination and dynamic games. In *International Economic Policy Coordination* (eds W. H. Buiter and R. C. Marston). Cambridge: Cambridge University Press.

Oudiz, G. and Sachs, J. (1985) International policy coordination in dynamic macroeconomic models. In *International Economic Policy Coordination*. (eds

W. H. Buiter and R. C. Marston). Cambridge: Cambridge University Press.

Takayama, A. (1974) *International Trade.* New York: Holt, Rinehart and Winston.

Taylor, J. B. (1985) International coordination in the design of macroeconomic policy rules, *European Economic Review,* 28, 53–82.

Turnovsky, S. J. and d'Orey, V. (1986) Monetary policies in interdependent economies with stochastic disturbances: a strategic approach. *Economic Journal,* 96, 696–721. Reprinted in this volume as chapter 13.

Index